Police Innovation

Second Edition

Over the last forty years, policing has gone through a period of significant change and innovation. The emergence of new strategies has also raised issues about effectiveness and efficiency in policing, and many of these proactive strategies have become controversial as citizens have asked whether they are also fair and unbiased. Updated and expanded for the second edition, this volume brings together leading police scholars to examine these key innovations in policing. Including advocates and critics of each innovation, this comprehensive book assesses the impacts of police innovation on crime and public safety, the extent of implementation of these new approaches in police agencies, the dilemmas these approaches have created for police management, and their impacts on communities.

David Weisburd is Distinguished Professor of Criminology, Law and Society at George Mason University and Walter E. Meyer Professor of Law and Criminal Justice at the Hebrew University. He has received many international awards recognizing his work on policing and criminology more generally, including the Stockholm Prize in Criminology, the Edwin Sutherland and August Vollmer Awards from the American Society of Criminology, and the Israel Prize. Professor Weisburd served as Chair of the National Academies of Sciences Committee on Proactive Policing.

Anthony A. Braga is a Distinguished Professor in and Director of the School of Criminology and Criminal Justice at Northeastern University. Between 2007 and 2013, Braga served as the Chief Policy Advisor to Commissioner Edward F. Davis of the Boston Police Department. His work with the Boston Police Department was recognized by the International Association of Chiefs of Police with its Excellence in Law Enforcement Research Award (2011).

Police Innovation

Contrasting Perspectives

Second Edition

Edited by

DAVID WEISBURD
George Mason University and Hebrew University

ANTHONY A. BRAGA
Northeastern University

CAMBRIDGE
UNIVERSITY PRESS

University Printing House, Cambridge CB2 8BS, United Kingdom

One Liberty Plaza, 20th Floor, New York, NY 10006, USA

477 Williamstown Road, Port Melbourne, VIC 3207, Australia

314–321, 3rd Floor, Plot 3, Splendor Forum, Jasola District Centre,
New Delhi – 110025, India

79 Anson Road, #06–04/06, Singapore 079906

Cambridge University Press is part of the University of Cambridge.

It furthers the University's mission by disseminating knowledge in the pursuit of
education, learning, and research at the highest international levels of excellence.

www.cambridge.org
Information on this title: www.cambridge.org/9781108417815
DOI: 10.1017/9781108278423

© Cambridge University Press 2019

First Published 2006
Second edition 2019

Printed and bound in Great Britain by Clays Ltd, Elcograf S.p.A.

A catalogue record for this publication is available from the British Library.

ISBN 978-1-108-41781-5 Hardback
ISBN 978-1-108-40591-1 Paperback

Contents

v

Figures

Tables

Notes on Contributors

Barak Ariel Hebrew University of Jerusalem and the University of Cambridge

Rachel Boba Santos Radford University

Anthony A. Braga Northeastern University

John E. Eck University of Cincinnati

John A. Eterno Molloy College

Jack R. Greene Northeastern University

Rosann Greenspan Berkeley Law, University of California

George L. Kelling Rutgers University

David M. Kennedy John Jay College of Criminal Justice

Christopher S. Koper George Mason University

Cynthia Lum George Mason University

Lorraine Mazerolle The University of Queensland

Stephen D. Mastrofski George Mason University

Tracey L. Meares Yale Law School

Emily Owens University of California, Irvine

Janet Ransley Griffith University

Jerry Ratcliffe Temple University

Dennis P. Rosenbaum University of Illinois at Chicago

Eli B. Silverman John Jay College of Criminal Justice

Wesley G. Skogan Northwestern University

William H. Sousa University of Nevada, Las Vegas

Ralph B. Taylor Temple University

David Thacher University of Michigan

Brandon Turchan Northeastern University

Tom R. Tyler Yale Law School

David Weisburd George Mason University and Hebrew University

Brandon C. Welsh Northeastern University

James J. Willis George Mason University

Christopher Winship Harvard University

Introduction

Understanding Police Innovation

David Weisburd and Anthony A. Braga

INTRODUCTION

Over the last decades of the twentieth century, American policing went through a period of significant change and innovation. In what is a relatively short historical time frame, the police began to reconsider their fundamental mission, the nature of the core strategies of policing, and the character of their relationships with the communities that they serve. Innovations in policing in this period were not insular and restricted to police professionals and scholars, but were often seen on the front pages of America's newspapers and magazines, and spoken about in the electronic media. Some approaches, like broken windows policing – termed by some as zero tolerance policing – became the subject of heated political debate. Community policing, one of the most important police programs that emerged during this period, was even used to give its name to a large federal agency – The Office of Community Oriented Policing Services – created by the Violent Crime Control and Law Enforcement Act of 1994.

Police scholars have argued that this period of change was the most dramatic in the history of policing (e.g., see Bayley, 1994). This claim does not perhaps do justice to the radical reforms that led to the creation of modern police forces in the nineteenth century, or even the wide-scale innovations in tactics or approaches to policing that emerged after the Second World War. However, observers of the police have invariably been struck by the pace and variety of innovation in this period. Whether this period of change is greater than those of previous generations is difficult to know since systematic observation of police practices is a relatively modern phenomenon. However, by the first decade of the new century, a Committee of the National Academy of Sciences concluded that in recent years we have "witnessed a remarkable degree of innovation in policing" (Skogan & Frydl, 2004: 82).

In this second edition of *Police Innovation: Contrasting Perspectives*, we bring together leading police scholars to examine the major innovations in policing that began to emerge during the last decades of the twentieth century and have continued into the twenty-first century. We update our 2004 edition both by revising earlier contributions, and by adding six additional chapters that cover three new innovations that have emerged since our first edition was published. We now focus on eleven police innovations that are concerned with change in police strategies and practices. These include eight innovations that were examined in the first edition: community policing, broken windows policing, problem-oriented policing, pulling levers policing, third-party policing, hot spots policing, CompStat, and evidence-based policing. We also examine three new police innovations: procedural justice policing, predictive policing, and policing focused on new technologies – termed technology policing in our volume. This is, of course, not an exhaustive list of innovations in policing during this period. For example, we do not examine innovations in tactics and strategies that affected only specialized units or were applied to very specific types of crimes. Our approach is to identify innovations that had influence on the broad array of police tasks and on the practices and strategies that broadly affect the policing of American communities.

We title the chapters examining each police innovation reviewed in this volume under the headings "Advocate" and "Critic." In this context, our book seeks to clarify police innovation in the context of chapters written by those who have played important roles in developing innovation, and those who have stood as critics of such innovation. Nonetheless, we do not take a debate format in our book. Authors did not respond to each other's papers, but rather sought to present a perspective that would clarify the benefits of the innovation examined, or the potential problems that the innovation raises for policing. The critics often identify promising elements of innovation while pointing out the difficulties that have been encountered in the application of innovations in the field. The advocates often note the drawbacks of particular strategies, while arguing that they should be widely adopted. Accordingly, our chapters represent serious scholarly examination of innovations in policing, recognizing that established scholars may disagree about the directions that policing should take while drawing from the same empirical evidence.

By design, the essays in this volume take a "micro" approach to the problem of police innovation, focusing on the specific components, goals, and outcomes associated with a specific program or practice. In this introductory chapter, we take a "macro" approach to the problem of police innovation that allows us to see how innovation more generally emerged and developed during this period. We do not think that the dramatic surge in police innovation of the last few decades occurred as a matter of chance. Our approach is to see the development of innovation in policing as a response to a common set of problems and dilemmas. This approach can also help us to understand the broad trends of police innovation that we observe.

The development of the chapters for the second edition of this edited volume occurred during a time of renewed concern over the strategies and tactics used by American police departments to control crime. Recent events involving the deaths of African-American men at the hands of police officers in Ferguson, MO; New York, NY; Chicago, IL; and elsewhere in the United States have exposed rifts in the relationships between the police and the communities they protect and serve. As suggested by the President's Task Force on 21st Century Policing (2015: 42), "[a]ny prevention strategy that unintentionally violates civil rights, compromises police legitimacy, or undermines trust is counterproductive." In public debate, specific kinds of police innovations have been nominated as contributing to poor police relationships with minority communities while others have been promoted as possible remedies to improve these strained relationships. In many of the revised and new advocate and critic contributions, authors consider how particular innovations may either improve or further damage police relationships with minority residents and communities more generally. These updated views on varying police innovations during this most recent crisis of confidence in American policing represent an important contribution of the second edition.

UNDERSTANDING INNOVATION AND POLICING

Many scholars seem to take for granted what strikes us as a central problem in understanding the broader phenomenon that our volume examines. Why did we observe a period of significant innovation in policing in the last decades of the twentieth century? One simple answer to this question would be to note that institutions change, and that when faced with new ideas that have potential to improve their functioning, they will naturally choose what is innovative. However, those who have studied the diffusion of innovation have been led to a very different view of the processes that underlie the adoption of new products, programs, or practices. Everett Rogers, who pioneered the scientific study of diffusion of innovation, argues, for example, that "more than just a beneficial innovation is necessary" to explain its widespread diffusion and adoption (1995: 8). Indeed, there are many examples of innovations that represent clear improvements over prior practice, yet fail to be widely adopted.

Rogers brings the example of the "Dvorak Keyboard," named after a University of Washington researcher who sought to improve on the "Qwerty" keyboard in use since the late nineteenth century. The "Qwerty" keyboard was engineered to slow down typists in the nineteenth century in order to prevent jamming of keys that was common in the manual typewriters of that period. However, as the engineering of typewriters improved in the twentieth century, there was no longer a need for a keyboard engineered to slow typists down. Indeed, it seemed natural that a better arrangement of the keyboard would be developed that would allow for quicker typing that would cause less fatigue. Dvorak developed such a keyboard in 1932 basing his arrangement of the keys on time and motion studies. Dvorak's keyboard was clearly an improvement on the Qwerty keyboard. It allowed for more efficient and faster typing, and led to less fatigue on the part of typists. But, today, more than eighty years after Dvorak's development of a better and more efficient keyboard, the Qwerty keyboard remains the dominant method. Indeed, Dvorak's keyboard is merely an interesting historical curiosity.

The diffusion of innovation requires that there be a "perceived need" for change in the social system in which an innovation emerges (Rogers, 1995: 11). That need can be created by industries or interest groups, for example, through advertisements that lead consumers to believe that they must have a particular new product or service. Often in social systems, the recognition that something must change is brought about by a period of crisis or challenge to existing programs or practices (see e.g., Rogers, 1995; Altschuler & Behn, 1997). In this context, we think that the key to understanding the emergence of a period of rapid innovation in policing in the last decades of the twentieth century lies in a crisis in policing that emerged in the late 1960s. Identifying that period of crisis can help us to understand not only why we observe so much police innovation in recent decades, but also why that innovation follows particular patterns of change.

The Crisis of Confidence in American Policing

The decade of the 1970s began with a host of challenges to the police as well as the criminal justice system more generally (LaFree, 1998). This was the case in part because of the tremendous social unrest that characterized the end of the previous decade. Race riots in American cities, and growing opposition, especially among younger Americans, to the Vietnam War, often placed the police in conflict with the young and with minorities. However, American fears of a failing criminal justice system were also to play a role in a growing sense of crisis for American policing. In 1967, a presidential commission report on the Challenge of Crime in a Free Society reinforced doubts about the effectiveness of criminal justice in combating crime in the United States:

In sum, America's system of criminal justice is overcrowded and overworked, under-manned, underfinanced, and very often misunderstood. It needs more information and more knowledge. It needs more technical resources. It needs more coordination among its many parts. It needs more public support. It needs the help of community programs and institutions in dealing with offenders and potential offenders. It needs, above all, the willingness to reexamine old ways of doing things, to reform itself, to experiment, to run risks, to dare. It needs vision. (President's Commission, 1967: 80–81)

Shortly after the presidential report on the Challenge of Crime in a Free Society, the Kerner Commission on Civil Disorders published a report, which also raised significant questions about the nature of criminal justice in the United States, and the organization of American policing. However, in this case, it was the question of race, and the relationship between police and minority communities, that was to have center stage. The challenges to patterns of American discrimination against African Americans were not focused primarily on the police, but the police, in addition to other criminal justice agencies, were seen as "part of the problem" and not necessarily working to help in producing a solution to difficult social issues:

In Newark, Detroit, Watts and Harlem, in practically every city that has experienced racial disruption since the summer of 1964, abrasive relationships between police and Negroes and other minority groups have been a major source of grievance, tension and ultimately disorder. (Kerner Commission, 1968: 157)

The concerns of the commission reports in the 1960s and the sense of growing alienation between the police and the public in the latter half of that decade led policymakers, the police, and scholars to question the nature of American policing, and, in particular, the strategies that were dominant in policing since World War II. A National Research Council Committee to Review Research on Police Policy and Practices termed these approaches in 2004 as the "standard model of policing" (Skogan & Frydl, 2004). Weisburd and Eck note:

This model relies generally on a "one size fits all" application of reactive strategies to suppress crime, and continues to be the dominant form of police practices in the United States. The standard model is based on the assumption that generic strategies for crime reduction can be applied throughout a jurisdiction regardless of the level of crime, the nature of crime, or other variations. Such strategies as increasing the size of police agencies, random patrol across all parts of the community, rapid response to calls for service, generally applied follow-up investigations, and generally applied intensive enforcement and arrest policies are all examples of this standard model of policing. (Weisburd & Eck, 2004: 44)

A number of important questions about the standard model of policing had been raised in the 1960s. Nonetheless, there was little serious academic inquiry into the impact of policing strategies on crime or on public attitudes. The need for such research was apparent, and in the 1970s serious research attention was to begin. One important impetus for such studies of the police came from the federal government. With the Omnibus Crime Control and Safe Streets Act of 1968, a research arm of the US Department of Justice was established, eventually to become the National Institute of Justice, which was to invest significant resources into research on police and other components of the criminal justice system. But important funding for research on policing was also to come from private foundations. Perhaps the most important contribution to policing was made by the Ford Foundation in 1970 when it established the Police Development Fund. The Fund, and the Police Foundation that it established, were to foster a series of large-scale studies on American policing. McGeorge Bundy, then-president of the Ford Foundation, argued in announcing the establishment of a Police Development Fund in 1970:

The need for reinforcement and change in police work has become more urgent than ever in the last decade because of rising rates of crime, increased resort to violence and rising tension, in many communities, between disaffected or angry groups and the police. (Bundy, 1970)

With the establishment of the Police Foundation and the newly established federal support for research on the criminal justice system, the activities of the police began to come under systematic scrutiny by researchers. Until this time, there had been a general assumption that policing in the post–World War II era represented an important advance over previous decades, and was effective in controlling crime.

For example, perhaps the dominant policing strategy in the post–World War II period was routine preventive patrol in police cars. It was drawn from a long history of faith in the idea of "police patrol" that had become a standard dogma of policing for generations. George Kelling and his colleagues wrote in their introduction to the Kansas City Preventive Patrol Experiment, a study conducted by the Police Foundation:

Ever since the creation of a patrolling force in 13th century Hangchow, preventive patrol by uniformed personnel has been a primary function of policing. In 20th century America, about $2 billion is spent each year for the maintenance and operation of uniformed and often superbly equipped patrol forces. Police themselves, the general public, and elected officials have always believed that the presence or potential presence of police officers on patrol severely inhibits criminal activity. (Kelling et al., 1974: 1)

Preventive patrol in police cars was the main staple of police crime prevention efforts at the beginning of the decade of the 1970s. As Kelling and colleagues noted in the Police Foundation report on the Kansas City study, "(t)oday's police recruits, like virtually all those before them, learn from both teacher and textbook that patrol is the 'backbone' of police work" (Kelling et al., 1974: 1). The Police Foundation study sought to establish whether empirical evidence actually supported the broadly accepted assumptions regarding preventive patrol. The fact that questions were raised about routine preventive patrol suggests that the concerns about the police voiced in the decade before had begun to impact the confidence of police managers. As Kansas City Police Chief Clarence M. Kelley, later to become director of the Federal Bureau of Investigation (FBI), said in explaining the need for the Kansas City experiment: "Many of us in the department had the feeling we were training, equipping, and deploying men to do a job neither we, nor anyone else, knew much about" (Murphy, 1974: v).

To understand the impact of the Kansas City study on police managers and researchers, it is important to recognize not only that the study examined a core police practice but that its methodological approach represented a radical departure from the small-scale evaluations of police practices that had come earlier. The Kansas City Preventive Patrol Experiment was a social experiment in policing on a grand scale, and it was conducted in a new Foundation that had significant resources and was backed by the well-established and respected Ford

Foundation. Patrick Murphy, the distinguished police manager, and president of the Police Foundation at the time, suggests just how much the Foundation itself saw the experiment as a radical and important change in the quality of police research:[1]

This is a summary report of the findings of an experiment in policing that ranks among the few major social experiments ever to be completed. The experiment was unique in that never before had there been an attempt to determine through such extensive scientific evaluation the value of visible police patrol. (Murphy, 1974: v)

This context, both in terms of the centrality of the strategy examined, the scale of the research, and the prestige of the institutions that supported the study, including the Kansas City Police Department and its chief, Clarence Kelley, were to give the findings of the study an impact that is in retrospect out of proportion to the actual findings. One study in one jurisdiction, no matter how systematic, cannot provide a comprehensive portrait of the effects of a strategy as broad as routine preventive patrol. Moreover, the study design was to come under significant academic criticism in later years (Minneapolis Medical Research Foundation, 1976; Larson & Cahn, 1985; Sherman & Weisburd, 1995). Nonetheless, in the context of the decade in which it was conducted, this study was to have a critical impact upon the police and police researchers. This was especially the case since the research findings were to be consistent with a series of other studies of core police practices.

Kelling and his colleagues, in cooperation with the Kansas City Police Department, took fifteen police beats and divided them up into three groups. In five of these, called "reactive" beats, "routine preventive patrol was eliminated and officers were instructed to respond only to calls for service" (Kelling et al., 1974: 3). In five others, defined as "control" beats, "routine preventive patrol was maintained at its usual level of one car per beat" (Kelling et al., 1974: 3). In the remaining five beats, termed "proactive" beats, "routine preventive patrol was intensified by two to three times its usual level through the assignment of additional patrol cars" (Kelling et al., 1974: 3). When Kelling and his colleagues published the results of their study in 1974, it shattered one of the bedrock assumptions of police practitioners – that preventive patrol was an effective way to prevent crime and increase citizens' feelings of safety. They concluded simply that increasing or decreasing the intensity of routine preventive patrol in police cars did not affect either crime, service delivery to citizens, or citizens' feelings of security.

Another large-scale study, conducted by William Spelman and Dale Brown and published in 1984, was also to challenge a core police assumption of that period – that improvement in rapid response to calls for service would lead to

---

[1] It is important to note that a number of large social experiments were conducted during this period (e.g., see Bell et al., 1980; Struyk & Bendick, 1981) and thus the Kansas City Preventive Patrol experiment can be seen as part of a larger effort to subject social programs to systematic empirical study.

improvements in crime fighting. This study was developed in good part because of the findings of a prior investigation in Kansas City that found little support for the crime control effectiveness of rapid response to calls for service (Kansas City Police Department, 1977). With support from the National Institute of Justice, Spelman and Brown interviewed 4,000 victims, witnesses, and bystanders in some 3,300 serious crimes in four American cities. This was another major study in terms of the resources brought to bear and the methods used. Again, it examined a strategy that was aided by technological advances in the twentieth century and that was a central dogma of police administrators – that police must get to the scene of a crime quickly if they are to apprehend criminal offenders. Spelman and Brown explained:

For at least half a century, police have considered it important to cut to a minimum their response times to crime calls. The faster the response, they have reasoned, the better the chances of catching a criminal at or near the scene of the crime. (Spelman & Brown, 1984: xxi)

Based on the data they collected, however, Spelman and Brown provided a very different portrait of the crime control effectiveness of rapid response to calls for service:

Rapid police response may be unnecessary for three out of every four serious crimes reported to police. The traditional practice of immediate response to all reports of serious crimes currently leads to on-scene arrests in only 29 of every 1,000 cases. By implementing innovative programs, police may be able to increase this response-related arrest rate to 50 or even 60 per 1,000, but there is little hope that further increases can be generated. (Spelman & Brown, 1984: xix)

These findings, based on a host of systematic data sources from multiple jurisdictions, provided little support for the strategy of rapid response as a police practice to do something about crime. Indeed, Spelman and Brown found that citizen reporting time, not police response time, most influenced the possibility of on-scene arrest. Marginal improvement in police response times was predicted to have no real impact on the apprehension or arrest of offenders.

The Kansas City Preventive Patrol Experiment and the National Institute of Justice study of police response time were not the only studies to "debunk" existing police practices. James Levine, for example, analyzed national crime data on the effectiveness of increasing the number of police in an article published in 1975. His title sums up his findings: "The Ineffectiveness of Adding Police to Prevent Crime." Despite the fact that this effort and many others that challenged conventional police practices did not represent the kind of systematic data collection or analysis of the Police Foundation and National Institute of Justice studies, they followed a similar "narrative" which became increasingly common as the 1990s approached. Levine, for example, begins by noting the broad consensus for the principle that adding more police will make cities safer. He then goes on to note that "(s)ensible as intensified policing may sound on the surface, its effectiveness in combating crime has yet to be demonstrated" (Levine, 1975: 523). Finally, drawing upon simple tabular data on police strength and crime rates over time, he concludes:

It is tempting for politicians and government leaders to add more police: it is an intuitively sensible and symbolically satisfying solution to the unrelenting problem of criminal violence . . . The sad fact is, however, that they receive a false sense of security; in most situations, they are just as vulnerable with these extra police as without them. (1975: 544)

Follow-up investigations were also the subject of critical empirical research during this period. The standard model of policing had assumed that general improvements in methods of police investigations would lead to crime control gains both because more active offenders would be imprisoned and thus unable to commit crime, and because potential offenders would be deterred by the prospect of discovery and arrest (Skogan & Frydl, 2004). But, a series of studies in the 1970s and early 1980s suggested that investigations had little impact upon crime (Greenwood et al., 1975; Greenwood, Petersilia & Chaiken, 1977; Skogan & Antunes, 1979; Eck, 1983). This was the case in good part because many crimes, especially property crimes, were found unlikely to be solved by police investigations. These studies consistently showed that if citizens did not provide information about suspects to first responding officers, follow-up investigations were unlikely to lead to successful outcomes.

In retrospect, many of these studies overstated what could be learned about standard police practices from the findings gained (Weisburd & Eck, 2004). And, in practice, there were evaluations in this period that produced more promising findings regarding standard police practices such as routine preventive patrol (e.g., see Press, 1971; Schnelle et al., 1977; Chaiken, 1978). Moreover, more recent research provides a more nuanced portrait of the crime control effectiveness of specific standard policing models.[2] Nonetheless, as the United States entered the decade of the 1990s, there appeared to be a consensus that traditional police practices did not work in preventing or controlling crime. As Michael Gottfredson and Travis Hirschi wrote in their classic book *A General Theory of Crime* in 1990: "No evidence exists that augmentation of patrol forces or equipment, differential patrol strategies, or differential intensities of surveillance have an effect on crime rates" (Gottfredson & Hirschi, 1990: 270). David Bayley wrote even more strongly in 1994:

---

[2] This is the case, for example, in considering whether police staffing levels influence levels of crime. Econometric studies have begun to show significant crime prevention gains for increases in the number of police in a city (see, e.g., Evans & Owens, 2007; Machin & Olivier, 2011). However, the conclusion that these studies reflect the impact of the standard model of policing has been criticized because they often examine the boost in police resources that comes from support for community policing or other proactive policing strategies (Lee, Eck & Corsaro, 2016). More generally, we think that it is time for police scholars to renew efforts to evaluate the standard model of policing in the context of improved evaluation methods.

The police do not prevent crime. This is one of the best-kept secrets of modern life. Experts know it, the police know it, but the public does not know it. Yet the police pretend that they are society's best defense against crime ... This is a myth. First, repeated analysis has consistently failed to find any connection between the number of police officers and crime rates. Secondly, the primary strategies adopted by modern police have been shown to have little or no effect on crime. (Bayley, 1994: 3)

This view of the ineffectiveness of policing strategies was reinforced by official crime statistics. These statistics, widely available to the public, suggested that the police were losing the "war on crime." In particular, in America's largest cities, with their well-established professional police forces, crime rates, and especially violent crime rates, were rising at alarming rates. Between 1973 and 1990, violent crime doubled (Reiss & Roth, 1993). It did not take a statistician to understand that the trends were dramatic. For example, in Figure 1.1 we report the trends in violent crime rates by city size per 100,000 population. Clearly, crime was on the rise, and the trend had been fairly consistent over a long period. Thus, not only were scholars showing that police strategies did little to impact upon crime, but the overall crime statistics commonly used by the government and community to define police effectiveness were providing a similar message.

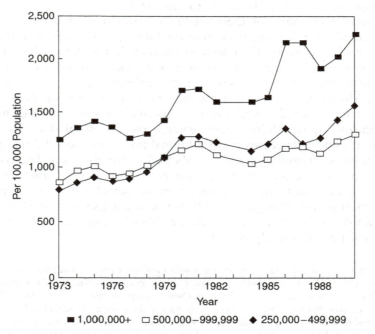

FIGURE 1.1 Total Violent Crime (trends in violent crime rates by city size)
Source: Reiss & Roth, 1993

CRISIS AND CHANGE IN AMERICAN POLICING

It is against this backdrop that the innovations we examine in this volume have developed. Our view is that the challenges to police effectiveness, rising crime rates, and concerns about the legitimacy of police actions that began to develop in the late 1960s created a perceived need for change in what some have described as the industry of American policing (Ostrom, Whitaker & Parks, 1978; Skogan & Frydl, 2004). Unfortunately, there is no hard empirical evidence that would allow us to make this link directly, since the study of the adoption of innovation has only recently become a subject of interest for police scholars (e.g., see Weiss, 1997; Klinger, 2003; Weisburd et al., 2003). Accordingly, there have been few systematic studies of these processes and scholars were generally not concerned about the emergence of innovation as a research problem when these innovations were being developed.

Nonetheless, we think it reasonable to make a connection between the perceived failures of the standard model of American police practices and the experimentation with innovation, and openness to the adoption of innovation that occurred in the last decades of the twentieth century. Certainly, such a link is made by many of those who fostered innovation in policing. For example, in his proposal for problem-oriented policing in 1979, Herman Goldstein referred directly to the growing evidence of the failures of traditional police practices:

Recently completed research questions the value of two major aspects of police operations – preventive patrol and investigations conducted by detectives. Some police administrators have challenged the findings; others are awaiting the results of replication. But those who concur with the results have begun to search for alternatives, aware of the need to measure the effectiveness of a new response before making a substantial investment in it. (1979: 240)

William Bratton (1998a) in describing the emergence of CompStat in New York City also refers to the failures of traditional approaches, and the need for innovation that would allow the police to be more effective in doing something about crime problems:

The effects of rapidly responding to crimes were muted because research showed it took people almost 10 minutes to decide to call the police in the first place. And police riding in air-conditioned squad cars, rapidly going from call to call, did not make people feel safer. In fact, it further separated the police from the public, the consumers of police services. Fortunately, the researchers and practitioners did not stop their work at finding what was not working, but began to look at how to think differently about crime and disorder and develop strategies that would work. (1998a: 31)

More generally, the turn of the last century was a period of tremendous change in police practices. This is perhaps most evident in the development of community-oriented policing, which was aided by financial support from the Office of Community Oriented Policing Services established in 1994. As Wesley Skogan reports in this volume (Chapter 1), community policing in some form has been adopted by most police agencies in the United States. In a Police Foundation survey conducted in 1997, 85 percent of surveyed police agencies reported they had adopted community policing or were in the process of doing so (Skogan, 2004). A Bureau of Justice Statistics survey conducted at the turn of the century found that more than 90 percent of departments in cities over 250,000 in population reported having full-time, trained community-policing officers in the field (Bureau of Justice Statistics, 2003).

The openness of police agencies to innovation is perhaps even more strongly illustrated by the sudden rise of CompStat as a police practice. CompStat was only developed as a programmatic entity in 1994, and was not encouraged financially by federally funded programs. Nonetheless, by the turn of the century, more than a third of larger police agencies had claimed to have implemented the program and a quarter of police agencies claimed that they were planning to adopt a CompStat program (Weisburd et al., 2003). In a recent review that covered many of the innovations we examine, the National Academy of Sciences Committee on Proactive Policing concluded that these approaches "are not isolated programs used by a select group of agencies but rather a set of strategies that have been diffused across the landscape of American policing" (Weisburd & Majmundar, 2018: 2–30).

A number of police scholars have suggested that the changes that such surveys observe are more cosmetic than substantive. Some studies have documented the "shallow" implementation of police innovations, and have suggested that in the end the police tend to fall back on traditional methods of conducting police work (e.g., see Clarke, 1998; Eck, 2000). For example, even in police agencies that have adopted innovations in problem-oriented policing, careful analysis of the activities of the police suggest that they are more likely to follow traditional police practices than to choose innovative approaches (Braga & Weisburd, Chapter 8 in this volume). Moreover, the main practices of the standard model of policing continue to dominate the work of most police agencies (Skogan & Frydl, 2004; Telep & Winegar, 2015).

While the depth of innovation over the last few decades remains a matter of debate, it is certainly the case that police agencies have become open to the idea of innovation, and that new programs and practices have been experimented with and adopted at a rapid pace over the last few decades. We think this openness can be traced to the crisis in police legitimacy and effectiveness that we have described.

UNDERSTANDING THE FORM AND CHARACTER OF POLICE INNOVATION

Recognizing the importance of the challenges to policing that began to emerge in the late 1960s can help us to understand not only the cause for a period of rapid innovation, but also the form and character of the innovations that we observe in this period and which are the focus of our volume. The innovations we study here represent different forms of adaptation to similar problems. Overall, they seek to find a solution to a set of challenges to the effectiveness and legitimacy of policing we have reviewed.

Community policing, which is examined in the next section of our volume, is one of the first new approaches to policing to emerge in this modern period of police innovation. Community policing programs were already being implemented and advocated in the 1980s (e.g., Trojanowicz, 1982; Goldstein, 1987; Cordner, 1988; Green & Mastrofski, 1988; Weisburd & McElroy, 1988; Trojanowicz, 1989), and by the 1990s, as we have already noted, the idea of community policing had affected most American police agencies. At the outset, community policing did not define crime reduction as a central element of its success (see, e.g., Klockars, 1988; Skolnick & Bayley, 1986). Indeed, it can be seen more directly in its early development as a response to the crisis of legitimacy of policing that developed from conflicts between the police and minority communities, and the more general alienation we have described between the police and the public in the 1960s and 1970s. While it may be argued that the community and police service to citizens was always an important part of American police work (see, e.g., Wilson, 1968), community-based policing legitimated a set of roles for the police that had previously been marginal to the police function, at least in terms of evaluations of police performance.

Community policing represented a radical departure from the professional model of policing that was dominant in the post–World War II period. For decades, the police had assumed that the main task of policing was to fight crime, and that the police, like other professionals, could successfully carry out their task with little help and preferably with little interference from the public. The police were the experts in defining the nature of crime problems and the nature of the solutions that could be brought to do something about them. The community, in this context, did not have a central role in the police function, and the responsibility for crime problems lay squarely in the hands of the policing industry. In community policing, the community was to be a co-producer of public safety, and the priorities of the police were to be defined in consultation with the community.

Kelling and Moore (1988: 4) argue that "during the 1950s and 1960s, police thought they were law enforcement agencies primarily fighting crime." In the "community era" or community policing era, the police function broadens and includes "order maintenance, conflict resolution, provision of services through problem solving, as well as other activities" (Kelling & Moore, 1988: 2). The justification for these new activities was drawn either from a claim that historically the police had indeed carried out such functions, or that the community from which the police gained legitimacy saw these as important functions of the police. David Bayley notes that this approach "creates a new role for police with new criteria for performance":

If police cannot reduce crime and apprehend more offenders, they can at least decrease fear of crime, make the public feel less powerless, lessen distrust between minority groups and the police, mediate quarrels, overcome the isolation of marginal groups, organize social services, and generally assist in developing "community." These are certainly worthwhile objectives. But are they what the police should be doing? They are a far cry from what the police were originally created to do. (1988: 228)

As Bayley suggests, one way to understand the early development of community policing is to recognize that it responds to the question: What is the justification for the police if they cannot prevent crime? And in developing a response to this question, community policing responded to another key part of the crisis of American policing we described, the alienation between the police and communities, and especially minority and disadvantaged communities. While crime fighting has increasingly become a central concern in community policing over the last two decades, an important contribution of community policing to police innovation was its recognition that there were many critical community problems that the police could address that were not traditionally defined as crime problems. The expansion of the police function was to become an important part of many of the innovations that are discussed in this volume. This definition of new tasks for policing can be seen in part as a response to the failure of police to achieve the crime control goals of the professional model of policing.

In this Second Edition, we include a more recent innovation in policing, procedural justice policing, in Part II of our book. Like community-oriented policing, this approach did not emerge as an innovation focused primarily on crime control. Rather, like community oriented policing, it sought to respond to a crisis in the relationship of the police to the public. The recent National Academy of Sciences report on proactive police noted that the "United States has once again been confronted by a crisis of confidence in policing" (Weisburd & Majmundar, 2018: ch. 8). Reminiscent of the conflicts between minority communities and the police in the 1960s we have seen large protests against what communities see as unfair police treatment or police violence. Procedural justice policing is a direct response to this old and new crisis in American policing. But procedural justice policing does not simply seek to improve the relationships between the police and the public, it predicts that such changes will enhance crime control. Indeed, some of its advocates have argued that it will in the long run yield stronger crime prevention gains than more traditional innovations that focus directly on crime control:

We argue that these changing goals and style reflect a fundamental tension between two models of policing: the currently dominant proactive risk management model, which focuses on policing to prevent crimes and makes promises of short-term security through the professional management of crime risks, and a model that focuses on building popular legitimacy by enhancing the relationship between the police and the public and thereby promoting the long-term goal of police community solidarity and, through that, public-police cooperation in addressing issues of crime and community order. (Tyler, Goff & MacCoun, 2015: 603)

This approach, like community policing, assumes that the police cannot succeed in their efforts to control crime without the support of the public. However, procedural justice policing focuses on how the police treat the public as individuals in everyday encounters, not on the coproduction of public safety. It expects public evaluations of police legitimacy to grow if the police give citizens a voice in police/citizen encounters; if they behave in a way that leads to citizens perceive their behavior as neutral in such encounters; if they treat citizens with dignity and respect; and if they behave in ways that lead citizen to assess their motives as trustworthy and fair. Procedural justice policing does not seek to define new strategic tactics of crime control. It does, however, seek to alter the relationships between the police and the public radically. In this policing model, changes in how police behave in encounters with citizens have the potential to alter not only the perceptions of the police of those directly affected but, through them, the community's perceptions of police legitimacy. With a change in such perceptions, they expect that individuals will be more willing to comply with police authority, and that they will cooperate more with the police by reporting crime and collaborating with the police in crime prevention. This police innovation, though a product of recent crises between the police and the public, also responds directly to the crisis of police legitimacy that helped spur police innovation four decades ago.

Broken windows policing, the subject of Part III of our volume, like community policing, also seeks to direct the police to problems that had often been ignored in standard police practices. The idea of broken windows policing developed out of a Police Foundation study, the Newark Foot Patrol Experiment (Kelling, Pate, Dieckman & Brown 1981). From that study, James Q. Wilson and George Kelling (1982) identified a link between social disorder and crime that suggested the importance of police paying attention to many problems that were seen in earlier decades as peripheral to the police function. Wilson and Kelling were impressed by the activities of the police officers who walked patrol in the Police Foundation study, and thought that what might be seen in traditional policing as inappropriate behavior actually held the key to public safety and crime reduction. Kelling and Coles write:

Most New Jersey police chiefs were dismayed when they learned from program evaluators what (anonymous) officers, who were supposed to be "fighting crime," were actually doing while on foot patrol. For example, after being called a second time during the same evening to end brawls in the same bar, one foot patrol officer had had enough: although the "bar time" was some hours away, he ordered the bar closed for business as usual. The bartender grumbled, closed up, and opened the next day for business as usual. When this incident was recounted to the chief of the department in which it occurred – disguised to protect the confidentiality of the officer, so that the chief believed it happened in another department – he responded, "that wouldn't happen in my department, the officer would be fired." (1996: 18)

Wilson and Kelling argued that concern with disorder was an essential ingredient for doing something about crime problems. Indeed, the broken windows thesis was that serious crime developed because the police and citizens did not work together to prevent urban decay and social disorder:

(A)t the community level, disorder and crime are usually inextricably linked, in a kind of developmental sequence. Social psychologists and police officers tend to agree that if a window in a building is broken *and is left unrepaired*, all of the rest of the windows will soon be broken. (1982: 31)

In the context of crime, Wilson and Kelling claim "that 'untended' behavior also leads to the breakdown of community controls":

A stable neighborhood of families who care for their homes, mind each other's children, and confidently frown on unwanted intruders can change in a few years or even a few months, to an inhospitable and frightening jungle. A piece of property is abandoned, weeds grow up, a window is smashed. Adults stop scolding rowdy children; the children emboldened, become more rowdy. Families move out, unattached adults move in … Such an area is vulnerable to criminal invasion. Though it is not inevitable, it is more likely here, rather than in places where people are confident they can regulate public behavior by informal controls. (1982: 31)

Broken windows policing encourages the police to be concerned with problems of disorder, and moves crime itself to a secondary or at least second-stage goal of the police. From the perspective of the crisis of policing we have described, broken windows policing again responds to the crisis of police effectiveness by expanding the goals of policing. On the one hand, it provides a theory for why police have failed in crime control in earlier decades. Crime is part of a developmental process and to reduce crime the police must intervene early in that process. On the other hand, it provides a new focus for policing – disorder – which allows the police to more easily focus prevention efforts, and through which they can more directly show success.

Problem-oriented policing, the subject of Part IV of our volume, also sought to broaden the problems that police approached. In Herman Goldstein's original formulation of problem-oriented policing in 1979, he argued that the "police job requires that they deal with a wide range of behavioral problems that arise in the community" (1979: 242). However, in this case, the solution for the crisis of policing was not found in the definition of new tasks for the police, but rather in a critique of traditional police practice. Goldstein assumed that the police could impact crime and other problems if they took a different approach, in this case, the problem-oriented policing approach. Accordingly, a second response to the crisis we have described is not to accept, as some academic criminologists had, that the police could not do something about crime and thus to search to define other important police functions as central (Gottfredson & Hirschi, 1990; Bayley, 1994), but to argue that the strategies of the standard policing model were flawed and that new more effective models could be developed.

Problem-oriented policing sought to redefine the way in which the police did their job. Goldstein argued that the police had "lost sight" of their primary task, which was to do something about crime and other problems, and instead had become focused on the "means" of allocating police resources. He identified this pathology as a common one in large organizations, and sought, through the model of problem solving, to develop a more successful method of ameliorating crime and other community problems.

Other innovations in policing that emerged fully around the turn of the century also take the approach that the police can be effective in doing something about crime if they adopt innovative police practices. Pulling levers policing discussed in Part V capitalizes on the fact that a large proportion of violent crime is committed by a relatively small group of high rate offenders. It adopts a problem-oriented approach to deal with these offenders, but provides a broader and more comprehensive combination of strategies than more traditional problem-oriented policing programs. Pioneered in Boston to deal with an "epidemic" of youth violence (Kennedy, Piehl & Braga, 1996), the pulling levers approach begins by drawing upon a collection of law enforcement practitioners to analyze crime problems and develop innovative solutions. It seeks to develop a variety of "levers" to stop high rate offenders from continuing criminal behavior that include not only criminal justice interventions, but also social services and community resources.

Third-party policing discussed in Part VI of this volume, offers another solution to the failures of the standard policing model. It follows suggestions made by Herman Goldstein (1979) that the "tool box" of police strategies be expanded. In this case, however, the resources of the police are expanded to "third parties" that are believed to offer significant new resources for doing something about crime and disorder.[3] The opportunity for a third-party policing approach developed in part from more general trends in the relationship between civil and criminal law (Mann, 1992; Mazerolle & Ransley, Chapter 11 in this volume). The expansion of the civil law and its use in other legal contexts as a method of dealing with problems that were once considered to be the exclusive province of criminal statutes, created important new tools for the police. Third-party policing asserts that the police cannot successfully deal with many problems on their own, and thus that the failures of traditional policing models may be found in the limits of police powers. Using civil ordinances and civil courts, or the resources of private agencies, third-party policing recognizes that much social control is exercised by institutions other than the police and that crime can be managed through agencies other than the criminal law.

Hot spots policing discussed in Part VII, was first examined in the Minneapolis Hot Spots Experiment (Sherman & Weisburd, 1995).

---

[3] The impetus for third-party policing does not necessarily come from the police. Mazerolle and Ransley (2006) argue that a variety of external demands have imposed third-party policing on the police industry.

The Minneapolis study was developed as a direct response to the findings of the Kansas City Preventive Patrol Experiment. Drawing upon empirical evidence that crime was clustered in discrete hot spots (e.g., see Pierce, Spaar & Briggs, 1986; Sherman, 1987; Sherman, Gartin & Buerger, 1989; Weisburd, Maher & Sherman, 1992), Sherman and Weisburd argued that preventive patrol might be effective if it was more tightly focused.

[If] only 3 percent of the addresses in a city produce more than half of all the requests for police response, if no police are dispatched to 40 percent of the addresses and intersections in a city over one year, and, if among the 60 percent with any requests the majority register only one request a year, then concentrating police in a few locations makes more sense than spreading them evenly through a beat. (1995: 629)

Hot spots policing does not demand that the police change their strategies, but requires that they focus them more carefully at places where crime is clustered.

In Part VIII of this volume, we examine predictive policing. The term predictive policing was first popularized in a symposium sponsored by the National Institute of Justice in 2009. William Bratton, then police commissioner of the LA police department, and the main developer of another innovation we will examine, CompStat, played a key role in raising this idea, again as a way for the police to focus in and improve on its crime control mission. Predictive policing is a strategy that uses predictive algorithms based on combining different types of data to anticipate where and when crime might occur and to identify patterns among past criminal incidents. The National Academies of Sciences Committee on Proactive Policing noted that "predictive policing overlaps with hot spots policing but is generally distinguished by its reliance on sophisticated analytics that are used to predict likelihood of crime incidence within very specific parameters of space and time and for very specific types of crime" (Weisburd & Majmundar, 2018: ch. 2).

CompStat, discussed in Part IX, also responds to the failures of the standard model of policing by critiquing the ways in which the police carry out their tasks. However, in the case of CompStat, the focus is less on the specific strategies that the police are involved in and more on the nature of police organization itself. Herman Goldstein noted in 1979 that the failures of the standard model of policing could be explained by the fact that police organizations were poorly organized to do something about crime. CompStat was designed to overcome that limitation. It sought to empower the police command structure to do something about crime problems. William Bratton, the New York City police chief who coined the term and developed the program wrote:

We created a system in which the police commissioner, with his executive core, first empowers and then interrogates the precinct commander, forcing him or her to come up with a plan to attack crime. But it should not stop there. At the next level down, it should be the precinct commander, taking the same role as the commissioner, empowering and interrogating the platoon commander. Then, at the third level, the platoon commander should be asking his sergeants ... all the way down until everyone in the entire organization is empowered and motivated, active and assessed and successful. It works in all organizations, whether it's 38,000 New York cops or Mayberry, R. F. D. (Bratton, 1998b: 239)

Evidence-based policing, discussed in Part X, also traces the failures of traditional policing practices to the ways in which the police carry out their tasks. It draws from a much wider set of public policy concerns, and a broader policy movement than other police innovations examined in this volume. There is a growing consensus among scholars, practitioners, and policymakers that crime control practices and policies should be rooted as much as possible in scientific research (Sherman, 1998; Cullen & Gendreau, 2000; MacKenzie, 2000; Sherman et al., 2002; Weisburd & Neyroud, 2011; Lum & Koper, 2017). Over the last two decades, there has been a steady growth in interest in the evaluation of criminal justice programs and practices reflected in part by the growth in criminal justice funding for research during this period (e.g., see Telep, Garner & Visher, 2015). Increasing support for research and evaluation in criminal justice may be seen as part of a more general trend toward utilization of scientific research for establishing rational and effective practices and policies. This trend is perhaps most prominent in the health professions where the idea of "evidence-based medicine" had gained strong government and professional support before the turn of the century (Millenson, 1997; Zuger, 1997), though the evidence-based paradigm has also developed in other fields (e.g., see Nutley & Davies, 1999; Davies, Nutley & Smith, 2000; Parsons, 2002; Victora, Habicht & Bryce, 2004). The evidence-based approach does not necessarily assume that the police can be more effective, but it argues that a reliance on evidence in the police industry is a prerequisite for the development of effective policing practices (Sherman, 1998). Weisburd and Neyroud (2011; see also Neyroud & Weisburd, 2014) argue that evidence-based policing is key to responding to the joint crises of effectiveness and police legitimacy in the context of increasing pressures to reduce funding for public services.

The final innovation we examine is also new to the Second Edition. Technologies in policing have advanced rapidly over the last few decades (Lum, Koper & Willis, 2016). Such technologies have not developed in a vacuum but have sought to reinforce police responses to the crises that motivated this now long period of developing police innovation to reduce crime and increase police legitimacy. Crime mapping, license plate reader technologies, and body cameras are all examples of technologies that have been integrated in policing with the goal of responding to challenges to police effectiveness in reducing crime, or increasing public trust in the police. This reliance on technology as a vehicle to improve policing seemed to us an important enough development to be included in a volume on key police innovations.

CONCLUSION

In our Introduction, we have traced the wide diffusion of innovations in the last decades of the twentieth century to a crisis of police practices that had begun to develop in the late 1960s, and has in specific ways reemerged in recent years (spawning new approaches that we have added to the Second Edition). We have argued that it is not accidental that so much innovation was brought to American policing during this period. Indeed, such innovation can be understood in the context of a series of challenges to American policing that created a perceived need for change among the police, scholars, and the public. We have also argued that the paths of police innovation can be understood in the context of the critiques that developed of standard policing models. In some cases, the innovations minimized the importance of crime fighting, which had been the focus of earlier policing models. Such innovations responded to the crisis of policing by defining a broader or new set of tasks that the police could perform more effectively. In many cases, such innovations focused on improving perceptions of police legitimacy and relationships more generally between the police and the public, another important component of the crisis we described. Other innovations, however, started with a critique of the methods used in the traditional policing models. These innovations assumed that the police could be more effective in preventing or controlling crime, if the tactics used were changed. These approaches, in turn, have been supplemented in recent years through such innovations as predictive policing, and new technologies have also been focused on efforts to improve police legitimacy (e.g., body cameras).

In the following chapters, prominent police scholars examine each of the innovations that we have discussed. The format of advocates and critics provides a broad framework for assessing these innovations and allows us to identify the major advantages and disadvantages of these approaches. In our conclusions, we try to draw more general lessons from these contributions, and discuss the possible directions that police innovation will take in the coming decades.

REFERENCES

Altschuler, A. A., & Behn, R. D. (eds.) (1997). *Innovation in American Government: Challenges, Opportunities, and Dilemmas.* Washington, DC: Brookings Institution Press.
Bayley, D. H. (1988). Community policing: A report from the devil's advocate. In J. R. Greene, & S. D. Mastrofski (eds.), *Community Policing: Rhetoric or Reality?* (pp. 225–238). New York: Praeger.
Bayley, D. (1994). *Police for the Future.* New York: Oxford University Press.
Bell, J. G., Robins, P. K., Spiegelman, R. G., & Weiner, S. (eds.) (1980). *A Guaranteed Annual Income: Evidence from a Social Experiment.* New York: Academic Press.

Bratton, W. J. (1998a). Crime is down in New York City: Blame the police. In W. J. Bratton, & N. Dennis (eds.), *Zero Tolerance: Policing a Free Society*. London: Institute of Economic Affairs Health and Welfare Unit.

Bratton, W. J. with Knobler, P. (1998b). *Turnaround: How America's Top Cop Reversed the Crime Epidemic*. New York: Random House.

Bundy, McGeorge. (1970, July). Press Conference. Presented in New York City, NY.

Bureau of Justice Statistics. (2003). *Local Police Departments 2000*. Washington, DC: Bureau of Justice Statistics, US Department of Justice.

Chaiken, J. (1978). What is known about deterrent effects of police activities. In J. Cromer (ed.), *Preventing Crime* (pp. 109–136). Beverly Hills, CA: Sage Publications.

Clarke, R. (1998). Defining police strategies: Problem solving, problem-oriented policing and community-oriented policing. In T. O'Connor Shelley, & A. C. Grant (eds.), *Problem-Oriented Policing: Crime-Specific Problems, Critical Issues, and Making POP Work*. Washington, DC: Police Executive Research Forum.

Cordner, G. (1988). A problem-oriented approach to community-oriented policing. In J. Greene, & S. Mastrofski (eds.), *Community Policing: Rhetoric or Reality?* New York: Praeger.

Cullen, F., & Gendreau, P. (2000). Assessing correctional rehabilitation: Policy, practice, and rospects. In J. Horney (ed.), *Policies, Processes, and Decisions of the Criminal Justice System: Criminal Justice 3*. Washington, DC: US Department of Justice, National Institute of Justice.

Davies, H. T. O., Nutley, S., & Smith, P. (2000). *What Works: Evidence-Based Policy and Practice in Public Services*. London: Policy Press.

Eck, J. E. (1983). *Solving Crime: A Study of the Investigation of Burglary and Robbery*. Washington, DC: Police Executive Research Forum.

Eck, J. E. (2000). Problem-oriented policing and its problems: The means over ends syndrome strikes back and the return of the problem-solver. Unpublished manuscript. Cincinnati, OH: University of Cincinnati.

Evans, W. N., & Owens, E. G. (2007). COPS and crime. *Journal of Public Economics*, *91*, 181–201.

Goldstein, H. (1979). Improving policing: A problem oriented approach. *Crime and Delinquency*, 24, 236–258.

Goldstein, H. (1987). Toward community-oriented policing: potential, basic requirements, and threshold questions. *Crime and Delinquency*, 25, 236–258.

Gottfredson, M., & Hirschi, T. (1990). *A General Theory of Crime*. Palo Alto, CA: Stanford University Press.

Greene, J., & Mastrofski, S. (eds.) (1988). *Community Policing: Rhetoric or Reality?* New York: Praeger.

Greenwood, P. W., Chaiken, J., Petersilia, M., & Prusoff, L. (1975). *Criminal Investigation Process, III: Observations and Analysis*. Santa Monica, CA: Rand Corporation.

Greenwood, P. W., Petersilia, J., & Chaiken, J. (1977). *The Criminal Investigation Process*. Lexington, MA: D.C. Heath.

Kansas City Police Department. (1977). *Response Time Analysis*. Kansas City, MO: Kansas City Police Department.

Kelling, G. L., & Coles, C. M. (1996). *Fixing Broken Windows: Restoring Order and Reducing Crime in Our Communities*. New York: The Free Press.

Kelling, G. L., & Moore, M. H. (1988). From political to reform to community: The evolving strategy of police. In J. R. Greene, & S. D. Mastrofski (eds.), *Community Policing: Rhetoric or Reality?* New York: Praeger.

Kelling, G. L., Pate, A., Dieckman, D., & Brown, C. E. (1974). *The Kansas City Preventive Patrol Experiment: Technical Report*. Washington, DC: Police Foundation.

Kelling, G. L., Pate, A., Ferrera, A., Utne, M., & Brown, C. E. (1981). *Newark Foot Patrol Experiment*. Washington, DC: The Police Foundation.

Kennedy, D., Piehl, A., & Braga, A. (1996). Youth violence in Boston: Gun markets, serious offenders, and a use-reduction strategy. *Law and Contemporary Problems, 59,* 147–196.

Kerner Commission. (1968). *National Advisory Commission on Civil Disorder*. Washington, DC: US Government Printing Office.

Klinger, D. A. (2003). Spreading diffusion in criminology. *Criminology and Public Policy, 2,* 461–468.

Klockars, C. B. (1988). The rhetoric of community policing. In J. R. Greene, & S. D. Mastrofski (eds.), *Community Policing: Rhetoric or Reality* (pp. 239–258). New York: Praeger.

LaFree, G. (1998). *Losing Legitimacy: Street Crime and the Decline of Social Institutions in America*. Boulder, CO: Westview Press.

Larson, R. C., & Cahn, M. F. (1985). *Synthesizing and Extending the Results of Police Patrols*. Washington, DC: US Government Printing Office.

Lee, Y., Eck, J. E., & Corsaro, N. (2016). Conclusions from the history of research into the effects of police force size on crime – 1968 through 2013: A Historical Systematic Review. *Journal of Experimental Criminology, 12,* 431–451.

Levine, J. P. (1975). Ineffectiveness of adding police to prevent crime. *Public Policy, 23,* 523–545.

Lum, C., & Koper, C. S. (2017). *Evidence-Based Policing: Translating Research into Practice*. Oxford, UK: Oxford University Press.

Lum, C., Koper, C. S., Willis, J., Happeny, S., Vovak, H., & Nichols, J. (2016). *The Rapid Diffusion of License Plate Readers in US Law Enforcement Agencies*. Fairfax, VA: Center for Evidence-Based Crime Policy, George Mason University.

Machin, S., & Olivier, M. (2011). Crime and police resources: The street crime initiative. *Journal of the European Economic Association, 9,* 678–701.

MacKenzie, D. (2000). Evidence-based corrections: Identifying what works. *Crime and Delinquency, 46,* 457–471.

Mann, K. (1992). Punitive civil sanctions: The middleground between criminal and civil law. *Yale Law Journal, 101,* 1795–1873.

Mazerolle, L. G., & Ransley, J. (2006). *Third-Party Policing*. Cambridge: Cambridge University Press.

Millenson, M. L. (1997). *Demanding Medical Excellence: Doctors and Accountability in the Information Age*. Chicago: University of Chicago Press.

Minneapolis Medical Research Foundation, Inc. (1976). Critiques and commentaries on Evaluation Research Activities – Russell Sage Reports. *Evaluation, 3,* 115–138.

Murphy, P. V. (1974). Foreword. In G. L. Kelling, T. Pate, D. Dieckman, & C. E. Brown, *The Kansas City Preventive Patrol Experiment: Technical Report*. Washington, DC: Police Foundation.

Neyroud, P., & Weisburd, D. (2014). Transforming the police through science: The challenge of ownership. *Policing*, 8(4), 287–293.

Nutley, S., & Davies, H. T. O. (1999). The fall and rise of evidence in criminal justice. *Public Money and Management*, 19, 47–54.

Ostrom, E., Whitaker, G., & Parks, R. (1978). Policing: Is there a system? In J. May, & A. Wildavsky (eds.), *The Policy Cycle*. New York: Russell Sage Foundation.

Parsons, W. (2002). From muddling through to muddling up: Evidence based policy making and the modernisation of British Government. *Public Policy and administration*, 17, 43–60.

Pierce, G., Spaar, S., & Briggs, L. R. (1986). *The Character of Police Work: Strategic and Tactical Implications*. Boston: Center for Applied Social Research, Northeastern University.

President's Commission on Law Enforcement and Administration of Justice. (1967). *The Crime Commission Report: The Challenge of Crime in a Free Society*. Washington, DC: US Government Printing Office.

President's Task Force on 21st Century Policing. (2015). *Final Report of the President's Task Force on 21st Century Policing*. Washington, DC: Office of Community Oriented Policing Services.

Press, S. J. (1971). *Some Effects of an Increase in Police Manpower in the 20th Precinct of New York City*. New York: New York City Rand Institute.

Reiss, A. J., Jr., & Roth, J. A. (eds.) (1993). *Understanding and Preventing Violence: Panel on the Understanding and Control of Violent Behavior*. Washington, DC: National Academies Press.

Rogers, E. M. (1995). *Diffusion of Innovations* (4th ed.). New York: Free Press.

Schnelle, J. F., Kirchner, R. E., Jr., Casey, J. D., Uselton, P. H., Jr., & McNees, M. P. (1977). Patrol evaluation research: A multiple-baseline analysis of saturation police patrolling during day and night hours. *Journal of Applied Behavior Analysis*, 10, 33–40.

Sherman, L. W. (1987). *Repeat calls to the police in Minneapolis*. Washington, DC: CrimeControl Institute.

Sherman, L. W. (1998). *Evidence-Based Policing. Ideas in American Policing Series*. Washington, DC: The Police Foundation.

Sherman, L. W., & Weisburd, D. (1995). General deterrent effects of police patrol in crime "hot-spots": A randomized controlled trial. *Justice Quarterly*, 12, 626–648.

Sherman, L. W., Gartin, P. R., & Buerger, M. E. (1989). Hot spots of predatory crime: Routine activities and the criminology of place. *Criminology*, 27, 27–56.

Sherman, L. W., Farrington, D., Welsh, B., & MacKenzie, D. (eds.) (2002). *Evidence Based Crime Prevention*. New York: Routledge.

Skogan, W. G. (2004). Impediments to community policing. In L. Fridell, & M. A. Wycoff (eds.), *Community Policing: The Past, Present and Future*. Washington, DC: Police Executive Research Forum.

Skogan, W. G., & Antunes, G. E. (1979). Information, apprehension, and deterrence: Exploring the limits of police productivity. *Journal of Criminal Justice*, 7, 217–241.

Skogan, W., & Frydl, K. 2004. *Fairness and Effectiveness in Policing: The Evidence*. Washington, DC: National Research Council.

Skolnick, J. H., & Bayley, D. H. (1986). *The New Blue Line: Police Innovation in Six American Cities*. New York: The Free Press.

Spelman, W., & Brown, D. K. (1984). *Calling the Police: Citizen Reporting of Serious Crime*. Washington: US Government Printing Office.

Struyk, R. J., & Bendick, M., Jr. (eds.) (1981). *Housing Vouchers for the Poor: Lessons from a National Experiment*. Washington, DC: The Urban Institute Press.

Telep, C. W., & Winegar, S. (2015). Police executive receptivity to research: A survey of chiefs and sheriffs in Oregon. *Policing: A Journal of Policy and Practice*, 10, 241–249.

Telep, C. W., Garner, J. H., & Visher, C. A. (2015). The production of criminological experiments revisited: The nature and extent of federal support for experimental designs, 2001–2013. *Journal of Experimental Criminology*, 11, 541–563.

Trojanowicz, R. (1982). *An Evaluation of the Neighborhood Foot Patrol Program in Flint, Michigan*. East Lansing: National Neighborhood Foot Patrol Center, Michigan State University.

Trojanowicz, R. (1989). *Preventing Civil Disturbances: A Community Policing Approach*. East Lansing: Michigan State University, National Center for Community Policing.

Tyler, T. R., Goff, P. A., & MacCoun, R. J. (2015). The impact of psychological science on policing in the United States: Procedural justice, legitimacy, and effective law enforcement. *Psychological Science in the Public Interest*, 16, 75–109.

Victora, C. G., Habicht, J. P., & Bryce, J. (2004). Evidence-based public health: moving beyond randomized trials. *American Journal of Public Health*, 94, 400–405.

Weisburd, D., & Eck, J. E. (2004). What can police do to reduce crime, disorder, and fear? *Annals of the American Academy of Political and Social Science*, 593, 42–65.

Weisburd, D., & Neyroud, P. (2011). *Police Science: Towards a New Paradigm*. Washington, DC: National Institute of Justice.

Weisburd, D., & Majmundar M. (eds.). (2018). *Proactive Policing: Effects on Crime and Communities*. Committee on Proactive Policing: Effects on Crime, Communities, and Civil Liberties. Washington, DC: The National Academies Press.

Weisburd, D., Maher, L., & Sherman, L. W. (1992). Contrasting crime general and crime specific theory: The case of hot-spots of crime. *Advances in Criminological Theory*, 4, 45–70.

Weisburd, D., Mastrofski, S. D., McNally, A. M., Greenspan, R., & Willis, J. J. (2003). Reforming to preserve: Compstat and strategic problem solving in American policing. *Criminology and Public Policy*, 2, 421–456.

Weisburd, D., & McElroy, J. E. (1988). Enacting the CPO (Community Patrol Officer) role: Findings from the New York City pilot program in community policing. In J. R. Greene, & S. D. Mastrofski (eds.), *Community Policing: Rhetoric or Reality?* New York: Praeger.

Weiss, A. (1997). The communication of innovation in American policing. *Policing*, 20, 292–310.

Wilson, J. Q. (1968). *Varieties of Police Behavior: The Management of Law and Order in Eight Communities*. Cambridge, MA: Harvard University Press.

Wilson, J. Q., & Kelling, G. L. (1982). Broken windows: The police and neighborhood safety. The Atlantic Monthly, March, 29–38.

Zuger, A. (1997). New way of doctoring: By the book. The New York Times. December 16.

PART I

COMMUNITY POLICING

I

Advocate

Community Policing

Wesley G. Skogan

The concept of community policing is very popular with politicians and the general public – so popular that few police chiefs want to be caught without some program they can call community policing. As early as 1997, a survey of police departments conducted by the Police Foundation found that 85 percent reported they had adopted community policing or were in the process of doing so (Skogan, 2005). The biggest reason they gave for not doing so was that community policing was "impractical" for their community. In my own tabulations of the data, this reply was mostly from small departments with only a few officers. Bigger cities included in the survey (those with populations greater than 100,000) all claimed to have adopted community policing – half (they recalled) by 1991 and the other half between 1992 and 1997. The most recent similar figures come from a national survey of departments conducted in 2013. In my tabulations, about 95 percent of the departments in cities of more than 250,000 in population that had an official mission statement included a commitment to community policing (Bureau of Justice Statistics, 2015).

What do cities that claim they are "doing community policing" actually do? They describe a long list of projects. Under the rubric of community policing, officers patrol on foot (in the 1997 survey, 75 percent listed this as a community policing activity), or perhaps on horses, bicycles, or Segways. Departments variously train civilians in citizen police academies, permanently assign officers to small geographical areas, open small neighborhood storefront offices, canvass door-to-door to identify local problems, publish newsletters, conduct drug education projects, and work with municipal agencies to enforce health and safety regulations. The 2013 survey found that two-thirds of larger departments utilized information from community surveys to assess the extent of neighborhood problems and evaluate their own performance (Bureau of Justice Statistics, 2015).

However, community policing is not defined by these kinds of activities. Activities, projects, and programs come and go, and they should as conditions change. Communities with different problems and varied resources to bring to bear against them should try different things. Community policing is not a set of specific programs. Rather, it involves changing decision-making processes and creating new cultures within police departments. It is an organizational *strategy* that leaves setting priorities and the activities that are needed to achieve them largely to residents and the police who serve in their neighborhoods. Community policing is a process rather than a product. Digging beneath the surface, it is defined by three ideas: citizen involvement, problem solving, and decentralization. In practice, these three dimensions turn out to be densely interrelated, and departments that shortchange one or more of them will not be very effective.

This essay sets the stage for a discussion of community policing. It reviews the three core concepts that define community policing, describes how they have been turned into concrete community policing programs, and reports some of what we know about their effectiveness. It draws heavily on my experience evaluating community programs in several cities, as well as on what others have reported. It summarizes some of the claims made for community policing, and some of the realities of achieving them in the real world.

COMMUNITY INVOLVEMENT

Community policing is defined in part by efforts to develop partnerships with community members and civic organizations that represent many of them collectively. It requires that police engage with the public as they set priorities and develop their tactics. Effective community policing requires responsiveness to citizen input concerning both the needs of the community and the best ways by which the police can help meet those needs. It takes seriously the public's definition of its own problems. This is one reason why community policing is an organizational strategy but not a set of specific programs – how it looks in practice *should* vary considerably from place to place, in response to unique local situations and circumstances.

Listening to the community can produce new policing priorities. Officers involved in neighborhood policing quickly learn that residents can be deeply concerned about problems that previously were not high on the police agenda. To a certain extent, they define things differently. The public often focuses on threatening and fear-provoking *conditions* rather than discrete and legally defined *incidents*. They can be more concerned about cars speeding down their residential streets and the physical decay of their community than they are about traditionally defined "serious crimes." They worry about graffiti, public drinking, and the litter and parking problems created by nearby commercial strips. The public sometimes defines their problem as people who need to be taught a lesson. In Chicago, a well-known social type is the "gangbanger," and people want them off the street. The police, however, are trained to recognize and organized to respond to crime incidents, and they have to know what people do, not their popular category. Given these differences, community residents are unsure if they can (or even should) rely on the police to help them deal with these problems. Many of these concerns thus do not generate complaints or calls for service, and, as a result, the police know surprisingly little about them. The routines of traditional police work ensure that officers will largely interact with citizens who are in distress because they have just been victimized, or with suspects and troublemakers. Accordingly, community policing requires that departments develop new channels for learning about neighborhood problems. And when they learn about them, they have to have systems in place to respond effectively (Skogan et al., 1999).

Civic engagement extends to involving the public in some way in efforts to enhance community safety. Community policing promises to strengthen the capacity of communities to fight and prevent crime on their own. The idea that the police and the public are "coproducers" of safety, and that officers cannot claim a monopoly over fighting crime, predates the community policing era. The community crime prevention movement of the 1970s was an important precursor to community policing. It promoted the idea that crime was not solely the responsibility of the police. Now police find that they are expected to lead community efforts. They are being called upon to take responsibility for mobilizing individuals and organizations around crime prevention. These efforts include neighborhood watch, citizen patrols, and education programs stressing household target hardening and the rapid reporting of crime. Residents are asked to assist the police by reporting crimes promptly when they occur and cooperating as witnesses. Community policing often involves increased "transparency" in how departments respond to demands for more information about what they do and how effective they are. A federal survey of police agencies found that by 1999, more than 90 percent of departments serving cities of 50,000 or more were giving residents access to crime statistics or even crime maps (Bureau of Justice Statistics, 2001). Even where efforts to involve the community were already well established, moving them to center stage as part of a larger strategic plan showcases the commitment of the police to community policing.

All of this needs to be supported by new organizational structures and training for police officers. Departments need to reorganize in order to provide opportunities for citizens to come into contact with their officers under circumstances that encourage these exchanges. There has to be a significant amount of informal "face time" between police and residents, so that trust and cooperation can develop between the prospective partners. To this end, many departments hold community meetings and form advisory committees, work out of storefront offices, survey the public, and create informational web sites. During the height of community involvement in Chicago's community policing effort, the city held about 250 small police–public meetings every month. These began in 1995, and, by the end of 2016, residents had shown up on more than one million occasions to attend almost 54,000 community meetings (author's tabulations). In some places, police share information with residents through educational programs or by enrolling them in citizen-police academies that give them in-depth knowledge of law enforcement. By 1999, almost 70 percent of all police departments – and virtually every department serving cities of 50,000 or more – reported regularly holding meetings with citizen groups (Bureau of Justice Statistics, 2001).

What are the presumed benefits of citizen involvement? Community policing aims at rebuilding trust in the community and ensuring support for the police among taxpayers. This is clearly a difficult target. Opinion polls document that Americans have given up thinking that politicians and government adequately represent them. For example, in 1961, almost 80 percent of Americans reported that they "trust the federal government to do what is right just about always, or / most of the time." By 2015, that figure had dropped to 19 percent (Pew Research Center, 2015). Police come off better than most government bodies when Americans are asked how much confidence they have in them; during the 1990s and 2000s, police stood above the President, the Supreme Court and most national institutions. In June 2016, Americans were most confident in the military (73 percent had "a great deal" or "quite a lot" of confidence in them), but police came next, at 56 percent. About one-quarter of Americans had that much confidence in the criminal justice system, and only 9 percent rated members of Congress positively (Gallup, Inc., 2015).

Community policing is especially about recapturing the legitimacy that police have in large measure lost in many of America's minority communities. The same opinion polls show that African Americans and recent immigrants have dramatically less confidence in the police. A 2016 analysis of national trends in opinion found that, while 58 percent of White respondents had a great deal or quite a lot of confidence in police, the comparable figure for African Americans was 29 percent. Blacks were much quicker to report that racial minorities were being treated unfairly by the police, and that police are corrupt (Gallup, Inc., 2016). Likewise, in surveys conducted in Chicago, African Americans and Hispanic immigrants were much more likely to believe that officers are brutal and corrupt (Skogan and Steiner, 2004). These groups are the only growing part of the population in a number of American cities, and civic leaders know that they have to find ways to incorporate them into the system. Police take on community policing in part because they hope that building a reservoir of public support may help them get through bad times when they occur (see the discussion of "nasty misconduct" below). Community policing might help police be more effective. It could encourage witnesses and bystanders to step forward in neighborhoods where they too often do not, for example. More indirectly, it might help rebuild the social and organizational fabric of neighborhoods that previously had been given up for lost, enabling residents to contribute to maintaining order in their community (Sampson, Raudenbush & Earls, 1997).

An important spin-off of civic engagement is that the adoption of community policing almost inevitably leads to an expansion of the police mandate, and this further expands the list of points on which it should be evaluated. Controlling serious crime by enforcing the criminal law remains the primary job of the police. But instead of seeing the police exclusively in these terms, and viewing activities that depart from direct efforts to deter crime as a distraction from their fundamental mission, advocates of community policing argue that the police have additional functions to perform, and different ways to conduct their traditional business. As a practical matter, when police meet with neighborhood residents in park buildings and church basements to discuss neighborhood problems, the civilians present are going to bring up all manner of problems. If the police who are present put them off, or have no way of responding to their concerns, they will not come back next month. Community policing takes seriously the public's definition of its own problems, and this inevitably includes issues that lie outside the traditional competence of the police. Officers can learn at a public meeting that loose garbage and rats in an alley are big issues for residents, but some other agency is going to have to deliver the solution to that problem. When police meet with residents in Chicago, much of the discussion focuses on neighborhood dilapidation (including problems with abandoned buildings and graffiti) and on public drinking, teen loitering, curfew and truancy problems, and disorder in schools. There is much more talk about parking and traffic than about personal and property crime, although discussion of drug-related issues comes up quite often (Skogan, 2006). The broad range of issues that concern the public requires, in turn, that police form partnerships with other public and private agencies that can join them in responding to residents' priorities. They could include the schools and agencies responsible for health, housing, trash pickup, car tows, and graffiti cleanups.

In practice, community involvement is not easy to achieve. Ironically, it can be difficult to sustain in areas that need it the most. Research on participation in community crime prevention programs during the 1970s and 1980s found that poor and high-crime areas often were not well endowed with an infrastructure of organizations that were ready to get involved, and that turnout for police-sponsored events was higher in places honeycombed with block clubs and community organizations (Skogan, 1988). In high crime areas, people tend to be suspicious of their neighbors, and especially of their neighbor's children. Fear of retaliation by gangs and drug dealers can undermine public involvement as well (Grinc, 1994). In Chicago, a study of hundreds of community meetings found that residents expressed concern about retaliation for attending or working with the police in 22 percent of the city's beats (Skogan, 2006). In addition, police and residents may not have a history of getting along in poor neighborhoods. Residents are as likely to think of the police as one of their problems as they are to see them as a solution to their problems. It probably will not be the first instinct of organizations representing the interests of poor communities to cooperate with police. Instead, they are more likely to press for an end to police misconduct. They will call for new resources from the outside to address community problems, for organizations rarely blame their own constituents for their plight (Skogan, 1988). There may be no reason for residents of crime-ridden neighborhoods to think that community policing will turn out to be anything but another broken promise; they are accustomed to seeing programs come and go, without much effect (Sadd & Grinc, 1994). They certainly will have to be trained in their new roles. Community policing involves a new set of jargon as well as assumptions about the new responsibilities that both police and citizens are to adopt. The 2000 survey of police departments by the federal government found that "training citizens for community policing" was common in big cities; in cities of more than 500,000, 70 percent reported doing so (Bureau of Justice Statistics, 2013).

In addition, community policing runs the risk of inequitable outcomes. In an evaluation of one of the very first programs, in Houston, Texas, I found that White and middle-class residents received most of the benefits of the program. They found it easy to cooperate with the police, and shared with the police a common view of whom the troublemakers were in the community. Blue-collar African Americans and Latinos remained uninvolved, on the other hand, and after a year they had seen no visible change in their lives (Skogan, 1990). Finally, the investment that police make in community policing is always at risk. Nasty episodes of police misconduct can undermine those efforts. When excessive force or killings by police become a public issue, years of progress in police–community relations can disappear. The same is true when there are of revelations of widespread corruption.

On the police side, there may be resistance in the ranks. Public officials' and community activists' enthusiasm for neighborhood-oriented policing encourages its detractors within the police to dismiss it as "just politics," or another passing civilian fad. Officers who get involved can become known as "empty holster guys," and what they do gets labeled "social work." Police officers prefer to stick to crime fighting. (For a case study in New York City of how this happens, see Pate & Shtull, 1994.) My first survey of Chicago police, conducted before that city's community policing program began, found that two-thirds of them disavowed any interest in addressing "non-crime problems" on their beat. More than 70 percent of the 7,500 police officers surveyed thought community policing "would bring a greater burden on police to solve all community problems," and also "more unreasonable demands on police by community groups" (Skogan & Hartnett, 1997). Police are often skeptical about programs invented by civilians, who they are convinced cannot possibly understand their job. They are particularly hostile to programs that threaten to involve civilians in setting standards or evaluating their performance, and they do not like civilians influencing their operational priorities. Police can easily find ways to justify their aloofness from the community; as one officer told me, "You can't be the friend of the people and do your job."

On the other hand, some studies point to positive changes in officer's views once they become involved in community policing. Lurigio and Rosenbaum

(1994) summarized twelve studies of this, and found many positive findings with respect to job satisfaction, perceptions of improved relations with the community, and expectations about community involvement in problem solving. Skogan and Hartnett (1997) found growing support for community policing among officers involved in Chicago's experimental police districts, in comparison to those who continued to work in districts featuring policing as usual.

PROBLEM SOLVING AND THE COMMUNITY

Community policing also involves a shift from reliance on reactive patrol and investigations toward a problem-solving orientation. In brief (for it is discussed in detail in other chapters of this book), problem-oriented policing is an approach to developing crime reduction strategies. Problem solving involves training officers in methods of identifying and analyzing problems. It highlights the importance of discovering the situations that *produce* calls for police assistance, identifying the causes which lie behind them, and designing tactics to deal with these causes. Problem solving is a counterpoint to the traditional model of police work, which usually entails responding sequentially to individual events as they are phoned in by victims. Too often this style of policing is reduced to driving fast to crime scenes in order to fill out pieces of paper reporting what happened. Problem solving, on the other hand, calls for examining patterns of incidents to reveal their causes and to help plan how to deal with them proactively. Problem-oriented policing also recognizes that the solutions to those patterns may involve other agencies and may be "non-police" in character; in traditional departments, this would be cause for ignoring them. The best programs encourage officers to respond creatively to the problems they encounter, or to refer them appropriately to other agencies (Eck, 2004).

Problem-solving policing can proceed without a commitment to community policing. The latter stresses civic engagement in identifying and prioritizing neighborhood problems; without that input, the former frequently focuses on patterns of traditionally defined crimes that are identified using police data systems. Problem-oriented community policing sometimes involves community members or organizations actually addressing particular issues, not just identifying them, but more often it is conducted by the police and allied city agencies. However, community policing involves neighborhood residents as an end in itself, and, in evaluation terms, it is important to count this as a "process success." The problem with relying on the data that is already in police computers is that when residents are involved they often press for a focus on issues that are not well documented by department information systems, such as graffiti, public drinking, and building abandonment. Effective programs must have systems in place to respond to a broad range of problems, through partnerships with other agencies. The 2013 national survey of agencies found that in cities of more than 250,000 residents, about 70 percent of departments reported they had formed problem-solving partnerships with community groups and local agencies (Bureau of Justice Statistics, 2015).

Is this easy to do? It is at least as hard as involving the community, for bureaucracies are involved, and interagency cooperation can easily fail. For a long list of familiar bureaucratic and political reasons, other city and state agencies usually think that community policing is the police department's program, not theirs. They resist bending their own professional and budget-constrained priorities to accommodate police officers who call on them for help. Making this kind of inter-organizational cooperation work turns out to be one of the most difficult problems facing innovative departments. When the chief of an East Coast city was new, he told me that he could handle things in his department; his biggest fear was that his mayor might not handle the city's other agencies, and that they would not provide the kind of support that community policing requires. If community policing is the police department's program, it may fail. Community policing must be the city's program.

It is also hard to involve police officers in problem solving. Cordner and Biebel (2003) did an in-depth study of problem-solving practice in a major American city. Although the department had been deeply committed to problem solving for more than fifteen years, they found that street officers typically defined problems very narrowly (e.g., one address, or one suspected repeat offender); their analysis of it consisted of making personal observations from their car; they crafted solutions from their own experience; and two-thirds of the time their proposed solution did not go past arresting someone. The study concluded that, after fifteen years of practice, this department's glass was only half full. What observers would classify as "full scale" problem solving was rarely encountered. Even the advocates of problem solving (you will hear from them in later chapters) admit that it requires a great deal of training, close supervision, and relentless follow-up evaluation to make it work. However, one important organizational function that often gets shortchanged is training. Training is expensive and officers have to be removed from the line – or paid overtime – to attend. And few departments are adequately staffed with supervisors who themselves were full-fledged problem solvers (Eck, 2004).

Community policing has also revived interest in systematically addressing the task of crime prevention. In the traditional model of policing, crime prevention was deterrence based. To threaten arrest, police patrol the streets looking for crimes (engaging in random and directed patrol), they respond quickly to emergency crime calls from witnesses and victims, and detectives then take over the task of locating offenders. Concerned residents, on the other hand, do not want the crime that drives these efforts to happen in the first place. Their instinct is to press for true prevention. Police-sponsored prevention projects are in place throughout the country. Problem solving has brought crime prevention theories to the table, leading police to tackle the routine activities of victims and the crucial roles played by "place managers" such as landlords or shopkeepers, and not just offenders (Eck & Wartell, 1998; Braga et al., 1999). When community policing came to Chicago, one of the first actions of a new district commander was to convince a bank to open an ATM machine in his police station, so residents had a safe place to go to transact business. An emphasis on "target hardening" has gotten police involved in conducting home security surveys and teaching self-defense classes. But when communities talk about prevention, they mostly talk about their children, and ways of intervening earlier with youths who seem on a trajectory toward serious offending. Much of the of work preventing the development of criminal careers lies with agencies besides the police, including family courts, children's protection agencies, parents, peer networks, and schools. To their efforts, the police add involvement in athletic and after school programs, DARE presentations in schools, special efforts to reduce violence in families, and initiatives that focus attention on the recruitment of youths into gangs.

DECENTRALIZATION

Decentralization is an organizational strategy that is closely linked to the implementation of community policing. Decentralization can be pursued at two levels. Typically, more responsibility for identifying and responding to chronic crime and disorder problems is to be delegated to mid-level commanders in charge of the geographical districts or precincts that make up a city. Departments have had to experiment with how to structure and manage a decentralization plan that gives mid-level managers real responsibility, and how to hold them accountable for measures of their success. Here, community policing intersects with another movement in policing (and the subject of another pair of chapters in this book), the emergence of a culture of systematic performance measurement and managerial accountability.

The idea is to devolve authority and responsibility further down the organizational hierarchy. Departments need to do this in order to encourage the development of local solutions to locally defined problems, and to facilitate decision-making that responds rapidly to local conditions. There may be moves to flatten the structure of the organization by compressing the rank structure, and to shed layers of bureaucracy within the police organization to speed communication and decision-making. In Chicago, most of the department's elite units – including detectives, narcotics investigators, special tactical teams, and even the organized crime unit – were required to share information and more closely coordinate their work with the geographical districts. The department's management accountability process called them on the carpet when they failed to serve as "support units" for uniformed patrol officers (Skogan, 2006). To flatten the organization, Chicago abolished the civil service position of captain, leaving the department with just three permanent ranks (Skogan & Hartnett, 1997).

At the same time, more responsibility for identifying and responding to community problems may be delegated to individual patrol officers and their sergeants, who are in turn encouraged to take the initiative in finding ways to deal with a broad range of problems specific to the communities they serve. Structurally, community policing leads departments to assign officers to fixed geographical areas, and to keep them there during the course of their day. This is known as adopting a "turf orientation." Decentralization is intended to encourage communication between officers and neighborhood residents, and to build an awareness of local problems among working officers. They are expected to work more autonomously at investigating situations, resolving problems, and educating the public. They are being asked to discover and set their own goals, and sometimes to manage their work schedule. This is also the level at which collaborative projects involving both police and residents can emerge. In 2013, a national survey of police departments found that assigning officers geographically was virtually the norm in cities over 250,000 (Bureau of Justice Statistics, 2015).

This pattern of dual decentralization is adopted not only so that police can become more proactive and more preventive, but also so that they can respond efficiently to problems of different magnitude and complexity. Under the professional model, marching orders for the police traditionally come from two sources: 911 calls from the public concerning individual problems, and initiatives or programs originating at police headquarters or even City Hall. Every experienced officer can tell stories of the crazy things officers sometimes have to do because "downtown" announced a citywide initiative that was irrelevant for their district. A Chicago commander once described to me how he was punished (he lost a day's pay) because – as a district commander – he assigned two officers to identifying abandoned cars and getting them towed, rather than the maximum of one officer that the rule book mandated. He used this story to good effect whenever officers complained in a meeting that the department was getting away from its traditional practices because of community policing.

Decentralization, paired with a commitment to consultation and engagement with local communities, also allows the police to respond to local problems that are important to particular communities. Police were not organized to respond to the organized groups and community institutions that make up "civil society." Now surveys of departments indicate that, as part of a community policing initiative, virtually all larger departments now consult local advisory boards representing specific communities.

Is decentralization easy to pull off? It is at least as hard as problem solving, and politically risky to boot. For all of the adoption of specific programs, researchers who track trends in police organization are skeptical that there has been much fundamental "flattening" of police hierarchies – which is, after all, about their jobs (Maguire et al., 2003; Greene, 2004). Resistance to reform does not just come from the bottom of the organization. Junior executives at police headquarters may resist having authority taken from them and pushed to lower levels in the organization. Managers at this level are in a position to act as a filter between the chief and operational units, censoring the flow of decisions and information up and down the command hierarchy (for a case study of how this can undermine community policing initiatives, see Capowich, 2005). This is one reason why special community policing units are often run from the chief's office, or housed in a special new bureau; this enables the department to get neighborhood officers on the street while bypassing the barons who dominate key positions at headquarters. Too often they are command- and control-oriented and feel most comfortable when everything is done by the book. Discussions of community policing often feature management buzz words like "empowerment" and "trust," and this makes them nervous because they also worry about inefficiency and corruption.

And, of course, these concerns are real. One of the dilemmas of community policing is that calling for more operational and street-level discretion runs counter to another trend in policing, which is to tighten the management screws and create an increasingly rule-bound corner in order to control police corruption and violence. Police do misuse their discretion, and they do take bribes. Ironically, however, *many* of the recent innovations discussed in this book go the other way; they recognize, widen, and celebrate the operational independence of individual officers. Community policing recognizes that problems vary tremendously from place to place, and that their causes and solutions are highly contextual. We expect police to use "good judgment" rather than somehow enforce "the letter of the law." Community policing stresses that workers at the very bottom of the organization are closest to the customer, and are to use their best judgment about how to serve the neighborhoods where they are assigned. It calls for the bottom-up definition of problems. Decentralizing, reducing hierarchy, granting officers more independence, and trusting in their professionalism are the organizational reforms of choice today, not tightening things up to constrain officer discretion.

Decentralization almost certainly puts new responsibilities on the shoulders of front-line supervisors, the sergeants, and others who watch over the daily activities of working officers. Traditionally, their role was to watch for infractions of the rule book. However, translating organizational policy into practice has become more complex than that. The chapters in this book provide an inventory of the many, and more complicated, things society is asking officers to do, and in this environment their immediate supervisors need to become teachers, coaches and mentors, as well as disciplinarians. Examining one of the first experiments with community policing, Weisburd, McElroy, and Hardyman (1988) observed that successful sergeants had to develop work plans, prioritize problems and encourage their officers to take the initiative, and then assess their successes and failures in light of the diverse and very particular problems facing the beats in which they worked. Recognizing this, when Chicago launched its community policing initiative, they paid special attention to sergeants. Sergeants received more training than anyone else in the organization, in order to backstop their teaching and coaching capabilities.

Beat officers working around the clock were assigned the same sergeant, whose tasks including building their team spirit, encouraging cross-shift communication among them, staffing monthly beat community meetings, and seeing to it that the formal plan they were to develop for their beat was put in motion (Skogan & Hartnett, 1997).

It may be difficult to pull off decentralization to the turf level because it takes too many people. Community policing is labor intensive, and may require more officers. Police managers and city leaders will have to find the officers required to staff the program. Finding the money to hire more officers to staff community policing assignments is hard, so departments may try to downsize existing projects. This can bring conflict with powerful unit commanders and allied politicians who support current arrangements. Research on changes in police organizational structure did find that their "spatial differentiation" increased during the 1990s, with the spread of storefront offices and the creation of more and smaller district stations (Maguire et al., 2003), but there was a price to be paid for this. Police departments also face "the 911 problem." Their commitment to respond to 911 calls as quickly as possible dominates how resources are deployed in every department. Community policing has encountered heavy political resistance when the perception arose (encouraged, to be sure, by its opponents) that resources previously devoted to responding to emergency calls were being diverted to this "social experiment."

Decentralization is also difficult to manage because evaluation of the effectiveness of many community policing initiatives is difficult. The management environment in policing today stresses "accountability for results" (Willis, Mastrofski & Kochel, 2010). In this model, units are not rewarded for their activities, however well meaning, but for declining crime. However, the public often wants action on things that department information systems do not account for at all. In decentralized departments, residents of different neighborhoods make different demands on police operations. They value the time officers spend meeting with them, and they like to see officers on foot rather than driving past on the way to a crime scene. Agencies committed to both community policing and CompStat-style accountability assessment seem to have to run their associated operations independently, so contrary are their managerial demands (Willis, Mastrofski & Kochel, 2010). As a result, both individual and unit performance is harder to assess in community policing departments (see also Mastrofski, 1998).

CAN IT WORK?

Because many different projects and activities take place under this conceptual umbrella, it has long been difficult to come to an overall assessment regarding whether or not community policing works. A further complexity has been that community policing aims at affecting different and more diverse outcomes than those that are targeted by routine proactive policing projects. Often these targets are not to be found in standard policing databases, increasing the complexity and expense of conducting studies of community policing effectiveness. The long-term character of many of the concerns addressed by community policing, and the patience that they require in dealing with them, provide additional challenges, as few studies have tracked community policing for longer than a year or so. Studies of the effectiveness of its major features across a broad range of outcomes took some time to accumulate.

The best evidence available on the impact of community policing was systematically reviewed in a report appearing in 2014 (Gill et al., 2014). It came to mixed conclusions. Across the evaluations that could be identified for analyses there was little sign that conventional measures of crime were much impacted by the effort, including in the subset of interventions that included a specific problem-solving component. Fear of crime showed mixed results depending on how it was measured, but overall was not greatly affected. However, survey measures of the extent of social and physical disorder – neighborhood problems that frequently go unrecognized without community input – were positively affected by community-oriented interventions. A 2017 review by a panel of the National Research Council concurred with this, noting that the highly variable set of activities undertaken as part of community policing initiatives can make it difficult to generalize about its possible effects on crime (Weisburd & Majmundar, 2018).

That said, I do not know of a single police department that adopted community policing because they thought that it was a *direct* route to getting the crime rate down. In any event, crime has dropped dramatically across the United States, while police continue to face a legitimacy crisis of major proportions. In addition to crime, efforts to evaluate it need to focus as well on the important community and governance processes that it is intended to set in motion, because they represent potentially important "wins" on their own. The extent of the public's trust and confidence in police is an obvious first issue. Here the reviewers found more evidence that community policing could make a difference. Satisfaction with the police went up significantly in three-quarters of the neighborhoods where it was tested. Measures of the legitimacy of the police improved in six of the ten studies in which it was assessed. The report concluded that community policing had clear effects on quality-of-life and "citizen-focused" outcomes that research suggests could have longer-term effects on crime through their community-building effects, if they could be tracked over time (Gill et al., 2014). The report did not consider possible racial and ethnic differences in outcome patterns, despite the fact that this is among the most significant policing issues of our time. For example, my own long-term evaluation of ten years of citywide community policing in Chicago found that resident's views of their police improved over time, in the end by 10–15 percentage points on measures of their effectiveness, responsiveness, and demeanor. Importantly, Hispanics, African Americans, and Whites all shared these improved views (Skogan, 2006).

Evaluators also should look into the "mobilizing" effects of programs, including the extent of parallel community self-help efforts and extending even to the possible development of organizational and leadership capabilities among newly activated residents. Most observers would agree that community factors are among the most important determinants of safety, not the vigor of police enforcement activities, and that is an important rationale for a community-building approach. Sociological research indicates that "collective efficacy" (a combination of trust among neighborhood residents and the expectation that neighbors will intervene when things go wrong) plays an important role in inhibiting urban crime. However, the same work indicates that it is mostly White, home-owning neighborhoods that currently have it, and researchers have yet to document how neighborhoods that do not have collective efficacy can generate it for themselves (Skogan, 2012). Many probably need help, and that is where community policing could step in. The 2017 National Research Council report – which found only mixed evidence, but not much of it – described how this *might* work:

Many expect that community-oriented policing should bring police and citizens closer together in common cause and should strengthen communication among various community groups as well as between police and public. It should invest residents with the necessary skills, resources, and sense of empowerment to mobilize against neighborhood problems. (Weisburd & Majmundar, 2018, 6–7)

Some survey studies, but not all, find a link between positive views or experiences with police and perceptions of stronger community responses to crime, but the jury is still out on the causal link between the two (Kochel, 2017). Certainly the community-building spirit of community policing, and its accomplishments in involving residents in anti-crime activites, point in this direction, and this should be an important focus of evaluation in this area. That it is actually focused on community building is another reason why evaluation studies need to be long term, able to assess the underlying logic of community policing: that focused police and city efforts can help revitalize community processes like collective efficacy. However, none of the comparisons of program and control areas considered in the most systematic review of community policing research looked at the effect of programs over a period longer than one year.

PROSPECTS

One unanswered question is whether community policing can survive the dual blows of plummeting federal financial support, plus the effects of the fiscal crises that engulfed many cities and their pension funds. Under the 1994 Violent Crime and Law Enforcement Act, the federal government spent billions of dollars to support community policing. Federal agencies sponsored demonstration projects designed to spur innovation and promote the effectiveness of community policing, and they promoted it heavily through national conferences and publication. The Act specified that one of the roles of these new officers should be "to foster problem solving and interaction with communities by police officers," and it also funded the creation of regional community policing centers around the country. But even where commitment to community policing is strong, maintaining an effective program can be difficult in the face of competing demands for scarce resources (Office of Community Oriented Policing Services, 2011). Critics call for returning to the "core functions" of policing, and even supporters of community policing have acquiesced to cutbacks in neighborhood units and closed storefront offices. Training appears to be continuing, at least selectively. In 2013, all or almost all new recruits in cities over 250,000 in population were receiving community policing training, but in-service retraining of experienced officers was much less frequent (Bureau of Justice Statistics, 2015).

Another issue is whether community policing can continue to survive CompStat. As I noted earlier, many of its features push in the opposition direction. To a significant extent, in the current management environment, what gets measured is what matters. The accountability process is about harnessing hierarchy to achieve top management's objectives, which are in turn driven by the data they have at hand, and those data usually say little about community priorities. Police researchers attribute many of the problems of contemporary policing to the mismatch between the formal hierarchical structure of police organizations and the true nature of their work, which is extremely decentralized, not amenable to "cookie cutter" solutions to problems, dependent on the skills and motivation of the individual officers handling it, and mostly driven externally by 911 calls rather than management strategies. Perhaps the accountability process has ridden to the rescue of the traditional hierarchical structure, trying again to impose that hierarchy on work that does not fit its demands.

The two certainly collide. James Willis and colleagues (2010) explored how community policing and CompStat might manage to coexist. They found that, at best, agencies attempting to deploy both essentially ran them in separate worlds. They concluded,

By operating them as systems mostly buffered from each other, the departments avoided having to confront in highly visible ways the dilemmas that would inevitably arise where the doctrines of the two reforms were at odds ... In contrast, a more integrated CompStat/community policing model would require much more radical changes to existing organizational routines, and such changes may have greater costs and risks and meet with considerable resistance from threatened parties. (Willis et al., 2010: 978)

Faced with this pressure, there is a risk that the focus of departments will shift away from community policing, back to the activities that better fit recentralizing management structures.

There are additional counter trends. One is renewed pressure from the federal government to involve local police extensively in enforcing immigration laws. This is often stoutly resisted by chiefs of police, who claim that it would be a great setback to their community involvement and trust-building projects with the burgeoning immigrant populations of many cities. We shall see if they can continue to resist (Skogan, 2009). Community policing also competes for attention, resources, and political interest with a number of "wars." These include the war on drugs, the global war on terror ("GWAT"), and zero-tolerance misdemeanor enforcement being pursued in the misguided belief that this is somehow broken windows policing (for more on broken windows, see the next section of this book). Most recently, stop and frisk has become the crime-prevention strategy of choice in American policing (see Chapter 9 and 10 of this book). The threats this policy poses for effective community policing include the high volume of unwarranted stops that generates, the extreme concentration of stops in minority communities, and the focused impact of these on the legitimacy of policing, and perhaps of the state. And the contrary effects all of these pale in significance in comparison to that of officer pushback against this and related reforms. When community policing, procedural justice initiatives, and other community-facing strategies come into conflict with police politics and culture, the latter threaten (in the words of President Obama's police reform commission) to "eat policy for lunch" (President's Task Force on 21st Century Policing, 2015: 11).

In summary, reform is difficult, and fragile. It is important to note that reports from cities that have – reluctantly, they say – cut back on their community policing units usually claim that they will continue doing it anyway, because it has become part of their agency's regular way of doing business. This signals that they see it as one of their significant claims on legitimacy. It is also entrenched in many places. Compared to many innovations considered in this book, community policing is a relatively old idea, but it is one that has legs. Community-oriented policing has taken off across the world, reshaping public service in many nations. In the end, it will be politics, in the form of broad grassroots support for community policing and elite concern regarding the continuing legitimacy crisis that threatens the stability of polity, that will rescue it.

REFERENCES

Braga, A. A., Weisburd, D. L., Waring, E. J., Mazerolle, L. G., Spelman, W., & Gajewski, F. (1999). Problem-oriented policing in violent crime places: A randomized controlled experiment. *Criminology*, 37, 541–580.
Bureau of Justice Statistics. (2001). *Community Policing in Local Police Departments 1997 and 1999*. Washington, DC: Bureau of Justice Statistics, US Department of Justice.

Bureau of Justice Statistics. (2015). *Local Police Departments, 2013: Personnel, Policies and Practices*. Washington, DC: Bureau of Justice Statistics, US Department of Justice.

Cordner, G., & Biebel, E. (2003). Research for practice: Problem-oriented policing in practice. National Institute of Justice, unpublished research report.

Capowich, G. E. (2005). A case study of community policing implementation: Contrasting success and failure. In K. R. Kerley (ed.), *Policing and Program Evaluation*, pp. 138–153. Upper Saddle River, NJ: Prentice Hall.

Eck, J. E. (2004). Why don't problems get solved? In W. G. Skogan (ed.), *Community Policing: Can It Work?* pp. 185–206. Belmont, CA: Wadsworth.

Eck, J. E., & Wartell, J. (1998). Improving the management of rental properties with drug problems: A randomized experiment. In L. G. Mazerolle, & J. Roehl (eds.), *Civil Remedies and Crime Prevention*, vol. 9, Crime Prevention Studies. pp. 161–185. Monsey, NY: Criminal Justice Press.

Gallup, Inc. (2015). *Americans' Confidence in Institutions Stays Low*. Washington, DC.

Gallup, Inc. (2016). *Public Opinion Context: Americans, Race and Police*. Washington, DC.

Gill, C., Weisburd, D., Telep, C. W., Vitter, Z., & Bennett, T. (2014). Community-oriented policing to reduce crime, disorder and fear and increase satisfaction and legitimacy among citizens: a systematic review. *Journal of Experimental Criminology*, 10, 399–428.

Greene, J. R. (2004). Community policing and police organization. In W. G. Skogan (ed.), *Community Policing: Can It Work?* Belmont, CA: Wadsworth, 30–54.

Grinc, R. M. (1994). 'Angles in marble': Problems in stimulating community involvement in community policing. *Crime & Delinquency*, 40, 437–468.

Kochel, T. R. (2017). Applying police legitimacy, cooperation, and collective security hypotheses to explain collective efficacy and violence across neighbourhoods. *International Journal of Comparative and Applied Criminal Justice*, 1–20.

Lurigio, A., & Rosenbaum, D. (1994). The impact of community policing on police personnel. In D. P. Rosenbaum (ed.), *The Challenge of Community Policing: Testing the Promises*, pp. 147–163. Thousand Oaks, CA: Sage Publications.

Maguire, E. R., Shin, Y., Jhao, J., & Hassel, K. D. (2003). Structural change in large police agencies during the 1990s. *Policing: An International Journal of Police Strategies and Management*, 26, 251–275.

Mastrofski, S. D. (1998). Community policing and police organization structure. In J. Brodeur (ed.), *How to Tecognize Good Policing: Problems and Issues*, pp. 161–189. Thousand Oaks, CA: Sage Publications.

Office of Community Oriented Policing Services. (2011). *The Impact of the Economic Downturn on American Police Agencies*. Washington, DC: US Department of Justice.

Pate, A. M., & Shtull, P. (1994). Community policing grows in Brooklyn: An inside view of the New York police department's model precinct. *Crime & Delinquency*, 40, 384–410.

Pew Research Center. (2015). *Beyond Distrust: How Americans View Their Government*. Washington, DC.

President's Task Force on 21st Century Policing. (2015). *Final Report of the President's Task Force on 21st Century Policing*. Washington, DC: Office of Community Oriented Policing Services.

Sadd, S., & Grinc, R. (1994). Innovative neighborhood oriented policing: An evaluation of community policing programs in eight cities. In D. P. Rosenbaum (ed.),

The Challenge of Community Policing: Testing the Promises. pp. 27–52. Thousand Oaks, CA: Sage Publications.

Sampson, R., Raudenbush, S., & Earls, F. (1997). Neighborhoods and violent crime. *Science*, 277, 918–924.

Skogan, W. G. (1988). Community organizations and crime. In M. Tonry, & N. Morris, (eds.), *Crime and Justice: An Annual Review*, pp. 39–78. Chicago: University of Chicago Press.

Skogan, W. G. (1990). *Disorder and Decline: Crime and the Spiral of Decay in American Cities.* New York: The Free Press.

Skogan, W. G. (2005). Community policing: Common impediments to success. In L. Fridell, & M. A. Wycoff (eds.), *Community Policing: The Past, Present and Future*, pp. 159–167. Washington, DC: Police Executive Research Forum.

Skogan, W. G. (2006). *Police and Community in Chicago.* New York: Oxford University Press.

Skogan, W. G. (2009). Policing Immigrant Communities in the United States. In W. F. McDonald (ed.), *Immigration, Crime and Justice*, pp. 189–204. Bingley, UK: Emerald Publishing.

Skogan, W. G. (2012). Collective action, structural disadvantage and crime. *Journal of Police Studies*, 25, 135–152.

Skogan, W. G., & Hartnett, S. M. (1997). *Community policing, Chicago style.* New York: Oxford University Press.

Skogan, W. G. Hartnett, S. M., DuBois, J., Comey, J. T., Kaiser, M., & Lovig, J. H. (1999). *On the Beat: Police and Community Problem Solving.* Boulder, CO: Westview.

Skogan, W. G., & Steiner, L. (2004). Crime, disorder and decay in Chicago's Latino Community. *Journal of Ethnicity in Criminal Justice*, 2, 7–26.

Weisburd, D., McElroy, J., & Hardyman, P. (1988). Challenges to supervision in community policing: Observations on a pilot project. *American Journal of Police*, 7, 29–50.

Weisburd, D., & Majmundar, M. K. (eds). (2018). *Proactive Policing: Effects on Crime and Communities.* Washington, DC: The National Academies Press.

Willis, J. J., Mastrofski, S. D., & Kochel, T. R. (2010). The co-implementation of Compstat and community policing. *Journal of Criminal Justice*, 38, 969–980.

2

Critic

Community Policing: A Skeptical View

Stephen D. Mastrofski

About three decades ago, a few American police leaders caught the wave of community policing reform, and now just about everybody has gone surfing. If recent nationwide polls of police are indicative, many lower-ranking officers are catching the community policing wave (Mastrofski, 2017). Early interest in this reform can be attributed to police anxieties in the 1960s and 70s about skyrocketing crime and urban violence, unmet rising expectations from the civil rights movement, and middle-class alienation from government authority (Fogelson, 1977: ch. 11). Like a "perfect storm" these forces converged, stimulating criticism from blue ribbon commissions and a daily drumbeat of negative press for police. Calls for change were issued, some radical: community control of policing, deprofessionalization, and reassignment of some core police tasks to other government agencies and the private sector. Alarmed and intent on ending this crisis of legitimacy (LaFree, 1998), progressive police and scholars began to explore ways to make American police both more effective and more democratic without losing many of the advances made in policing in the previous half century (Goldstein, 1977; 1990; Trojanowicz & Bucqueroux, 1990; Wilson & Kelling, 1982). The resulting community policing reforms were influenced by fashions in organization development intended to make agencies less bureaucratic, more responsive to the "customer," and more results oriented (Mastrofski, 1998; Mastrofski and Ritti, 2000). Although early twenty-first-century concerns about the threat of terrorism may have dissipated federal financial support for community policing, highly publicized events featuring violence between police and the community have stoked alarm about the state of police–community relations, resulting in a national blue-ribbon commission document that once again advances community policing as a key to American policing that is more effective and legitimate (President's Task Force, 2015: 43): "Recommendation: Community policing should be infused throughout the culture and organizational structure of law enforcement agencies."

Unlike some reforms that narrow their focus over time, community policing has remained multifaceted and diverse. Some departments emphasize "broken-windows," others feature problem-oriented policing, and still others stress policing that establishes stronger police–public partnerships (Mastrofski et al., 1995: 540–541; Cordner, 2014). Much of the reform literature suggests that all of these are desirable and compatible. Whether or not that is so, it is clear that different elements of community policing appeal to different audiences, leading to debates over what community policing really means. In fact, ambiguity and flexibility give community policing its all-things-to-all-people character and has contributed to its political viability, embraced by public leaders across the political spectrum. However, this diversity makes it difficult to conduct a rigorous inquiry into the merits of community policing, a finding noted by the panel on police policies and practices organized by the National Research Council (NRC) to assess, among other things, this reform (Skogan & Frydl, 2004: 232–233). It concluded that community policing was simply too amorphous a concept to submit to empirical evaluation and recommended that researchers evaluate it by breaking it down into more specific components.

The editors of this volume seem to have taken the NRC panel's recommendation. They have organized chapters around a number of specific reforms that have been widely construed as important elements of community policing: problem-oriented policing, broken-windows policing, third-party policing, pulling-levers policing, and procedural justice policing. Therefore, to minimize overlap, as much as possible, I will focus my discussion on those efforts that try to link the police more closely to the community in "partnership" arrangements: joint activities to coproduce services and achieve desired outcomes, giving the community a greater say in what the police do, or simply engaging each other to produce a greater sense of police–community compatibility.

I will fulfill my critic role by offering a skeptical view. The skeptic is a thoughtful doubter, reflecting the methodology, not the conclusion. To the extent that community policing is a good thing, it should withstand the careful scrutiny of thoughtful doubters. Reformers have raised a wide range of expectations about community policing. I will address four of them: (1) What forms has it taken? (2) Has it introduced more democracy into the processes of policing? (3) What has it contributed to the reduction of crime and disorder? (4) Has it increased public satisfaction with and support for the police?

THE FORM OF COMMUNITY POLICING: ORGANIZATION AND PRACTICE

I consider three ways in which the form of community policing may manifest itself: programs and structural features of the organization, the culture or outlook of police officers, and changes in practice at the street level.

Community Policing Programs and Structures

Observers and advocates of community policing have argued that it should not be defined as a series of programs, as police executives are wont, but rather as an "organizational strategy" that may employ a wide range of efforts designed to change decision-making processes involving the police and members of the community (Kelling & Moore, 1988; Skogan, 2006b). There is a growing consensus (promoted by scholars and federal funding agencies) that the core of what distinguishes community policing is citizen involvement, problem solving, and organizational decentralization (Skogan, 2006b).[1] The underlying argument for these three features goes something like this. Citizen involvement enlists more resources in whatever police and their constituents are attempting to accomplish and increases the chances that community members will accept and support these practices and the police organization in general. Problem solving is intended to make the processes of policing more effective by being smarter (police-led, preventive, creative, based on scientific knowledge and continuous evaluation) than traditional reactive methods. And decentralized organization structures are expected to facilitate the sort of organizational flexibility and creativity that makes effective community engagement and problem solving possible. This perspective lends greater coherence to the innovation, but it does not render the programmatic and structural elements any less important, for they are still the presumed means to the ends of the reform.

Despite reformers' admonition that community policing is not defined as a set of programs, program implementation is the most common strategy for its accomplishment. Programs tell us who is to do what and to what ends. Programs are visible and offer a way to append something that promises innovation onto well-established structures and processes that will experience minimal disruption. Neighborhood Watch, community meetings, citizen police academies, citizen surveys, door-to-door canvassing, non-auto patrols, storefront offices, youth sports programs, hotlines, victim assistance, and the establishment of special community policing units are some examples of programs that are often appended to the existing organization to facilitate desirable police–citizen communication (Roth, Roehl & Johnson, 2004). In addition, a department may adopt certain decentralized structures thought to *facilitate* police–community partnerships, such as drawing beat boundaries to coincide with neighborhood boundaries, permanent assignment of officers to beats, and delegating decision-making to the lowest level (e.g., "teams") to enable a more fine-tuned responsiveness to community preferences and needs (Roth et al., 2004). The adoption of such programs has been variable, but nonetheless widespread across the American landscape (Maguire &

[1] See Cordner (2014) for a more expansive definition that spans multiple dimensions: philosophical, strategic, tactical, and organizational.

Mastrofski, 2000; Roth et al., 2000; Maguire & Katz, 2002). Most importantly, in a relatively short time, the number of police agencies adopting such programs has grown significantly (Roth et al., 2004). However, these types of studies tend to indicate that the *partnership* aspects of community policing are the most weakly implemented (Maguire & Katz, 2002; Maguire & King, 2004; Roth et al., 2004). A recent analysis of quasi-experimental or experimental evaluations of community policing in the United States and other nations provided an appendix that showed that only nineteen of the forty-five sites studied had features that attended to all three of the core elements of community policing (community engagement, problem solving, and decentralization; Gill et al., 2014).[2] It is not clear how representative this sample is of the population of all community policing efforts launched, but it seems fair to say that programmatically, community policing remains a diverse and inchoate innovation, compared to some of the others reviewed in this volume.

At least as important as its direction is the scope and intensity of community policing's implementation: its coverage (proportion of the community exposed to it) and dosage (intensity of exposure). Certainly there are organizational surveys inquiring whether community policing has been adopted and with what features (e.g., Morabito, 2010). One of these national surveys, for example, asked agency respondents to judge the degree to which community policing had permeated the organization's structure and operations (Mastrofski, Willis & Kochel, 2007). Fifty-nine percent indicated that community policing had become a major part; 32 percent indicated a moderate part; and only 9 percent indicated a minor or no part. Of course, such responses are impressionistic and highly subjective, fraught with reactivity to the social desirability of embracing a reform that has become popular, at least in principle. Learning what portions of the organization and community are covered by community policing and the complexities of the implementation process are not easily captured by simple questionnaires, especially when respondents have incentives for reporting strong implementation of a popular innovation (Maguire & Mastrofski, 2000; Roth et al., 2004: 4).

We might have greater faith in indirect measures of structural change in police organizations – debureaucratizing changes deemed instrumental to the accomplishment of community policing, but based on measures arguably less susceptible to the reactivity of the desirability of reform (Maguire, 1997; Mastrofski, 1998; Mastrofski & Ritti, 2000; Greene, 2004). One analysis found mixed results between 1993 and 1998 and is largely confirmed by more recent research (Maguire et al., 2003; Maguire, 2014: 80–82). Large municipal police agencies moved significantly toward the community policing ideals of decentralization, lower administrative intensity, and greater civilianization. Some aspects of spatial differentiation did increase (more police stations and

---

[2] Analysis performed by author.

mini-stations), but the number of beats did not. On the other hand, hierarchical flattening did not occur, nor did hierarchical segmentation, and vertical differentiation continued to increase. Police agencies also failed to become less formalized and less functionally differentiated. Overall, the researchers typified the changes as "quite small" (Maguire et al., 2003: 271). An analysis of structural changes between 1993 and 2000 found largely consistent results. With the exception of a 15 percent increase in daytime patrol beats, researchers found "remarkable stability" in American policing structure during this period (Zhao, Ren & Lovrich, 2010: 222). Expecting basic structural changes over the course of even a couple of decades may be unrealistic (Mastrofski & Willis, 2010), but reform advocates anticipating a sea change in these aspects of police organizations are surely disappointed.

A distinct structural trend in American policing that appears counter to the goals of community policing is "militarization," a development emphasized by Maguire (2014). During the first half of the community policing reform era, the percent of agencies with paramilitary units shot up from 59 percent in 1982 to 89 percent in 1995. And police have increased the power of their armament, as well as military technologies, such as surveillance, communications, and computing. Thus, while the velvet glove of community policing has seen little structural change, the iron fist of militaristic structures and technologies has grown substantially. The juxtaposition of these trends raises the unanswered question of whether American police organizations attempt to use the community policing approach to guide and limit the forceful and intrusive aspects of police militarism, or whether they operate independently of each other.

A more reliable approach to measuring the extent of community policing program implementation is extended and intensive on-site observation, but here we lack a sufficiently large, representative sample of organizations monitored over time. What we have instead are a small collection of on-site case studies and cross-sectional comparisons of departments, most of which were selected because they were thought to exemplify good community policing implementation, likely overstating the case for strong implementation. Some of these have claimed successes in implementing community policing (Roth et al., 2000: ch. 7), but a substantial number have also documented failures and disappointments (Greene, Bergman & McLaughlin, 1994; Sadd & Grinc, 1994; Tien & Rich, 1994; Rosenbaum & Wilkinson, 2004). One group conducted 3–5-day site visits between 2000 and 2003 at a dozen local agencies thought to be among the more successful in implementing community policing (Maguire & Wells, 2009). They found a mixture of implementation successes, partial successes, and failures in a dozen departments around the nation. The studied organizations mounted new structures and launched new technologies, but it was not yet clear the extent to which these changes actually promoted problem solving and community engagement. Problem-solving was not widely dispersed among police officers and was typically performed in a shallow way compared to the reform ideals. Some departments created new structures to facilitate community engagement with important stakeholder groups (businesses, racial and ethnic minorities, other government agencies), but others fielded efforts that amounted merely to repackaging old ways of doing things. Commitment to community engagement that gave citizens a role in setting priorities and devising responses to problems was infrequently observed.

Perhaps the most intensive analysis of community policing orientation is that performed by Skogan over a decade at the Chicago Police Department. Chicago is widely regarded as a big-city national leader in commitment to community policing during the 1990s and into the millennium, due in no small part to continual pressure from a powerful mayor to make it happen (Skogan & Hartnett, 1997; 2006a). At the end of the city's tenth year with community policing, evaluators gave implementation a mixed set of "grades": public involvement (B), partnership with other agencies (A), internal reorganization, such as decentralization and accountability (A), and problem solving (C) (Skogan et al., 2004: 154–155). Of course, it is difficult to know what to make of these grades, as they have a large subjective element (especially the standards to which performance is held). However, it is instructive to note the difficulties Chicago had, even with the elements for which they received top marks. For example, a key feature of Chicago's internal reorganization was structurally facilitating the establishment of a neighborhood "turf" orientation among some Chicago officers, which meant that community policing "beat team" specialists would be able to spend lots of time getting to know and work with neighborhood residents (Skogan, 2006a: 59–65). Approximately 25 percent of the patrol force was assigned to beat teams. Their calls-for-service workload was to be lessened and concentrated in their assigned beat (Skogan, 2006a: 82). The remaining members of the patrol force continued to engage intensively in standard response to calls for service and preventive patrol, roaming throughout the district to deal with the workload so that beat officers could concentrate their time in their assigned beats. Beat team officers were expected to remain assigned to a given beat for at least one year, with the goal that 70 percent of their dispatched calls would be to locations within the assigned beat; after four years the department was able to document a 66 percent average. Skogan details the challenges that made doing so very difficult: changing well-established complex shift/area assignment procedures which kept officers from continually working the same areas for extended time periods, the need for more resources to maintain calls-for-service responsiveness while freeing up time for community policing, accommodating fluctuations in the workload distribution across beats, and dealing with political pressure on realigning beat boundaries in ways contrary to these purposes.

Another intensive evaluation of a somewhat different community policing-type program in the United Kingdom yielded similar results (Tuffin et al., 2006). Six different agencies were evaluated between 2003 and 2005 in terms of the extent to which they implemented "reassurance policing," which required police to focus on "signal crimes and disorders" about which the public has special interest. Intervention elements included community engagement, problem solving, partnerships, and foot patrol. Implementation fidelity was rated like a traffic-light system. Two sites established a "green" level throughout or mid-way through the project; the other four were rated "amber," suggesting that some elements were not fully achieved. The national program funding averaged slightly above a rather modest £100,000 per site. Even so, there was considerable motivation and support among participants for program success. But, as with Chicago, most agencies remained challenged to implement the program fully. Thus, many departments either fail to try to make structural changes needed to facilitate community policing, or they try and fail (Skogan, 2006a: 65). The challenge for researchers is that without more intensive implementation studies such as this, it is difficult to know with much precision just how exceptional Chicago's community policing effort was.

Here is one lesson to draw from these efforts to establish well-implemented community policing: it is not a walk in the park, and even mixed accomplishments are hard-won and extraordinary. Like running a sub-four-minute mile, we know it can be done, but we also know that few have the will and ability to do it. Early adopters may have that degree of commitment, but later adopters often rely upon the notoriety of the early adopters' success, and fail to attend to the challenges that must be overcome to secure that success in their case (Tolbert and Zucker, 1983; Ritti & Mastrofski, 2002). In fact, it seems likely that many police departments and their communities are unwilling or unable to make the sorts of commitments it takes to go beyond the fairly superficial transformations that come from adopting canned programs that are pale replicas of the real deal. Even as early as 1993, only half of the top executive respondents to a national survey indicated that community policing would require major changes in policies, goals, mission statements, and training, and only 27 percent indicated that it would require extensive reorganization (Wycoff, 1994). Thus, it seems unlikely that large numbers were committed to the kind of effort that Chicago's experience suggests is necessary to show substantial gains.

The complexities of rearranging police organizations to support community policing have made it difficult for researchers to offer broad, empirically based implementation assessments. A recent National Academies review found that training for the various elements of community policing (especially problem solving with the community) was typically modest, lasting only a few days (Weisburd & Majmundar, 2018: ch. 5). Few studies examine in depth the extent to which first-line supervisors reinforce and extend training lessons, ignore, or even resist them (but see Engel & Worden, 2006). As community policing emerged in the 1980s, it was clear that it called for different modes of first-line supervision that supported the creativity and flexibility essential to effective community outreach and problem solving (Weisburd, McElroy &

Hardyman, 1988), yet there is little research that tells us how and how much police supervisors and middle managers have found ways to accommodate the largely unchanged bureaucratic policing structures to the demands of community policing. The extent to which police agencies have made excellence in community policing a viable career advancement pathway (by offering recognition, promotions, desirable assignments, etc.) is virtually unexplored except for a relatively small number of intensive on-site case studies, such as those described.

Whether other reforms a department has implemented are reinforcing community policing or detracting from it is also a concern. One assessment based on site visits of a few days noted that CompStat shares some goals and methods with community policing, but that it also has some important differences and in any event is usually implemented in a "stove-piped" fashion that makes it difficult to harness its centralized management accountability processes to the decentralized nature of community policing, or to square the rigid accountability demands of CompStat with the need for the trial-and-error processes of problem-oriented policing (Willis, Mastrofski & Kochel, 2010). One in-depth case analysis has noted concerns that CompStat in Chicago would redirect attention away from neighborhood concerns to the traditional crime statistics that departments use (Skogan, 2006a: 99). This issue was of sufficient concern to the COPS Office that it has supported an in-progress project to explore the development of ways to integrate community policing into the CompStat framework.[3] Currently there is no rigorous evidence that both of these divergent reforms can be closely integrated successfully. In sum, creating the proper structural environment for community policing is no slam dunk, so skepticism is warranted when a department reports that it has a fully implemented, smoothly running operation in a short time period. The regrettable reality is that we really do not have rigorous knowledge of the state of structural change across a wide swath of American communities.

Community Policing Culture

"Community policing is a philosophy, not a program" (Roth et al., 2000: 183) is a popular phrase among academics and practitioners. To what extent have police embraced the community policing philosophy? Many community policing advocates anticipated that it would be difficult to get large numbers of police to embrace the community policing philosophy (Sparrow, Moore & Kennedy, 1990; Moore, 1992: 150), and early on-site studies confirmed the difficulties of changing police culture (e.g., Herbert, 1998; Sadd & Grinc, 1994). Skogan and Hartnett (1997: 106) reported "modest opinion shifts" among officers in the early years of Chicago's effort, with more positive attitudes among those who had been part of the community policing

---

[3] www.policefoundation.org/?s=Compstat+2.0.

prototype districts. Positive results were also noted in other cities (Skogan & Hartnett, 1997: 76), but there were also locations where exposure to a community policing program was followed by a distinct decline in support for community policing (Rosenbaum & Wilkinson, 2004). A 2006 national survey of departments with 100 or more officers revealed that 45 percent found it extremely or very challenging to get the support of rank-and-file officers, although nearly as many indicated that they experienced no such challenge or were successful in overcoming it (Mastrofski et al., 2007).

However, by the third decade of reform, there is evidence that support for community policing among America's police is now the norm, not the exception. The National Police Research Platform's 2014–15 survey focusing on departments of 100–3,000 sworn plus a small number of very large departments, found that 73 percent of more than 12,000 officers indicated some or strong support for community policing, while only 8 percent opposed it (Mastrofski, 2017).[4] Across the eighty-nine departments in this sample, the average indicating some or strong support was 75 percent, and the portion in the 25th percentile doing so was not that much less at 68 percent. This does not appear to be a timing fluke (pre-Ferguson, MO). A follow-up 2016 Platform survey conducted by the Pew Research Center in fifty-four of the Platform sites used sample weightings to reflect precisely the national distribution of departments (Mastrofski, 2017; Morin et al., 2017). It found that 88 percent of officer respondents found community policing somewhat or very useful. There still may well be pockets of resistance (one 2014–15 Platform department had as low as 44 percent support for community policing), but the substantial majority of officers in most departments appears to have incorporated community policing into their value system as something positive. An optimist could interpret this support as a change in the hearts and minds of police. A pessimist would suspect that community policing, once experienced, proved not to be much of a change from the way things had been done in the past, and, hence, met with broader acceptance and approval. To get a better sense of that, we turn to the practice of community policing at the street level.

Street-Level Practice

Although the current level of officer support for community policing is remarkable, this does not guarantee translation of a more positive cultural disposition to a robust display of actual police behavior. It is the particulars of everyday police work that determine how much community policing is experienced by most citizens. Assessments of the linkage between police attitudes and behavior have shown the relationship to be quite modest in size

---

[4] The survey defined community policing for the respondents as, "The police being responsive to community concerns and working in close partnership with the community to solve problems."

(Worden, 1989; Skogan & Frydl, 2004; Worden & McLean, 2014). An analysis of Platform survey data from approximately 3,000 rank-and-file patrol officers found only small correlations (in the expected direction) between support for procedural justice and the self-reported frequency with which officers engaged in procedural justice practices in traffic stops (Mastrofski, 2017). Some field observation studies of police–citizen encounters have shown that pro-community policing officers were generally more likely to resort to procedural justice methods and less inclined to act unjustly (Mastrofski, Snipes & Supina, 1996: 290; McCluskey, Mastrofski & Parks 1999). One field observation study found that those officers most strongly committed to community policing were also those who committed the largest share of constitutional search and seizure violations, perhaps because of their strong commitment to ridding the neighborhood of troublemakers (Gould & Mastrofski, 2004). Thus the evidence here is mixed.

One expectation of reformers is that community policing will bring officers face-to-face with the public more frequently and that during these encounters, officers will learn more about people and their problems, solve their problems, or at least comfort them when problems cannot be solved. A systematic observation of patrol officers in the mid-1990s found that community policing specialists in Indianapolis and St Petersburg spent *less* time in face-to-face encounters with the public than did the patrol generalists, whose traditional job remained responding to calls for service and engaging in preventive patrol (Parks, Mastrofski & Gray, 1999: 499–500). The specialists did spend more time than generalists at community meetings, but the difference was not large. Officers of both types found it difficult to spend extended periods of time in their assigned beats (Parks et al., 1998: 2–18). And the community policing specialists spent more of their time with citizens who were more respectable and less likely to present them with elevated emotions (Parks et al., 1999).

Many expect that community policing will cause officers to become less reliant on traditional forms of law enforcement or coercive methods and more inclined to a service-oriented style that attends to a wide array of problems but uses informal methods more frequently (Wilson, 1968). Officers who embrace community policing may make fewer arrests (Mastrofski et al., 1995: 552), but the researchers were unable to illuminate the mechanisms by which management achieved these results, and they were unable to determine whether making fewer arrests was a good thing (Mastrofski, 2004). Subsequent analysis suggested that pro-community policing officers underused their authority at a rate almost twice that of anti-community policing officers according to the dictates of a service-oriented approach associated with community policing (Mastrofski, 2009). Using similar observational protocols in a different city, other researchers found that officers whose special job assignment was to do community policing were less inclined to arrest suspects than traditional beat officers, but the difference was not statistically significant (Novak et al., 2002). There were no statistically significant differences in the patterns of influence on the arrest decision, except that community policing specialists were less inclined than traditional beat officers to arrest when the suspect was intoxicated. Some systematic field research shows that the style of community policing embraced by management may influence the use of verbal and physical coercion in some ways but not others (Terrill & Mastrofski, 2004: 127).[5] A study of situations where officers were seeking citizen compliance showed that officers positively disposed to community policing were not statistically distinguishable from negatively disposed officers in their resort to coercion (Mastrofski et al., 1996: 291). The limited evidence suggests that community policing has not had profound effects on the use of coercion, albeit the most useful analysis would examine effects for segments of the population most at risk (e.g., young African-American males).

Summary on Organization and Practice of Community Policing

Community policing is now embedded in various ways in the vast majority of America's local police departments, and a sizable majority of officers views it positively, at least in abstract terms. Many community policing programs have been fielded, but research has not yet made clear how widely dispersed within the community or intensive their application has been. Fundamental structural changes appear to be somewhat mixed in direction and, perhaps not surprisingly, modest in scope. Field studies of actual police practice – especially regarding the uniformed patrol function – have produced a mixed bag of relationships between various forms of community policing effort and the experiences of the police and the community when they engage each other in routine encounters. In the main, community policing does not appear to have stimulated a radical shift in the form or practice of police work, but rather a broad array of modest, incremental steps, which is not to underestimate the effort required to accomplish these changes. Perhaps it is reasonable to think of community policing as the icing on the cake of the organization and practice of policing in the twenty-first century. But sometimes even modest changes can produce meaningful consequences. We now turn to several of these.

DEMOCRACY IN POLICING

Numerous advocates of community policing have wanted to use it to infuse more "democracy" into the processes of policing. This can mean many things,

[5] Officers' attitudes toward developing partnerships with the community had no significant bearing on their inclination to use verbal or physical force with suspects in the two departments studied. The effects of training and community policing specialist assignment did not show consistent effects in the two departments.

ranging from increasing the transparency and public's knowledge of policing, community participation in and influence over decision making about policing, and community coproduction, which means the public's involvement in the actual work of policing. Underlying motivations run the gamut: increasing community control of policing – especially for socio-economic groups with little prior influence, enhancing the legitimacy of and support for the police, and increasing police effectiveness and efficiency. The relative strength of these expectations is important, because they determine the standards of success. Much of the academic literature, as well as the program literature, speaks of "police–community engagement" without getting into the nitty-gritty of how much change is expected of both the police and the community, in how and how much they "engage," and to what ends. To the extent that the police must change, then democratic principles require the creation and sustenance of mechanisms for the expression of community preferences, increases in the receptivity of police for community involvement in decisions and activities that have become the "professional" and therefore exclusive domain of the police, and ways to hold police accountable to the community for their performance. To the extent that the community must change, it is expected to develop a more sophisticated awareness of the potential and limits of what police can and should do; the community must develop its own willingness and capacity to engage with the police in decision making, and find a willingness to embrace a role in actually executing plans to improve the community.

How much democracy has community policing infused into the nation's communities? Given the importance of this, the evidence is remarkably thin. Much of what is available comes from the extended study of Chicago's community policing effort since the 1990s (Skogan, 2006a: ch. 5). This analysis nicely summarizes a major democratic policing issue: which partner dominates – the police/government leaders or the constellation of community interest groups that have their own agendas? Despite efforts of the local organized interest groups, the resolution of this political tug of war fell decidedly on the side of the police/government leaders in Chicago. Beat meetings were designated the principal mechanism for developing and enacting the police–citizen partnership. The boundaries of these beats and the location/timing of meetings were all determined by the police. Which police officers were assigned to the beat was a determination made by the department. The police, not the community, selected residents to co-lead meetings with an officer, and more often than not, the officer ran the meeting. Attendees did not vote on issues, and no public record of meeting actions was kept, making external accountability difficult. In sum, those desiring a grassroots form of local political control to emerge out of Chicago's community policing effort were disappointed. The police are clearly in charge and the residents and other stakeholders are the subordinate partner, fulfilling Klockars' (1988: 250) prophecy: "[Community policing] . . . is totally dependent upon, organized by, and controlled by police themselves."

That does not necessarily mean that Chicago's experiment failed to increase democratic influence in policing. Community members did get involved in beat meetings, and although their average number represented a very small portion (0.4 percent) of the city's population (Skogan, 2006a: 149), these meetings constituted the only opportunity available to all residents to give input. A good meeting attracted thirty community participants, but very few of those were frequent attenders, which surely diluted their influence. High crime did not suppress participation, but rather was associated with high participation. As expected, there was a strong establishment (e.g., property owners, higher education) bias in *who* participated, they were more positive about the police, and they were more concerned about neighborhood problems than the larger population of people living in the beat. Despite these biases, the nature of problems nominated by meeting participants tended to reflect the priorities of the larger resident population of the area, and the police also tended to agree with the community priorities expressed at the meeting (p. 164). During the meeting, citizens took an active role in nominating problems for consideration, and eventually the police department established a procedure for reporting police progress on these problems to attendees, so there was an element of accountability introduced into the process. Participants noted improved access to information about what police were doing. One area where meetings were judged deficient was their inability to stimulate high levels of citizen participation in actually getting engaged in coproductive problem-solving activities. On the other hand, beat meetings seemed to provide a real alternative to traditional modes of influence for Chicago's neighborhoods to mobilize the police and city government to deal with their problems. In the typically less-well-off neighborhoods, where informal social control, collective efficacy, neighborhood mobilization, and political influence were weakest, that is where the beat meeting attendance rate was strongest (p. 171). Further, the attendance rates and priorities of participants were found to exert a substantial effect independent of these other modes of influence (p. 207). In much of this analysis, Latinos benefited least, compared to African American and White citizens.

Thus, Chicago's community policing effort produced a mixed bag of "democratic" improvements. It did not make citizens coequal with the police, much less the dominant deciders of personnel, policy, and practice, but it paved a way for citizens to give voice to their concerns, to learn what police were doing, to voice complaints, and to participate in coproductive activities, should they so choose.

There are several things worth noting about Chicago's experience. First, it took tremendous effort – not only resources, but a willingness to engage in trial-and-error learning to adapt and overcome numerous failures. Second, it is not clear that other police agencies were willing and able to sustain this commitment, especially when the competition for scarce government resources in an anemic nationwide financial recovery and the threat of terrorism demanded attention too (Cordner, 2014: 160). Early in the reform's ascendance Houston (Skogan, 1990), Birmingham, Oakland (Kerley & Benson, 2000), Seattle (Lyons, 1999), and elsewhere (Sadd & Grinc, 1994) found it especially challenging for police to increase substantially community engagement that promotes and sustains democratic processes. Some skeptics voiced concern that community policing programs used the community to laud the police, not to govern them (Murphy, 1993: 20–21). In the assessments of community policing in the 1990s and early 2000s, police leaders "remained reluctant to give the community real authority and responsibilities" (Roth et al., 2004: 10). And finally, there simply is insufficient research that tells us with reliability what features of police departments, community policing programs, and communities themselves will promote the infusion of democracy into policing.

REDUCING CRIME AND DISORDER

Community policing is prized, not only for what it is, but for what it may yield. As the community policing movement gathered steam in the 1990s, advocates increasingly shifted their attention to its potential to reduce crime and disorder, a national political issue, and one of the central justifications for the distribution of federal funds through the COPS Office in the US Department of Justice. Beginning in the late 1990s, there have been four major efforts to assess the crime control performance of community policing (Sherman, 1997 and updated in Sherman & Eck, 2002; Skogan & Frydl, 2004: ch. 6; Gill et al., 2014; Weisburd & Majmundar, 2018). Although they differ in some of the particulars, all four show consistency in pointing to a pattern of largely disappointing conclusions about what available scientific research shows. What follows draws heavily on the analysis of the 2017 National Academies review.

Studies do not identify a consistent or strong crime control effect issuing from community policing. The systematic review of this literature for the Campbell Collaboration showed that only seventeen of forty-seven tests of outcomes yielded a conclusion that community policing was shown to be effective in reducing officially recorded crime relative to comparison groups (Gill et al., 2014: 413). Further, the research is plagued by weaker evaluation designs; the stronger studies among them tend not to show crime control effects. A small group of studies with methodological rigor do show with consistency a crime reduction effect for problem-oriented policing, which serves as one of the elements of community policing in many agencies. However, research has not been structured to determine the separate effects of problem-oriented policing from other community policing elements that may or may not be present (community engagement and decentralization).

The National Academies analysis (Weisburd & Majmundar, 2018: ch. 4) led to the conclusion that the crime control effects of community policing were inconsistent. This was accompanied by a host of other cautions and complaints about the quality and quantity of extant research. Community policing efforts varied tremendously in terms of what constituted the community policing intervention – from relatively modest door-to-door canvassing or newsletters and storefront operations to the establishment, promotion, and participation in community beat associations on a monthly basis with continuing involvement in problem-solving projects. Reviews of this literature were unable to illuminate which aspects of community policing were most influential, and in the face of such program heterogeneity, they were unable to offer insights as to which combinations of elements were most and least promising. Further, community policing was often implemented in tandem with other distinctly non-community policing program elements (for example the aggressive enforcement element of "weeding" combined with the community development element of "seeding" in the 1990s), but evaluations were unable to disaggregate effects of the two strikingly different approaches. Most studies examined the effects of community policing over a relatively short time period, typically a year or less. And many studies were conducted relatively early in the department's history with community policing, leaving open the possibility that the program had not sufficiently matured or been in effect long enough to make substantial impacts. The reviews were unable to control systematically for the critical factor of implementation fidelity, so it is difficult to know if inconsistent effects were due to inconsistencies in implementation or that community policing just is not a reliable remedy for crime in principle. And there is a paucity of rigorous research that considers whether targeting community policing at the micro-place level (e.g., block faces) substantially improves the prospects of desired crime control effects (Weisburd, Morris & Ready, 2008).

A recent systematic review measured community policing's effect size using official crime data in nineteen independent tests where it was possible to make these calculations. It found very modest average effects – odds ratios of 1.05 and 1.10, depending on what kind of crimes were included in the analysis (Gill et al., 2014: 413).[6] The most positive aspects of the currently available knowledge issuing from research reviews is the promise of problem-oriented policing as an element of community policing. The reader is referred to this volume's chapters on POP (Part IV) for a detailed discussion of that strategy, but in the context of this chapter, it seems reasonable to expect that the one feature of community policing that focuses on solving problems (most often crime problems) would show the greatest promise in actually achieving those results, as opposed to the features that are at best only indirectly related (community engagement and organization decentralization).

---

[6] Although the latter effect (on violent crime only) was significant, the researchers discounted it because of imprecision in crime statistics, large confidence intervals, great inter-study heterogeneity and the sensitivity of results to a small number of studies.

Thus, the current body of research is not all that encouraging about the likelihood or size of community policing crime control benefits, but attention to the many limitations in that research could leave open the possibility of more positive conclusions in the future.

PUBLIC SATISFACTION AND SUPPORT OF THE POLICE

For many, the bottom-line test of community policing is whether it pleases the public and causes its members to support the police, a major concern of the President's Task Force (2015). The public's reaction to community policing has been a matter of considerable interest to researchers, and so there is growing body of evidence available to make judgments about community policing's contributions. Community reactions can be of different sorts: how people feel about community safety and their quality of life (e.g., fear of crime, perceptions of disorder), how people feel about the policing they are receiving (general satisfaction or judgments of competence) or specific events or dimensions of performance, and the degree of support or deference they are willing to offer (trust in the police, willingness to accede to their authority). A recent systematic review of studies included a review of sixteen independent measures of perceived disorder, eighteen of fear of crime, twenty-three of citizen satisfaction, and ten of police legitimacy (Gill et al., 2014: 413). Based on this systematic review and the National Academies review of empirical research (Weisburd & Majmundar, 2018: ch. 6), it is appropriate to judge the prospects of community policing for increasing public satisfaction and support of police as more positive than those offered by research on crime and disorder, although many research limitations were also noted and findings were qualified. The National Academies findings are summarized as follows.

Compared to control groups, citizens exposed to community policing treatments tended to have more positive reactions, albeit the difference tended to be moderate.[7] These effects were most reliable for measures of citizen satisfaction and much less so for perceptions of disorder, fear of crime, and judgments of police legitimacy. Community policing backfire effects were rarely noted, leaving the National Academies committee to conclude that community policing offered some prospects of modest gains in community reactions with little danger of negative consequences.

There is little empirical research on the effects of community policing on community collective efficacy and cooperation with the police (e.g., reporting crimes), and what is available shows no clear pattern of effectiveness.

---

[7] The Gill et al. (2014: 415–417) meta-analysis yielded a statistically significant 37 percent increase in the odds of citizen satisfaction based on a sample of seventeen independent quasi-experimental studies. They noted a 28 percent average increase in the odds of citizens' perceptions of legitimacy (trust and confidence in police) across ten studies, but this did not achieve a level of statistical significance.

The strongest available study on collective efficacy was conducted in the United Kingdom (Tuffin et al., 2006), and failed to show statistically significant effects for measures of social cohesion, feelings of trust toward neighbors, and involvement in voluntary activity.

Problem-solving, as a community policing strategy, mirrored the pattern of effects for community policing in general, with fairly consistent positive impacts on citizen satisfaction, but mixed effects on other community reaction indicators and a near absence of backfire effects. The committee found few studies – with mixed effects – for the broken-windows approach to community policing, preventing it from offering conclusions, except to suggest that when broken windows was harnessed to a problem-solving approach, it showed more positive results than the variety that employed traditional enforcement measures.

As with research on community policing's effects on crime and disorder, the National Academies committee itemized a list of limitations to the research on community reactions (Weisburd & Majmundar, 2018: ch. 6). In general, there were few randomized control trials among the available studies, so the ability to rule out alternative influences on community policing was not as strong as one might wish. The content of the community policing treatment appeared to vary widely and was not controlled in comparative reviews. The breadth and intensity of treatment were not well documented, which makes the comparison of findings across studies difficult. Outcomes were conceptualized and measured differently across studies, undermining generalizations about patterns of effects across different sorts of community reactions. There are relatively few rigorous studies of community policing's effects in small towns and rural areas, most instead concentrating in larger, urban areas. The notion of community is often left vague conceptually, but operationally is nearly always aggregated into people who reside in a designated area, even though they may be divided into subgroups that have remarkably different experiences and views of the police (e.g., victims vs. suspects). Some may have frequent, high-intensity contacts with police, while others have relatively little contact. An exception to this is the research on Chicago, which showed how varied effects could be across racial/ethnic groups (African Americans, Latinos, and Whites; Skogan, 2006a). And very few studies examine the effects of community policing on community reactions for more than a year or so. The absence of long-term studies over many years means that our knowledge of the reform's accomplishments and limitations remains rather superficial. What does a sustained commitment to community policing change in community dynamics? Again, research in Chicago is the exception, with a decade-long analysis available. Fear of crime retreated across a broad range of socio-economic groups, although the amount of decline varied (e.g., by race/ethnic group). Notably, a quality-of-service index based on citizens' perceptions plateaued at about the sixth year (Skogan, 2006a: 280). What one takes from this lengthy list of weaknesses in available knowledge is the need for considerable caution in what one should expect from any given community policing program being considered for launch or discontinuation.

CONCLUSION

It is difficult to reject the ideals of community policing, but the devil is in the details (Klockars, 1988). The idea of community policing appears to be accepted by substantial majorities of police up and down the hierarchies of America's police agencies. The idea of community policing has sustained popularity, even with the persistent concern about countering terrorism in the world and a shrinkage of federal financial support in the last decade. While the scope and intensity of community policing implementation across the nation is still not well illuminated, available field reports suggest that after three decades there is scant evidence of a broad scale "quiet revolution," a "new blue line," or a "paradigm shift." Those hoping for a vital infusion of community hands-on democracy into policing processes will find the enhanced "advisory role" tepid tea, even where opportunities for participation have been raised through police-organized neighborhood and beat meetings. The anemic level of community policing's crime and disorder control effects, noted in the Committee to Review Research 2004 report, remain after another decade of studies. A more positive note can be sounded for community policing's impact on public satisfaction with police, although even here the results do not extend with high consistency to other indicators of the public's views (fear of crime, perceptions of disorder, and legitimacy). The best one can predict with confidence is a moderate improvement in community satisfaction.

The question that naturally arises from this state of affairs is whether these benefits justify the costs of engaging in community policing. This is a complex issue that cannot be answered definitively based on available evidence (Gascon & Foglesong, 2010). But there are a few points we can consider. First, the creation of the COPS Office as a mechanism for the distribution of financial awards to state and local agencies to promote community policing signaled that community policing imposes substantial financial costs. This is reinforced by a national survey of police agencies that found that the most frequently indicated challenge to implementing community policing was acquiring resources (Mastrofski et al., 2007). An example of this cost dynamic is given by the need of many programs to create specialized community policing jobs or units, and freeing personnel time to engage in many aspects of community policing (e.g., keeping beat officers in their small assigned beats instead of dispatching them outside of beats to maintain a low response time). This requires cutting back resources devoted to other "standard" operations (e.g., responding to calls for service, conducting criminal investigations), acquiring additional resources, or achieving greater efficiency to free up existing resources. Thus, we have good reason to suspect that the resource costs of community policing are substantial, and that in turn raises the question of whether these create substantial opportunity costs to investing in community policing, as opposed to other strategies that are more promising and/or less costly. Definitive answers are not available from evaluation research, but it is worth noting that the "standard model" of reactive policing through responding to calls for service and follow-up crime investigations (Skogan & Frydl, 2004: ch. 6) continues to dominate the allocation of resources, quite possibly because police leaders and their government overseers perceive, correctly, that public support rests heavily on the police delivering these tangible, highly valued, and widely distributed services far more than the less easily observed and more selectively distributed benefits community policing is expected to render (Mastrofski & Willis, 2010: 85).

So what does this skepticism demand? Skeptics can begin by directing much of their doubting to the body of available research, which has offered a far-from-sufficient set of empirical tests of community policing's implementation and impact. The usual call for more and better research is apropos. The recent National Academies (Weisburd & Majmundar, 2018) report calls for a long list of improvements. We need better knowledge of the coverage and dosage of police innovations as they are distributed across the nation's communities. More conceptual clarity and measurement quality are needed on the specific features that comprise the hodgepodge of its programs, techniques, and philosophies. Stronger designs to increase confidence in estimating the actual impact of community policing is required, along with better documentation and assessment of the costs imposed. Studies that simultaneously measure well those impacts across the wide range of outcomes people care about will increase knowledge of trade-offs between such objectives as crime control and community trust in the police. Long-term longitudinal studies are needed to test the capacity of police organizations to sustain their efforts and to learn their cumulative effects over many years. When the next edition of this volume is published, complaints about the quantity and quality of relevant evidence need to be many fewer.

The available evidence should not suggest to skeptics that community policing was necessarily the wrong direction for police in the late twentieth and early twenty-first centuries, but there is reason to call for trying more daring pathways to move in that direction. Too many community policing programs seem designed to adjust the community to the police way of doing things, rather than adjusting the police to the community's perspective. To adapt Gertrude Stein's famous line, there is often so little *there* there. We need an era of more profound experimentation with the innovative elements of community policing. What happens if community members are given a greater say in who patrols their neighborhood? What happens if officers engaged in community policing are assigned to work an area for several years, rather than rotated annually or more frequently? What if officer performance evaluations include how well the officer knows the people and customs of his/her assigned turf? What if the availability of career advancement were to depend heavily on how well officers perform on things that are essential to community policing, rather than the usual arrests, clearances, and calls answered statistics? What happens if community stakeholders have a significant role in training officers about serving their constituents (Kringen & Kringen, 2017)? What if the principles and tactics of community policing become the guiding force for all units in the police department, not just patrol or specialist community-oriented units? What if officers and community members are given extensive training and ongoing support to engage in community outreach and problem solving? What if policing structures, procedures, and practices are actually transformed to promote community policing, rather than merely tolerate it? If there is a community policing way to make use-of-force decisions, then this needs to be vigorously incorporated into training, performance evaluation, and disciplinary protocols. It is not clear that community policing can blunt the outrage felt by ethnic minorities over police abuses of authority, but finding ways to make both the courts and the police department more transparent will be an important step, one that needs to go well beyond merely finding a role for selected community members in the review of complaints against the police, such as independent authority, disciplinary accountability, auditing of policy and practices (not just individual cases), transparency, due process for officers, and ready public filing access (Ofer, 2016). This sort of change will create risk taking of a major sort. Our police have long struggled, often with good reason, to build effective buffers from community pressure (Reiss, 1992), and it is not always clear that enough citizens are willing to commit the necessary effort, especially in the most afflicted areas. But Americans need to know more about what more invigorated versions of community policing will produce.

ACKNOWLEDGMENTS

The author thanks David Weisburd and Anthony Braga for their helpful suggestions in the preparation of this manuscript.

REFERENCES

Cordner, G. (2014). Community policing. In M. D. Reisig, & R. J. Kane (eds.), *Police and Policing* (pp. 148–171). New York: Oxford University Press.

Engel, R. S., & Worden, R. E. (2006). Police officers' attitudes, behavior, and supervisory influences: An analysis of problem solving. *Criminology*, 41(1), 131–66.

Fogelson, R. M. (1977). *Big City Police*. Cambridge: Harvard University Press.

Gascon, G., & Foglesong, T. (2010). *Making Policing More Affordable. New Perspectives in Policing*. Washington, DC: National Institute of Justice.

Gill, C., Weisburd, D., Telep, C. W., Vitter, Z., & Bennett, T. (2014). Community-oriented policing to reduce crime, disorder and fear and increase satisfaction and legitimacy among citizens: A systematic review. *Journal of Experimental Criminology*, 10, 399–428.

Goldstein, H. (1977). *Policing a Free Society*. Cambridge, MA: Ballinger Publishing Company.

Goldstein, H. (1990). *Problem-Oriented Policing*. New York: McGraw-Hill.

Gould, J. B., & Mastrofski, S. D. (2004). Suspect searches: Assessing police behavior under the Constitution. *Criminology and Public Policy*, 3, 316–362.

Greene, J. R. (2004). Community policing and organization change. In W. G. Skogan (ed.), *Community Policing: Can It Work?* (pp. 30–53). Belmont, CA: Wadsworth.

Greene, J. R., Bergman, W. T., & McLaughlin, E. J. (1994). Implementing community policing: Cultural and structural change in police organizations. In D. Rosenbaum (ed.), *The Challenge of Community Policing: Testing the Promises* (pp. 92–109). Thousand Oaks, CA: Sage.

Herbert, S. (1998). Police subculture reconsidered. *Criminology*, 32(2), 343–370.

Kelling, G. L., & Moore, M. H. (1988). From political to reform to community: The evolving strategy of police. In J. R. Greene, & S. D. Mastrofski (eds.), *Community Policing: Rhetoric or Reality* (pp. 3–25). New York: Praeger.

Kerley, K. R., & Benson, M. (2000). Does community-oriented policing help build stronger communities? *Police Quarterly*, 3(1), 46–69.

Klockars, C. B. (1988). The rhetoric of community policing. In J. R. Greene, & S. D. Mastrofski (eds.), *Community Policing: Rhetoric or Reality?* (pp. 239–258). New York: Praeger.

Kringen, A. L., & Kringen, J. L. (2017). Outside the academy: Learning community policing through community engagement. *Ideas in American Policing* 20. Washington, DC: Police Foundation.

LaFree, G. (1998). *Losing Legitimacy: Street Crime and the Decline of Institutions in America*. Boulder, CO: Westview Perseus.

Lyons, W. (1999). *The Politics of Community Policing: Rearranging the Power to Punish*. Ann Arbor: University of Michigan Press.

Maguire, E. R. (1997). Structural change in large municipal police organizations during the community policing era. *Justice Quarterly*, 14, 547–576.

Maguire, E. R. (2014). Police organizations and the iron cage of rationality. In M. D. Reisig, & R. L. Kane (eds.), *The Oxford Handbook of Police and Policing* (pp. 68–98). New York: Oxford University Press.

Maguire, E. R., & Katz, C. M. (2002). Community policing, loose coupling, and sensemaking in American police agencies. *Justice Quarterly*, 19, 501–534.

Maguire, E. R., & King, W. R. (2004). Trends in the policing industry. *The Annals of the American Academy of Political and Social Science*, 593, 15–41.

Maguire, E. R., & Mastrofski, S. D. (2000). Patterns of community policing in the United States. *Police Quarterly*, 3, 4–45.

Maguire, E. R., Shin, Y., Zhao, J., & Hassell, K. D. (2003). Structural change in large police agencies during the 1990s. *Policing: An International Journal of Police Strategies and Management*, 26, 251–275.

Maguire, E., & Wells, W. (2009). *Implementing Community Policing: Lessons from 12 Agencies*. Washington, DC: Office of Community Oriented Policing Services.

Mastrofski, S. D. (1998). Community policing and police organization structure. In J. Brodeur (ed.), *Community Policing and the Evaluation of Police Service Delivery* (pp. 161–189). Thousand Oaks, CA: Sage.

Mastrofski, S. (2004). Controlling street-level police discretion. *The Annals of the American Academy of Political and Social Sciences*, 593, 100–118.

Mastrofski, S. (2009). Measuring the quality of street-level police work. Paper presented at the Centre of Excellence in Policing and Security Policing Symposium: New Directions for Policing Serious and Complex Crime. March 10. Sydney, AU: CEPS.

Mastrofski, S. D. (2017). The receptivity of the police to community-oriented reforms. *ACJS Today*, 42(3), 107–117.

Mastrofski, S. D., & Ritti, R. R. (2000). Making sense of community policing: A theoretical perspective. *Police Practice and Research Journal*, 1, 183–210.

Mastrofski, S., Snipes, J., & Supina, A. (1996). Compliance on demand: The public's response to specific police requests. *Journal of Research in Crime and Delinquency*, 33, 269–305.

Mastrofski, S. D., & Willis, J. J. (2010). Police organization continuity and change: Into the Twenty-first Century. *Crime and Justice: A Review of Research*, 39, 55–144.

Mastrofski, S. D., Willis, J. J., & Kochel, T. R. (2007). The challenges of implementing community policing in the United States. *Policing: A Journal of Policy and Practice*, 1 (2), 223–234.

Mastrofski, S. D., Worden, R. E., & Snipes, J. B. (1995). Law enforcement in a time of community policing. *Criminology*, 33, 539–563.

McCluskey, J. D., Mastrofski, S. D., & Parks, R. B. (1999). To acquiesce or rebel: Predicting citizen compliance with police requests. *Police Quarterly*, 2, 389–416.

Moore, M. H. (1992). Problem-solving and community policing. In M. Tonry, & N. Morris (eds.), *Modern Policing* (pp. 99–158). Chicago: University of Chicago Press.

Morabito, M. S. (2010). Understanding community policing as an innovation: Patterns of adoption. *Crime and Delinquency*, 56(4), 564–587.

Morin, R., Parker, K., Stepler, R., & Mercer, A. (2017). *Behind the Badge. Social & Demographic Trends*. Washington, DC: Pew Research Center. www.pewsocialtrends.org/2017/01/11/reimagining-the-police-through-training-and-reforms/.

Murphy, C. (1993). The development, impact and implications of community policing in Canada. In J. Cacko, & S. E. Nankoo (eds.), *Community Policing in Canada* (pp. 13–26). Toronto: Canadian Scholars Press.

Novak, K. J., Frank, J., Smith, B. W., & Engel, R. S. (2002). Revisiting the decision to arrest: Comparing beat and community officers. *Crime and Delinquency*, 48(1), 70–98.

Ofer, U. (2016). Getting it right: Building effective civilian review boards to oversee police. *Seton Hall Law Review*, 46, 1033–1062.

Parks, R. B., Mastrofski, S. D., DeJong, C., & Gray, M. K. (1999). How officers spend their time with the community. *Justice Quarterly*, 16, 483–518.

Parks, R. B., Mastrofski, S. D., Reiss, A. J., Jr., Worden, R. E., Terrill, W. C., DeJong, C., Stroshine, M., & Shepard, R. (1998). *St. Petersburg Project on Policing Neighborhoods: A Study of the Police and the Community*. Report to the National Institute of Justice. Bloomington, IN: Indiana University.

President's Task Force on 21st Century Policing. (2015). *Final Report of the President's Task Force on 21st Century Policing*. Washington, DC: Office of Community Oriented Policing Services.

Reiss, A. J., Jr. (1992). Police organization in the twentieth century." In M. Tonry, & N. Morris (eds.), *Modern Policing* (pp. 51–98). Chicago: University of Chicago Press.

Ritti, R. R., & Mastrofski, S. D. (2002). The institutionalization of community policing: A study of the presentation of the concept in two law enforcement journals. Final report to the National Institute of justice. Manassas, VA: George Mason University.

Rosenbaum, D. P., & Wilkinson, D. L. (2004). Can police adapt? Tracking the effects of organizational reform over six years. In W. Skogan (ed.), *Community Policing: Can It Work?* (pp. 79–108). Belmont, CA: Wadsworth.

Roth, J. A., Roehl, J., & Johnson, C. C. (2004). Trends in community policing. In W. Skogan (ed.), *Community Policing: Can It Work?* (pp. 3–29). Belmont, CA: Wadsworth.

Roth, J. A., Ryan, J. F., Gaffigan, S. J., Koper, C. S., Moore, M. H., Roehl, J., Johnson, C. C., Moore, G. E., White, R. M., Buerger, M. E., Langston, E. A., & Thacher, D. (2000). *National Evaluation of the COPS Program – Title I of the 1994 Crime Act.* Washington, DC: National Institute of Justice.

Sadd, S., & Grinc, R. (1994). Innovative neighborhood oriented policing: An evaluation of community policing programs in eight cities. In D. Rosenbaum (ed.), *The Challenge of Community Policing: Testing the Promises* (pp. 27–52). Sage: Thousand Oaks.

Sherman, L. W. (1997). Policing for crime prevention. In L. W. Sherman, D. Gottfredson, D. MacKenzie, J. Eck, P. Reuter, & S. Bushway (eds.), *Preventing Crime: What Works, What Doesn't, What's Promising?* (pp. Ch. 8: 1–58). Washington, DC: National Institute of Justice.

Sherman, L. W., & Eck, J. E. (2002). Policing for crime prevention. In L. W. Sherman, D. P. Farrington, B. C. Welsh, & D. L. MacKenzie (eds.), *Evidence-Based Crime Prevention* (pp. 295–329). New York: Routledge.

Skogan, W. G. (1990). *Disorder and Decline: Crime and the Spiral of Decay in American Cities.* New York: The Free Press.

Skogan, W. G. (2004). Representing the community in community policing. In W. G. Skogan (ed.), *Community Policing: Can It Work?* (pp. 57–75). Belmont, CA: Wadsworth.

Skogan, W. G. (2006a). *Police and Community in Chicago: A Tale of Three Cities.* New York: Oxford University Press.

Skogan, W. G. (2006b). The promise of community policing. In D. Weisburd, & A. A. Braga (eds.), *Police Innovation: Contrasting Perspectives* (pp. 27–43). New York: Cambridge University Press.

Skogan, W., & Frydl, K. (2004). *Fairness and Effectiveness in policing: The Evidence.* (Committee to Review Research on Policy and Practices, Committee on Law and Justice, Division of Behavioral and Social Sciences and Education). Washington, DC: The National Academies Press.

Skogan, W. G., & Hartnett, S. M. (1997). *Community Policing, Chicago Style.* New York: Oxford.

Skogan, W. G., Steiner, L., Benitez, C., Bennis, J., Borchers, S., DuBois, J., Gondocs, R., Hartnett, S., Kim, S. Y., & Rosenbaum, S. (2004). *Community Policing in Chicago, Year Ten: An Evaluation of Chicago's Alternative Policing Strategy.* Springfield, IL: Illinois Criminal Justice Information Authority.

Sparrow, M. K., Moore, M. H., & Kennedy, D. M. (1990). *Beyond 911: A New Era for Policing.* New York: Basic Books.

Terrill, W., & Mastrofski, S. D. (2004). Working the street: Does community policing matter? In W. G. Skogan (ed.), *Community Policing: Can It Work?* (pp. 109–135). Belmont, CA: Wadsworth.

Tien, J. M., & Rich, T. F. (1994). The Hartford COMPASS Program: Experiences with a weed and seed-related program. In D. Rosenbaum (ed.), *The Challenge of Community Policing: Testing the Promises* (pp. 192–206). Thousand Oaks, CA: Sage.

Tolbert, P. S., & Zucker, L. G. .(1983). Institutional sources of change in the formal structure of organizations: The diffusion of civil service reform 1880–1935. *Administrative Science Quarterly*, 28, 22–39.

Trojanowicz, R. C., & Bucqeroux, B. (1990). *Community Policing: A Contemporary Perspective*. Cincinnati, OH: Anderson Publishing Company.

Tuffin, R., Morris, J., & Poole, A. (2006). *An Evaluation of the Impact of the National Reassurance Policing Programme* (HORS 296). London, UK: Home Office Research, Development and Statistics Directorate. www.gov.uk/government/uploads/system/uploads/attachment_data/file/115825/hors296.pdf.

Weisburd, D., & Majmundar, M. K. (2018). *Proactive Policing: Effects on Crime and Communities* (Committee on Proactive Policing: Effects on Crime, Communities and Civil Liberties, Committee on Law and Justice, Division of Behavioral and Social Sciences and Education). Washington, DC: The National Academies Press.

Weisburd, D., McElroy, J., & Hardyman, P. (1988). Supervision in Community Policing: Observations on a Pilot Project. *American Journal of Police*, 7(2), 29–50.

Weisburd, D., Morris, N. A., & Ready, J. (2008). Risk focused policing at places: An experimental evaluation. *Justice Quarterly*, 25(1), 163–200.

Willis, J. J., Mastrofski, S. D., & Kochel. T. R. (2010). The Co-Implementation of Compstat and Community Policing. *Journal of Criminal Justice*, 38, 969–980.

Wilson, J. Q. (1968). *Varieties of Police Behavior*. Cambridge, MA: Harvard University Press.

Wilson, J. Q., & Kelling, G. L. (1982). Broken windows: The police and neighborhood safety. *Atlantic Monthly*, 249, 29–38.

Worden, R. E. (1989). Situational and attitudinal explanations of police behavior: A theoretical reappraisal and empirical assessment. *Law & Society Review*, 23, 667–711.

Worden, R. E., & McLean, S. J. (2014). Police discretion in law enforcement. In G. Bruinsma, & D. Weisburd (eds.), *Encyclopedia of Criminology and Criminal Justice* (pp. 3596–3607). New York, NY: Springer-Verlag.

Wycoff, M. A. (1994). *Community Policing Strategies: Draft Final Report*. Washington, DC: Police Foundation.

Zhao, J., Ren, L., & Lovrich, N. (2010). Police organizational structures during the 1990s: An application of contingency theory. *Police Quarterly*, 13(2), 209–232.

PART II

PROCEDURAL JUSTICE POLICING

3

Advocate

Procedural Justice Policing

Tom R. Tyler and Tracey L. Meares

INTRODUCTION

The goal of procedural justice policing is to promote long-term crime reduction through creating and maintaining widespread popular legitimacy among the people in policed communities. This trust in the police has a set of desirable consequences. First, it lowers the rate of crime because those who view the law as legitimate are less likely to break it. Second, it transforms the relationship between the police and the public from coercive to consensual, with people more likely to willingly accept and defer to police authority. Third, it promotes voluntary cooperation, facilitating police efforts to manage social order. And finally, it promotes community development by creating a climate of reassurance within which people more willingly engage with others, leading to economic, social, and political vibrancy. This climate helps communities to develop out of the conditions promoting crime, rather than trying to arrest their way forward.

This effort is based first on the evidence-informed finding that popular legitimacy motivates the previously mentioned behaviors. It is further developed by reference to studies making clear that there are mechanisms through which the police can create and maintain popular legitimacy. This research points to evaluations of the justice or injustice or the procedures through which the police exercise their authority (i.e., procedural justice) as the key antecedents of legitimacy. Hence, if the police build their policies and practices with sensitivity to their impact upon evaluations of procedural justice, they can advance the goal of popular legitimacy. Such efforts can proceed in parallel with crime control, leading to both public safety and legitimate policing.

There are several ways that this approach is distinct. First, it defines popular legitimacy as of equal importance to crime control. And, it argues that there are policing approaches that can achieve both objectives at the same time. Second, it is targeted at the long-term goal of crime reduction, rather at short-term crime control. Through heightened acceptance of the law, criminal behavior is lower, cooperation is higher, and the basis is created for supporting community development. Community development both lessens the motivations for criminal activity and heightens the resiliency of communities to combat social disorder through feelings of collective efficacy and via stronger informal social networks.

POLICING AND CRIME CONTROL

Crime in America today is at historically low levels. There have been steep and steady declines in both violent and nonviolent crime across the United States. According to the Bureau of Justice Statistics the violent crime rate in 2015 is 23 percent of what it was in 1993, while the property crime rate is 32 percent of what it was. The benefits of these low crime rates are obvious.

As you would expect in an era of declining and relatively low crime, recent discussions about policing in America are not focused on crime rates. The public does not believe that crime is high or out of control. And the public generally believes that the police can and have controlled crime. This current era of low crime is important because it provides an opportunity to step back from a focus on crime control and to reexamine the role that we want the police to play in our democratic society. In particular, it provides an opportunity to address issues of popular legitimacy.

POPULAR LEGITIMACY

What is popular legitimacy? Scholars use the term popular legitimacy to refer to public judgments about whether the police are entitled to exercise authority and the public is obligated to defer to and accept police decisions. As it is commonly measured by empirical researchers, legitimacy has three components. The first is perceived obligation. If people feel that the police are entitled to exercise authority, they conversely endorse the obligation to defer to them. The second is trust. Those who believe that the police are honest and motivated to act for the good of the community are more likely to defer to the police. The third is normative alignment. If people feel that they agree with the police about the basic values that guide police actions, they are more likely to accept police authority. These three elements are typically found to be intertwined and each distinctly leads to particular desirable law-related actions (Tyler & Jackson, 2014). Our suggestion is that policing in a democratic society needs to be attuned to the issues shaping public trust.

A beginning point for discussing public trust is noting that declining crime rates have not led to increases in public trust in the police. In 1993, 52 percent of Americans indicated that they trust the police and in 2016, the percentage was 56 percent. So even though crime rates have declined significantly over the last twenty-five years, trust the police has not changed. Between 1993 and 2016, the percentage of Americans reported by Gallup polls to trust the police has ranged from 50 to 60 percent. Similarly, recent Reuters poll found that 37 percent of all Americans believe that "police officers tend to unfairly target minorities," while 31 percent believe that "police officers routinely lie to serve their own interests" (Schneider, 2015).

The key question is whether we can identify a vision for policing that leads to *both* crime control and high levels of trust in the police. Since the police have generally defined their mission as crime control, it is striking that declining crime rates have not enhanced popular legitimacy. Police leaders have generally assumed that the public primarily holds them to account for lowering the rate of crime and that, as a result, if they do control crime they will have public support. They have, consequently, been surprised that lower crime rates have not led to heightened public support. This lack of connection between crime rates and police legitimacy raises questions about how the public evaluates the police, an issue we will address in this chapter. Effectiveness in lowering crime ought to lead to public trust and support, but evidence suggests that it does not. Research explains this finding by showing that neither estimates of the rate of crime nor evaluations of police effectiveness in controlling crime are primary factors shaping public trust.

DOES THE PUBLIC TRUST THE POLICE?

There is today considerable controversy about the police in the United States but it is about a different set of issues than crime rates. The degree of public controversy has been at such a high level that there was a recent National Presidential Taskforce on 21st Century Policing. As would be expected when crime is not a salient public concern, these recent controversies are not focused on whether or not the police can control crime. There are, of course, some exceptions: for example, the ongoing public concern about high-visibility gun-related deaths in Chicago. However, as a general matter, the issue that has dominated recent discussions about policing is not crime but public trust in the police.

The more salient issues about policing in America today are centered around the widespread evidence not of trust but of a high level of public distrust. For example, in the aftermath of police shootings, the police typically promise a fair investigation and urge public caution. Those assurances have been greeted with skepticism in several recent incidents. On a national level, these issues have led Federal authorities and national police leaders to identify distrust as a central concern in policing, as evidenced by the testimony before and the conclusions reached by the President's Task Force on 21st Century Policing.

Issues about the police have historically been, and are today, intertwined with issues of race relations. African Americans are found to be 25 to 30 percent less trusting of the police than are Whites. This gap has existed for decades and continues to exist today. It is, therefore, not surprising that the type of mistrust noted above is particularly strongly felt in the minority community. The PEW Center, for example, found that in 2014, 36 percent of Whites had confidence in the police not to use excessive force and only 18 percent of African-Americans (PEW, 11/26/2014). In response to the Ferguson, Missouri, shooting of Michael Brown, 52 percent of Whites trusted the police to investigate the shooting and only 18 percent of African-Americans (PEW, 8/18/2014).

Irrespective of what is central to public concerns, it is important to consider what is most desirable in American policing. There are clearly differing views about this issue, with some leaders arguing that the police should restrict their focus to developing and implementing strategies for effectively managing crime, an issue about which they are particularly knowledgeable. Others suggest that it is important to engage more directly with public concerns to address the sources of distrust. A broader effort would lead to the need for the police to address issues beyond those related to how to manage crime.

PROCEDURAL JUSTICE AND POLICING

How is procedurally just policing related to these issues? Procedural justice is a model for how to police. Its desirability flows from research suggesting that public trust is a key concern that ought to influence how the police behave so the police need to understand how their actions shape public views. Research then makes procedural justice important by demonstrating that public trust is rooted in procedural justice. This finding is first important because it helps to explain why crime control does not lead to trust. Trust is not established by lowering the crime rate or by being seen to be effective in managing crime. Trust develops from a different set of evaluations and those are related to the procedural fairness through which the police exercise their authority.

Procedural justice refers to four aspects of the exercise of police authority. First, people want a voice. The public wants the police to allow people to express their views or tell their side of the story before determining policies or making decisions. Second, people care about neutrality. People want the police to act in a transparent and impartial manner by making decisions based upon facts, not prejudices. Neutrality is also related to whether the police explain what their policies are and how they are being applied. Third, people want interpersonal respect. The public wants the police to treat people with courtesy and respect. This includes respect for people's rights as citizens and for their dignity as people. People care about whether the police treat them in ways that communicate that they are viewed as good citizens and not suspects, deviants, or marginal members of their community. Fourth, people care about trustworthy motives. It is important to people to feel that the police are motivated to do what is good for the people in their community. They want to believe that the police are sincere and benevolent, focused on the needs and concerns of the public, and willing to acknowledge and address people's concerns.

These four elements – voice, neutrality, respect, and trustworthy motives – are central to public judgments about how fairly the police are exercising their authority in the communities they police.

WHY PROCEDURAL JUSTICE?

Why is being treated fairly or unfairly by the police important to community residents. As community authorities, the police, like any representatives of the society, give people messages about inclusion and status in the community. When the police humiliate and demean people, they tell them that they are marginal members of the community. Most people in any community are not actively involved in criminal activity and feel devalued if they are treated as suspects, deviants, and potential criminals. Even those who are involved in crime want to experience decency from people who represent the community and respect for their humanity even if their actions are condemned and they are punished. An important aspect of any contact with an authority is that their actions communicate identity-relevant information and that information has an impact upon people feelings of self-worth and self-esteem, as well as everyday anxiety and even symptoms of PTSD (Geller et al., 2014; Tyler, Fagan & Geller, 2014; Tyler, 2017a). This identity-based element of authority reflects the role of relational issues in the connection between people and legal authorities (Tyler & Lind, 1992).

WHY DOES LEGITIMACY MATTER?

Why would popular legitimacy matter to the police? Beyond the currently high salience of incidents of police misconduct and the problems they cause for communities, the argument for the value of a focus on popular legitimacy exists on several levels. The first is that because popular legitimacy shapes law-related behavior, building legitimacy is a desirable crime-fighting strategy. And, as such a strategy, it has the advantage of building willing acceptance of the law and consent to legal authority, which reduces the need to create and maintain a viable surveillance presence on the part of the police. Policing based upon surveillance and possible apprehension to create risk perception and compliance is not based upon willing acceptance and depends upon the continued presence of the police. Policing based upon legitimacy supports rule following and deference to police authority via consent.

A focus only on compliance with the law as the goal of policing obscures the potential for a more consensual model of legal regulation, a model that depends upon the ability of trust and confidence to generate public cooperation with the police to comanage social order and to further motivate public engagement in, and identification with, communities, which motives community development.

The first point is that a recurrent complaint among the police toward the community is the lack of public cooperation in fighting crime. This includes reporting criminals and crimes, identifying criminals as a witness, and testifying in court when needed. It also includes being a juror and working with the police in community meetings and with groups such as neighborhood watch to support police efforts to maintain social order. All of these forms of citizen behavior are enhanced by trust in the police (Tyler & Fagan, 2008; Tyler & Jackson, 2014). The first important point that develops from these findings is that the efforts of the police to manage crime in the community are aided by having the public's trust.

Beyond fighting crime, the long-term pay off of popular legitimacy is realized in the connection between policing and the economic, social and political development of communities. Trust in the police promotes a climate of reassurance, which motivates identification with one's community and engagement in that community (Tyler & Jackson, 2014). Police leaders frequently note that you cannot arrest your way out of crime. The finding that trust in the police promotes the goal of community development is an additional advantage.

WHAT SHAPES LEGITIMACY?: THE CENTRALITY OF PROCEDURAL JUSTICE

Legitimacy-based models of policing are desirable forms of institutional design but their viability depends upon being able to create and maintain a reservoir of legitimacy within the population. At this time, the procedural justice model is the most theoretically developed and empirically supported model for achieving the goal of legitimacy-based policing. Hence, it is the most promising framework within which to conceptualize changes in the goals of policing and move from a "police force" model to a "police service" model in American policing.

What empirical evidence supports the procedural justice model? Hagan and Hans (2017) note that there is today a large literature on procedural justice, ranging across a variety of authorities and institutions. As an example, they note that there have been over 30,000 references to research on this issue in the last five years prior to theie review, and it has played an important role in policy reform discussions (Meares, 2014) culminating in the President's Task Force on 21st Century Policing.

The Social Psychology of Procedural Justice

Support for the initial procedural justice model is found in the literature in social psychology (Thibaut & Walker, 1975; Leventhal, 1980). The first research efforts in this area are those of John Thibaut and Laurens Walker. Their research program is summarized in their book *Procedural Justice* (1975) and their research is reviewed in *The Social Psychology of Procedural Justice* (Lind & Tyler, 1988). The first important point about these studies is that they are well-designed randomized control trials (RCTs). They are built around variations in courtroom procedures and they demonstrate that different procedures are rated differently in terms of their perceived procedural justice. Procedural variations are also shown to shape a variety of types of evaluations of judicial procedures and/or authorities. These procedural justice findings are replicated in a series of experimental studies conducted within this research group (Thibaut, Walker & Lind, 1972; Lind, Thibaut & Walker, 1973; Thibaut, Walker, LaTour & Houlden, 1974; Walker, LaTour, Lind & Thibaut, 1974; Thibaut & Walker, 1975; Houlden et al., 1978; LaTour, 1978; Lind et al., 1978). The studies have high internal validity, but were conducted in laboratory contexts so they involve college students (Damaska, 1975; Hayden & Anderson, 1979). They also often lack measurement of legitimacy as an outcome of experience and, in the context of this report, lack a focus on the police. On the other hand, their experimental nature means that they have high internal validity in connecting objective variations in what authorities and institutions do to whether people feel fairly treated.

The psychological literature on procedural justice has been reviewed by Miller (2001) and MacCoun (2005). Miller discusses two behavioral consequences of procedural injustice. The first is a lower willingness to comply with authorities. The second is a diminished motivation to pursue group goals and concerns. In addition, Miller notes the absence of any downside consequences of fair procedures. He further notes that research valuably expands the universe of goals beyond compliance, something central to law, to include enhancing the viability of organizations. When the MacCoun (2005) review was conducted, the psychological literature had over 700 articles on the topic of procedural justice. His review of this literature suggests that, across the wide range of types of authority considered, procedural justice is consistently found to shape compliance and cooperation with authorities. In particular, these effects are found with both experimental and correlational research designs. The author notes that "the sheer heterogeneity of tasks, domains, populations, designs, and analytic methods provides remarkable convergence and triangulation (MacCoun, 2005: 173)" in support of the core propositions of procedural justice. This is particularly important in the light of subsequent methodological critiques of this literature (Nagin & Telep, 2017).

Procedural Justice in Management

The central arguments of procedural justice models have subsequently been tested in management settings and a distinct literature on procedural justice has developed within organizational psychology/organizational behavior. An early example is a study by Earley and Lind (1987) in which workers were randomly assigned to work under different procedures varying in their perceived fairness. These differences were found to influence perceived justice and employee performance on the job. The literature on procedural justice in work settings has expanded broadly to include variations in many aspects of work organizations and their impact upon a number of dependent variables, including but not limited to adherence to rules and work requirements. A particular advantage of studies in work settings is that they also look at employee engagement and extra-role (e.g., nonrequired) behavior.

Cohen-Charash and Spector (2001) reviewed 190 studies (148 field studies and 42 laboratory studies) and found that variations in workplace characteristics reliably shaped perceived fairness in both field studies (p. 293; r = 0.52) and laboratory studies (p. 293; r = 0.38). The studies provide direction for efforts to create policing procedures that build trust by showing that providing voice in procedures for work assignment, pay appraisal, grievance management, and other similar issues is especially central to perceived fairness. They further show that procedural justice is reliably related to a number of evaluations, including satisfaction with one's job, pay, supervisor, management, and performance appraisal procedures (their table 7, p. 299). Procedural justice is also related to employee commitment to the job, normative commitment, trust in the organization, trust in one's supervisor, and turnover intentions (their table 7, p. 300).

Their review further suggests that variations in the workplace characteristics associated with differences in perceived fairness are found to have an uneven relationship to required workplace behaviors. Studies show a connection to workplace performance for field studies (p. 296; r = 0.45), but not for lab studies (r = 0.11, not significant). The studies consistently find a relationship to voluntary extra-role behavior (organization citizenship behavior) (p. 297; r = 0.23) and to undermining work behaviors (r = −0.28; i.e., more fairness leads to less shirking, sabotage, etc.).

Colquitt, Conlon et al. (2001) review the justice literature and Colquitt, Scott et al. (2013) re-review the original and the new literature and identify 493 distinct studies. In the larger re-review, they find significant overall influences of procedural justice on trust in authorities (Colquitt, Scott et al., 2013: 210), organizational citizenship behavior (p. 207), task performance (p. 208) and (negatively) on counterproductive work behavior, i.e., rule breaking and destructive actions (p. 209). The review finds equally strong relationships for studies that focus upon particular personal experiences and those that make overall evaluations of the procedural justice of the workplace. This includes their own workplace and the overall organization (Tyler & Blader, 2000). It is particularly striking that both the justice of the particular workplace and the overall justice of the organization are important and distinct contributors to overall evaluations. For example, workers in a large multi-site organization are influenced by the fairness of the actions of a remote central leader, as well as to the justice of the actions of their immediate superior.

Perhaps most importantly, in terms of the model outlined, Colquitt et al. (2013) conducted a mediational analysis and found that the relationship between the organizational justice of the work organization and relevant employee behaviors was significantly, but not completely mediated by "social exchange quality" (see their figure 1, p. 217). Social exchange quality was measured as a combined index that includes trust, mutual respect, perceived management support, and commitment. It is in many ways similar to the idea of legitimacy in a management context. This type of mediating role is also identified in more recent studies of management settings (Ma, Liu & Liu, 2014).

In the case of compliance with rules, there are several studies illustrating workplace factors that have an influence on compliance, something which is treated in this literature as an aspect of task performance in this research. Greenberg (1994) manipulates the fairness of the enactment of smoking ban in a work setting and finds resulting compliance variations. Greenberg (1990) varies the fairness of pay changes and finds a later impact on employee theft. Lind et al. (1993) conduct a field study involving interviews with disputants and find that perceived fairness shapes the subsequent acceptance of arbitration awards. Dunford and Devine (1998) and, Greenberg, Scott, and Welchans (2000) interview employees and find that variations in the perceived fairness of termination procedures predict whether people later file lawsuits. In a multinational setting, Kim and Mauborgne (1993) conduct a survey-based study and find that rule following is linked to perceived management fairness.

Procedural Justice in the General Criminal Justice System

Another prior literature deals with criminal justice, but not with the police. Several studies deal with the courts, linking trust and confidence in courts to procedural justice (Kitzmann & Emery, 1993; Wemmers, 2013; Tyler, 2001; Farole, 2007; Abuwala & Farole, 2008). This effect is also found for willingness to accept court decisions (MacCoun et al., 1988; Tyler & Huo, 2002). Other studies deal with the government authorities more broadly (Poythress, 1994; Wenzel, 2002; Murphy, 2004; Tyler, 2011; Vainio, 2011).

In the case of recidivism following a court procedure, Gottfredson et al. (2007) study the influence of drug courts compared to traditional courts on later recidivism and find an impact that is mediated by procedural justice. Similarly, the Red Hook community court, which has features associated with procedural justice, lowers recidivism (Lee et al., 2014), and Wales et al. (2010) indicate similar recidivism effects in a mental health court. A study by Canada and Hiday (2014) indicates that procedural justice influences whether people terminate program participation.

Summary: Procedural Justice Outside Policing

In summary, the theoretical model underlying the procedural justice approach has been widely supported in studies varying in their context and their methodology. What is striking is the convergence of the findings of these widely varied studies. Many studies, including experimental variations in procedures suggest that it is possible to reliably create policies and practices that influences perceived procedural justice. Studies also suggest that such variations shape not only perceived procedural justice but also compliance, cooperation, and a variety of other types of organizationally relevant behaviors. This echoes the MacCoun (2005) suggestion that variations in method or the type of authority do not change the basic conclusions reached.

Of particular importance is the finding that those studies that do conduct mediational analyses indicate that the impact of procedural justice upon behavior is mediated by social orientations toward the relevant authority or organization. It is important to acknowledge that procedural justice effects are sometimes direct and do not flow through broader attitudes or values about an organization. In particular, being treated fairly or unfairly by a particular authority often directly shapes behavioral reactions toward that authority irrespective of whether or not it influences broader views about the organization of which they are members. For example, a study of Muslims living in the UK found that the procedural justice of police actions directly shaped the willingness to cooperate, but that the influence was not mediated by changes in legitimacy (Huq, Tyler & Schulhofer, 2011).

Procedural Justice in Policing

In the case of the police, a number of studies suggest that perceptions of the procedural justice of police actions are a key evaluation that shapes the popular legitimacy of both particular police officers and the police as an overall organization (Kitzmann & Emery, 1993; Wemmers, 1996; Tyler, 2006a; Farole, 2007; Hinds, 2007; Hinds & Murphy, 2007; Abuwala & Farole, 2008; Tyler & Fagan, 2008; Tor, Gazal-Ayal & Garcia, 2010; Elliott, Thomas & Ogloff, 2011; Hasisi & Weisburd, 2011; Jonathan-Zamir & Weisburd, 2013; Mazerolle et al., 2012; Myhill & Bradford, 2012). Donner and colleagues (2015) review twenty-eight studies of the police and conclude that procedural justice activities during police interactions with the public positively influence public views of police legitimacy and trust in the police. This conclusion is supported both by studies that use subjective measures assessing orientations toward cooperation (see Mazerolle et al., 2012; Wolfe et al., 2016) and objective measures of citizen cooperation (Mastrofski et al., 1996; Dai et al., 2011; Mazerolle et al., 2013). Procedural justice also affects willingness to defer to police authority as measured by self-report in surveys (Tyler & Fagan, 2008; Tyler & Huo, 2002).

There is also an emerging body of experimental studies of the impact of procedurally just treatment on citizen attitudes toward the police. These studies do not provide a clear conclusion regarding whether manipulations in the procedural justice of treatment by the police can improve perceptions of police legitimacy and cooperation. Mazerolle and colleagues (2013) examine police stops in Australia and find that a single experience of heightened procedural justice generalizes to shape trust in the police in the community. The Queensland Community Engagement Trial (QCET) was a randomized controlled trial that provides for an experimental treatment in the form of scripted traffic checks for drunk driving. Officers were trained to follow a protocol designed to maximize the procedural justice of the brief interactions occasioned by the random breath testing (RBT). Scripts were formulated to incorporate the components of procedural justice into officers' administration of the RBT. During thirty of sixty RBT operations, officers were directed to use the experimental script, and senior officers monitored their compliance with the protocol. These police–citizen encounters were quite brief: ordinarily (i.e., the control condition), they were "very systematic and often devoid of anything but compulsory communication" (Mazerolle et al., 2013: 40). This is about twenty seconds in duration. The scripted procedurally just encounters were longer, at ninety-seven seconds on average, but still quite brief. Each driver who was stopped during these sixty RBT operations was given a survey to be completed later and returned to the researchers. The procedural justice treatment had the hypothesized effects on citizens' judgments. However, response rates, for both experimental and control drivers, were about 13 percent, raising concerns about the validity of the findings.

The QCET's design, but not its results, have been replicated (MacQueen and Bradford, 2015). MacQueen and Bradford (2015) used a block-randomized design with pre- and post-test measures. The treatment was a police-stop procedure that involved key messages built around procedural justice and a leaflet to motorists that emphasized similar themes. The study found no significant improvements in general trust in the police or perceived police legitimacy. Similarly, a recent experiment using traffic stops in Turkey (Sahin et al., 2016) found that behavior during stops shaped views about the particular police officers involved, but did not generalize to overall perceptions about the traffic police. And Lowrey and colleagues (2016), who studied street stops by having observers view video clips of traffic stops, found an impact upon specific evaluations of the stop, including obligation to obey and trust and confidence in the officers, but not on generalizations to broader attitudes about the police.

The particular forms of police contact used in the studies noted are highly scripted and therefore do not vary in the ways that other forms of police contact do. Worden and McLean (2016: 34) comment: "Traffic checkpoints that involve very brief encounters between police and citizens are susceptible to such prescriptions, but police–citizen encounters in most domains of police work – and especially in those with the strong potential for contentious interactions – do not lend themselves to such experimental or administrative manipulation." Studies of the police emphasize that the police normally deal with a wide variety of situations and have very different styles of addressing each one (Muir, 1977). Epp, Maynard-Moody, and Haider-Markel (2014) argue that it is investigatory street stops, not traffic stops, that are central to creating feelings of injustice, since street stops are routinized and linked to understandable violations of known laws. Hence, such street stops are much less likely to create variations in perceived unfairness in treatment and are less likely to differentially impact upon perceived legitimacy. In other words, it is important not to overstate the importance of either the positive impact of the Mazerolle findings or of their subsequent disconfirmation in other studies.

In the case of assessing the impact of police contact on later willingness to cooperate with the police, Mazerolle and colleagues (2013) create a combined measure of self-reported behavior summarizing ongoing compliance and future willingness to cooperate. They evaluate five experimental studies that provide eight outcome measures. In three of eight cases there is a significant influence of police intervention upon compliance/cooperation. Mazerolle and colleagues (2013: 261) conclude that the results suggest that the "interventions had [a] large, significant, positive association with a combined measure of compliance and cooperation." Mazerolle et al. (2014) further contains an extended meta-analysis on procedural justice effects. In reviewing community policing efforts that contain procedural justice elements, the authors find four studies exploring influence upon compliance/cooperation and report three significant relationships in the expected direction (p. 28). With restorative justice conferencing, they find four studies examining influence on compliance/cooperation and four significant relationships (p. 29). The authors conclude that procedural justice has positive effects upon perceived legitimacy, and that these jointly shape self-reported compliance/cooperation.

Recent studies also suggest that perceived procedural justice may impact identification with the community, social capital, and engagement in the community (Kochel, 2012; Tyler and Jackson, 2014). Kochel (2012) studies the police in Trinidad and Tobago through interviews with 2,969 people in thirteen police districts and finds that the nature of police–citizen interactions had an impact on collective efficacy. Collective efficacy is particularly strongly linked to judgments about the quality of police services, a combined measure that includes satisfaction with services, and judgments about whether the police are competent, respectful, capable of maintaining order, and willing to help citizens with their problems. Tyler and Jackson (2014) conduct a national survey and find that procedural justice and legitimacy policing is associated with identification with the community, collective efficacy and behaviors such as likelihood of shopping in the community and participating in local politics. This suggests that the perceived fairness of policing can have an impact beyond the arena of crime and criminal justice – it can also more broadly affect communities and their well-being.

The central conclusion of the procedural justice literature is that, when people deal with authorities, their evaluations of the perceived fairness of the procedures through which authority is exercised influence legitimacy more strongly than does the perceived outcome of the encounter (Tyler, 2006a; Tyler, Fagan & Geller, 2014; Tyler & Jackson, 2014). Similarly, when people are making overall assessments of the legitimacy of a criminal justice institution in their community, they focus upon how members of that institution generally deal with the public (Sunshine & Tyler, 2003; Tyler, 2006a; Tyler, Fagan & Geller, 2014; Tyler & Jackson, 2014).

Objective Coding of Police Behavior

It is important to note that, in addition to subjective perceptions of police treatment along the four dimensions that matter to perceived legitimacy, researchers have also observed and coded officer conduct to determine how officer actions relate to subjective perceptions. That is, rather than relying upon the research subject's personal perceptions and judgments about how the police treated him/her, researchers construct a protocol for observing and classifying officer behavior that satisfies the definition of procedural justice. This requires sufficiently clear and detailed instructions to create reliable measures of officer conduct that trained third-party observers can replicate reliably from situation to situation and across observers (Worden & McLean, 2014).

Interestingly, the relatively few studies that have explored objective measures of the components of perceived procedural justice have found that, unlike subjective measures, the elements of procedural justice are only modestly related, suggesting that they are best conceived as a formative index (Jonathan-Zamir et al., 2013; Worden & McLean, 2014). Further, the only study (Worden & Mclean, 2014) to have compared objective and subjective measures of officer conduct along these dimensions found that the objective and subjective measures are themselves related but the magnitude of that connection varies across dimensions (see discussion as follows).

The Nagin-Telep Critique

While there are a number of studies that support the argument that procedural justice influences legitimacy and that legitimacy shapes law-related behavior, a recent critique of this literature (Nagin & Telep, 2017) highlights several important points. First, most of the research on policing to date is nonexperimental. While a number of studies provide experimental support for the ideas concerning procedural justice and legitimacy that have been outlined, most are not on the police. Hence, further *experimental* research is needed on procedural justice and legitimacy in policing. That experimental research is already occurring and it is encouraging that recent experimental studies support the argument that police procedural justice shapes police legitimacy and decision acceptance when dealing with the police (Reisig, Mays & Telep, 2018).

Second, the existing studies on policing do not test the complete proposed causal model (procedural justice → legitimacy → behavior) within a single study; nor do they demonstrate that there is not a reverse causal flow, for example, with prior legitimacy shaping the perceived procedural justice of an experience. For these reasons, it is important to recognize the need for further experimental research on procedural justice in policing.

In responding to this critique, Tyler (2017c) suggests that the reason procedural justice models have drawn the attention of criminal justice authorities is that they reflect the most promising model for understanding how to build trust in the police. Because policing has focused so heavily upon models of crime control, there is very little research in policing on how to build public trust in the police. Procedural justice models, therefore, draw heavily upon findings outside policing to justify their validity and the need for any viable models of legitimacy in policing is what is motivating their widespread adoption. Future research on policing will hopefully provide more direct evidence in support of this model. It is also important for police researchers to explore other potential mechanisms for building trust.

The National Academies of Sciences recently released a consensus study report on Proactive Policing (Weisburd & Majmundar, 2018). That review of the literature reached conclusions similar to those already outlined. The report concludes that already available evidence from areas outside policing suggests that the procedural justice → legitimacy → behavior model receives strong experimental support in many areas of authority. However, the report notes that, at this time, there is very little experimental support demonstrating the effectiveness of this model in the area of policing. That is not to say that there is no evidence. There is already an abundance of nonexperimental research that supports this model (Tyler, Goff & MacCoun, 2015). However, further experimental studies are needed.

WHAT IS PROCEDURAL JUSTICE?

The psychological literature on perceived procedural justice has identified the already outlined four elements of experience that are linked to whether people evaluate them as being procedurally just. Those dimensions are not normatively identified by legal scholars. Rather, they have been drawn from research on the criteria that people themselves use to rate their experiences (Tyler, 1988). Importantly, studies suggest that there is substantial agreement across race, gender, and income levels in the criteria that define a fair procedure (Tyler & Huo, 2002).

Two of the elements identified are linked to how police officers are perceived to make decisions. Two other elements are linked to how the police are viewed as treating people.

The key to understanding this model is that the elements are focused upon how people experience policing, i.e., whether they feel they have a voice, whether they think the procedures are neutral, whether they feel respected, and whether they infer that the police are trustworthy. The underlying argument is that the way people perceive these features of police action shapes whether people do or do not judge the police to be legitimate.

In its subjective form, procedural justice has been typically assessed in one or both of two ways. The first is to ask people how fairly decisions were made or how they were treated. The second is to ask about the four aspects of procedural justice that emerge from studies of the meaning of procedural justice (Tyler, 1988). When studies assess subjective voice, neutrality, respect, and trust, they typically find that these dimensions are highly intercorrelated and that all four dimensions correlate strongly with evaluations of overall justice in decision-making and treatment (Tyler, 1988; Tyler & Fagan, 2008; Worden & McLean, 2014).

This finding suggests that it is possible to view subjective procedural justice as an overall dimension, although it is equally possible to distinguish the four dimensions. Empirical studies indicate that people distinguish more strongly among these four dimensions when they are evaluating their personal experiences than when they are making ratings of general police behavior in their community (Tyler, 2006).

There are several ways that the utility of these elements of procedural justice can be assessed. One way is to train officers along the lines of these elements and see if they are experienced as fairer and more legitimate. The Australian work on police stops does this and shows impact on perceived legitimacy. Similarly, studies in management settings show that organizations can be proactively designed to heighten employee feelings of fairness, just as studies in court design support the finding that courts can be created that will be generally experienced as fairer by those who go through them. At the same time, it has proven more challenging to link the ratings of the fairness of police behavior by observers in street interactions with the police to the perceptions of the people involved in those interactions. More research is needed before a clear set of police actions can be consistently linked to subjective justice judgments about police officers or the police more broadly.

INTERNAL DEPARTMENT DYNAMICS

Another approach to improving policing that also draws upon procedural justice is to focus on creating fairer internal dynamics within police departments. When officers feel more fairly treated by their superiors, they act more fairly when dealing with the public (Farmer, Beehr & Love, 2003;

DeAngelis and Kupchik, 2007, 2009; Tyler et al., 2007; Taxman and Gordon, 2009; Wolfe and Piquero, 2011; Harris & Worden, 2014; Bradford et al., 2013). These studies show that officers who feel fairly treated are more likely to view their department, as well as its policies and leaders, as legitimate and to comply with organizational rules and policies; to feel organizational commitment; to want to stay with the department; and to work cooperatively with their supervisors (Trinkner & Tyler, 2016).

Central to discussions of officer stress is the parallel finding that officers working in departments low in the procedural justice of their department culture experience higher levels of job-related stress. Working in stressful situations within a department that does not have the elements of procedural justice contributes to a set of occupational hazards associated with policing: suicide, alcoholism, divorce, depression, etc. This argument is supported by a large literature on how the general organizational climate of workplaces shapes health. The core health-related argument is that creating procedurally just organizational conditions promotes well-being and when such conditions are not present, stress is high.

The physical and mental ailments resulting from workplace stress include taking sick days, becoming ill, using drugs, drinking, experiencing marital problems, and even suicide. The public health literature on the influence of workplace conditions on stress has widely documented these as consequences of working within an unfair environment. While the focus of the studies varies, they all show a connection between unfair management practices and poor employee health (for a review, see Robbins, Ford & Tetrick, 2012). Studies indicate that, in particular, poor relationships between workers and their immediate supervisors produce stress on the job.

What is the connection between the fairness of the experience that officers have in their stationhouse and what they do on the street? A recent study by Bradford and colleagues (2013) indicates that those officers who experience fair process and procedures in their department are not only more likely to comply with department rules and more likely to be committed to organization goals, but they are also more likely to be supportive of community policing models that emphasize cooperation with the community and building positive working relationships with community members. Trinkner and colleagues (2016) find the same results in a study of Chicago police officers. They link procedural justice in the department directly to stress levels among officers.

SELF-LEGITIMACY

While there have not been studies of the police that focus upon issues of identity and status in policing, in particular studies that identify police actions shaping these judgments, several studies have argued for the importance of identity issues. Murphy and colleagues (2015) use longitudinal data to study the influence of procedural justice upon tax payments. They find that the effects are mediated by impact upon social identity as reflected through taxpayer identification with the government. Bradford and colleagues (2015) study traffic offenders and find that social identity, as evidenced by their identification with their community, mediates between procedural justice and self-reported propensity to offend. Finally, in a sample of the residents of England and Wales, Bradford (2014) found a strong association between police procedural fairness, social identity and police legitimacy. On the other hand, police unfairness undermines the sense of shared identity with the police (Reicher et al., 2004).

One especially important aspect of police officer identity is self-legitimacy (Bradford & Quinton, 2014). Do officers feel confident in their own authority? Bradford and Quinton (2014) suggest that when officers identify with their organization, they feel legitimate in their role. This, in turn, supports a commitment to democratic modes of policing.

IMPLICATIONS FOR POLICING

Why should the police care about procedural justice? The procedural justice model argues that focusing on procedural justice matters if the police want popular legitimacy. And, they should want popular legitimacy because it facilitates doing their jobs in more desirable ways. This is the case because procedural justice builds and maintains legitimacy, which promotes obeying the law and cooperating with the police. Although it is possible to seek to exercise social control by the threat or use of force, and although the police are well equipped to do so because they are vested with instruments of force (guns, tasers, clubs, etc.), it is in fact not most desirable for the police to approach situations with a force orientation or to use force in their interactions. This approach defines situations as conflicts and frames them as force based. If officers instead focus on acting fairly, they build legitimacy and gain voluntary deference. Such deference is not based upon force, but upon obligation and responsibility. Hence, the issue of power and force is minimized, and conflict is avoided as much as possible and, when it exists, it is deescalated as much as is possible.

But the broader point from our perspective is why society should care about how the police act when dealing with the community? Society's goal ought not to be the maintenance of large police forces, especially in an era of low crime and when local budgets are working for scraps. Rather it should be to determine the most effective way to balance managing public safety against other goals. A dollar used to fund the police is a dollar that is not used to repair a bridge, fund a school, or help people with healthcare. Is that dollar being well spent? It is not an argument in favor of high crime to ask this question. It is valuable to point to evidence that other types of policing besides those that dominate America today are equally effective in managing crime and more effective in advancing other community goals like community engagement and solidarity, as well as engagement in efforts to promote economic, social, and political goals.

One important emerging research finding is that focused policing (hot spots policing) is particularly effective in reducing crime (Weisburd & Majmundar, 2018). Parallel to this development the ability to identify criminals through mechanisms such as network analysis has allowed for an increasing focus on the small group of violence offenders in any given community (Green, Thibaut & Papachristos, 2017; Sierra-Arevalo & Papachristos, 2017). These evidence-informed advances in policing practice further suggest that the size of police forces might reasonably decline. And this could happen without crime rates rising if those officers who remained were deployed strategically.

Ironically, it was fifty years ago that policing last received national attention on the level it is seeing today. President Johnson convened the Commission on Law Enforcement and Administration of Justice (Katzenbach Commission, 1967) and the National Advisory Commission on Civil Disorders (Kerner Commission, 1968). These reports argued that the police should become more involved in social welfare functions. The same issue is important today. Police leaders resist efforts to transform the police into an agency that deals with a broader range of social problems and express frustration that they must deal with issues such as mental health populations on the street. On the other hand, they resist efforts to reduce the size of police forces, although the crime rate has dramatically declined since the 1970s.

At this time, there are several paths that the police might choose (Tyler, 2017b). One is to focus on building popular legitimacy and to become involved in efforts to build the social, economic, and political viability of communities. The studies already outlined indicate that changes in police philosophy (from a police force to a police service) could result in contacts that build trust. The future of policing could be about building trust. This would move the police more in the direction of performing tasks that address social issues. Policing would not be focused largely or solely upon harm reduction via crime control. On normative democratic grounds, it is important to recognize that the police are, at the end of the day, public servants and the community residents they deal with are their clients. Our structure of government in particular emphasizes that that police and other government agencies should intrude only sparingly into our lives and only when justified to protect people and communities from crime and disorder.

As it stands, studies suggest that the general impact of contact with the police, especially among juveniles, is to lower perceived legitimacy (Petrosino, Guckenburg & Turpin-Petrosino, 2010; Tyler, Fagan & Geller, 2014). Hence, another approach would be to minimize public contact with a harm-reduction oriented police force and thereby minimize alienation and distrust. Some communities already seek to minimize police intrusion or to at least limit investigatory stops. This approach creates another problem in leaving vulnerable people without protection. And, as we have noted, it raises the question of what to do with the police forces that have grown in past decades to combat much higher crime rates. Is there enough political will to reduce such forces and reallocate social resources?

The feasibility of advancing the goal of transforming the mission of the police develops out of the movement of evidence-informed law. It draws from theoretical models in the social sciences that define alternative ways of organizing the relationship between the police and the community and provides evidence for the value of those approaches. These findings both point to new directions for policing goals and for the policies and practices of the police and suggest the importance of theory-based research on the police.

REFERENCES

Abuwala, R., & Farole, D. J. (2008). *The Effects of the Harlem Housing Court on Tenant Perceptions of Justice.* New York: Center for Court Innovation.

Bradford, B. (2014). Policing and social identity: procedural justice, inclusion and cooperation between police and public. *Policing & Society, 24*, 22–43.

Bradford, B., Hohl, K., Jackson, J., & MacQueen, S. (2015). Obeying the rules of the road: Procedural justice, social identity and normative conflict. *Journal of Contemporary Criminal Justice, 3*(2), 171–191.

Bradford, B., & Quinton, P. (2014). Self-legitimacy, police culture and support for democratic policing in an English constabulary. *British Journal of Criminology, 54*, 1023–1046.

Bradford, B., Quinton, P., Myhill, A., & Porter, G. (2014). Why do "the law" comply? Procedural justice, group identification and officer motivations in police organizations. *European Journal of Criminology, 11*(1), 110–131.

Canada, K. E., & Hiday, V. A. (2014). Procedural justice in mental health court: An investigation of the relation of perception of procedural justice to non-adherence and termination. *Journal of Forensic Psychiatry and Psychology, 25*(3), 321–340.

Cohen-Charash, Y., & Spector, P. E. (2001). The role of justice in organizations: A meta-analysis. *Organizational Behavior and Human Decision Processes, 86*, 278–321.

Colquitt, J. A., Conlon, D. E., Wesson, M. J., Porter, C. O. L. H., & Ng, K. Y. (2001). Justice at the millennium: A meta-analytic review of 25 years of organizational justice research. *Journal of Applied Psychology, 86*, 425–445.

Colquitt, J. A., Scott, B. A., Rodell, J. B., Long, D. M., Zapata, C. P., Conlon, D .E., & Wesson, M. J. (2013). Justice at the millennium, a decade later: A meta-analytic test of social exchange and affect-based perspectives. *Journal of Applied Psychology, 98*(2), 199–236.

Dai, M., Frank, J., & Sun, I. (2011). Procedural justice during police–citizen encounters. *Journal of Criminal Justice, 39*(2), 159–168.

Damaska, M. (1975). Presentation of evidence and fact finding precision. *University of Pennsylvania Law Review, 123*(5), 1083–1106.

De Angelis, J., & Kupchik, A. (2007). Citizen oversight, procedural justice, and officer perceptions of the complaint investigation process. *Policing, 30*, 651–671.

De Angelis, J., & Kupchik, A. (2009). Ethnicity, trust, and acceptance of authority among police officers. *Journal of Criminal Justice*, *37*, 273–279.

Donner, C., Maskaly, J., Fridell, L., & Jennings, W. G. (2015). Policing and procedural justice. *Policing*, *38*, 153–172.

Dunford, B., & Devine, D. (1998). Employment at-will and employee discharge: A justice perspective on legal action following termination. *Personnel Psychology*, *51*(4), 903–934.

Earley, P. C., & Lind, E. A. (1987). Procedural justice and participation in task selection. *Journal of Personality and Social Psychology*, *52*(6), 1148–1160.

Elliott, I., Thomas, S. D., & Ogloff, J. R. (2011). Procedural justice in contacts with the police: Testing a relational model of authority in a mixed methods study. *Psychology, Public Policy, and Law*, *17*, 592–610.

Epp, C. R., Maynard-Moody, S., & Haider-Markel, D. P. (2014). *Pulled Over: How Police Stops Define Race and Citizenship*. Chicago: University of Chicago Press.

Farmer, S. J., Beehr, T. A., & Love, K. G. (2003). Becoming an undercover police officer. *Journal of Organizational Behavior*, *24*, 373–387.

Farole, D. J. (2007). *Public Perceptions of New York's Courts. The NY State Residents Survey*. New York: Center for Court Innovation.

Gottfredson, D. C., Kearley, B. W., Najaka, S. S., & Rocha, C. M. (2007). How drug treatment courts work. *Journal of Research in Crime and Delinquency*, *44*(1), 3–35.

Green, B., Thibaut H., & Papachristos, A. V. (2017). The social contagion of gunshot violence in co-offending networks. *Journal of American Medical Association Internal Medicine*, *177*(3), 326–333.

Greenberg, J. (1990). Employee theft as a reaction to underpayment inequity: The hidden cost of pay cuts. *Journal of Applied Psychology*, *75*(5), 561–568.

Greenberg, J. (1994). Using socially fair treatment to promote acceptance of a work site smoking ban. *Journal of Applied Psychology*, *79*(2), 288–297.

Hagan, J., & Hans, V. P. (2017). Procedural justice theory and public policy. *Annual Review of Law and Social Science*, *13*, 1–3.

Harris, C., & Worden, R. (2014). The effect of sanctions on police misconduct. *Crime and Delinquency*, *60*, 1258–1288.

Hasisi, B., & Weisburd, D. (2011). Going beyond ascribed identities: The importance of procedural justice in airport security screening in Israel. *Law and Society Review*, *45*, 867–892.

Hayden, R., & Anderson, J. (1979). On the evaluation of procedural systems in laboratory experiments. *Law and Human Behavior*, *3*(1/2), 21–38.

Hinds, L. (2007). Building police–youth relationships: The importance of procedural justice. *National Association Youth Justice*, *7*, 195–209.

Hinds, L., & Murphy, K. (2007). Public satisfaction with police: Using procedural justice to improve police legitimacy. *The Australian & New Zealand Journal of Criminology*, *40*, 27–42.

Houlden, P., LaTour, S., Walker, L., & Thibaut, J. (1978) Preference for modes of dispute resolution as a function of process and decision control. *Journal of Experimental Social Psychology*, *14*, 13–30.

Huq, A., Tyler, T. R., & Schulhofer, S. J. (2011). Mechanisms for eliciting cooperation in counterterrorism policing: Evidence from the United Kingdom. *Journal of Empirical Legal Studies*, *8*, 728–761.

Jonathan-Zamir, T., & Weisburd, D. (2013). The effects of security threats on antecedents of police legitimacy: Findings from a quasi-experiment in Israel. *Journal of Research in Crime and Delinquency, 50*, 3–32.

Kim, W. C., & Mauborgne, R. A. (1993). Procedural justice, attitudes, and subsidiary top management compliance with multinationals' corporate strategic decisions. *Academy of Management, 36*(3), 502–526.

Kitzmann, K., & Emery, R. (1993). Procedural justice and parents' satisfaction in a field study of child custody dispute resolution. *Law and Human Behavior, 17*, 553–567.

Kochel, T. R. (2012). Can police legitimacy promote collective efficacy? *Justice Quarterly, 29*, 384–419.

LaTour, S. (1978). Determinations of participant and observer satisfaction with adversary and inquisitorial modes of adjudication. *Journal of Personality and Social Psychology, 36*(12), 1531–1545.

Lee, C. G., Cheesman, F., Rottman, D., Swaner, R., Lambson, S., Rempel, M., & Curtis, R. (2014). *A Community Court Grows in Brooklyn: A Comprehensive Evaluation of the Red Hook Community Justice Center Final Report.* National Center for State Courts.

Leventhal, G. S. (1980). What should be done with equity theory? New approaches to the study of fairness in social relationships. In K. Gergen, M. Greenberg, and R. Willis (eds.), *Social Exchange* (pp. 27–55). New York: Plenum.

Lind, E. A., Erickson, B. E., Friedland, N., & Dickenberger, M. (1978). Reactions to procedural models for adjudicative conflict resolution: A cross-national study. *Journal of Conflict Resolution, 2*, 318–341.

Lind, E. A., Greenberg, J., Scott, K., & Welchans, T. D. (2000). The winding road from employee to complainant: Situational and psychological determinants of wrongful-termination claims. *Administrative Science Quarterly, 45*(3), 557–590.

Lind, E. A., Kulik, C. T., Ambrose, M., & de Vera Park, M. (1993). Individual and corporate dispute resolution. *Administrative Science Quarterly, 38*, 224–251.

Lind, E. A., Thibaut, J., & Walker, L. (1973). Discovery and presentation of evidence in adversary and non-adversary proceedings. *Michigan Law Review, 71*, 1129–1144.

Lind, E. A., & Tyler, T. R. (1988). *The Social Psychology of Procedural Justice.* New York: Plenum.

Lowrey, B., Maguire, E., & Bennett, R. (2016). Testing the effects of procedural justice and overaccommodation in traffic stops: A randomized experiment. *Criminal Justice and Behavior, 43*(10), 1430–1449.

Ma, B., Liu, S., & Liu, D. (2014). The impact of organizational identification on the relationship between procedural justice and employee work outcomes. *Social Behavior and Personality: An International Journal, 42*(3), 437–444.

MacCoun, R. (2005). Voice, control, and belonging: The double-edged sword of procedural fairness. *Annual Review of Law and Social Sciences, 1*, 171–201.

MacCoun, R. J., Lind, E. A., Hensler, D. R., Bryant, D. L., & Ebener, P. A. (1988). *Alternative Adjudication.* Santa Monica, CA. Rand.

MacQueen, S., & Bradford, B. (2015), Enhancing public trust and police legitimacy during road traffic encounters: Results from a randomised controlled trial in Scotland. *Journal of Experimental Criminology, 11*, 419–443.

Mastrofski, S., Snipes, B., & Supina, A. E. (1996). Compliance on demand: The public's response to specific police requests. *Journal of Research in Crime & Delinquency, 33*, 269–305.

Mazerolle, L., Antrobus, E., Bennett, S., & Tyler, T. R. (2013). Shaping citizen perceptions of police legitimacy: A randomized field trial of procedural justice. *Criminology, 51*, 33–64.

Mazerolle, L., Bennett, S., Davis, J., Sargeant, E., & Dunning, M. (2013). Procedural justice and police legitimacy. *Journal of Experimental Criminology, 9*, 245–274.

Mazerolle, L., Bennett, S., Antrobus, E., & Tyler, T. R. (2012). Shaping citizen perceptions of police legitimacy: A randomized field trial of procedural justice. *Criminology, 51*, 1–31.

Mazerolle, L., Sargeant, E., Cherney, A., Bennett, S., Murphy, K., Antrobus, E., & Martin, P. (2014). *Procedural Justice and Legitimacy in Policing.* Springer.

Meares, T. (2014). The law and social science of stop and frisk. *American Review of Law and Social Sciences, 10*, 335–342.

Miller, D. (2001). Disrespect and the experience of injustice. *Annual Review of Psychology, 52*, 527–553.

Muir, W, Jr. (1977). *Police: Streetcorner Politicians.* Chicago: University of Chicago Press.

Murphy, K. (2004). Procedural justice, shame and tax compliance. Working paper 50. Center for Tax System Integrity. Australian National University. Canberra.

Myhill, A., & Bradford, B. (2012). Can police enhance confidence in improving quality of service? *Policing and Society, 22*, 397–425.

Nagin, D. S., & Telep, C. W. (2017). Procedural justice and legal compliance. *Annual Review of Law and Social Science, 13*, 5–28.

Petrosino, A., Guckenburg, S., & Turpin-Petrosino, C. (2010) *Formal System Processing of Juveniles: Effects on Delinquency.* Oslo, Norway: Campbell Collaboration.

PEW. Polls, 11/26/2014.

PEW. Polls, 8/18/2014.

Poythress, N. (1994). Procedural preferences, perceptions of fairness, and compliance with outcomes: A study of alternatives to the standard adversary trial procedure. *Law and Human Behavior, 18*(4), 361–376.

President's Commission on Law Enforcement and the Administration of Justice (Katzenbach Commission). (1967). US Government Printing Office.

Reicher S., Stott, C., Cronin, P., & Adang, O. (2004). An integrated approach to crowd psychology and public order policing. *Policing: An International Journal of Police Strategies & Management, 27*(4), 558–572.

Reisig, M. D., Mays, R. D., & Telep, C. W. (2017). The effects of procedural injustice during police-citizen encounters: A factorial vignette study. *Journal of Experimental Criminology, 14*, 49–58.

Report of the National Advisory Commission on Civil Disorders (Kerner Commission). (1968). New York: Bantam Books.

Robbins, J., Ford, M. T., & Tetrick, L. E. (2012). Perceived unfairness and employee health: A meta-analytic integration. *Journal of Applied Psychology, 97*(2), 235–272.

Sahin, N., Braga, A., Apel, R., & Brunson, R. (2016). The impact of procedurally-just policing on citizen perceptions of police during traffic stops: The Adana Randomized Controlled Trial. *Journal of Quantitative Criminology*, 1–26.

Schneider, B. (January 15, 2015). Do Americans trust their cops to be fair and just? New poll contains surprises. *Reuters US edition.*

Sierra-Arevalo, M., & Papachristos, A. V. (2017). Social Networks and Gang Violence Reduction. *Annual Review of Law and Social Science, 13*, 373–393.

Sunshine, J., & Tyler, T. R. (2003). The Role of Procedural Justice and Legitimacy in Shaping Public Support for Policing. *Law & Society Review*, 37 (3), 513–548.

Taxman, F. S., & Gordon, J. A. (2009). Do fairness and equity matter? An examination of organizational justice among correctional officers in adult prisons. *Criminal Justice and Behavior*, 36, 695–711.

Thibaut, J., & Walker, L. (1975). *Procedural Justice: A Psychological Analysis*. Hillsdale, NJ: Erlbaum.

Thibaut, J., Walker, L., LaTour, S., & Houlden, P. (1974). Procedural justice as fairness. *Stanford Law Review*, 26, 1271–1289.

Thibaut, J., Walker, L., & Lind. E. A. (1972). Adversary presentation and bias in legal decision-making. *Harvard Law Review*, 86, 386–401.

Tor, A., Gazal-Ayal, O., & Garcia, S. M. (2010). Fairness and the willingness to accept plea bargain offers. *Journal of Experimental Legal Studies*, 7, 97–116.

Trinkner, R., Tyler, T. R., & Goff, P. A. (2016). Justice from within: The relations between a procedurally just organizational climate and police organizational efficiency, endorsement of democratic policing, and officer well-being. *Psychology, Public Policy and Law*, 22, 158–172.

Tyler, T. R. (1988). What is procedural justice? Criteria used by citizens to assess the fairness of legal procedures. *Law and Society Review*, 22, 103–135.

Tyler, T. R., (2001). Public trust and confidence in legal authorities: What do majority and minority group members want from the law and legal institutions? *Behavioral Sciences and the Law*, 19, 215–235.

Tyler, T. R. (2006a). *Why People Obey the Law*. Princeton, NJ: Princeton University Press.

Tyler, T. R. (2006b). Psychological perspectives on legitimacy and legitimation. *Annual Review of Psychology*, 57, 375–400.

Tyler, T. R. (2011). *Why People Cooperate: The Role of Social Motivations*. Princeton, NJ: Princeton University Press.

Tyler, T. R. (2016). Police contact and legitimacy. Unpublished manuscript, Yale Law School.

Tyler, T. R. (2017a). Can the police enhance their popular legitimacy through their conduct? *University of Illinois Law Review*, 2017, 1971–2008.

Tyler, T. R. (2017b). From harm reduction to community engagement: Redefining the goals of American policing in the twenty-first century. *Northwestern University Law Review*, 111, 1537–1564.

Tyler, T. R. (2017c). Procedural justice and policing: A rush to judgment. *Annual Review of Law and Social Science*, 13, 29–53.

Tyler, T. R., & Blader, S. (2000). *Cooperation in Groups: Procedural Justice, Social Identity, and Behavioral Engagement*. Philadelphia, PA: Psychology Press.

Tyler, T. R., Callahan, P. E., & Frost, J. (2007). Armed, and dangerous (?): Motivating rule adherence among agents of social control. *Law & Society Review*, 41(2), 457–492.

Tyler, T. R., & Fagan, J. (2008). Legitimacy and cooperation: Why do people help the police fight crime in their communities? *Ohio State Journal of Criminal Law*, 6, 230–274.

Tyler, T. R., Fagan, J., & Geller, A. (2014). Street stops and police legitimacy. *Journal of Empirical Legal Studies*, 11(4), 751–785.

Tyler, T. R., Goff, P. A., & MacCoun, R. J. (2015). The impact of psychological science on policing in the United States: Procedural justice, legitimacy, and effective law enforcement. *Psychological Science in the Public Interest, 16*, 75–109.

Tyler, T. R., & Huo, Y. J. (2002). *Trust in the Law. Encouraging Public Cooperation with the Police and Courts.* New York: Russell Sage Foundation.

Tyler, T. R., & Jackson, J. (2014). Popular legitimacy and the exercise of legal authority: Motivating compliance, cooperation and engagement. *Psychology, Public Policy and Law, 20*, 78–95.

Tyler, T. R., & Lind, E. A. (1992). A relational model of authority in groups. In M. Zanna (ed.), *Advances in experimental social psychology* (vol. 25, pp. 115–191). New York: Academic Press.

Vainio, A. (2011). Why are forest owners satisfied with forest police decisions? Legitimacy, procedural justice, and perceived uncertainty. *Social Justice Research, 24*, 239.

Wales, H. W., Virginia, A., & Bradley, R. (2010). Procedural justice and the mental health court judge's role in reducing recidivism. *International Journal of Law and Psychiatry, 33*, 265–271.

Walker, L., LaTour, S., Lind, A., & Thibaut, J. (1974). Reactions of participants and observers to modes of adjudication. *Journal of Applied Social Psychology, 4*, 295–310.

Weisburd, D., & Majmundar, M. K. (2018). *Proactive Policing: Effects on Crime and Communities.* National Academies of Science.

Wemmers, J. M. (1996). *Victims in the criminal justice system: A study into the treatment of victims and its effect on their attitudes and behavior* (Doctoral dissertation).

Wemmers, J. M. (2013). Victims' experiences in the criminal justice system and their recovery from crime. *International Review of Victimology, 19*, 221–233.

Wenzel, M. (2002). The impact of outcome orientation and justice concerns on tax compliance: The role of taxpayers' identity. *Journal of Applied Psychology, 87*(4), 629–645.

Wolfe, S. E., Nix, J., Kaminski, R., & Rojek, J. (2016). Is the effect of procedural justice on police legitimacy invariant? *Journal of Quantitative Criminology, 32*, 253–282.

Wolfe, S. E., & Piquero, A. R. (2011). Organizational justice and police misconduct. *Criminal Justice and Behavior, 38*, 332–353.

Worden, R. E., & McLean, S. J. (2014). *Assessing Police Performance in Citizen Encounters: Police Legitimacy and Management Accountability.* Albany, NY: John Finn Institute for Public Safety.

Worden, R. E., & McLean, S. J. (2016). Measuring, managing, and enhancing procedural justice in policing. *Criminal Justice Policy Review, 29*(2), 149–171.

4

Critic

The Limits of Procedural Justice

David Thacher

Police are society's last resort. We grant them broad authority to force solutions on urgent problems when less coercive tactics have failed. We always hope they will be able to resolve those problems peacefully; the whole point of concentrating the authority to use force in a single institution is to professionalize it – to ensure that it will be used less intensively and more responsibly than it otherwise would be (Bittner, 1990: 257ff.). But even when police successfully resolve an emergency without resorting to overt coercion, the covert threat of doing so if "voluntary" compliance fails always lies in the background.

This aspect of policing seems destined to make a free society uneasy. It can be tempting to downplay, ignore, or deny the essential role that coercion plays in police work. "How," Egon Bittner asked, "can we arrive at a favorable or even accepting judgment about an activity which is, in its very conception, opposed to the ethos of the polity that authorizes it? Is it not well nigh inevitable that this mandate be concealed in circumlocution?" (1990: 131). Reform programs that succumb to this temptation end up reforming only the least significant aspects of policing, and they may obscure more urgent questions about when police should use their unique authority (Klockars, 1988).

The procedural justice agenda for policing sits uneasily with these concerns. Its guiding motivation over more than three decades has been to develop a robust alternative to the coercive model of law – to show that legal authorities can usually secure compliance more easily by treating people fairly than by threatening them with force (Schulhofer, Tyler & Huq, 2011: 350ff. Schauer, 2015: ch. 5; Tyler, 2016). That agenda has real potential to advance the mission of policing by reducing the need to resort to coercion (Tyler & Huo, 2002: 1–5), but we should not lose sight of how much lies outside its scope.

First, by design, it excludes questions about when police should use the coercive authority that makes them unique. Advocates of procedural justice argue that people usually care more about process than outcomes, and their reform agenda mainly focuses on how, not when, police should intervene in community life. By contrast, when police officers decide whether to stop, search, arrest, or physically restrain someone, they are making decisions about outcomes; they are deciding whose freedom will be restricted in what circumstances. To make those decisions well, they need to rely on more substantive principles of justice, including those embodied in the diverse bodies of law that regulate police work (Harmon, 2012), in administrative guidelines about the proper use of police authority (Goldstein, 1967; Davis, 1975), in project-specific decisions about the appropriate use of police discretion (Thacher, 2016), and in professional expertise within policing (Klockars, 1996). Police reform can and should strive to refine this complex body of substantive principles, particularly by searching for new ways to minimize the use of coercive authority (e.g., Klockars, 1996; Thacher, 2015a; Harmon, 2016). At best, the procedural justice agenda does not address these substantive questions about the circumstances in which the use of police authority is necessary and appropriate. At worst, it obscures them and diverts valuable attention elsewhere.

Second, advocates for procedural justice often overstate its potential to reduce the need for coercion. The case for procedural justice rests on an empirical claim – that procedurally fair practices affect public cooperation and compliance with police requests – but such claims are vulnerable to two challenges. First, the concepts and causal relationships they rely on are very complex, and comparably intricate causal relationships in other contexts have often turned out to be too weak, unstable, and elusive to provide a firm basis for public policy (Rein & Winship, 1999; Thacher, 2004). More than three decades of social science research have amassed considerable evidence that perceptions of procedural fairness are associated with the perceived legitimacy of legal authorities, but so far this work has provided little evidence for the stronger causal and interpretive claim that police reform efforts must rely on – that deliberate efforts to encourage procedurally fair policing will substantially improve public cooperation with the police (Nagin & Telep, 2017; Weisburd & Majmundar, 2018: 329ff.). Second, by framing the study of procedural fairness as a purely empirical matter, policing scholars have obscured important moral questions about it (Thacher, 2015b). To the extent that procedural justice research *does* identify tactics that make people more likely to comply with police authority, those tactics need moral and legal scrutiny, not just empirical analysis; otherwise there is no way to distinguish illicit manipulation from appropriate deference to authority (Miller, 2016). "Voluntary" compliance may be less benign and more coercive than it appears, so police still need clear substantive standards about when they can justifiably seek it.

This essay develops these concerns in three steps. The first section clarifies the meaning of procedural justice and distinguishes it from a more substantive agenda for police reform. The rest of the essay turns to the main normative claim that procedural justice scholars seem to be making – that the pursuit of procedural justice should be a central priority for police reform because it is the best way to generate public trust, cooperation, and deference to police authority. The second section considers the empirical case for this claim, and the third section considers its moral logic.

PROCEDURAL JUSTICE AND ITS ALTERNATIVES

Procedural justice did not begin as a fully developed policing strategy but as a theoretical perspective in academic psychology – a theory of how various psychological attitudes and judgments interrelate. Most models of human psychology across the social sciences have emphasized the role of self-interest in explaining human judgments and behavior, but a variety of social psychologists have argued that moral concerns have more influence on our relationships with social organizations. People do not mainly cooperate with groups and institutions because they think that is the best way to advance their material self-interest; they care more about whether they are being treated fairly, since fair treatment signals their value and status within the community (Lind & Tyler, 1988).

As a guide for criminal justice practice, this account suggests that legal authorities may be able to gain public cooperation more easily by exercising their authority in a procedurally fair manner than by using the threat of force and sanctions (Sunshine & Tyler, 2003; Tyler & Huo, 2002). Consider the President's Task Force on 21st Century Policing, which described procedural justice as "the guiding principle" for police reform (President's Task Force, 2015: 12). The Task Force's final report advised police leaders to reform "the ways officers and other legal authorities interact with the public" in order to increase public trust in police. Police should aim to treat people in a dignified and respectful manner, give them an opportunity to tell their side of the story, make decisions in a neutral and transparent way, and convey "trustworthy motives" (p. 10).

These ideas have implications for many different organizational practices, including management's relationship with the agency's own workforce (President's Task Force, 2015: 14), public input into police strategy (Kunard & Moe, 2015: 8), and the agency's response to citizen complaints (Fischer, 2014). So far, however, documented procedural justice initiatives focus mainly on the character of street-level interactions between patrol officers and the public. Leading training programs have encouraged officers to treat members of the public "fairly and with respect as human beings" – for example, by explaining the reason why an officer conducted a pedestrian stop, listening empathetically to the citizen's side of the story during an encounter, avoiding rude and insensitive comments, and showing concern for the welfare of the people they interact with (Skogan, van Craen & Hennessy, 2015: 321–323; Gilbert, Wakeling & Crandall, 2015). Similarly, a leading field study of procedural justice instructed officers to explain why they were conducting a sobriety checkpoint, tell drivers that they had been stopped at random, solicit the drivers' ideas about police priorities, and thank them for their time and cooperation (Mazerolle et. al., 2013).

Former Chicago Police Superintendent Garry McCarthy has been one of the most visible police leaders to embrace procedural justice, and his work illustrates more concretely what procedural justice initiatives look like in practice. McCarthy summarized his own understanding of procedural justice with an aphorism: "It's not what you do, it's how you do it" (Wildeboer, 2013). That view guided the stop-and-frisk strategy he developed in Chicago, which was a centerpiece of the department's approach to crime prevention; street stops surged during the first three years of his tenure (Skogan, 2017). Shortly after taking office in 2011, McCarthy wrote a white paper outlining that strategy. That document acknowledged the need to ensure that officers only conduct stops when they are lawful, but it mainly focused on the need to change the way officers interact with the public during a stop:

It is imperative that police officers explain the logic behind the street stop and take the individual through the process step by step. This includes greeting the pedestrian respectfully, explaining the reason for the stop, explaining the stop within the context of the department's overall crime reduction strategy, and then taking the pedestrian through each step of the stop as it proceeds. Explaining the logic behind the stop, or "selling" it to the pedestrian, encourages the officer to treat the pedestrian with respect and explain departmental policy and strategy. Even if a stop results in an arrest, that pedestrian and his or her fellow community members can distinguish between an encounter in which the pedestrian was treated with procedural fairness and one in which he or she was not. The law enforcement officer's demeanor and interaction with the pedestrian (the selling of the stop) is the most important determinant in whether the pedestrian and bystanders will believe the stop was legitimate. (McCarthy, 2012: 39)

Chicago soon embarked on a major effort to train thousands of patrol officers in the procedural justice philosophy (Skogan et al., 2015). The goal, as McCarthy explained it to a reporter, was to maintain community support for the heavy use of street stops as a crime prevention strategy: "So you can stop somebody but . . . you explain to them why you stopped them" (Wildeboer, 2013).[1] This perspective is consistent with academic studies of procedural justice, which have suggested that "if stops are carefully initiated, police would not have to reduce their frequency" (Schulhofer, Tyler & Huq, 2011: 352), that "it is not stops per se that undermine legitimacy, but the behavior of the police during those stops" (Tyler, Fagan & Geller, 2014: 760), and that fair treatment will raise the odds that the public will grant police the authority "to decide whom to stop, question, and ticket" (Sunshine & Tyler, 2003: 518).

---

[1] McCarthy brought this approach (and the language of "selling the stop") from Newark, where he had developed a stop and frisk strategy based on procedural justice ideas (Lachman, La Vigne &, Matthews, 2012: 8; Baker, 2010).

What does this perspective leave out? In McCarthy's language, it leaves out questions about what police do as opposed to how they do it – how often and in what circumstances police invoke their authority to stop, search, cite, arrest, physically restrain, and otherwise coerce people. Those questions implicate substantive justice as well as procedural justice; they are questions about fair outcomes, not just fair process.[2]

Most simply, procedural justice leaves out lawfulness. Advocates for procedural justice draw this contrast repeatedly; One of their central claims is that procedural justice defines an important dimension of good policing that is distinct from the traditional concern for lawfulness (e.g., Meares, 2015). McCarthy's agenda for pedestrian stops illustrates a strategy of policing that heavily emphasized that dimension. Although he briefly acknowledged that stops should be lawful (McCarthy, 2012: 41), his action plan overwhelmingly emphasized procedural fairness: It aimed to reform how officers conducted their stops rather than when they conducted them (except to say they should do so more often).[3] By contrast, civil rights organizations like the American Civil Liberties Union and the Civil Rights Division of the US Department of Justice have repeatedly called on police departments to strengthen legal controls over investigative stops, mainly by providing more rigorous training about what the law requires and better monitoring of how well officers comply with it. For example, the class action settlement for a lawsuit that challenged stop and frisk practices in New York public housing required the NYPD to revise its patrol guide and training to provide more detailed guidance about the behaviors and circumstances that do and do not provide "reasonable suspicion" for a pedestrian stop (Davis v. New York, 2015). Earlier patrol guides said little about that topic, and critics alleged that lack of training and oversight gave police free reign to question almost anyone in public housing. As a result, they believed, police were detaining and frisking people who should have been left alone. The main goal of this reform was to regulate what police do – who they stop in what circumstances – rather than how they do it.

---

[2] They may also be questions about effectiveness and raw politics, but I focus here on the moral evaluation of police work to which procedural justice scholars have rightly tried to redirect attention. As I discuss here, the distinction that procedural justice scholars draw between substance and procedure is not always clear, and their treatment of "substantive" (or "distributive" or "outcome") justice has been particularly thin. Given the central role this distinction plays in procedural justice literature and the notorious difficulties involved in distinguishing "procedures" and "substance" in other contexts, the failure to clarify it is surprising.

[3] Civil rights organizations argued that the latter question remained urgent in both Chicago and Newark during McCarthy's leadership. Records of Terry stops in Chicago were too haphazard to assess easily, but an ACLU analysis suggested that nearly half did not record reasonable suspicion (Ramos, 2013) and that officers received no post-academy training on how to conduct a stop and frisk lawfully (ACLU, 2015: 8). Shortly after McCarthy left Newark, DOJ investigators concluded that agency managers lacked any evidence that three-quarters of the department's pedestrian stops complied with the constitution and that agency policies and training failed to adequately instruct officers about the requirements of reasonable suspicion (USDOJ, 2014: 8–11).

Procedural justice leaves out other aspects of substantive fairness as well. Students of procedural justice have rightly observed that lawfulness is a weak constraint. As Tracey Meares succinctly explained: "People do not automatically approve of a stop just because an officer is legally entitled to make one" (2015: 5). On her view, procedural fairness is the additional consideration that people use to distinguish lawful but unacceptable stops from fully acceptable stops. There are other possibilities. During the last major crisis of police legitimacy in the 1960s, scholars also concluded that lawful policing was not enough; the criminal law had become so broad that it justified police intervention in an alarmingly wide range of circumstances (Thacher, 2016: 540–541). Instead of procedural fairness, however, they called for substantive guidance about when police should actually invoke the authority that was legally available to them (Goldstein, 1967; Davis, 1975). The legacy of their agenda survives today in administrative guidelines for the use of police discretion (Kelling, 1999; Friedman, 2017: 63ff.), in agency policies governing the use of force (Walker & Archbold, 2014: ch. 3), and in tailored strategies for resolving community problems at particular times and places (Thacher, 2016). Substantive fairness is not just a matter of whether people get "what they deserve under the law" (Sunshine & Tyler, 2003: 541). It is also a matter of whether moral and practical considerations beyond the law itself support the decision to invoke police authority under the circumstances – and particularly whether less coercive forms of intervention could accomplish police goals successfully.

The Milwaukee police department under chief Edward Flynn illustrates this aspect of substantive fairness. Like McCarthy, Flynn sought to increase police–citizen contacts in Milwaukee dramatically, particularly by paying more attention to traffic violations, but he recognized that these stops could aggravate enforcement burdens on the residents of high-crime neighborhoods – the very people his strategy aimed to protect. Citizen satisfaction surveys had found that even among city residents who had been stopped by police, support for the department varied considerably depending on the outcome of the stop (for example, whether the driver got a ticket) and the degree of burden it imposed (for example, whether the car was searched or whether a pedestrian was patted down). Recognizing all this, the department de-emphasized the use of formal sanctions and searches, encouraging officers to use warnings rather than citations and arrests whenever possible and to minimize intrusive searches. The goal was to keep coercive intervention to a minimum, not just to carry it out in a procedurally fair manner. Police should stop drivers who break relatively minor traffic rules and question pedestrians acting suspiciously, but they should usually let the driver off with a warning rather than a ticket, and they should not exploit the stop to rifle through their cars and pockets. Department policy and training did encourage officers to treat people with dignity and respect and to convey their neutrality and benevolent motives, but the agency's main goal was to minimize unfavorable outcomes even when the law authorized them (Milwaukee Police, 2017; Cera & Coleman, n.d.).[4]

Milwaukee's strategy aimed to minimize the volume of arrests, citations, and intrusive searches that a high rate of stops might generate, but stops themselves are a form of coercive intervention even when they do not lead to sanctions. In particular, pedestrian stops and frisks can be emotionally jarring, physically invasive, and even sexually humiliating (Butler, 2017: ch. 3). Minimizing the sheer volume of stops is arguably an important goal. In principle, administrative guidelines could aim to do that by specifying more parsimoniously the circumstances in which police should invoke their broad legal authority to conduct a stop. I am not aware of any police department that has refined its stop and frisk strategy in that way, but the approach is common in other contexts. Use of force policies often prohibit the use of force in situations where the law permits it (Walker & Archbold, 2014), and order-maintenance guidelines often define the behavior that warrants police attention more narrowly than the law itself (for example, that jaywalking usually isn't worth police attention or that discreet public drinking should be ignored in some locations) and instruct police to use the least intrusive method possible to control it even when the law authorizes more forceful intervention (Kelling, 1999).

These strategies all aim to refine and enforce substantive standards that specify when various forms of coercive intervention are justified. Procedural justice sets that contentious task aside in order to focus on *how* police exercise their authority once they have decided to invoke it. As psychologist Tom Tyler put it in one provocative essay, the goal is to find a way to build community support for legal authority, "even though their decisions are possibly contrary to peoples' feelings about what is right," so that legal authorities "can gain acceptance from both the winners and the losers in a policy debate" (Tyler, 2000: 988; cf. 2006: 66). As Tyler emphasizes, pluralistic societies that lack a shared moral framework sometimes have no alternative, but it is not the only way to cope with moral disagreement. Sometimes it is possible to identify more refined principles for legal intervention that a wider range of moral views can endorse (Rawls, 1993; Sunstein, 1995), decentralize decision-making so that broad legal standards can be adapted to the expectations and circumstances of diverse communities (Cohen & Sabel, 1997; Dorf & Sabel, 1998), or narrow the scope of state authority over individual and community life (Mill, 1859/1978; Larmore, 1987: 42ff.). If the mismatch between law and personal morality cannot be eliminated entirely, at least it can be minimized; and when

---

[4] In 2017, the ACLU filed a class action lawsuit alleging that Milwaukee police had done too little to ensure that their investigative stops were lawful. I take no position on that allegation. My claim is not that Milwaukee's strategy is appropriate, all things considered; I claim only that it illustrates an often-ignored dimension of policing practice that is distinct from both lawfulness and procedural justice.

law must override personal views about right and wrong, it can strive to intervene as parsimoniously as possible (Thacher, 2015a). When legal authorities refine and enforce the law according to these principles, the people subject to it have no legitimate objection to their fate. Where procedural justice tries to build support for the law and law enforcement *in spite of* some peoples' reasonable belief that legal authorities are intervening unjustifiably, substantive justice aims to reshape legal intervention so that it is less likely to offend those beliefs in the first place.

I have tried not to define procedural justice too narrowly. Critics sometimes suggest that it demands nothing more than polite and respectful treatment during street-level interactions, but its advocates rightly point out that procedural justice also requires high quality decision-making – including careful consideration of relevant facts, a sincere concern for community well-being, and a determined effort to keep the officer's personal biases at bay (e.g., Meares, 2017: 1898). But even this broader understanding of procedural justice does not encompass the substantive considerations I have described, such as those contained in the post-*Davis* patrol guides (which define more clearly when pedestrian stops and trespassing arrests should and should not be conducted in public housing), and the Milwaukee traffic patrol guidelines (which instruct officers to avoid citations and arrests in most circumstances). Those considerations focus on outcomes, not procedures. They focus on whether people behaving in particular ways in particular circumstances should be stopped, arrested, cited, or otherwise coerced. If procedural justice did encompass those factors, the distinction at the heart of one of the literature's core claims – that "people typically care much more about how law enforcement agents treat them than about the outcome of the contact" (Meares, 2015: 5) – would unravel, and the claim itself would lose meaning.

THE EMPIRICAL CASE FOR PROCEDURAL JUSTICE

The argument that procedural justice deserves a central place in police reform rests mainly on an empirical claim: that procedurally fair policing is the most effective strategy for improving community trust and support for the police.[5] Despite dramatic reductions in crime since the early 1990s, public confidence in the police remains strained in many communities, and police sometimes have a hard time getting the cooperation and deference they need to do their jobs (Tyler & Huo, 2002: 5). Procedural justice researchers aim to diagnose the reasons for these tensions. By identifying what the public expects from police beyond successful crime reduction, these researchers aim to identify the

---

[5] Some procedural justice advocates also make the more ambitious claim that peoples' perceptions of fair treatment affect the likelihood that they will obey the law in the first place (esp. Tyler, 2006). The questions and concerns I raise in this section apply even more strongly to that claim (cf. Weisburd & Majmundar, 2018: 155–163).

elements that need to be part of an effective strategy for building community trust (Sunshine & Tyler, 2003: 515–516; Tyler, 2014: 16). Their conclusions are by now well known. People view legal authorities as legitimate when they think they behave in a procedurally fair manner, and perceptions of legitimacy lead to cooperation, deference, and obedience of the law. Procedural fairness seems to matter more than the threat of sanctions does, and more than judgments about distributive justice, fair outcomes, or lawfulness.

While the vast body of research that supports these conclusions is impressive, it has repeatedly encountered several challenges. Those challenges involve familiar concerns about causal inference, but they also involve a variety of less-widely recognized concerns, including interpretive concerns about the meaning of key concepts and ontological concerns about the scope of the causal powers that researchers have investigated. Consider each of these challenges in turn.

Challenges of Causal Inference

The most familiar concern involves the challenge of distinguishing correlation from causation. Most procedural justice research in policing documents the "antecedents" of legitimacy and compliance without demonstrating that those antecedents cause the relevant outcomes. Research shows that people who think police act fairly tend to trust them and comply with their authority, but that may not mean that their perceptions have a causal effect on trust and compliance. For example, people who trust the police may have developed a strong commitment to the social order early in life, and perhaps such people tend both to view police behavior through rose-colored glasses and to defer to legal authority. If so, then perceptions of fair treatment may track deference to the law not because the former causes the latter but because both are affected by personality (cf. Worden & McLean, 2017: 51).

Daniel Nagin and Cody Telep (2017) recently argued that this kind of problem is pervasive in procedural justice research, and it affects both attitudinal studies based on survey research (e.g., Sunshine & Tyler, 2003) and observational studies in the field (e.g., Mastrofski, Snipes & Supina, 1996). A few recent studies have tried to address it by conducting experiments, both in the field and in the lab – for example, by asking respondents to watch randomly selected videos of police-citizen encounters or by conducting sobriety checkpoints guided by randomly assigned protocols. Some of these studies have found modest effects of procedurally fair policing on perceptions of procedural justice and self-reported compliance (at least among the small subset of people who responded to the surveys; *e.g.*, Mazerolle et. al., 2013), but others have not (e.g., MacQueen & Bradford, 2015, though this negative finding may have been the result of failed implementation). A thorough review of this literature by the National Academies of Science, Engineering, and Medicine recently concluded that "the research base is currently insufficient to draw conclusions about whether procedurally just policing causally influences either perceived legitimacy or cooperation" (Weisburd & Majmundar, 2018: 248).

Some commentators have argued that rigorous psychology experiments in other fields lend indirect support to the procedural justice hypothesis in policing (Tyler, 2017; Weisburd & Majmundar, 2018: 232). The extensive body of procedural justice research conducted in a wide range of other contexts is clearly an impressive intellectual achievement. Still, it is important to recognize how police authority differs from authority in other domains. For example, police–citizen interactions tend not to be repeat interactions to the same degree as employee–supervisor interactions, and that difference may affect the relative importance of outcomes and procedures. People may care more about the process used to reach a decision than the decision itself when they expect their fate to be determined by that same process many more times, but they may feel differently when they view the decision as a one-off; they may also feel more confident about their ability to evaluate a process (and therefore more willing to rely on such evaluations) the more often they encounter it. More fundamentally, police authority is typically more momentous than authority in other fields because police hold a monopoly on the legally sanctioned use of coercive force. To use that authority in circumstances where it is avoidable or unjustified is uniquely troubling, so it would not be surprising if we used distinctive standards to evaluate it. Differences like these make it unclear how well findings about the causal impact of procedural justice in other domains will carry over to policing. So far, we do not know (Weisburd & Majmundar, 2018: 248).

Challenges of Interpretation

Even when researchers convincingly demonstrate that one of the factors they have measured has a causal effect on another, it may not be clear what exactly each factor represents, and therefore how it relates to the concrete tactics and priorities relevant to policing. One of the most influential studies of procedural justice in policing measured perceptions of *distributive* fairness partly by asking respondents whether minority residents "receive a lower quality of service than do whites," but it used similar-sounding questions to measure perceptions of *procedural* fairness, such as whether the police "treat everyone in your community equally." Another question about distributive fairness asked respondents whether people get "what they deserve under the law," while another question about procedural fairness asked whether police "accurately understand and apply the law" (Sunshine & Tyler, 2003). Do survey respondents distinguish carefully among these questions? Do they interpret their meaning the same way that researchers do? Is it appropriate to describe their answers as statements about the "outcomes" and "process" of police intervention? Unless the answer to all of these questions is "yes," the study's conclusion that people care more about procedural justice than distributive justice is hard to interpret.

Several important statistical, observational, ethnographic, and philosophical analyses give reasons to question whether procedural justice research has successfully isolated the complex attitudes it attempts to study and how those attitudes relate to concrete policing practices. The most prominent study of construct validity in procedural justice research found that the attitudes tapped by commonly used survey questions do not seem to be entirely distinct (Reisig, Bratton & Gertz, 2007); it is not possible to conclude that "procedural justice" matters more than "distributive justice" from research that relies on them.[6] A major observational study that reviewed video footage of police–citizen encounters found that survey responses cannot be taken as a reasonable interpretation of actual police behavior, and the observed level of procedural justice had less influence on trust in the police than substantive factors like whether the officer used force or conducted a search (Worden & McLean, 2017: ch. 7). Ethnographic work that probes people's attitudes toward the police in depth has repeatedly found that their judgments encompass many considerations other than procedural fairness (Epp, Maynard-Moony & Haider-Markel, 2014; Futterman, Hunt & Kalven, 2016; Bell, 2017); when we listen closely to what people say about police in their own words (rather than their responses to standardized survey questions), they seem care quite a bit about what police do, not just how they do it. The most careful conceptual analysis of procedural justice research has concluded that the concept of legitimacy it employs represents a fairly narrow motivation for legal compliance, and most empirical studies in the field have not successfully isolated it; to act in a way that is consistent with the law is not the same as *obeying* the law, and people who act that way may simply be doing what they think is right regardless of what legal authorities have asked them to do (Schauer, 2015). In short, a diverse range of careful analyses of what it means to say that procedures have more impact than outcomes on police legitimacy and cooperation have raised significant doubts about whether the evidence cited in support of that statement has adequately tapped into the relevant concepts.

---

[6] By dropping these questions from the survey, the authors produced new composite measures of procedural and distributive justice that seemed to make better psychometric sense, and an analysis using these revised measures of procedural and distributive justice replicated some (but not all) of the literature's main findings. But what does the new, stripped-down measure of each variable represent? The fact remains that widely used survey questions that directly ask survey respondents about central elements of procedural justice as researchers have long articulated them – whether officers "make decisions based on their own personal feelings" (neutrality) and whether they "listen to all citizens involved before deciding what to do" (voice) – yielded answers that appeared much more closely related to distributive justice. The decision to drop these questions rather than repurpose them as additional measures of distributive justice was not dictated by factor analysis alone but by the observation that "these items were originally designed to measure different factors" (Reisig, Bratton & Gertz, 2007).

The comparative claim that procedural fairness matters *more* than outcomes raises further challenges. A reasonable test of that claim would not only need to compare fair procedures with unfair procedures, it would also need to compare fair outcomes with unfair outcomes. Consider the aspect of "outcome fairness" associated with lawfulness. Police often fail to understand and follow the law (Gould & Mastrofski, 2004), but procedural justice research has rarely studied both lawful and unlawful policing directly.[7] For example, the field experiments discussed earlier (such as the sobriety checkpoint study) do not vary the lawfulness of police behavior, so even if they convincingly demonstrated that procedural justice matters, they would not have demonstrated that it matters more than lawfulness.

Moreover, fair outcomes are not just a matter of lawfulness. Milwaukee's approach to traffic stops and street stops differs from Chicago's mainly because Milwaukee's command staff discouraged arrests and citations in favor of warnings. Assuming that both departments were equally lawful and effective, Milwaukee's strategy arguably led to fairer outcomes because it imposed a lighter enforcement burden. It is not clear that procedural justice research has really shown that an approach like Milwaukee's has less impact on community confidence than an approach like Chicago's. (As noted earlier, Milwaukee's own data about public perceptions of the police suggested that outcomes mattered considerably, and survey research in Chicago supports the same conclusion; Skogan, 2017: 260–262.) In practice, efforts to use police authority in more restrained ways have sometimes proven revolutionary for police–community relations. When police in High Point, North Carolina, decided not to arrest most of the drug dealers who sustained the city's worst

---

[7] One sophisticated recent study attempted to fill this gap. Researchers showed video recordings of police encounters and provided a narrative description of how the encounter came about, and they attempted to vary both the procedural justice of the encounter (for example, whether the officer listened to the citizen) and "the actual legality of police behavior" (Meares, Tyler & Gardener, 2015: 138). It is unclear, however, whether the study varied the second factor successfully. The researchers deliberately did not tell respondents that police had behaved unlawfully; instead they provided contextual information intended to signal that fact – for example, a statement that "the individual in the video was stopped after the police officer observed him walking down the street late at night" or that the man driving the car was stopped "while he was driving appropriately and within the speed limit" (Meares, Tyler & Gardener, 2015: 341, 322). Did the respondents assume that the absence of a clearly stated legal reason for these stops meant that the police had stopped the driver or pedestrian illegally, as the researchers apparently intended? Or did they assume that some unstated reason justified the stop – that the pedestrian matched the description of a suspect, for example, or that the driver had expired tags or a broken headlight (which would not be covered by the statement that he was "driving appropriately and within the speed limit")? In any case, this study is apparently the only one that has investigated variation in lawfulness directly, and whether its findings can be replicated beyond the specific (laboratory) context where it was conducted remains an open question. Survey-based studies potentially tap into natural variation in police lawfulness, but when they operationalize it using survey questions they suffer from the kind of problems discussed in the previous paragraph and later in this chapter.

overt drug market but instead to "bank" the cases against them and give them an ultimatum, the officers' forbearance profoundly affected many community members. One NAACP leader told the audience at a community meeting about the project: "I never would have believed that the police would hold our young men in their hands, able to put them in prison, and not do it" (Kennedy, 2008: 154–155).

Challenges of Application

A final set of concerns has to do with the scope of the causal powers that researchers have studied, and therefore the use to which their findings can be put. Procedural justice researchers often make general claims that people care more about procedures than outcomes (e.g., Lind & Tyler, 1988: 1–2; Tyler, 2014: 35; Meares, 2015: 5), but the preferences they study may be more contingent than this sweeping language suggests. Some research in social psychology does seem to tap into stable features of human cognition that vary little across contexts – for example, our tendency to overestimate the probability that vivid, frightening events will occur and underestimate the probability of hard-to-visualize threats, or our tendency to give too much weight to the final moments of an experience and ignore its duration when we remember how well we liked it (Kahneman, 2011: chs. 12, 35). It is not clear whether procedural justice researchers intend to uncover invariant features of the mind like these; their conclusions often sound more like empirical reports of the preferences that particular people in particular places currently have. Tyler has defended the value of observational research in the real word (as opposed to the psychology lab) on this basis. Stressing "the futility of trying to draw an overall conclusion about how important one factor is, alone or relative to others," he observes that "surveys of natural settings are important because they tap into the strength of each factor within a particular setting" (Tyler, 2016: 517). He and others have noted how the meaning and importance of procedural justice may vary across cultures (e.g., Tyler, 2007; Tankebe, 2009). What general claims are left to make? Whether someone cares more about procedural justice than fair outcomes presumably depends on many things – not just on that person's cultural and demographic identity but also on the actual state of policing in her community. In a city where police have recently been accused of theft, smuggling, and kidnapping (Phippen, 2016), a predominant focus on procedural justice rather than police lawfulness might be insulting. When we need to decide whether our local police department should focus scarce energy on procedural justice, lawfulness, or more parsimonious use of discretionary authority, what can we learn by consulting general social science findings that we cannot learn by conducting a community dialogue?

If the value of procedural justice depends on context, then the question is not so much whether process-based policing is a viable strategy for rebuilding community trust but under what conditions it is effective – what background factors and support structures need to be in place to make procedural justice work (Cartwright & Hardie, 2012: 61ff.). The research strategy that has dominated the procedural justice literature is not well suited to that question. Its methodological and conceptual framework comes from social psychology and criminology, where researchers typically aim to explain why some people trust police more than others do – and especially how their level of trust depends on (their perception of) the way police treat them. Reformers then craft a strategy by combining the styles of policing that are associated with higher levels of trust across individuals. That approach faces at least two problems. First, practices that "work" to build trust when individual officers use them on their own initiative may have very different effects once a department makes them part of a deliberate and sustained program of action (cf. Cartwright & Hardie, 2012: 30–32). For example, the public may catch on quickly when police begin to deliberately design procedures that only appear fair. They may begin to see canned explanations, comment cards, and empty opportunities for voice as cynical ploys to mask the injustice of a substantively inappropriate practice (cf. Lind & Tyler, 1988: 76). Second, even if researchers can identify front-line practices that inspire public confidence in the police, there is no guarantee that police managers can get their officers to use them; there is no guarantee, in other words, that managers can create the organizational context those practices need to thrive. In one of the few recent studies of procedural justice that has paid close attention to the organizational environment of police work, Robert Worden and Sarah McLean (2017: 5) conclude that procedurally just policing is ambiguous and difficult to monitor, and they express skepticism about the ability of police departments to successfully encourage officers to carry it out as intended. A new wave of research has begun to investigate the impact of procedural justice training programs in policing, and some early findings suggest that training may affect officers' attitudes (e.g., Skogan et al., 2015); two studies provide evidence (albeit equivocal) that training may modestly affect their decisions in the field (Weisburd & Majmundar, 2018: 160). Overall, however, the National Academies review of proactive policing strategies concluded that "evidence is extremely limited for the effectiveness of training or other policy levers in affecting police behavior vis-à-vis procedural justice" (Weisburd & Majmundar, 2018: 161). To date, no study has shown that a deliberate effort to encourage officers to treat people more fairly can substantially affect the attitudes and behavior of the people police interact with.

A full understanding of these complex organizational and community dynamics requires a different kind of research than psychologists and criminologists usually conduct, particularly historical and case study research that investigates comprehensive efforts to shore up an agency's legitimacy over a long stretch of time. Procedural justice has not been studied systematically from that more holistic perspective, but relevant historical work seems to provide little support for the claim that police agencies can successfully overcome severe legitimacy deficits by focusing mainly on procedural fairness. Wilbur Miller's research is particularly relevant because he has studied police legitimacy more directly than most historians, and he has worked within the same Weberian tradition as Tyler (Miller, 1977: 222). In a study of the Bureau of Internal Revenue agents who enforced federal liquor tax laws in the late nineteenth century, Miller found that Bureau officials initially faced a severe legitimacy crisis that made it very difficult to do their jobs. Neighbors warned moonshiners when tax collectors were on their way, and few would willingly serve as informants, witnesses, or jurors. The Bureau eventually gained the cooperation and deference it needed by accepting significant restraints on the scope of its authority, including a tacit agreement to restrict enforcement to brazen scofflaws, extensive provisions for clemency, and limits on asset forfeiture (Miller, 1991: 52–59). The key to agency legitimacy involved what officers did, not how they did it. In a study of the early New York City police, Miller similarly found that police tried to gain legitimacy (and to a halting and uneven degree succeeded) by using their discretion to tailor general legal rules to local expectations. Police work in this environment "called for flexibility in the administration of justice – taking individual circumstances into account when making decisions and rendering substantive rather than merely formal justice" (Miller, 1977: 21). A neighborhood officer "would not win much respect if he consistently contradicted local standards and expectations in favor of impersonal bureaucratic ideals" (Miller, 1977: 23). I know of no historical evidence that procedural fairness has played a comparably large role in a sustained effort to build public support for police in other agencies.

Researchers have sometimes suggested that Robert Peel's vision for the early London police reflects key principles of procedural justice and that the success of that force illustrates the value of his approach. Peel stressed the need for officers to demonstrate "impartial service to law," "courtesy," and other key elements of procedural justice, and under Richard Mayne's long and influential leadership the London police tried to put that vision into practice by cultivating an impersonal demeanor that would make officers into "models of restraint and politeness" (Miller, 1977: 38–42). All of this does seem to resonate with core ideas of procedural justice. On closer examination, however, the long-run success of even London's police required close attention to what the police did, not just how they did it (e.g., Miller, 1977: 48, 55, 62–63, 132–138). In Michael Ignatieff's words:

To win this cooperation, the police manipulated their powers of discretion. They often chose not to take their authority to the letter of the law, preferring not to "press their luck" in return for tacit compliance from the community. In each neighbourhood, and sometimes street by street, the police negotiated a complex, shifting, largely unspoken "contract." They defined the activities they would turn a blind eye to, and those which they would suppress, harass, or control ... This was the microscopic basis of police legitimacy. (1979: 445)

As Peel's "Blue Locusts" spread throughout the rest of the country, resistance arose not from a failure to achieve Peel and Mayne's ideal of neutrality and politeness but from the substantive restrictions on individual freedom they imposed. Riots erupted in response to police involvement in strike-breaking, crackdowns on popular recreation, interference in political activity, and the arrest and pursuit of well-loved members of the community (Storch, 1975: 72). Community support (or at least tolerance) came only when police tailored the scope of their substantive authority more closely to local expectations. British citizens cared deeply about what police did, not just how they did it.

THE MORAL LIMITS OF PROCEDURAL JUSTICE

Whether or not the process-based elements of Peel's strategy played a significant role in building legitimacy for the British police, what may be most notable about them was the degree to which they were an adaptation to an undemocratic legal system. The London police represented a vigorous effort to assert the legal framework of an aristocratic society on the inhabitants of its largest city, and later on the rest of the country. Compared with the police forces that soon took shape in America, London's police were more numerous, more powerful, more centralized, and more insulated from popular influence – accountable not to municipal officials but to the Home Office, and organized around precincts that had been deliberately mismatched to existing political divisions (Reith, 1943: 51; Miller, 1977: 12; Walker, 1977: 15). Peel had first thought about the police function in an even less democratic context as Chief Secretary for Ireland during the early years of its vexed union with Britain; his problem, in effect, was to develop a system of policing that could successfully impose British authority on the United Kingdom's new and reluctant Catholic subjects (Reith, 1943: 35; Palmer, 1988: 193–236; Vitale, 2017). In both contexts, his task was to build support and deference for an agency enforcing laws that he knew lacked broad public support.

Advocates for procedural justice obviously do not describe their own goals that way, but the agenda they have pursued is uncomfortably well suited to it. Procedural justice aims to provide legitimacy to legal institutions regardless of the content of the laws they enforce. As Tyler recently put it: "If people think they ought to obey the law, they obey it irrespective of what it says they should or should not do" (2016: 511). Tyler is speaking here about legitimacy in general, but the sentiment applies more clearly to legitimacy based on procedural fairness than legitimacy based on substantive fairness (i.e., on a belief that the law represents a reasonable accommodation of the moral convictions and interests of a diverse society). Civil disobedients who believe they have a duty to obey the law *unless* it is morally outrageous do not think legitimacy is content independent in this sense (e.g., King, 1964). People who refuse to cooperate as witnesses, jurors, or the compliant subjects of consent searches because they think the relevant laws are unjust are not indifferent to the outcomes the law pursues; they do not cooperate irrespective of what legal authorities say they and their neighbors should or should not do (e.g., Butler, 2010). They believe cooperation is appropriate only when legal authorities exercise coercive authority in circumstances where it is justified.[8]

Procedural justice research has no place for these considerations because it studies the antecedents of a form of legal authority that has no substantive boundaries. The most widely cited study of procedural justice in policing measured the consequences of legitimacy partly by asking respondents whether they agree that "the police should have the right to stop and question people on the street" (the question does not mention a need for reasonable suspicion), that "the police should have the power to do whatever they think is needed to fight crime," and that "the police should be able to search peoples' homes without having to get permission from a judge if they think stolen property or drugs are inside" (Sunshine & Tyler, 2003: 542, 546). A study like this investigates the style of policing that will lead people to accept police intervention regardless of whether that intervention is legally or morally appropriate.

Students of procedural justice have applied this morally agnostic attitude to the concept of "procedural fairness" itself. Researchers do not consider what makes a procedure fair according to law or morality. Instead, they ask survey respondents to report whether they are satisfied with the procedure they experienced. Using this approach, researchers have suggested that police should provide people with an opportunity to tell their side of the story, but that they can satisfy this demand when they "show an honest interest in what people have to say, even if it is not going to change anything" (Skogan et al., 2015: 325) or when the topic the officer asks about is irrelevant to the decision she is making (Mazerrole et. al., 2013: 41). These studies analyze procedural justice and legitimacy in a manner that is "thoroughgoing in its empiricism" (Meares, Tyler & Gardener, 2015: 305), aiming to document how the research subjects actually understand these ideas regardless of whether their understanding is coherent or defensible. "It is beyond the scope of this book to evaluate whether those studied 'ought' to be more or less satisfied than they are with legal authorities," Tyler explained in *Why People Obey the Law* (2006: 148).[9] That research strategy is intellectually coherent, but the terminology it uses can be misleading. The words that researchers use to describe their central concepts ("procedural justice," "legitimate," "defer") make them sound like they refer to morally attractive things, but we must always remember that researchers have disclaimed any responsibility for moral evaluation. People

---

[8] Tyler seems to suggest that legal authorities cannot rely on this kind of consideration as a basis for compliance – for example, when he asserts that "authorities cannot plan based on the assumption that personal morality will support compliance with their actions" (2006: 65) – but the lesson of the historical examples I have just given is that officials can and do try to adapt the law and its enforcement to prevailing moral sentiment.

[9] Tyler adopts this value-neutral approach to legitimacy from Weber. For critiques and alternatives, see Selznick (1992: 268–273), Pitkin (1973: 280ff.), Beetham (1991).

who "defer" to "legitimate authority" in this morally agnostic sense may not be impressed by a well-founded sense of moral rightness so much as they are confused, deceived, or weary. Those who continue to defy the authorities may expect officers to pander to their whims.

When social scientists strip the moral connotations out of the concepts they use, we cannot responsibly apply their findings to practice until we put those moral considerations back in (Thacher, 2015b). Businesses sometimes use psychological research to sell us things we don't need, and politicians sometimes use it to get us to support causes and vote for candidates who won't serve our interests. More benevolent authorities hope to nudge us in the direction that they judge to be best for us or for society. All of these officials exploit predictable quirks in human cognition to manipulate the choices people will make. In doing so, they raise important ethical concerns about manipulation, transparency, and freedom (Sunstein, 2016).

Those concerns also apply to procedural justice research, which generates psychological knowledge about how human beings tend to respond to various cues in their environment. It tells us what people respond to, not necessarily what they truly value. According to Tyler's "group value" theory, procedurally fair treatment apparently does have intrinsic value. It is a way of recognizing and expressing a person's status in the group and her dignity as an individual (e.g., Tyler & Blader, 2000). Psychologist Allen Lind provides a different interpretation. People do not value fair treatment for its own sake but instead use it as a decision heuristic. People ultimately care about fair outcomes, but when they don't have enough information to evaluate whether an outcome is fair they rely on procedural cues to guess (e.g., van den Bos, Lind & Wilke, 2001). When a person gets stopped by the police, she often has no idea whether the officer really had a good, lawful reason for a stop, but if the officer treats her with dignity and respect she may give the officer the benefit of the doubt (Tyler 2014: 12; Meares, Tyler & Gardener, 2015: 331). She does not defer because she believes that all stops conducted respectfully are legitimate. She defers because she thinks stops made for good, lawful reasons are legitimate, and she assumes that respectful officers probably have such reasons.

The ethical concern arises when the officers' managers have encouraged them through aggressive performance management to push and perhaps exceed the limits of reasonable suspicion (Skogan, 2017) while equipping them with interpersonal skills they can use to persuade citizens to give them the benefit of the doubt (Skogan et al., 2015). Like marketers and political campaigners trying to sell a product or a candidate, their police leaders are strategically using a known decision-making heuristic to "sell" the stops their officers make. If the stops are unjustified, that effort may at best be a distraction from more important priorities.

These are not new concerns for policing. Eric Miller observes that police have used tactics "identical or akin to procedural justice" for years. For decades, modern interrogation techniques have used empathy and a non-confrontational, respectful tone to encourage suspects to cooperate (Miller, 2016: 354–366), and since at least the 1980s, patrol officers have used psychological insights to gain consent for voluntary searches (Epp et al., 2014: 39). Both strategies represent progress from a brutal past – the Reid method is better than the third degree, and consent searches are better than lawless raids and shakedowns – but both remain controversial (Friedman, 2017: 8; Hager, 2017). Critics argue that they replace physical coercion with psychological manipulation, and they maintain that the people who "voluntarily" comply with police requests often believe they have no choice. This subtle form of coercion may be harder to regulate than more blatant forms; it is harder even to perceive (Miller, 2016: 360; Weisburd & Majmundar, 2018: 114).

Procedural justice may reduce the need for police to use overtly coercive tactics, but any "consent" it brings about cannot single-handedly justify police intervention. Policing is always potentially coercive, and police should intervene only when coercion is justified. The use of procedurally fair tactics does not alter that basic reality (though it may conceal it). We should not want a strategy of policing that convinces citizens to acquiesce to unreasonable requests for compliance. We should want a strategy that refuses to make such requests in the first place. The most important goal of police reform is to develop and enforce appropriate substantive guidelines about when police should even try to exert their authority. Because the conceptual framework of procedural justice replaces questions about the moral and legal justification of police action with questions about community satisfaction with the police (Weisburd & Majmundar, 2018: 113–115; cf. Lind & Tyler, 1988: 3–5), it systematically excludes many of the intellectual resources that those who want to pursue that goal need to rely on.

CONCLUSION

It is better for police officers to treat the people they encounter with dignity and respect than to treat them badly, and it is better for them to enforce the law in a neutral and trustworthy manner than to do the opposite. Procedural justice research has usefully called attention to these vital dimensions of police work. They are most important in agencies that already follow the law, minimize and properly regulate the use of force and arrest, and seek community input about how they should use their discretionary authority, but where something about the manner in which officers interact with the public makes many people believe otherwise. Advocates of procedural justice rightly observe that even when police exercise their authority responsibly, officers may still need to persuade the public of their integrity; they may also be right that a visible display of procedural fairness can sometimes help with that task (Meares, Tyler & Gardener, 2015: 319). What I question is whether the need for such displays can really serve as "the guiding principle" of police reform (President's Task Force, 2015: 12).

The case for procedural justice rests on an empirical claim: that procedurally fair policing can strengthen police legitimacy, and in turn improve public cooperation, deference, and law-abiding behavior. As in many other areas of criminal justice, the evidence for this complex causal and interpretive claim is more equivocal than the most enthusiastic accounts suggest. It turns out to be difficult to justify policy ideas on the basis of their long-run consequences (Rein & Winship, 1999; Thacher, 2004). In the meantime, we should not lose sight of the important moral considerations that this empirical claim sets aside even if it turns out to be true. Police intervention is always potentially coercive, and the decision about when coercive intervention is justified is one of the most difficult decisions any society must make. A reform agenda that mostly sets that decision aside to focus on how police behave once the decision to intervene has already been made is at best incomplete.

On what basis should police make such momentous decisions? The law provides one source of guidance, and we cannot assume that police already make the best possible use of it – not because most police deliberately break the law but because legal standards are complex and infinitely demanding, and because new developments in police strategy always have to be carefully adjusted to evolving legal constraints. Moreover, the law is not the only source of guidance for the police. American criminal law gives police remarkably broad authority to arrest, detain, and use force, and it is simply not true that all possible uses of this expansive legal authority are equally appropriate as long as police use it in a procedurally fair manner. The most important task for police reform may be to provide better guidance about when, not just how, police should invoke the profound authority the law has granted them.

If we view procedural justice as a supplement to this more substantive agenda for police reform, it can make an important contribution to American policing. The advocates of procedural justice are undoubtedly right to point out that the public's beliefs about procedural fairness are important. But when they insist on the stronger claim that perceptions of procedural justice matter *more* than outcomes, and *more* than lawfulness, they may give the impression that procedural justice is a substitute rather than a supplement for the alternative agenda I have described. In the process, they risk blinding police leaders to the difficult but centrally important questions that demand their attention – questions about when it is appropriate to use the coercive authority entrusted to the police at all. A rare window to reshape American policing may have opened up over the past five years. It would be a shame to use it to pursue an agenda that simply set those questions aside.

REFERENCES

ACLU of Illinois (2015). *Stop and Frisk in Chicago.*
Baker, A. (2010). Selling the "Stop" in "Stop and Frisk," *The New York Times*, Sept. 16, 2010.

Beetham, D. (1991). The Legitimation of Power. London: Macmillan.
Bell, M. (2017) Police reform & the dismantling of legal estrangement. *Yale Law Journal*, 126, 2054–2150.
Bittner, E. (1990). *Aspects of Police Work*. Boston: Northeastern University Press.
Butler, P. (2010). *Let's Get Free: A Hip Hop Theory of Justice*. New York: The New Press.
Butler, P. (2017). *Chokehold: Policing Black Men*. New York, The New Press.
Cartwright, N., & Hardie, J. (2012). *Evidence-Based Policy: Doing It Better*. New York: Oxford University Press.
Cera, J., & Coleman, A. (n.d.). City of Milwaukee Citizen Satisfaction Survey, Center for Urban Initiatives and Research.
Cohen, J., & Sabel, C. (1997). Directly deliberative polyarchy. *European Law Journal*, 3, 313–342.
Davis, K. C. (1975). *Police Discretion*. St. Paul: West Publishing.
Davis v. *New York*, 10 Civ. 0699 (S.D.N.Y.) (SAS) (2015). Stipulation of Settlement and Order.
Dorf, M., & Sabel, C. (1998). A constitution of democratic experimentalism. *Colombia Law Review*, 98, 267–473.
Epp, C., Maynard-Moody, S., & Haider-Markel, D. (2014). *Pulled Over: How Police Stops Define Race and Citizenship*. Chicago: University of Chicago Press.
Fischer, C. (2014). *Legitimacy and Procedural Justice: The New Orleans Case Study*. Washington, DC: Police Executive Research Forum.
Friedman, B. (2017). *Unwarranted: Policing without Permission*. New York: Farrar, Strauss, and Giroux.
Futterman, C., Hunt, C., & Kalven, J. (2016). Youth/police encounters on Chicago's South Side: Acknowledging the realities. *University of Chicago Legal Forum*, 2016, 125–211.
Gilbert, D., Wakeling, S., & Crandall, V. (2015). *Procedural Justice and Police Legitimacy: Using Training as a Foundation for Strengthening Police-Community Relationships*. Oakland: California Partnership for Safe Communities.
Goldstein, H. (1967). Police policy formulation: A proposal for improving police performance. *Michigan Law Review*, 65, 1123–46.
Gould, J., & Mastrofski, S. (2004) Suspect searches: Assessing police behavior. *Criminology & Public Policy*, 3, 315–362.
Hager, E. (2017). The seismic change in police interrogations. *The Marshall Project*, March 7, 2017.
Harmon, R. (2012). The problem of policing. *Michigan Law Review*, 110, 768–818.
Harmon, R. (2016). Why arrest? *Michigan Law Review*, 115, 307–64.
Ignatieff, M. (1979). Police and the people: The birth of Mr. Peel's "Blue Locusts." *New Society*, 443–446.
Kahneman, D. (2011). *Thinking, Fast and Slow*. New York: Farrar, Strauss, and Giroux.
Kelling, G. (1999). *Broken Windows and Police Discretion*. Washington, DC: National Institute of Justice.
Kennedy, D. (2008). *Deterrence and Crime Prevention*. Oxon: Routledge.
King, M. L., Jr. (1964). Letter from a Birmingham Jail. In *Why We Can't Wait*. New York: Harper and Row.
Klockars, C. (1988). The rhetoric of community policing. In J. Greene & S. Mastrofski (eds.), *Community Policing: Rhetoric or Reality* (pp. 239–258). New York: Praeger.

Klockars, C. (1996). A theory of excessive force and its control. In W. Geller & H. Toch (eds.), *Police Violence: Understanding and Controlling Police Abuse of Force* (pp. 1–22). New Haven: Yale University Press.

Kunard, L., & Moe, C. (2015). *Procedural Justice for Law Enforcement: An Overview.* Washington, DC: Office of Community Oriented Policing Services.

Lachman, P., La Vigne, N., & Matthews, A. (2012). Examining law enforcement use of pedestrian stops and searches. In N. La Vigne, P. Lachman, A. Matthews, & S. R. Neusteter (eds.), *Key Issues in the Police Use of Pedestrian Stops and Searches* (pp. 1–11). Washington, DC: Urban Institute.

Larmore, C. (1987). *Patterns of Moral Complexity.* New York: Cambridge University Press.

Lind, A., & Tyler, T. (1988). *The Social Psychology of Procedural Justice.* New York: Plenum.

MacQueen, S., & Bradford, B. (2015). Enhancing public trust and police legitimacy during road traffic encounters: Results from a randomized controlled trial in Scotland. *Journal of Experimental Criminology,* 11, 419–443.

Mastrofski, S., Snipes, J., & Supina, A. (1996). Compliance on demand: The public's response to specific police requests. *Journal of Research in Crime and Delinquency,* 33, 269–305.

Mazerolle, L., Antrobus, E., Bennett, S., & Tyler, T. (2013). Shaping citizen perceptions of police legitimacy: A randomized field trial of procedural justice. *Criminology,* 51, 33–63.

McCarthy, G. (2012). Using stop and frisk powers responsibly. In N. La Vigne, P. Lachman, A. Matthews, & S. R. Neusteter (eds.), *Key Issues in the Police Use of Pedestrian Stops and Searches* (pp. 37–43). Washington, DC: Urban Institute.

Meares, T. (2015). Rightful Policing. *New Perspectives in Policing Bulletin.* Washington, DC: National Institute of Justice, 2015.

Meares, T., Tyler, T., & Gardener, J. (2015). Lawful or fair? How cops and laypeople perceive good policing. *Journal of Criminology and Criminal Law,* 105, 297–344.

Meares, T. (2017). This land is my land? *Harvard Law Review,* 130, 1877–1900.

Mill, J. S. (1859/1978). *On Liberty.* Indianapolis: Hackett.

Miller, E. (2016). Encountering resistance: Contesting policing and procedural justice, *University Chicago Legal Forum,* 2016, 295–368.

Miller, W. (1977). *Cops and Bobbies: Police Authority in New York and London, 1830–1870.* Chicago: University of Chicago Press.

Miller, W. (1991). *Revenuers and Moonshiners: Enforcing Federal Liquor Law in the Mountain South, 1865–1900.* Chapel Hill: University of North Carolina Press.

Milwaukee Police. (2017). Milwaukee Police Chief Refutes Claims Made in Lawsuit, Feb. 22, www.youtube.com/watch?v=1mVHfR-aF70&feature=youtu.be.

Nagin, D., & Telep, C. (2017). Procedural justice and legal compliance. *Annual Review of Law and Social Science,* 13, 5–28.

Palmer, S. (1988). *Police and Protest in England and Ireland, 1780–1850.* New York: Cambridge University Press.

Phippen, J. W. (2016). What's wrong with the police department in Calexico, California? *The Atlantic,* May 19.

Pitkin, H. (1973). *Wittgenstein and Justice.* Berkeley: University of California Press.

President's Task Force on 21st Century Policing. (2015). *Final Report of the President's Task Force on 21st Century Policing*. Washington, DC: Office of Community Oriented Policing Services.

Ramos, E. (2013). Poor data keeps Chicago's stop and frisk hidden from scrutiny, *WBEZ News*, September 12, 2013.

Rawls, J. (1993). *Political Liberalism*. New York: Columbia University Press.

Rein, M., & Winship, C. (1999). The dangers of strong causal reasoning. *Society*, 36, 38–46.

Reisig, M., Bratton, J., & Gertz, M. (2007). The construct validity and refinement of process-based policing measures. *Criminal Justice and Behavior*, 34, 1005–1028.

Reith, C. (1943). *The British Police and the Democratic Ideal*. New York: Oxford University Press.

Schauer, F. (2015). *The Force of Law*. Cambridge: Harvard University Press.

Schulhofer, S., Tyler, T., & Huq, A. (2011). American policing at a crossroads: Unsustainable policies and the procedural justice alternative. *The Journal of Criminal Law & Criminology*, 101, 335–374.

Selznick, P. (1992). *The Moral Commonwealth*. Berkeley: University of California Press.

Skogan, W. (2017). Stop-and-frisk and trust in police in Chicago. In D. Oberwittler & S. Roché (eds.), *Police-Citizen Relations: A Comparative Investigation of Sources and Impediments of Legitimacy around the World* (pp. 247–265). Oxon: Routledge.

Skogan, W. (2017). La méthode du « stop-and-frisk » en tant que stratégie organisationnelle : leçons tirées à partir des exemples des villes de New York et Chicago. Stop and frisk as an organizational strategy: Lessons from New York and Chicago. *Cahiers de la Sécurité et de la Justice*, 40, 54–62.

Skogan, W., Van Craen, M., & Hennessy, C. (2015). Training police for procedural justice. *Journal of Experimental Criminology*, 11, 319–334.

Storch, R. (1975). The plague of blue locusts: Police reform and popular resistance in Northern England, 1840–57. *International Review of Social History*, 20, 61–90.

Sunshine, J., & Tyler, T. (2003). The role of procedural justice and legitimacy in shaping public support for policing. *Law and Society Review*, 37, 513–548.

Sunstein, C. (1995). Incompletely theorized agreements. *Harvard Law Review*, 108, 1733–1772.

Sunstein, C. (2016). *The Ethics of Influence*. New York: Cambridge University Press.

Tankebe, J. (2009). Public Cooperation with the Police in Ghana: Does Procedural Fairness Matter? *Criminology*, 47, 1265–1293.

Thacher, D. 2004. Order maintenance reconsidered. *The Journal of Criminal Law and Criminology*, 94, 381–414.

Thacher, D. (2015a). Olmsted's police. *Law and History Review*, 33, 577–620.

Thacher, D. (2015b). Perils of value neutrality. *Research in the Sociology of Organizations*, 44, 317–352.

Thacher, D. (2016). Channeling police discretion: The hidden potential of focused deterrence. *University of Chicago Legal Forum*, 2016, 533–578.

Tyler, T.(2000). Multiculturalism and the willingness of citizens to defer to law and to legal authorities. *Law and Social Inquiry*, 25, 983–1019.

Tyler, T. (2006). *Why People Obey the Law*. Princeton: Princeton University Press.

Tyler, T., ed. (2007). *Legitimacy and Criminal Justice: An International Perspective*. New York: Russell Sage Foundation.

Tyler, T. (2014). What are legitimacy and procedural justice in policing? and why are they becoming key elements of police leadership? In C. Fischer (ed.), *Legitimacy and Procedural Justice: A New Element of Police Leadership*. Washington: US Department of Justice.

Tyler, T. (2016). Understanding the force of law, *Tulsa Law Review*, 51, 507–519.

Tyler, T. (2017). Procedural justice and policing: A rush to judgment?, *Annual Review of Law and Social Science*, 13, 29–53.

Tyler, T., & Blader, S. (2000). *Cooperation in Groups*. Philadelphia: Psychology Press.

Tyler, T., & Huo, Y. (2002). *Trust in the Law*. New York: Russell Sage.

Tyler, T., Fagan, J., & Geller, A. (2014). Street stops and police legitimacy. *Journal of Empirical Legal Studies*, 11, 751–785.

United States Department of Justice, Civil Rights Division (2014). *Investigation of the Newark Police Department*, July 22.

van den Bos, K., Lind, A., & Wilke, H. (2001). The psychology of procedural and distributive justice viewed from the perspective of fairness heuristic theory. In R. Cropanzano (ed.), *Justice in the Workplace: From Theory to Practice* (vol. 2, pp. 49–66). Mahwah, NJ: Lawrence Erlbaum Associates Publishers.

Vitale, A. (2017). The myth of liberal policing, *The New Inquiry*, April 5.

Walker, S., & Archbold, C. (2014). *The New World of Police Accountability*. Thousand Oaks: Sage.

Weisburd, D., and M. K. Majmundar, eds. (2018). *Proactive Policing: Effects on Crime and Communities*. Washington, DC: The National Academies Press.

Wildeboer, R. (2013). 8,000 Chicago cops now a little friendlier. *WBEZ-News*, Dec. 21.

Worden, R., & McLean, S. (2017). *The Mirage of Police Reform: Procedural Justice and Police Legitimacy*. Berkeley: University of California Press.

PART III

BROKEN WINDOWS POLICING

5

Advocate

Of "Broken Windows" Criminology and Criminal Justice

William H. Sousa and George L. Kelling

INTRODUCTION: A FEW UP FRONT DISCOURSES

Despite attacks from the criminological, legal, and academic left, "broken windows" theory is a robust policy option in criminal justice practice and crime prevention. It has not only fueled the community policing movement, it has also informed the evolution of community courts, community prosecution, and community probation and parole. The Mid-town Manhattan Community Court, to give just one example, emphasizes broken windows' ideas in its philosophy and practice. Moreover, the ideas embodied in broken windows have moved beyond criminal justice and criminology to areas like public health, education, parks, and business improvement districts (BIDs).

The original article (Wilson & Kelling, 1982), published in the *Atlantic*, has had surprising "legs." Although exact figures are not available, circulation staff of the *Atlantic* have told both James Q. Wilson and Kelling (one of the authors of this paper), that "Broken Windows" has been reproduced more than any other article in *Atlantic's* history. Moreover, familiarity with broken windows is widespread internationally: *Fixing Broken Windows*, published by Kelling and Catherine M. Coles in 1996, has been translated into Spanish, Polish, and Japanese. The vast publicity, of course, associated with both the restoration of order in New York's subways during the early 1990s and the crime reduction in the city itself in the mid-1990s contributed to the popularization of broken windows, especially since both then Mayor Rudolph Giuliani and Police Commissioner William Bratton repeatedly identified it as a key part of their policing strategy.

OF METAPHORS

As background, the term "broken windows" is a metaphor. Briefly, it argues that just as a broken window left untended is a sign that nobody cares and invites more broken windows, so disorderly behavior left untended is a sign that nobody cares and leads to fear of crime, more serious crime and, ultimately, urban decay. ("Broken windows policing" refers to a police emphasis on disorderly behavior and minor offenses, often referred to as "quality of life" offenses like prostitution, public urination, and aggressive panhandling.)

Its expression as a metaphor partially explains the rapid spread of ideas embodied in broken windows. A metaphor, as defined in the *Oxford English Dictionary*, is "(T)he figure of speech in which a name or descriptive term is transferred to some object different from, but analogous to, that to which it is properly applicable" (OED, 1989: 676). Its origins are from the Greek, "to transfer," "to carry," or "to bear." Breaking it down, the broken windows metaphor transfers the "common wisdom" that a minor happening like a broken window can lead to increased damage if not taken care of, to the presumed consequences of uncivil and petty criminal behaviors: fear, serious crime, and urban decay.

The strength of a good metaphor is that it puts forward complex and nuanced ideas in simple and original ways that are easily communicated and readily recalled. When fresh and vivid, metaphors shock readers into attention. Criminal justice and criminology are riddled with metaphors – "white collar" crime, criminal justice "system," "wars" against crime and drugs, "blind justice," and the "thin blue line" are just a few examples. Metaphors, however, cut both ways. As the poet Robert Frost has noted: "All metaphor breaks down somewhere. That is the beauty of it. It is touch and go with the metaphor, and until you have lived with it long enough you don't know where it is going. You don't know how much you can get out of it and when it will cease to yield. It is a very living thing."[1]

Using metaphors, as a consequence, is risky. Because they simplify, metaphors distort as well as reveal. They mask complexity; they call attention to some aspects of an issue and ignore others; they age; they "break down somewhere" as Frost puts it; and soon, "everybody knows what they mean," regardless of whether everybody does or does not. As a result, metaphors also easily lend themselves both to misstatement or misrepresentation, either out of ignorance or to serve some purpose.

Complicating this issue for a metaphor like broken windows, is that the ideas in broken windows have policy implications and have come to be *practiced*: that is, the broken windows metaphor is expressed not just in words, but in day-to-day action by agencies – most often by public police, but by other sectors as well. The extent to which these practices adhere to the spirit, philosophy, and intent of the original broken windows argument is, of course, open to debate. We have seen many applications of what is called a broken windows approach that we have found worrisome. We have also seen and participated in applications of

---

[1] This quote is taken from Frost's "Education by Poetry." It can be found on page 41 of *Selected Prose of Robert Frost*, ed. Hyde Cox and Edward Connery Lathem (Holt, Rinehart, and Winston; New York).

broken windows of which we are proud: the New York City subway, to give just one example.

OF BROKEN WINDOWS: WHAT ARE THE IDEAS OF BROKEN WINDOWS?

Although one can find many of the core ideas of broken windows in earlier works by James Q. Wilson and Kelling (Wilson, 1968; Kelling et al., 1981) – as well as many other authors (see, for example, Jacobs, 1961; Glazer, 1979) – the most important presentation was the *Atlantic* article. What are these core ideas?

1. Disorder and fear of crime are strongly linked; (pp. 29–30)
2. Police (in the examples given, foot patrol officers) negotiate rules of the street. "Street people" are involved in the negotiation of those rules; (30)
3. Different neighborhoods have different rules; (30)
4. Untended disorder leads to breakdown of community controls; (31)
5. Areas where community controls break down are vulnerable to criminal invasion; (32)
6. "The essence of the police role in maintaining order is to reinforce the informal control mechanisms of the community itself." (34)
7. Problems arise not so much from individual disorderly persons as it does from the congregation of large numbers of disorderly persons; (35) and,
8. Different neighborhoods have different capacities to manage disorder. (36)

Additionally, the article raises some of the complexities associated with order maintenance. They include:

1. To what extent can order maintenance be shaped by the rules of neighborhoods rather than criminal law? (34)
2. How do we ensure equity in the enforcement of ordinances so "that police do not become the agents of neighborhood bigotry"? (35)
3. How is the balance maintained between individual rights and community interests? (36)
4. How do we ensure that community controls do not turn into neighborhood vigilantism? (36)

In 1996, these ideas and issues were again discussed in considerable detail in *Fixing Broken Windows* by Kelling and Catherine M. Coles (1996, with a Foreword by James Q. Wilson). *Fixing* not only restated these ideas, it discussed in detail many of the complexities and issues raised by the ideas of broken windows and their implementation in many communities. For example chapter 2, "The Growth of Disorder," is a detailed discussion of the historical and legal issues involved in defining disorder and balancing individual rights with community interests. We will not bother here to provide more details about *Fixing* except to make two points: first, *Fixing* explicitly located order maintenance within the context of community policing and the emerging community prosecution movement. (It will be remembered that community policing was in inchoate stages in 1981 when the original article was written.) Second, it heavily emphasized the differential strengths of neighborhoods – the important consequence of this was that order maintenance policies and activities were highly discretionary, from administrative policymaking to officers on the street.

An important question here is: do we (Wilson, Kelling, Coles, and, more recently, Sousa [see Kelling & Sousa, 2001; Sousa, 2010; 2015]) own these ideas? Obviously not, in two senses: first, many authors and programs emphasized police order maintenance long before the original article was written. Second, the ideas in broken windows are now "out there" and readers, academicians, and policymakers are free to make of them what they wish. Ideas have a life of their own and such is as it should be. The fact that some broken windows programs are a far cry from anything any of us ever had in mind is simply what happens in the policy arena. On the other hand, we do have a special claim when critics attack our written work. Critics, at least academic critics, of broken windows are obligated to "second order agreement": that is, the obligation to reproduce the ideas under question faithfully, if not enthusiastically. This is not only a matter of good scholarship; it is also a matter or professional ethics. Alas, this has not always happened.

Indeed, many of the academic and legal critiques have not only distorted broken windows, but they have done so with considerable zeal and passion. Among other charges, broken windows gives rise to "wars" on the poor, racism, and police brutality. For one author, Wilson and Kelling are "aversive racists" (Stewart, 1998). Another argues that Wilson's and Kelling's main policy recommendation to police is that they should "kick ass" (Bowling, 1999). Some activist groups have also accepted these distortions of broken windows. Campaign Zero (an affiliation of the Black Lives Matter movement), for example, lists ending broken windows policing as one of its policy solutions for police reform, arguing that the tactic is responsible for police killings of citizens (Campaign Zero, 2017). The question is: Why such misrepresentation and passion?

OF THE SPECIAL IRE OF CRIMINOLOGISTS

To answer the question posed above some background is needed. The dominant criminological and criminal justice paradigm of the past half-century is that formulated by President Lyndon Johnson's Presidential Commission on Law Enforcement and the Administration of Justice. Its 1967 publication, *The Challenge of Crime in a Free Society*, endorsed the "system" model of criminal justice and gave rise to, and framed, criminal justice education to this day (President's Commission, 1967).[2] The underlying assumption that

---

[2] The idea of a criminal justice "system" was first promulgated by the American Bar Foundation during the 1950s. Many of the staff persons of the Bar Foundation, e.g., Lloyd Ohlin, Frank

shapes the entire report and its policy and educational consequences is that crime is caused by structural features of society: racism, poverty and social injustice – the "root causes" of crime.

The assumed causal links among poverty, racism, and crime are woven throughout the President's Commission reports. Moreover, the report is laced with recommendations that deal with such broad societal problems: schools should be improved; youth should be prepared for employment; barriers to employment posed by discrimination should be eliminated; housing and recreational facilities should be improved; minimum family income should be provided – many, if not all, highly desirable social policies with which we have no quarrel.

The criminal justice "system" in this model is largely reactive. Police may patrol neighborhoods, but they do so in a largely non-intrusive fashion: in cars, remaining "in-service," – that is driving around in a random fashion – to ensure that they are available for calls. As the "front end" of the system, their primary responsibility is to respond to serious crime through enhanced communication systems. In this view, minor offenses are either formally decriminalized or virtually decriminalized as a matter of priorities and policies. Finally, the report is basically silent on the role of citizens and the community (except to support police), takes no notice of private security, and disregards the private sector. Crime control is achieved through broad social/political action to redress the structural inequities in society and by the activities of a public criminal justice system that processes offenders.

Crime *prevention* in this model is equated with grand ideas of social change: basic societal problems will have to be resolved. As the report indicates:

Warring on poverty, inadequate housing, and unemployment is warring against crime. A civil rights law is a law against crime. Money for schools is money against crime. Medical, psychiatric, and family-counseling services are services against crime. More broadly and most importantly every effort to improve life in the "inner city" is an effort against crime. A community's most enduring protection against crime is to right the wrongs and cure the illnesses that tempt men to harm their neighbors. (President's Commission, 1967: 6)

In this view then, we are left with two policy options: change society and/or process cases. Liberals and conservatives (they have their own macro approach – restore the family and its values) alike largely accept this framework. Thus we get extensive debates about sentencing, capital punishment, the exclusionary rule, mandatory sentencing, "three strikes you're out," prison construction, and so forth, but virtually the entire debate is within the bounds of the paradigm first put forward by President Johnson's Crime Commission.

Remington, and Herman Goldstein, were important contributors to the President's Commission report.

As such, the criminal justice system paradigm was integral to the 1960s Great Society.[3] Government *could* solve the problems of poverty, racism, and social injustice. The Great Society was not just a set of programs, linked as it was to civil rights, it was a moral cause to which social scientists were intensely committed and in which they were deeply involved. Crime prevention was to be a by-product of solving society's major problems. In the opinion of many championing this view, disloyalty to the root causes theory is evidence that one disregards the problems of poverty, racism, and social injustice. The liberal/left fear is that if disorder, fear, and crime are uncoupled from root causes, society's motivation to manage its ills will be reduced. Whether intended or not, crime prevention is held hostage to the pursuit of extremely broad social goals, some of which are only attainable over decades at best.

So then to return to the question, what explains the special attention that broken windows has gotten from critics? First, broken windows defies root cause orthodoxy: that is, to prevent crime one must alleviate these social ills. It also questions corollary issues and policies: decriminalization, deinstitutionalization, "victimless" crime, and the views that only individuals and not neighborhoods can be victims and that individual rights almost always trump community interests. Second, broken windows and crime control success in New York City came out of the political right (e.g., James Q. Wilson and Mayor Rudolph Giuliani). This was a hard dose for liberal social scientists to swallow. Hence, the heated debates about why crime declined in New York City.[4] Finally, because of New York City, broken windows has become widely known, both in professional circles and in the popular media. It has become so well known that often when cited in the popular media it is neither attributed nor defined. Consequently, a press release or title that "refutes" broken windows, or implies something like it, is more likely to gather attention than it would otherwise. In other words, some authors are "piggybacking" on broken windows. We have no quarrel with this – we are in a marketplace of ideas; we would just caution such authors to represent broken windows and its implications accurately.

OF RESEARCH INTO BROKEN WINDOWS

Research on broken windows can be loosely divided into two categories. The first includes studies that examine the theoretical underpinnings of the hypothesis, such as the link between disorder and fear or the association

[3] Lloyd Ohlin, e.g., was not only the author (with Richard Cloward) of *Delinquency and Opportunity: A Theory of Delinquent Gangs* (1960), one of the key works giving rise to the War on Poverty and the Great Society, he was also a member of the President's Commission on Law Enforcement and the Administration of Justice.

[4] It is interesting that neither the work of Ronald Clarke in *situational crime prevention* nor Marcus Felson in *routine activities* has engendered the hostility that broken windows has: both are as equally dismissive of root cause and motivational theories of crime control.

between incivilities and serious crime. The second includes research that evaluates policies that are derived from or otherwise influenced by broken windows, such as quality-of-life programs or order maintenance enforcement practices. We briefly discuss these two categories.

Broken Windows Research: The Disorder-Fear and Disorder-Crime Connections

Broken windows argues that disorderly conditions and behaviors are linked both to citizen fear and to serious crime. Few criminologists have concern with this disorder-fear portion of the hypothesis, and a fair amount of empirical research – some of which goes as far back as research conducted by the President's Commission during the 1960s – demonstrates an association between incivilities and fear (see Skogan & Maxfield (1981) and Ross & Jang (2000) for two examples). Some debate continues regarding measurement concerns, causal order, and individual versus ecological level influences on fear. LaGrange, Ferraro, and Supancic (1992), for instance, suggest that while incivility is related to fear, the effect is mediated through perceptions of risk. Taylor (2001) concludes that the incivility–fear connection is stronger at the individual level (one's perception of incivilities in the neighborhood has a greater impact than the actual amount of incivilities in the neighborhood) and that the connection is weak when examined longitudinally (incivilities influence later changes in fear, but not as strongly or consistently as other factors). Overall, however, much research to date agrees that disorder is, at least in some way, positively associated with fear.[5]

Unlike the disorder-fear hypothesis, the disorder-serious crime connection is more controversial. Skogan (1990) was the first to find support for the link empirically in *Disorder and Decline*. Using primarily survey data from forty neighborhoods in six cities (Chicago, Atlanta, San Francisco, Philadelphia, Houston, and Newark, NJ), Skogan found a highly significant disorder-crime connection while taking into account other factors such as poverty, instability, and race. Harcourt (1998) has since challenged these findings, claiming among other concerns that Skogan's inclusion of several neighborhoods with particularly strong disorder-crime connections (from the city of Newark) manipulated the overall results. After reproducing the analyses and removing these neighborhoods from Skogan's dataset, Harcourt finds that the relationship between disorder and serious crime disappears.[6] Harcourt's

---

[5] Interestingly, research has produced mixed results in terms of whether managing disorder reduces fear – see Hinkle & Weisburd (2008) and Weisburd et al. (2015) – although this may be due to different methods of disorder management.

[6] After reproducing Skogan's study, but before removing the Newark neighborhoods from the analysis, Harcourt acknowledges a statistically significant connection between disorder and robbery. When he eliminates the Newark neighborhoods, this disorder-robbery connection disappears.

methods, however, have also been questioned (see Xu, Fiedler & Flaming, 2005). Harcourt removed several neighborhoods from the analysis to produce the no-association result, but the removal of several *different* neighborhoods from the dataset may have *strengthened* the disorder-crime connection found by Skogan (Eck & Maguire, 2000; Xu et al., 2005). Harcourt's analysis, therefore, does less to disprove Skogan's results and more to point out a limitation to the original dataset: its sensitivity to outliers (Eck & Maguire, 2000).

Often cited as convincing evidence against the disorder-crime association (and to the broken windows hypothesis overall) is Sampson and Raudenbush's (1999) assessment of the relationship between "collective efficacy," disorder, and serious crime.[7] The authors use a variety of methods for their investigation, including systematic social observations designed to capture disorderly behaviors and conditions on the streets of Chicago. They challenge the connection between disorder and serious crime by suggesting that while disorder is moderately correlated with predatory crime, once antecedent neighborhood constructs (such as collective efficacy) are considered, the direct relationship between the two all but disappears. Sampson and Raudenbush conclude that the level of collective efficacy is a strong predictor of both disorder and predatory crime and that the relationship between incivilities and crime is spurious except for officially measured robbery. According to the authors, these results "contradict the strong version of the broken windows thesis" (1999: 637).[8]

We have several difficulties with the Sampson and Raudenbush study that involve the authors' methodological decisions (such as their failure to observe night-time activities) and their interpretation of the data (such as their casual dismissal of the robbery finding) (see Kelling, 2001), but others have challenged their analyses as well (see Xu et al., 2005). Jang and Johnson (2001), for example, argue that Sampson and Raudenbush have not tested the broken windows theory at all because they misinterpreted the original thesis and therefore mis-specified their analyses. As Jang and Johnson point out, broken windows postulates that disorder *indirectly* leads to crime via weakened community and neighborhood controls (stated somewhat differently, Wilson and Kelling (1982) argue that disorder, *left unchecked by community and neighborhood controls*, will lead to more serious crime). Sampson and Raudenbush, however, assume the thesis proposes that disorder is *directly* associated with crime, and so test a model in which disorder mediates the effects of neighborhood characteristics (including collective efficacy) on crime

---

[7] Collective efficacy is defined as "the linkage of cohesion and mutual trust with shared expecta-tions for intervening in support of neighborhood social control" (Sampson & Raudenbush, 1999: 612–613). For purposes of their study, the collective efficacy measure was created by combining two measures from survey data: shared expectations for informal social control (represented by five survey items asking respondents to report the likelihood that their neighbors would take action given certain scenarios) and social cohesion / trust (represented by five survey questions asking residents to report on the trustworthiness, helpfulness, and collegiality of their neighbors).

[8] What "the strong version of the broken windows thesis" is remains a mystery to us, but so be it.

rather than neighborhood characteristics mediating the effects of disorder (Jang & Johnson, 2001). Taking into account this misinterpretation, Jang and Johnson estimate that Sampson and Raudenbush's assessment actually provides *positive* rather than negative support for broken windows.[9]

In any event, the debate over the link between disorder and crime remains contentious, research on the topic has produced mixed results, and further research is required to better understand the underlying mechanisms proposed in broken windows (i.e., connections between fear, disorder, collective efficacy, and crime) (see Weisburd et al., 2015). Interestingly enough, Taylor's (2001) examination of the incivility-crime connection seems to verify the inconsistency of previous research. His longitudinal assessment of Baltimore neighborhoods provides qualified support for the idea that "grime" leads to crime. He finds, however, that while disorder influences some later changes in criminal activity (as well as changes in neighborhood decline and fear), the results differ across indicators (types of disorder) and across outcomes (types of crime). Additionally, Taylor finds that other indicators, such as initial neighborhood status, are more consistent predictors of later crime.[10]

Broken Windows Research: Policy Evaluation

A primary policy implication derived from the original *Atlantic* article is that if police and communities are able to manage minor disorders, the result can be a reduction in criminal activity. As such, activities that can be classified as broken windows policing, which emphasize the assertive enforcement of minor offenses, continue to be implemented in communities across the country.[11] Subsequent evaluations of broken windows policing activities and their impact on crime typically consider whether measures of minor offense enforcement are significantly related with measures of serious crime reduction.[12]

---

[9] Jang and Johnson (2001) themselves find support for broken windows, indicating in their analysis that neighborhood disorder is significantly related to illicit drug use among adolescents. However, individual "religiosity" (one's commitment to religion) and social networks weaken the effect of disorder on drug use.

[10] Some research on the geographic distribution of crime also confirms the complex nature of the minor offense / serious offense relationship. Weisburd, Maher and Sherman (1993), for example, suggest that calls for service for minor offenses (public morals, drunks) correlate more strongly with certain serious offenses (i.e., robberies) than with others in crime "hot spots."

[11] We use the terms "broken windows," "quality-of-life," and "order maintenance" interchangeably to describe a policing style that emphasizes the management of minor offenses. For reasons that are evident in this paper, we do not consider "zero-tolerance" to be synonymous with these terms. We are also careful to distinguish between order maintenance tactics as performed by NYPD in the 1990s and NYPD's "stop-and-frisk" practices as implemented during the 2010s.

[12] As noted above, some studies have also considered whether disorder management is associated with fear of crime (Hinkle & Weisburd (2008); Weisburd, Hinkle, Famega & Ready (2011); Weisburd et al. (2015)). Weisburd et al. (2011), for example, determined that order maintenance practices had a minimal impact on public perceptions of fear or perceptions of crime.

The New York City Police Department during the 1990s and early 2000s provides perhaps the most obvious example of a macro policy of order maintenance, as it is well known that officers were asked to be more assertive in the management of minor offenses (i.e., typically those offenses that were virtually ignored in the past).[13] That an increase in minor offense enforcement accompanied a reduction in serious crime in New York helped to spark a continuing debate: did the strategy contribute to the reduction, or were other factors involved?

Numerous factors have been offered as potential causes for crime reduction in New York and elsewhere: changes in demographic and economic trends, shifts in drug use patterns, statistical regression to the mean, changes in the cultural values of at-risk populations, and many others.[14] Several studies have examined the extent to which a general order maintenance strategy has contributed to the crime drop relative to other factors. Previously, we found that NYPD order maintenance activities in the 1990s had a significant effect on violence reduction in New York net of economic, demographic, and drug use variables (Kelling & Sousa, 2001). Others have also found these crime reduction benefits of order maintenance tactics in New York (Corman & Mocan, 2005; Rosenfeld, Fornango & Rengifo, 2007; Messner et al., 2007; Cerdá et al., 2009), and in other places (Worrall, 2002; Berk & MacDonald, 2010; see also Braga, Welsh & Schnell, 2015). Some analysts, however, are either unable to find such an effect or are generally more hesitant in terms of crediting order maintenance practices with reductions in crime (Harcourt & Ludwig, 2006; Zimring, 2012; Baumer & Wolff, 2014; Greenberg, 2014).

Investigations of general broken windows strategies can offer policy insight, but the data available for such analyses are often less than ideal. The limitations of macro-level data – often put forward by the authors themselves – therefore prohibit conclusive statements from these analyses alone (see Weisburd, Telep & Lawton (2014) for a discussion of the limitations of macro-level data when addressing this issue). Several field evaluations, however, have examined the effectiveness of the strategy as implemented in focused, place-specific initiatives. Braga et al. (1999), for instance, designed a field experiment in Jersey City, NJ, to assess the impact of problem-oriented policing strategies focused on social and physical disorders in violent places. They concluded that these strategies were associated with decreases in observed disorders, citizen calls for service, and criminal incidents. Similarly, Braga and Bond (2008) analyzed data from a randomized experiment in Lowell, MA, designed to assess the impact of

---

[13] In respects, the idea that "everyone knows" that NYPD was an "order maintenance" department is unfortunate. While it is true that the management of minor offenses was an important strategy in New York, the strategy was most prominent when used to support focused problem-solving activities that are often driven by the CompStat process (Kelling & Sousa, 2001).

[14] For a review of the potential causes of crime reduction in New York and elsewhere during the 1990s, see generally Karmen (1999) and Blumstein and Wallman (2000). See also Karmen (2000) and Kelling and Sousa (2001).

a general disorder management strategy on crime in hot spots, concluding that the effort resulted in decreases in calls for service for crime and disorder with little evidence of displacement.

Other field studies, though perhaps less detailed than those of Braga et al. (1999) and Braga and Bond (2008), are less supportive of broken windows policies. Novak, Hartman, Holsinger, and Turner (1999) analyzed a police enforcement effort designed to reduce specific disorders – primarily alcohol and traffic-related offenses – in a community in a Midwestern city (although it was not designed to necessarily impact serious crime). The authors determined that the effort was not associated with a decrease in either robbery or burglary (the two serious crimes they analyzed) at the target site, although they acknowledge the result may be due to the duration (one month) and dosage level of the intervention. Katz, Webb, and Schaefer (2001) evaluated the impact of a police quality-of-life program in Chandler, AZ, designed to reduce social and physical disorders with the intent of decreasing serious crime. The authors found that, in general, the program had an impact on public morals disorders (such as prostitution and public drinking) and physical disorders in the target area. However, the impact on serious crime was minimal and changes in criminal activity varied by section of the target area.

DISCUSSION

Whether regarding theory or policy, empirical research on broken windows has produced mixed results. Some academics, attorneys, and criminologists, however, have used the "mixed" results to mount offensives against the thesis. Their argument goes something like the following:

Studies are inconsistent when it comes to broken windows. Some find the necessary link between disorder and crime, some do not, and some find it only in certain places and/or for certain types of criminal activity. Because there are statistically better predictors of crime – such as neighborhood collective efficacy, neighborhood stability, etc. – policies should concentrate on improvements in those areas rather than on "fixing broken windows." Policies based on these better predictors can be more effective and are less morally objectionable than the management of minor offenses.

We argue three points in the remainder of this paper: (1) broken windows may have merit beyond the link between disorder and crime; (2) claims that broken windows is morally objectionable, to date, are based on little actual knowledge of order maintenance in practice; (3) despite criticisms, broken windows offers a viable policy option within communities.

Broken Windows and Strong Causal Reasoning

The concepts of disorder and serious crime each capture extremely complex sets of activities – the fact that research is inconsistent concerning the link between the two is of little wonder. Indeed, it is difficult for us to argue that all instances of serious crime are the result of social and/or physical incivilities. Our guess is that as investigations continue into the relationship between disorder and crime, research will find stronger or weaker associations as both concepts are disaggregated into their numerous components. Some research has already foreshadowed this conclusion. In several studies, for example, robbery has been linked to disorder where other serious crimes have not (Skogan, 1990; Harcourt, 1998; Sampson & Raudenbush, 1999; but see Taylor, 2001). We also suspect that even different types of robbery are more or less associated with disorderly conditions and/or behaviors.[15]

In any event, debates will likely continue as to the strength of the causal connections between disorder and crime and the policy relevance behind these connections. But as Thacher (2004) indicates, both proponents and opponents of "broken windows" have become preoccupied with the search for strong causal relationships between disorder and criminal activity – a type of connection that is rarely (if ever) clearly understood in criminology despite the best efforts of objective social science. Thacher suggests that by basing the merits of order maintenance on the results of causal connection studies, criminology avoids a more important moral question: Is the management of minor offenses justified regardless of its indirect effects on crime? In other words, is the direct effect of order maintenance on public order a legitimate public policy goal?

In his analysis, Thacher argues that at least some types of order maintenance policing practices are important as ends unto themselves – regardless of their impact on serious crime – because "they address important instances of accumulative harms and offenses" (2004: 101). Evidence from field experiments suggests that managing minor offenses can prevent the spread of further disorder (see Keizer, Lindenberg, & Steg, 2008). Indeed, some police order maintenance strategies are implemented with no original intent to reduce serious crime but instead with the goal of restoring public order. Restoration of order in the New York City subway provides an example. While evidence indicates that reductions in both disorder and serious crime (i.e., robberies)

---

[15] From our perspective, a finding that disorder is linked to robbery in these studies is both interesting and important for policy. Others, however, in their apparent zeal to disprove broken windows, gloss over the robbery finding. Because *only* robbery is related to disorder, so the argument goes, the thesis is inherently flawed (never mind that robbery is a "bellwether" crime and general gauge of violence in many communities). We believe that those who hold the disorder-crime connection up to such lofty standards suffer from a similar affliction as those who believe in what Hirschi and Selvin refer to as the first false criterion of causality: "Insofar as a relation between two variables is not perfect, the relation is not causal" (1966: 256). Among other reasons, Hirschi and Selvin argue that this criterion is false because perfect relations are virtually unknown in criminology. We agree, and thus those who will settle for little less than a perfect relationship between disorder and crime as "proof" of broken windows are not likely to find this proof in past, present, or future research.

were linked to police order maintenance efforts (especially against fare-beating and aggressive begging), the policing effort was initially implemented as an attempt to bring control to an environment that had grown chaotic (Kelling & Coles, 1996). Similarly, the disorder-reduction program described by Novak et al. (1999) did not have a substantial impact on serious crime, but it was only intended to reduce specific incivilities (primarily alcohol and traffic violations) in response to community complaints about these minor offenses (unfortunately, the authors were unable to assess the intervention's impact on these disorders). Even when an order maintenance intervention that is designed to reduce serious crime fails to do so, this does not necessarily mean the intervention is without merit. For instance, although Katz et al. (2001) concluded that a disorder reduction program did not have the intended impact on serious crime, they suggest that the intervention may still have been worthwhile because it had a significant effect on both social and physical disorders in the target area.

Broken Windows and Morally Complex Policing

Of course, even if we build an argument that public order is a legitimate goal for public policy and that order maintenance policing can directly benefit public order, this still leaves the question of whether such a policing strategy is morally appropriate (Thacher, 2004). It is true that broken windows is morally complex. In the original *Atlantic* article – as we outlined above – Wilson and Kelling were greatly concerned with the ambiguities, complexities, and controversies concerning order maintenance. Likewise Kelling and Coles discussed the legality and constitutionality of order maintenance throughout chapter two – the longest chapter in *Fixing Broken Windows*. Some critics of broken windows, however, have literally ignored what was written in the original article and in *Fixing* and have instead argued that order maintenance is morally reprehensible. Among other concerns, they claim that order maintenance policies encourage heavy-handed, "zero-tolerance" police tactics, or that they criminalize relatively innocuous behaviors deemed acceptable in communities, or that they disproportionately affect citizens living in poor and minority neighborhoods.

The difficulty with critics' arguments, however, is that their assertions are based on little actual knowledge of order maintenance as implemented by police managers or as performed by line officers. Thacher (2004) makes this point strongly. Certainly many critics claim to "know" about broken windows policing, but their understanding of it appears to come from dramatized media accounts and either deliberate or careless distortions of the broken windows metaphor.[16] In fact, few have actually examined order maintenance

---

[16] An example of this comes from Greene (1999) who criticizes New York's order maintenance policing as brutal compared to other departments such as San Diego: "[the comparison] between

in practice. Most criminologists/lawyers, for example, who have attacked the NYPD's 1990s era practices, claimed that broken windows as practiced was morally reprehensible, and dismissed New York's crime reductions as due to structural variables, have spent little or no time "on the ground" either in neighborhoods or with police.

We analyzed broken windows policing in New York City as it was implemented during the early 2000s (Kelling & Sousa, 2001; Sousa, 2010). One of us (Sousa) spent considerable time riding with NYPD and recording observations of officers as they performed various tasks including those that can be considered order maintenance. The observations suggest that order maintenance, at least as performed by NYPD at that time, can best be described as officers *paying attention* to minor offenses that were essentially ignored in the past. Sometimes "paying attention" to minor offenses involved formal action – such as arrest or citation – but more often than not it involved no official action at all. While officers did not ignore disorderly behavior, they were much more likely to informally warn, educate, scold, or verbally reprimand citizens who committed minor offenses. Contrary to the claims of critics, we concluded that officers were mindful of the moral complexities behind their activities, considered the contexts and circumstances surrounding incivilities and minor offenses before taking action, and exercised careful discretion while performing order maintenance tasks.

All may not agree with our assessment of order maintenance as it was performed in New York and all are free to disagree with our interpretations of the observations. The point however, is that these observations were made with the intent to develop a more thorough understanding of broken windows in

New York City and San Diego offers compelling evidence that cooperative police-community problem solving can provide effective crime control through more efficient and humane methods" (1999: 185). Comparing New York to San Diego is troublesome at best, but even if such a comparison were possible, much of Greene's evidence for New York's less "humane" methods is based on little first-hand knowledge and comes instead from questionable and unreliable sources. For example, she cites politician Mark Green's opinions as authoritative on the subject of New York's order maintenance policing, but fails to mention Green's transparent agenda as one of Giuliani's chief political rivals of the 1990s. Additionally, while she correctly points out that complaints against the police increased when order maintenance was introduced in New York (evidence that she claims supports the New York brutality position), Greene fails to place this point in its proper context. First, complaints against the police did increase from 1992 to 1995, but the number of officers also increased by nearly 10,000 during the same time period. Second, order maintenance policing necessarily requires more frequent contacts between officers and citizens – often in situations where the citizen is suspected of some sort of legal violation. Considering the number of officers added, combined with the increased frequency of contacts between police and citizens, one might be surprised if the number of complaints against police did not increase. Third, while the number of complaints against the police increased until 1995, the number *decreased* throughout the rest of the 1990s despite the fact that assertive enforcement of minor offenses continued. Greene's analysis exemplifies a general lack of knowledge of broken windows policing – particularly in New York – by those who claim a competency of it.

practice – at least in New York. We share with Thacher (2004) the view that the merits of broken windows should be evaluated less on causal connection studies (which are unlikely to produce definitively conclusive advice for policy) and more on detailed descriptions of order maintenance as it is practiced. Only the accumulation of more detailed investigations is likely to shed light on the ethical considerations of applied order maintenance and its impact on disorder in communities. Critics rightly point out that broken windows policies are morally complex, but until they begin to develop a more substantive understanding of that which they criticize, their claims that order maintenance policies are objectionable are nothing more than assertions based on questionable media accounts, dubious suspicions, and often politically driven speculations. In the end, research may find that order maintenance, as interpreted by some police departments or implemented by some police officers, is morally questionable, but for critics to condemn the practice without sufficient knowledge of it or on the basis of media representations is professionally irresponsible.

Broken Windows and Policy Options

Finally in this section, we wish to briefly address two points made by some critics of broken windows. The first is that other policy options, such as problem-oriented policing, situational crime prevention, and community crime prevention, are available in lieu of broken windows policies. The second is that because there are better indicators of crime and crime reduction – e.g., "collective efficacy," neighborhood stability, etc. – focus should be on policy improvements in those areas rather than on policies derived from broken windows.

Regarding the first point, we want to acknowledge that research continues to show that crime control efforts resulting from problem-solving, situational crime prevention, and community crime prevention demonstrate potential at reducing crime and restoring order in communities.[17] We do not, nor have we ever, suggested that order maintenance policing should be implemented instead of these efforts. Quite the contrary, we believe that order maintenance should represent a policy option in support of police and community efforts to be implemented as problem analysis and problem solving dictate.[18] In fact, close examination reveals that this is the reality even in an organization that had a reputation as an "order maintenance" department: we found numerous examples of successful NYPD problem-solving efforts driven by the CompStat process – some of which had virtually no order maintenance quality to them at all (Kelling & Sousa, 2001).

[17] For a review of this research, see Eck and Maguire (2000) and Weisburd and Eck (2004).
[18] A recent National Academies of Sciences report suggests that broken windows interventions are more effective when integrated with place-based, problem-oriented practices (Weisburd & Majmundar, 2018).

Regarding the second point, we wish to point out that many of the "better" statistical predictors of crime essentially offer little in the way of policy options. No one will argue, for example, against the desire to improve neighborhood "collective efficacy," but notions such as this are nebulous in both concept and practice. Easing unemployment, poverty, and racial tensions are highly desirable goals to be sure, but the methods by which these goals are to be attained are far from certain. Even if practitioners possessed the knowledge, skill, and resources to effect change in these areas, it is unclear whether, when, and to what extent these changes would later impact crime. The "better" statistical predictors of crime may be intellectually informative, but they represent vague concepts and/or unachievable goals to the practitioner who is tasked with implementing realistic crime control policies. Broken windows policies, in contrast, are *practical options*. They can be implemented as part of a larger problem-solving agenda, can be employed in a timely fashion, and can offer the potential for timely results.

CONCLUSION: OF CRIME, CRIMINOLOGY, AND CRIMINAL JUSTICE

The contrast between the response to broken windows by policymakers and practitioners, on the one hand, and a good portion of criminologists, on the other, is stark. In the world of policy and practice, broken windows has become, for the most part, integral to the conventional wisdom of community justice – whether it be policing, prosecution, probation and parole, or community courts. The same largely holds true for the BID movement and the neighborhood community anti-crime movement.[19] Indeed, many of our policymaking and practitioner colleagues find the responses of many criminologists to broken windows mystifying – for them a sign that criminologists are simply out of touch with the real world. They have a point. In fact, they have several points.

First, the root cause ideology has locked criminology and criminal justice into a practical dead end (it probably is a theoretical dead end as well, but that is another story). Until the past twenty or twenty-five years or so, criminology and criminal justice has had little more to offer to crime prevention than political advocacy/action to achieve a liberal/left version of a "just society." If one thinks of the "big ideas" in criminal justice that have enriched the recent past, the story is telling. *Community policing* had its origins in the work of the American Bar Foundation, the early Police Foundation (1970–1980), and policing itself. *Problem-solving*, too, had its origins in the work of the American Bar Foundation, but as refined and articulated by Herman Goldstein, a public

---

[19] For an interesting discussion regarding the impact of BIDs on disorder and crime management, see Cook and MacDonald (2011).

administrator. *Situational crime prevention* was originated and largely formulated by a psychologist, Ronald Clarke. *Pulling levers* – the ideas that led to the dramatic drop in gang killings in Boston – was largely the product of line police in the Boston Police Department and shaped by public policy scholar, David Kennedy. *CompStat* – the administrative mechanism that addresses problems of information sharing and accountability in policing – was a product of the private sector and an entrepreneurial police chief, William Bratton and some of his closest colleagues in the NYPD (Simons, 1995). *Broken windows* grew out of work by a political scientist, James Q. Wilson, and a social worker turned police researcher, Kelling. It can be argued that the notion of *hot spots* was developed and broadly promulgated through the work of contemporary criminologists (see Sherman, 1989; Sherman, Gartin & Buerger, 1989; Weisburd et al., 1993), but much of the initial work, both theoretical and practical, was rooted in the work of Glenn Pierce and developed outside traditional criminological/criminal justice circles (see Pierce, Spaar & Briggs 1984). With few exceptions, it is difficult to come up with recent criminal justice innovations that have their origins in criminology.[20]

Second, and this is closely linked to the first, criminology, with its special interest in *why* people commit crimes, has co-opted schools of criminal justice. We have no quarrel with the academic study of why people commit crimes, it is a legitimate and important inquiry; however, we believe it should be properly lodged within sociology (within which criminology is a specialty). Why criminal justice has been co-opted by criminology is complex but includes the newness of criminal justice as a field, the status and tenure structures of universities, the ascendancy of "Great Society" theoreticians in crime control thinking, and the dominance of root causes ideology during the post–President's Commission era. Nonetheless, the idea that university units dedicated to crime control – after all, it was the crime problem that spurred their origin under the 1970s Law Enforcement Assistance Administration – should be dedicated to criminological pursuits, rather than crime control, was a turn of events that mired such units into relatively fruitless pursuits – at least from a public policy point of view.

Finally, criminology and criminal justice have confused scientific standards of evidence with the evidence that policy makers and practitioners require in the real world. To be sure, policy makers would love to live in a world where they were 95 percent certain that implementing particular policies or practices would have the desired outcome. As a matter of fact, they do not and will not. Policymakers live in a world in which they have to make decisions – many of

---

[20] We do not mean to dismiss the contributions of contemporary criminologists to the development and/or furtherance of these innovations. (Anthony Braga, for example, was highly influential with David Kennedy in the crafting of the *pulling levers* violence reduction initiative.) Our point here is simply that many modern criminal justice ideas are heavily influenced by those outside the discipline of criminology.

them, life and death – in which they are confronted with mixes of problems and programs that do not lend themselves to clean experiments, bad data, and often conflicting and/or uncertain research findings. In such a world, 70 or 80 percent certainty would be a happy thing. Broken windows looks pretty good in this world: if properly done, it will most probably be approved of by neighborhood residents, it may reduce their fear of crime, and it looks like it will reduce some street crimes. Not a bad bet for policymakers and practitioners.

ACKNOWLEDGMENTS

We wish to thank Anthony Braga and David Weisburd for their helpful comments on earlier drafts of this paper.

REFERENCES

Baumer, E. P., & Wolff, K. T. (2014). Evaluating contemporary crime drop(s) in America, New York City, and many other places. *Justice Quarterly, 31*(1), 5–38.

Berk, R., & MacDonald, J. (2010). Policing the homeless: An evaluation of efforts to reduce homeless-related crime. *Criminology & Public Policy, 9*(4), 813–840.

Blumstein, A., & Wallman, J. (eds.). (2000). *The Crime Drop in America.* Cambridge, UK: Cambridge University Press.

Bowling, B. (1999). The rise and fall of New York murder: Zero tolerance or crack's decline? *British Journal of Criminology, 39*(4), 531–554.

Braga, A. A., & Bond, B. J. (2008). Policing crime and disorder hot spots: A randomized controlled trial. *Criminology, 46*(3), 577–607.

Braga, A. A., Weisburd, D. L., Waring, E. J., Green Mazerolle, L., Spelman, W., & Gajewski, F. (1999). Problem-oriented policing in violent crime places: a randomized controlled experiment. *Criminology, 37*(3), 541–580.

Braga, A. A., Welsh, B. C., & Schnell, C. (2015). Can policing disorder reduce crime? A systematic review and meta-analysis. *Journal of Research in Crime and Delinquency, 52*(4), 567–588.

Campaign Zero. (2017). *End Broken Windows Policing.* Retrieved from www .joincampaignzero.org/brokenwindows.

Cerdá, M., Tracy, M., Messner, S. F., Vlahov, D., Tardiff, K., & Galea, S. (2009). Misdemeanor policing, physical disorder, and gun-related homicide: A spatial analytic test of "broken-windows" theory. *Epidemiology, 20*(4), 533–541.

Cloward, R. A., & Ohlin, L. E. (1960). *Delinquency and Opportunity: A Theory of Delinquent Gangs.* New York: The Free Press.

Cook, P. J., & MacDonald, J. (2011). Public safety through private action: An economic assessment of BIDs. *The Economic Journal, 121*(May), 445–462.

Corman, H., & Mocan, N. (2005). Carrots, sticks, and broken windows. *Journal of Law and Economics, 48*, 235–262.

Eck, J. E., & Maguire, E. R. (2000). Have changes in policing reduced violent crime? An assessment of the evidence. In A. Blumstein, & J. Wallman (Eds.), *The Crime Drop in America.* Cambridge, UK: Cambridge University Press.

Glazer, N. (1979). On subway graffiti in New York. The Public Interest, 54 (Winter), 3–11.

Greenberg, D. F. (2014). Studying New York City's crime decline: Methodological issues. *Justice Quarterly*, 31(1), 154–188.

Greene, J. A. (1999). Zero tolerance: a case study of police policies and practices in New York City. *Crime & Delinquency*, 45(2), 171–187.

Harcourt, B. E. (1998). Reflecting on the subject: a critique of the social influence conception of deterrence, the broken windows theory, and order-maintenance policing New York style. *Michigan Law Review*, 97, 291–389.

Harcourt, B. E., & Ludwig, J. (2006). Broken windows: New evidence from New York City and a five-city experiment. *University of Chicago Law Review*, 73, 271–320.

Hinkle, J. C., & Weisburd, D. (2008). The irony of broken windows policing: A micro-place study of the relationship between disorder, focused police crackdowns and fear of crime. *Journal of Criminal Justice*, 36(6), 503–512.

Hirschi, T., & Selvin, H. C. (1966). False criteria of causality in delinquency research. *Social Problems*, 13, 254–268.

Jacobs, J. (1961). *The Death and Life of Great American Cities*. New York, NY: Vintage Books.

Jang, S. J., & Johnson, B. R. (2001). Neighborhood disorder, individual religiosity, and adolescent use of illicit drugs: a test of multilevel hypotheses. *Criminology*, 39(1), 109–144.

Karmen, A. (ed.). (1999). *Crime and Justice in New York City*. New York, NY: Primis Custom Publishing.

Karmen, A. (2000). *New York Murder Mystery: The True Story Behind the Crime Crash of the 1990s*. New York, NY: New York University Press.

Katz, C. M., Webb, V. J., & Schaefer, D. R. (2001). An assessment of the impact of quality-of-life policing on crime and disorder. *Justice Quarterly*, 18(4), 825–876.

Keizer, K., Lindenberg, S., & Steg, L. (2008). The spreading of disorder. *Science*, 322, 1681–1685.

Kelling, G. L. (2001). Broken windows and the culture wars: A response to selected critiques. In R. Matthews, & J. Pitts (eds.), *Crime, Disorder, and Community Safety*. London, UK: Routledge.

Kelling, G. L., & Coles, C. M. (1996). *Fixing Broken Windows: Restoring Order and Reducing Crime in Our Communities*. New York, NY: The Free Press.

Kelling, G. L., Pate, A., Ferrara, A., Utne, M., & Brown, C. E. (1981). *Newark Foot Patrol Experiment*. Washington, DC: Police Foundation.

Kelling, G. L., & Sousa, W. H. (2001). *Do Police Matter? An Analysis of the Impact of New York City's Police Reforms*. Civic Report No. 22. New York, NY: Manhattan Institute.

LaGrange, R. L., Ferraro, K. F., & Supancic, M. (1992). Perceived risk and fear of crime: Role of social and physical incivilities. *Journal of Research in Crime and Delinquency*, 29(3), 311–334.

Messner, S. F., Galea, S., Tardiff, K. J., Tracy, M., Bucciarelli, A., Piper, T. M., Frye, V., & Vlahov, D. (2007). Policing, drugs, and the homicide decline in New York City in the 1990s. *Criminology*, 45(2), 385–414.

Novak, K. J., Hartman, J. L., Holsinger, A. M., & Turner, M. G. (1999). The effects of aggressive policing of disorder on serious crime. *Policing: An International Journal of Police Strategies & Management*, 22(2), 171–190.

Oxford English Dictionary, 2nd ed. (1989). Oxford: Clarendon Press.

Pierce, G. L., Spaar, S. A., & Briggs, L. R. (1984). *The Character of Police Work: Implications for the Delivery of Services.* Boston, MA: Center for Applied Social Research, Northeastern University.

President's Commission on Law Enforcement and the Administration of Justice. (1967). *The Challenge of Crime in a Free Society.* Washington, DC: US Government Printing Office.

Rosenfeld, R., Fornango, R., & Rengifo, A. F. (2007). The impact of order-maintenance policing on New York City homicide and robbery rates: 1981–2001. *Criminology, 45* (2), 355–384.

Ross, C. E., & Jang, S. J. (2000). Neighborhood disorder, fear, and mistrust: The buffering role of social ties with neighbors. *American Journal of Community Psychology, 28*(4), 401–420.

Sampson, R. J., & Raudenbush, S. W. (1999). Systematic social observations of public spaces: A new look at disorder in urban neighborhoods. *American Journal of Sociology, 105,* 603–651.

Sherman, L. W. (1989). Repeat calls for service: Policing the "hot spots." In D. J. Kenney (ed.), *Police and Policing: Contemporary Issues.* New York, NY: Praeger.

Sherman, L. W., Gartin, P. R., & Buerger, M. E. (1989). Hot spots of predatory crime: routine activities and the criminology of place. *Criminology, 27*(1), 27–55.

Simons, R. (1995). Control in an age of empowerment. *Harvard Business Review* (March-April), 80–88.

Skogan, W. G. (1990). *Disorder and Decline: Crime and the Spiral of Decay in American Neighborhoods.* New York, NY: The Free Press.

Skogan, W. G., & Maxfield, M. G. (1981). *Coping with Crime: Individual and Neighborhood Reactions.* Beverly Hills, CA: Sage.

Sousa, W.H. (2010). Paying attention to minor offenses: Order maintenance policing in practice. *Police Practice and Research: An International Journal, 11*(1), 45–59.

Sousa, W. H. (2015). What passes for scholarship these days: A response to broken windows critic Bernard Harcourt, (vol. Autumn). City Journal, New York, NY: Manhattan Institute.

Stewart, G. (1998). Black codes and broken windows: the legacy of racial hegemony in anti-gang civil injunctions. *Yale Law Journal, 107*(7), 2249–2279.

Taylor, R. B. (2001). *Breaking Away from Broken Windows.* Boulder, CO: Westview Press.

Thacher, D. (2004). Order maintenance reconsidered: moving beyond strong causal reasoning. *The Journal of Criminal Law & Criminology, 94*(2), 101–133.

Weisburd, D., & Eck, J. E. (2004). What can police do to reduce crime, disorder, and fear? *The Annals, 593,* 42–65.

Weisburd, D., Hinkle, J.C., Braga, A.A., & Wooditch, A. (2015). Understanding the mechanisms underlying broken windows policing: The need for evaluation evidence. *Journal of Research in Crime and Delinquency, 52*(4), 567–588.

Weisburd, D., Hinkle, J.C., Famega, C., & Ready, J. (2011). The possible "backfire" effects of hot spots policing: An experimental assessment of impacts on legitimacy, fear and collective efficacy. *Journal of Experimental Criminology, 7,* 297–320.

Weisburd, D., Maher, L., & Sherman, L. (1993). Contrasting crime general and crime specific theory: The case of hot spots of crime. *Advances in Criminological Theory, 4,* 45–70.

Weisburd, D., & Majmundar, M. K. (eds.). (2018). *Proactive Policing: Effects on Crime and Communities.* Washington, DC: The National Academies Press.

Weisburd, D., Telep. C. W., & Lawton, B. (2014). Could innovations in policing have contributed to the New York City crime drop even in a period of declining police strength?: The case of stop, question and frisk as a hot spots policing strategy. *Justice Quarterly*, 31(1), 129–153.

Wilson, J. Q. (1968). *Varieties of Police Behavior*. Cambridge, MA: Harvard University Press.

Wilson, J. Q., & Kelling, G. L. (1982). Broken windows: the police and neighborhood safety. *The Atlantic Monthly*, March, 29–38.

Worrall, J. L. (2002). *Does "Broken Windows" Law Enforcement Reduce Serious Crime?* CICG Research Brief. Sacramento, CA: California Institute for County Government.

Xu, Y., Fiedler, M. L., & Flaming, K. H. (2005). Discovering the impact of community policing: the broken windows thesis, collective efficacy, and citizens' judgment. *Journal of Research in Crime and Delinquency*, 42(2), 147–186.

Zimring, F. E. (2012). *The City That Became Safe: New York's Lessons for Urban Crime and Its Control*. New York, NY: Oxford University Press.

6

Critic

Incivilities Reduction Policing, Zero Tolerance, and the Retreat from Coproduction: Even Weaker Foundations and Stronger Pressures

Ralph B. Taylor

> The district attorneys from Brooklyn, the Bronx, Manhattan and Queens moved to dismiss 644,000 outstanding arrest warrants stemming from minor offenses at least 10 years old, more than a third of the city's 1.6 million outstanding summons warrants. This backlog stems from the now-discredited belief that petty offenses, like riding a bike on the sidewalk or drinking in public, could lead to more serious crimes. The result was the blanketing of minority neighborhoods with criminal summonses that forced hundreds of thousands of people to live with a constant threat of jail time for minor infractions.
>
> (The New York Times Editorial Board August 11, 2017)

A 2002 *New Yorker* cartoon depicts two grizzled prisoners whiling away the day on their bunks in their cell. The one on the bottom bunk, presumably in reply to a question from the inmate in the top bunk, explains, "There might have been some carelessness on my part, but it was mostly just good police work." The inmate on the top bunk seems startled by the admission.

Is broken windows policing, aka incivility reduction policing, good police work? And if answering in the affirmative, the follow up question is: good in what sense? Such problem-driven police work, in contrast to incident-driven police work (Wilson & Kelling, 1989), seems less likely to land the honest criminal mentioned above in prison. So, what are the measurable outcomes of interest that would make this "good police work"? Reduced resident fear of crime and stronger local social dynamics (Weisburd et al., 2015)? Less serious crime in the community (Braga, Welsh & Schnell, 2015)? More confidence in police, and/or the broader criminal justice system (Taylor & Lawton, 2012)?

An additional, equally crucial follow up question is: if incivilities reduction policing is effective, does it spawn negative externalities (Meares, 2015b)? What are the adverse side effects? Reducing citizens' willingness to assist the police in solving crimes? Deepening civilians' suspicions that the police force and other criminal justice institutions are unfair, unjust, and perhaps corrupt?

The first version of this chapter (Taylor, 2005) worried that zero tolerance policing, ostensibly "justified by the incivilities thesis" could be "exacerbating the very problems [in police–community relations] these earlier policing innovations sought to reduce" (p. 110). Developments since have transformed worry into serious misgivings.

Most concerning have been numerous questionable civilian deaths at the hands of police and possible links between those deaths and order maintenance policing activities. One case was linked both to order maintenance policing and resisting arrest. The death of Eric Garner at the hands of NYPD officers trying to take him into custody on Staten Island in July 2014, for illegally selling "loosies" (single cigarettes) that may have been smuggled into New York City (Campbell, 2015) rekindled debate about broken windows policing.

Today, controversy over their [Wilson & Kelling's] metaphorical "broken windows" theory is reverberating again after Eric Garner, a Staten Island man, died of a chokehold last month while being taken into custody for illegally selling cigarettes. Critics denounce the theory as neoconservative pablum resulting in overpolicing and mass incarceration for relatively minor offenses that disproportionately target poor, black and Hispanic people. Moreover, they say it was not derived from scientific evidence and its connection to the city's drastic decline in major crime remains unproven. (Roberts, 2014)

In response to concerns about questionable, unjustified deaths of civilians of color at the hands of police, scholars wonder if police have exhibited a "Ferguson effect" (MacDonald, 2016), becoming increasingly reluctant to engage in discretionary policing, including order maintenance policing, or to engage with the community, thereby perhaps increasing crime rates. The scholarly evidence on this question, so far at least, turns out to be complex and nuanced (Pyrooz et al., 2016; Wolfe & Nix, 2016; Shjarback et al., 2017).

Other developments prove relevant as well. Policing research on and concerns about procedural justice have exploded (Mazerolle et al., 2013; Donner et al., 2015). Which returns us to the negative externalities point surfaced earlier: do order maintenance policing actions adversely affect the perceived legitimacy of police? Second, empirical evidence about impacts of broken windows policing has accumulated. That evidence, however, is accompanied by foundational questions about broken windows policing and ongoing methodological questions (Weisburd et al., 2015). Third, in the field, police department have taken controversial roles in immigration enforcement (Koper et al., 2013). Fourth, in the courts, judges have handed down high profile and controversial rulings about stop-and-frisk practices (Meares, 2015a), the latter sometimes linked to order maintenance policing.

Broken windows policing is conceptually grounded on the incivilities thesis (Taylor, 2001). The incivilities thesis, although it comes in several different guises, suggests that physical deterioration and disorderly social conduct encountered in places near one's home or in places one regularly frequents, each contribute independently to personal safety concerns, related community sentiments, and neighborhood structural decline and crime. By implication, incivility positive-reducing initiatives will contribute to neighborhood structural stability, an enhanced sense of personal safety including lower fear of crime, and other outcomes. To the extent that this logic model is inaccurate, inadequate, or potentially misleading, incivilities reduction as a set of policing strategies may fail to deliver. Supporters of incivilities reduction policing policies sometimes become impatient with concerns about clarifying causal dynamics, arguing these concerns are unrelated to policy effectiveness (Sousa & Kelling, 2005). But understanding the relevant processes, and how they unfold over time, is crucial to identifying relevant intervention points for policies and practices. Simply put, theory is central to crime prevention (Welsh, Zimmerman & Zane, 2017) and to other types of prevention as well.

The next section provides a capsule statement of how the incivilities thesis has evolved, and provides more detail on the socio-ecologic dynamics hypothesized by the broken windows version. Attention turns to a short summary of what is known about impacts of incivilities and incivilities reduction policing. Various earlier and more current concerns are highlighted. The discussion then broadens context in two ways: first, providing an alternate historical outline of where broken windows policing came from and, second, outlining the elements of a police–citizen coproduced process of public safety. Given that context, it sketches one crucial, specific challenge facing successful coproduction *over time* in an urban residential context.

INCIVILITIES THESIS

Evolution

The evolution of the incivilities thesis has been summarized elsewhere (Taylor, 1999; Taylor, 2001: 93–114; Link et al., 2017).[1] In essence, what started out as a psychological, individual-level model of reactions to crime-linked local disorderly conditions (Wilson, 1975; Garofalo & Laub, 1978) became progressively social psychological, and then ecological, eventually applying to entire communities. During the same time frame, the thesis became longitudinal, describing the impacts of changing incivilities. Outcomes of interest expanded as well. Ultimately, the thesis sought to explain not only changes in personal safety concerns among individuals and in neighborhoods, but also changes in neighborhood structural viability and safety (Skogan, 1990) and, even more recently, urban health (Mooney et al., 2017).

---

[1] More details on this material appear in Taylor (1999; 2001).

The Broken Windows Version

A public policy scholar, the late James Q. Wilson, and a well-known policing scholar, George L. Kelling, introduced the intermediate version of the incivilities thesis: broken windows. It is intermediate in its geographic and temporal scopes. They introduced a *specific* group- and place-based series of processes explaining how physical and social incivilities taking place on urban neighborhood streets or seen from the streets, if *not* "fixed" by someone, can affect residents and regular street users. Appearing incivilities, if they are not resolved when they surface, and if they are key to residents' interpretation of their surroundings (Innes, 2014), will affect residents and regular users. Spatial behaviors (e.g., residents spend less discretionary time on the front), personal safety concerns (e.g., residents feel more vulnerable), and willingness to intervene (e.g., residents become less willing to tell loud teens late at night to knock it off) (Taylor, 2001: 98–100), can all be affected. In the next step in the model, low-grade problems with unsupervised but now emboldened local youth will lead, over time, to big problems with serious street offenders moving in. Street crimes like robberies go up. The model frames the following solutions. Police can play important roles in reducing crime by responding to incivilities. Conditions are improved, local informal control is "reinforced," and crime increases forestalled. "The essence of the police role in maintaining order is to reinforce the informal control mechanisms of the community itself. The police cannot, without committing extraordinary resources, provide a substitute for that informal control" (Wilson & Kelling, 1982). These dynamics, they point out, are most likely observed in "teetering" neighborhoods; neighborhoods where structural changes there or nearby, or crime changes there or nearby, make residents especially alert to and concerned both about their personal safety and future neighborhood viability.

Wilson and Kelling (1982; 1989) point out the numerous challenges with incivilities reduction policing. Whose order do the police maintain? How do they avoid becoming agents of bigotry? Further, "getting effective community organizations started in the most troubled neighborhoods" proves challenging (Wilson & Kelling, 1989).

Empirical Evidence

Skogan (2015) reviews major empirical work on the incivilities thesis, emphasizing work linked to his version of the thesis, disorder and decline. Among his important conclusions are the following: incivilities can impact reactions to crime, like fear, independent of the impacts of local crime or crime perceptions; they also can affect neighborhood structural stability and abrade residents' informal control. Further, effects of incivilities on neighborhood crime changes are not always consistent, but when they do occur the process may be direct, or it may be indirect occurring via personal safety concerns and/or local social dynamics. He also highlights the numerous questions about alternate operationalizations of incivilities indicators, and the relevant range of phenomena qualifying as disorders. Skogan also points out the expansion of outcomes of interest to concerns beyond criminology and criminal justice, for example, impacts of incivilities on stress or healthy behaviors like walking (Mooney et al., 2017).

The recent NAS report provides an additional review that questions whether broken windows policing works. "The impacts of broken windows policing are mixed across evaluations, again complicating the ability of the committee to draw strong inferences" (National Academies of Sciences, 2017: S6). Further, "The evidence was insufficient to draw any conclusions regarding the impact of broken windows policing on community social controls" (S7–S8).

Complementing these two reviews, recent work highlights three additional points. First, research continues to illuminate the properties of perceived incivilities indicators. One of the most central perceived social incivility indicators according to the broken windows version, is problems with local groups of unsupervised teens. Examinations of its construct validity prove both supportive and unsupportive. The item does and does not link as expected to the relevant underlying conditions. It does reflect local gang presence (Blasko, Roman & Taylor, 2015). This favors the idea that it is telling us about problematic behaviors of local youth and young adults. But its expected connection to another troublesome youth indicator, local delinquency rates, washes out once neighborhood socioeconomic status is considered (Taylor et al., 2011). Of course, delinquency rates themselves are enormously complicated productions (Taylor, 2015: 38–47) and that may be responsible in part for the washing out of the connection with the incivility indicator.

Turning to the standard "how big a problem" rating format often used for survey-based indicators of perceived incivilities, recent scholarship deepens concerns about how to interpret racial and age differences on these indicators. Different types of survey respondents literally use response categories differently when rating some local perceived social and physical incivilities (Ward, Link & Taylor, 2017). This raises questions about studies relying solely on perceived incivility indicators.

Third, on the theoretical side, part of the causal ordering may be incorrect. Link and colleagues (Link et al., 2017) found longitudinal impacts of perceived incivilities on later changes in perceived crime risk in some ways proved stronger than the impacts of perceived risk on perceived incivilities. This would fit with Innes' (2014) concept of signal crimes and signal disorders. Some residents on a street, for important local and personal reasons, were more attuned to local incivilities, leading over time to forming more sobering interpretations of their own personal crime risks. This links to the broader point, made by Weisburd et al. (2015), that researchers have yet to document how the proposed psychological, social psychological, and ecological *dynamics* invoked by the model, actually operate.

INCIVILITIES REDUCTION POLICING: IMPACTS

What we know about incivilities reduction policing is that it works – if it is community-based. Braga and colleagues' (Braga et al., 2015) systematic review found that "policing disorder strategies" (568) did reduce crime if those strategies were based on problem-focused efforts shaped by community policing, rather than "aggressive order maintenance strategies that target individual disorderly behaviors" (568).

The community problem-solving programs, which accounted for 20 of the 30 tests, usually attempted to engage residents, local merchants, and others in the identification of local crime and disorder problems and the development and implementation of appropriate responses. As such, the community problem-solving programs often involved a varied set of disorder reduction strategies designed to change criminogenic dynamics generated by social and physical disorder problems in very specific places. (p. 574)

The stronger impacts of the community-based strategies "suggest that, when considering a policing disorder approach, police departments should adopt a 'community coproduction model' rather than drift toward a zero-tolerance policing model" (Braga et al., 2015: 581). We turn to that community coproduction model later.

But when broken windows policing strategies are considered more broadly, as noted above, the recent NAS report raises numerous questions: about effectiveness, about fairness, and about legality (National Academies of Sciences, 2017).

Theoretical Concerns

Space limitations preclude more than a brief summary of the major theoretical concerns raised by the incivilities thesis, and of the programs put into place based in part on its tenets. Some of these points are covered by Taylor (2001: 95–122) or Harcourt (2001: 123–216), and Welsh and colleagues (Welsh, Braga & Bruinsma, 2015) surface additional concerns.

Do the Processes Work as Hypothesized?

Do the multi-step, place-based, meso-level dynamics unfold over time as envisioned by Wilson and Kelling? Although it seems unimaginable, there are no longitudinal, empirical works to date, with either observational studies using a representative sample of streets in a jurisdiction or community, or panel data with samples of residents on samples of streets, or experiments, or simulations, gauging the validity of the *specific* sequence proposed in the broken windows version of the incivilities thesis. We have some interesting tests of cross-time relationships between reported incivilities and crime at the census tract level (O'Brien & Sampson, 2015), and some connections between incivilities, social climate, and crime at the neighborhood level (Sampson, 2012). But the specific longitudinal, streetblock-level sequence proposed by Wilson and Kelling remains un-tested. The model provides us with a proposed sequence of how small groups living on or regularly using certain streetblocks, and the individuals in those groups, respond as incivilities shift. We simply don't know if the longitudinal sequences portrayed are accurate.

A recent retrospective on the first twenty-five years of broken windows research and policy pointed out many areas needing future attention (Welsh et al., 2015). The above question deserves to be on that list, perhaps at the very top. Weisburd et al. (2015) highlight the same concern.

We know a lot about place-based informal control dynamics, and their links to local crime, reactions to crime, and person-place bonds (Sampson, 2012; Groff, 2015). It is possible that some of the theoretical perspectives predating the broken windows thesis describe the same dynamics with equal adequacy (Weisburd et al., 2015). Therefore, we need to document the hypothesized ecological, social psychological, and psychological longitudinal processes specified by broken windows. Once we have done that we can learn whether the broken windows model is needed. Can broken windows explain the changes observed, and the links between those changes, *better* than alternate theoretical frames? As of this writing, no one knows.

Placing Broken Windows within Community Criminology
The broken windows version of the incivilities thesis, and broken windows policing, exist within a broader portion of criminology called community criminology. "Community criminology theories address crime ... at the community level ... either as a predictor or an outcome, and impacts of community features on crime or a crime related attribute at the individual, group, or community levels" (Taylor, 2015: 4). This perspective highlights how broader community factors affect small group dynamics, and how small group dynamics affect individuals, and the reverse of both of these. That leads to two vital questions for broken windows. How are these street dynamics dependent on broader neighborhood conditions and outside-neighborhood factors? This is the "teetering neighborhoods" setting condition discussed by Wilson and Kelling (1982). Understanding these links seems especially crucial for developing a sounder understanding of the locations where incivilities reduction policing would prove a more efficient use of police resources.

Further, how do these street dynamics affect individuals? Relatedly, how do individual changes shape group changes? The *longitudinal* interplay between intra-individual psychological and behavioral dynamics, and related group dynamics, remains unexamined.

What Disorder Where
As Wilson and Kelling (1982) originally anticipated, it is difficult to define one type of disorder deserving police attention in all locations. The focus of order maintenance policing efforts since they began, have been context sensitive. Presumably, the order focus that does emerge will be driven in large part by the officers' communications with citizen and business leaders in the

community. These dynamics are simply part of the broader discretionary fabric of policing (Kelling, 1999). To say police will focus on different non-crime problems in different locations is nothing new. It does, however, create challenges for police supervisors, and it does place a premium on police being closely enough connected with local citizen and business leaders that they have a sense of what is most disturbing to the community. As will be shown below, absent a broader neighborhood government structure in a locale, forging the needed links in the most troubled neighborhoods proves impossible.

Collapse of the Harm Principle

Harcourt (2001) suggests elevating minor misdemeanors to arrest-worthy behaviors – making the merely annoying dangerous because of its anticipated long-term, harmful impacts to the community – results in a collapse of the harm principle. Stated differently, previously accepted orderings differentiating more vs. less serious criminal or deviant behavior get collapsed, creating confusion rather than changing normative views toward minor misdemeanors. For example, a May 11, 2001, AP story reported a fifth grader handcuffed and taken from Oldsmar Elementary School in Florida for drawing pictures of guns.

Increasing Inequality

Offenses where officers have the most discretion have the greatest potential to be policed in a racially biased manner. Citations and summonses for minor misdemeanors may introduce even greater levels of racial inequality into criminal justice processing if, unattended, they become warrants for arrest (Tonry, 1995). Increasing police activity around misdemeanors seems likely to increase overall racial inequality in this "front end" portion of criminal justice processing.

This point seems even more relevant, given the shifting legal status of cannabis use. Geller and Fagan (2010) argue that police routinely use cannabis use as part of the reasonable articulable suspicions leading to civilian stops. "The racial imbalance in marijuana enforcement in Black neighborhoods suggests a 'doubling down' of street-level policing" (Geller & Fagan, 2010: abstract).

Subject Creation

Focusing policing efforts on disorderly people widens the social gap between the haves and the have-nots, making the latter seem less deserving, more criminal, and more dangerous than they are. It creates an "uncritical dichotomy between disorderly people and law abiders" (Harcourt, 2001: 7). Such a binary schema is not only inaccurate, but also encourages further social divisiveness. The societal implications are disturbing.

Construct Validating Key Survey-Based Perceived Incivilities Indicators

Others (Taylor, 1999; Skogan, 2015) have commented both on questions about how different types of incivility indicators, as well as different incivility indicators within a type, do or do not connect to one another. Some of the most recent work does and does not support a broken windows interpretation of perceptions of unsupervised teen groups, a key perceived social incivility indicator. It does link to nearby gang presence (Blasko et al., 2015) but under some conditions does not connect to local delinquency rates (Taylor et al., 2011). Questions about how to interpret demographic differences in mean perceived incivilities deepen given recent work finding that different groups literally use the response categories for rating incivilities in different ways (Ward et al., 2017). The "meaning" of specific incivilities indicators is likely to continue to be an active area of inquiry, as is the question about links between incivilities and broader ideas of disorder. Kubrin (2008) argues we need more conceptual clarity around terms like incivilities and disorder. She is right.

WHERE DOES BROKEN WINDOWS POLICING COME FROM?

George Kelling and others have placed the development of broken windows policing in a specific historical context (Kelling & Coles, 1996; Kelling, 1999). That perspective sees police in the 1970s and 1980s as hamstrung, unable to take care of witnessed minor infractions they saw because of concerns about citizen complaints and lack of court follow-through.

An alternate view starts with the urban disorders of the 1960s, and the various types of policing innovations that followed as part of subsequent reform responses. This amounts to further expanding the above descriptive context by placing the theoretical evolution of the broken windows thesis in a broader set of evolving police-citizen coproduction strategies. If this *mis en scene* is correct, then for broken windows policing to work, the essentials of the coproduction process first need attention. Second, the special longitudinal challenges for police–community partnership posed by the urban residential and organization fabric need consideration as well.

Before getting to the history, a quick note. What is a coproduced public good like safety? "'Coproduction' of public services ... involves a mixing of the productive efforts of consumer/citizens and of their official producers ... [it means] citizens and their officials working together" (Ostrom, 2010: 10). More details follow.

Although it is Flintstone-era ancient history to anyone younger than 65 in 2015, urban disorders rocked dozens of major US cities in the 1960s. Kathryn Bigelow's movie *Detroit*, playing in theatres at the time of this revision, puts one element of the Detroit riots – the Algiers Motel incident (Hersey, 1968) involving the deaths of three Blacks at the hands of police – under a microscope. Looting and citizen riots in many cities, and police riots in some cities were later put under the analytical microscope by high profile commissions or sociologists (Fogelson, 1968). One of the most widely quoted reports from the time, the Kerner Commission concluded that policing practices had contributed in part to some of the outbreaks (Kerner, 1968).[2] The

---

[2] Of course, this is not the only decade of the twentieth century in which police activity has been linked to urban riots.

Commission also pinpointed increasing segregation and structural inequality as additional facilitating factors, although these were perhaps less remediable. Rothstein (2017) provides the policy explanation for these structural patterns.

Consequent concerns about police practices inspired not only federal initiatives seeking to further professionalize the police, like LEEP (Law Enforcement Education Program) funds sending thousands of police officers to college (Gaines & Kappeler, 2008: 114). They also encouraged braoder thinking about ways police department structures and practices could reduce the distrust and antagonism between police officers and citizens, especially citizens of urban communities of color.

Structural changes emerging from such thinking included the expansion of police-organized community relations councils, often staffed by a community relations sergeant but already in place in some jurisdictions at the time of the riots (Kerner, 1968: 283); additional police–citizen review commissions with some oversight over some range of police matters; and, later, citizen police academies. Whether these changes were just "window dressing" or more substantive, and why degree of citizen review or oversight varied across locales are interesting questions, but not ones pursued given the focus here.

More relevant to our focus are a host of strategies first appearing in the very early 1970s. These can be roughly grouped into two classes – those emphasizing citizens' and citizen groups' roles, and those emphasizing how patrolling police interact with citizens. Strategies emphasizing citizens' roles included a broad range of community crime prevention activities: Neighborhood Watch, Citizens on Patrol, Operation ID, security surveys, and Operation Whistlestop, to name a few (Rosenbaum, 1988). Although the origins of some of these go back to Winchester, England, and the 1200s, the key feature as these emerged in the 1970s was a neighborhood-based coordinating group working with a designated police officer. The latter was often a crime prevention specialist or a community relations officer. Much has been written about whether these programs were successful or not, for what crimes, and under what types of conditions (Rosenbaum, 1988).

A second class of strategies also emerging in the early and mid-1970s addressed patrolling officers' relations with citizenry more generally. Many departments sought to develop more "stable" relationships between patrolling officers, local citizens, and local small business personnel. Patrolling officers were assigned to particular neighborhoods for an extended period of time with team policing and geographic- or neighborhood-based policing. The hope was that, over time, officers would develop a corruption-free understanding of how local residents and business leaders viewed crime and related problems in those locations (Greene & Pelfrey, 1997). To deepen this understanding, in the late 1970s, researchers like the late Robert Trojanowicz suggested flattening the tires on the patrol cars, giving the police Nikes, and getting them out of their cars. Foot patrolling officers also were tasked to work cooperatively with local business and citizen leaders and identify the specific crimes, crime locations, and crime-related problems deserving attention. Police–citizen contact, coordination, and coproduction were seen as critical conditions for success (Greene & Taylor, 1988). This model, in contrast to the typical community crime prevention model, links numerous police officers simultaneously with numerous local citizens and local business personnel without an intervening neighborhood organization.

Progressing into the 1980s and 1990s, these models morphed into related labels including third party policing (Mazerolle, Kadleck & Roehl, 1997; Buerger & Mazerolle, 1998), problem-oriented policing (Spelman & Eck, 1987), and, most difficult to define, community policing (Cordner, 1997). Despite widespread disagreement about what constitutes community policing, and what its goals are (Greene & Mastrofski, 1988), most would agree on the following underlying principles (Skogan & Hartnett, 1997): "organizational decentralization" (p. 6) permitting more autonomy to those officers most directly involved with the locals, and easier police-public communication; "a commitment to . . . problem-oriented policing" (p. 7); "responsiveness to citizen input" (p. 8); and building neighborhood capacity to prevent crime or solve crime-related problems, i.e., to help neighborhood groups become coproducers of safety (p. 8).

Within this broader evolution, the development of both the practice and theory behind incivilities reduction policing proves intriguing as well. On the practice side, the initial policing focus was a variant of problem-oriented policing (Wilson & Kelling, 1982). Following a problem-oriented SARA (Scanning, Analysis, Response, and Assessment) approach (Spelman & Eck, 1987), police would identify troublesome conditions in a locale, and work with citizenry and other agencies to resolve those. Oakland's "Beat Health" program is just one excellent example of such an approach (Mazzerolle, Kadleck & Roehl, 1998). In short, broken windows policing clearly started out as a coproduction model. Citizens were involved in problem identification, and other agencies were involved in problem resolution. It was not presumed the police would board up the abandoned houses themselves. To better understand this coproduction component, the following section outlines its essential elements.

COPRODUCTION

Police rely on citizens and other agencies in numerous ways. Most simply, citizens must report incidents to the police if the police are not right there to see the crime taking place. So fundamentally, producing public safety is a coproduction process, wherein police and citizens, and other organizations working with the police all contribute to the outcome (Ostrom et al., 1979). Ostrom (1996) defines coproduction as "the process through which inputs used to provide a good or service are contributed by individuals who are not 'in' the same organization ... Coproduction implies that citizens can play an active role in producing public goods and services of consequence to them" (1996: 1073).

Various factors make coproduction more or less effective than a service provision model for achieving the intended outcome. Service recipients – in this case neighborhood residents, neighborhood leaders, and local business personnel – need to be active participants in the process (Ostrom, 1996: 1079). In addition "both parties must be legally entitled to take decisions, giving them both some room for maneuver ... [and] participants need to build credible commitments to one another (e.g., through contractual obligations, based on trust or by enhancing social capital)" (Jeffery & Vira, 2001: 9).

Reputations, trust, and reciprocity play pivotal roles in increasing cooperation between members of the partnership (Ostrom, 1998). A coproductive relationship between citizen leaders and police may create policing which is more responsive and more favorably viewed, and a citizenry more willing to report to the police (Ostrom & Whitaker, 1973).

Clearly, significant structural impediments beyond the control of police departments limit the possibilities of effective police–citizen coproduction. Most importantly, police, in contrast to other public sector agencies, are charged with maintaining social control, and administering "law" (Black, 1980). Reciprocity cannot emerge given such a condition, although mutual responsiveness can. In addition, the citizenry in locations where effective coproduction is most needed – low income, urban communities of color – are exactly the same places where distrust between the police and citizens is most profound (Weitzer, 1999; Weitzer & Tuch, 1999) and police are seen as least effective (Taylor, Wyant & Lockwood, 2015). The trust requisite for maximally effective coproduction will take much longer to grow in these locations.

The above limitations aside, in key ways, police innovations emerging since the 1970s contained elements of a coproduction model. They attempted to increase citizen–police trust, to facilitate stable relationships between police and local leaders and citizens, and, by tuning police to local concerns, increase locality-based police responsiveness.

ZERO-TOLERANCE POLICING AND BACK WHERE WE STARTED

Unfortunately, some current police practices relying on the incivilities thesis as justification have rejected the coproduction idea. The popular zero tolerance policing is a case in point. When police focus just on that subset of social incivilities – disorderly or drunk people, rowdy groups of teens, panhandlers, or street vagrants – and seek to remove them from the street, either through aggressive policing, or fines, or even arrests, we have zero tolerance policing (Ismaili, 2003; McArdle & Erzin, 2001).

These behaviors are aggressively targeted by police in the belief that suppressing these street activities will reduce the occurrence of more serious crimes in those places. The primary focus is on social incivilities with less attention given to physical conditions. Legal and political scrutiny of these stop practices has resulted in fewer stops in New York City and elsewhere (Keys, 2017; The New York Times Editorial Board, 2017).

The movement toward zero tolerance strategies and away from coproduction has taken place gradually over the last thirty years (McArdle & Erzin, 2001). This changing emphasis within the incivilities thesis may be driven in part by wider societal changes (Garland, 2002; Ismaili 2003: 262). Putting the policing shifts in a broader context, we may be seeing a historic shift in American and Canadian policing back to the social control model of the late nineteenth century, and away from the crime control model which dominated in the second quarter of the twentieth century (Monkkonen, 1981; Boritch & Hagan, 1987).

Kelling (1999: 3) has recognized that incivilities models are used to support zero tolerance strategies, but he argues against such a connection: "it is an equation that I have never made." He clearly plants broken windows policing within community policing.

Broken windows policing is a tactic of community policing – highly discretionary, easy to abuse, but when conducted properly contributes enormously to the quality of urban life. Above all, however, it grows out of close interaction between police and citizens in neighborhoods, who work together to maintain order and reduce crime. Inevitably, even in the best of police departments, something will go wrong, that is, an officer will make a mistake or be incompetent with tragic consequences. It is under these circumstances that police and community need a strong relationship that sustains itself during periods of crisis. Somehow this has been lost in policing in many American cities today. (Kelling, 2015: 628)

Nevertheless, zero tolerance policing policies *are* widely accepted because they are legitimated, in the minds of many, by the incivilities thesis. Over time, the police and the public expect these strategies to reduce serious crime rates. Police *themselves* believe this (see Kelling & Sousa, 2001, ethnographic observation 2A).

At the same time, the best, most-recent review of zero tolerance does not accept constitutionally problematic aspects of zero tolerance policing. The recent NAS (2017: S3-S4) report raises questions about whether research has firmly established adverse legal impacts of zero tolerance policies. For example, the panel concludes "empirical evidence is insufficient ... to support any conclusion about whether proactive policing strategies [like zero tolerance, among others] systematically promote or reduce constitutional violations." The panel does admit, however, "such strategies may raise concerns about deeper legal values."

Despite the recent NAS report's dismissal of constitutional violations associated with zero tolerance, the recent deaths of civilians arising in part from zero tolerance policing actions, coupled with numerous court actions in major cities around stop-question-and-frisk actions that police often initiate because of witnessed incivilities or minor infractions, both point to the dark side of zero tolerance policing.

And therein lies the irony. The final stage in the evolution of strategies originally intended to defuse police–community conflicts has accelerated police actions that, instead, deepen and widen these same conflicts. Post-urban-disorder policing innovations spanning at least four decades sought to defuse police–community antagonisms by moving closer to coproduction models. Scrutiny of police–community relations following the disorders of the 1960s led to a variety of coproduction models. With community crime prevention initiatives, police sought to coordinate with citizenry through local citizen-led groups, while the members of those groups would serve as the "eyes and ears" of the police. In return, the police would keep those groups informed about local crime patterns. Geographic and team policing were department-based organizational strategies intended to increase trust of the police among local citizens, citizen leaders, and business personnel. In the mid-1980s, departments sought closer connections with communities through community policing partnerships; they also sought to increase their effectiveness through third party policing and problem-oriented policing initiatives. These latter innovations required police to coordinate much more closely than they had in the past with other local agencies. Such coordination was in recognition of the limits of police powers, coupled with the hope that solving problems related to crime could make residents feel better and might even reduce crime itself.

But at the same time, in the last few decades, social or physical incivilities, in part because of broader trends (White, 2001; Enns, 2016), have increased as well, putting more pressure on police to do *something*. Although many of these incivilities require the police to coordinate with other agencies, like housing or licensing and inspections, there is a subset of social incivilities against which the police can act directly: people being disorderly. And they have, armed with zero tolerance policies.

Thus, this series of innovations has come full circle. Zero tolerance policies – ostensibly in the minds of some justified by the incivilities thesis, a thesis formulating a way for police to respond to community concerns – instead endorse and entrench aggressive policing. It was such aggressive policing that the Kerner Commission tagged as a contributor to the urban disorders in the first place. Despite the ongoing debate about the sources inspiring this evolution, from the individual police department up to the changing social fabric; despite scholars' refutation of the incivilities thesis–zero tolerance connection; and despite the empirical weaknesses and theoretical vagaries of the incivilities thesis, zero tolerance policing is currently widely practiced and thought to be justified by that thesis.

Could some jurisdictions be turning away from zero tolerance? In New York City, a high profile stop and frisk ruling in 2013, and the election of Mayor De Blasio has been followed by markedly lower stop rates (Baker, 2017). Rates also have dropped markedly in Chicago (Keys, 2017). MacDonald (2016) thinks a

"Ferguson effect" is partly responsible for dropping stop and frisk rates. The broader reach of a racialized view of the criminal justice system in the United States (Tonry, 1995), driven in part by recent well-known work by Michelle Alexander (2010) and others (Coates, 2015) are probably contributing as well. It is not clear at this time, however, given the political and law enforcement developments since the 2016 election, whether there is a broad turn across many jurisdictions in this country away from broken windows policing, and away from police focusing aggressively on social incivilities.

RETURNING POLICING INNOVATIONS TO A
COPRODUCTION MODEL

Perhaps increased public scrutiny of police departments, deepening concerns about officer–civilian shooting incidents, elevated officer wariness, the introduction of body-worn cameras, mounting legal pressures on some police departments, and the popularizing of racialized views of the criminal justice system are all contributing, in some locations, to recent turns away from aggressive police responses to social incivilities. But a firmer, more positive rationale is needed to re-orient incivilities reduction policing.

What is needed at this juncture is to return community-based policing innovations and, more generally, to a coproduction model (Ostrom et al., 1979). That said, there are, of course, major impediments to such a reorientation: political, organizational, and economic. One crucial challenge is finding representative and organized community organizations with which the police can partner (Wilson & Kelling, 1982).

To expand on this last point, part of the community partner challenge arises from the longitudinal texture of the urban residential fabric. The related stumbling blocks, and the empirical evidence pointing them out, are described in more detail elsewhere. In brief, the main points are this. Neighborhood boundaries and names can change over time. In Baltimore during one period, both type and extent of change often linked to local racial differences, socioeconomic status (Taylor, 2001: 303–357), or political agendas from beyond the neighborhood itself (Logan & Molotch, 1987). Those changes create substantial difficulties for police–citizen coproduction of public safety.

Further, neighborhoods where stable police partnerships were most needed were those where local political ecologies changed quickly (Taylor, 2001: 303–357). Significant changes in both boundaries and representing organizations were most rapid in those communities most in need of a workable police–community partnership. In such locales, police working with community leaders were in danger of collaborating with decreasingly representative community groups, or of being confused about the relevant spatial domain, or both.

Ideally, community-police partnerships should be organized at the neighborhood level. To do so would increase citizens' buy-in and stake in the outcome. Partnerships organized around police beats or districts (e.g., Skogan & Hartnett, 1990) end up working with a cluster of local leaders in each beat, whose constituencies only partially overlap the police organizing unit. In these situations, it is not surprising that local leaders' commitments often rapidly wane.

If police are to move to a neighborhood-based framework for organizing partnerships, some sort of stability of the neighborhood organizational framework would seem to be required. Ongoing neighborhood changes decrease police willingness to move to that organizing framework, and create difficulties in establishing working relationships between police and citizens. If police are to engage in problem reduction, and to be effective and respond in ways that best benefit the overall community, they need to understand a single spatial arena and the key players. It takes time working in one locale with one set of stakeholders to develop such understanding. Understanding, trust, and some element of reciprocity are key ingredients for effective coproduction (Ostrom, 1998).

Given the volume and diversity of neighborhood boundary and name changes observed (Taylor, 2001: 303–357), and the understandable urban dynamics driving these changes (Hunter, 1974), it appears that successful police–community coproducing relationships could be developed only in urban or suburban locations with strong overarching neighborhood governance structures. Many cities have such structures (Hallman, 1984; Ferman, 1996). To attempt to stabilize such partnerships *without* that broader, organizing and legitimizing political structure, effectively dooms these partnerships. It limits them to being no more than anemic relationships with no real commitment either from police or citizen leaders. According to the coproduction model, it is extremely difficult, if not impossible, to coproduce community safety in such settings without that broader infrastructure.

SUMMARY

After the urban disorders of the 1960s, in the 1970s and 1980s police departments adopted a range of strategies involving the community and grounded in a coproduction model. That led ultimately to the incivilities thesis, including the broken windows version of that thesis, and the latter spawned aggressive zero tolerance policing of social incivilities. The latter is a repudiation of the coproduction model, and exacerbates the very police-community tensions the last five decades of reform strategies sought to address. The setting-dependent, specific set of longitudinal streetblock-level processes hypothesized by the broken windows version of the incivilities thesis remain unverified. If the outcome focus is just on street crime, it is not clear that the broken windows version of the incivilities thesis is needed, given other available and potentially relevant models of informal control and crime patterns. Offsetting these concerns is a limited degree of empirical validity. Empirical studies show that incivilities reduction policing, particularly if organized around community problem-solving rather than aggressive misdemeanour-focused, stop-based policing, is effective at reducing crime. Numerous questions remain. How do we *jointly* evaluate crime reduction benefits of these policies alongside associated negative externalities? How do we trace the links between these adverse impacts and the incivilities reduction or zero tolerance strategies themselves?

Are proactive policing policies like zero tolerance *inherently* problematic

Most importantly, what's the way out? (1) Local governments can help police departments solve the stable community partner problem. (2) Political leaders and key stakeholders can create the pressures, the opportunities, and the backing so that police and community leaders can return to a true coproduced model of public safety. Until incivilities reduction policing returns to its roots as a *true* coproduced product, it could continue to create more problems than it solves.

ACKNOWLEDGMENTS

The author thanks the two editors and Ron Davis for helpful comments on earlier drafts of the chapter. Address correspondence to RBT, Department of Criminal Justice, Gladfelter Hall, Temple University, 1115 West Berks Street, Philadelphia, PA 19122 (ralph.taylor @ temple.edu).

REFERENCES

Alexander, M. (2010). *The New Jim Crow*. New York City: The New Press.
Baker, A. (2017). Street stops by New York City Police have plummeted. *New York Times*, May 30. Retrieved from www.nytimes.com/2017/05/30/nyregion/nypd-stop-and-frisk.html].
Black, D. (1980). *The Behavior of Law*. New York: Academic Press.
Blasko, B. L., Roman, C. G., & Taylor, R. B. (2015). Local gangs and residents' perceptions of unsupervised teen groups: Implications for the incivilities thesis and neighborhood effects. *Journal of Criminal Justice*, 43(1): 20–28. doi:http://dx.doi.org/10.1016/j.jcrimjus.2014.11.002.
Boritch, H., & Hagan, J. (1987). Crime and the changing forms of class control: Policing public order in "Toronto the Good," 1859–1955. *Social Forces*, 66(2): 307–335.
Braga, A. A., Welsh, B. C., & Schnell, C. (2015). Can policing disorder reduce crime? A systematic review and meta-analysis. *Journal of Research in Crime and Delinquency*, 52(4): 567–588. doi: 10.1177/0022427815576576.
Buerger, M., & Mazerolle, L. G. (1998). Third-party policing: A theoretical analysis of an emerging trend. *Justice Quarterly*, 15: 301–328.
Campbell, J. April 7 (2015). Smuggled, untaxed cigarettes are everywhere in New York City. *The Village Voice*. Retrieved from www.villagevoice.com/2015/04/07/smuggled-untaxed-cigarettes-are-everywhere-in-new-york-city/].
Coates, Ta-Nehisi. (2015). *Between the World and Me*. New York: Spiegel & Grau.

Cordner, G. (1997). Community Policing. In R. G. Dunham, & G. P. Alpert (eds.), *Critical Issues in Policing: Contemporary Readings*. Prospect Heights, IL: Waveland Press.

Donner, C., Maskaly, J., Fridell, L., & Jennings, W. G. (2015). Policing and procedural justice: A state-of-the-art review. *Policing: An International Journal of Police Strategies & Management*, 38(1): 153–172. doi: 10.1108/pijpsm-12-2014-0129.

Enns, P. K. (2016). *Incarceration Nation*. Cambridge: Cambridge University Press.

Ferman, B. (1996). *Challenging the Growth Machine: Neighborhood Politics in Chicago and Pittsburgh*. Lawrence: University of Kansas Press.

Fogelson, R. M. (1968). From resentment to confrontation: The police, the Negroes, and the outbreak of the nineteen-sixties riots. *Political Science Quarterly*, 83(2): 217–247.

Gaines, L. K., & Kappeler, V. E. (2008). *Policing in America*. Newark, NJ: LexisNexis.

Garland, D. (2002). *The Culture of Control: Crime and Social Order in Contemporary Society*. Chicago: University of Chicago Press.

Garofalo, J., & Laub, J. (1978). The fear of crime: Broadening our perspective. *Victimology*, 3: 242–253.

Geller, A., & Fagan, J. (2010). Pot as pretext: Marijuana, race, and the new disorder in New York City street policing. *Journal of Empirical Legal Studies*, 7(4): 591–633. doi: 10.1111/j.1740-1461.2010.01190.x.

Greene, J. R., & Mastrofski, S. (eds.). (1988). *Community Policing: Rhetoric and Reality*. New York: Praeger.

Greene, J. R., & Pelfrey, W. V. (1997). Shifting the balance of power between police and community. In R. G. Dunham, & G. P. Alpert (eds.), *Critical Issues in Policing: Contemporary Readings*. Prospect Heights, IL: Waveland Press.

Greene, J. R., & Taylor, R. B. (1988). Community-based policing and foot patrol: Issues of theory and evaluation. In J. R. Greene, & S. D. Mastrofski (eds.), *Community Policing: Rhetoric or Reality?* (pp. 195–224). New York: Praeger.

Groff, E. R. (2015). Informal social control and crime events. *Journal of Contemporary Criminal Justice*, 31(1): 90–106. doi: 10.1177/1043986214552619.

Hallman, H. W. (1984). *Neighborhoods: Their Place in Urban Life*. Beverly Hills: Sage.

Harcourt, B. E. (2001). *Illusion of Order: The False Promise of Broken Windows Policing*. Cambridge, MA: Harvard University Press.

Hersey, John. (1968). *The Algiers Motel Incident*. New York: Knopf.

Hunter, A. (1974). *Symbolic Communities*. Chicago: University of Chicago Press.

Innes, M. (2014). *Signal Crimes: Social Reactions to Crime, Disorder, and Control*. Oxford: Oxford University Press.

Ismaili, K. (2003). Explaining the cultural and symbolic resonance of zero tolerance in contemporary criminal justice. *Contemporary Justice Review*, 6(3): 255–264.

Jeffery, R., & Vira, B. (2001). Introduction. In R. Jeffery, & B. Vira (eds.), *Conflict and Cooperation in Particiaptory Natural Resource Management* (pp. 1–16). New York: Palgrave MacMillan.

Kelling, G. L. (1999). "Broken Windows" and Police Discretion. US Department of Justice, Office of Justice Programs.

Kelling, G. (2015). An author's brief history of an idea. *Journal of Research in Crime and Delinquency*, 52(4): 626–629. doi: 10.1177/0022427815578175.

Kelling, G. L., & Coles, C. M. (1996). *Fixing Broken Windows: Restoring Order and Reducing Crime in Our Communities*. New York: Free Press.

Kelling, G. L., & Sousa, W. H., Jr. (2001). Do Police Matter?: An Analysis of the Impact of New York City's Police Reforms. *Manhattan Institute Civic Report, No. 22.*

Kerner, O. (1968). *Report of the National Advisory Commission on Civil Disorders.* New York: Bantam.

Keys, A. (2017). The Consultant's First Semiannual Report on Investigatory Stop and Protective Pat Down Agreement for the Period January 1, 2016 – June 30, 2016. Chicago.

Koper, C. S., Guterbock, T. M., Woods, D. J., Taylor, B., & Carter, T. J. (2013). The effects of local immigration enforcement on crime and disorder. *Criminology & Public Policy,* 12(2): 239–276. doi: 10.1111/1745-9133.12022.

Kubrin, C. E. (2008). Making order of disorder: A call for conceptual clarity. *Criminology & Public Policy,* 7(2): 203–214.

Link, N. W., Kelly, J. M., Pitts, J. R., Waltman-Spreha, K., & Taylor, R. B. (2017). Reversing broken windows: Evidence of lagged, multilevel impacts of risk perceptions on perceptions of incivility. *Crime & Delinquency,* 63(6): 659–682. doi: 10.1177/0011128714555606.

Logan, J. R., & Molotch, H. (1987). *Urban Fortunes.* Berkeley: University of California Press.

MacDonald, H. (2016). *The War on Cops.* New York: Encounter Books.

Mazerolle, L., Bennett, S., Davis, J., Sargeant, E., & Manning, M. (2013). Procedural justice and police legitimacy: A systematic review of the research evidence. *Journal of Experimental Criminology,* 9(3): 245–274. doi: 10.1007/s11292-013-9175-2.

Mazzerolle, L. G., Kadleck, C., & Roehl, J. (1998). Controlling drug and disorder problems: The role of place managers. *Criminology,* 36: 371–404.

McArdle, A., & Erzin, T. (eds.). (2001). *Zero Tolerance: Quality of Life and the New Police Brutality in New York City.* New York: New York University Press.

Meares, T. L. (2015a). Programming errors: Understanding the constitutionality of stop-and-frisk as a program, not an incident. *University of Chicago Law Review,* 82: 159–180.

Meares, T. (2015b). Broken windows, neighborhoods, and the legitimacy of law enforcement or why i fell in and out of love with Zimbardo. *Journal of Research in Crime and Delinquency,* 52(4): 609–625. doi: 10.1177/0022427815583911.

Monkkonen, E. H. (1981). *Police in Urban America, 1860–1920.* Cambridge: Cambridge University Press.

Mooney, S. J., Joshi, S., Cerda, M., Kennedy, G. J., Beard, J. R., & Rundle, A. G. (2017). Neighborhood disorder and physical activity among older adults: A longitudinal study. *Journal of Urban Health-Bulletin of the New York Academy of Medicine,* 94 (1): 30–42. doi: 10.1007/s11524-016-0125-y.

National Academies of Sciences, Engineering, and Medicine. (2017). *Proactive Policing: Effects on Crime and Communities.* Washington, DC: National Academies Press. doi: https: doi.org/10.17226/24928.

O'Brien, D. T., & Sampson, R. J. (2015). Public and private spheres of neighborhood disorder. *Journal of Research in Crime and Delinquency,* 52(4): 486–510. doi: 10.1177/0022427815577835.

Ostrom, E., & Whitaker, G. (1973). Does local community control of police make a difference? Some preliminary findings. *American Journal of Political Science,* 17(1): 48–76.

Ostrom, E., Parks, R. B., Whitaker, G. P., & Percy, S. L. (1979). The public service production process: A framework for analysing police services. In R. Baker, & F. A. Meyer, Jr. (eds.), *Evaluating Alternative Law Enforcement Policies* (pp. 65–73). Lexington: DC Heath.

Ostrom, E. (1996). Crossing the great divide: Coproduction, synergy and development. *World Development*, 24(6): 1073–1088.

Ostrom, E. (1998). A behavioral approach to the rational choice theory of collective action: Presidential Address, American Political Science Association, 1997. *American Political Science Review*, 92(1): 1–22.

Ostrom, E. (2010). A long polycentric journey. *Annual Review of Political Science*, 13 (1): 1–23. doi:10.1146/annurev.polisci.090808.123259.

Pyrooz, D. C., Decker, S. H., Wolfe, S. E., & Shjarback, J. A. (2016). Was there a Ferguson effect on crime rates in large U.S. cities?. *Journal of Criminal Justice*, 46: 1–8. doi: https://doi.org/10.1016/j.jcrimjus.2016.01.001.

Roberts, S. August 10 (2014). Author of "Broken Windows" policing defends his theory. *New York Times*. Retrieved from www.nytimes.com/2014/08/11/nyregion/author-of-broken-windows-policing-defends-his-theory.html?_r=0</i>.

Rosenbaum, D. P. (1988). Community crime prevention: A review and synthesis of the literature. *Justice Quarterly*, 5(3): 323–395.

Rothstein, R. (2017). *The Color of Law: A Forgotten History of How Our Government Segregated America*. New York: W. W. Norton.

Sampson, R. J. (2012). *Great American City: Chicago and the Enduring Neighborhood Effect*. Chicago: University of Chicago Press.

Shjarback, J. A., Pyrooz, D. C., Wolfe, S. E., & Decker, S. H. (2017). De-policing and crime in the wake of Ferguson: Racialized changes in the quantity and quality of policing among Missouri police departments. *Journal of Criminal Justice*, 50: 42–52. doi:https://doi.org/10.1016/j.jcrimjus.2017.04.003.

Skogan, W. G. (1990). *Disorder and Decline: Crime and the Spiral of Decay in American Cities*. New York: Free Press.

Skogan, W. G., & Hartnett, S. (1997). *Community Policing, Chicago Style*. New York: Oxford University Press.

Skogan, W. (2015). Disorder and decline: The state of research. *Journal of Research in Crime and Delinquency*, 52(4): 464–485. doi: 10.1177/0022427815577836.

Sousa, W. H., & Kelling, G. (2005). Of "broken windows," criminology and criminal justice. In D. Weisburd, & A. A. Braga (eds.), *Police Innovation: Contrasting Pespectives* (pp. 77–97). Cambridge: Cambridge University Press.

Spelman, W., & Eck, J. E. (1987). *Problem-Oriented Policing*. Washington, DC: National Institute of Justice.

Taylor, R. B. (1999). The incivilities thesis: Theory, measurement and policy. In R. L. Langworthy (ed.), *Measuring What Matters* (pp. 65–88). Washington, DC: National Institute of Justice / Office of Community Oriented Policing Services.

Taylor, R. B. (2001). *Breaking Away from Broken Windows: Evidence from Baltimore Neighborhoods and the Nationwide Fight against Crime, Grime, Fear and Decline*. New York: Westview Press.

Taylor, R. B. (2005). Incivilities Reduction Policing, Zero Tolerance, and the Retreat from Coproduction: Weak Foundations and Strong Pressures. In D. Weisburd, & A. A. Braga (eds.), *Innovations in Policing* (pp. 98–114). Cambridge: Cambridge University Press.

Taylor, R. B. (2015). *Community Criminology: Fundamentals of Spatial and Temporal Scaling, Ecological Indicators, and Selectivity Bias*. New York: New York University Press.

Taylor, R. B., Harris, P. W., Jones, P. R., Garcia, R. M., & McCord, E. S. (2011). Ecological origins of shared perceptions of troublesome teen groups: Implications for the basic systemic model of crime, the incivilities thesis, and political economy. *Journal of Research in Crime and Delinquency*, 48(2): 298–324. doi: 10.1177/0022427810391537.

Taylor, R. B., & Lawton, B. A. (2012). An integrated contextual model of confidence in local police. *Police Quarterly*, 15(4): 414–445. doi: 10.1177/1098611112453718.

Taylor, R. B., Wyant, B. R., & Lockwood, B. (2015). Variable links within perceived police legitimacy?: Fairness and effectiveness across races and places. *Social Science Research*, 49.

The New York Times Editorial Board. August 11 (2017). Editorial: Another Course Correction for City Policing. *New York Times*. Retrieved from www.nytimes.com/2017/08/10/opinion/nyc-summonses-prosecutors-petty-crimes.html?ref=opinion&_r=0]</i>.

Tonry, M. H. (1995). *Malign Neglect: Race, Crime and Punishment in America*. New York: Oxford University Press.

Ward, J. T., Link, N. W., & Taylor, R. B. (2017). New windows into a broken construct: A multilevel factor analysis and DIF assessment of perceived incivilities. *Journal of Criminal Justice*, 51: 74–88. doi: http://dx.doi.org/10.1016/j.jcrimjus.2017.06.004.

Weisburd, D., Hinkle, J. C., Braga, A. A., & Wooditch, A. (2015). Understanding the mechanisms underlying broken windows policing: The need for evaluation evidence. *Journal of Research in Crime and Delinquency*, 52(4): 589–608. doi: 10.1177/0022427815577837.

Weitzer, R. (1999). Citizens' perceptions of police misconduct: Race and neighborhood context. *Justice Quarterly*, 16: 819–846.

Weitzer, R., & Tuch, S. A. (1999). Race, class, and perceptions of discrimination by the police. *Crime & Delinquency*, 45(4): 494–507.

Welsh, B. C., Braga, A. A., & Bruinsma, G. J. N. (2015). Reimagining broken windows: From theory to policy. *Journal of Research in Crime and Delinquency*, 52(4): 447–463. doi: 10.1177/0022427815581399.

Welsh, B. C., Zimmerman, G. M., & Zane, S. N. (2017). The centrality of theory in modern day crime prevention: Developments, challenges, and opportunities. *Justice Quarterly*, 35(1): 1–23. doi: 10.1080/07418825.2017.1300312.

White, G. F. (2001). Homeownership: Crime and the tipping and trapping processes. *Environment & Behavior*, 33(3): 325–342.

Wilson, J. Q. (1975). *Thinking About Crime*. New York: Basic.

Wilson, J. Q., & Kelling, G. L. (1982). Broken Windows. *Atlantic Monthly*, 211 (March):29–38.

Wilson, J. Q., & Kelling, G. L. (1989). Making neighborhoods safe. Atlantic February: 46–52.

Wolfe, S. E., & Nix, J. (2016). The alleged "Ferguson Effect" and police willingness to engage in community partnership. *Law and Human Behavior*, 40(1): 1–10.

PART IV

PROBLEM–ORIENTED POLICING

7

Advocate

Why Problem-Oriented Policing

John E. Eck

> Shot while playing basketball, a teenager lay bleeding to death just steps away from a hospital as emergency room workers refused to treat him, saying it was against policy to go outside. Hospital officials rescinded the policy later today.
>
> (Associated Press, 1998)

Why would a hospital have such a policy? This is question Herman Goldstein (1979) asked, but he asked it of policing. His answer was that, "All bureaucracies risk becoming preoccupied with running their organizations and getting so involved in their method of operating that they lose sight of the primary purposes for which they were created. The police seem unusually susceptible to this phenomenon" (1979: 236–237). He called this phenomenon the "means over ends syndrome" (p. 238). Although Goldstein gave numerous examples of the means over ends syndrome in policing, he emphasized the overuse of law enforcement, particularly arrests and the use of the criminal justice system. The law, and its enforcement, are tools to solve problems, according to Goldstein. They are not ends in themselves. They are one of numerous means for accomplishing something greater. Enforcing the law should no more define policing than the claw hammer defines carpenters, the toilet plunger defines plumbers, the drafting table defines architects, or Power Point slides define college professors.

Today, well into the twenty-first century, the controversies around the police use of force are just as relevant as when Goldstein identified the challenges of the means over ends syndrome some forty years ago. Addressing these challenges requires confronting at least two important questions. How can police in a democratic society be most effective while minimizing the intrusion of government power into the daily lives of its citizens? How can governments apply policing without burdening particular groups more than other groups?

Problem-oriented policing was Goldstein's answer. He redefined the ends of policing, and then suggested the mean police could use to achieve them. Police should focus on problems. They should examine these problems in depth. They should expand their ideas of possible solutions to include the actions of other institutions. They should carefully determine if these solutions work. This chapter describes the implications of Goldstein's insights.

It is easy to get lost in the questions problem-oriented policing creates. Among these questions are: Should a specialized unit carry out problem solving, or should all police officials contribute? What is the role of crime analysis? How should the police involve community members? How can the police best collaborate with other government agencies, non-profits, and businesses? What is the role of academic researchers in assisting in problem solving? These are important questions. Nevertheless, we should recognize right now at the beginning, that these are questions about the means for solving problems. For this reason, I will ignore them, mostly.

Problem-oriented policing is based on the premises that (a) the public brings a wide variety of troubles to the police, (b) that the causes of these troubles are often complex, (c) that the police should make systematic enquiries into these complexities, (d) these enquires help police better address the troubles, and (e) learning from successful and unsuccessful innovations makes police more effective. The validity of these premises becomes obvious if we pause to look at their opposites: (a') the public demands little of the police, (b') the causes of these demands are simple, (c') so systematic inquiry into the demands is of little use, (d') better approaches to handling the publics' demands are not needed, and (e') examining police success and failures will not improve policing. None of these contrarian points stand up to close scrutiny.

So why is problem-oriented policing so often misinterpreted? One reason is that it reorients the police mission to a new unit of work: the problem. It shifts policing to a scientific approach to preventing crime and away from the routine application of the law. And it replaces the notion of the police as gatekeepers to the criminal justice system with the idea that the police are central to many networks that affect public well-being.

WHAT IS PROBLEM-ORIENTED POLICING?

Herman Goldstein (1979) created problem-oriented policing to address police discretion. Police officers are given wide latitude to handle incidents. This gives them the ability to tailor decisions to the specific needs of situations, but it also allows officers to take inappropriate actions. Unguided discretion is at the heart of most of the maladies facing policing – for example, over and improper use of force, ineffective crime reduction procedures, corruption, and discriminatory practices. Goldstein claimed that officers should be provided with meaningful guidance in how to use their discretion, thus reducing the chances of inappropriate actions. To produce this guidance, police need to know more about the types of problems they handle. Unfortunately, police administrators focus disproportionately on what the police do rather than on what the police are supposed to accomplish. This is the aforementioned means over ends syndrome (Goldstein, 1979).

The means over ends syndrome is most obvious in police use of the law. In the mid-1990s, I listened to a new police chief speak to my community group. After talking, he took questions. One resident asked why the police were arresting so many homeless men in the old downtown. The chief asked rhetorically, "Were they drunk in public? If they were, they were violating the law and should be arrested." That was it. The chief did not try to show how these arrests would address any of the legitimate concerns that the public might have with homeless men – from unsightliness, to aggressive panhandling, to the health of the homeless men themselves. Whether he meant to or not, the chief confused the problems the community wanted addressed with the particular means – law enforcement – he wanted his officers to use. A year later, despite the arrests, there was no decline in the problems of the homeless in my community. As in this example, police and the public often confuse applying the law with reduction in troublesome circumstances. Law enforcement is one of numerous tools, according to Goldstein (1979), not a goal.

What are the ends that the police should address? The police role is to address the bewildering array of troublesome circumstances brought to them by the public. Goldstein called these circumstances "problems." How should these problems be addressed? If there are numerous tools, in addition to law enforcement, how can the police select the right tools for each problem? The answer is to study the problem, learn why it occurs and continues, then select tools that fit the problem. Success should be measured by problem reduction – fewer, less serious, and less harmful problems – rather than the particular action taken.

Notice that problem-oriented policing contains two arguments. The *normative* argument is that the police are supposed to reduce problems rather than simply respond to incidents and apply the relevant law. Given that the public demands that the police address a wide range of troublesome circumstances, and given that these various troubles have a wide variety of causes, then it is important that the police understand these causes to develop appropriate responses. I will come back to this point later.

The *empirical* argument relies on evidence that problem solving works to reduce problems. Later, I will summarize the evidence supporting the use of problem-oriented policing. In the concluding section of this chapter, I will apply both normative and empirical arguments to compare problem-oriented policing to alternative policing strategies. But before examining these arguments, it is important to describe problem-oriented policing in detail.

HOW HAS PROBLEM-ORIENTED POLICING EVOLVED?

Problem-oriented policing has evolved in four ways: its definition of "problem"; its theoretical underpinnings; processes for problem solving; and how problem solving should be organized within police agencies.

Problem Definition

Problem-oriented policing is unique among police improvement strategies. Goldstein created an entirely new unit of work for policing: the problem. The term "problem" was shorthand for the wide array of troubles the public calls upon the police to handle. Despite its centrality, Goldstein left "problem" undefined. A more precise definition was needed to operationalize problem-oriented policing. So Ronald Clarke and I defined a problem as a reoccurring set of similar events, harmful to members of communities, that the public expect the local police to address. This definition is summarized by the acronym, CHEERS, for *Community, Harm, Expectations, Events, Recurring*, and *Similarity* (Clarke & Eck, 2003). A problem, then, is anything that meets all six CHEERS criteria.

To get a better understanding of the CHEERS criteria, let's expand the example of the drunk homeless men. As articulated by this chief, drunk homeless men in the downtown do not meet all the CHEERS criteria. It occurred in the community. There were public expectations that the police should be involved. Drunkenness and homelessness seemed to be recurring troubles. And it probably involved similar men in a similar area. Missing from the chief's depiction was any description of what harms were being created, and the sorts of events that created the trouble.

In fact, there may have been several problems. Drunk homeless men in the downtown may have engaged in aggressive panhandling – events that fall close to but just short of robbery. If so, the harm is the fear imposed on pedestrians and the events are the encounters between pedestrians and panhandlers. Or, the homeless could be harming themselves: drug and alcohol abuse, living on the street, and related actions jeopardizing their health. These health-related harms could have been marked by events such as drug overdoses, emergency room admissions, or deaths. Or, the problem could have been that the drunk homeless were victims of predatory crime, either by other homeless men or by people who enjoy abusing those who are helpless. In this case, the events were the attacks and the harms were injury and fear.

Though these three problems overlap, they are distinct. This becomes clearer if one considers the actions police should take to address the problems. If the problem was homeless men harming themselves, then arresting them makes little sense. Police partnering with health and service agencies, as well as local businesses (around which these men congregate) makes more sense. If the problem was aggressive panhandling, arrests might be useful, but not because of drunkenness. If the problem was mostly about the victimization of the homeless, any law enforcement should be directed at those who prey upon them.

Problem Theory

Problem-oriented policing requires a theory of problems (Eck & Madensen, 2012). By 1987, the link between problem solving and routine activity theory had become apparent (Eck & Spelman, 1987). By the early 1990s, routine activity theory (Felson, 2016) became incorporated within problem-solving training through the "problem-analysis triangle." The problem triangle, based on routine activity theory (Felson, 2016), aids problem analysis and response development by highlighting the basic elements of problems (Eck, 2003). The triangle is now a standard part of problem analysis (Read, Tilley & Webb, 2000; Clarke & Eck, 2003; Braga, 2008). Problem-oriented policing uses a variety of concepts, tools, and procedures from environmental criminology: repeat victim and place analysis, examining property ownership and street configurations, and situational crime prevention and crime mapping, to name but a few (Clarke & Eck 2003; Braga, 2008).

Environmental criminology theory, practice, and evidence has been incorporated in publications providing police with problem-solving guidance. These include general-purpose guides (Office of Community Policing, 1998; Bynum, 2001) as well as Anthony Braga's (2008) in-depth text on problem-oriented policing. There is a library of introductions to specific technical areas, such as surveys (Eck & LaVigne, 1993; Weisel, 1999), evaluations (Eck, 2017), and mapping (Harries, 1999; Eck, Chainey & Cameron, 2005). The Jill Dando Institute for Crime Sciences, with funding from the Home Office, published a guide to problem solving for crime analysts (Clarke & Eck, 2003). The US Department of Justice funded a US version (Clarke & Eck, 2005). These manuals have been translated into over twenty languages. In 2004, the Center for Problem-Oriented Policing implemented a theory-based on-line decision framework, the Problem Analysis Module (PAM), to facilitate individual and group problem solving (Center for Problem-Oriented Policing, 2004). There are over seventy problem-specific guides to aid in diagnosing and solving problems ranging from abandoned buildings to animal cruelty to child abuse and neglect to commercial robbery to abuse of 911.

Problem Solving Process

The transition of problem-oriented policing from police theory to police practice necessitated the development of detailed guidance. The SARA process (Scanning, Analysis, Response, Assessment) was one of the first efforts in this direction (Eck & Spelman, 1987). It has become almost synonymous with problem-oriented policing (Scott, 2000; Sidebottom & Tilley, 2011).

Scanning represents police routinely identifying possible problems, verifying them (and rejecting those that are not problems), and developing a definition of them. The CHEERS criteria are used here.

Analysis is the systematic inquiry into the causes of a problem to reveal leverage points that will suggest useful solutions. The problem-analysis triangle is most useful here. Though some aspects of analysis (and scanning) involve crime mapping and statistical analysis, much analysis involves talking to people and making direct observations. Police themselves often have a wealth of undocumented knowledge about problems, and these informal insights should be examined to help discover what to do with the problem. The same can be said of members of the community around the problem, employees of government agencies and non-profits who deal with aspects of the problem, and business owners whose operations touch on the problem (Goldstein, 1979, 1990).

At the third stage, response, the police use their knowledge developed in the earlier stages to develop a potential solution. The police should examine a wide array of possible interventions. Sometimes this means working with other groups and organizations to improve their capacity to address the public's concerns. For example, if the homeless problem in the earlier example were largely about where people slept and obstruction of sidewalks, then partnering with homeless shelters and other aid agencies and non-profits might be useful. Just because the public expects the police to be involved, does not make the problem something that the police handle alone.

The final step, assessment, involves determining if that solution was actually implemented as planned and if it reduced the problem as hoped. Given that the focus of policing should be on reducing harms from problems, it is critical that the police determine the degree to which their actions – and the actions of their partners – lead to improvements.

Although described as a linear, step-by-step approach, in practice police often move back and fourth among the SARA steps as they learn more, or find that their first attempts were not successful.

Organization

Goldstein wanted to locate problem-oriented policing in police headquarters. This unit would examine problems with the goal of providing advice to the police command as to what officers should do to improve their handling of these troublesome circumstances. A succession of pilot tests in Madison, Wisconsin (Goldstein & Susmilch, 1982), London (Hoare, Stewart & Purcell, 1984), Baltimore County, Maryland (Cordner, 1986), and Newport News, Virginia (Eck & Spelman, 1987) moved the location of analysis from a headquarters operation to police officers assigned to operational units.

Decentralization of problem solving had consequences. It expanded the number of problems that could be handled by expanding the number of people who could address them. This reduced the scale of problem analysis from problem classes to individual manifestations of problem classes – from how to handle street prostitution in general, for example, to how to handle street prostitution on a particular street. Decentralization and reduction in scale truncated inquiry into problems, from the extensive analysis Goldstein envisioned, to limited probing by busy street cops. These changes reduced the quality of the average problem-solving effort.

Although the average quality may have declined, the range of quality probably widened. At the upper levels, some important inquiries have been undertaken, resulting in reductions of serious problems: for example, Boston's youth homicide reduction effort (Kennedy, Braga & Piehl, 1997; Braga et al., 2001), Liverpool's reduction of glass bottle injuries (Hester & Rice, 2001), the California Highway Patrol's project to reduce farm workers' highway deaths (Helmick, 2002), and Cincinnati's reduction in deaths from vehicle crashes (Corsaro et al., 2012). At the bottom level, what is called "problem solving" may simply be targeted enforcement or referrals to other agencies.

Recently, there has been renewed interest in centralized problem inquiries to improve quality. Advances in crime analysis have propelled these units to the center of problem-oriented policing, both as support for line officers engaged in problem solving, but also as leaders of major enquires (Boba, 2003; Clarke & Eck, 2003). Examples of this include the crime analysis unit of the Chula Vista (California) Police Department's work to regulate nuisance motels (Bichler, Schmerler & Enriquez, 2013), and the efforts of the Paducah (Kentucky) Police Department's crime analyst to curb Walmart's excessive use of police services (Zidar, Schaefer & Eck, 2018).

Almost forty years since it was first articulated, important changes have taken place in the concept of "problem," the theory of problem-oriented policing, the guidance provided to police officials, and the organizational location of problem-oriented policing. Except for organizational location, all of these changes have been toward increasing specificity. This stands in stark contrast to other proposed police strategies, such as community policing, broken-windows theory, and CompStat, which have become less defined over time (Eck & Rosenbaum, 1994; Harcourt, 2001; Weisburd et al., 2003) as their proponents attempt to generalize from a singular case to achieve universal appeal.

SHOULD POLICE ADOPT A PROBLEM-ORIENTED APPROACH?

As I noted earlier, there are two basic arguments in favor of problem-oriented policing. The first is a *normative* argument. The second is an *empirical* argument. For simplicity, I will describe each separately, although, in reality, these arguments are intertwined.

Problem-Oriented Policing as a Values Statement

The decision to assert that the goal of the police is to address problems entails a choice from among alternative values. One could claim that the police *should* only provide emergency services. The prevention of crime, disorder, and other troublesome circumstances *should* be left to individuals, community organizations, private markets, other professions, or other government entities.

One could argue that policing *should* be about fighting crime – both handling its aftermath and reducing future occurrences. Everything else is a sideshow created by historical happenstance, poor city administration, and other arbitrary factors. Police have shed many functions and so police *should* shed remaining non-crime functions.

One could also argue that the police *should* focus on separating law violators from non-violators and help to bring the violators before the courts. Further, the prevention of crime is not a police function but is the responsibility of others. If the police prevent crime, it is only an unintended side benefit of a focus on justice.

Clearly, to choose a problem-oriented approach is to reject these alternatives. This choice has nothing to do with evidence. It's a choice of values. Taking a problem-oriented approach is an assertion that the police *should* focus on limiting the harm from the diverse array of concerns brought to police attention. It is a recognition that people legitimately demand a great deal of the police, often because other institutions fail. It is a recognition that the police are the single government agency that takes the lead in addressing these concerns, and preventing future occurrences because they are the sole 24-hour general-purpose public trouble-shooting agency available (Bittner, 1980).

From a normative perspective, addressing problems is what the police *should* be doing. There is a need for an organization that deals with things that go wrong. Fixing many of these failures often raises the possibility that force may be required. So a general-purpose agency with the ability to use the coercive powers of the state is required (Bittner, 1980). And if we desire policing to be effective and responsive to the public, then scientific examination of problems is necessary.

A Problem-Oriented Approach as Effective Policing

The normative perspective tells us whether problem-oriented policing is desirable in principle; that it could help us achieve socially desirable goals. But it does not tell us if it will work. Fortunately, there have been a number of tests of police problem-solving effectiveness. When crime hot spots are randomly assigned to problem-solving or standard policing, the hot spots receiving the problem solving improve more on average than those receiving standard policing (Weisburd & Green, 1995; Braga et al., 1999). Based on the published descriptions, however, the analysis undertaken in the experimental treatment of hot spots was relatively limited.

The evaluations of problem solving by police have been systematically reviewed by David Weisburd and colleagues (2010). Systematic reviews, and meta-analysis findings are important because they assess the totality of the evidence across all available studies, and do not rely on a single study for their conclusions. Weisburd et al. (2010) found that although not every attempt succeeded, most efforts were effective, and that, overall, problem-oriented policing was more effective at reducing problems than alternatives.

There is additional evidence from meta-analysis evaluations of other policing strategies. Problem solving is often, though not always, used in conjunction with other policing strategies, such as community policing, hot spots patrols, and broken windows policing. Adding problem solving to community policing efforts might improve its effectiveness, though this is uncertain, based on a meta-analysis review of community policing studies (Gill et al., 2014). The difficulty is that community policing has only minor impact on crime or disorder, and it is unclear how thoroughly problem solving was implemented when it was used. More impressive findings come from a meta-analysis of hot spots policing. Braga, Papachristos, and Hureau (2014) found that although hot spots policing was effective, it was demonstrably more effective if problem solving tactics were used instead of merely having police patrol crime or disorder hot spots.

Broken windows theory claims that police should address disorder because that will help drive down crime. The theory is not specific about how this should be done. Although many of its advocates rely on law enforcement, the original authors extolled problem solving for reducing disorder (Wilson & Kelling, 1989). It turns out, based on yet another meta-analysis of many evaluations, that if the police address disorder using problem solving tactics, they are more likely to reduce these problems than if they use enforcement (Braga, Welsh & Schnell, 2015).

One of the hallmarks of a problem-oriented approach is the emphasis on finding alternatives to the use of law enforcement to reduce crime, disorder, and other problems. The utility of alternatives can be found in a variety of areas. Repeat victimization interventions typically use non-traditional interventions and sometimes explicitly use law enforcement approaches as a last resort (see Anderson, Chenery & Pease, 1995). There are a number of quasi-experiments pointing to the effectiveness of combining a repeat victimization analysis with the use of alternative approaches to prevention. These studies often result in reductions in crime (Grove et al., 2012).

Evidence from other programs show that diversifying police action beyond enforcement has payoffs. Crackdowns on drug hot spots produce small to modest crime or disorder reduction (Sherman et al., 1995). But when coupled with landlord interventions, the impact is larger (Hope, 1994; Green, 1995; Eck & Wartell, 1998; Mazerrole, Roehl & Kadleck, 1998). Matthews (1993) noticed a similar phenomenon with prostitution. Early enforcement resulted in short-term improvements but not sustained change. When enforcement was coupled with changes in street layout, he noted longer-lasting and deeper impacts (Matthews, 1993). Cohen and colleagues (2003) found that police crackdowns on illegal drug dealing at bars had noticeable but temporary effects. What would have occurred if the intervention had targeted the bar owners using a wider variety of interventions? There is a small but useful set of evaluations suggesting that the impact would have been greater (Homel et al., 1997; Eck & Guerette, 2012).

In conclusion, police should embrace a problem-oriented approach. First, it upholds the fundamental value that governments should seek minimally intrusive ways to address the diverse needs of the public. If one agrees with the basic ideas that the public come to the police with a variety of legitimate problems, and that the police mission is to find ways to reduce these problems, then problem-oriented policing is sensible. Further, the evidence consistently shows that the police are able to address problems and that the application of problem solving works better than alternatives.

IS THERE AN ALTERNATIVE TO PROBLEM-ORIENTED POLICING?

Should police select problem-oriented policing as their overall departmental strategy? Values and evidence suggest so. However, police do not select a strategy in abstract. Their choices are always relative to alternatives. And their choices are usually based on multiple criteria. First, a strategy should address the full range of problems the public brings to the police, not just those involving crime and disorder. Second, a strategy should not rely solely on law enforcement. Third, the strategy should encourage partnerships with non-police agencies, non-governmental organizations, and communities. Fourth, the strategy should encourage shifting the responsibility of problems to entities better equipped to address them, or who are responsible for their creation. Fifth, given the increasing need to understand problems, a strategy should embrace the collection and analysis of data describing problems and possible solutions. Sixth, since police officials often develop considerable experience and expertise in handling problems, a strategy should tap this expertise. Seventh, a strategy should give highest priority to what it is supposed to accomplish and then to how this is to be done. In short, it should not risk running afoul of the means over ends syndrome. Finally, a strategy should be well supported by evidence.

Table 7.1 applies these eight criteria to problem-oriented policing and ten other strategies.

Not surprising, problem-oriented policing scores well on all eight. Equally unsurprising, standard policing – reliance on criminal investigation, random patrolling, and rapid response to calls from the public (Weisburd & Eck, 2004) – scores poorly. This was the style of policing Goldstein was reacting to when he created problem-oriented policing. The other strategies fall in between these two extremes.

Community policing does well for the first three criteria. However, though it embraces the idea of partnerships, there is little in the theory of community policing that suggests shifting problems from police to those who create them, or who are better able to address them. Although community policing can make use of officer expertise, it is not particularly analytical. Most writing about community policing describes tactics that should be used, rather than what should be accomplished. Finally, the evidence suggests we must be skeptical about its use as a crime or disorder reducing strategy, whatever other merits it has (Gill et al., 2014).

TABLE 7.1 *Summary Comparison of Policing Strategies*

	Pop	Standard	Cop*	Broken windows	Third party	CompStat	Hot spot*	Predictive	Intelligence led**	Focused deterrence	Evidence based
1. Addresses full range of community demands	full range	crime & emergencies	full range	crime & disorder	unclear	no	crime & disorder	crime	crime	crime	Possible, depends on evidence available
2. Relies mostly on law enforcement	no	yes	no	usually	no	usually	yes	yes	usually	yes	no
3. Encourages partnerships	yes	no	yes	no	yes	no	no	no	variable	yes	if it works
4. Can shift problems to those responsible	yes	no	no	no	yes	no	no	no	no	no	if it works
5. Uses an analytical approach	yes	no	no	no	unknown	yes	yes	yes	yes	limited	yes
6. Relies on officer expertise	yes	no	yes	unclear	unclear	no	no	no	yes	unclear	unclear
7. Ends or means emphasized	ends	means	means	ends	means	means	means	means	mixed	means	means & ends
8. Evidence for effectiveness	yes	no	no	no	yes	no	yes	unclear-insufficient evidence	unclear-insufficient evidence	yes	no

* Strategy applied without problem solving

** Some versions overlap substantially with a problem-oriented approach (Ratcliffe, 2016)

Broken windows policing fares even worse. If implemented without problem solving, using enforcement only, it fails most of these criteria. The possible exception is officer expertise. Wilson and Kelling (1982) highlight the local knowledge of beat officers and how this can be used to reduce disorder. To its credit, broken windows theory focuses more on ends than means. However, it is unclear if broken windows policing can be applied to the full range of demands on policing.

Third party policing is a relatively flexible strategy that might be able to address a broad range of community demands, though this is not clear. It does not exclusively rely on law enforcement and it explicitly does encourage partnerships. And it does seek to shift responsibility for problems from the police. It is unclear how analytical it is, or how much it uses officer expertise. It is a means-focused strategy, emphasizing a particular form of solution to problems. The evidence in support of its effectiveness is encouraging (Mazerolle & Ransley, 2005).

The principle value of CompStat is that it applies an analytical approach. But by centralizing authority, it reduces the ability of a police agency to handle a wide range of concerns, relies too heavily on enforcement, does not embrace partnerships, seems unable to shift problems to where they belong, and does not draw on officer expertise (Weisburd et al., 2003). CompStat, as a set of command and control practices, is largely about administration rather than what is to be achieved. Finally, there is no evidence that it reduces crime and disorder.

Hot spots policing and predictive policing are closely related, if the predictions are of where and when crimes will occur. The principle difference may simply be the use of advanced analytics for predictions, rather than more common crime analysis methods. Both are analytical. Though the goal is to drive crime or disorder down, both strategies emphasize a particular means for doing so, usually patrolling. Hot spots policing has been well tested and shown to be effective (Braga et al., 2014). The number of studies of predictive policing is too limited to draw strong conclusions. On all other criteria, however, both strategies are weak.

Intelligence-led policing has developed over the last two decades. Though it can overlap considerably with problem-oriented policing (Ratcliffe, 2016), it tends to focus mostly on crime. To date, most descriptions emphasize enforcement, but do not strongly embrace partnerships or shifting responsibility. Descriptions of intelligence-led policing emphasize analytical methods, but include the use of more qualitative sources of information as well. That is why I gave it a "yes" for using officer expertise. Like hot spots policing, the emphasis is on the means for analyzing crime problems. Unlike hot spots policing, it is less concerned with how this is accomplished. There are insufficient tests of the strategies to know how effective it is.

Focused deterrence is a product of problem-oriented policing, originally designed to address gang-involved homicides. Though it has been applied to other crimes, it is not a general strategy for policing. Rather, it is a class of solutions that will apply to some problems and not others. The principle mechanism for achieving its results is the use of enforcement. It does partner with other police agencies, prosecutors, correctional agencies, and community members. Focused deterrence does use some analytical techniques – social network analysis, for example – but analysis is not a strong part of the approach. It is not clear how much it relies on officer expertise. By emphasizing a particular set of deterrence practices, focused deterrence emphasizes means relative to ends. Nevertheless, there is very good evidence that it works well to reduce specific crimes (Braga & Weisburd, 2012).

Evidence-based policing draws attention to the scientific evidence supporting the use of an intervention. In principle, it could address a broad range of community demands, but evidence about what works to address these demands is often very limited or absent. It is agnostic about the utility of enforcement: it depends on the evidence. It is similarly agnostic about the use of partnerships and shifting responsibility. It does encourage analysis, particularly in evaluating responses. Because it relies heavily on published scientific evidence, it is less reliant on officer field experience. This can pose a difficulty if there is little evidence available concerning a particular problem. Nevertheless, some of the techniques suggested by Lum and Koper (2017) imply this could be overcome. I have listed it as both means and ends based. It focuses on selecting interventions that work, thus is ends based. It also emphasizes a type of intervention (ones with evidence), so it is means based. Finally, there are no scientific studies showing that police agencies consistently using evidence produce better outcomes for their publics. This limitation may seem peculiar. However, there are no strong experiments of police use of evidence, nor are there any systematic reviews or meta-analyses of this strategy. So, although the assumption that if an agency uses evidence-based practices, it will be more effective seems very plausible, it is still an untested assumption.

Since strategy selection is in part dependent on the alternative strategies available, this comparison is necessary to determine if problem-oriented policing is useful. We have already seen that problem-oriented policing addresses particular values and it is based on evidence. With this comparison, we can see that, based on eight reasonable criteria, it is theoretically more sound than alternatives. Consequently, if one wants a general purpose, ends-oriented, and evidence-based policing strategy, it is problem-oriented policing. This comparison is based on the assumption that the strategies are mutually exclusive.

However, if we dispense with this assumption, the options are greater. Many of these strategies could be used in conjunction with problem-oriented policing. At its core, problem-oriented policing is evidence based (see Lum & Koper (2017: 15–20) for a good discussion of this). It not only calls on police to conduct a broad search for remedies, and examine evidence, it demands that the police evaluate the remedies it selects. It is the only strategy that explicitly builds in testing of solutions (the Assessment stage of SARA). Community policing and third-party policing, emphasizing different types of partnerships, are particularly compatible. Intelligence-led policing overlaps considerably with problem-oriented policing (Ratcliffe, 2016). Many hot spots policing projects use problem solving at hot spots, as do some broken windows policing efforts (Braga et al., 2014). Focused deterrence can be used as a particular solution to some problems. Even CompStat might be adapted to provide an administrative mechanism to promote problem solving (Weisburd et al., 2003; Willis, Mastrofski & Kochel, 2010).

Ultimately, we have to ask ourselves, what we want of our police. Consider this scenario, based on a composite of recent news accounts.

Sighting the third young Black male in a week crossing in the middle of the same busy thoroughfare, the patrol officer ...

a) once again, stopped the youth, asked him for ID, lectured him on the dangers of crossing mid-block, and issued him a citation. He then continued his patrolling. Or,
b) slowed traffic to allow the youth to safely cross, and then asked himself, why is this occurring on this street and how can the city change things to make it safer for pedestrians to cross? The next day, he requested a list of pedestrian-vehicle accidents from the crime analysis unit, and began systematically observing pedestrian traffic on the block.

Which set of actions is most likely to reduce harm to the public? Which type of policing do you want?

REFERENCES

Anderson, D., Chenery, S., & Pease, K. (1995). *Preventing Repeat Victimization: A Report on Progress in Huddersfield*. London: Home Office, Police Research Group.

Associated Press. (1998, May 19). As dying teen bleeds nearby, hospital staff stays inside – incident prompts change in policy. *Washington Post*, A9.

Bichler, G., Schmerler, K., & Enriquez, J. (2013). Curbing nuisance motels: An evaluation of police as place regulators. *Policing: An International Journal of Police Strategies and Management*, 36(2), 437–462.

Bittner, E. (1980). *The Functions of Policing in Modern Society*. Rockville, MD: National Institutes of Mental Health.

Boba, R. (2003). *Problem Analysis in Policing*. Washington, DC: Police Foundation.

Braga, A. A. (2008). *Problem Oriented Policing and Crime Prevention*. 2nd edition. Monsey, NY: Criminal Justice Press.

Braga, A. A., Kennedy, D. M., Waring, E. J., & Piehl, A. M. (2001). Problem-oriented policing, deterrence, and youth violence: An evaluation of Boston's operation ceasefire. *Journal of Research in Crime and Delinquency*, 38(3), 195–225.

Braga, A. A., Papachristos, A. V., & Hureau, D. M. (2014). The effects of hot spots policing on crime: An updated systematic review and meta-analysis. *Justice Quarterly*, 31(4), 633–663.

Braga, A. A., & Weisburd, D. L. (2012). The effects of focused deterrence strategies on crime: A systematic review and meta-analysis of the empirical evidence. *Journal of Research in Crime and Delinquency*, 49(3), 323–358.

Braga, A. A., Weisburd, D. L., Waring, E. J., Mazerolle, L. G., Spelman, W., & Gajewski, F. (1999). Problem-oriented policing in violent crime places: A randomized controlled experiment. *Criminology*, 37(3), 541–580.

Braga, A. A., Welsh, B.C., & Schnell, C. (2015). Can policing disorder reduce crime? A systematic review and meta-analysis. *Journal of Research in Crime and Delinquency* 52(4), 567–588.

Bynum, T. (2001). *Using Analysis for Problem-Solving: A Guidebook for Law Enforcement*. Washington, DC: Office of Community Oriented Policing Services.

Center for Problem-Oriented Policing. (2004) *Problem analysis module*. www .popcenter.org/learning/PAM/default.cfm. Accessed June 24, 2017.

Clarke, R. V., & Eck, J. E. (2003). *Becoming a Problem-Solving Crime Analyst: In 55 Small Steps*. London: Jill Dando Institute of Crime Science.

Clarke, R. V., & Eck, J. E. (2005). *Crime Analysis for Problem Solvers. In 60 Small Steps*. Washington, DC: Office of Community Oriented Policing.

Cohen, J., Gorr, W., & Singh, P. (2003). Estimating intervention effects in varying risk settings: Do police raids reduce illegal drug dealing at nuisance bars? *Criminology*, 41, 257–292.

Cordner, G. W. (1986). Fear of crime and the police: An evaluation of a fear reduction strategy. *Journal of Police Science and Administration*, 14(3), 223–233.

Corsaro, N., Gerard, D. W., Engel, R. S., & Eck, J. E. (2012). Not by accident: An analytical approach to traffic crash harm reduction. *Journal of Criminal Justice*, 40(6), 502–514.

Eck, J. E. (2017). *Assessing Responses to Problems: Did It Work?* (Tool Guide no. 1, second edition). Washington, DC: Bureau of Justice Assistance.

Eck, J. E. (2003). Police problems: The complexity of problem theory, research and evaluation. In J. Knutsson (ed.), *Problem-Oriented Policing: From Innovation to Mainstream* (vol. 15, pp. 79–113). Monsey, NY: Criminal Justice Press.

Eck, J. E., Chainey, S., & Cameron, J. (2005). *Mapping Crime: Understanding Hot Spots*. Washington, DC: US Department of Justice, National Institute of Justice.

Eck, J. E., & Guerette, R. T. (2012). Place-based crime prevention: Theory, evidence, and policy. In B. Welsh, & D. Farrington (eds.), *The Oxford Handbook of Crime Prevention* (pp. 354–383). New York: Oxford University Press.

Eck, J. E., & LaVigne, N. G. (1993). *A Police Guide to Surveying Citizens and Their Environment*. Washington, DC: Bureau of Justice Assistance.

Eck, J. E., & Madensen, T. (2012). Situational crime prevention makes problem-oriented policing work: The importance of interdependent theories for effective Policing. In N. Tilley, & G. Farrell (eds.), *The Reasoning Criminologist: Essays in Honour of Ronald V. Clarke* (pp. 80–92). New York: Routledge.

Eck, J. E., & Rosenbaum, D. P. (1994). The new police order: Effectiveness, equity, and efficiency in community policing. In *The Challenge of Community Policing: Testing the Promises* (pp. 3–23). Thousand Oaks, CA: Sage.

Eck, J. E., & Spelman, W. (1987). Who ya gonna call? The police as problem-busters. *Crime and Delinquency*, 33(1), 31–52.

Eck, J. E., & Wartell, J. (1998). Improving the management of rental properties with drug problems: A randomized experiment. In L. G. Mazerolle, & J. Roehl (eds.), *Civil Remedies and Crime Prevention* (pp. 161–185). Monsey, NY: Criminal Justice Press.

Felson, M. (2016). The routine activities approach. In R. Wortley, & M. Townsley (eds.), *Environmental Criminology and Crime Analysis* (2nd ed., pp. 87–97). New York: Routledge.

Gill, C., Weisburd, D., Telep, C. W., Vitter, Z., & Bennett, T. (2014). Community-oriented policing to reduce crime, disorder and fear and increase satisfaction and legitimacy among citizens: A systematic review. *Journal of Experimental Criminology, 10*(4), 399–428.

Goldstein, H. (1979). Improving policing: A problem oriented approach. *Crime and Delinquency, 25*(2), 236–258.

Goldstein, H. (1990). *Problem-Oriented Policing.* New York: McGraw Hill.

Goldstein, H., & Susmilch, C. E. (1982). *Experimenting with the Problem-Oriented Approach to Improving Police Service: A Report and Some Reflections on Two Case Studies.* Madison: University of Wisconsin Law School.

Green, L. (1995) Policing places with drug problems: The multi-agency response team approach. In J. E. Eck, & D. Weisburd (eds.), *Crime and Place*, 4 (pp. 199–216). Monsey, NY: Criminal Justice Press.

Grove, L. E., Farrell, G., Farrington, D. P., & Johnson, S. (2012). *Preventing Repeat Victimization: A Systematic Review.* Stockholm, Sweden: Brå – The Swedish National Council for Crime Prevention.

Harcourt, B. (2001). *Illusion of Order: The False Promises of Broken Windows Policing.* Cambridge, MA: Harvard University Press.

Harries, K. (1999). *Mapping Crime: Principles and Practice.* Washington, DC: National Institute of Justice.

Helmick, D. O. (2002). *Safety and Farm Labor Vehicle Education Program.* Sacramento, CA: California Highway Patrol.

Hester, J., & Rice, K. (2001). *Operation Crystal Clear: In an Effort to Reduce Glass Related Street Violence, the Message Remains "Crystal Clear."* Liverpool, UK: Merseyside Police.

Hoare, M. A., Stewart, G., & Purcell, C. M. (1984). *The Problem Oriented Approach: Four Pilot Studies.* London: Metropolitan Police, Management Services Department.

Homel, R., Hauritz, M., McIlwain, G., Wortley, R., & Carvolth, R. (1997). Preventing alcohol-related crime through community action: The surfer's paradise safety action project. In R. Homel (ed.), *Policing for Prevention: Reducing Crime, Public Intoxication and Injury*, 7 (pp. 35–90). Monsey, NY: Criminal Justice Press.

Hope, T. (1994). Problem-oriented policing and drug market locations: Three case studies. In R. V. Clarke (ed.), *Crime Prevention Studies*, 2 (pp. 5–31). Monsey, NY: Criminal Justice Press.

Kennedy, D. M., Braga, A. A., & Piehl, A. M. (1997). The (un)known universe: Mapping gangs and gang violence in Boston. In D. Weisburd, & T. McEwen (eds.), *Crime Mapping* (pp. 219–262). Monsey, NY: Criminal Justice Press.

Lum, C., & Koper, C. S. 2017. *Evidence-Based Policing: Translating Research into Practice.* New York: Oxford University Press.

Matthews, R. (1993). *Kerb-Crawling, Prostitution and Multi-Agency Policing.* London: Home Office.

Mazerolle, L. G., & Ransley, J. (2005). *Third Party Policing*. New York: University of Cambridge Press.

Mazerolle, L. G., Roehl, J., & Kadleck, C. (1998). Controlling social disorder using civil remedies: Results for a randomized field experiment in Oakland, California. In L. G. Mazerolle, & J. Roehl (eds.), *Civil Remedies and Crime Prevention*, 9 (pp. 141–159). Monsey, NY: Criminal Justice Press.

Office of Community Oriented Policing Services. (1998). *Problem-solving tips: A guide to reducing crime and disorder through problem-solving partnerships*. Washington, DC: US Department of Justice, Office of Community Oriented Policing Services.

Ratcliffe, J. H. (2016). *Intelligence-Led Policing* (2nd edition). New York: Routledge.

Read, T., Tilley, N., & Webb, E. B. (2000). *Not Rocket Science? Problem-Solving and Crime Reduction*. London: Home Office.

Scott, M. S. (2000). *Problem-Oriented Policing: Reflections on the First 20 Years*. Washington, DC: US Department of Justice, Office of Community Oriented Policing Services.

Sherman, L. W., Rogan, D. P., Edwards, T., Whipple, R., Shreve, D., Witcher, D., & Bridgeforth, C. A. (1995). Deterrent effects of police raids on crack houses: A randomized, controlled experiment. *Justice Quarterly*, 12(4), 754–781.

Sidebottom, A., & Tilley, N. (2011). Improving problem-oriented policing: The need for a new model? *Crime Prevention and Community Safety*, 13(2), 79–101.

Weisburd, D., & Eck, J. E. (2004). What can police do to reduce crime, disorder, and fear? *The Annals of the American Academy of Political and Social Sscience*, 593(May), 42–65.

Weisburd, D. L., & Green, L. (1995). Policing drug hot spots: The Jersey City drug market analysis experiment. *Justice Quarterly*, 12(4), 711–735.

Weisburd, D., Mastrofski, S. D., McNally, A. M., Greenspan, R., & Willis, J. J. (2003). Reforming to preserve: Compstat and strategic problem solving in American policing. *Criminology and Public Policy*, 2(3), 421–456.

Weisburd, D. L., Telep, C. W., Hinkle, J., & Eck, J. E. (2010). Is problem-oriented policing effective in reducing crime and disorder? *Criminology and Public Policy*, 9(1), 139–172.

Weisel, D. (1999). *Conducting Community Surveys: A Practical Guide for Law Enforcement Agencies*. Washington, DC: Bureau of Justice Statistics and Office of Community Oriented Policing Services.

Willis, J. J., Mastrofski, S. D., & Kochel, T. R. (2010). *The Co-Implementation of Compstat and Community Policing*. Fairfax, VA: Center for Justice Leadership and Management, George Mason University.

Wilson, J. Q., & Kelling, G. L. (1982). Broken windows: The police and neighborhood safety. *The Atlantic Monthly*, 249(3), 29–38.

Wilson, J. Q., & Kelling, G. L. (1989). Making neighborhoods safe. *The Atlantic Monthly* (February), 46–52.

Zidar, M., Shafer, J. G., & Eck, J. E. (2018). The role of the crime analysis in problem solving: Some problems are just freaking obvious. *Policing: A Journal of Policy and Practice*, 12(3), 316–331.

8

Critic

Problem-Oriented Policing: The Disconnect between Principles and Practice

Anthony A. Braga and David Weisburd

Problem-oriented policing works to identify *why* things are going wrong and to frame responses using a wide variety of innovative approaches (Goldstein, 1979). Using a basic iterative approach of problem identification, analysis, response, assessment, and adjustment of the response, this adaptable and dynamic analytic approach provides an appropriate framework to uncover the complex mechanisms at play in crime problems and to develop tailor-made interventions to address the underlying conditions that cause crime problems (Eck & Spelman, 1987; Goldstein, 1990). Many police departments have experimented with the approach and the available evaluation evidence suggests that problem-oriented policing is a fundamentally sound approach to controlling crime and disorder problems (Skogan & Frydl, 2004; Weisburd & Eck, 2004; Braga, 2008; Weisburd et al., 2010). The US National Academies of Science, Engineering, and Medicine Committee on Proactive Policing recently reviewed the more rigorous evaluations of problem-oriented policing and concluded that these programs lead to short-term reductions in crime and disorder (Weisburd & Majmundar, 2018).

But is the "problem-oriented policing" that researchers have evaluated similar to the model of problem-oriented policing that its originators proposed? There is substantial evidence that, too often, the principles envisioned by Herman Goldstein are not being practiced in the field. Deficiencies in current problem-oriented policing practices exist in all phases of the process. A number of scholars have identified challenging issues in the substance and implementation of many problem-oriented policing projects, including the tendency for officers to conduct only a superficial analysis of problems and rushing to implement a response, the tendency for officers to rely on traditional or faddish responses rather than conducting a wider search for creative responses, and the tendency to completely ignore the assessment of the effectiveness of implemented responses (Cordner, 1998; but also see Clarke, 1998; Read & Tilley, 2000; Scott & Clarke, 2000). Indeed, the research literature is filled with a long history of cases where problem-oriented policing programs tend to lean toward traditional methods and where the problem-solving process is weak (Goldstein & Susmilch, 1982; Eck & Spelman, 1987; Buerger, 1994; Capowich, Roehl & Andrews, 1995; Read & Tilley, 2000). In his review of several hundred submissions for the Police Executive Research Forum's Herman Goldstein Award for Excellence in Problem-Oriented Policing, Clarke (1998) laments that many problem-oriented policing projects bear little resemblance to Goldstein's original definition. Eck (2000) comments that contemporary problem-oriented policing is but a shadow of the original concept.

In this chapter, we examine the nature of problem solving and problem-oriented policing as it is practiced in the field. Our main conclusion is that there is a disconnect between the rhetoric and reality of problem-oriented policing, and that this is not likely to change irrespective of the efforts of scholars and policy makers. Indeed, we take a very different approach to this problem than others who have examined the deficiencies of problem-oriented approaches. We argue that there is much evidence that what might be called "shallow" problem solving can be effective in combating crime problems. This being the case, we question whether the pursuit of problem-oriented policing, as it has been modeled by Goldstein and others, should be abandoned in favor of the achievement of a more realistic type of problem solving. While less satisfying for scholars, it is what the police have tended to do, and it has been found to lead to real crime prevention benefits.

DEFINING THE PROBLEM

To understand our argument, it is useful to review the problems that police encounter at each stage of the well-known SARA model (Scanning, Analysis, Response, Assessment) that was developed in Newport News, Virginia, to crystallize the problem-oriented process (Eck & Spelman, 1987). It is worth noting here that other models have been developed to guide police officers in their problem-solving efforts. For instance, Ekblom (2005) proposed the "5Is" (Intelligence, Intervention, Implementation, Involvement, Impact) as a better way to capture what problem-oriented policing calls for and ideally does. SARA, however, remains the most influential model for implementing problem-oriented policing. In practice, many problem-oriented policing projects that follow the SARA model do not follow its linear stepwise approach. Rather, the steps tend to occur simultaneously or in a fashion by which officers move back and forth between scanning, analysis, and responses (Capowich & Roehl, 1994; Braga, 1997; Cordner & Biebel, 2005). Nevertheless, the model provides a useful way to structure our discussion of the disconnect between principles and practice in the problem-oriented policing process.

Scanning

Scanning involves the identification of problems that are worth looking at because they are important and amenable to solution. Herman Goldstein (1990) suggests that the definition of problems be at the street level of analysis and not be restricted by preconceived typologies. Goldstein further clarifies what is meant by a problem by specifying the term as "a cluster of similar, related, or recurring incidents rather than a single incident; a substantive community concern; or a unit of police business" (1990: 66). To ensure that problems are specified correctly, it is important to break down larger categories of crime into more specific kinds of offenses (Clarke, 1997). For example, auto theft should be further specified into particular types of auto theft such as "joy riding" or "stripping for auto parts." Close analysis of these specific problems may lead to very different types of intervention that might be more appropriate for each component of an auto theft problem when compared to a more general approach.

There are many ways a problem might be nominated for police attention. A police officer may rely upon his or her informal knowledge of a community to identify a problem that he or she thinks is important to the well-being of the community. Another approach to identifying problems is through consultation with community groups of different kinds, including other government agencies. Another possibility is to identify problems from the examination of citizen calls for service coming in to a police department. This approach is implicitly recommended by those who advocate "repeat call analysis" in the identification of crime "hot spots" (Sherman & Weisburd, 1988; Sherman, Gartin & Buerger, 1989; Weisburd & Mazerolle, 2000). The notion is that citizens will let the police know what problems are concerning them by making calls as individuals. Problems can be identified by examining the distribution of crime incidents at specific public or private places such as stores, bars, restaurants, shopping malls, ATM locations, apartment buildings, and other facilities (Clarke & Eck, 2007).

Crime mapping remains a very popular way for police departments to identify existing crime problems (Weisburd, Mastrofski & Greenspan, 2001) and, relatedly, hot spots policing has diffused widely among police departments as a strategy to address identified high-crime places (Weisburd & Lum, 2005). Problem-oriented policing has been applied to address crime hot spots with the available evaluation evidence suggesting stronger crime prevention impacts relative to simply increasing traditional policing activities in targeted high-crime places (Braga, Papachristos & Hureau, 2014).

Relative to their performance in other phases of the process, police officers are generally good at identifying problems (Bynum, 2001). However, Clarke (1998) suggests that problem-oriented police officers often fail to make appropriate specifications of the problems they are addressing in one of two ways: they either undertake a project that is too small or too big. Small, beat-level projects, such as dealing with a confused lonely old man who is seeking some daily companionship by repeatedly calling the police for a variety of concerns, may be better handled as a citywide project addressing older citizens who live alone and generate a large number of calls for trivial matters (Clarke, 1998). Some overly ambitious initiatives, such as dealing with "gang delinquency" or focusing on a "problem neighborhood," do not represent a single problem, but a collection of problems. For example, in the "problem neighborhood," there could be a diverse set of problems such as drug markets, auto theft, and domestic violence. These are separate problems that require individual attention. Problems in problem-oriented policing programs are often broadly identified; this destroys the discrete problem focus of the project and leads to a lack of direction at the beginning of analysis (Clarke, 1998).

Analysis

The analysis phase challenges police officers to analyze the causes of problems behind a string of crime incidents or substantive community concern. Once the underlying conditions that give rise to crime problems are known, police officers develop and implement appropriate responses. The challenge to police officers is to go beyond the analysis that naturally occurs to them; namely, to find the places and times where particular offenses are likely to occur, and to identify the offenders who are likely to be responsible for the crimes. Although these approaches have had some operational success, this type of analysis usually produces directed patrol operations or a focus on repeat offenders. The idea of analysis was intended to go beyond this. Unfortunately, as Boba (2003) observes, while problem-oriented policing has blossomed in both concept and practice, problem analysis has been the slowest part of the process to develop. In his twenty-year review of problem-oriented policing, Michael Scott (2000) concludes that problem analysis remains the aspect of problem-oriented policing that is most in need of improvement. The Police Executive Research Forum's national assessment of the US Community Oriented Policing Services (COPS)-sponsored "Problem Solving Partnerships" program also found that problem analysis was the weakest phase of the problem-oriented policing process (PERF, 2000).

Bynum (2001) suggests that police have difficulty clearly defining problems, properly using data sources, conducting comprehensive analyses, and implementing analysis-driven responses. Some officers skip the analysis phase or conduct an overly simple analysis that does not adequately dissect the problem or does not use relevant information from other agencies (such as hospitals, schools, and private businesses) (Clarke, 1998). Based on his extensive experience with police departments implementing problem-oriented policing, Eck (2000) suggests that much problem analysis consists of a simple examination of police data coupled with the officer's working experience with the problem. In their analysis of problem-oriented initiatives in forty-three police departments in England and Wales, Read and Tilley (2000) found that problem analysis was generally weak with many initiatives accepting the definition of a problem at face value, using only short-term data to unravel the nature of the problem, and failing to adequately examine the genesis of the crime problems.

Analyzing problems at crime hot spots may present a particularly vexing challenge to problem-oriented police officers. Given the contemporary popularity of crime mapping in the identification of problems worthy of police attention, we feel that it is important to highlight the difficulties in analyzing problems at hot spots. High-activity crime places tend to have multiple problems and the problems at crime places can be quite complex and involved. In their close analysis of hot spots in Minneapolis, Weisburd and his colleagues (1992) suggest that a heterogeneous mix of crime types occur at high activity crime places rather than a concentration of one type of crime occurring at a place. In their examination of problem-oriented policing in San Diego, Capowich and Roehl (1994: 144) observed that multiple problems tend to coincide at places and report, "at the beat level, there are no pure cases in which the problem can be captured under a single classification. The range of problems is wide, with each presenting unique circumstances." In Oakland's Beat Health program to deal with drug nuisance locations, officers encountered difficulties unraveling what was happening at a place and deciding how it should be addressed (Green, 1996). Evaluations of problem-oriented policing programs to control crime hot spots in Lowell (Braga & Bond, 2008) and Boston (Braga, Hureau & Papachristos, 2011), Massachusetts, also noted the multitude of identified problems at each crime place and the challenges faced by officers in analyzing these problems.

In the Jersey City (NJ) problem-oriented policing in violent crime hot spots experiment, the number of identified problems per place ranged from three to seven, with a mean of 4.7 problems per place (Braga, 1997; Braga et al., 1999). Table 8.1 presents the problems identified by officers for further analysis and the key characteristics of violent crime hot spots in the Jersey City problem-oriented policing experiment. From their training and the reading materials made available to them, the problem-oriented officers expected that they would be preventing violence at each place by focusing on very specific underlying characteristics or situational factors. After examining places closely, the officers observed that they would be controlling a multitude of crime problems. All twelve places were perceived to suffer from social disorder problems such as loitering, public drinking, and panhandling; eleven places suffered from physical disorder such as trash-filled streets, vacant lots, and abandoned buildings. Seven places had problems with illicit drug selling and three places had problems with property crimes.

Across and within places in the Jersey City problem-oriented policing experiment, few problems were analyzed thoroughly (Braga, 1997). Eck and Spelman (1987) suggest two classifications for the depth of problem analysis:

TABLE 8.1 *Problems and Characteristics of Twelve Violent Crime Places*

Place	Problems	Relevant Characteristics
1	Assault and robbery of commuters	Train and bus terminals
	Shoplifting	Restaurants and retail stores
	Pick-pocketing	Abandoned buildings
	Drug selling	Abandoned automobiles
	Homeless loitering and panhandling	Holes in fences around terminal
	Disorderly groups of youths	Poor lighting
	Physical disorder	Piles of lumber used by loiterers
		Piles of trash deposited by illegal dumpers
2	Street fights	Major thoroughfare
	Drug market	Bodega
	Public drinking and drug use	Tavern
	Disorderly groups of youths	Abandoned buildings
	Physical disorder	Vacant lot
3	Assault and robbery of college students	College campus
	Burglary and larceny on campus	Multiple bus stops
	Loitering	Trash-strewn vacant lot with tall weeds
	Minor drug selling	Low-income apartment building
	Physical disorder	Trash-strewn alley
		Poor lighting
4	Assault and robbery of students	Grammar/middle school
	Car jacking	Community college
	Homeless loiterers	Retail stores
	Disorderly groups of youths	Major intersection
5	Robbery of retail stores	Retail stores
	Street fights	Restaurants
	Disorderly groups of youths	Major thoroughfare
	Public drinking	Poor lighting
	Physical disorder	
6	Drug market	Liquor store
	Loitering	Major thoroughfare
	Public drinking	Poor lighting
	Physical disorder	
7	Robbery of elderly	Senior citizen housing complex
	Disorderly groups of youths	Low-income housing project
	Physical disorder	Interstitial area between middle- and lower-class neighborhoods
		Poor lighting
		Bus stop
8	Drug market	Large low-income apartment building
	Street fights	Tavern
	Bar fights	Retail stores

(continued)

TABLE 8.1 (*continued*)

Place	Problems	Relevant Characteristics
	Disorderly groups loitering	
	Public drinking	
	Physical disorder	
9	Active indoor and outdoor drug market	Abandoned buildings
	Street fights	Low-income apartment building
	Loitering	Major thoroughfare
	Public drinking	Vacant lots
	Physical disorder	
10	Robbery of convenience stores	Retail stores
	Disorderly groups of youths	Major thoroughfare
	Loitering	Trash-strewn streets
	Burglaries	
	Physical disorder	
11	Street fights	Abandoned buildings
	Drug market	Residential neighborhood
	Public drinking	Poor lighting
	Loitering	Vacant lots
	Physical disorder	Graffiti
		Trash-strewn streets
12	Drug market	Park
	Bar fights	Taverns
	Street fights	Poor lighting
	Public drinking	Retail stores and restaurants
	Loitering	Trash-strewn streets
	Disorderly groups of youths	
	Physical disorder	

limited analysis and extended analysis. Eck and Spelman (1987) grouped problem-solving efforts by the Newport News (VA) Police Department by determining whether there were obvious information sources that were not used, given the nature of the problem; if there were not any obvious unused sources, the effort was classified as extended. Using these definitions, slightly less than one third (31.1 per cent; 19 of 61) of the identified problems in the Jersey City study received what could be described as an extended analysis. It must be noted that, for certain problems, a superficial analysis was all that was necessary (e.g., alleviating a trash problem by recognizing that there were not any trash receptacles at the place). Weak problem analyses occurred for two reasons. First, at ten of twelve places, the officers believed that they "knew what was going on" based on their working knowledge and "on the spot" appraisals of problems. Second, the officers believed that most of the street crime at the place could be linked directly or indirectly to the physical and social disorder of a place. From their problem-oriented policing training, the officers were familiar with the "broken windows" thesis and much preferred the simplicity of a general plan to restore order and reduce crime at places over the specifics of the SARA model to control the multiple and interrelated problems of a place. Rather than conducting rigorous analysis of crime problems and developing tailor-made solutions, the officers generally attempted to control their places via aggressive order maintenance and making physical improvements such as securing vacant lots or removing trash from the street.

Responses

After a problem has been clearly defined and analyzed, police officers confront the challenge of developing a plausibly effective response. The development of appropriate responses is closely linked with the analysis that is performed. The analysis reveals the potential targets for an intervention, and it is at least partly the idea about what form the intervention might take that suggests important lines of analysis. As such, the reason police often look at places and times where crimes are committed is that they are already imagining that an effective way to prevent the crimes would be to get officers on the scene through directed patrols. The reason they often look for the likely offender is that they think that the most effective and just response to a crime problem would be to arrest and incapacitate the offender. However, the concept of "problem-oriented policing" as envisioned by Herman Goldstein (1990), calls on the police to make a much more "uninhibited" search for possible responses and not to limit themselves to getting officers in the right places at the right times, or identifying and arresting the offender (although both may be valuable responses). Effective responses often depend on getting other people to take actions that reduce the opportunities for criminal offending, or to mobilize informal social control to drive offenders away from certain locations.

Newer intelligence-led policing and predictive policing models overlap with problem-oriented policing in the analysis of crime problems to drive decision-making on police deployments and crime prevention strategies. Intelligence-led policing challenges police departments to enhance criminal intelligence and crime data collection and analysis techniques to improve the strategic management of crime problems, especially those generated by prolific and serious offenders (Ratcliffe, 2016). Predictive policing uses statistical algorithms that draw on different types of data to anticipate where and when crime might occur and to identify patterns among past criminal incidents (Perry et al., 2013; Ratcliffe, 2014). To date, unfortunately, most police crime prevention strategies generated through enhanced analyses in intelligence-led and predictive policing models have been comprised of traditional enforcement activities rather than nuanced responses rooted in underlying conditions and dynamics that give rise to recurring crime problems (Eck, Chapter 7 in this volume; Boba, Chapter 16 in this volume).

The available research evidence suggests that the responses of many problem-oriented policing projects rely heavily upon traditional police tactics (such as arrests, surveillance, and crackdowns) and neglect the wider range of available alternative responses (Clarke, 1998). Many evaluations of problem-oriented policing efforts have documented a preponderance of traditional policing tactics (see, e.g., Capowich & Roehl, 1994; Cordner, 1994). Read and Tilley (2000) found that officers selected certain responses prior to, or in spite of, analysis; failed to think through the need for a sustained crime reduction; failed to think through the mechanisms by which the response could have a measurable impact; failed to fully involve partners; narrowly focused responses, usually on offenders; as well as a number of other weakness in the response development process. Cordner (1998) observed that some problem-oriented policing projects gravitate toward faddish responses rather than implementing a response that truly fits the nature of the problem.

As suggested above, the complexity of problems at crime hot spots may discourage police officers from developing innovative responses. For example, frustrated narcotics officers may choose to chase drug dealers at a place rather than implementing a plan to change the multiple underlying characteristics of a place that make it an attractive spot for illicit drug sales (Green, 1996; Eck & Wartell, 1998; Taylor, 1998). In the Jersey City problem-oriented policing experiment, the numerous responses implemented at the violent crime hot spots mirrored the complexity of the problems they were intended to control (Braga, 1997). Twenty-eight types of responses were implemented across the places (Table 8.2). The number of responses per place ranged from one to twelve, with a mean of 6.7 responses per place. Traditional policing tactics were used at all places and comprised between 14 percent (Place 7) and 100 percent (Place 4 and Place 10) of the responses per place. On average, almost a third (31.1 per cent) of the responses implemented per place involved traditional enforcement. Situational interventions intended to modify the characteristics of a place were implemented at ten of twelve treatment places. The situational strategies varied according to the nuances of the problems at places (e.g., razing an abandoned building or the code inspection of a tavern). However, at all locations, a package of aggressive order maintenance interventions was used to control the social disorder of the places. These tactics included repeat foot and radio car patrols, dispersing groups of loiterers, issuing summons for public drinking, "stop and frisks" of suspicious persons, and so on. At nine places, drug enforcement was used to disrupt drug sales at the place. The officers believed that an increased presence and the harassment of illicit users of the place would quell egregious social disorder, at least temporarily, until a better plan could be developed and implemented. According to the officers, aggressive order maintenance was a treatment that could affect all illicit activity no matter what the variation: drug selling, loitering by disorderly youth, homeless panhandlers, predatory robbers – all could be affected by an increased presence in a bounded geographical area. The Jersey

TABLE 8.2 *Responses to Problems at Violent Crime Places*

Place	Responses
1	Aggressive order maintenance to disperse loitering homeless and disorderly youths
	Drug enforcement to disrupt street-level drug sales around train and bus terminal
	Robbery investigation to apprehend robbery crew
	Public works removed trash at place to discourage illegal dumping
	Hung "No dumping – Police take notice" sign to discourage illegal dumping
	Fixed holes in fence to secure access to the bus and train terminal
	Boarded and fenced abandoned buildings to prevent drug activity and squatting
	Helped homeless find shelter and substance abuse treatment
	Dispensed crime prevention literature to commuters
	Removed piles of lumber to discourage loitering
2	Aggressive order maintenance to disperse groups of disorderly youths
	Drug enforcement to disrupt street-level drug sales on street corner and from bodega
	Required store owners to clean trash from store fronts
	Erected fences to secure vacant lot from illicit drug activity
	Cleaned vacant lot
	Boarded and fenced abandoned buildings to prevent drug activity
	Removed drug-selling crew's stashed guns
	Housing code enforcement to repair dilapidated building
	Eviction of drug seller from low-income apartment at place
	Surveillance of drug offenders using videotapes
3	Aggressive order maintenance to disperse loiterers from vacant lot and apartment building area
	Drug enforcement to disrupt street-level drug sales from vacant lot, alley, and apartment building
	Robbery investigation to apprehend robbery crew
	Cut weeds and removed trash from vacant lot
	Erected fence around vacant lot to prevent drug sales and robberies
	Public works removed trash and drug paraphernalia from alley
	Public works trimmed trees to increase lighting around vacant lot, alley, and apartment building
	Dispensed crime prevention literature to students and campus security
	Improved apartment building security by adding new door locks; prevented access to drug dealers
4	Aggressive order maintenance to disperse vagrants and groups of disorderly youths
	Directed patrol before and after school hours
	Robbery investigation to apprehend robbery crew
5	Aggressive order maintenance to disperse groups of disorderly youths
	Required store owners to clean store fronts

(*continued*)

TABLE 8.2 (*continued*)

Place	Responses
	Changed style of trash cans to prevent loitering
6	Aggressive order maintenance to disperse loiterers
	Drug enforcement to disrupt street-level drug sales in front of liquor store
	Required store owners to clean store fronts
	Opened and cleaned vacant lot to allow neighborhood kids to play basketball
	Repaired street lights to increase lighting in area
	Housing code enforcement to clean apartment building used as stash house
7	Aggressive order maintenance to disperse loitering groups of disorderly youths
	Housing code enforcement to remove trash from within housing project
	Evicted squatters and drug sellers from unoccupied apartments in low-income housing project
	Public works removed trash from around low-income housing project
	Improved housing project security by adding new locks to doors; prevented access to drug dealers
	Improved lighting around housing project by installing floodlights and replacing streetlights
	Enforced parking ordinances around housing project to impound cars of drug sellers and buyers
8	Aggressive order maintenance to disperse loiterers
	Intensive drug enforcement to disrupt street-level sales and dismantle major drug organization
	Required store owners to clean store fronts
	Code investigation of taverns
9	Aggressive order maintenance to disperse loiterers
	Drug enforcement to disrupt street-level drug sales
	Housing code enforcement to clean up low-income property
	Evicted drug sellers from low-income apartment building
	Boarded and fenced abandoned buildings to prevent drug activity
	Razed abandoned buildings
	Cleaned vacant lots
	Public works removed trash from street
	Erected fences around vacant lots to secure from drug activity
	Surveillance of offenders at place using video tapes
	Hung sign "No drug selling – Area under video surveillance by police"
10	Aggressive order maintenance to disperse groups of disorderly youths
11	Aggressive order maintenance to disperse loiterers
	Drug enforcement to disrupt street-level drug sales
	Surveillance of offenders at place using video tapes
	Hung sign "No public drinking – Area under video surveillance by police"
	Public works trimmed trees to increase lighting in area
	Boarded and fenced abandoned buildings to prevent drug activity
	Cleaned vacant lot
	Erected fence around vacant lot to secure from drug activity

TABLE 8.2 *(continued)*

Place	Responses
	Removed graffiti from building
	Mobilized residents to keep streets clean in front of their homes
	Public works removed trash from street
	Added trash receptacles to prevent litter
12	Aggressive order maintenance to disperse loiterers and groups of disorderly youth
	Drug enforcement to disrupt drug sales at park and in and around bars
	Code investigation of taverns; one bar shut down and other bar owners discontinue sales of "take-out" alcohol
	Required storeowners to clean storefronts

City officers much preferred this strategy to the additional work necessary to implement alternative situational responses (Braga, 1997).

Assessment

The crucial last step in the practice of problem-oriented policing is to assess the impact the intervention has had on the problem it was supposed to solve. Assessment is important for at least two different reasons. The first is to ensure that police remain accountable for their performance and for their use of resources. Citizens and their representatives want to know how the money and freedom they surrendered to the police are being used, and whether important results in the form of less crime, enhanced security, or increased citizen satisfaction with the police has been achieved. A second reason assessment is important is to allow the police to learn about what methods are effective in dealing with particular problems. Unless the police check to see whether their efforts produced a result, it will be hard for them to improve their practices.

The degree of rigor applied to the assessment of problem-oriented initiatives will necessarily vary across the size and overall importance of the problems addressed (Clarke, 1998). Serious, large and recurrent problems such as controlling gang violence or handling domestic disputes deserve highly rigorous examinations. Other problems that are less serious, or common, such as a lonely elderly person making repeat calls to the police for companionship, are obviously not worth such close examinations. Unfortunately, Scott and Clarke (2000) observe that assessment of responses is rare and, when undertaken, it is usually cursory and limited to anecdotal or impressionistic data.

Clarke's (1998: 319–320) review of submissions for the Herman Goldstein award provides a good summary of the common limitations of assessments performed by police departments engaged in problem-oriented policing projects:

- Police report reductions in calls for service or arrests without relating the results to specific actions taken. In other words, the police frequently fail to examine whether variations in "dosage levels" of the response correlate with variations in relevant crime statistics.
- Police consider assessment only as an afterthought, rather than building it into the original outline of the project.
- Police fail to present any control data. For example, if some action has been taken in one location that appears to have produced a decrease in the number of calls for service, the police do not generally document what, if anything, happened in a similar nearby location where no action was taken.
- On the rare occasion when control data are presented, police fail to ensure that the control is adequate. For example, the control location may be so different from the original site that it is impossible to conclude anything from the comparison.
- Police fail to study displacement. Many agencies do not realize that their response may simply have pushed the problem elsewhere.

It is worth noting here that the existing program evaluation evidence base for problem-oriented policing largely consists of weaker evaluation studies while rigorous studies comprise a very small group (Braga, 2010; Weisburd & Majmundar, 2018). Indeed, Weisburd et al. (2010) only identified ten evaluations that met the minimum methodological standards of their systematic review – a comparison group that did not receive the problem-oriented policing treatment. Their systematic review also identified forty-five before/after intervention studies without a strong control or comparison group. Weak evaluations, unfortunately, provide less valid answers to policy questions when compared to well-designed quasi-experiments and randomized controlled trials (Weisburd, Lum & Petrosino, 2001; Shadish, Cook & Campbell, 2002). When the evaluation evidence base is largely informed by weak designs, practitioners risk implementing certain treatments or programs as effective crime prevention practices when they are not; this can lead to significant economic and social costs (see, e.g., Boruch, 1975; Weisburd, 2003). Beyond improving officer assessments of specific problem-oriented policing projects implemented by local police departments, the rigor of more formal problem-oriented policing program evaluations needs to be improved.

Is "Shallow" Problem Solving Enough?

Despite the gap between the desired application of the approach and its actual implementation, there is considerable evidence that problem-oriented policing is effective in preventing crime (see, e.g., Skogan & Frydl, 2004; Weisburd & Eck, 2004; Braga, 2008; Weisburd et al., 2010; Weisburd & Majmundar,

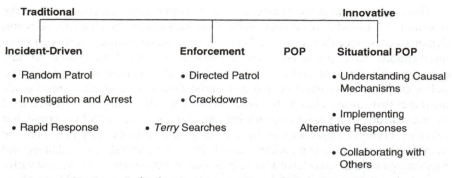

FIGURE 8.1 Continuum of Police Strategies to Control High-Crime Places

2018). This suggests that problem-oriented policing interventions may not need to be implemented in the ways envisioned by Herman Goldstein in order to produce a crime prevention effect. Perhaps, simply focusing police resources on identifiable risks that come to the attention of problem-oriented policing projects, such as high-activity offenders, repeat victims, and crime hot spots, may be enough to produce crime control gains. Therefore, we think that it is critically important to refine and extend current definitions of police crime prevention efforts.

Given the long police tradition of responding to high-crime locations and the current popularity of hot spots policing, our concluding discussion focuses on police crime efforts at high-crime places. These concepts could also be applied to offender- and victim-focused responses. Figure 8.1 presents a continuum of strategies, ranging from traditional to innovative, that police can use to control crime at high-crime places. At one extreme, police departments use traditional, incident-driven strategies to control crime in the community. Although these activities coincidentally cluster in space and time, these ad-hoc enforcement strategies are not specifically targeted at problem places and the limitations of this approach are, by now, well known. Based on Eck's (1993) examination of alternative futures for problem-oriented policing, problem-solving efforts can be divided into "enforcement" and "situational" problem-oriented policing programs. "Enforcement" problem-oriented policing interventions have moved the police response forward by focusing mostly traditional tactics at high-risk times and locations. Although these programs are "problem-oriented" in a global way, their tactics do not employ the individualized treatments to crime problems advocated by Herman Goldstein (1990). These interventions have included optimizing patrol time in hot spots (Koper, 1995; Sherman & Weisburd, 1995), conducting aggressive *Terry* searches for guns in areas that are known for high levels of firearms violence (Sherman, Shaw & Rogan, 1995), and implementing systematic crackdowns in street-level drug markets (Weisburd & Green, 1995).

These enforcement problem-oriented policing interventions focus mainly on the time and location of crime events, rather than focusing on the characteristics and dynamics of a place that make it a hot spot for criminal activity. Although these interventions have produced crime control gains and have added to law enforcement's array of crime prevention tools, it is commonly assumed that police could be more effective if they focused their efforts on the criminogenic attributes that cause a place to be "hot." In other words, adding an increased level of guardianship at a place by optimizing patrol is a step in controlling crime, but reducing criminal opportunities by changing site features, facilities, and the management at a place (e.g., adding streetlights, razing abandoned buildings, and mobilizing residents) may have a more profound effect on crime. At the innovative end of the continuum is Goldstein's (1990) vision of "situational" problem-oriented policing: members of police agencies undertake thorough analysis of crime problems at places, collaborate with community members and other city agencies, and conduct a broad search for situational responses to problems.

Similar to other studies, translating problem-oriented policing theory into practice was difficult for Jersey City problem-oriented police officers. On the continuum of police strategies to control high-activity crime places, the program as implemented would fit between enforcement and situational problem-oriented interventions (see Figure 8.1). Despite falling short of Goldstein's vision, the Jersey City problem-oriented policing program was still found to be effective in preventing crime (Braga et al., 1999). Some scholars would describe the efforts of the Jersey City police officers as "problem solving" rather than problem-oriented policing (Cordner, 1998). Problem solving is a "shallow" version of problem-oriented policing as these efforts are smaller in scope, involve rudimentary analysis, and lack formal assessments. According to Cordner (1998), problem solving better describes what an officer does to handle a particular dispute or drug house rather than initiatives to deal with problems of substantial magnitude like prostitution in a downtown area and thefts from autos in parking lots. Enforcement problem-oriented initiatives would also fit what we would consider shallow problem solving. When the complexities of crime problems at places and the difficulties police officers experience in unraveling these problems and implementing individualized responses are considered, shallow problem solving can be a very practical way for police departments to prevent crimes at places. And, as suggested by a growing evidence base, shallow problem-solving efforts to control high-crime locations do seem to control crime and disorder problems (e.g., see Braga & Bond, 2008; Braga, Hureau & Papachristos, 2011).

Should We Expect Police Agencies to Develop More In-Depth Problem Solving?

Problem-oriented policing advocates lament the state-of-the-art in problem solving and offer a laundry list of suggestions to improve the capacity of police agencies to engage strategic problem solving (see, e.g., Scott, 2000; Boba, 2003; Braga, 2008). Is it realistic to expect police agencies to develop their capacity to conduct more in-depth problem-oriented policing so their officers can go beyond the shallow problem solving that is practiced in the field? Cordner and Biebel (2005) found that, despite fifteen years of national promotion and a concerted effort at implementation within the San Diego Police Department, problem-oriented policing as practiced by ordinary police officers fell far short of the ideal model. Cordner and Biebel (2005) suggest that it may be unreasonable to expect every police officer to continuously engage in full-fledged problem-oriented policing.

We believe that it is unlikely that police agencies will enhance their problem-solving efforts in the foreseeable future. There seems to be, at least, two obstacles. First, the hierarchical organizational structure of policing in itself tends to inhibit innovation and creativity. In their close examination of CompStat, Willis, Mastrofski, and Weisburd (2004) found that, while the program holds out the promise of allowing police agencies to adopt innovative technologies and problem-solving techniques, it actually hindered innovative problem solving while strengthening the existing hierarchy through the added pressure of increased internal accountability. Officers were reluctant to brainstorm problem-solving approaches during CompStat meetings for fear of undermining authority or the credibility of their colleagues. Moreover, the danger of "looking bad" in front of superior officers discouraged middle managers from pursuing more creative crime strategies with a higher risk of failure.

Second, the organizational culture of policing is resistant to this in-depth approach to problem solving. The community policing movement that emerged in the 1980s stressed greater police recognition of the role of the community and emphasized "decentralization" and "debureaucratization" to empower rank and file officers to make decisions about how to better serve the neighborhoods to which they were assigned (Skolnick & Bayley, 1986; Mastrofski, 1998). Weisburd and his colleagues (2003) suggest that the popularity and rapid diffusion of CompStat programs across larger police departments in the United States during the 1990s could be interpreted as an effort to maintain and reinforce traditional police structures rather than an attempt to truly reform American policing. The rapid rise of CompStat within police agencies did not enhance their strategic problem-solving capacity at the beat level as CompStat departments were found to be reluctant to relinquish power that would decentralize some key elements of decision making such as allowing middle managers to determine beat boundaries and staffing levels, enhancing operational flexibility, and risk going beyond the standard tool kit of police tactics and strategies (Weisburd et al., 2003). The overall effect of the spread of CompStat, whether intended or not, was to reinforce the traditional bureaucratic model of command and control.

More generally, the type of in-depth problem solving that Goldstein and other problem-oriented policing advocates have proposed seems unrealistic in the real world of policing, especially at the street level where it is often envisioned. In the real world of police organizations, community and problem-oriented police officers rarely have the latitude necessary to assess and respond to problems creatively. As William Bratton (1998: 199) observed in his assessment of community policing in New York City at the beginning of his tenure, "street-level police officers were never going to be empowered to follow through." CompStat was offered as a solution to this problem, but the ability of the rank and file officer to make decisions changed little as middle managers were held accountable for achieving organizational goals of successful crime control (Willis et al., 2004). Of course, decentralizing decision-making power to line-level officers does not guarantee effective problem solving. In their assessment of problem solving in Chicago, a police department well known for its efforts to decentralize their organization to facilitate community policing, Skogan and his colleagues (1999: 231) gave a failing grade ranging from "struggling" to "woeful" for problem solving efforts in 40 per cent of the beats they studied. Inadequate management, poor leadership and vision, lack of training, and weak performance measures were among the operational problems identified as affecting problem solving in the poorly performing beats (Skogan et al., 1999).

CONCLUSION

Problem-oriented policing represents an important innovation in American policing. However, as we have illustrated, the practice of problem-oriented policing too often falls short of the principles suggested by Herman Goldstein (1990). Given the extensive literature on the gap between principles and practice, it seems unrealistic to expect line-level officers to conduct in-depth problem-oriented policing as their routine way of dealing with crime problems. Successful applications of problem-oriented policing usually involve larger-scale problems, the involvement of academic researchers and crime analysis units, and the solid support of the police command staff to implement alternative responses. The Boston Police Department's Operation Ceasefire intervention to prevent gang violence (Braga et al., 2001; Braga, Hureau & Papachristos, 2014), the Newport News Police Department's efforts to reduce thefts from cars parked in shipyard parking lots (Eck & Spelman, 1987), and the Charlotte-Mecklenburg Police Department's program to reduce theft from construction sites (Clarke & Goldstein, 2002) involved resources that were far beyond the reach of the rank and file police officer.

Research evidence suggests that shallow problem-solving efforts, ranging from focused enforcement efforts in high-risk places and at high-risk times to problem solving with weak analyses, mostly traditional responses, and limited assessments, are enough to prevent crime. Perhaps it is time to stop trying to achieve the ideal of strategic problem-oriented policing at the street level and embrace the reality of what has been shown to lead to real crime prevention value – ad hoc shallow problem-solving efforts that focus police on high-risk places, situations, and individuals. We suggest that line-level officers should be encourageD to problem solve at the beat level and more sophisticated problem-oriented policing projects should be engaged higher up in the organization with the support of a crime analysis unit and in collaboration with other criminal justice agencies, academic researchers, and community-based groups. However, it is time for police practitioners and policy makers to set aside the fantasy of street-level problem-oriented policing and embrace the reality of what they can expect from the beat officer in the development of crime prevention plans at the street level.

REFERENCES

Boba, R. (2003). *Problem Analysis in Policing*. Washington, DC: Police Foundation.
Boruch, R. (1975). On common contentions about randomized field experiments. In R. Boruch, & H. Reicken (eds.), *Experimental Testing of Public Policy: The Proceedings of the 1974 Social Sciences Research Council Conference on Social Experimentation*. Boulder, CO: Westview Press.
Braga, A. A. (1997). Solving Violent Crime Problems: An Evaluation of the Jersey City Police Department's Pilot Program to Control Violent Places. Doctoral Dissertation, Rutgers University. Ann Arbor, MI: University Microfilm International.
Braga, A. A. (2008). *Problem-Oriented Policing and Crime Prevention*. Second edition. Monsey, NY: Criminal Justice Press.
Braga, A. A. (2010). Setting a higher standard for the evaluation of problem-oriented policing initiatives. *Criminology & Public Policy*, 9(1), 173–182.
Braga, A. A., & Bond, B. (2008). Policing crime and disorder hot spots: A randomized controlled trial. *Criminology*, 46(3), 577–608.
Braga, A. A., Kennedy, D., Waring, E., & Piehl, A. (2001). Problem-oriented policing, deterrence, and youth violence: An evaluation of Boston's Operation Ceasefire. *Journal of Research in Crime and Delinquency*, 38, 195–225.
Braga, A. A., Hureau, D., & Papachristos, A. (2011). An ex-post-facto evaluation framework for place-based police interventions. *Evaluation Review*, 35(6), 592–626.
Braga, A. A., Hureau, D., & Papachristos, A. (2014). Deterring gang-involved gun violence: Measuring the impact of Boston's Operation Ceasefire on street gang behavior. *Journal of Quantitative Criminology*, 30(1), 113–139.
Braga, A. A., Papachristos, A., & Hureau, D. (2014). The effects of hot spots policing on crime: An updated systematic review and meta-analysis. *Justice Quarterly*, 31(4), 633–663.
Braga, A. A., Weisburd, D., Waring, E., Green-Mazerolle, L., Spelman, W., & Gajewski, F. (1999). Problem-oriented policing in violent crime places: A randomized controlled experiment. *Criminology*, 37, 541–580.
Bratton, W. (1998). *Turnaround: How America's Top Cop Reversed the Crime Epidemic*. New York: Random House.
Buerger, M. (1994). The problems of problem-solving: Resistance, interdependencies, and conflicting interests. *American Journal of Police*, 13, 1–36.
Bynum, T. (2001). *Using Analysis for Problem-solving: A Guidebook for Law Enforcement*. Washington, DC: Office of Community Oriented Policing Services, US Department of Justice.

Capowich, G., & Roehl, J. (1994). Problem-oriented policing: Actions and effectiveness in San Diego. In D. Rosenbaum (ed.), *The Challenge of Community Policing: Testing the Promises*. Thousand Oaks, CA: Sage Publications.

Capowich, G., J. Roehl, & C. Andrews. (1995). *Evaluating Problem-Oriented Policing Outcomes in Tulsa and San Diego*. Final Report to the National Institute of Justice. Alexandria, VA: Institute for Social Analysis.

Clarke, R. (ed.). (1997). *Situational Crime Prevention: Successful Case Studies*. 2nd edition. Albany, NY: Harrow and Heston.

Clarke, R. (1998). Defining police strategies: Problem solving, problem-oriented policing and community-oriented policing. In T. O'Connor Shelley, & A. C. Grant (eds.), *Problem-Oriented Policing: Crime-Specific Problems, Critical Issues, and Making POP Work*. Washington, DC: Police Executive Research Forum.

Clarke, R., & Eck, J. E. (2007). *Understanding Risky Facilities*. Problem-Oriented Guides for Police, Problem Solving Tools Series, no. 6. Washington, DC: US Department of Justice, Office of Community Oriented Policing Services.

Clarke, R., & Goldstein, H. (2002). Reducing theft at construction sites: Lessons from a problem-oriented project. In N. Tilley (ed.), *Analysis for Crime Prevention*. New York: Criminal Justice Press.

Cordner, G. (1994). Foot patrol without community policing: Law and order in public housing. In D. Rosenbaum (ed.), *The Challenge of Community Policing: Testing the Promises*. Thousand Oaks, CA: Sage Publications.

Cordner, G. (1998). Problem-oriented policing vs. zero tolerance. In T. O'Connor Shelley, & A. C. Grant (eds.), *Problem-Oriented Policing: Crime-Specific Problems, Critical Issues, and Making POP Work*. Washington, DC: Police Executive Research Forum.

Cordner, G., & Biebel, E. (2005). Problem-oriented policing in practice. *Criminology & Public Policy*, 4(1), 155–180.

Eck, J. E. (1993). Alternative futures for policing. In D. Weisburd, & C. Uchida (eds.), *Police Innovation and Control of the Police: Problems of Law, Order, and Community*. New York: Springer-Verlag.

Eck, J. E. (2000). Problem-oriented policing and its problems: The means over ends syndrome strikes back and the return of the problem-solver. Unpublished manuscript. Cincinnati, OH: University of Cincinnati.

Eck, J. E., & Spelman, W. (1987). *Problem-Solving: Problem-Oriented Policing in Newport News*. Washington, DC: Police Executive Research Forum.

Eck, J. E., & Wartell, J. (1998). Improving the management of rental properties with drug problems: A randomized experiment. In L. Green-Mazerolle, & J. Roehl (eds.), *Civil Remedies and Crime Prevention*. Monsey, NY: Criminal Justice Press.

Ekblom, P. (2005). The 5Is framework: Sharing good practice in crime prevention. In E. Marks, A. Meyer, & R. Linssen (eds.), *Quality in Crime Prevention*. Hanover, MD: LPR.

Goldstein, H. (1979). Improving policing: A problem-oriented approach. *Crime and Delinquency*, 25, 236–258.

Goldstein, H. (1990). *Problem-Oriented Policing*. Philadelphia, PA: Temple University Press.

Goldstein, H., & Susmilch, C. (1982). The drinking-driver in Madison: A study of the problem and the community's response. Madison: University of Wisconsin Law School.

Green, L. (1996). *Policing Places with Drug Problems*. Thousand Oaks, CA: Sage Publications.

Koper, C. (1995). Just enough police presence: Reducing crime and disorderly behavior by optimizing patrol time in crime hot spots. *Justice Quarterly*, 12, 649–672.

Mastrofski, S. (1998). Community policing and police organization structure. In J. Brodeur (ed.), *How to Recognize Good Policing: Problems and Issues*. Thousand Oaks, CA: Sage Publications.

Perry, W., McInnis, B., Price, C., Smith, S., & Hollywood, J. (2013). *Predictive Policing: The Role of Crime Forecasting in Law Enforcement Operations*. Washington, DC: RAND Corporation.

Police Executive Research Forum (PERF). (2000). *PSP National Evaluation Final Report*. Washington, DC: Police Executive Research Forum.

Ratcliffe, J. (2014). What is the future ... of predictive policing? *Translational Criminology*, 4–5.

Ratcliffe, J. (2016). *Intelligence-Led Policing*. Second edition. Portland, OR: Willan.

Read, T., & Tilley, N. (2000). *Not Rocket Science? Problem-Solving and Crime Reduction*. Crime Reduction Series Paper 6. London: Policing and Crime Reduction Unit, Home Office.

Scott, M. (2000). *Problem-Oriented Policing: Reflections on the First 20 Years*. Washington, DC: US Department of Justice, Office of Community Oriented Policing Services.

Scott, M., & Clarke, R. V. (2000). A review of submission for the Herman Goldstein Excellence in Problem-Oriented Policing Award. In C. Sole Brito, & E. Gratto (eds.), *Problem Oriented Policing: Crime-Specific Problems, Critical Issues, and Making POP Work* (vol. 3). Washington, DC: Police Executive Research Forum.

Shadish, W., Cook, T., & Campbell, D. (2002). *Experimental and Quasi-Experimental Designs for Generalized Causal Inference*. Belmont, CA: Wadsworth.

Sherman, L. W., Gartin, P., & Buerger, M. (1989). Hot spots of predatory crime: Routine activities and the criminology of place. *Criminology*, 27, 27–56.

Sherman, L. W., Shaw, J., & Rogan, D. (1995). *The Kansas City Gun Experiment*. Washington, DC: National Institute of Justice, US Department of Justice.

Sherman, L. W., & Weisburd, D. (1988). Policing the hot spots of crime: A redesign of the Kansas City Preventive Patrol Experiment. Research proposal submitted to the US National Institute of Justice, Program on Research in Public Safety and Security.

Sherman, L. W., & Weisburd, D. (1995). General deterrent effects of police patrol in crime hot spots: A randomized controlled trial. *Justice Quarterly*, 12, 625–648.

Skogan, W., & Frydl, K. (eds.). (2004). *Fairness and Effectiveness in Policing: The Evidence*. Committee to Review Research on Police Policy and Practices. Committee on Law and Justice, Division of Behavioral and Social Sciences and Education. Washington, DC: The National Academies Press.

Skogan, W., Hartnett, S., DuBois, J., Comey, J., Kaiser, M., & Lovig, J. (1999). *On the Beat: Police and Community Problem Solving*. Boulder, CO: Westview Press.

Skolnick, J., & Bayley, D. (1986). *The New Blue Line: Police Innovations in Six American Cities*. New York: Free Press.

Taylor, R. (1998). Crime and small-scale places: What we know, what we can prevent, and what else we need to know. In *Crime and Place: Plenary Papers of the 1997 Conference on Criminal Justice Research and Evaluation*. Washington, DC: National Institute of Justice, US Department of Justice.

Weisburd, D. (2003). Ethical practice and evaluation of interventions in crime and justice: The moral imperative for randomized trials. *Evaluation Review*, 27, 336–354.

Weisburd, D., & Eck, J. E. (2004). What Can Police Do to Reduce Crime, Disorder, and Fear? *Annals of the American Academy of Political and Social Science*, 593, 42–65.

Weisburd, D., & Green, L. (1995). Policing drug hot spots: The Jersey City DMA experiment. *Justice Quarterly*, 12, 711–736.

Weisburd, D., & Lum, C. (2005). The diffusion of computerized crime mapping policing: Linking research and practice. *Police Practice and Research*, 6(5), 433–448.

Weisburd, D., Lum, C., & Petrosino, A. (2001). Does research design affect study outcomes in criminal justice? *The Annals of the American Academy of Social and Political Sciences*, 578, 50–70.

Weisburd, D., Maher, L., & Sherman, L. W. (1992). Contrasting crime general and crime specific theory: The case of hot spots of crime. *Advances in Criminological Theory*, 4, 45–69.

Weisburd, D., & Majmundar, M. (eds.). (2018). *Proactive Policing: Effects on Crime and Communities*. Committee on Proactive Policing: Effects on Crime, Communities, and Civil Liberties. Washington, DC: The National Academies Press.

Weisburd, D., Mastrofski, S., & Greenspan, R. (2001). *Compstat and Organizational Change*. Washington, DC: Police Foundation.

Weisburd, D., Mastrofski, S., McNally, A. M., Greenspan, R., & Willis, J. (2003). Reforming to preserve: Compstat and strategic problem solving in American policing. *Criminology and Public Policy*, 2(3), 421–456.

Weisburd, D., & Mazerolle, L. (2000). Crime and disorder in drug hot spots: Implications for theory and practice in policing. *Police Quarterly*, 3(3), 331–349.

Weisburd, D., Telep, C., Hinkle, J., & Eck, J. (2010). Is problem-oriented policing effective in reducing crime and disorder? Findings from a Campbell systematic review. *Criminology & Public Policy*, 9(1), 139–172.

Willis, J., Mastrofski, S., & Weisburd, D. (2004). Compstat and bureaucracy: A case study of challenges and opportunities for change. *Justice Quarterly*, 21(3), 463–496.

PART V

PULLING LEVERS (FOCUSED DETERRENCE) POLICING

9

Advocate

Policing and the Lessons of Focused Deterrence

David M. Kennedy

INTRODUCTION

Pity the poor soul who, more than twenty years ago, would have predicted that hard-core street cops would be sitting down with serious violent offenders, telling them politely to cease and desist, asking them what they and their families need, and going to extreme lengths to keep them safe and out of jail. Exactly that has in fact become standard practice with police officers nationally; beyond that, and not coincidentally, that standard practice is increasingly understood to work very well indeed. The "focused deterrence" strategies piloted in Boston in the mid-1990s and implemented since then in a range of other jurisdictions are racking up impressive results in preventing violent crime and have become essentially mainstream. What was once seen as at best innovative – but more often to be fringe bordering on the bizarre, as in the face-to-face meetings between authorities and offenders that the Boston strategy invented – is now standard practice and routine not just for special interventions but as a philosophy of policing: it is, one hears police chiefs say, "what we do."

"Focused deterrence" is one fruit of the problem-oriented policing movement. The approach first emerged as part of the Boston Gun Project, a problem-oriented policing project aimed at "gang" violence in Boston, and has since spread to other jurisdictions, settings, and substantive problems (Kennedy, 1997, 1998, 2002a; Kennedy & Braga, 1998; Braga et al., 2001; Braga, Kennedy & Tita, 2002; Dalton, 2003; McGarrell & Chermak, 2003; Tita et al., 2003; Wakeling, 2003; Papachristos, Meares & Fagan, 2007; Hawken & Kleiman, 2009; Corsaro, Brunson & McGarrell, 2010; Corsaro et al., 2012; Kilmer et al., 2013; Warner, Pacholke & Kujath, 2014; Corsaro & Engel, 2015; Papachristos & Kirk, 2015; Sechrist, Weil & Shelton, 2016; Sierra-Arevalo, Charette & Papachristos, 2017; Braga, Weisburd & Turchan, 2018). It was, in that sense, straight from the problem-oriented copybook: it focused on a relatively narrow problem, utilized a wide variety of information sources and analytic techniques, relied heavily on the experience and insight of front-line law enforcement and community actors, and sought a strategic intervention that would have a substantial impact (Goldstein, 2002). It has grown in part by repeating that process with a focus on different substantive problems. It is also one of a growing number of policing interventions that combines a set of relatively traditional tactics with a new strategic focus, and adds to that mix new operational tools, resulting in a strategy that looks both very traditional and quite new and different (Weisburd & Eck, 2004).

The best news about these strategies is that they seem to have worked in a number of jurisdictions against serious crime problems that have traditionally been regarded as intractable, and even, in principle, impossible for criminal justice actors to address. But beyond that, they suggest a bridge between traditional and powerful – but often, in practice, unhappily limited – ideas and actions, and variations on those ideas and actions that can lead to potent, practical applications. And in recent years they have suggested a bridge between constituencies that have frequently been in opposition and whose underlying norms and aspirations have been seen as necessarily in opposition. This article looks at the experience to date with focused deterrence strategies. It is not a review of the operational idea, its intellectual roots, particular interventions, or the formal evaluation of impacts; those things have been done elsewhere. Rather, it treats another set of concerns: what these strategies seem to have meant to police departments and other criminal justice agencies, to communities, and to those interested in criminal justice reform; and why; and what that experience suggests about next steps.

WHAT IT IS

Focused deterrence strategies deploy enforcement, social services and other supports, the moral voice of communities, and deliberate communication in order to create a powerful deterrent to particular behavior by particular high-risk groups and individuals. Focused deterrence strategies have tended to follow a basic framework that includes the following:

- Selection of a particular crime problem, such as youth homicide or street drug dealing;
- Pulling together an interagency enforcement group, typically including police, probation, parole, state and federal prosecutors, and sometimes federal enforcement agencies;
- Conducting research, usually relying heavily on the field experience of front-line police officers, to identify key offenders – and frequently *groups* of offenders, such as street gangs, drug crews, and the like – and the context of their behavior;
- Framing a special enforcement operation directed at those offenders and groups of offenders, and designed to substantially influence that context,

for example by using any and all legal tools (or "levers") to sanction groups such as crack crews whose members commit serious violence;

- Matching those enforcement operations with parallel efforts to direct services and the moral voices of affected communities to those same offenders and groups;
- Communicating directly and repeatedly with offenders and groups to let them know that they are under particular scrutiny, what acts (such as shootings) will get special attention, when that has in fact happened to particular offenders and groups, and what they can do to avoid enforcement action. One form of this communication is the "forum," "notification," or "call-in," in which offenders are invited or directed (usually because they are on probation or parole) to attend face-to-face meetings with law enforcement officials, service providers, and community figures.

In Boston, for example, probation officers pulled members of street drug groups into meetings with authorities, service providers, and community figures where they were told that violence had led to comprehensive enforcement actions against several violent groups, that violence by their groups would provoke the same enforcement actions, that services were available to those who wished them, that the affected communities desperately wanted the violence to stop, and that groups that did not act violently would not get such unusual, high-level enforcement attention. Similar efforts in other jurisdictions soon followed. Focused deterrence was a central theme in the Justice Department's Strategic Approaches to Community Safety Initiative and Project Safe Neighborhoods initiatives, and the basic ideas began showing up in local operations (Dalton, 2003). Virtually all of this work was in the original group-related homicide and gun violence frame. In around the mid-2000s, however, the theory of focused deterrence began to evolve from a relatively narrow one associated largely with that particular problem to a rather fully realized elaboration on traditional deterrence theory (Kennedy, 2008; Kleiman, 2009), and to expand to address other substantive problems.

Perhaps the most important element of that broader view is its recognition of the critical importance of *legitimacy*: the perception of the public of the police and the law, and the importance of that perception to compliance and offending (Tyler, 2006; Meares, 2009). Simply put, it is now well understood that – particularly in the most challenging community settings – as legitimacy goes up, crime goes down, and as legitimacy goes down, crime goes up. Attention to legitimacy has had a profound impact on the understanding of how the approach should frame relationships, messages, communications, and interactions between practitioners and offenders and potential offenders (Mazerolle et al., 2012; Papachristos & Kirk, 2015). While always present in the practice of pulling levers, legitimacy theory and research has underscored the need to treat call-in participants and others subject to interventions with respect, to emphasize the goal of protecting them and keeping them out of the criminal justice system, to stress the desire of criminal justice authorities to be direct and transparent about their actions and intentions, and even to design and implement call-ins and other engagements in ways that model respect and fairness. Some scholars have framed such interventions around legitimacy and procedural justice rather than deterrence (Papachristos et al., 2007; Wallace et al., 2015). More broadly, several of the key figures in the development of focused deterrence theory have argued that it is distal enough from received ideas about deterrence, and includes so many different theoretical and practical elements, that the label is fundamentally misleading. "When taking focused deterrence as a label for a now reasonably well-defined and understood body of crime-prevention theory and associated operational crime-prevention ... it should be recognized that the label fails to capture, and in fact distorts, both that theory and that practice" (Kennedy, Kleiman & Braga, 2017: 159). A recognition of the historical roots of community alienation and their impact on legitimacy has even led to notions of the need for formal racial reconciliation work between police and communities (Kennedy, 2009; Mentel, 2012), and to such work in practice (National Initiative for Building Community Trust and Justice, 2017).

The practice of focused deterrence has expanded to include interventions aimed at individual gun and violent offenders (Papachristos et al., 2007), drug markets (McGarrell, Corsaro & Brunson, 2010), intimate partner violence (Kennedy, 2002b; Sechrist et al., 2016), probation supervision (Hawken & Kleiman, 2009), prison safety and security (Warner et al., 2014), drunk driving (Kilmer et al., 2013), and to serious violence in non-US settings (Williams et al., 2014; National Network for Safe Communities, 2018). Such particular applications of the core theory continue to develop.

WHAT COPS KNOW

The implementation and evolution of focused deterrence strategies have been necessarily dependent on the willingness of criminal justice practitioners – particulary police departments and officers – to employ them. As odd and apparently self-defeating as these strategies may have seemed at the outset, and for some time thereafter – just try telling a grizzled street cop that the way to stop violent crime is to tell hard-core offenders exactly what your enforcement plans are – their originally conditional and now enthusiastic appeal to practitioners makes a certain amount of sense. These are interventions that are based on what cops (and many others in law enforcement) know to be true. The whole of the strategy is certainly not familiar, and frequently met with deep skepticism: the idea that offenders will pay any attention to a "stop it" message, for example – no matter how direct, credible, and backed up by action – often provoked stark disbelief. At the same time, though, much of what goes into these operations, and what sets them apart from other operations, is knowledge and outlook deeply ingrained in enforcement circles. Those sensibilities have shaped both the strategies and law enforcement's response to adopting them.

Police officers (and prosecutors, probation officers, and the like) know, for example, that for many crime problems, repeat offenders and repeat victims are at the center of the action. They know that much of that action is in particular neighborhoods, and particular places within those neighborhoods. They know that different kinds of groups, and various kinds of problems within and between those groups, drive a lot of what happens. They know that these groups and their members commit vast numbers of crimes, probation and parole violations, and other offenses, from failing to show up in court to not paying fines and child support to drinking and drugging to driving illegally. They know this not from reading criminology and social science – though all these threads are to be found there (Kennedy, 2003) – but from their own experience. They know that if those groups and individual offenders were controlled, it would make a big difference. Experienced practitioners know that our usual attempts to shape offenders' behavior, whether through traditional enforcement or through services, counseling, social work, or such means, are hugely ineffective: most experienced law enforcement personnel hold out little or no hope that serious offenders will be influenced by anything short of a cop standing at arm's length. That frequently, perhaps usually, makes them despair of doing *anything* effective. But they want to, and their inclination is to do so through enforcement: police officers and their kin in other agencies believe in good guys and bad guys, and they believe in the exercise of authority, and they want to draw lines in the sand and enforce them. Focused deterrence interventions speak to this orientation. It suits cops to say, stop it. They need to be persuaded that it can work, but this mindset at least opens the door.

Operationally, the wealth of very particular street knowledge at the front lines of these agencies is an invaluable resource. Police officers, in particular – but also frequently probation and parole officers, line prosecutors, the sheriff's officers who manage jail populations, and others – frequently have extraordinary insight into who is doing what, and why, and very often what will happen next. What from even a small distance looks chaotic, senseless, and unpredictable is often known to these practitioners as comprehensible and, in its own way, coherent. They know who is in what street groups, and who is fighting with whom; what last year's antecedent to yesterday's shooting was; who is committing the drug robberies that are not even being reported to the police; who is selling drugs on the corners; what mid-level dealer is running the crack houses operated only by juveniles; what turf is claimed by which groups, and who is allowed there and who is not; which domestic violence offenders are currently most dangerous to what women. Police departments and other enforcement agencies generally make little or no use of this front-line knowledge, partly because it is often of no use in making cases – an unreported drug robbery, to take a particularly clear example, cannot be prosecuted – and partly because of the top-down management typical of police agencies. As a result, what is common knowledge at the street level can be utterly obscure just a few steps away. In Washington, DC, for example, even some career homicide prosecutors argued vehemently that that city's extraordinary homicide rate was the product of solo gunslingers bumping into each other on the streets: there was, they believed, no more sense to it than that, and no logic or context beyond chaotic social breakdown. That was what they saw in the formal fact patterns they reviewed and presented in prosecutions. Police officers were incredulous, and for good reason: a review of homicide incidents based on front-line knowledge showed clearly that homicide was rooted in very patterned behavior by a fairly small number of very active and well-known, mostly neighborhood-based drug crews (Travis et al., 2003). But until what they knew was deliberately gathered and recorded, it had no formal existence and could not shape policy or operations.

Qualitative research can draw this information out. These methods – incident reviews, gang and group mapping exercises, systems to gather front-line knowledge about "hidden" crimes like drug robberies and domestic violence – have become central both to unpacking particular crime problems and to implementing "pulling levers" interventions (Kennedy, Braga & Piehl, 1997; Kennedy & Braga, 1998; Dalton, 2003; McGarrell & Chermak, 2003; Wakeling, 2003). The information they produce is vital, and frequently astonishes both agency executives and outsiders. In San Francisco, for example, a surge in homicide that shocked the city and led to, among other things, a high-profile public forum by the mayor was the product, by front-line consensus, of perhaps a hundred or fewer particularly dangerous, influential – and quite well-known – offenders. The process of gathering and utilizing such knowledge honors the front lines and greatly enhances the salience of subsequent operations.

RECLAIMING DETERRENCE: FUTILITY AND DISPLACEMENT

The Boston operation and what followed were deterrence strategies. Most criminal justice practitioners, most of the time, did not believe in deterrence. That the strategies work, and beyond that work with offenders and crime problems that have demonstrably been particularly resistant to ordinary enforcement, has helped reclaim the idea of, and shaped new understandings regarding the real operation and practice of, deterrence.

The failure of deterrence is everywhere in law enforcement. Practitioners certainly believe that it is operating at some level – if police shut down operations, crime would certainly go up – but they do not much believe that it is operating at the margin. They do not believe that offenders, particularly serious offenders, much care about official consequences for their crimes or that those consequences can be increased such that offenders will care. The evidence for this is manifest. Many offenders are arrested and sanctioned repeatedly, and continue to offend. Many commit crimes such as drug dealing in full public view. Many routinely violate the terms and conditions of probation and parole. And many, by their actions and words, show their apparent disregard for extreme and predictable consequences of their behavior, such as being hurt or killed on the street. When offenders don't mind dying, authorities frequently say, what can we possibly do that they will care about?

This does not undercut the faith police and other authorities have in *enforcement*. But it severely limits the ways in which they think enforcement can be effective. It may work to swamp an area with officers: as long as that persists, offenders will keep their heads down. It will certainly work to take an offender off the streets: while he's inside, he won't commit any crimes outside. But authorities tended to have little or no faith in their ability to persuade offenders to change their behavior, or in fact to do anything at all: one of the predictable hurdles in implementing early Boston-style focused deterrence operations was police officers' conviction that probationers would not even bother to show up when directed to appear at call-ins. They violate their probation all the time, and nothing ever happens, officers say; why should this be any different? (In fact, compliance at call-ins is routinely very high, and, in practice, seeing probationers appear often opened the first chink in line officers' skepticism about the larger strategy.)

Closely linked is an absolute, nearly theological belief in displacement: that anything short of incarceration will simply move offenders around. The research on this point is by now pretty persuasive: displacement is far less universal than has long been thought, is virtually never complete, and in fact enforcement efforts frequently produce a "diffusion of benefits," the opposite of displacement (Clarke & Weisburd, 1994; Braga, 2002). Police and other enforcement practitioners remain unmoved. This is not what they see, and they do not believe it.

One of the most important results of the manifest impact of focused deterrence strategies, then, is that the basic idea of deterrence – a big and important idea – has been rehabilitated. The facts are quite clear: in jurisdiction after jurisdiction, the worst of offenders – gang members, violent offenders, shooters – are substantially changing their behavior without being taken off the street; probationers comply; meth addicts stop using; recidivist drunk drivers stop drinking. It was but a short step to the provocative thought that it is not that offenders cannot be deterred, but that what we were normally doing was simply not deterring them: and that quite possibly we can do better. The framing and mechanisms for in fact doing better were built into the theory and became practically available: focus on one or a few important things, not on everything; focus on a small number of extreme high-risk groups and networks, not on everyone; focus on creating real consequences, not on threatening essentially false ones; work with community and civic resources; seek to understand and even respect the situations of the high-risk; understand the way official practice and malpractice do damage and undercut compliance;

and build communication and relationship with those whom one seeks to influence.

THE SALIENCE OF GROUPS AND NETWORKS

The first "pulling levers" interventions focused on various kinds of groups and networks: gangs, drug crews, and the like. The next main iteration focused on overt community drug markets, a setting where collective dynamics between dealers and buyers were central (Kennedy, 1990). This is not necessarily an essential part of the framework. As has been noted, applications of the core theory have been developed for individuals: gun and violent offenders, probationers and parolees, intimate partner offenders, and drunk drivers. But much of the work of focused deterrence has been on homicide and serious violence in urban settings, and, in practice, those problems are overwhelmingly concentrated in groups and networks of chronic offenders (Kennedy, 1997, 1998, 2002a; Kennedy & Braga, 1998; Braga et al., 2001; Braga et al., 2002; Dalton, 2003; McGarrell & Chermak, 2003; Tita et al., 2003; Wakeling, 2003). Various sorts of groups of offenders representing a tiny fraction of the population have repeatedly been shown to be responsible for most homicides and large shares of other violent crime (Kennedy, 2003). The operational strategies have simply followed that presentation of the problem. Once again, the salience of groups and networks is a commonplace in the literature, and also a commonplace on the front lines. It has not, however, been a commonplace in official accounts of these problems or, frequently, in operational responses to them. Elevating their recognition and the attention paid to them is an important development.

There are a number of reasons groups and networks have gotten far less attention than they should have in law enforcement practice. Police and other authorities recognize the existence of gangs, but outside a few jurisdictions most of these groups and networks are not what are generally thought of as gangs (Kennedy, 2002a). Legal avenues rarely allow a group or network to be held legally responsible for a criminal act; a loose-knit drug group cannot in practice be charged collectively for the shooting committed by one of its members. Homicide investigators and prosecutors responsible for uncovering and presenting the fact pattern will themselves frequently not know about the rest of the group or the larger context of the shooting. Those who know the most about the group and its behavior, such as conflicts with other groups, will frequently be narcotics and precinct officers and have no role in the investigation or in the gathering and interpreting of departmental intelligence. What results is a kind of open secret in which the existence of offender groups and networks, and the significance of their behavior, is both very well known to some practitioners and neither recognized nor acted upon elsewhere. In New Haven, for example, authorities concerned about gun crime insisted that gangs were not an issue: the Latin Kings, who had previously been a presence, had been eliminated through federal prosecutions. Work with front-line police officers, however, brought to the surface what they already knew: that loose neighborhood-based groups of chronic offenders were responsible for most of the violence (Dalton, 2003). Similar findings are invariable in other jurisdictions.

Some of the implications are immediate and practical. These groups can in fact be attended to as groups, even when something like a conspiracy case or a RICO prosecution cannot be brought: a hand-to-hand drug buy from each member can put the whole group out of action. The prospect of using the many such legal avenues is in fact the origin of the "pulling levers" label. Once recognized, these groups can also be communicated with: they can be told, for example, that a shooting by one of their number will result in action against all. Their relations with other groups can be identified and monitored, so that allies and enemies in a simmering group-on-group vendetta get special attention.

A particularly interesting possibility – less immediate, but perhaps no less practical – is recognizing that such groups and networks of groups produce and enforce their own codes, rules, and expectations. This, again, is classic sociology, criminology, and psychology, which have always placed great emphasis on norms (Kennedy, 2003). Police and other authorities have rarely matched this recognition. A drive-by shooting will typically be viewed as an expression of the shooter's character and choice, or more remotely as the product of more global forces such as neighborhood, class, or racial and ethnic factors. Authorities rarely consider that something intermediate might be operating, such as the imposition by the shooter's crew of norms that demand violence in certain circumstances, and the real benefits and risks that go along with complying or failing to comply. Nor do they consider the possibility of deliberately countering or even changing those norms, as by letting all group members know that violence by one will impose costs on all, or by mobilizing respected community voices to challenge them. In Lowell, Massachusetts, for example, police responded to shootings by young Asian gang members, against whom they had very little legal leverage, by cracking down on the gambling parlors operated by older gang members and telling them explicitly that the shooting had triggered the crackdowns. The police could not control the shooters, but the older members could and did (Braga, McDevitt & Pierce, 2005). Recognizing groups and group processes opens up an enormous range of analysis and action that operates in between, and may be more productive than, the usual very particular attention to individuals and very broad attention to social factors.

Recent and important work on *social network analysis* has brought a new set of methods for identifying and understanding high-risk networks and violence dynamics (Green, Horel & Papachristos, 2017), and has cemented and expanded the original idea that groups and group processes are at the heart of street homicide and gun violence. Powerful computer tools can draw on widely existing criminal justice administrative data such as shooting incident reports and arrest records to construct victim and offender networks and facilitate the identification of extraordinarily high-risk groups even within those networks (Papachristos, Braga & Hureau, 2012). Analyzing those networks over time can identify ways in which violence "cascades" through the network along lines of relationship, capturing precisely and graphically the influence of risk, vendetta, "beef," and retaliation (Green et al., 2017). Such tools and insight greatly sharpen the ability to focus pulling levers (and other) interventions.

THE STRATEGIC USE OF TRADITIONAL ENFORCEMENT

Law enforcement likes enforcing the law. For better or for worse, the appeal of the traditional operational toolkit – patrol, rapid response, investigation, arrest, prosecution, jail, prison, and the like – remains strong. A large body of academic and, beyond that, practical experience suggesting that these tools are often very weak indeed has done little to change their primacy (Braga, 2002; Weisburd & Eck, 2004). Their failure in practice is much more likely to be ascribed to system or social failure – we're making the arrests, the prosecutors are letting us down; what can we do when nobody in the neighborhood is finishing school or working – than it is to lead to fundamental reconsideration of how business is or ought to be done. Police, prosecutors, and others believe, even in the midst of great frustration, in what they do.

Focused deterrence strategies appeal to practitioners partly because they make a virtue of those beliefs and of existing agency capacities. These tools, *as deployed*, are usually unsatisfactory. Deploying them in new ways may be very different. Law enforcement personnel, and many others, think that the logic and the actions of enforcement should matter. People should seek to avoid being arrested, should avoid going to prison, should not want probation officers in their bedrooms. The manifest failure of existing tools to win compliance from offenders fuels the common conclusion that they are, on that evidence, irrational. But what if here, too, there is a middle ground? It is true that chronic offenders are frequently arrested and sanctioned. But it is also true – and, again, well understood both from research and from practical experience – that most crimes are not reported, most that are reported are not cleared, most that are cleared are not met with stiff sanctions, sanctions such as probation are generally not rigorously enforced, and so on (Kennedy, 2003). It is thus possible for there to be a great deal of enforcement without that enforcement being consistent, predictable, or very meaningful to offenders. A street drug dealer may have been arrested a number of times. But each day, when he considers whether to go work his corner, the chance that he will be arrested *today* will be both small and essentially random. This can be true even for very serious crimes. In one of the most violent areas of Washington, DC, nearly three-quarters of homicides go unsolved (M. Miranda, Office of the United States Attorney, personal communication). Police and others very often know what happened, but they cannot put cases together, and so there are no official consequences (Braga, Piehl & Kennedy, 1999).

Law enforcement personnel understand very well – better than most others, short of offenders – that this is in fact true. Their usual responses, which have to do with resources, dramatically altering the behavior of various criminal justice agencies and judges, and the willingness of the public to come forward, and the like, are hopeless, and they know that as well. Focused deterrence strategies offer a way out. It is in fact possible to warn each of sixty street gangs in a jurisdiction that the first to commit a homicide will get overwhelming attention, and to back that promise up. Experience shows that when offenders believe that promise, their behavior changes. And the more the practical work has shown that – that even chronic drunk drivers will stay sober when they know they will be breath-tested twice a day and that failure will be met with a small but immediate sanction – the more criminal justice practitioners have come to understand that even apparently incorrigible "offenders" are in fact very often rational and can be reached.

This is very much old wine in new bottles: traditional building blocks assembled in common sense but original ways. It bows in both directions: to the conviction on the part of police and other authorities that enforcement is (or should be) powerful, justified, and important, and to the painfully clear fact that enforcement as usual too often simply does not work. Many in criminal justice have long been aware of the latter without being willing or able to give up the former. These strategies, at least to some extent, offer a way forward.

COMMUNICATION, RELATIONSHIP, AND COMMON GROUND

Communication with offenders is a central element in focused deterrence strategies. Communication and persuasion have long been recognized as essential elements in the deterrence process: sanctions offenders do not know about cannot deter them, and sanctions offenders do not believe in will not deter them (Zimring & Hawkins, 1973; Kennedy, 2003). Communication has in practice gotten very little attention, however, either theoretically or practically. We tend to assume what we know in fact to be false: that offenders understand the complicated and often rapidly shifting enforcement environment they face. One central lesson of focused deterrence operations is the clear power of direct communication with offenders. A city's-worth of drug crews may utterly ignore the fact – may not collectively even be aware of the fact – that one crew has just been taken off the street. But tell them all that this has happened, and beyond that that attention to groups is now standard operating procedure, and beyond that that the next group that commits violence will be treated likewise, and beyond that that enforcement attention will be heightened if groups are active in street drug sales – and matters may change. The evidence is that matters do change.

As experience with these strategies has accumulated, two related themes have emerged. One is that *relationships* between authorities and offenders matter a great deal. There is no acceptable place for this notion in traditional enforcement thinking. The operational and legal conventions of traditional law enforcement and case processing – call by call, incident by incident, case by case – run counter. The atmosphere and resonances of policing and much of the rest of law enforcement, with its division of the world into white hats and black hats, also very much run counter. Where the idea of relationship does have a place, as is sometimes true in probation and parole, there is a tendency to partition out the exercise of authority: leading, for example, to the framing of supervisees as "clients," which leads to much eye-rolling by the more enforcement-minded.

Focused deterrence strategies structure a very different kind of relationship. Authorities meet with offenders, as in call-ins, in a setting that is respectful, civil, but also unabashedly about, in part, authority and consequences. Such contacts are often repeated. They are often supplemented as needed in other settings, such as pointed warnings on the street when front-line intelligence suggests that trouble is brewing between particular groups. They include other elements, such as the offering of services and impassioned statements by community figures. One of the most striking features of call-ins for police officers and other enforcement figures is that offenders tend to be well behaved, attentive, and often visibly moved by what ministers, mothers who have lost their children to the street, and neighborhood elders have to say to them. It is not uncommon for offenders to applaud authorities who speak to them uncompromisingly but also respectfully. Once the call-in process becomes known on the streets, offenders sometimes show up uninvited and ask to be allowed to sit in. The contrast with the conventional wisdom – that offenders are wild, self-destructive, unreachable, and the like – is graphic.

It is but a short step to the idea that there is in fact *common ground* between authorities and offenders. There is also no place for this in traditional enforcement thinking, which assumes a constant, zero-sum struggle between the forces of good and bad. In fact, there is a great deal of common ground. Offenders do not wish to die; they for the most part do not wish to be arrested and go to prison; they do not want their mothers to grieve; they do not want their younger siblings following in their footsteps or walking deadly streets; they would, all else being equal, prefer to do their business quietly and safely. These are, at least sometimes, goals authorities and offenders can seek together. Each gang may put down its guns if it understands that all are putting them down. Drug dealers may shift the ways in which they do business if they understand that police will be paying particular attention to the street markets and crack houses that most damage and endanger communities. Such common ground is certainly not absolute, or always to be found, but it is also not unknown. The clear fact that offenders respond to, and sometimes quite evidently welcome, the new rules established in focused deterrence strategies is beginning to suggest to authorities that offenders might *want* things to be different, or at least that they may be far less resistant than invariably assumed. It is, like the rest of the focused framework, a notion that is both common-sensical and radical.

Criminal Justice Reform

In recent years, sentiment in the United States around criminal justice has shifted profoundly. America's extraordinary rate of incarceration – exceptional both historically for the nation and comparatively internationally – and the racial disparity built into it has come to be recognized as a crisis, with wide agreement across the political spectrum that the situation is profoundly unacceptable (National Research Council, 2014; Lee, 2015). The damaging impact of even "low level" criminal justice contact such as police stops (Gelman, Fagan & Kiss, 2007) and the even more profound impact of incarceration and concentrations of incarceration on individuals, families, and communities has become widely acknowledged (Clear, 2009). Widely accepted and even preferred – in some circles – policing strategies such as high levels of stop and frisk have become the focus not only of policy debate but of political salience: in New York City, the most powerful exponent of the practice, it came under legal attack and was a central issue in the 2013 mayoral election, with the winning candidate pledging to curtail the practice (De Blasio, 2013). Police violence, especially the shooting of unarmed black men, has become a core public and civil rights issue, leading to and driven by the emergence of new activist movements such as Black Lives Matter (Joseph, 2017). Riots have been sparked by outrage over police shootings in several American cities. There have been a number of high-profile assassinations of police officers (Karimi, 2016; Mueller & Baker, 2017).

At the federal level, the Obama Administration spoke out about police violence directed at black men, made investigation and supervision of police misbehavior a top Department of Justice priority, issued guidelines intended to limit the use of draconian federal sentencing power, took steps to release nonviolent drug offenders from federal prison, convened a high-level panel on police policy and reform, and launched an initiative to bring "Smart Policing" to municipalities (President's Task Force on 21st Century Policing, 2015). Early steps in the Trump Administration have reversed some of these policies, leading to criticism from police organizations and even cities and police departments subject to the previous administration's investigations (Williams & Oppel, 2017).

Roughly in parallel, there have been significant increases in homicide and serious violence in a number of American cities (Economist, 2017). Some of these have been in cities that have experienced some of the highest-profile incidents of police violence and associated protests, leading to concerns of, on the one hand, "depolicing" leading to increased violence, and, on the other, a worsening legitimacy crisis leading to increased violence (Beck, 2016; Rosenfeld, 2016). Taken together, the United States is in a fundamentally new, fraught, and undefined place with respect to race, violence prevention, policing, and criminal justice.

Focused deterrence has emerged as an important element in responding to this moment. In a time of heightened homicide and gun violence, it currently represents, as will be explored below, the most effective evidence-based approach to that issue. It represents a clear alternative to what have been competing policing models, such as "zero tolerance," as communities become unwilling to accept, and police agencies become unwilling to carry out, those strategies. It is associated with reductions in arrest and subsequent criminal justice contact: exactly what the reform agenda is calling for. It is predicated on an empirical analysis that says explicitly that "dangerous communities" are not dangerous as such, but are in fact remarkably mainstream and resilient communities with a relatively small number of very high-risk people in them, with the clear corollary that those communities should not be demonized on the basis of racial or other such factors. It frames those high-risk people first and foremost in terms of their risk of death and victimization, rather than as "offenders," and begins its contact with them first with community moral engagement, then with social service support, then with an attempt to deter, and only after that with actual law enforcement. And it is, as has been noted, now explicitly framed in terms of legitimacy, the failure of legitimacy, and attempts to repair and enhance legitimacy.

Built into that framing is a developing but explicit recognition of the ways in which historical racism and oppression under color of law, including by the police, have done grave damage to blacks and black communities in the United States; how that reality and community understandings and narratives have shaped distrust of the police and damaged legitimacy; how profligate and intrusive policing strategies like "zero tolerance" have continued that damage and played into those understandings and narratives; and how explicit acknowledgement of those realities by the police and clear commitments to doing differently and even repairing the damage done must be part of effective and legitimate strategies going forward (Office of Community Oriented Policing Services, 2014; Kennedy, 2011).

A conception of this process within focused deterrence strategies as frank "reconciliation" work – with resonance with similar work in South Africa and other such settings – began with the development of the focused deterrence drug market intervention (DMI) and researchers' ethnographic experience of the ways in which street drug enforcement both failed to address drug markets and did enormous damage in the eyes of communities; the ways in which those realities were understood in the affected communities in terms of historical oppression and deliberate damage under color of law; the ways in which communities were in turn demonized by police; and the need for explicit attention to these dynamics (Kennedy, 2009). In this analysis, the history of racial oppression and resulting experience and narratives were a powerful impediment to legitimacy, community informal social control, and effective community/police partnerships, and thus needed explicit attention and corrective action.

Once framed in theory and piloted in small-scale practice in DMI interventions, the idea made its way more broadly into pulling levers thinking and into discourse and practice within policing (Meares, 2009; Kennedy, 2011; Office of Community Oriented Policing Services, 2014). Acknowledgments of the reality of the racially oppressive historic role of police have in fact become remarkably common in American policing, such as the 2016 acknowledgement by International Association of Chiefs of Police Terrance Cunningham of the "dark side of our shared history" and that "the first step in this process is for law enforcement and the IACP to acknowledge and apologize for the actions of the past and the role that our profession has played in society's mistreatment of communities of color." Focused deterrence strategies have thus emerged in the current American moment around race, race relations, and criminal justice not only as a way to do a better job of producing public safety while doing less harm, but also as a vehicle for surfacing, acknowledging, and addressing – with an active and positive role for police and policing – core racial issues.

EVIDENCE OF IMPACT

The body of evaluation research has grown and evolved considerably. A now substantial number of evaluations has solidified evidence that the original "Operation Ceasefire" group-violence approach consistently produces substantial impact (Braga, 2008; Braga et al., 2008; McGarrell et al., 2006; Engel, Corsaro & Tillyer, 2010; Braga, Hureau & Papachristos, 2014; Corsaro & Engel, 2015; Papachristos & Kirk, 2015; Sierra-Arevalo, Charette & Papachristos, 2017). Systematic reviews of this body of evaluation research, and of the literature on the prevention of serious violent crime more generally, have found strong evidence for overall impact and for the primacy of the approach in addressing homicide and gun violence. A 2012 Campbell Collaboration study found evidence of impact across ten pulling levers program evaluations, most of which (but not all) were group violence interventions (Braga & Weisburd, 2012). A subsequent Campbell Collaboration systematic review addressed twenty-four evaluations, including interventions focused on groups, individuals, and drug markets; found broad evidence of impact; and concluded that focused deterrence interventions "generate noteworthy crime reduction impacts and should be part of a broader portfolio of crime reduction strategies available to policy makers and practitioners" (Braga et al., 2018). A meta-analysis of forty-three reviews, including more than 1,400 studies, of the broader violence prevention literature concluded that "focused deterrence ... has the largest direct impact on crime and violence of any intervention in this report" (Abt & Winship, 2016).

A systematic review of strategies to prevent gang violence concluded that "pulling-levers' strategies ... are the most consistently effective solution to gang-related delinquency" (Wong et al., 2012). A systematic review of the violence prevention and rehabilitation literature found focused deterrence effective in reducing gun violence, with the largest effect sizes and strongest evidence base (Weisburd, Farrington & Gill, 2016). And while "gold standard" random control trials are difficult to implement in focused deterrence settings, particularly with respect to group-focused interventions designed to use communication to influence groups and networks not subjected to direct contact, an RCT evaluating a focused deterrence intervention with individual probationers found impact on their general offending behavior (Hamilton, Rosenfeld & Levin, 2017).

Most of these impact evaluations focused on the core question of whether the evaluation produced violence reduction. Research is beginning to look beyond that, however, to explore mechanisms within the "black box" of the intervention and effects beyond pure crime impacts. An evaluation of a later version of Ceasefire in Boston, for example, found evidence for deterrent rather than enforcement effects – gangs not subject to actual criminal justice attention also showed violence reduction (Braga, Apel & Welsh, 2013) – and an evaluation of an intervention in Cincinnati found that it was associated with substantial reductions in both crime and arrests (University of Cincinnati Policing Institute, 2009).

CONCLUSION

As this record and the range of interventions suggest, the approach has become increasingly mainstream – it is no longer "fringe" or controversial but has become, for the most part, an accepted way of thinking about addressing especially violent crime. It has been applied in scores of cities nationally (Braga & Weisburd, 2012) and is of increasing interest internationally (Williams et al., 2014; Densley & Squier Jones, 2016; Abt & Winship, 2016). The three American cities generally considered most significant when it comes to crime and crime control – New York, Chicago, and Los Angeles – are all currently employing it. Importantly, as the approach has developed and spread, the core ideas that inform it have also become increasingly mainstream. It has become routine, for example, for policymakers to articulate that a very small core group of high-risk people is at the heart of violent crime problems. New Orleans mayor Mitch Landrieu, for example, said recently that "the majority of murders in New Orleans were committed by a small and identifiable set of people in a few neighborhoods as the result of petty disputes" (Landrieu, 2014). It has also become widely understood that much of that violence is about social friction, not about making money; that that is at heart a group-related issue (Vasquez et al., 2015); and there has emerged broad willingness to focus community voices, social services, and deterrence on such problems.

Understanding and endorsing the framework and the approach has moved beyond the original small networks of scholars and criminal justice practitioners to, for example, community organizers and reform advocates (PICO National Network and Law Center to Prevent Gun Violence, 2016).

The pulling levers approach thus finds itself well adrift of any common conception of deterrence, focused or otherwise. Informal social control, primacy for social services and other facilitative interventions, attention to not imposing the harms that accompany other and more traditional policing and law enforcement approaches, conscious attention to reducing enforcement and incarceration, explicit attention to race, the incorporation of frank reconciliation processes, and an approach to deterrence dominated by communication rather than the actual application of law and sanction is not really anybody's ordinary sense of deterrence (though, in fact, all of these things can be linked to and understood through an emerging new deterrence theory; Kennedy, 2008). What is clear is that a school of thought and action born out of the intersection of many kinds of existing scholarly theory and research, immersion in communities and front-line practice, and concrete engagements with important substantive problems continues to evolve and bear fruit. That process seems unlikely to stop where it is.

REFERENCES

Abt, T., & Winship, C. (2016). *What Works in Reducing Community Violence: A Meta-Review and Field Study for the Northern Triangle*. Washington, DC: US Agency for International Development.

Beck, C. (2016, February 11). Charlie Beck: The real Ferguson effect in L.A. *Los Angeles Times*. www.latimes.com/opinion/op-ed/la-oe-0211-beck-ferguson-effect-lapd-20160211-story.html.

Braga, A. A. (2002). *Problem-Oriented Policing and Crime Prevention*. Monsey, NY: Criminal Justice Press.

Braga, A. A. (2008). Pulling levers focused deterrence strategies and the prevention of gun homicide. *Journal of Criminal Justice*, 36(4), 332–343.

Braga, A. A., Apel, R., & Welsh, B. C. (2013). The spillover effects of focused deterrence on gang violence. Evaluation Review, 37(3–4), 314–342.

Braga, A. A., Hureau, D., & Papachristos, A. V. (2014). Deterring gang-involved gun violence: Measuring the impact of Boston's Operation Ceasefire on street gang behavior. *Journal of Quantitative Criminology*, 30(1), 113–139.

Braga, A. A., Kennedy, D. M., & Tita, G. (2002). New approaches to the strategic prevention of gang and group-involved violence. In C. R. Huff (ed.), *Gangs in America*, 3rd edition. Thousand Oaks, CA: Sage Publications.

Braga, A. A., Kennedy, D. M., Waring, E., & Piehl, A. (2001). Problem-oriented policing, deterrence, and youth violence: An evaluation of Boston's Operation Ceasefire. *Journal of Research in Crime and Delinquency*, 38, 195–225.

Braga, A. A., McDevitt, J., & Pierce, G. (2005). Understanding and preventing gang violence: Problem analysis and response development in Lowell, Massachusetts. *Police Quarterly*, 8.

Braga, A. A., Piehl, A., & Kennedy, D. M. (1999). Youth homicide in Boston: An assessment of supplementary homicide report data. *Homicide Studies*, *3*, 277–299.

Braga, A. A., Pierce, G. L., McDevitt, J., Bond, B. J., & Cronin, S. (2008). The strategic prevention of gun violence among gang-involved offenders. *Justice Quarterly*, *25*(1), 132–162.

Braga, A. A., & Weisburd, D., (2012). *The Effects of "Pulling Levers" Focused Deterrence Strategies on Crime*. Oslo, Norway: Campbell Systematic Reviews.

Braga, A. A., Weisburd, D., & Turchan, B. (2018). Focused deterrence strategies and crime control: An updated systematic review and meta-analysis of the empirical evidence. *Criminology and Public Policy*, *17*(1). doi: 10.1111/1745-9133.12353.

Clarke, R., & Weisburd, D. (1994). Diffusion of crime control benefits: Observations on the reverse of displacement. *Crime Prevention Studies*, *2*, 165–184.

Corsaro, N., Brunson, R., & McGarrell, E. (2010). Problem-oriented policing and open-air drug markets: Examining the Rockford pulling levers strategy. *Crime and Delinquency*. doi: 10.1177/0011128709345955.

Corsaro, N., & Engel, R.S. (2015). Most challenging of contexts: Assessing the impact of focused deterrence on serious violence in New Orleans. *Criminology & Public Policy*, *14*(3).

Corsaro, N., Hunt, E., Hipple, N. K., & McGarrell, E. (2012). The impact of drug market pulling levers policing on neighborhood violence: An evaluation of the High Point Drug Market Intervention. *Criminology & Public Policy*, *11*, 167–200.

Clear, T. R. (2009). *Imprisoning Communities: How Mass Incarceration Makes Disadvantaged Communities Worse*. Oxford: Oxford University Press.

Dalton, E. (2003). *Lessons in Preventing Homicide*. Project Safe Neighborhoods Report. Lansing: School of Criminal Justice, Michigan State University.

De Blasio, B. (2013). Stop-and-frisk can only work after real police reform. *The Guardian*. www.theguardian.com/commentisfree/2013/may/13/stop-and-frisk-new-york-bill-de-blasio.

Densley, J., & Squier Jones, D. (2016). Pulling levers on gang violence in London and St. Paul. In C. L. Maxson, & F-A. Esbensen, (eds.), *Gang Transitions and Transformations in an International Context* (pp. 291–305). New York: Springer.

Economist. (2017). Murder rates in 50 American cities. Economist.com. www.economist.com/blogs/graphicdetail/2017/02/daily-chart-3.

Engel, R. S., Corsaro, N., & Tillyer, M. S. (2010). *Evaluation of the Cincinnati Initiative to Reduce Violence (CIRV)*. Cincinnati, OH: University of Cincinnati Policing Institute.

Gelman, A., Fagan, J., & Kiss, A. (2007). An analysis of the New York City police department's "stop-and-frisk" policy in the context of claims of racial bias. *Journal of the American Statistical Association*, *102*(479), doi: 10.1198/016214506000001040.

Goldstein, H. (2002). On further developing problem-oriented policing: The most critical need, the major impediments, and a proposal. In J. Knutsson (ed.), *Mainstreaming Problem-Oriented Policing*. Monsey, New York: Criminal Justice Press.

Green, B., Horel, T., & Papachristos, A. V. (2017). Modeling contagion through social networks to explain and predict gunshot violence in Chicago, 2006 to 2014. *JAMA Internal Medicine*, *177*(3), 326–333. doi:10.1001/jamainternmed.2016.8245.

Hamilton, B., Rosenfeld, R., & Levin, A. (2017). Opting out of treatment: Self- selection bias in a randomized controlled study of a focused deterrence notification meeting. *Journal of Experimental Criminology*. https://doi.org/10.1007/s11292-017-9309-z.

Hawken, A., & Kleiman, M. (2009). *Managing Drug Involved Probationers with Swift and Certain Sanctions: Evaluating Hawaii's HOPE*. Los Angeles: NCJRS.

Joseph, P. E. (2017). Why Black Lives Matter still matters. *New Republic*. https://newrepublic.com/article/141700/black-lives-matter-still-matters-new-form-civil-rights-activism.

Karimi, F. (2016). Dallas sniper attack: 5 officers killed, suspect identified. CNN.com. www.cnn.com/2016/07/08/us/philando-castile-alton-sterling protests/index.html.

Kennedy, D. M. (1990). *Fighting the drug trade in Link Valley. Case C16-90–935.0*. Cambridge, MA: John F. Kennedy School of Government, Harvard University.

Kennedy, D. M. (1997). Pulling levers: Chronic offenders, high-crime settings, and a theory of prevention. *Valparaiso University Law Review, 31*, 449–484.

Kennedy, D. M. (1998). Pulling levers: Getting deterrence right. *National Institute of Justice Journal, July*, 2–8.

Kennedy, D. M. (2002a). A tale of one city: Reflections on the Boston gun project. In G. Katzmann (ed.), *Securing Our Children's Future: New Approaches to Juvenile Justice and Youth Violence*. Washington, DC: Brookings Institution Press.

Kennedy, D. M. (2002b). *Controlling Domestic Violence Offenders. Report submitted to the Hewlett-Family Violence Prevention Fund*. Cambridge, MA: John F. Kennedy School of Government, Harvard University.

Kennedy, D. M. (2003). *Reconsidering deterrence*. Final report submitted to the US National Institute of Justice. Cambridge, MA: John F. Kennedy School of Government, Harvard University.

Kennedy, D. M. (2008). *Deterrence and Crime Prevention: Reconsidering the Prospect of Sanction*. London: Routledge.

Kennedy, D. M. (2009). Drugs, race and common ground: Reflections of the High Point Intervention. *National Institute of Justice Journal, 262*, 12–17.

Kennedy, D. M. (2011). *Don't Shoot: One Man, a Street Fellowship, and the End of Violence in Inner-City America*. USA: Bloomsbury.

Kennedy, D. M., & Braga, A. A. (1998). Homicide in Minneapolis: Research for problem solving. *Homicide Studies, 2*, 263–290.

Kennedy, D. M., Braga, A. A., & Kleiman, M. (2017). Beyond deterrence: Strategies of focus and fairness. In N. Tilley, & A. Sidebottom (eds.), *Handbook of Crime Prevention and Community Safety*. New York: Routledge.

Kennedy, D. M., Braga, A. A., & Piehl, A. (1997). The (un)known universe: Mapping gangs and gang violence in Boston. In D. Weisburd, & J. T. McEwen (eds.), *Crime Mapping and Crime Prevention*. Monsey, NY: Criminal Justice Press.

Kilmer, B., Nicosia, N., Heaton, P., & Midgette, G. (2013). Insights from South Dakota 24/7 sobriety project. *American Journal of Public Health, 103*(1), 37–43.

Kleiman, M. (2009). *When Brute Force Fails: How to Have Less Crime and Less Punishment*. Princeton, NJ: Princeton University Press.

Landrieu, M. (2014). New Orleans' top priority: Cut its murder rate. *CNN Money*. http://money.cnn.com/2014/12/09/news/economy/new-orleans-landrieu/index.html.

Lee, T. (2015). America's incarceration problem hits bipartisan sweet spot. MSNBC.com. www.msnbc.com/msnbc/incarceration-bipartisan-sweet-spot.

Mazerolle, L., Bennett, S., Davis, J., Sargeant, E., & Manning, M. (2012). *Legitimacy in Policing*. Oslo, Norway: Campbell Systematic Reviews.

McGarrell, E., & Chermak, S. (2003). *Strategic approaches to reducing firearms violence: Final report on the Indianapolis Violence Reduction Partnership*. Final report submitted to the U.S. National Institute of Justice. East Lansing: School of Criminal Justice, Michigan State University.

McGarrell, E., Chermak, S., Wilson, J., & Corsaro, N. (2006). Reducing homicide through a "lever-pulling" strategy. *Justice Quarterly, 23,* 214–229.

McGarrell, E., Corsaro, N., & Brunson, R. K. (2010). The drug market intervention approach to overt drug markets. *VARSTVOSLOVJE, Journal of Criminal Justice and Security, 12*(4), 397–407.

Meares, T. L. (2009). The legitimacy of police among young African-American men. *Marquette Law Review, 92*(4), 651–666.

Mentel, Z. (2012). *Racial Reconciliation, Truth-Telling, and Police Legitimacy*. Washington, DC: US Department of Justice, Office of Community Oriented Policing Services.

Mueller, B., & Baker, A. (2017). Police officer is "murdered for her uniform" in the Bronx. *New York Times.* www.nytimes.com/2017/07/05/nyregion/nypd-bronx-police-shooting.html.

National Initiative for Building Community Trust and Justice. (2017). 2017 Interim Status Report. Trustandjustice.org. https://trustandjustice.org/pilot-sites.

National Network for Safe Communities. (2018). International Initiatives. Nnscommunities.org. https://nnscommunities.org/our-work/strategy/international-initiatives.

National Research Council. (2014). *The Growth of Incarceration in the United States: Exploring Causes and Consequences.* Committee on Causes and Consequences of High Rates of Incarceration. J. Travis, B. Western, & S. Redburn (eds.), Committee on Law and Justice, Division of Behavioral and Social Sciences and Education. Washington, DC: The National Academies Press.

Office of Community Oriented Policing Services. (2014). *Strengthening the Relationship Between Law Enforcement and Communities of Color: Developing an Agenda for Action.* Washington, DC: US Department of Justice, Office of Community Oriented Policing Services.

Papachristos, A. V., Meares, T. L., & Fagan, J. (2007). Attention felons: Evaluating Project Safe Neighborhoods in Chicago. *Journal of Empirical Legal Studies, 4,* 223–272.

Papachristos, A. V., Braga, A. A., & Hureau, D. (2012). Social networks and the risk of gunshot injury. *Journal of Urban Health: Bulletin of the New York Academy of Medicine, 89*(6), 992–1003.

Papachristos, A. V., & Kirk, D. S. (2015). Changing the street dynamic: Evaluating Chicago's group violence reduction strategy. *Criminology and Public Policy, 14* (3), 1–34.

PICO National Network and Law Center to Prevent Gun Violence. (2016). *Healing Communities in Crisis: Lifesaving Solutions to the Urban Gun Violence Epidemic.* http://smartgunlaws.org/wp-content/uploads/2016/04/Healing-Communities-in-Crisis-4–3.pdf.

President's Task Force on 21st Century Policing. (2015). *Final Report of the President's Task Force on 21st Century Policing*. Washington, DC: US Department of Justice, Office of Community Oriented Policing Services.

Rosenfeld, R. (2016). *Documenting and Explaining the 2015 Homicide Rise: Research Directions*. Washington, DC: US Department of Justice, National Institute of Justice.

Sechrist, S., Weil, J., & Shelton, T. (2016). *Executive Summary of the Evaluation of the Offender Focused Domestic Violence Initiative (OFDIV) in High Point, NC & Replication in Lexington, NC*. Greensboro: University of North Carolina, Greensboro and the North Carolina Network for Safe Communities.

Sierra-Arevalo, M., Charette, Y., & Papachristos, A. V. (2017). Evaluating the effect of project longevity on group-involved shootings and homicides in New Haven, Connecticut. *Crime and Delinquency*, 63(4), 446–467. doi:10.1177/0011128716635197.

Tita, G., Riley, K. J., Ridgeway, G., Grammich, C., Abrahamse, A., & Greenwood, P. (2003). *Reducing Gun Violence: Results From an Intervention in East Los Angeles*. Santa Monica, CA: Rand Corporation.

Travis, J., Kennedy, D., Roman, C., Beckman, K., Solomon, A., & Turner, E. (2003). *An Analysis of Homicide Incident Reviews in the District of Columbia*. Unpublished report. Washington, DC: Urban Institute, Justice Policy Center.

Tyler, T. (2006). *Why People Obey the Law*. Princeton, NJ: Princeton University Press.

University of Cincinnati Policing Institute. (2009). *Implementation of the Cincinnati Initiative to Reduce Violence (CIRV): Year 2 Report*. Cincinnati, OH: University of Cincinnati Policing Institute.

Vasquez, E.A., Wenborne, L., Peers, M., Alleyne, E., & Ellis, K. (2015). Any of them will do: In-group identification, out-group entitativity, and gang membership as predictors of group-based retribution. *Aggressive Behavior*, 41, 242–252. doi:10.1002/ab.21581.

Wakeling, S. (2003). *Ending Gang Homicide: Deterrence Can Work*. Perspectives on Violence Prevention, vol. 1. Sacramento: California Attorney General's Office and the California Health and Human Services Agency.

Wallace, D., Papachristos, A. V., Meares, T. L., & Fagan, J. (2015). Desistance and legitimacy: The impact of offender notification meetings on recidivism among high risk offenders. *Justice Quarterly*, 33(7), 1237–1264.

Warner, B., Pacholke, D., & Kujath, C. (2014). *Operation Place Safety: First Year in Review*. Washington Department of Corrections. www.nnscommunities.org/uploads/Operation_Place_Safety_First_Year_Report_2014.pdf

Weisburd, D., & Eck, J. (2004). What can police do to reduce crime, disorder, and fear? *Annals of the American Academy of Political and Social Science*, 593, 42–65.

Weisburd, D., Farrington, D., & Gill, C. (eds.). (2016. *What Works in Crime Prevention and Rehabilitation: Lessons from Systematic Reviews*. New York: Springer-Verlag.

Williams, D. J., Currie, D., Linden, W., & Donnelly, P. (2014). Addressing gang-related violence in Glasgow: A preliminary pragmatic quasi-experimental evaluation of the community initiative to reduce violence (CIRV). *Aggression and Violent Behavior*, 19(6), 686–691.

Williams, T., & Oppel, R. (2017). Police chiefs say Trump's law enforcement priorities are out of step. *New York Times.* www.nytimes.com/2017/02/12/us/police-chiefs-trump-law-enforcement-priorities.html.

Wong, J., Gravel, J., Bouchard, M., Morselli, C., & Descormiers, K. (2012). *Effectiveness of Street Gang Control Strategies: A Systematic Review and Meta-Analysis of Evaluation Studies.* Public Safety Canada.

Zimring, F., & Hawkins, G. (1973). *Deterrence: The Legal Threat in Crime Control.* Chicago, IL: University of Chicago Press.

Critic

Partnership, Accountability, and Innovation: Clarifying Boston's Experience with Focused Deterrence

Anthony A. Braga, Brandon Turchan, and Christopher Winship

Pioneered in Boston as part of its Operation Ceasefire strategy to halt serious youth violence in the 1990s, focused deterrence approaches (also known as "pulling levers" policing) have been embraced by police departments in the United States and other countries as an effective approach to crime prevention (Travis, 1998; Dalton, 2002; Deuchar, 2013). In its simplest form, the approach consists of selecting a particular crime problem, such as youth homicide; convening an interagency working group of law enforcement practitioners; conducting research to identify key offenders, groups, and behavior patterns; framing a response to offenders and groups of offenders that uses a varied menu of sanctions to stop them from continuing their violent behavior; focusing social services and community resources on targeted offenders and groups to match law enforcement prevention efforts; and directly and repeatedly communicating with offenders to make them understand why they are receiving this special attention (Kennedy, 1997; Kennedy, Chapter 9 in this volume). Although the goal of focused deterrence strategies is to prevent crime by changing offender perceptions of sanction risk, other complementary crime prevention mechanisms seem to support the crime control efficacy of these programs (Braga & Kennedy, 2012; Kennedy, Kleiman & Braga, 2017). These strategies are also intended to change offender behavior by mobilizing community action, enhancing procedural justice, and improving police legitimacy.

A growing body of rigorous scientific evidence suggests focused deterrence strategies have been useful in preventing violence beyond the Boston experience (Braga, Weisburd & Turchan, 2018). A recent review by the US National Academies of Sciences concluded that focused deterrence strategies generate noteworthy crime control impacts when applied to gang and group-related violence, disorderly street drug markets, and repeat offender problems (Weisburd & Majmundar, 2018). However, Boston has been challenged to sustain the implementation of the Ceasefire strategy over extended time periods (Braga, Hureau & Winship, 2008). High profile replications of the Boston approach have experienced similar challenges. In Baltimore, local political problems undermined the implementation process (Braga, Kennedy & Tita, 2002). In Minneapolis, the strategy was abandoned as the participating agencies returned to their traditional methods of dealing with violence (Kennedy & Braga, 1998).

We believe that the difficulties experienced in Boston and by other jurisdictions stem from a limited understanding of the larger Ceasefire story. Boston's success in reducing youth violence has been attributed to a wide variety of programs and strategies: public health interventions, police–probation partnerships, enhanced federal prosecutions, police–black minister partnerships, and the Ceasefire focused deterrence strategy. Many observers have suggested that these are isolated and competing explanations. For example, in his discussion of Operation Ceasefire and the Boston Police Department's collaboration with activist black ministers, Fagan (2002: 136) describes these as "two distinct and contrasting narratives [that] comprise the Boston story."

In reality, the Boston story consists of multiple interconnected layers. As we discuss below, the implementation of Ceasefire was possible because of newly formed relationships among the police and other law enforcement and social service agencies and between the police and the community, with the latter creating important mechanisms for police accountability. Thus, although available quantitative evidence suggests that Operation Ceasefire was the key initiative associated with a significant reduction in youth violence, a fuller and more nuanced description of the Boston experience is needed. A narrow and inappropriate interpretation of Boston's success as simply being due to Operation Ceasefire creates the danger of unrealistic expectations of success, serious implementation problems in replicating the Ceasefire program, and an inability to sustain implemented violence prevention programs.

In order to understand the innovations that took place in Boston's policing strategies during the 1990s, it is necessary to examine the importance of two key elements that created the foundation that made change possible. First, in order for the Boston Police to develop an innovative program involving a variety of partners, it was essential to have established a "network of capacity" consisting of dense and productive relationships that partners could be drawn from. Second, because of the long history of perceived racism on the part of the Boston Police, a new mechanism of police accountability was necessary in order to create trust that new programs would be beneficial to the community. This trust was essential for establishing needed community and political support for innovative efforts by the Boston Police. Operation Ceasefire simply could not have been launched without either a network of partners who were a central component of its design or the trust that derived from accountability.

This chapter begins by briefly describing the key elements of Ceasefire. It then examines the available evidence on Ceasefire's effect on serious violence in Boston and elsewhere. It subsequently discusses the implementation of Ceasefire within the changing political context of police–community relationships and evolving police partnerships with other agencies. It then analyzes the implications of the fuller Boston story for replicating and sustaining the Boston approach in other jurisdictions. Finally, the chapter reviews implementation challenges in applying focused deterrence in other jurisdictions and presents some key strategies for maintaining and ensuring program integrity.

THE BOSTON GUN PROJECT AND OPERATION CEASEFIRE

Like many American cities during the late 1980s and early 1990s, Boston suffered an epidemic of youth violence that had its roots in the rapid spread of street-level crack-cocaine markets (Kennedy, Piehl & Braga, 1996). The Boston Gun Project was a problem-oriented policing project aimed at preventing and controlling serious youth violence. The problem analysis phase of the Project began in early 1995 and the Operation Ceasefire strategy was implemented in mid 1996. The trajectory of the Project and of Ceasefire has been extensively documented (see, e.g., Kennedy et al., 1996; Kennedy, Braga & Piehl, 2001; Kennedy, Chapter 9 in this volume). Briefly, a problem-solving working group of law enforcement personnel, youth workers, and researchers diagnosed the youth violence problem in Boston as one of patterned, largely vendetta-like hostility amongst a small population of highly active criminal offenders, and particularly amongst those involved in some sixty loose, informal, mostly neighborhood-based gangs. Based on the problem analysis findings, the Boston Gun Project working group crafted the Operation Ceasefire initiative that was tightly focused on disrupting ongoing conflicts among youth gangs.

The Boston Police Department's Youth Violence Strike Force (YVSF), an elite unit of some forty officers and detectives, coordinated the actions of Operation Ceasefire. An interagency working group, comprised of law enforcement personnel, youth workers, and members of Boston's TenPoint Coalition of activist black clergy, was convened on a bi-weekly basis to address outbreaks of serious gang violence. Operation Ceasefire's "pulling levers" strategy was designed to deter gang violence by reaching out directly to gangs, saying explicitly that violence would no longer be tolerated, and backing up that message by "pulling every lever" legally available when violence occurred (Kennedy, 1997). These law enforcement levers included disrupting street-level drug markets, serving warrants, mounting federal prosecutions, and changing the conditions of community supervision for probationers and parolees in the targeted group. Simultaneously, youth workers, probation and parole officers, and clergy offered gang members services and other kinds of help. If gang members wanted to step away from a violent lifestyle, the Ceasefire working group focused on providing them with the services and opportunities necessary to make the transition.

The Ceasefire working group delivered their anti-violence message in formal meetings with gang members, through individual police and probation contacts

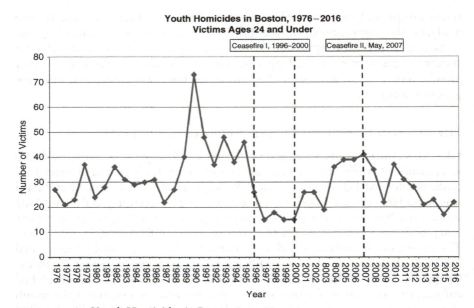

FIGURE 10.1 Youth Homicides in Boston, 1976–2016

with gang members, through meetings with inmates of secure juvenile facilities in the city, and through gang outreach workers (Kennedy et al., 2001). The deterrence message was not a deal with gang members to stop violence. Rather, it was a promise to gang members that violent behavior would evoke an immediate and intense response. If gangs committed other crimes but refrained from violence, the normal workings of police, prosecutors, and the rest of the criminal justice system dealt with these matters. But if gang members shot and killed people, the working group focused its enforcement actions on the violent gang.

A large reduction in the yearly number of Boston youth homicides (victims twenty-four years of age or younger) followed immediately after Operation Ceasefire was implemented in mid-1996. This reduction was sustained for the next five years (see Figure 10.1). The Ceasefire program, as designed, was in place until 2000 (Braga et al., 2008). During the early years of new millennium, the Boston Police experimented with a broader approach to violence prevention by expanding certain Ceasefire tactics to a broader range of problems such as serious repeat violent gun offenders, the re-entry of incarcerated violent offenders back into high-risk Boston neighborhoods, and criminogenic families in hot spot areas. These new approaches were known broadly as "Boston Strategy II" and seemed to diffuse the ability of Boston to respond to ongoing conflicts among gangs (Braga et al., 2008). Youth homicide, most of which was gang related, returned as a serious problem for the City of Boston in 2004 and this rise continued through 2007.

The Boston Police Department and its partners reinstated the Operation Ceasefire approach in mid-2007 to address this concerning increase in serious youth violence (Braga, Hureau & Papachristos, 2014). The reconstituted Ceasefire program was highly focused on addressing ongoing violent conflicts among gangs, drew upon the violence prevention principles of the original strategy, and effectively engaged the existing network of criminal justice, social service, and community-based partners in Boston. Once again, youth homicide decreased after the implementation of the Ceasefire focused deterrence regime (Figure 10.1).

EVIDENCE ON THE IMPACT OF CEASEFIRE ON SERIOUS VIOLENCE

A US Department of Justice (DOJ)-sponsored evaluation of Operation Ceasefire implemented during the 1990s used a non-randomized control group design to analyze trends in serious violence between 1991 and 1998. The evaluation reported that the 1990s Ceasefire intervention was associated with a 63 percent decrease in monthly number of Boston youth homicides, a 32 percent decrease in monthly number of shots-fired calls, a 25 percent decrease in monthly number of gun assaults, and, in one high-risk police district given special attention in the evaluation, a 44 percent decrease in monthly number of youth gun assault incidents (Braga et al., 2001). The evaluation also suggested that Boston's significant youth homicide reduction associated with Operation Ceasefire was distinct when compared to youth homicide trends in most major US and New England cities.

Other researchers, however, have observed that the some of the decrease in homicide may have occurred without the Ceasefire intervention in place as violence was decreasing in most major US cities (Fagan, 2002; Levitt, 2004). The National Academies' Panel on Improving Information and Data on Firearms concluded that the Ceasefire evaluation was compelling in associating the intervention with the subsequent decline in youth homicide (Wellford, Pepper & Petrie, 2005). However, the Panel also suggested that many complex factors affect youth homicide trends and it was difficult to specify the exact relationship between the Ceasefire intervention and subsequent changes in youth offending behaviors. While the DOJ-sponsored evaluation controlled for existing violence trends and certain rival causal factors such as changes in the youth population, drug markets, and employment in Boston, there could be complex interaction effects among these factors not measured by the evaluation that could account for some meaningful portion of the decrease. The evaluation was not a randomized, controlled experiment. Therefore, the non-randomized control group research design cannot rule out these internal threats to the conclusion that Ceasefire was the key factor in the youth homicide decline.

Like the Panel, we believe that Ceasefire was responsible for a meaningful proportion of the youth homicide decline during the 1990s. However, it is difficult to determine the exact contribution of Ceasefire to the decline. Clearly, other factors were responsible for some of the decline. Braga, Hureau, and Papachristos (2014) conducted a more rigorous quasi-experimental evaluation of the reconstituted Boston Ceasefire program implemented during the mid-2000s. Propensity scores were used to match treated Boston gangs to untreated Boston gangs who were not connected to the treated gangs through rivalries or alliances. Differences-in-differences estimators in growth-curve regression models were used to assess the impact of Ceasefire by comparing gun violence trends for matched treatment gangs relative to matched comparisons gangs during the 2006 through 2010 study time period. The evaluation reported that total shootings involving directly treated Ceasefire gangs were reduced by 31 percent relative to total shootings involving comparison gangs. Using similar evaluation methods, Braga, Apel, and Welsh (2013) found that the Ceasefire strategy also created spillover deterrent effects onto other gangs that were socially connected to targeted gangs through rivalries and alliances. Total shootings involving these "vicariously treated" gangs were also decreased by 24 percent relative to total shootings by matched comparison gangs.

It is important to note that the findings from the mid-2000s Ceasefire evaluation yielded a much more conservative violence reduction estimate when compared with program impacts reported in the 1990s Ceasefire quasi-experimental evaluation. It is well known among social scientists that program evaluations with more rigorous research designs tend to result in smaller and null effects (Rossi, 1987). Nonetheless, we believe it is problematic to implement programs that falsely raise citizen expectations of large violent-crime reductions and dramatic changes in the quality of residential life in neighborhoods suffering from persistent drug and violent crime problems. It is much more prudent to take a skeptical approach to policy interventions until a portfolio of proven practices has been developed. The available focused deterrence evaluation evidence suggests that the approach does indeed reduce crime (Weisburd & Majmundar, 2018). Nevertheless, as the quality of program evaluations continues to improve, the impacts of focused deterrence programs seem to be much more modest relative to the large violence reduction and quality-of-life improvements described in earlier accounts (for a discussion, see Braga et al., 2018).

THE LARGER BOSTON STORY I: THE DEVELOPMENT
OF A "NETWORK OF CAPACITY"

Missing from the account of Operation Ceasefire reported in most law enforcement circles is the larger story of an evolving collaboration that spanned the boundaries that divide criminal justice agencies from one another, criminal justice agencies from human service agencies, and criminal justice agencies from the community. Such collaborations are necessary to legitimize, fund, equip, and operate complex strategies that are most likely to succeed in both controlling and preventing youth violence (Moore, 2002). The solid working relationships that were at the heart of the interagency working group process were developed long before the Boston Gun Project commenced in 1995. In essence, Boston created a very powerful "network of capacity" to prevent youth violence (Moore, 2002). This network was well positioned to launch an effective response to youth violence because criminal justice agencies, community groups, and social service agencies coordinated and combined their efforts in ways that could magnify their separate effects. Ceasefire capitalized on these existing relationships by focusing the network on the problem of serious gang violence.

Criminal justice agencies work largely independent of each other, often at cross-purposes, often without coordination, and often in an atmosphere of distrust and dislike (Kennedy, 2002). Until the height of the youth violence epidemic, this observation was certainly true in Boston. It was painfully apparent that no one agency could mount a meaningful response to the gang violence that was spiraling out of control in the city. The crisis forced Boston criminal justice agencies to work together and develop new approaches to deal with the violence problem. YVSF officers and detectives and line-level workers from other criminal justice agencies collaborated on a variety of innovative programs, including: "Operation Nightlight" – a police–probation partnership to ensure at-risk youth were abiding by the conditions of their release into the community (Corbett, Fitzgerald & Jordan, 1998); "Safe Neighborhoods Initiatives" – a community prosecution program that was rooted in a partnership between the Suffolk County District Attorney's Office, the Boston Police, and community members in hot spot neighborhoods (Coles & Kelling, 1999); and a partnership between the Boston Police, the Bureau of Alcohol, Tobacco, and Firearms (ATF), and the US Attorney's Office to identify and apprehend illegal gun traffickers who were providing guns to violent gangs (Kennedy et al., 1996).

The YVSF also formed working relationships with social service and opportunity provision agencies. For certain prevention initiatives, the YVSF was the lead agency involved in the program, such as the "Summer of Opportunity" program that provides at-risk youth with job training and leadership skills that could be transferred to workplace, school, or home settings. More often, however, the police supported the activities of youth social service providers from community-based organizations such as the Boston Community Centers' streetworker program and the Dorchester Youth Collaborative. YVSF officers and detectives would encourage at-risk youth to take advantage of these resources and also consider the input of youth workers in determining whether certain gang-involved youth would be better served by prevention and intervention actions rather than enforcement actions.

When the Boston Gun Project was initiated, the YVSF had already developed a network of working relationships that could be powerfully channeled by a more focused initiative like Operation Ceasefire. Criminal justice agency partnerships provided a varied menu of enforcement options that could be tailored to particular gangs. Without these partnerships, the available "levers" that could be pulled by the working group would have been limited. Social service and opportunity provision agencies were also integrated into Ceasefire interventions to provide a much-needed "carrot" to balance the law enforcement "stick." The inclusion of prevention and intervention programs in the Ceasefire intervention was vitally important in securing community support and involvement in the program. We believe that the legitimacy conferred upon the Ceasefire initiative by key community members was an equally important condition that facilitated the successful implementation of this innovative program.

THE LARGER BOSTON STORY II: ACCOUNTABILITY AND POLICE–COMMUNITY RELATIONS

There was a radical change in the relationship between the Boston Police and Boston's minority communities that pre-dated Ceasefire and had a profound influence on the trajectory of the Ceasefire intervention. This collaborative relationship, led by Ten Point Coalition activist black ministers, developed in the context of a high level of community dissatisfaction with policing strategies and tactics engaged in by the Boston Police (Winship & Berrien, 1999). When the violence epidemic started in the late 1980s, the Boston Police was ill equipped to deal with the sudden increase in serious youth violence. The Boston Police relied upon highly aggressive and reportedly indiscriminate policing tactics to deal with street gang violence (Winship & Berrien, 1999; Berrien & Winship, 2002; 2003). A series of well-publicized scandals emanating from an indiscriminate policy of stopping and frisking all black males in high-crime areas outraged Boston's black community. Perhaps the most important was the 1989 murder of Carol Stuart, a pregnant white woman on her way home from Boston City Hospital. Initially, Charles Stuart, the victim's husband who was the actual murderer, led Boston Police investigators to believe that the murderer was a black male. The police responded by blanketing the Mission Hill housing projects for a suspect. Abusive police conduct was reported to be widespread as coerced statements led to the wrongful arrest of a black male. The black community and the local media were outraged and condemned the discriminatory actions of the investigating officers. The Carol Stuart case and other scandals lead to the establishment of the St Clair Commission, an independent committee appointed to investigate the policies and practices of the Boston Police. In 1992, it released its report, which cited extensive corruption and incompetent management and called for extensive reform including the replacement of top personnel.

In response, the Boston Police overhauled its organization, mission, and tactics during the early 1990s. The existing command staff, including the Commissioner, were replaced with new officers who were known to be innovative and hardworking; investments were made to improve the department's technology to understand crime problems; a neighborhood policing plan was implemented; and beat-level officers were trained in the methods of community and problem-oriented policing. In 1991, the Anti-Gang Violence Unit (AGVU) was created and charged with disrupting ongoing gang conflicts rather than mounting an aggressive campaign to arrest as many offenders as possible. By 1994, the AGVU evolved into the YVSF and its mandate was broadened beyond controlling outbreaks of gang violence to more general youth violence prevention. While these changes were important in creating an environment where the police could collaborate with the community, residents of Boston's poor minority neighborhoods remained wary of and dissatisfied with a police department that had a long history of abusive and unfair treatment.

In 1992, a loosely allied group of activist black clergy formed the Ten Point Coalition after a gang invasion of the Morningstar Baptist Church. During a memorial for a slain rival gang member, mourners were attacked with knives and guns (Winship & Berrien, 1999; Kennedy et al., 2001; Berrien & Winship, 2002; 2003). In the wake of that outrage, the Ten Point Coalition ministers decided they should attempt to prevent the youth in their community from joining gangs, and also that they needed to send an anti-violence message to all youth, whether gang-involved or not.

Initially, the ministers assumed an adversarial role to the Boston Police and were highly critical in the public media of police efforts to prevent youth violence. However, as the ministers worked the streets, they started to form effective relationships with particular YVSF officers and develop a shared understanding of the nature of youth violence in Boston: only a small number of youth in the neighborhoods were involved in violence, many of these gang-involved youth were better served by intervention and prevention strategies, and only a small number of these gang-involved youth needed to be removed from the streets through arrest and prosecution strategies.

The Ten Point ministers also sheltered the police from broad public criticism while the police were engaged in activities the ministers deemed to be of interest to the community and its youth. In 1995, Paul McLaughlin, a local gang prosecutor who was white, was murdered on his way home from work. The initial description of the assailant ("young black male wearing a hooded sweatshirt and baggy pants") was vague enough to cause concern by many in the black community that an "open season on young black males" similar to that during the Carol Stuart investigation would occur (Grunwald & Anand, 1995). Fortunately, these initial fears were unfounded as the black ministers and the Boston Police supported each other in the handling of the media and the ensuing investigation. The black ministers publicly praised the police for showing restraint in their conduct and the police praised the ministers for their willingness to provide help and keep the community calm (Berrien & Winship, 2002, 2003).

Prior to Ceasefire, the Ten Point ministers also helped the Boston Police manage negative publicity by the local media after several potentially explosive events ranging from the beating of a black undercover officer by uniformed police officers (Chacon, 1995) to the accidental death of seventy-five-year-old retired minister who suffered a fatal heart attack after a botched drug raid (Mallia & Mulvhill, 1994). In these cases, the ministers took two positions. First, they demanded that the police department take responsibility for its actions, investigate incidents thoroughly, and hold those involved accountable. Second, after it was clear that the Boston Police was accepting responsibility, the ministers communicated to the community that the police were in fact reacting appropriately. This, in turn, prevented these situations from becoming racially explosive and provided the police with the continued political support they needed in order to undertake policy innovations, such as Ceasefire. In more recent years, the ministers have continued to play this dual role with regards to fatal police shootings, eight of which occurred over a twenty-two-month period between 2000 and 2002 (Tench, 2002).

While the TenPoint ministers were not involved in the design of the Ceasefire intervention, they were influential as an informal "litmus test" of the types of enforcement actions that would and would not be tolerated by the community. The youth workers participating in the design of Ceasefire would voice their concerns about community reaction to any proposed enforcement tactics that could be viewed as overly aggressive. However, what usually ended discussions was the recognition of the political vulnerability of the Boston Police to the consequences of the TenPoint ministers potentially reporting any questionable practices to local media and, more importantly, exerting pressure on the Mayor's Office to deal with perceived inappropriate actions by the Department. For example, while discussing plausible interventions, the working group considered the notable gun violence reduction results of the Kansas City Gun Experiment, which involved intensive enforcement of laws against illegally carrying concealed firearms via safety frisks during traffic stops, plain view, and searches incident to arrest in gun violence hot spot areas (Sherman & Rogan, 1995). After some discussion, the working group rejected the idea of engaging a hot spots policing strategy as the Boston Police did not want to adopt an enforcement program that could be viewed by the Ten Point ministers as a return to the indiscriminate "stop and frisk" policies of the past.

When Ceasefire was ready to be implemented, the commander of the YVSF presented the program to key black ministers to obtain their approval of, and involvement in, the initiative. The Boston Police knew that they would need the political support of the Ten Point Coalition to pursue aggressive enforcement actions against hard-core gang members central to violent conflicts. While the Ceasefire initiative was a violence prevention campaign, given the Carol Stuart case and other incidents, the community and local media could have easily misunderstood the enforcement tactics as simply another law enforcement initiative designed to arrest large numbers of young black men. The ministers recognized the value of the Ceasefire approach to violence prevention as it was carefully focused only on violent gang-involved youth and provided social services and opportunities to gang youth who desired them. After Ceasefire was implemented, Ten Point Coalition ministers became regular members of the working group. Ministers played key roles in working with the police to identify dangerous gang-involved youth, communicating the anti-violence deterrence message to all youth and, with the help of social service providers, offering assistance to gang youth who wanted to step away from their violent lifestyles. By including the ministers in the Ceasefire working group, the Boston Police developed a mechanism for transparency and accountability that was very desirable to Boston's minority community. Through their involvement in Ceasefire, the ministers became part of the process of determining which gang interventions would be done and when. In addition, they, along with others, gave gangs members the message that they had a choice: stop the "gang banging" and they would be helped – with school, a job, family; continue and the full weight of the law (and the community) would come down on them, with every possible lever being used to see that they were incarcerated. At a more general level, a shared understanding of the reality of youth violence and the actions that were necessary to prevent and control that violence emerged (Berrien & Winship, 2002; 2003). The transparency and involvement in the enforcement process built trust and further solidified a functional working relationship between the community and the Boston Police. In turn, by engaging a process through which they were meaningfully and appropriately accountable to the community, the Boston Police created the political support, or "umbrella of legitimacy," that it needed to pursue more focused and perhaps more aggressive intervention than would have been possible otherwise (Berrien & Winship, 2002).

IMPLICATIONS OF THE LARGER BOSTON STORY FOR OTHER JURISDICTIONS

Operation Ceasefire became a nationally recognized model for youth violence reduction programs and many jurisdictions quickly started to experiment with the approach (Kennedy, Chapter 9 in this volume). Unfortunately, despite some initial promising results, many of these replications were never fully implemented or were eventually abandoned. Braga has been involved in replication efforts in a number of cities, including Baltimore, Minneapolis, and San Francisco, and these jurisdictions simply did not have an adequate network of capacity in place before adopting a Ceasefire-like approach to youth violence. Operation Ceasefire was a "relationship intensive" intervention based on trust and the ability of a diverse set of individuals to work together toward a common goal. The narrow description of Ceasefire that currently circulates in criminal justice circles is, in many ways, a recipe for frustration and eventual failure as it simplifies the trajectory of the Boston experience. And, as suggested by the cessation of the Ceasefire in Boston during the early 2000s, it can be challenging to keep these networks focused on specific problems over extended time periods.

Effective collaborations and the trust and accountability that they entail are essential in launching a meaningful response to complex youth violence problems. However, the fact that such collaborations are needed does not guarantee that they inevitably rise or, once developed, that they are sustained. There are many significant obstacles to their development and maintenance such as giving up control over scarce resources that could compromise agencies' traditional missions, aligning agencies' individual work efforts into a functional enterprise, and developing a collective leadership among a group of individuals aligned with the needs of their individual organizations (Bardach, 1998).

A central problem in creating and managing effective capacity-building collaborations is overcoming the problem of distrust (Bardach, 1998). Distrust corrodes the creative process that criminal justice agencies and community-based organizations are necessarily engaged in. Like most cities, distrust characterized the relationship among criminal justice agencies and between criminal justice agencies and the inner city community in Boston. Practitioners and community members in Boston were able to overcome their historical distrust and form productive working relationships. These relationships existed before Ceasefire and were the foundation upon it was built. Of course, working groups can be forced together and, sometimes, can implement short-term programs that have promising initial results. However, if the initiative is not based on a shared understanding of the problem and cemented through functional partnerships, the initiative will fall apart. These are key issues for other jurisdictions to consider in replicating Operation Ceasefire and in sustaining the collaborative effort once it has been launched.

In many community and problem-oriented policing projects, community members serve as informants who report to the police on unacceptable community conditions and the particulars of crime problems (Skogan & Hartnett, 1997; Braga, 2008). They are rarely engaged as "partners" or "coproducers" of public safety. Police officers remain the "experts" on crime who are primarily responsible for developing and managing interventions to address crime problems. Through their collaboration with Ten Point ministers, the Boston Police discovered a system whereby they were accountable to the community. This accountability to the community became a great asset to the police. By engaging the ministers in their violence prevention efforts and creating a sense of joint ownership of the youth violence problem, the Boston

Police created the political support necessary for both innovation and more focused and aggressive intervention. With the Ten Point's approval of and involvement in Operation Ceasefire, the community supported the approach as a legitimate violence prevention campaign. Police strategies can acquire true legitimacy within the inner city only if the community partner supports police tactics when they are appropriate as well as publicly criticizes activities that are not (Berrien & Winship, 2002; 2003). Given the potentially harsh law enforcement levers that can be pulled as part of a Ceasefire-like program, we feel that community involvement is critical in replicating and sustaining such intensive violence-prevention initiatives. Without the political support of the community, the police cannot pursue an innovative enforcement strategy that targets truly dangerous youth at the heart of urban youth violence problems.

IMPLEMENTATION CHALLENGES IN OTHER JURISDICTIONS

The multifaceted and interagency structure of focused deterrence interventions presents a number of opportunities for implementation challenges and threats to treatment integrity. Evidence suggests the extent to which focused deterrence strategies are effective in controlling crime and violence is contingent on their fidelity to core prevention principles and program activities. A national assessment of US DOJ-sponsored Project Safe Neighborhoods (PSN) initiatives in eighty-two cities, which encouraged local sites to embrace the focused deterrence approach, found greater implementation fidelity was associated with more robust crime control gains (McGarrell et al., 2010). Unfortunately, implementation challenges have been found to threaten the integrity of gang and group violence reduction, DMI, and individual offender focused programs alike. Indeed, nearly one-third of the twenty-four evaluations included in the Braga et al. (2018) review of focused deterrence strategies reported at least one potential threat to treatment integrity.

Beyond the implementation challenges in Baltimore, Boston, Minneapolis, and San Francisco mentioned earlier, other gang and group-based initiatives have also experienced noteworthy program management challenges. For instance, the robustness of the Rochester Ceasefire intervention was limited by uncertain enforcement actions, poor inter-agency communication and coordination, and deficiencies in marketing the deterrence message to the targeted audience (Delaney, 2006). The Kansas City No Violence Alliance group violence reduction strategy had to overcome early problems stemming from a lack of leadership and poor communication among participating agencies before the intervention took hold (Fox, Novak & Yaghoub, 2015).

A high-risk individual offender variation of the Boston model was applied in Chicago, Illinois, as part of the PSN initiative. Gun- and gang-involved parolees returning to two highly dangerous Chicago Police Department districts went through "offender notification forums," where they were informed of their vulnerability as felons to federal firearms laws with stiff mandatory minimum sentences; offered social services; and addressed by community members and ex-offenders. Initial program evaluation evidence suggested that PSN generated sharp violent crime decreases in the two treated police districts and reduced recidivism among treated individuals (see Papachristos, Meares & Fagan, 2007; Wallace et al., 2016). This initial success spurred the aggressive expansion of the PSN intervention to 24 percent of the city's police districts. Unfortunately, this expansion was not accompanied by increased resources and the resulting program was not well coordinated or supported in the expansion areas. Not surprisingly, the expanded PSN effort was not associated with any discernible crime control gains in the treated areas relative to comparison areas (Grunwald & Papachristos, 2017).

Focused deterrence programs implemented to reduce crime driven by street-level drug markets are generally called "drug market intervention" (DMI) strategies (Kennedy & Wong, 2009). DMI focused deterrence strategies identify street-level dealers, immediately apprehend violent drug offenders, and suspend criminal cases for non-violent dealers. DMI strategies then bring together non-violent drug dealers, their families, law enforcement and criminal justice officials, service providers, and community leaders for a meeting that makes clear the dealing has to stop, the community cares for the offenders but rejects their conduct, help is available, and renewed dealing will result in the activation of the existing case. Evaluation research has shown the DMI approach to be effective in controlling crime in High Point, North Carolina (Corsaro et al., 2012; Saunders et al., 2015) and elsewhere (Corsaro, Brunson & McGarrell, 2009; Corsaro & McGarrell, 2009).

As a result of the early success of the drug market intervention approach, the US Bureau of Justice Assistance (BJA) funded an effort to systematically replicate the DMI strategy in thirty-two sites around the United States (Saunders, Robbins & Ober, 2017). Of the thirty-two sites that attempted a DMI, only seven implemented a program with enough integrity to warrant a formal evaluation.[1] However, these seven sites also experienced difficulty implementing the DMI program properly. Deficiencies ranged from a lack of support from partnering agencies and community groups to uncertain identification of key players in targeted drug markets to diminished follow-up on enforcement and social service promises after completed call-ins with drug offenders (Saunders et al., 2016). Two of the seven sites failed to make it past the planning phase of the intervention while only four sites conducted at least one call-in and completed all five phases.

The BJA-supported evaluation of these seven sites found that DMI programs with greater implementation fidelity experienced the largest reductions in crime (Saunders et al., 2017). Similarly, Braga, Weisburd, and Turchan (2018) attributed the smaller effect sizes observed for DMI programs in their

---

[1] The seven sites included: Flint, Michigan; Guntersville, Alabama; Jacksonville, Florida; Gary, Indiana; Montgomery County, Maryland; New Orleans, Louisiana; and Roanoke, Virginia.

systematic review and meta-analysis to compromises in the DMI treatment as delivered in the reviewed studies. We believe that the collective BJA DMI experience, as well as the other problematic applications of focused deterrence more generally, affirms the importance of developing a network of capacity that is rooted in trust and accountability among the collaborating agencies to ensure proper implementation.

SYSTEMATIC EFFORTS TO IMPROVE THE IMPLEMENTATION OF FOCUSED DETERRENCE

As focused deterrence programs have gained increasing prominence as a key component of a balanced portfolio of interventions to prevent urban violence, there have been systematic efforts to promote the proper implementation of these strategies. Most notably, the National Network for Safe Communities (NNSC) at the John Jay College of Criminal Justice have developed a variety of practitioner-oriented resources that structure program activities to ensure treatment integrity in focused deterrence strategies. For instance, NNSC (2016) recommends that after a focused deterrence call-in is held:

(1) The working group should meet to recap the call-in and plan future project activities.
(2) Data analysis should be ongoing and performance metrics continuously tracked.
(3) Follow through on promises made at call-ins must materialize (e.g., enforcement actions, connecting clients to social services, and continuing to engage with the moral voices of the community).
(4) Communication with clients should be ongoing via holding additional call-ins, conducting custom notifications at the residences of clients, contacting high-risk individuals not under community supervision, and interrupting escalating violence.

In addition to maintaining and ensuring treatment integrity from the outset of implementation, local jurisdictions should focus on developing accountability structures and sustainability plans before focused deterrence programs commence. Accountability and sustainability in focused deterrence initiatives can be threatened by personnel turnover due to its reliance on a number of key actors required across multiple agencies and groups to successfully execute the strategy. The continuity of the original Boston Ceasefire intervention was seriously hindered by personnel turnover among key criminal justice managers and important community stakeholders involved in the process (Braga et al., 2008). There are, however, ways that the consequences of personnel turnover could be minimized. For example, in response to substantial turnover of key staff involved with the Chicago PSN program, project coordinators conducted "reboot" trainings with new replacement staff to ensure buy-in and maintain treatment integrity (Grunwald & Papachristos, 2017: 142).

The National Network for Safe Communities (2016) outlined two ways that program sustainability and accountability could be enhanced: (1) establishing a governing structure that extends beyond the working group and (2) creating a performance maintenance system for intelligence gathering and analysis as well as continually keeping partners engaged in the project. The most comprehensive approach to address sustainability concerns through establishing a formal multi-level governance structure was undertaken by the Cincinnati Initiative to Reduce Violence (CIRV). Prior to the initiation of the intervention, CIRV staff recruited local business executives and social science researchers to participate in the planning process and provide input that would increase long-term viability of the intervention (Tillyer, Engel & Lovins, 2012). The three primary ways these outside experts assisted with the overall design of the CIRV was via "(a) development of an organizational structure, (b) utilization of corporate strategic planning principles for managing the work, and (c) systematic data collection to assist in decision making and outcome evaluation" (Tillyer et al., 2012: 978).

Three tiers made up the CIRV organizational structure (Engel, Tillyer & Corsaro, 2013). At the top was a *Governing Board* composed of high-ranking city officials who were responsible for overseeing the project, providing resources, and overcoming obstacles encountered during implementation. Reporting to the Governing Board was a *Strategy and Implementation Team* comprised of spokespersons, heads of individual strategy teams, consultants, and an executive director, and this body was responsible for daily operations, strategy development, and monitoring results. There were four *Individual Strategy Teams* that were responsible for carrying out particular aspects of the intervention and these included a law enforcement team, social services team, community engagement team, and systems team. In this tiered organizational structure, the governing board offers a stabilizing presence when there is personnel turnover among team leaders, consultants, and members of individual strategy teams.

The second area where outside experts contributed to the CIRV was incorporating corporate principles into project planning and implementation. Utilizing corporate principles was intended to help project participants organize, prioritize, and assign tasks needing to be accomplished (Tillyer et al., 2012). These assignments, along with corresponding performance measures, were tracked using "balanced scorecards" in order to promote accountability among teams for short-term performance assessments while also linking metrics to the overall strategy (Tillyer et al., 2012: 980). Tillyer and colleagues (2012) noted that there was initial resistance to this form of oversight among participating law enforcement and social service providers but its value was demonstrated when some team members began experiencing "mission creep" and the tool helped as a corrective influence realigning them with the intervention's goals and objectives.

Systematic data collection was the final area where outside experts assisted with the CIRV. The purpose of establishing systematic data collection is to provide project managers and decision makers with the most thorough and accurate possible depiction of the problem. In addition to impact measures (e.g., the number of homicides or group-involved shootings), data collection efforts for the CIRV also incorporated several process measures in order to assess treatment fidelity (Tillyer et al., 2012). Process measures that were examined included "the extent to which the message was delivered to the target population, the level of law enforcement action that was being taken against violent groups linked to a homicide, and details regarding the delivery of services to those who were requesting help" (Tillyer et al., 2012: 981–982).

One particular data collection tool that has proven valuable in gang and group-based focused deterrence interventions is the shooting scorecard. A shooting scorecard tracks the number of shootings committed by groups in a given area over a defined period of time (e.g., weeks, months, or years). Convening appropriate individuals (e.g., detectives, patrol officers, crime analysts, etc.) to collectively review shooting scorecards at regular meetings offers a number of benefits: it presents timely information on gun violence to project personnel, it provides police with a better understanding of the dynamics of gun violence in their jurisdiction, and it assists management with identifying the most frequently offending and high-risk groups and ensuring that resources are distributed accordingly (Braga & Hureau, 2012; Braga et al., 2014). Shooting scorecards have been found to be an effective tool in cities seeking implement and track group violence interventions, such as Boston, Massachusetts; Newark, New Jersey; Oakland, California; and Salinas, California (see Braga & Hureau, 2012; Braga et al., 2014; Conroy, Harmon & Roehl, 2015).

CONCLUSION

Existing program evaluation evidence suggests that focused deterrence strategies generate significant crime reduction impacts when applied to gang and group-related violence, disorderly street drug markets, and repeat offender problems (Braga et al., 2018; Weisburd & Majmundar, 2018). Some observers suggest focused deterrence strategies hold great promise in improving strained relationships between minority neighborhoods and the police departments that serve them through the inclusion of community members in the strategy, engagement of offenders in procedurally just offender notification sessions, and the provision of service and opportunities to offenders (Meares, 2009; Brunson, 2015). However, focused deterrence programs need to be implemented properly to generate these desirable crime control gains and police–community relations benefits. The available program evaluation evidence reviewed here suggests that it is difficult for local jurisdictions to achieve successful program implementations that remain robust over time.

A careful analysis of the implementation of focused deterrence in Boston suggests that jurisdictions need to ensure that a vibrant network of capacity that is grounded in trust and accountability needs to be in place when these programs commence. Experiences in other jurisdictions affirm the larger Boston story and offer a broader knowledge base to consider the development of accountability structures and sustainability plans to make certain that programs remain potent and appropriately focused beyond the initial implementation. Without such a priori planning and structure development, focused deterrence programs will not achieve their desired crime control goals. And, equally concerning, the inappropriate implementation of these programs could exacerbate poor police–community relations and generate collateral harms through the increased surveillance and harsh enforcement if these strategies are not appropriately focused (Griffiths & Christian, 2015). Focused deterrence strategies have been described elsewhere as exercises in "getting deterrence right" (e.g., Braga, 2012); we think it is critically important for jurisdictions experimenting with these strategies to be equally committed to the exercise of "getting implementation right."

REFERENCES

Bardach, E. (1998). *Getting Agencies to Work Together*. Washington, DC: Brookings Institution Press.

Berrien, J., & Winship, C. (2002). An umbrella of legitimacy: Boston's police department – Ten Point Coalition collaboration. In G. Katzmann (ed.), *Securing Our Children's Future: New Approaches to Juvenile Justice and Youth Violence*. Washington, DC: Brookings Institution Press.

Berrien, J., & Winship, C. (2003). Should we have faith in the churches? The Ten-Point Coalition's effect on Boston's youth violence. In B. Harcourt (ed.), *Guns, Crime, and Punishment in America*. New York: New York University Press.

Braga, A. (2008). *Problem-Oriented Policing and Crime Prevention*. 2nd edition. Monsey, NY: Criminal Justice Press.

Braga, A. (2012). Getting deterrence right? Evaluation evidence and complementary crime control mechanisms. *Criminology and Public Policy*, 11(2), 201–210.

Braga, A., Apel, R., & Welsh, B. (2013). The spillover effects of focused deterrence on gang violence. *Evaluation Review*, 37(3–4), 314–342.

Braga, A., & Hureau, D. M. (2012). Strategic problem analysis to guide comprehensive gang violence reduction strategies. In E. Gebo, & B.J. Bond (eds.), *Looking Beyond Suppression: Community Strategies to Reduce Gang Violence*. Lexington, MA: Lexington Books.

Braga, A., Hureau, D. M., & Grossman, L. S. (2014). *Managing the Group Violence Intervention: Using Shooting Scorecards to Track Group Violence*. Washington, DC: US Department of Justice, Community Oriented Policing Services.

Braga, A., Hureau, D. M., & Papachristos, A. V. (2014). Deterring gang-involved gun violence: Measuring the impact of Boston's Operation Ceasefire on street gang behavior. *Journal of Quantitative Criminology*, 30, 113–139.

Braga, A., Hureau, D. M., & Winship, C. (2008). Losing faith? Police, Black Churches, and the resurgence of youth violence in Boston. *Ohio State Journal of Criminal Law*, 6, 141–172.

Braga, A., & Kennedy, D. (2012). Linking situational crime prevention and focused deterrence strategies. In N. Tilley, & G. Farrell (eds.), *The Reasoning Criminologist: Essays in Honour of Ronald V. Clarke*. London, UK: Taylor and Francis.

Braga, A., Kennedy, D., & Tita, G. (2002). New approaches to the strategic prevention of gang and group-involved violence. In C. R. Huff (ed.), *Gangs in America*, 3rd edition. Thousand Oaks, CA: Sage Publications.

Braga, A., Kennedy, D., Waring, E., & Piehl, A. (2001). Problem-oriented policing, deterrence, and youth violence: An evaluation of Boston's Operation Ceasefire. *Journal of Research in Crime and Delinquency*, 38, 195–225.

Braga, A., Weisburd, D., & Turchan, B. (2018). Focused deterrence strategies and crime control: An updated systematic review and meta-analysis of the empirical evidence. *Criminology & Public Policy*, 17(1).

Brunson, R. (2015). Focused deterrence and improved police-community relations: Unpacking the proverbial "black box". *Criminology and Public Policy*, 14(3), 507–514.

Chacon, R. (1995). Boston Police investigators seek cause of undercover officer's injuries. The Boston Globe, February 4: 22.

Coles, C., & Kelling, G. (1999). Prevention through community prosecution. *The Public Interest*, 136, 69–84.

Conroy, A., Harmon, R., & Roehl, J. (2015). Implementing a comprehensive smart on crime strategy. *United States Attorneys' Bulletin*, March, 22–44.

Corbett, R., Fitzgerald, B., & Jordan, J. (1998). Boston's Operation Night Light: An emerging model for police-probation partnerships. In J. Petersilia (ed.), *Community Corrections: Probation, Parole, and Intermediate Sanctions*. New York: Oxford University Press.

Corsaro, N., Brunson, R. K., & McGarrell, E. F. (2009). Problem-oriented policing and open-air drug markets: Examining the Rockford pulling levers strategy. *Crime & Delinquency*, 59(7), 1085–1107.

Corsaro, N., Hunt, E. D., Kroovand Hipple, N., & McGarrell, E. F., (2012). The impact of drug market pulling levers policing on neighborhood violence: An evaluation of the High Point drug market intervention. *Criminology and Public Policy*, 11(2), 167–199.

Corsaro, N., & McGarrell, E. F. (2009). *An evaluation of the Nashville drug market initiative (DMI) pulling levers strategy*. East Lansing: Michigan State University, School of Criminal Justice.

Dalton, E. (2002). Targeted crime reduction efforts in ten communities: Lessons for the Project Safe Neighborhoods Initiative. *US Attorney's Bulletin*, 50, 16–25.

Delaney, C. (2006). *The Effects of Focused Deterrence on Gang Homicide: An Evaluation of Rochester's Ceasefire Program*. Rochester, NY: Rochester Institute of Technology.

Deuchar, R. (2013). *Policing Youth Violence: Transatlantic Connections*. London, UK: IEP Press.

Engel, R. S., Tillyer, M. S., & Corsaro N. (2013). Reducing gang violence using focused deterrence: Evaluating the Cincinnati Initiative to Reduce Violence (CIRV). *Justice Quarterly*, 30, 403–439.

Fagan, J. (2002). Policing guns and youth violence. *The Future of Children*, 12, 133–151.

Fox, A. M., Novak, K. J., & Yaghoub, M. B. (2015). *Measuring the Impact of Kansas City's No Violence Alliance*. Kansas City: University of Missouri; Kansas City, Department of Criminal Justice and Criminology.

Griffiths, E., & Christian, J. (2015). Considering focused deterrence in the age of Ferguson, North Charleston, and beyond. *Criminology & Public Policy*, 14, 573–581.

Grunwald, M., & Anand, G. (1995). Authorities praised; Some Blacks wary. The Boston Globe, September 30: 80.

Grunwald, B., & Papachristos, A. V. (2017). Project Safe Neighborhoods in Chicago: Looking back a decade later. *Journal of Criminal Law and Criminology*, 107, 131–160.

Kennedy, D. (1997). Pulling levers: Chronic offenders, high-crime settings, and a theory of prevention. *Valparaiso University Law Review*, 31, 449–484.

Kennedy, D. (2002). A tale of one city: Reflections on the Boston Gun Project. In G. Katzmann (ed.), *Securing Our Children's Future: New Approaches to Juvenile Justice and Youth Violence*. Washington, DC: Brookings Institution Press.

Kennedy, D., & Braga, A. (1998). Homicide in Minneapolis: Research for problem solving. *Homicide Studies*, 2, 263–290.

Kennedy, D., Braga, A., & Piehl, A. (2001). Developing and implementing operation ceasefire. In *Reducing Gun Violence: The Boston Gun Project's Operation Ceasefire*. Washington, DC: National Institute of Justice, US Department of Justice.

Kennedy, D., Kleiman, M., & Braga, A. (2017). Beyond deterrence: Strategies of focus and fairness. In N. Tilley, & A. Sidebottom (eds.), *Handbook of Crime Prevention and Community Safety* 2nd ed. New York, NY: Routledge.

Kennedy, D., Piehl, A., & Braga, A. (1996). Youth violence in Boston: Gun markets, serious offenders, and a use-reduction strategy. *Law and Contemporary Problems*, 59, 147–196.

Kennedy, D. M., & Wong, S. (2009). *The High Point Drug Market Intervention Strategy*. Washington, DC: US Department of Justice, Office of Community Oriented Policing Services.

Levitt, S. (2004). Understanding why crime fell in the 1990s: Four factors that explain the decline and six that do not. *Journal of Economic Perspectives*, 18, 163–190.

Mallia, J., & Mulvihill, M. (1994). Minister dies as cops raid wrong apartment. The Boston Herald, March 26: 1.

McGarrell, E. F., Corsaro, N., Hipple, N. K., & Bynum, T. S. (2010). Project Safe Neighborhoods and violent crime trends in US Cities: Assessing violent crime impact. *Journal of Quantitative Criminology*, 26, 165–190.

Meares, T. (2009). The legitimacy of police among young African American men. *Marquette Law Review*, 92(4), 651–666.

Moore, M. (2002). Creating networks of capacity: the challenge of managing society's response to youth violence. In G. Katzmann (ed.), *Securing Our Children's Future: New Approaches to Juvenile Justice and Youth Violence*. Washington, DC: Brookings Institution Press.

National Network for Safe Communities. (2016). *Group Violence Intervention: An Implementation Guide*. Washington, DC: US Department of Justice, Community Oriented Policing Services.

Papachristos, A. V., Meares, T., & Fagan, J. (2007). Attention felons: Evaluating Project Safe Neighborhoods in Chicago. *Journal of Empirical Legal Studies*, 4, 223–272.

Rossi, P. (1987). The iron law of evaluation and other metallic rules. *Research in Social Problems and Public Policy*, 4, 3–20.

Saunders, J., Lundberg, R., Braga, A., Ridgeway, G., & Miles, J. (2015). A synthetic control approach to evaluating place-based crime interventions. *Journal of Quantitative Criminology*, 31(3), 413–434.

Saunders, J., Ober, A. J., Kilmer, B., & Greathouse, S. M. (2016). *A Community-Based, Focused-Deterrence Approach to Closing Overt Drug Markets: A Process and Fidelity Evaluation of Seven Sites, Appendix G*. Santa Monica, CA: RAND Corporation.

Saunders, J., Robbins, M., & Ober, A. J. (2017). Moving from efficacy to effectiveness: Implementing the drug market intervention across multiple sites. *Criminology & Public Policy*, 16, 787–814.

Sherman, L., & Rogan, D. (1995). Effects of gun seizures on gun violence: "Hot spots" patrol in Kansas City. *Justice Quarterly*, 12, 673–694.

Skogan, W., & Hartnett, S. (1997). *Community Policing, Chicago Style*. New York: Oxford University Press.

Tench, M. (2002). Group offers support for Evans, Points to progress in curbing violence. The Boston Globe, September 21: 34.

Tillyer, M. S., Engel, R. S., & Lovins, B. (2012). Beyond Boston: Applying theory to understand and address sustainability issues in focused deterrence initiatives for violence reduction. *Crime & Delinquency*, 58, 973–997.

Travis, J. 1998. Crime, Justice, and Public Policy. Plenary presentation to the American Society of Criminology, Washington, DC, November 12. http://www.ojp.usdoj.gov/nij/speeches/asc.htm.

Wallace, D., Papachristos, A. V., Meares, T., and Fagan, J. (2016). Desistance and Legitimacy: The Impact of Offender Notification Meetings on Recidivism among High Risk Offenders. *Justice Quarterly*, 33(7), 1–28.

Weisburd, D., & Majmundar, M. (eds.). (2018). *Proactive Policing: Effects on Crime and Communities*. Committee on Proactive Policing: Effects on Crime, Communities, and Civil Liberties. Washington, DC: The National Academies Press.

Wellford, C., Pepper, J., & Petrie, C. (eds.). (2005). *Firearms and Violence: A Critical Review*. Committee to Improve Research Information and Data on Firearms. Committee on Law and Justice, Division of Behavioral and Social Sciences and Education. Washington, DC: The National Academies Press.

Winship, C., & Berrien, J. (1999). Boston cops and Black Churches. *The Public Interest*, 136, 52–68.

PART VI

THIRD–PARTY POLICING

11

Advocate

Third-Party Policing

Lorraine Mazerolle and Janet Ransley

INTRODUCTION

In Third-Party Policing (hereafter TPP), police partner with others to proactively reduce crime and disorder, often focusing on places with recurrent crime problems, or people at high risk of offending. Partnerships in policing are not new. Police have always sought out and formed partnerships with a range of different entities to tackle a myriad of different types of problems. What is new for police is the *expectation,* and sometimes the legislated mandate, that they will partner with others. In the United States, the emphasis for police is on partnerships with communities to co-produce public safety (see President's Task Force on 21st Century Policing, 2015). In the United Kingdom, police are compelled by law to involve local authorities in setting priorities and developing plans (see Police Reform and Social Responsibility Act 2011; Police and Fire Reform (Scotland) Act 2012), and numerous reports (see Independent Police Commission, 2013: 14–15; and National Debate Advisory Group, 2015, ch. 2) have expressed a vision for policing in which partnerships are central to most policing functions.

TPP is just one form of partnership policing, characterized by police engaging with entities that have access to legal levers in order to enhance their capacity to control and prevent crime. The key mechanism of TPP is the activating or escalating of latent legal processes. These legal options are often underutilized or dormant (at least from a crime control perspective) until police initiate, foster, remind, and encourage their partners to use them. One of the central tenets of TPP is that third parties possessing a legal mandate (i.e., an existing power or sanction from legislation, regulation, contract, or other source) are likely to make better crime control partners than partners lacking access to a legal lever (Mazerolle, 2014). In TPP, therefore, partnerships are theorized to be effective and sustainable because of the existing legal powers that underpin the foundations for collaboration.

Evidence supporting the effectiveness of partnership approaches for addressing crime and disorder is well established (see Green, 1996; Eck & Wartell, 1998; Dunworth & Mills, 1999; Fleming, 2005; Johnson, 2005; McGarrell et al., 2006; Berry et al., 2011 for a review; Braga, Papachristos & Hureau, 2014; Corsaro & Engel, 2015; see also Mazerolle, Soole & Rombouts, 2007 for a review), suggesting that partnerships are effective because they create greater capacity than the police might otherwise possess. Rosenbaum (2002) suggests that partnerships increase the capacity of police and their partners to target criminogenic risk factors in a multifaceted manner while also efficiently pooling and executing resources (see also Cherney, 2008; Rosenbaum & Schuck, 2012). Similarly, Bond and Gittell (2010: 119) suggest that multiagency partnerships can coproduce positive outcomes by facilitating coordination through "frequent high-quality communication supported by relationships of shared goals, shared knowledge, and mutual respect" (see also Gittell, 2006; 2011; Gittell et al., 2000; Gittell et al., 2008).

In TPP, Mazerolle and her colleagues (see Buerger & Mazerolle, 1998; Mazerolle & Ransley, 2005) argue that a third party's legal powers, activated in the context of a crime control partnership with police, provide the key mechanism that motivates actors to contribute to the coproduction of crime control benefits (see also Mazerolle, 2014). TPP is thus defined as police efforts to persuade or coerce organizations or non-offending persons, such as public housing agencies, property owners, parents, health and building inspectors, and business owners, to take some responsibility for preventing crime or reducing crime problems (Buerger & Mazerolle, 1998: 301). Often these efforts overlap with other proactive policing strategies, such as place-based and problem-oriented approaches (National Academies of Sciences, Engineering, and Medicine, 2017). But the unique feature of TPP is that the approach uses a third party's laws to systematically expand, and potentially optimize, the capacity of police to bring non-police partners into the business of crime control. Police do this by convincing or coercing third parties to target and focus their laws and resources on the geographic, situational, and/or individual factors that underlie crime and disorder problems.

Central to TPP is that police operate within a legal and regulatory framework that enables them to draw on the authority and powers of their partners. These partners may be voluntary, co-opted or coerced to help control crime problems. Cooperative consultation by police with community members, parents, inspectors, and regulators might encourage and convince those third parties to take on more crime control or prevention responsibility. Such consultation encourages partners to help alter underlying conditions that police believe might lead to future crime problems. In these situations, police coercion and sanctioning is not required. Instead, police rely on their persuasive powers, while being consciously aware, or even unaware, of alternative methods of coercion that they could resort to if the third-party target proves to be an unwilling participant. At other times, the police use coercive means with third parties, which might reduce crime problems, but also potentially undermine their legitimacy (see Meares, 2006; Ransley, 2016). At this coercive end of the engagement continuum, the police engage third parties by threatening or actually initiating actions that compel the third party's participation in the crime-control activity. This type of coercion in order to engage third parties' legal levers creates the potential for the intervention to backfire, causing unintended consequences, such as re-victimizing victims or marginalized groups, or damaging the legitimacy of police or their partners (see Mazerolle & Ransley, 2005; Desmond & Valdez, 2013; Stuart, Armenta & Osborne, 2015; Swan, 2015). There is also the potential for the privacy of third parties to be adversely affected (National Academies of Sciences, Engineering, and Medicine, 2017).

The proliferation of TPP has not occurred in a vacuum, nor as an idea born at the grassroots of policing, nor because more police have improved their proactive crime control efforts. Rather, we argue that the pace, context, and prominence of TPP initiatives have escalated in recent years as one of the many consequences of the move from centralized state control to a system of decentralized networks of governance and crime control agents. The proliferation and development of TPP is, we suggest, reflective of external pressure and the general transformation of government and governance taking place in contemporary society.

In this chapter, we provide an analysis of the TPP approach to crime control. We begin by situating TPP in the broader governance and regulatory literature. We then examine the dimensions of TPP, focusing on TPP partnerships and the broad range of legal levers used in TPP. The evaluation evidence pertaining to TPP is then presented before we explore the potential long-term effects of partnerships used in a TPP context. We conclude with a discussion about the future of TPP, including recognition of the potential backfire effects of policing in partnership with third parties.

GOVERNANCE, REGULATION, AND THIRD-PARTY POLICING

We have previously argued (Mazerolle & Ransley, 2005) that the rise of TPP is part of a pattern of major change, indeed a transformation, of government and governance that began in the second half of the twentieth century. This political, legal, economic, and social transformation affected the institutions of government and civil society and approaches to crime, its prevention, and its control (Braithwaite, 2000). Big, organizing themes like governance, risk, and plurality affected crime control and policing, along with what has been described as the "punitive turn" (Garland, 2001) and the governance of communities through crime and crime control techniques (Simon, 2007).

These trends have had four major impacts on police: the first is seen in a diversification or pluralization of crime control providers, expanding policing efforts to include, alongside mainstream police, broad networks of public, private, and non-government agencies, including private security providers, insurers, loss control specialists, and security hardware providers (see Bayley & Shearing, 1996; 2001; Loader, 2006; Crawford, 2009; Sparrow, 2015). Second, there has been a growth in administrative and regulatory agencies that have some crime or disorder control functions, adding overlapping networks of control, and in some cases discipline, onto policing, including, for example, housing, social welfare, child protection, and immigration enforcement bodies (see Crawford, 2006; Wood, 2006; Kemshall, 2014).

The third impact of changing governance on policing has been the importance of risk frameworks in shaping police practice (O'Malley, 1992; 2000; 2016; Kemshall, 2014). Indeed, Ericson and Haggerty (1997) have argued that police work was revolutionized by the rise of the risk society, and that as a result the police function fundamentally changed from a focus on dealing with law-breakers to collecting and brokering the knowledge needed to deal with risks. This analysis complemented the actuarial justice thesis of Feeley and Simon (1992; 1994), which suggested an increasing trend for the criminal justice system to focus on risky people, places, and activities to prevent future offending, rather than on investigating and sanctioning past offending.

Fourth, the tendency to increased punitiveness has extended the contexts in which crime control occurs and the tools and practices that can be drawn upon. Not only are more people directly caught up in the criminal justice system – seen most clearly in rising rates of incarceration in countries like the United States (Simon, 2007) and Australia (Weatherburn, 2016) – but that system has also extended into new fields, including schools, and increasingly, homes (Swan, 2015). Further, the increased hybridization of the criminal and civil legal systems (see Mazerolle & Ransley, 2005; Ransley, 2014; Stuart et al., 2015) gives the criminal justice system, specifically police, access to a much broader range of tools and sanctions.

To these transformative forces in governance has been added a drive for austerity and efficiency, particularly since the global financial crisis (Eck & Eck, 2012; Kemshall, 2014). Police officers are an expensive commodity, and the need for economy is affecting how they are used and deployed (Crawford, 2017), so having non-offending third parties assume some of the responsibility and costs of controlling and preventing crime is a major appeal of the new approach for governments (Cheh, 1998; Eck & Eck, 2012), as well as giving police access to new levers and remedies, such as civil orders and injunctions, property closures, parental responsibility contracts, and asset forfeiture schemes. A second appeal of measures like TPP to governments is that by relying on non-criminal measures, some of the restrictions and protections of the criminal justice system, such as high evidentiary standards and burdens of proof, can be avoided, thereby simplifying criminal justice enforcement (Crawford, 2009; Ransley, 2016). A third appeal, arguably, is that by broadening participation in crime reduction, police legitimacy can be enhanced. The United Kingdom legislative schemes already referred to have driven the idea of crime control partnerships, with police mandated to partner with other agencies, groups, and individuals to prevent and reduce crime. Such partnerships are driven not just by operational needs, but also by the idea that they can be more effective than police alone in reducing crime problems, and better reflect community priorities. Thus, they are seen as contributing to enhanced community support and legitimacy. However, there is still relatively little evidence to support the connection between partnership and community approaches and enhanced police legitimacy (National Academies of Sciences, Engineering, and Medicine, 2017). Further, as will be discussed, police partnerships can also weaken public acceptance and legitimacy, particularly when third-party participation is achieved more by coercion than cooperation.

Some examples show these transformative forces in action. O'Malley (2016) describes policing road traffic in an Australian state, where the detection and assessment of offending, issuance of notices and penalties, and enforcement are overwhelmingly conducted by non-police-operated cameras, computers, and agencies. The policing role, in this context, no longer involves the police, or at least they have a much-reduced role, and the sanctioning almost entirely involves civil and not criminal law (see also Parness, 2010 about similar US schemes). Justice has become routinized, and mediated through surveillance and information technologies. In the United States, the rise of Business Improvement Districts (BIDs) sees police partner with private security entities to deliver enhanced services to business and property owners, who pay levies for this purpose (Cook & MacDonald, 2011; National Academies of Sciences, Engineering, and Medicine, 2017). Here, private operatives, along with enhanced CCTV and other forms of surveillance, supplement the role of the public police to increase crime control efforts for the benefit of BID members.

While police play a less prominent role in some traditional areas of crime control, other forms of social control have become increasingly criminalized. Stuart, Armenta, and Osborne (2015) use the example of immigration enforcement in the United States to show the increased criminalization of formerly regulatory systems of control, and the responsibilization of employers and communities to remove opportunities that might support undesirable immigrant populations. Australia goes further, by subjecting particular classes of new arrivals to mandatory detention, often off-shore, in facilities run by private prison operators (Gerard & Pickering, 2013). And Kemshall (2014) describes how, in the United Kingdom, the management of welfare-dependent families increasingly involves a convergence between social policy and the management of crime and criminals, with children and their families seen as "repositories of risk factors, with predetermined risk trajectories ripe for intervention" (Kemshall, 2008, cited in Kemshall, 2014: 401). In this environment, police partner with other agencies of control to assess risk, responsibilize children and their parents, and use civil legal powers to sanction noncompliance.

The overall impact of these trends has been to change the focus from state responsibility for investigating and correcting criminal behavior to a system where crime control and prevention networks are responsible for identifying and managing risks. Public police form one node of these networks, with private police, insurance companies, regulatory agencies, communities, schools, and parents as other nodes. These networks may exist within legislated frameworks, but are often episodic and ad hoc. The prime concern of police and the criminal justice system is less with the detection and rehabilitation of individual offenders, and more with identifying and corralling risky groups such as repeat offenders, sex offenders, drug users, and homeless or mentally ill people. New technologies involve systematic identification of target groups or places (Eck & Weisburd, 1995), and then new forms of surveillance, preventive detention, and incapacitation via longer or mandatory sentences. Along with these changes to policing, there has been an expansion of the regulatory function of contemporary governments, and in many places globally, a new approach to regulation (see Stiglitz, 2010; Braithwaite, 2011). Many contemporary regulators rely on techniques ranging from voluntary and enforced self-regulation through to selective use of command and control techniques and sanctions. They work with industry bodies, and increasingly as part of globalized regulatory networks (Braithwaite & Drahos, 2000). The practical effect is a shift in the regulatory model: from state control to market models, from hierarchical systems of command and control to responsive regulation. The new forms of governance require state control of the direction of regulation and risk management, with many of the operational regulatory and compliance functions then shifted out to the market, community, and other social institutions (Braithwaite, 2013; Grabosky, 2013).

The scope of regulation has also been expanding significantly since the 1960s, creating an extensive network of opportunities for crime control. In recent years, traditional areas of regulation (such as health, education, and taxation) have been joined by new forms of social regulation (such as occupational health and safety, building codes, consumer protection and environmental regulation). In many of these areas, formal regulation, or law, has been only one form of social control, with self, peer, and professional regulation also being significant. Recognition of this plurality of regulatory methods, coupled with ideologically inspired shrinkage of state activities, has led to a departure from reliance on command and control as the only way of securing compliance with regulation.

For many years now, the regulatory pyramid (Ayres & Braithwaite, 1992; Parker, 2013; Drahos, 2017) has set out a tiered ranking of techniques, beginning with persuasion and self-regulation, progressing through professional discipline, adverse publicity and fines, through to prosecution and the withdrawal of occupational licenses. Responsive regulation rests on a logical working through of these techniques, resulting in use of the most coercive only in a small number of cases of intransigence. Hence, regulation becomes a layered web, with strands contributed by public regulatory agencies, professional and community organizations and individuals, and international organizations.

The impact of using these responsive methods has been to turn regulatory agencies from reactive, hierarchical command structures to problem-oriented, team-based units focused on risk management (Sparrow, 1994; 2000). The emphasis moves from after-the-event use of formal legal sanctions, to cooperation, persuasion, and the creation of incentives for compliance. The attraction for the regulated is the comfort that the "big stick" of coercive sanctions will only be used as a last resort, and that those who are regulated will have some input into the rule-making and compliance processes.

Drawing from the regulatory literature (see Braithwaite, 2006; 2011), Mazerolle and her colleagues (Mazerolle, Higginson & Eggins, 2013; Mazerolle & Ransley, 2005) identify how much of TPP draws on the efficiencies of the pyramid escalation structure in response to noncompliance. It is assumed, therefore, that most escalations in TPP should not proceed far beyond the lower levels of the pyramid because, as Braithwaite (2011) suggests, the use of responsive regulation is likely to foster voluntary compliance through perceptions of legitimacy. Whether or not this is a fair assumption is open to debate, particularly once regulation has become co-opted for crime control purposes. For Braithwaite (2011), the lower levels of the pyramid are about reform and repair, or restorative justice, and only when this fails to change behavior in the way desired should there be resort to punishment and deterrence.

Emerging evidence from both the United States and United Kingdom suggests these principles of responsive regulation are not always applied in practice. Desmond and Valdez (2013), for example, describe a TPP initiative in which the lever of choice against perceived disorder problems was a punitive response to domestic violence victims, when a responsive regulation approach would first have sought more restorative solutions focused on helping victims. Similarly, Stuart, Armenta, and Osborne (2015: 239) describe how in Seattle, local ordinances permit police to issue civil trespass admonishments that expel problem people for extended periods, including from private property, with violation of the order then a criminal offense. The civil mechanism has been used to target the homeless, minorities, and people with alcohol and substance abuse histories, disproportionately affecting Blacks and Native Americans, and does nothing to address the underlying problems on which a properly developed TPP intervention would have focused. And Swan (2015) analyses local government ordinances prescribing parental liability for the conduct of their children, crime-free provisions in tenancy agreements, and nuisance ordinances as three classes of TPP intervention that contribute to increased criminalization, stigmatization, and other backfire effects. These examples may partly reflect regulatory culture in the United States, and the importance placed on rule-making, formal sanctions, and litigation (Morriss, Yandle & Dorchak, 2005). However, the United Kingdom experience of antisocial behavior orders is similar, despite the different regulatory culture. There, a range of new civil tools were introduced under the Crime and Disorder Act 1998 (UK), subsequently replaced by the Anti-Social Behaviour, Crime and Policing Act 2014 (UK). The measures were directed at perceived problems of troublesome youth, and concerns of chronic and persistent nuisance impacting on people's quality of life, but have been criticized for their impacts on marginalized groups, unintended consequences, and net-widening effects (see Crawford, 2009; Johnstone, 2017).

These changes in societal context have far-reaching implications for police and the organization of police work. One oft-cited effect of the shift in regulation has been the movement away from state dominated policing to the situation where most developed economies have more private than state police (Bayley & Shearing, 2001; Prenzler, Sarre & Kim, 2017). As private security guards replace police in BIDs, other public and private buildings, community centers, even public space, and as private prison administration proliferates, the role of the state increasingly becomes one of regulating standards rather than actually controlling policing and criminal justice functions. The end result is a "reconstitution of policing as a mechanism of governance oriented to the *management* of conduct across civil society, and the advent of a loosely coupled network of policing agencies" (Loader, 2000: 333–334, *emphasis added*) and a partial shift in the control of policing away from the state toward political sub-centers (Shearing, 1996).

Perhaps the most pervasive impact of the shift in governance is the assumption now that the public police no longer (if they ever did) have a monopoly over responding to and preventing crime, but are expected to work in partnership with a range of other institutions, agencies, and individuals. There is no clear framework for these types of partnership, but rather a set of expectations that police will work cooperatively with their partners (what we define as "third parties") in identifying and responding to crime, in ways that are likely to vary from community to community and problem to problem. We have already noted that the notion of police partnerships is now entrenched in legislation in the United Kingdom with the requirement for police and local authorities to cooperatively develop crime-reduction policies. In many other places, the expectation of police partnerships is articulated in strategic plans, policies, and operational documents.

Police have become, in Ericson and Haggerty's terms (1997), the brokers for these partnerships – coordinating, providing information and resources, responding to the risks. Risks are identified through the analysis of statistical data and technologies like computerized crime mapping systems and utilized systematically by the police through management systems like CompStat (see Weisburd et al., 2003). Inter-agency task forces and intervention teams with multi-agency membership all utilize these technologies for crime control purposes.

We argue that the proliferation of TPP is an intrinsic outcome of these transformations in governance and the rise of the new regulatory state. TPP is the result of global, regulatory processes and the accompanying pressures on the police to conform to contemporary regulatory practice. It is no coincidence that cooperation, risk-management, problem identification and solving, and partnerships are the new primary focus for regulatory practice, as well as policing.

DIMENSIONS OF THIRD-PARTY POLICING

The partnerships in TPP are defined and distinguished from other models of policing through the intrinsic links they have with transformations in governance more generally and in regulatory trends more particularly. The general form of TPP includes the police forming partnerships and using legal levers to control and prevent crime. The third party is valuable to police because it has access to legal provisions (i.e., legal levers) that are (or could be) applied to control or prevent a crime or disorder problem. TPP thus involves three key players: (1) the police ("first party"); (2) a crime or disorder problem ("second party"), which could be a problem place, problem people, or a situation where criminogenic places, times, and people converge; and (3) an external entity ("third party") that police partner with to control or prevent the crime or disorder problem (see Mazerolle, 2014).

In TPP, the first party is defined as the public police. Public police work in partnership with a third party for the purposes of controlling or preventing a crime and/or disorder problem. Partnerships may be forged in an ad hoc, episodic manner (see Mazerolle & Ransley, 2005), through a program of crime control activities (e.g., pulling levers policing, see Braga & Weisburd, 2012; problem-oriented policing, see Weisburd et al., 2010), and/or because the partnership is mandated by law (e.g., the UK Crime and Disorder Act, 1998; the Scottish Police and Fire Reform Act of 2012).

The second party in TPP is defined as the ultimate crime control or prevention target, which could be a problem person, situation, or place (see Buerger & Mazerolle, 1998; Mazerolle & Ransley, 2005). The third party is an entity – a person, an agency, organization, or business – that has legal powers and/or responsibilities. These are the third-party partners that create increased capacities for police, and who are theorized (and empirically found) to improve the crime control and prevention outcomes for police (e.g., see Green, 1996; Mazerolle & Ransley, 2005).

TPP PARTNERS

The TPP Partnership Matrix (see Mazerolle et al., 2013) captures the different types of TPP partnerships along two continuums: the number of partners involved in the initiative and the level and type of engagement. In terms of the number of partners in a TPP initiative, numerous examples exist of dyad partnerships formed between police and other entities. These include police partnerships with schools, with regulatory agencies like liquor enforcement, or with particular businesses. Oftentimes, police form more complex partnerships with multiple entities such as through liquor accords (Mazerolle et al., 2012; Miller et al., 2014; Shepherdson et al., 2014) and purpose-built task force teams such as the Specialized Multi-Agency Response Teams in Oakland, California (see Green, 1996). These third-party partnerships offer a range of different foci: some partnerships focus on particular places with recurrent crime problems while other partnerships focus on the people or groups seen as having a heightened risk of offending (e.g., repeat offenders, parolees, young or homeless people in public places).

The engagement continuum is, arguably, the controversial part of TPP. Mazerolle and her colleagues (2013) describe the engagement strategies with third-party partners ranging from collaborative to coercive (see also Mazerolle & Ransley, 2005). At the benign, collaborative end of the continuum, police adopt consultative or amicable approaches that aim to engender willing cooperation from a third party. This is when police make informal requests for cooperation, when they respectfully increase awareness about their partner's legal responsibilities, or when they provide incentives or rewards for cooperation (see, for example, Mazerolle et al., 2017).

At the coercive end of the engagement continuum, police use forceful techniques or tactics by threatening or actually imposing negative consequences or removing benefits in order to compel a third party to cooperate (see Raven, 2008), by publicly shaming the third party, withdrawing services, or initiating civil actions against the third party for failure to meet their statutory responsibilities (e.g., prosecuting bar owners who serve alcohol to minors). Mazerolle and Ransley (2005) describe these coercive engagement tactics as a "sledge-hammer" approach to policing. Buerger (1998: 95) goes further, arguing that by using coercive civil measures, police are in fact creating a new, not-politically-sanctioned form of public duty, bypassing normal legitimizing channels. Applying this approach to the examples previously discussed of TPP interventions with problematic outcomes (Desmond & Valdez, 2013; Stuart et al., 2015; Swan, 2015), it can be argued that rather than TPP itself being the cause of backfire effects, in each case it was the nature and extent of coercion that was problematic. By skipping the lower levels of the regulatory pyramid involving restorative and cooperative approaches, police moved straight to punishment and coercion, often directed at already victimized and marginalized individuals. Undue coercion also brings with it a danger of regulatory creep that extends legal interventions into new areas, and uses civil measures to evade appropriate criminal justice principles and protections. This in turn can lead to a net-widening effect as socially disadvantaged people are drawn within a broad criminal justice net simply because of where they live or whom they associate with, rather than actual illegality. These unintended consequences can be minimized by a better understanding of the need to begin with cooperative approaches before escalating to coercion, and also an acknowledgment of what Meares (2015) refers to as "rightful policing," the notion that there is a third way to understand policing, apart from its effectiveness at crime reduction, and its strict lawfulness. The third way focuses on legitimacy, and policing, in a way that maximizes this outcome.

There are many potential partners in TPP, including education authorities who prosecute the parents of truants, bar owners who work with police to reduce street drunkenness, and property owners who screen potential tenants and maintain the physical condition of their properties. However, a predominant group involved with police in TPP networks comprises regulatory authorities. These are government agencies or officials with a function of regulating and maintaining standards in some legal activity, such as housing, building, business, or industry. Typical regulatory officials who might become involved in TPP include building and health and safety inspectors and environmental protection officers. These officials are attractive to police because their functions are often accompanied by coercive powers to enter properties, inspect and search, issue closure orders, or take other retaliatory action against people in breach of the regulatory scheme. For police, partnering with such officials can act as a defacto extension of their own powers, as well as increasing their potential weapons and sanctions against people they suspect of involvement in criminal activity. But it is important to remember that crime control and prevention is not the primary aim of regulators, who instead have specific statutory functions to fulfill.

LEGAL LEVERS

Mazerolle and Ransley (2005) describe the second necessary mechanism of TPP interventions as the activation, escalation, or redirection of a third party's legal levers. Legal levers are broadly defined as the legal powers possessed by third parties that create a crime control or crime prevention capacity that is otherwise unavailable to police (see Buerger & Mazerolle, 1998). Smith and Mazerolle (2013) identify a myriad of municipal ordinances, codes, or by-laws that regulate the uses of property, particularly around construction, protection against fire, and other types of safety hazards. Civil sanctions and remedies vary greatly, and include court-ordered repairs of properties, fines, forfeiture of property or forced sales to meet fines and penalties, eviction, padlocking or temporary closure (typically up to a year) of a rented residential or commercial property, license restrictions and/or suspensions, movement restrictions, lost income from restricted hours, and ultimately arrest and incarceration (see Mazerolle et al., 1998). These are the types of laws that police, in partnership with their third party, can activate and use for crime-control purposes.

Much of what we describe as TPP has arisen as an unintended consequence of the law – or the "shadow of the law" – rather than as its specific object (notable exceptions include Britain's Police Reform and Social Responsibility Act 2011 and Anti-Social Behaviour, Crime and Policing Act 2014, which specifically mandate police partnerships and networks). TPP is influenced by the law, uses the law where necessary, is limited in scope by the law, but often occurs in practice as an extra-legal activity.

As Ransley (2014) suggests, the range of legal levers that could be used in TPP interventions is extensive. Our preliminary review of TPP literature (see Mazerolle & Ransley, 2005) indicates that most legal levers utilised in TPP interventions align closely with Braithwaite's (2006; 2011) concept of the regulatory pyramid. That is, legal levers are activated by initiation of more benign consequences to encourage compliance (e.g., education, warning letter) and then sequentially escalate to more punitive consequences to coerce compliance (e.g., infringement notices, to fines, to license revocation), with the ultimate sanctions at the tip of the pyramid. It is this codified and stipulated process for regulating conduct that differentiates TPP from other policing processes: unlike other partnership-type policing approaches (e.g., community-oriented, networked, plural or pulling levers policing), it is a necessary condition for TPP that partners possess a legal lever that is otherwise unavailable to police.

In TPP, compliance is obtained through the threat, or actual use, of some type of legislative provision. As such, a key defining feature of TPP is that there must be some sort of legal basis (statutes, delegated or subordinate legislation or regulations, contractual relationships, torts laws) that shapes police coercive efforts to engage a third party to take on a crime prevention or crime control role. The most common legal basis of TPP includes local, state, and federal statutes (including municipal ordinances and town by-laws), health and safety codes, uniform building standards, drug nuisance abatement laws, and liquor licensing (Mazerolle & Ransley, 2005). We point out that the legal basis does not necessarily need to be directly related to crime prevention or crime control. Indeed, most TPP practices utilize laws and regulations that were not designed with crime control or crime prevention in mind (e.g. Health and Safety codes, Uniform Building Standards). For the vast majority of TPP activities, the statutory basis that provides the coercive power for police to gain the "cooperation" of third parties derives from delegated legislation and obscure, noncriminal sources.

The partnerships between police and third parties occur within a legal framework that authorizes the conduct of the third party – the building inspector, local authority, licensing agency, or parent. This legal framework establishes the source of authority of the third party, the extent to which they can partner with police, the contexts in which they can do that, the types of action they can take against targets (criminogenic places and individuals), and the limits of their legal ability to cooperate with, or be coerced by, police.

In TPP, laws and legal mechanisms are directed at willing or unwilling non-offending third parties, with the object of facilitating or coercing them into helping to control the behavior of offending ultimate targets. The types of law used can be criminal or civil, and the distinction between these two categories is becoming increasingly blurred (see also Cheh, 1991). The laws or legal devices used may be established specifically for the relevant crime control purpose, or may be directed at some other issue but co-opted, by police, community groups, victims, or regulators, to achieve crime control or prevention goals.

EVALUATION EVIDENCE

Mazerolle and Ransley (2005) used systematic review techniques to locate, assess, and describe the extant TPP evaluation literature (see also the Mazerolle et al., 2013 Campbell Collaboration protocol to update this review). More than a decade ago, we identified a large pool of studies that varied in terms of methodological rigor, type of third party, type of legal lever, and type of crime problem targeted by the intervention. On the basis of mostly positive effect sizes across individual studies, Mazerolle and Ransley (2005) concluded that TPP appeared to be an effective policing strategy for reducing a wide range of crime and disorder problems.

Mazerolle and Ransley (2005) categorized the studies into five groups: the use of TPP in controlling drugs, violent crimes, property crime, youth problems, and crimes at criminogenic places. Our search strategies resulted in the identification of seventy-seven studies that included an evaluation component and also involved a TPP tactic. Of these, only twelve studies included sufficient data to calculate effect sizes (see Table 11.1). These twelve studies generated twenty-three effect sizes (odds ratios and standardized mean differences) across the variety of outcome measures (calls for service, arrests, field contacts, observations). The heterogeneous units of analysis and the variety of ways researchers had operationalized their outcome measures precluded calculation of mean effect sizes. As such, the individual outcomes were examined independently (see Mazerolle & Ransley, 2005). Table 11.1 summarizes the evaluation evidence.

As Table 11.1 shows, it appears that TPP is an effective mechanism to control drug problems. It is likely that it is an effective strategy for controlling violent crime and for dealing with young people. While the number and quality of the reported outcomes limit our assessment of the effectiveness of TPP, Table 11.1 also indicates that TPP is somewhat ineffective at controlling property crime problems. Our review suggests that the majority of evidence collated about TPP involves property owners (commercial property owners in particular) as third parties. We were also able to uncover limited, yet important, evidence that identifies parents, local councils, housing authorities, and victims as third parties.

TABLE 11.1 *Summary of Third-Party Policing Evaluation Evidence*

	All Studies N % 77 100	Studies where an effect size was calculated N % 12 100	Effect size outcomes (N = 23)	Most common third party from all 77 studies	Most common type of legal lever
1 Drugs	21 27.3	8 66.7	13/18 (72%) outcomes were *desirable*	Residential and commercial property owners	Municipal ordinances (e.g., building and health & safety codes, nuisance abatement)
2 Violent crime	21 27.3	2 16.7	2/2 (100%) outcomes were *desirable*	Licensed premises owners	Code of practice with restrictions on serving of alcohol
3 Places	15 19.4	0 0	NA	Local councils	Municipal ordinances
4 Young people	11 14	1 8.3	1/1 (100%) outcome was *desirable*	Parents	Curfews
5 Property Crime	9 12	1 8.3	2/2 (100%) outcomes were *undesirable*	Business owners	Theft-prevention policies

(Source: Mazerolle & Ransley, 2005)

Over the last ten years, evidence supporting the effectiveness of partnership approaches for addressing crime and disorder continues to grow (see Berry et al., 2011 for review). Rosenbaum and Schuck (2012) argue that partnerships are increasingly popular because they increase the capacity for police to target crime problems by using scarce resources efficiently (see also Cherney, 2008).

LONG-TERM OUTCOMES

In her Academy of Experimental Criminology Joan McCord lecture, Mazerolle (2014) argues that the failure of police to sustain their short-term suppressive benefits creates both a challenge and an opportunity for police. Statements about the role of police in contemporary society typically imply that the police have (or should have) responsibility for sustaining crime control benefits over the long run. The Report of the Independent Police Commission (*Policing for a Better Britain*), released in late 2013, for example, explicates a long-term, social justice role for police in preventing and suppressing crime. If reforms are adopted throughout Britain as a result of the Commission Report, police would be expected to build social cohesion and legitimacy, forge collaborations and partnerships, and consider how short-term interventions might play out in the long run. For British policing, the social justice model of policing is no longer aspirational, but rather a foundation for policing at a time when "the police have experienced sharp budget cuts and face a period of fiscal constraint that is likely to continue for the foreseeable future" (Independent Police Commission, 2013: 13). Weisburd and Telep (2014: 212) similarly argue that "causal mechanisms underlying developmental patterns of crime at a place ... suggest that strategies that focus on long-term social change should be added to the tool box of crime prevention at places."

Mazerolle (2014) argues that the crime control gains of policing could be sustained over the long term if productive partnerships (that are based on mutual respect, relational coordination, and legitimacy) use and only escalate legal levers under circumstances where every effort has been made to gain willing cooperation. In an experimental test of TPP, for example, Mazerolle and her colleagues (2017) found that legitimate and functional crime-control partnerships alter a third party's awareness and attitude toward their own legal levers when those third parties use and only escalate (under rare circumstances) legal lever sanctions in a way originally envisioned by Braithwaite's regulatory pyramid.

Clearly, however, there are both positive and negative outcomes of the resultant net-widening generated by third parties escalating their regulatory activity on all steps of the regulatory pyramid. On the one hand, a TPP intervention can address a wider range of complex motivations for compliance than can criminal law approaches. On the other hand,

Mazerolle and Ransley (2005) enumerate a range of negative consequences of this broadened base of control (see also Desmond & Valdez, 2013).

CONCLUSIONS

TPP is identified as one of eight key policing innovations of the 21st century (Weisburd & Braga, 2006) that enables police to target the places, people, situations, and/or times that disproportionately contribute to crime and disorder problems. More recently, the National Academies of Sciences, Engineering, and Medicine's Committee on Proactive Policing (2017) identified TPP as one proactive policing approach that shows a "small but rigorous body of evidence suggest[ing] that third party policing generates short-term reductions in crime and disorder" (National Academies of Sciences, Engineering, and Medicine, 2017: Conclusion 4–6). We know little, however, of the long-term impacts or jurisdictional outcomes of policing through third-party partnerships.

In this chapter, we have described how TPP expands the capacity of police to target crime and disorder clusters in two distinct ways: (1) by creating a partnership between police and non-police third parties that (2) harnesses the third party's resources and legal powers to control or prevent a crime or disorder problem. In TPP, police partner with external entities (third parties) – such as government regulators and inspectors, housing authorities, licensing authorities, and business owners – to use the partner's legal powers and responsibilities to regulate or alter the underlying social, physical, temporal, and/or situational conditions that generate crime and disorder problems (Buerger & Mazerolle, 1998; Mazerolle & Roehl, 1998; Mazerolle & Ransley, 2005). In TPP, the police indirectly address crime and disorder problems by working through (and with) their third party partners and those partners' range of legal levers.

We began the chapter by situating TPP in the broader governance and regulatory literature. We argued that changes in governance and regulation have affected policing by pluralizing crime-control providers, harnessing a range of non-criminal-justice regulators to help control problems – both at problem places and directed at problem people – reconstituting much police work as risk identification, management, and communication, and reconfiguring criminal justice to include a much broader range of social, cultural, and economic concerns than was once the case, as societies have increasingly been "governed through crime" (Simon, 2007).

We then examined the dimensions of TPP, describing the two key elements of TPP: partnerships and the broad range of legal levers used in TPP. Finally, we provided a summary of the existing evaluation evidence and examined how TPP is likely to be a policing innovation that sustains the long-term gains of police efforts to control and prevent crime problems. Yet we also recognize the potential backfire effects of policing in partnership with third parties, particularly when coercive practices are used to elicit compliance. In an era where police legitimacy is front and center of the reform agenda, TPP in its cooperative form of engagement is an innovation that holds promise in an ever-complex policing environment.

REFERENCES

Ayres, I., & Braithwaite, J. (1992). *Responsive Regulation: Transcending the Deregulation Debate*. New York: Oxford University Press.

Bayley, D. H., & Shearing, C. D. (1996). The future of policing. *Law & Society Review*, 30(3), 585–606.

Bayley, D., & Shearing, C. (2001). *The New Structure of Policing*. Washington, DC: National Institute of Justice.

Berry, G., Briggs, P., Erol, R., & van Staden, L. (2011). The effectiveness of partnership working in a crime and disorder context: A rapid evidence assessment (Research Report No. 52). London: Home Office.

Bond, B. J., & Gittell, J. H. (2010). Cross-agency coordination of offender reentry: Testing collaboration outcomes. *Journal of Criminal Justice*, 38(2), 118–129.

Braga, A. A, & Weisburd, D. L. (2012). *The effects of "pulling levers" focused deterrence strategies on crime*. Campbell Systematic Reviews, 2012(6). doi: 10.4073/csr.2012.6.

Braithwaite, J. (2000). The new regulatory state and the transformation of criminology. *British Journal of Criminology*, 40, 222–238.

Braithwaite, J. (2006). The regulatory state. In R. A. W. Rhodes, S. A. Binder, & B. A. Rockman (eds.), *The Oxford Handbook of Political Institutions* (pp. 407–430). Oxford: Oxford University Press.

Braithwaite, J. (2011). The essence of responsive regulation. *University of British Columbia Law Review*, 44(3), 475–420.

Braithwaite, J. (2013). Relational republican regulation. *Regulation & Governance*, 7, 124–144.

Braithwaite, J., & Drahos, P. (2000). *Global Business Regulation*. Melbourne: Cambridge University Press.

Braga, A. A., Papachristos, A. V., & Hureau, D. (2014). The effects of hot spots policing on crime: An updated systematic review and meta-analysis. *Justice Quarterly*, 31(4), 633–663.

Buerger, & Mazerolle, L. G. (1998). Third party policing: A theoretical analysis of an emerging trend. *Justice Quarterly*, 15(2), 301–328.

Buerger, M. (1998). The politics of third party policing. In L. G. Mazerolle, & J. Roehl (eds.) *Civil Remedies and Crime Prevention*. Crime Prevention Studies 9. Monsey, NY: Criminal Justice Press.

Cheh, M. (1991). Constitutional limits on using civil remedies to achieve criminal law objectives: Understanding and transcending the criminal-civil law distinction. *Hastings Law Journal*, 42, 1325–1413.

Cheh, M. (1998). Civil remedies to control crime: Legal issues and constitutional challenges. In L. G. Mazerolle, & J. Roehl (eds.), *Civil Remedies and Crime Prevention: Crime Prevention Studies* (vol. 9, pp. 45–66). New York: Criminal Justice Press.

Cherney, A. (2008). Harnessing the crime control capacities of third parties. *Policing: An International Journal of Police Strategies & Management*, 31, 631–647.

Cook, P., & MacDonald, J. (2011). Public safety through private action: An economic assessment of BIDs. *The Economic Journal*, 121(552), 445–462.

Corsaro, N., & Engel, R. S. (2015). Most challenging of contexts: Assessing the impact of focused deterrence on serious violence in New Orleans. *Criminology & Public Policy*, 14(3), 471–505.

Crawford, A. (2006). Networked governance and the post-regulatory state? Steering, rowing and anchoring the provision of policing and security. *Theoretical Criminology*, 10(4), 449–479.

Crawford, A. (2009). Governing through anti-social behaviour: Regulatory challenges to criminal Justice. *British Journal of Criminology*, 49(6), 810–831.

Crawford, A. (2017). Research co-production and knowledge mobilisation in policing. In J. Knutsson, & L. Thompson (eds.), *Advances in Evidence-Based Policing* (pp. 195–213). Abingdon: Routledge.

Desmond, M., & Valdez, N. (2013). Unpolicing the urban poor: Consequences of third-party policing for inner-city women. *American Sociological Review*, 78(1), 117–141.

Drahos, P. (2017). *Regulatory Theory: Foundations and Applications*. Canberra: Australian National University Press.

Dunworth, T., & Mills, G. (1999). *National evaluation of Weed and Seed*. National Institute of Justice Research in Brief (June). Retrieved from www.ncjrs.gov/App/abstractdb/AbstractDBDetails.aspx?id=175685.

Eck, J. E., & Eck, E. B. (2012). Crime place and pollution: Expanding crime reduction options through a regulatory approach. *Criminology & Public Policy*, 11(2), 281–316.

Eck, J., & Spelman, W. (1987). *Problem Solving: Problem-Oriented Policing in Newport News*. Washington, DC: Police Executive Research Forum and National Institute of Justice.

Eck, J., & Wartell, J. (1998). Improving the management of rental properties with drug problems. In L. Green Mazerolle, & J. Roehl (eds.), *Civil Remedies and Crime Prevention: Crime Prevention Studies* (vol. 9, pp. 161–183). Monsey, NY: Criminal Justice Press.

Eck, J., & Weisburd, D. (1995) *Crime Prevention Studies: Crime and Place* (vol 4). Monsey, NY: Criminal Justice Press.

Ericson, R. V., & Haggerty, K. D. (1997). *Policing the Risk Society*. Toronto: Toronto University Press.

Feeley, M., & Simon, J. (1992). The new penology: Notes on the emerging strategy of corrections and its implications. *Criminology*, 30(4), 449–474.

Feeley, M., & Simon, J. (1994). Actuarial justice: The emerging new criminal law. In D. Nelken (ed.), *The Futures of Criminology* (pp. 173–201). London: Sage.

Fleming, J. (2005). "Working together": Neighbourhood watch, reassurance policing and the potential of partnerships. *Trends & Issues in Crime and Criminal Justice*, 303 (September).

Garland, D. (2001). *The Culture of Control: Crime and Social Order in Contemporary Society*. Oxford: Oxford University Press.

Gerard, A., & Pickering, S. (2013). Crimmigration: criminal justice, refugee protection and the securitisation of migration. In H. Bersot, & B. Arrigo (eds.), *The Routledge Handbook of International Crime and Justice Studies*. London: Routledge.

Gittell, J. H. (2011). New directions for relational coordination theory. In G. M. Spreitzer, & K. S. Cameron (eds.), *The Oxford Handbook of Positive Organizational Scholarship*. Oxford Handbooks Online. Retrieved from www .oxfordhandbooks.com/view/10.1093/oxfordhb/9780199734610.001.0001/ oxfordhb-9780199734610-e-030.

Gittell, J. H. (2006). Relational coordination: Coordinating work through relationships of shared goals, shared knowledge and mutual respect. In O. Kyriakidou, & M. Ozbilgin (eds.), *Relational Perspectives in Organizational Studies: A Research Companion* (pp. 74–94). Cheltenham, UK: Edward Elgar Publishers.

Gittell, J. H., Fairfield, K., Bierbaum, B., Jackson, R., Kelly, M., Laskin, R., ... Zuckerman, J. (2000). Impact of relational coordination on quality of care, postoperative pain and functioning, and length of stay: A nine-hospital study of surgical patients. *Medical Care, 38,* 807–819.

Gittell, J. H., Weinberg, D. B., Pfefferle, S., & Bishop, C. (2008). Impact of relational coordination on job satisfaction and quality outcomes: A study of nursing homes. *Human Resource Management Journal,* 18, 154–170.

Grabosky, P. (2013). Beyond responsive regulation: The expanding role of non-state actors in the regulatory process. *Regulation & Governance,* 7, 114–123.

Green, L. (1996). *Policing Places with Drug Problems.* Thousand Oaks, CA: Sage.

Independent Police Commission (2013). *Policing for a Better Britain.* Retrieved from www.lse.ac.uk/socialPolicy/Researchcentresandgroups/mannheim/pdf/ policingforabetterbritain.pdf.

Johnson, H. (2005). Experiences of crime in two selected migrant communities. *Trends & Issues in Crime and Criminal Justice,* (302), 1–6.

Johnstone, C. (2017) Penalising presence in public space: Control through exclusion of the "difficult" and "undesirable." *International Journal for Crime, Justice and Social Democracy,* 6(2), 1–16.

Kemshall, H. (2008). Risks, rights and justice: Understanding and responding to youth risk. *Youth Justice,* 8(1), 21–37.

Kemshall, H. (2014). Conflicting rationalities of risk: Disputing risk in social policy – Reflecting on 35 years of researching risk. *Health, Risk & Society,* 16(5), 398–416.

Loader, I. (2000). Plural policing and democratic governance. *Social and Legal Studies,* 9 (3), 323–345.

Loader, I. (2006). Fall of the "Platonic Guardians": Liberalism, criminology and political responses to crime in England and Wales, *British Journal of Criminology,* 46, 561–581.

Mazerolle, L. (2014). The power of policing partnerships: Sustaining the gains. *Journal of Experimental Criminology,* 10(3), 341–365.

Mazerolle, L., Bennett, S., Antrobus, E., & Eggins, E. (2017). The co-production of truancy control: Results from a randomized trial of a police–schools partnership. *Journal of Research in Crime and Delinquency.* Advance online publication. doi: 10.1177/0022427817705167.

Mazerolle, L., Higginson, A., & Eggins, E. (2013). Registration for a systematic review: Third party policing for reducing crime and disorder: A systematic review. *The Campbell Collaboration Library of Systematic Reviews.*

Mazerolle, L. G., Kadleck, C., & Roehl, J. (1998). Controlling drug and disorder problems: The role of place managers. *Criminology,* 36, 371–404.

Mazerolle, L., & Ransley, J. (2005). *Third Party Policing.* Cambridge: Cambridge University Press.

Mazerolle, L. G., & Roehl, J. (1998). Civil remedies and crime prevention: An introduction. In L. Green Mazerolle, & J. Roehl (eds.), *Civil Remedies and Crime Prevention: Crime Prevention Studies* (vol. 9, pp. 1–20). Monsey, NY: Criminal Justice Press.

Mazerolle, L., Soole, D. W., & Rombouts, S. (2007). Street-level drug law enforcement: A meta-analytical review. *Campbell Collaboration Library of Systematic Reviews,* 2007(2). doi: 10.4073/csr.2007.2.

Mazerolle, L., White, G., Ransley, J., & Ferguson, P. (2012). Violence in and around entertainment districts: A longitudinal analysis of the impact of late-night lockout legislation. *Law & Policy,* 34(1), 55–79.

McGarrell, E. F., Chermak, S., Wilson, J. M., & Corsaro, N. (2006). Reducing homicide through a "lever-pulling" strategy. *Justice Quarterly,* 23(2), 214–231.

Meares, T. (2006). Third party policing: A critic. In D. Weisburd, & A. D. Braga (eds.), *Police Innovation: Contrasting Perspectives* (pp. 207–221). Cambridge: Cambridge University Press.

Meares, T., with Neyroud, P. (2015). *Rightful Policing. New Perspectives in Policing.* National Institute of Justice Report. www.ncjrs.gov/pdffiles1/nij/248411.pdf.

Miller, P., Curtis, A., Palmer, D., Busija, L., Tindall, J., Droste, N., . . . Wiggers, J. (2014). Changes in injury-related hospital emergency department presentations associated with the imposition of regulatory versus voluntary licensing conditions on licensed venues in two cities. *Drug and Alcohol Review,* 33(3), 314–322.

Morriss, A., Yandle, B., & Dorchak, A. (2005). Choosing how to regulate. *Harvard Environmental Law Review,* 29, 179–250.

National Academies of Sciences, Engineering, and Medicine. (2017). *Proactive Policing: Effects on Crime and Communities.* Washington, DC: The National Academies Press. Retrieved from https://doi.org/10.17226/24928.

National Debate Advisory Group. (2015). Reshaping policing for the public. Retrieved from www.npcc.police.uk/documents/reports/Reshaping%20policing%20for%20the%20public.pdf

O'Malley, P. (1992). Risk, power and crime prevention. *Economy and Society,* 21(3), 252–275.

O'Malley, P. (2000). Risk, crime and prudentialism revisited. In K. Stenson, & R. Sullivan (eds.), *Risk, Crime and Justice: The Politics of Crime Control in Liberal Democracies* (Ch. 5). London: Willan.

O'Malley, P. (2016). "Policing the Risk Society" in the 21st century. *Legal Studies Research Paper. Sydney Law School,* 16(11).

Parker, C. (2013). Twenty years of responsive regulation: An appreciation and appraisal. *Regulation & Governance,* 7, 2–13.

Parness, J. (2010). Beyond red light enforcement against the guilty but innocent: Local regulations of secondary culprits. *Willamette Law Review,* 47, 259.

Prenzler, T., Sarre R., & Kim, D.W. (2017). Reforming security industry training standards: An Australian case study. *International Journal of Comparative and Applied Criminal Justice,* DOI: 10.1080/01924036.2017.1326392.

President's Task Force on 21st Century Policing. 2015. *Final Report of the President's Task Force on 21st Century Policing.* Washington, DC: Office of Community

Oriented Policing Services. Retrieved from cops.usdoj.gov/pdf/taskforce/ TaskForce_FinalReport.pdf.

Ransley, J. (2014). Legal frameworks for Third-Party Policing. In *Encyclopedia of Criminology and Criminal Justice* (pp. 2906–2915). New York: Springer.

Ransley, J. (2016). Policing through third parties: Increasing coercion or improving legitimacy? In *The Politics of Policing: Between Force and Legitimacy* (pp. 41–58). Bingley, UK: Emerald Group Publishing Limited.

Raven, B. H. (2008). The bases of power and the power/interaction model of interpersonal influence. *Analysis of Social Issues and Public Policy*, 8, 1–22. doi: 10.1111/j.1530-2415.2008.00159.x

Rosenbaum, D. P. (2002). Evaluating multi-agency anti-crime partnerships: Theory, design and measurement issues. In N. Tilley (ed.) *Evaluation for crime prevention* Crime Prevention Studies (vol. 14, pp. 171–225). Monsey, NY: Criminal Justice Press.

Rosenbaum, D. P., & Schuck, A. M. (2012). Comprehensive community partnerships for preventing crime. *Oxford Handbooks Online.* doi: 10.1093/oxfordhb/ 9780195398823.013.0012

Shearing, C. (1996). Reinventing policing: Policing as governance. In O. Marenin (ed.), *Policing Change, Changing Police: International Perspectives. Current Issues in Criminal Justice* (vol. 4, pp. 285–308). New York: Garland.

Sheperdson, P., Clancey, G., Lee, M., & Crofts, T. (2014). Community safety and crime prevention partnerships: Challenges and opportunities. *International Journal for Crime, Justice and Social Democracy*, 3(1), 107–120.

Simon, J. (2007). *Governing through Crime: How the War on Crime Transformed American Democracy and Created a Culture of Fear*. Oxford University Press.

Smith, M. J., & Mazerolle, L. (2013). *Using Civil Actions against Property to Control Crime Problems (Problem-Oriented Guides for Police, Response Guide Series No. 11)*. Washington, DC: Center for Problem-Oriented Policing, US Department of Justice.

Sparrow, M. (1994). *Imposing Duties: Government's Changing Approach to Compliance*. Westport: Praeger.

Sparrow, M. (2000). *The Regulatory Craft: Controlling Risks, Solving Problems, and Managing Compliance*. Washington, DC: Brookings Press.

Sparrow, M. K. (2015). *Measuring Performance in a Modern Police Organization. New Perspectives in Policing*. Harvard Executive Session on Policing and Public Safety. Washington, DC: National Institute of Justice, US Department of Justice.

Stiglitz, J. (2010). Government failure vs. market failure: principles of regulation. In E. Balleisen, & D. Moss (eds.), *Government and Markets: Towards a New Theory of Regulation*. Cambridge, NY: Cambridge University Press.

Stuart, F., Armenta, A., & Osborne, M. (2015). Legal control of marginal groups. *Annual Review of Law and Social Science*, 11, 235–254.

Swan, S. (2015). Home Rules. *Duke Law Journal*, 64, 823–900.

Weisburd, D., & Braga, A. A. (eds.). (2006). *Police Innovation: Contrasting Perspectives*. Cambridge: Cambridge University Press.

Weisburd D., Mastrofski, S. D., McNally, A. M., Greenspan, R., & Willis, J. J. (2003). Reforming to Preserve: Compstat and Strategic Problem Solving in American Policing. *Criminology and Public Policy*, 2(3), 421–456.

Weisburd, D., & Telep, C. (2014). Hot spots policing: What we know and what we need to know. *Journal of Contemporary Criminal Justice*, 30(2), 200–220.

Weisburd, D., Telep, C. W., Hinkle, J .C., & Eck, J. E. (2010). Is problem-oriented policing effective in reducing crime and disorder? *Criminology and Public Policy*, 9, 139–172.
Wood, D. M., Ball, K., Lyon, D., Norris, C., & Raab, C. (2006). *A report on the surveillance society*. Surveillance Studies Network, UK.

12

Critic

Third-Party Policing: A Critical View

Tracey L. Meares and Emily Owens

According to Lorraine Mazerolle and Janet Ransley (2003), "third-party policing" describes police efforts to persuade or to coerce third parties, such as landlords, parents, local government regulators, community organizations, and business owners to take on some responsibility for preventing crime or reducing crime problems. Obviously, this definition seeks to distinguish policing directed at those who are and who might be criminal offenders from policing efforts directed at non-offending "others." Third-party policing also takes less punitive forms. For example, local governments are increasingly granting groups of businesses and homeowners the right to levy taxes in order to engage in infrastructure investment and surveillance activities in certain areas. Thus, the definition emphasizes the affinities that third-party policing has with other forms of civil regulation and with trends toward privatization of services previously monopolized, or heavily regulated, by state or local governments. Examples of such regulation abound. In an effort to ensure that corporations do not defraud stockholders, regulators place constraints – both civil and criminal – on accountants and lawyers. In an effort to make sure that employers do not violate civil rights laws, legislators have structured statutes so that violators pay plaintiffs' attorneys fees should the plaintiffs win. In this way, plaintiffs are persuaded to become "private attorneys general" helping public officials to enforce the law. Similarly, the rise of the modern "gig" economy has seen private groups directly competing with government agents in areas as varied as regulating taxi services to space travel.

Given the pervasive forms of such regulation today, that "third- party" efforts are becoming common in the enterprise of street crime control should hardly be surprising. We can redescribe even those efforts typically conceptualized as directed primarily at offenders in terms of third-party controls. Common consequences of criminal offending are sanctions in the form of a prison sentence or fine. However, it is silly to think that only the offender suffers the opprobrium that accompanies such sanctions. Families of the offender, as well as friends, can also suffer (e.g., Braman, 2004). In a world in which the costs associated with formal punishment extend beyond the actual offender to non-offenders, we should expect such third parties to engage in efforts to persuade, or even informally coerce, potential offenders to refrain from crime. And, social theorists have long explained how informal norms combine with formal sanctions to effect deterrence.[1] When informal social controls are supported by legal sanctions, social costs are made more salient so to better regulate behavior.

Importantly, informal controls are not relevant simply when they support formal legal sanctions. Informal controls also involve the normative processes and ethics of social interaction that regulate everyday social life, as well as the mobilization of community that occurs in response to problem behaviors (Sharkey 2018; Fagan & Meares, 2008; Doyle & Luckenbill, 1991). Thus, informal social controls are effective in several ways: inhibition of problem behaviors, facilitation of conformity, and restraint of social deviance once it appears. The key is to see that that evaluation of the deterrent effect of a policy cannot depend simply on the likely impact of formal punishment, but, rather, must also include some kind of assessment of the reciprocity between legal and social controls. It is not enough to ask whether a potential offender will be persuaded not to offend by assessing how he will compare the costs of potential formal punishment against the benefit of engaging in the crime. We also need to know about the potential offender's community context and social role to be able to begin to make assessments regarding the potential effectiveness of a planned formal legal sanction.

Our task here is not to bring all policing efforts under the potentially commodious umbrella of third-party policing, however. While it should be clear that much of traditional criminal law enforcement and policing can be described as "third-party policing," in this volume the meaning of the term is more limited. Contributors to this volume have pinpointed third-party policing as those efforts by many policing agencies that recognize that much social control is exercised by institutions other than the police and that crime can be managed through agencies besides those concerned primarily with dispensing criminal justice, such as the police. Specific examples include nuisance abatement, anti-gang loitering laws, business improvement districts, and public housing eviction policies, among others (Mazerolle & Ransley, Chapter 11 in this volume).

The primary purpose of this chapter is to review the arguments made by the critics of third-party policing efforts. Although the concerns of most of these critics are based in constitutional law, some critics make a special effort to explicate the potentially destructive racial dynamics of some third-party policing strategies. These arguments target the distributional effects of exactly

---

[1] Zimring and Hawkins (1997) explain this point by distinguishing the educative and deterrent effects of punishment. Likewise, Williams and Hawkins (1992) explain the conceptual differences between the deterrent effect of legal sanctions and social control through informal mechanisms.

which groups bear the burden of third-party law enforcement. After reviewing these arguments, this chapter will conclude by attempting to address the costs and benefits of third-party policing strategies with special emphasis on the race-based critiques of these approaches.

CIVIL LIBERTARIAN CRITIQUE

One basic criticism of government targeting of third-party non-offenders to persuade or informally coerce the so-called "real offenders" to refrain from lawbreaking, is that by targeting third parties the government uses its power to restrict the liberty of those who "really aren't doing anything wrong." The essence of civil libertarianism is that coercive government power should be deployed only in those instances in which it is necessary to protect individuals from the use of force or fraud by others. Under this view, a threat to levy a civil fine against a landlord in order to persuade her to better scrutinize and identify potential drug-dealing renters, as documented in Desmond and Valdez (2013), is patently impermissible. According to libertarian beliefs, state power ought to be trained upon the drug dealer, not the landlord, as the dealers are the true wrongdoers.

Private groups, legislators, and other governmental officials have an answer to this foundational criticism. Criminal offenders are sometimes difficult to locate and bring to justice through the conventional criminal justice apparatus. In fact, criminal liability itself has, over time, expanded to address this problem. We punish offenders not only for the crime of robbery, but also for the offense of attempted robbery. Further, prosecutors often utilize offenses such as conspiracy and solicitation in order to ferret out and punish crime before it takes place. Neither the doctrine of conspiracy nor of solicitation actually requires that the prohibited act occur. The doctrines require simply that a person agrees with another to commit a criminal offense (conspiracy), or request that another engage in conduct that constitutes a crime (solicitation).[2] Additionally, we punish those who assist others in criminal offending under the doctrine of accomplice liability even when the accomplice has not himself or herself committed any act that many would deem criminal. According to the doctrine of accomplice liability, individuals can be punished when they make a decision to further the criminal act of another and engage in an act that

---

[2] A person is guilty of conspiracy with another person to commit a crime if with the purpose of promoting or facilitating its commission he: (a) agrees with such other person or persons that they or one of them will engage in conduct which constitutes such crime or an attempt or solicitation to commit such crime; or (b) agrees to aid such other person or persons in the planning or commission of such crime (Model Penal Code, § 5.03). A person is guilty of solicitation to commit a crime if with the purpose of promoting or facilitating its commission he commands, encourages, or requests another person to engage in specific conduct which would constitute such crime or an attempt to commit such crime or which would establish his complicity in its commission or attempted commission (Model Penal Code, § 5.02).

furthers the principal's criminal act. In addition to all of this, civil remedies have long been used to hold offenders to account outside of the traditional criminal justice context.

Prophylactic measures, combined with civil remedies, provide law enforcers with a wider range of alternatives to crime control that are less costly than traditional criminal justice approaches. Third-party policing, then, is simply a small extension of this approach. There is, however, one basic difference between third-party policing efforts and prophylactic criminal and civil remedies directed at wrongdoers: those co-opted into enforcement efforts are not themselves wrongdoers in the usual sense.

This basic difference is a central one for critics of third-party policing concerned with civil liberties. Such critics might point to *Bennis v. Michigan* as a paradigmatic case of third-party policing gone awry. In *Bennis*, a car was seized from Mr. Bennis after he had been convicted of committing an indecent act with a prostitute while the two were in the car. Mrs. Bennis claimed that her interest in the car could not be forfeit to the State of Michigan because she was completely unaware of her husband's activities. The United States Supreme Court, in a plurality opinion, nonetheless ruled against her. As a result of the Court's decision, the State of Michigan was allowed to keep the Bennis family 1977 Pontiac, which was paid for primarily with money Mrs. Bennis earned from babysitting.

The *Bennis* plurality stated that there was a long history of permitting forfeiture against innocent owners in order to prevent further use of illicit property. The reasoning is obvious: if an innocent owner knows that there is a risk that her property might be forfeit if someone else uses the property for illegal purposes, she likely will take greater care than she otherwise would to ensure that her property is not so used. That is, she will become a third-party police officer.[3]

The problem with this reasoning, according to civil libertarians, is not whether the procedure works or not; rather, the problem is that the forfeiture process is fundamentally unfair under basic principles of due process of law. For one thing, the deterrence rationale that applies to Mrs. Bennis potentially implies that Michigan can punish Mrs. Bennis for her husband's crime. Such punishment is clearly inconsistent with due process. The Supreme Court has recognized the due process right of an innocent person to be free of punishment.[4] Mrs. Bennis was not tried and convicted before her punishment – the forfeiture of her interest in the family car – was meted out by the state. Indeed, she could not possibly have been convicted for the crime her

---

[3] Note that one dissenter in *Bennis*, Justice Stevens, clearly disagrees with this point (see *Bennis* at 1009, Stevens, J., dissenting). Justice Stevens declares that the goal of deterrence is not served by punishing "a person who has taken all reasonable steps to prevent an illegal act."

[4] In fact, the court, relying on substantive due process principles, held that once a criminal is found "not guilty" of a crime, the State may not impose punishment (*Foucha v. Louisiana*).

husband committed or any prophylactic offenses associated with it. Mrs. Bennis had no awareness of her husband's activities, so she possessed no criminal intent to engage in the offense or to further it in any way. Moreover, Mrs. Bennis had engaged in no act that could be considered criminal. While her husband was involved with a prostitute, Mrs. Bennis was simply waiting for her husband to come home for dinner.

Even if one was convinced that Michigan's actions in this case were not punitive, but instead were merely regulatory, one might still conclude that the state's action offended due process.[5] Deterring an activity such as prostitution is, of course, a legitimate aim of a state's police powers; however, due process principles require that government respect the rights of property owners and afford them procedural protections under civil law as well as criminal law. The Constitution's text is clear: government may not deprive individuals of life, liberty, or property without providing due process of law. Unfortunately for Mrs. Bennis and for others similarly situated, the procedural protections required to satisfy constitutional minimums are, in fact, minimal.[6] Still, the fact that a particular procedure meets the minimum requirements of procedural due process does not mean that critics are without recourse. Critics often contend that an enforcement operation like that in *Bennis* is inconsistent with substantive due process even when the operation meets the constitutional requirements of procedural due process. As Mary Cheh (1994: 25) has described the difference. Substantive due process analysis ordinarily proceeds along two tracks. Almost all laws touching social and economic matters are judged under a lenient rational-basis test, while laws that interfere with certain intimate and personal rights, such as child rearing, marriage and divorce, and use of contraceptives, are judged under a vigorous strict-scrutiny test. The rational-basis test is easily satisfied. Ordinary social and economic regulation is presumed constitutional, and so long as the law serves any permissible police power objective, it will be upheld. Legislatures are free to decide, without court interference, how they will tax, regulate, and control behavior. Under these analyses, a litigant must prove either that the forfeiture is so unreasonable as to fail rational basis, or that there is a protected interest at

---

[5] *Salerno vs. United States* describes preventive detention as regulatory rather than punitive and thus requiring more lenient procedural protection under the Due Process Clause.

[6] For example, see 18 USC. 981 (1988 & Supp. V 1993) for a discussion of the government's civil money laundering forfeiture provision or 21 U.S.C. 881 (1988 & Supp. V 1993) which authorizes the civil forfeiture of property connected to narcotics activity. Forfeiture is authorized in more than 140 federal statutes and most states have one or more laws permitting forfeiture (Steven L. Kessler [1994]. Civil and Criminal Forfeiture: Federal and State Practice 2.01, at 2–1). Typically, the government can effect its seizure without notice to the owner and without giving the owner a prior opportunity to object. See, for example, 19 USC. 1609–1615 (1988 & Supp. V 1993), the US Customs Service's procedures for seizure, forfeiture, and recovery of seized property.

issue such that the more rigorous strict-scrutiny test applies. Both of these types of arguments fail more often than they succeed.

This review of *Bennis* and related constitutional doctrines might suggest that it is futile for civil libertarians to adopt these constitutional arguments to block third-party policing efforts. This conclusion would be mistaken. Consider litigation against anti-gang loitering ordinances and curfews, which some consider third-party policing tools, and which have become increasingly popular in municipalities. Loitering and curfew ordinances are designed to keep teens from congregating at night to attract the ire of rival gang members and pick fights, or standing on corners to help friends hidden in alleys to sell drugs. By enforcing these laws, it is thought that police can help adults simply by acting as additional eyes and ears in the neighborhood. Some of these laws also are designed to make parents more accountable by penalizing parents whose children violate the ordinance. These laws have been met with resistance and constitutional challenge, and, in many cases, the civil libertarian critics have been successful. Chicago's first anti-gang loitering law was deemed unconstitutionally vague, a fate shared by numerous "loitering with intent" statutes around the country. Curfews in Washington, DC (*Hutchins v. District of Columbia*), San Diego (*Numez v. City of San Diego*), and other cities (e.g., *City of Maquoketo v. Russell*) have likewise been deemed to abridge the due process rights of teens and their parents. Local anti-nuisance ordinances have also come under constitutional scrutiny; *Groton v. Piro* (2017) found that nuisance violations which do not clearly distinguish between facilitating and reporting crime have the effect of limiting the First Amendment right of victims to contact police, and are therefore facially invalid. Here, the New Jersey Village of Grotton identified properties as "public nuisances" based on a predetermined point system; a property accumulated points based on police activity generally, including, for example, if a tenant called 911 to report individuals yelling threats outside her door, this would result in points being levied on her.

Ultimately the civil libertarian critique of government agencies involved in third-party policing boils down to one basic point: a concern with the scope of accountable government power. Civil libertarian critics believe, with some justification, that the greater the government's power, the more difficult it is to control; therefore, we all are better off if government power is limited as much as possible. One suspects that these critics would not be so concerned if they could be persuaded government power in these areas was utilized in a rational and transparent manner. Unfortunately, to the extent that preferred strategies utilize civil justice and political mechanisms as controls, as opposed to criminal justice mechanisms, it becomes that much more difficult to keep track of government activity and to limit it. Police discretion, always a powerful tool even when confined to criminal justice processing, potentially grows to almost unrecognizable proportions once it is no longer confined to the criminal justice cage.

RACIAL EQUITY CRITIQUE

Some critics of third-party policing strategies have complained about a specific problem that could be considered a subset of the critique detailed above. Namely, these critics are worried that, as third-party policing strategies loosen the reins on governmental discretion regarding whom to engage as the law is enforced, such discretion inevitably will be exercised more often against poor and minority-race citizens than against those who are not poor and/or of minority race.

Consider, as an example, Professor Dorothy Roberts's (1999) race-based critique of an anti-gang loitering law adopted by the City of Chicago in 1992. The ordinance exhibited unique third-party policing features. The Chicago City Council passed the ordinance to restrict gang-related congregations in public ways (Chicago, Il., Code § 8–4-015 1992). The ordinance was designed to respond to the grievances of citizens concerned about commonly occurring criminal street gang activity in their neighborhoods, such as drive-by shootings, fighting, and open-air drug dealing. By loitering in alleyway entrances and on street corners, drug dealers both solicited business and warned hidden compatriots of police patrols. The ordinance empowered designated police officers in specified areas to approach groups of three or more people loitering "with no apparent purpose" provided that those officers had reasonable cause to believe that at least one member of the group was a street gang member and ask the group to move along. If the group refused, then the officer was entitled to arrest the group. The third-party policing aspect is clear. Even those individuals whom the police had no reason to suspect were gang members, were potentially subject to arrest merely because of the company those individuals chose to keep (and where they chose to keep that company). By subjecting non-gang members to liability, municipal regulators incentivized them to help police constrain the behavior of their gang-involved compatriots.

Professor Roberts's (1999: 775) assessment of the law is blunt: "expansive and ambiguous allocations of police discretion are likely to unjustly burden members of unpopular or minority groups." In support of this claim, Roberts (1999: 785) points to the fact that in 1995, 46.4 percent of people arrested for vagrancy across US cities were black, even though blacks made up only 13 percent of the nation's population. No doubt a critic such as Roberts would also take data compiled by Justin Ready, Lorraine Mazerolle, and Elyse Revere (1998), demonstrating that 91 percent of the tenants evicted from public housing developments in Jersey City as part of a civil remedy program to achieve greater level of order in those developments were black, as evidence of the unjust burden suffered by minorities as third-party policing strategies are implemented.

Desmond and Valdez (2013) provide further evidence that third-party policing can have racially disparate impacts. In their study of Milwaukee, WI, they demonstrate that the likelihood that a property will be cited for nuisance violations is strongly correlated with the fraction of neighborhood residents who are black, over and above the influence of local crime or calls for service. Further, they argue that affected landlords overwhelming choose eviction, or some other "landlord-initiated forced move" in order to avoid further legal sanction.

An assumption that minorities are unfairly burdened by third-party policing strategies that are designed to give law enforcers more flexibility to address crime and disorder is based upon a fundamental premise – the weak political power of minority groups. Consider a famous *Yale Law Journal* article written in 1960 by William O. Douglas. In the piece, Douglas railed against the argument that anti-loitering laws were beyond constitutional reproach. It was naïve to trust contemporary communities to apply such laws evenhandedly, Douglas asserted, because those arrested under such laws typically came "from minority groups" with insufficient political clout "to protect themselves" and without "the prestige to prevent an easy laying-on of hands by the police" (Douglas, 1960: 13). When the Court did ultimately deem traditionally worded loitering laws unconstitutionally vague in *Papachristou v. City of Jacksonville* about ten years later, Douglas wrote the court's opinion.

Unlike the more general strategy of civil libertarians, advocates of constitutional arguments designed to protect minority groups from overweening police power have achieved more success in the Supreme Court and lower courts. In the 1960s, the prevailing sense of the court was that the coercive incidence of law enforcement, in both the North and South, was concentrated most heavily on minority citizens, who, by virtue of their exclusion from the political process, had no say about whether those policies were just. The result was the systematic devaluation of both the liberty of individual minority citizens and the well-being of minorities as a group. By insinuating courts deeply into the process of criminal-law enforcement, the federal constitutionalization of state police procedures was intended to correct this imbalance (Klarman, 1991). Similarly, in the political context of the 1960s, law enforcement officials were accountable only to representatives of the white majority. Indeed, for precisely this reason, the police predictably used their discretion to harass and repress minorities. Insisting that law-enforcement authority be exercised according to hyper-precise rules was a device for impeding the responsiveness of law enforcers to the demands of racist white political establishments. Such rules also made it much easier for courts to detect and punish racially motivated abuses of authority.

Thus, by pointing to racial imbalances in the enforcement of loitering laws, curfews, public housing evictions, and nuisance abatement laws, modern critics intentionally draw upon the particularized racial history of such strategies – and the courts' pointed disfavor of them. But, one question is whether the costs of such strategies, even considering the specific race-based arguments offered by critics such as Dorothy Roberts, outweigh their benefits.

COSTS AND BENEFITS

As noted above, police departments across the country have turned to third-party policing strategies as seemingly low-cost alternatives to traditional criminal justice apparatus to prevent crime. If such strategies are successful, the benefits are clear: reduced crime for (presumably) less money, as civil justice mechanisms typically are less costly than criminal justice ones. There is a dearth of available evaluations, but the initial studies are promising. For example, Jeffrey Grogger (2002) has found, through an empirical analysis of civil injunctions designed to reduce gang violence, that in the first year after the injunctions are imposed, violent crime falls by 5 to 10 percent. Moreover, Lorraine Mazerolle and her colleague (Mazerolle & Roehl, 1998) collect studies of various civil remedy programs designed to control drug problems. Most of the studies contained in the volume point to the effectiveness of such programs at reducing levels of targeted drug offenses. A handful of studies also point to the crime-reducing benefits of Business Improvement Districts (BIDs) that facilitate private investment in a menu of potentially crime-reducing activities, including physical infrastructure improvements and hiring private security guards. Brooks (2008) estimated that crime in Los Angeles, California, fell by between 6 and 10 percent in BIDs, an estimate later replicated by MacDonald and colleagues (2009; 2010) and Cook and MacDonald (2011). Further, Cook and MacDonald (2011) also found that arrests in BIDs fell by a third, suggesting that these private actions likely induced important behavioral changes on the part of potential criminals. However, MacDonald and colleagues (2009) present evidence that the crime-reducing benefits of BIDs in Los Angeles may not be equally distributed across area residents, as they found little evidence of a reduction in the violence victimization of juveniles.

The case for third-party policing, then, might be made on this evidence. Note, however, that many third-party policing strategies are place-based programs. And, if such place-based programs caused crime reduction in the targeted areas while simply diverting crime elsewhere, that would be an obvious cost. Geographic displacement of crime is a serious concern when place-oriented interventions are employed (Committee to Review Research, 2004: 240; National Academies of Sciences, 2017). Interestingly, the small body of research pertaining directly to this issue with respect to third-party policing indicates the opposite – a diffusion of crime control benefits (e.g., Mazerolle & Roehl, 1998; Mazerolle, Price & Roehl, 2000; Cook & MacDonald, 2011) to areas contiguous to the places targeted for third-party policing interventions.

Still, the fact that a few studies indicate some benefit through reduction in crime does not resolve the accounting for costs and benefits in favor of the benefit side of the ledger. Moreover, to be confident about a cost-benefit analysis, one must ask in this context whether such crime-reduction benefits would be achieved through more traditional policing methods – methods that are less likely to raise the hackles of civil liberties proponents (Caulkins, 1998).

This is the approach taken in some recent evaluations (e.g., Mazerolle, Price & Roehl, 2000), but not all (e.g., Cook & MacDonald, 2011). Without such results, police departments and other governmental entities ought to tread lightly before embarking on strategies that present the kinds of grave risks to civil liberties discussed earlier. Critics of third-party policing have a point when they assert that third-party policing interventions cannot be justified on crime reduction, even if substantial, alone.

Presumably, the critics whose arguments are sound in racial equity concerns would agree with this assessment. Urban minority residents face more crime than other non-minority groups, so such residents would likely benefit in the form of reduced crime, nuisance, and the like in their communities. However, such residents may not believe that reductions in, say, observable open-air drug selling are worth the costs in terms of civil liberties incursions.[7] The case for benefits needs more.

An additional argument pertaining to the benefits side is that third-party strategies potentially can help to change the social dynamics of neighborhoods in ways that promote crime-reducing norms. One way to do this is to point out that traditional criminal law enforcement methods potentially can impede a community's ability to resist and reduce crime. Traditional law enforcement methods rely on criminal justice processing and punishment – especially incarceration – to achieve crime reduction. Scholars have articulated theories describing how mass incarceration concentrated at the community or neighborhood level could hamper institutions of informal social control (Nagin, 1998; Rose & Clear, 1998). Drawing on Shaw and McKay's (1969) foundational work on the relationship between the social disorganization of neighborhoods and the persistence of high crime rates at the community level, these scholars have focused on various social processes, including (1) the prevalence, strength, and interdependence of social networks; (2) the extent of collective supervision by neighborhood residents and the level of personal responsibility they assume for addressing neighborhood problems; and (3) the rate of resident participation in voluntary and formal organizations (Sampson & Wilson, 1995; Wilson, 1996; Rose & Clear, 1998). The hypothesis is straightforward: When the processes of community social organization are prevalent and strong, crime and delinquency should be less prevalent, and vice versa. Burgeoning research suggests that mass incarceration following from traditional law enforcement methods inhibits social processes that support crime reduction and prevention (Lynch & Sabol, 2004); thus, law enforcement that does not rely heavily on incarcerative approaches, like third-party policing strategies, may be less harmful than traditional law enforcement

---

[7] I should acknowledge here that a reduction in open-air drug selling and a reduction in many of the harms associated with drug use do not necessary proceed in step. That is, it is certainly possible to imagine a world in which there is much less open-air drug selling and a simultaneous increase in consumption.

approaches to fragile urban poor community structures and may indeed support those structures in ways that lead to less crime. Brayne (2014) offer some pushback against this idea. Specifically, Brayne documents that youth who have initial contact with police officers are, on average, less likely to engage with social institutions that are most likely to participate in third-party policing (e.g., banks or hospitals).

Specifically, civil remedies can be democratizing in a sense. Such remedies typically are not reactive; rather, they are proactive. Neighborhood residents who have been (or feel they have been) underserved by policing organizations historically often turn to civil remedies as an alternative to traditional strategies. Indeed, an argument can be made that third-party strategies are especially empowering to residents of disadvantaged neighborhoods in a way that traditional policing often is not. That is, state-sponsored strategies that encourage individuals to work with one another can help to sustain a healthy social organization dynamic that can be harnessed in favor of crime reduction and resistance (Meares, 2002). Such forces can in themselves be supportive of neighborhood collective efficacy, which itself is associated with lower crime at the neighborhood level (Sampson, Raudenbush & Earls, 1997).

Finally, there may be normative concerns that can be arrayed against the civil libertarians' own arguments, whether those arguments are grounded in individual libertarian concerns or take on a more group-based, race-specific aspect. It is important to pay attention to where the groundswell of support for many third-party policing strategies lies. In no small number of cases, the support for these strategies comes from the residents of high-crime neighborhoods who are themselves often members of minority groups – the very people who face a heightened risk of criminal victimization and who live with the destructive impact of crime on the economic and social life of their communities and who feel the pinch of these laws in a meaningful way.

There is often little room in either the general civil libertarian critique or the more specifically racialized critique for the voice of this group of people, but it should be clear that, as a normative matter, their voices and votes ought to count for something. Of course, deciding that one ought to listen to the people who are most affected by third-party policing strategies does not guarantee a "right answer" to balancing issues inherent in these debates. There is no perspective-free way to determine whether the general structure of third-party approaches violates the Constitution. Some individual or set of individuals, judging the question in the light of their own experiences and values, must decide whether particular policies embody a reasonable balance between liberty and order. The question is who should decide.

To illustrate, consider an exchange from the City Council hearings on the Chicago gang-loitering ordinance. At the hearings, dozens of inner-city residents – from church leaders, to representatives of local neighborhood associations, to ordinary citizens – testified in favor of the proposed law. Harvey Grossman, Illinois director of the ACLU, testified against it:

I am a lawyer, and I spend a great deal of time doing nothing more than reviewing ordinances and statutes, and it turns into a little bit of a long exam game. ... We pick apart the statute. We focus on [a] word or [a] phrase, and we try to say why that phrase might or might not be constitutional. (Transcript of Meeting before Chicago City Council Committee on Police and Fire 107. May, 18, 1992)

He then proceeded to "pick apart" the gang-loitering ordinance, demonstrating the tension between it and various judicial precedents.

Alderman William Beavers, a council member who represented a poor and high-crime minority district on Chicago's south side, objected to this bookish conception of how to appraise the constitutionality of the law. "I don't know if you are attuned to what's going on in these neighborhoods," he told Grossman. "Maybe I need to take you out there and show you what's really going on" (Police and Fire, 107: 119). Grossman replied that that wouldn't be necessary:

I think our ability to come together and to try to resolve issues [like this] really doesn't ... depend on if I see what's happening in your neighborhood or you see what's happening in my neighborhood. [Rather, it depends on] one, empathy or ability to understand what's happening to other people and, two, some commitment, some intellectual integrity and some commitment to principle. And the principle that I am suggesting to you is inviolate. It doesn't change. (p. 120)

The tough issues surrounding the new community policing obviously aren't an "exam game" for the median inner-city voter. The people who experience both law enforcement and crime are people who think empathy is motivated by "inviolate" "intellectual" "principles" and just "doesn't depend," "really," on "see[ing] what's happening in [inner-city] neighborhood[s]." The values at stake and the difficult tradeoffs that must be made are not abstractions. They are real. This perhaps is a place where critics and advocates can come together. Procedural justice scholars have suggested that a reliance on procedures is useful when correct outcomes are not obvious to disparate members of a group. Groups may not always decide on an outcome, but they can almost always decide on procedures that everyone finds satisfying (Lind & Tyler, 1988). Thus, to the extent that we achieve very little agreement on constitutional substance, perhaps the best strategy to adopt as third-party policing goes forward is to insure that those most affected are insinuated into the political process and that their voices are heard.

CONCLUSION

One might say that a hallmark of twenty-first century policing is its commitment to policing strategies that were once denominated non-traditional – at least among the most progressive police executives considered to be leaders in the field. For example, the group Law Enforcement Leaders to Reduce Crime and Incarceration, which is composed of over 200 current and former law enforcement leaders from all 50 states and across the political spectrum, is committed to solutions to reduce crime *and* incarceration, disfavoring crime reductions strategies that rely upon arrest, jail, and prison. Thus, it is safe to say that approaches to policing will continue to include strategies that appear to stray from criminal justice norms. The third-party policing strategies reviewed in this volume clearly are congenial to these approaches.

The question remains, however, whether these approaches adequately recognize the values that American citizens have always held dear. Civil liberties proponents fear they do not, but perhaps such critics have not taken adequate account of the instrumental benefits to be obtained through the new policing. Instrumental benefits aside, both critics and proponents of third-party policing seem to have overlooked the potential for political engagement that the new policing strategies can offer to citizens – especially to crime-beleaguered citizens of poor urban communities. Whatever else may be said about these approaches in terms of crime reduction, the normative benefits of expanded political participation for those who have traditionally been shut out of governmental processes may be worth the cost of these controversial programs.

Expanded political participation is one hallmark of a more robust democracy, which itself can be a product of greater legitimacy of key government institutions. Since the first volume of this book was published, there has been a deep and sustained interest in research related to how the public understands its relationship to key institutions such as police, courts, and schools. We know after decades of research that people place much more emphasis – in making the determination of whether institutions are fair and can be trusted – on assessing the quality of their relations with representatives of the relevant institution as opposed to evaluating outcomes produced by those institutions (Tyler, 2006; National Academies, 2017). And we also know, for example, when people perceive police to be legitimate as understood in these terms, they are more likely to participate in civic activities in their communities by engaging in activities such as voting (Tyler & Jackson, 2014). These theories of popular legitimacy provide reasons to be optimistic about the potential for third-party policing to produce the kinds of benefits that civil libertarians should welcome, but we await empirical validation.

REFERENCES

Braman, D. (2004). *Doing Time on the Outside: The Hidden Effects on Families and Communities*. Ann Arbor: University of Michigan Press.
Brayne, S. (2014). Surveillance and system avoidance. *American Sociological Review*, 79 (3), 367–391.
Brooks, L. (2008) Volunteering to be taxed: Business improvement districts and the extra-governmental provision of public safety. *Journal of Public Economics*, 92(1–2), 388–406.
Caulkins, J. P. (1998). The cost effectiveness of civil remedies: The case of drug control interventions. In L. G. Mazerolle, & J. Roehl (eds.), *Civil Remedies and Crime Prevention*, 9. Monsey, NY: Criminal Justice Press.

Cheh, M. M. (1994). Can something this easy, quick, and profitable also be fair? Runaway civil forfeiture stumbles on the Constitution. *New York Law School Law Review*, 29, n1.

Cook, P. J., & MacDonald, J. (2011). Public safety through private action: An economic assessment of BIDs. *The Economic Journal*, 121(552), 445–462.

Committee to Review Research on Police Policy and Practices. (2004). *Fairness and Effectiveness in Policing: The Evidence*. Washington, DC: National Academies Press.

Desmond, M., & Valdez, N. (2013). Unpolicing the urban poor: Consequences of third-party policing for inner-city women. *American Sociological Review*, 78, 117–141.

Douglas, W. O. (1960). Vagrancy and arrest on suspicion. *Yale Law Journal*, 70 (n1), 1–14.

Doyle, D. P., & Luckenbill, D. F. (1991). Mobilizing law in response to collective problems: A test of Black's Theory Of Law. *Law & Society Review*, 25, 103–116.

Fagan, J., & Meares, T. (2008). Punishment, deterrence and social control: The paradox of punishment in minority communities. *Ohio St. Law Journal*, 6, 173–229.

Grogger, J. (2002). The effects of civil gang injunctions on reported violent crime. *Journal of Law and Economics*, 45, 69.

Klarman, M. J. (1991). The puzzling resistance to political process theory. *Virginia Law Review*, 77, 747–766.

Lind, E. A., & Tyler, T. R. (1988). *The Social Psychology of Procedural Justice*. New York: Plenum Press.

Lynch, J. P., & Sabol, W. J. (2004). Assessing the effects of mass incarceration on informal social control in communities. *Criminology and Public Policy*, 3, 267–294.

MacDonald, J., Blumenthal, R., Golinelli, D., Kofner, A., Stokes, R. J., Sehgal, A., Fain, T., & Beletsky, L. (2009). *Neighborhood Effects on Crime and Youth Violence: The Role of Business Improvement Districts in Los Angeles*. Santa Monica, CA: RAND Corporation.

MacDonald, J., Golinelli, D., Blumenthal, R., & Stokes, R. J. (2010). *The Effect of Business Improvement Districts on the Incidence of Violent Crimes*. Injury Prevention, 327–332.

Mazerolle, L., & Ransley, J. (2003). Third-party policing: Prospects, challenges and implications for regulators. Paper presented at the Current Issues In Regulations: Enforcement and Compliance Conference, Melbourne.

Mazerolle, L. G., & Roehl, J. (eds.). (1998). *Civil remedies and crime prevention*. Monsey, NY: Criminal Justice Press.

Mazerolle, L. G., Price, J. F., & Roehl, J. (2000). Civil remedies and drug control: A randomized field trial in Oakland, California. *Evaluation Review*, 24(2), 212–241.

Meares, T. L. (2002). Praying for community policing. *California Law Review*, 90, 1593–1634.

Nagin, D. (1998). Criminal deterrence research at the outset of the twenty-first century. In M. Tonry (ed.), *Crime and Justice: A Review of Research*. Chicago: University of Chicago Press.

National Academies of Sciences, Engineering, and Medicine. 2017. *Proactive Policing: Effects on Crime and Communities*. Washington, DC: The National Academies Press.

Ready, J., Mazerolle, L. G., & Revere, E. (1998). Getting evicted from public housing: An analysis of the factors influencing eviction decisions in six public housing sites. In L. G. Mazerolle, & J. Roehl (eds.), *Civil Remedies and Crime Prevention*. Monsey, NY: Criminal Justice Press.

Roberts, D. (1999). Foreword: Race, vagueness, and the social meaning of order maintenance policing: Supreme Court issue. *Journal of Criminology and Criminal Law*, 89, (n3), 776–785.

Rose, D., & Clear, T. (1998). Incarceration, social capital and crime: Implications for social disorganization theory. *Criminology*, 36, 441–480.

Sampson, R. J., & Wilson, W. J. (1995). Toward a theory of race, crime and urban inequality. In J. Hagan, & R. Peterson (eds.), *Crime and Inequality*. Stanford: Stanford University Press.

Sampson, R. J., Raudenbush, S. W., & Earls, F. (1997). Neighborhoods and violent crime: A multilevel study of collective efficacy. *Science*, 277, 918–925.

Sharkey, P. (2018). *Uneasy Peace: The Great Crime Decline, the Renewal of City Life, and the Next War on Violence*. New York: Norton.

Shaw, C. R., & McKay, H. D. (rev. ed. 1969). *Juvenile Delinquency and Urban Areas: A Study of Rates of Delinquency in Relationship to Differential Characteristics of Local Communities in American Cities*. Chicago: University of Chicago Press.

Tyler, Tom R. (2006) *Why People Obey The Law*. Princeton: Princeton University Press.

Tyler, Tom R., & Jackson, Jonathan. (2014) Popular legitimacy and the exercise of legal authority: Motivating compliance, cooperation and engagement. *Psychology, Public Policy and Law*, 20, 78–95,

Transcript of Meeting before Chicago City Council Committee on Police and Fire 107 (1992, May 18).

Williams, R., & Hawkins, R. (1992). Wife assault, costs of arrest, and the deterrence process. *Journal of Research in Crime and Delinquency*, 29(n3), 292–294.

Wilson, W. J. (1996). *When Work Disappears: The World of the New Urban Poor*. New York: Knopf.

Zimring, F. E., & Hawkins, G. (1997). *Crime Is Not the Problem: Lethal Violence in America*. New York: Oxford University Press.

CASES CITED

Bennis v. Michigan, 116 S. Ct. 994 (1996).

City of Maquoketa v. Russell, 484 N.W.2d 179 Iowa (1992).

Foucha v. Louisiana, 504 US 71, 95–98 (1992).

Hutchins v. District of Columbia, 942 F. Supp. 665 D.D.C. (1996).

Nunez v. City of San Diego, 114 F.3d 935 9th Cir. (1997).

Salerno v. United States, 481 US 739 (1987).

STATUTES CITED

18 USC. 981 (1988 & Supp. V 1993).

19 USC. 1609–1615 (1988 & Supp. V 1993).

21 USC. 881 (1988 & Supp. V 1993).

Chicago, Il., Code § 8-4-015 (1992).

PART VII

HOT SPOTS POLICING

13

Advocate

Hot Spots Policing as a Model for Police Innovation

David Weisburd and Anthony A. Braga

Looking at the major police innovations of the last few decades, what is most striking from a criminologist's perspective is the extent to which new programs and practices have been developed without reference to either criminological theory or research evidence. Some institutional theorists might argue that this is understandable given the limited ability of police agencies to reliably demonstrate their successes, and the political environments within which police agencies must operate (Meyer & Rowan, 1977; Mastrofski & Ritti, 2000; Willis, Mastrofski & Weisburd, 2004). However, this reality is very much at odds with a model of policing that would seek to draw new policies and practices from a solid research base (Sherman, 1998; Weisburd & Neyroud, 2011), and suggests an approach to policing that is based more on intuition and luck than on research and experimentation. Studies of the adoption of police innovation reinforce this problematic portrait of American police innovation. Widely touted programs such as community policing or CompStat have been widely diffused across the landscape of American policing absent any reliable evidence that they accomplish the goals that they set out to achieve (Weisburd et al., 2003; Weisburd & Eck, 2004).

In this context, "hot spots policing" represents a particularly important innovation on the American police scene. Its origins can be traced to innovations in criminological theory, and it was subjected to careful empirical study before it was diffused widely across American police agencies. In the following pages, we describe the origins of hot spots policing in theory and basic research, and the research evidence that has been developed to support hot spots policing practices. We will argue that there is strong theoretical justification for hot spots policing, and that evaluation evidence provides a solid empirical basis for continued experimentation and development of this approach. We also review what the empirical evidence says about key criticisms of hot spots policing, and discuss gaps in the existing knowledge base. In concluding, we examine research that suggests that the wide spread adoption of hot spots policing followed the development of basic and applied research suggesting its effectiveness.

FROM THEORY TO PRACTICE: AN EVIDENCE-BASED MODEL

The idea of hot spots policing can be traced to critiques of traditional criminological theory. For most of the last century, criminologists focused their understanding of crime on individuals and communities (Nettler, 1978; Sherman, 1995). In the case of individuals, criminologists sought to understand why certain people, as opposed to others, become criminals (e.g., see Hirschi, 1969; Akers, 1973; Gottfredson & Hirschi, 1990; Raine, 1993), or to explain why certain offenders become involved in criminal activity at different stages of the life course and cease involvement at other stages (e.g., see Moffitt, 1993; Sampson & Laub, 1993). In the case of communities, criminologists often tried to explain why certain types of crime or different levels of criminality are found in some communities as contrasted with others (e.g., see Shaw & McKay, 1972; Sampson & Groves, 1989; Bursik & Grasmick, 1993; Agnew, 1999) or how community-level variables, such as relative deprivation, low socioeconomic status, or lack of economic opportunity affect individual criminality (e.g., see Cloward & Ohlin, 1960; Wolfgang & Ferracuti, 1967; Merton, 1968; Agnew, 1992).

In most cases, research on communities focused on the macro level, often studying states (Loftin & Hill, 1974), cities (Baumer et al., 1998), and neighborhoods (Sampson, 1985; Bursik & Grasmick, 1993). This is not to say that criminologists did not recognize that the opportunities found at more micro levels of place could influence the occurrence of crime. For example, Edwin Sutherland, whose main focus was upon the learning processes that bring offenders to participate in criminal behavior, noted in his classic criminology textbook that the immediate situation influences crime in many ways: "a thief may steal from a fruit stand when the owner is not in sight but refrain when the owner is in sight; a bank burglar may attack a bank which is poorly protected but refrain from attacking a bank protected by watchmen and burglar alarms" (Sutherland, 1947: 5). Nonetheless, Sutherland, as other criminologists, did not see micro-geographic places as a relevant focus of criminological study. This was the case, in part, because crime opportunities provided by such places were assumed to be so numerous as to make concentration on specific places of little utility for theory or policy. In turn, criminologists traditionally assumed that situational factors played a relatively minor role in explaining crime as compared with the "driving force of criminal dispositions" (Clarke & Felson, 1993: 4; Trasler, 1993). Combining an assumption of a wide array of criminal opportunities, and a view of offenders that saw them as highly motivated to commit crime, it is understandable that criminologists paid little attention to the problem of the development of crime at micro levels of place.

While the focus on individuals and communities has continued to play a central role in criminological theory and practice, traditional theories and approaches were subjected to substantial criticism beginning in the 1970s. Starting with Robert Martinson's critique of rehabilitation programs in 1974, a series of studies documented the failures of traditional crime prevention initiatives (e.g., Sechrest, White & Brown, 1979; Whitehead & Lab, 1989). In policing, as well, there was substantial criticism of traditional approaches. For example, there was no more visible approach to crime prevention in policing in the 1970s, or one that involved greater cost, than preventive patrol in cars. The idea that police presence spread widely across the urban landscape was an important method for preventing crime and increasing citizens' feelings of safety was a bedrock assumption of American policing. But, in a major evaluation of preventive patrol in Kansas City, Missouri, the Police Foundation concluded that increasing or decreasing the intensity of preventive patrol did not affect either crime, or service delivery to citizens, or citizens' feelings of security (Kelling et al., 1974). Similarly, rapid response to emergency calls to the police was considered to be a crucial component of police effectiveness. Yet in another large-scale study, Spelman and Brown (1984) concluded that improvement in police response times has no appreciable impact on the apprehension or arrest of offenders.

These and other studies in the 1970s and 1980s led scholars to challenge the fundamental premise of whether the police could have a significant impact on crime (see also Levine, 1975; Greenwood, Petersilia & Chaiken, 1977). By 1994, the distinguished police scholar David Bayley (1994: 3) was able to write:

The police do not prevent crime. This is one of the best-kept secrets of modern life. Experts know it, the police know it, but the public does not know it. Yet the police pretend that they are society's best defense against crime ... This is a myth. First, repeated analysis has consistently failed to find any connection between the number of police officers and crime rates. Secondly, the primary strategies adopted by modern police have been shown to have little or no effect on crime.

A number of scholars argued that the failures of traditional crime prevention could be found in the inadequacies in program development and research design in prior studies (e.g., Farrington, Ohlin & Wilson, 1986; Goldstein, 1990). Other reviews stressed that there are examples of successful offender-focused crime prevention efforts, which can provide guidance for the development of more effective prevention policies (Farrington, 1983; Lipsey, 1992). Nonetheless, even those scholars who looked to improve such policies, came to recognize the difficulties inherent in trying to do something about criminality (Visher & Weisburd, 1998). Summarizing the overall standing of what they define as traditional "offender-centered" crime prevention, Patricia and Paul Brantingham (1990: 19) wrote: "If traditional approaches worked well, of course, there would be little pressure to find new forms of crime prevention. If traditional approaches worked well, few people would possess criminal motivation and fewer still would actually commit crimes."

Cohen and Felson (1979) introduced one influential critique of traditional criminological approaches to understanding crime that had a strong influence on the development of hot spots policing. They argued that the emphasis placed on individual motivation in criminological theory failed to recognize the importance of other elements of the crime equation. They noted that for criminal events to occur there is need not only of a criminal, but also of a suitable target and the absence of a capable guardian. They showed that crime rates could be affected by changing the nature of targets or of guardianship, irrespective of the nature of criminal motivations. Cohen and Felson's suggestion that crime could be affected without reference to the motivations of individual offenders was a truly radical idea in criminological circles in 1979. The routine activities perspective they presented established the context of crime as an important focus of study.

Drawing upon similar themes, British scholars led by Ronald Clarke began to explore the theoretical and practical possibilities of situational crime prevention (Clarke, 1983; Cornish & Clarke, 1986; Clarke, 1992; 1995). Their focus was on criminal contexts and the possibilities for reducing the opportunities for crime in very specific situations. Their approach, like that of Cohen and Felson, turned traditional crime prevention theory on its head. At the center of their crime equation was opportunity. Moreover, they sought to change opportunity rather than reform offenders. In situational crime prevention, more often than not "opportunity made the thief" (Felson & Clarke, 1998). This was in sharp contrast to the traditional view that the thief simply took advantage of a very large number of potential opportunities. Importantly, in a series of case studies, situational crime prevention advocates showed that reducing criminal opportunities in very specific contexts can lead to crime reduction and prevention (Clarke, 1992; 1995).

One natural outgrowth of these perspectives was that the specific places where crime occurs would become an important focus for crime prevention researchers (Eck & Weisburd, 1995; Taylor, 1997). While concern with the relationship between crime and place goes back to the founding generations of modern criminology (Guerry, 1833; Quetelet, 1842), the micro approach to places emerged only in the last few decades of the twentieth century (e.g., see Brantingham & Brantingham, 1975; Duffala, 1976; Mayhew et al., 1976; Rengert, 1980; Brantingham & Brantingham, 1981; Rengert, 1981; LeBeau, 1987; Hunter, 1988).[1] Places in this micro context are specific locations within the larger social environments of communities and neighborhoods (Eck & Weisburd, 1995). They are sometimes defined as buildings or addresses (see Sherman, Gartin & Buerger, 1989; Green, 1996), sometimes as block faces or street segments (see Sherman & Weisburd, 1995; Taylor, 1997), and sometimes

---

[1] It should be noted that a few early criminologists did examine the "micro" idea of place as discussed here (see Shaw & Myers, 1929). However, interest in micro places was not sustained and did not lead to significant theoretical or empirical inquiry.

as clusters of addresses, block faces, or street segments (see Block, Dabdoub & Fregly, 1995; Weisburd & Green, 1995).

In the mid to late 1980s, a group of criminologists began to examine the distribution of crime at micro places. Their findings radically altered the way many criminologists understood the crime equation, drawing them into a new area of inquiry that has important implications for police practice. Perhaps the most influential of these studies was conducted by Lawrence Sherman and his colleagues (Sherman, Buerger & Gartin, 1989; see also Sherman, 1987). Looking at crime addresses in the city of Minneapolis, they found a concentration of crime at places that was startling. Only 3 percent of the addresses in Minneapolis accounted for 50 percent of the crime calls to the police. Similar results were reported in a series of other studies in different locations and using different methodologies, each suggesting a very high concentration of crime in micro places (e.g., see Pierce, Spaar & Briggs, 1986; Weisburd, Maher & Sherman, 1992; Weisburd & Green, 1994; Weisburd et al., 2004). More recent research has reinforced this idea of crime concentrations (Braga, Andresen & Lawton, 2017; Telep & Weisburd, 2018), leading Weisburd (2015) to argue that there is a "law of crime concentration" at places showing not just that crime is concentrated, but that it is concentrated at similar levels across cities and across time.

Importantly, such concentration of crime at discrete places does not necessarily follow traditional ideas about crime and communities. There were often discrete places free of crime in neighborhoods that were considered troubled, and crime hot spots in neighborhoods that were seen generally as advantaged and not crime prone (Weisburd & Green, 1994; for more recent confirmation of these observations, see Weisburd, Groff & Yang, 2012). This empirical research reinforces theoretical perspectives that emphasize the importance of crime places, and suggested a focus upon small areas, often encompassing only one or a few city blocks that could be defined as "hot spots of crime" (Sherman & Weisburd, 1988; Sherman, Gartin & Buerger, 1989).

The Emergence of Hot Spots Policing

These emerging theoretical paradigms and empirical findings led Sherman and Weisburd (1995) to explore the practical implications of the hot spots approach for policing.[2] With cooperation from the Minneapolis Police Department, they

---

[2] Weisburd and Sherman came together at Rutgers University in the late 1980s where Weisburd was a faculty member and Sherman a distinguished visiting professor. Weisburd's interest in hot spots of crime developed from observations made during a study of the NYPD's community policing pilot program (Weisburd, 2015a; Weisburd, 2018). He observed that while assigned to larger beats, police officers given discretion to focus on community problems spent most of their time on a few specific blocks, and that street level crime and disorder seemed to decline in those places. Sherman observed in analyzing data in Minneapolis that crime calls were strongly

developed a large experimental field study of "police patrol in crime hot spots."
They sought to challenge the conclusions of the Kansas City Preventive Patrol
Experiment noted earlier, then well established, that police patrol has little
value in preventing or controlling crime. But, they also sought to show that
the focus of police efforts on crime hot spots presented a new and promising
approach for police practice.

The idea of focusing police patrol on crime hot spots represented a direct
application of the empirical findings regarding the concentration of crime in
micro places. The Kansas City Preventive Patrol Experiment had looked at the
effects of police patrol in large police beats. However, if "only 3 percent of the
addresses in a city produce more than half of all the requests for police response,
if no police are dispatched to 40 percent of the addresses and intersections in
a city over one year, and, if among the 60 percent with any requests the majority
register only one request a year (Sherman et al., 1989), then concentrating police
in a few locations makes more sense that spreading them evenly through a beat"
(Sherman & Weisburd, 1995: 629).

Nonetheless, the application of these findings to police practice raised
significant questions about the overall crime control benefits of a hot spots
approach. How would one know if crime prevention benefits gained at hot
spots would not simply be displaced to other areas close by? Sherman and
Weisburd noted that displacement was a potential but not necessarily certain
occurrence. However, they argued that the first task for researchers was to
establish that there would be any deterrent effect of police presence at the hot
spots themselves:

The main argument against directing extra resources to the hot spots is that it would
simply displace crime problems from one address to another without achieving any
overall or lasting reduction in crime. The premise of this argument is that a fixed supply
of criminals is seeking outlets for the fixed number of crimes they are predestined to
commit. Although that argument may fit some public drug markets, it does not fit all
crime or even all vice . . . In any case, displacement is merely a rival theory explaining *why*
crime declines at a specific hot spot, if it declines. The first step is to see whether crime can
be reduced at those spots at all, with a research design capable of giving a fair answer to
that question. (1995: 629)

The results of the Minneapolis Experiment stood in sharp distinction to
those of the earlier Kansas City study. The study used a rigorous
experimental design including randomization of 110 crime hot spots of
about a city block to treatment and control conditions. The treatment sites
received on average between two and three times as much preventive patrol
as the control sites. For the eight months in which the study was properly
implemented, Sherman and Weisburd found a significant relative

---

concentrated in crime hot spots (see Sherman et al., 1989). These intersecting observations led to
the Minneapolis Hot Spots Patrol Experiment (Sherman & Weisburd, 1988).

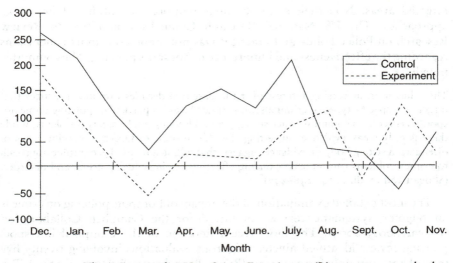

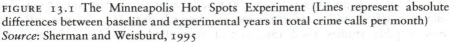

FIGURE 13.1 The Minneapolis Hot Spots Experiment (Lines represent absolute differences between baseline and experimental years in total crime calls per month) *Source*: Sherman and Weisburd, 1995

improvement in the experimental as compared to control hot spots both in terms of crime calls to the police and observations of disorder. Indeed, the effects of the program on crime, as measured by the difference between crime calls in the pre-experimental and experimental years, was found to be stable across the eight-month period (December through July) in which the program was properly implemented (see Figure 13.1). Crime, or at least crime calls and disorder, appeared to be prevented in the treatment as opposed to the control locations. Sherman and Weisburd (1995: 645) concluded that their results show "clear, if modest, general deterrent effects of substantial increases in police presence in crime hot spots." They noted that it was time for "criminologists to stop saying 'there is no evidence' that police patrol can affect crime" (1995: 647).

THE EMPIRICAL EVIDENCE FOR CRIME PREVENTION OUTCOMES IN HOT SPOTS POLICING

The Minneapolis Hot Spots Experiment led to a series of federal government supported studies of hot spots policing. These findings, in turn, provided what is perhaps the strongest weight of empirical evidence for the introduction of any policing practice (see Skogan & Frydl, 2004; Weisburd & Eck, 2004; Weisburd & Majmundar, 2018). Moreover, subsequent studies began to examine the displacement impacts of policing crime hot spots. For the most part, this was in terms of immediate spatial displacement, or displacement to areas close to the targeted areas. Nonetheless, the findings reinforce the utility of hot spots approaches. The US National Research Council's Committee to Review Research on Police Policy and Practices was not ambiguous in its conclusions regarding the effectiveness and importance of hot spots policing. The committee noted:

There has been increasing interest over the past two decades in police practices that target very specific types of criminals, and crime places. In particular, policing crime hot spots has become a common police strategy for addressing public safety problems. While there is only weak evidence suggesting the effectiveness of targeting specific types of offenders, a strong body of evidence suggests that taking a focused geographic approach to crime problems can increase policing effectiveness in reducing crime and disorder. (Skogan and Frydl, 2004: 246–247)

The most detailed examination of the impact of hot spots policing on crime is an ongoing systematic review conducted for the Campbell Collaboration (Braga, 2001; 2005). The most recent iteration of the Campbell hot spots policing review identified nineteen rigorous evaluations involving twenty-five tests of hot spots policing programs (Braga, Papachristos & Hureau, 2014). Ten eligible studies used quasi-experimental research designs (52.6 percent) and nine eligible studies used randomized controlled trials (47.4 percent) to evaluate the effects of hot spots policing on crime. The nineteen eligible studies were:

Minneapolis Repeat Call Address Policing (RECAP) Program (Sherman et al., 1989)*
New York Tactical Narcotics Teams (Sviridoff et al., 1992)
St. Louis Problem-Oriented Policing in 3 Drug Market Locations Study (Hope, 1994)
Minneapolis Hot Spots Patrol Program (Sherman & Weisburd, 1995)*
Jersey City Drug Markets Analysis Program (DMAP) (Weisburd & Green, 1995)*
Kansas City Gun Project (Sherman & Rogan, 1995a)
Kansas City Crack House Police Raids Program (Sherman & Rogan, 1995b)*
Beenleigh Calls for Service Project (Criminal Justice Commission, 1998)
Jersey City Problem-Oriented Policing at Violent Places Project (Braga et al., 1999)*
Houston Targeted Beat Program (Caeti, 1999)
Oakland Beat Health Program (Mazerolle, Price & Roehl, 2000)*
Pittsburgh Police Raids at Nuisance Bars Program (Cohen, Gorr & Singh, 2003)
Buenos Aires Police Presence after Terror Attack Study (DiTella & Schargrodsky, 2004)
Philadelphia Drug Corners Crackdowns Program (Lawton, Taylor & Luongo, 2005)

Jersey City Displacement and Diffusion Study (Weisburd et al., 2006)
Lowell Policing Crime and Disorder Hot Spots Project (Braga & Bond 2008)*
Jacksonville Policing Violent Crime Hot Spots Project (Taylor, Koper & Woods, 2011)*
Philadelphia Foot Patrol Program (Ratcliffe et al., 2011)*
Boston Safe Street Teams Program (Braga, Hureau & Papachristos, 2011)
* = randomized controlled trial

A noteworthy majority of the hot spots policing evaluations concluded that hot spots policing programs generated significant crime control benefits in the treatment areas relative to the control areas. Twenty of the twenty-five tests (80 percent) of hot spots policing interventions reported noteworthy crime-control gains associated with the approach. The five tests that did not report crime-control benefits were the Minneapolis RECAP treatment at commercial addresses, the New York Tactical Narcotics Team in the 70th Precinct, the Beenleigh Calls for Service Project, the Houston Targeted Beat Program's problem-oriented policing intervention, and the Jacksonville direct-saturation patrol intervention.

Meta-analysis is a method of systematic reviewing designed to synthesize empirical outcomes of studies, such as the effects of a specific crime prevention intervention on criminal offending behavior (Wilson, 2001). Meta-analysis uses specialized statistical methods to analyze the relationships between findings and study features (Lipsey & Wilson, 2001). The "effect size statistic" is the index used to represent the findings of each study in the overall meta-analysis of study findings and represents the strength and direction (positive or negative) of the relationship observed in a particular study (e.g., the size of the treatment effect found) (Lipsey & Wilson, 2001). The "mean effect size" represents the average effect of treatment on the outcome of interest across all eligible studies in a particular area, and is estimated by calculating a mean that is weighted by the precision of the effect size for each individual study. Due to limited information in the original evaluation reports, the Campbell Collaboration review meta-analysis only included effect sizes for twenty main effects tests and thirteen displacement and diffusion tests in sixteen eligible studies. All thirteen displacement and diffusion tests were limited to examining immediate spatial displacement and diffusion effects; that is, whether focused police efforts in targeted areas resulted in crime "moving around the corner" or whether these proximate areas experienced unintended crime control benefits.

The forest plots in Figure 13.2 show the standardized difference in means between the treatment and control or comparison conditions (effect size) with a 95 percent confidence interval plotted around them for all tests. Points plotted to the right of 0 indicate a treatment effect; in this case, the test showed a reduction in crime or disorder. Points to the left of 0 indicate a backfire effect where control conditions improved relative to treatment conditions.

Combined Effect Sizes for Study Outcomes

Study name	Outcome	Statistics for each study			Std diff in means and 95% CI
		Std diff in means	Standard error	p-Value	
KC Gun	Gun crimes	0.866	0.275	0.002	
Phila. Drug Corners	Combined	0.855	0.258	0.001	
Buenos Aires Police	Motor vehicle theft incidents	0.617	0.169	0.000	
JC Disp. Prost.	Prostitution events	0.525	0.149	0.000	
JC Disp. Drug	Drug events	0.441	0.131	0.001	
Minn. RECAP Resid.	Total calls	0.369	0.132	0.005	
Boston SST	Total violent incidents	0.341	0.020	0.000	
Oakland Beath Health	Drug calls	0.279	0.056	0.000	
JC DMAP	Combined	0.147	0.270	0.585	
Low ell POP	Total calls	0.145	0.034	0.000	
JC POP	Combined	0.143	0.043	0.001	
Phila. Foot Patrol	Violent incidents	0.525	0.021	0.000	
Pittsburgh Bar Raids	Drug calls	0.525	0.038	0.001	
NYC TNT 67	Combined	0.525	0.077	0.257	
Minn. Patrol	Total calls	0.525	0.015	0.000	
KC Crack	Total calls	0.051	0.039	0.188	
Minn. RECAP Comm.	Total calls	0.015	0.137	0.913	
Jacks onville POP	Combined	-0.005	0.092	0.959	
NYC TNT 70	Combined	-0.027	0.080	0.739	
Jacks onville Patrol	Combined	-0.055	0.096	0.568	
		0.184	0.035	0.000	

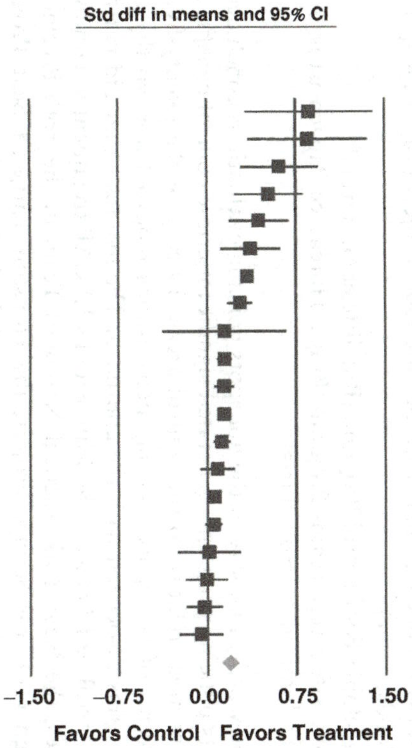

Favors Control   Favors Treatment

Meta-Analysis Random Effects Model, Q = 184.021, df = 19, p < 0.000

FIGURE 13.2 Meta Analysis of Effects of Hot Spots Policing Programs on Crime
Source: Braga, Papachristos, and Hureau (2014), p. 655

The meta-analysis of main effect sizes found a statistically-significant overall mean effect in favor of hot spots policing strategies (0.184). Nine of the thirteen displacement/diffusion tests reported effect sizes that favored diffusion effects over displacement effects. Only the Philadelphia Foot Patrol experiment reported a statistically significant displacement effect. The displacement/ diffusion meta-analysis suggests a small but statistically significant overall diffusion of crime control benefits effect (0.104) generated by the hot spots policing strategies.

IMPACTS ON COMMUNITIES

Traditional police strategies are generally focused on large geographic areas. Hot spots policing does not reinforce this community-focused idea of police services. Rather, it pushes the police to think of bad places rather than bad communities. In this context, police resources are not focused at communities but at specific hot spot places where crime is concentrated. This approach not only increases the dosage of policing that can be brought to problem places, it also reduces arbitrary allocations of police services. Such careful targeting of the allocation of policing can reduce the interventions of police in the everyday lives of people who live in high-crime communities, focusing those interventions on the specific streets where increased policing is needed.

Critics of hot spots policing have often ignored this benefit (e.g., see Rosenbaum, 2006; Kochel, 2011), focusing instead on the potential for hot spots policing to increase alienation of citizens at the places where hot spots policing tactics are applied. Despite arguments that intensive interventions, such as hot spots policing, will have negative impacts on citizen perceptions, there is very little evidence to support this position. A number studies show that residents in crime hot spots who are subject to focused police attention welcome the concentration of police efforts in problem places (e.g., see Sherman & Rogan, 1995a; Chermak, McGarrell & Weiss, 2001; Corsaro et al., 2012). For example, in the Kansas City Gun Experiment (Shaw, 1995; Sherman & Rogan, 1995a) the community at and near hot spots strongly supported the intensive patrols and perceived an improvement in the quality of life in the treatment neighborhood.

One recent study by Anthony Braga and Brenda Bond (2009) examined community reaction to the problem-oriented policing at crime and disorder hot spots initiative in Lowell, Massachusetts. Data from interviews showed that the community perceived improvements in social and physical disorder and had an increased number of contacts with the police. However, no statistically significant differences were found in fear of crime or perceptions of police tactics or demeanor. Recent experimental research from three cities in San Bernardino County, California, also found that a broken windows style intervention (in which the police focused on reducing incivilities) at hot spots had no impact on resident perceptions of fear of crime or police legitimacy

(Weisburd et al., 2011). A randomized experiment in Illinois found that though there were initial declines in legitimacy from intensive police patrols and problem-solving at hot spots, those effects withered quickly (Kochel & Weisburd, 2017). Importantly, the study found no evidence of increases in perceived abuse by police in the hot spots that received the experimental interventions.

Of course, hot spots policing practices in the field may include abusive policing practices in specific cases. But, as the National Academies of Sciences Committee on Proactive Policing concluded, "Existing research suggests that place-based policing strategies rarely have negative short-term impacts on community outcomes" (Weisburd & Majmundar, 2018: 208).

WHAT WE NEED TO KNOW

While the evidence for the effectiveness of hot spots policing is convincing, we think it important to note that there are still significant gaps in our knowledge about the effects of these interventions.[3] There is emerging evidence that certain broad categories of hot spots policing are more effective than others. Braga, Papachristos & Hureau (2014), for example, find in their systematic review that problem-oriented hot spots policing programs have larger effect sizes than approaches that simply increase police patrol But we know little about which specific hot spots strategies work best in which specific types of situations. Clearly, the effectiveness of strategies will depend on the specific types of crimes and types of places that are the focus of police attention. But we still do not have enough studies to provide detailed answers to these types of questions.

More generally, there is still a vast array of hot spots strategies that have not been rigorously tested (Weisburd & Telep, 2014). Koper (2014) notes drawing from a survey of agencies of various sizes that departments use a wide variety of strategies to address high-crime places. While some of the most popular strategies used by respondents have been well evaluated (e.g., problem-solving and directed patrol), other common responses have not been the subject of extensive rigorous research. For example, many agencies identified targeting known offenders as an effective strategy for shooting and homicide hot spots. To date, only limited research has evaluated a focus on known offenders as a hot spots strategy, but the results for this approach are very promising (see Ratcliffe et al., 2011). Buy-and-bust and reverse sting operations were identified by a number of respondents as effective approaches in drug violence hot spots, but these strategies have not been rigorously evaluated thus far. Other strategies frequently used by agencies that have not yet been researched extensively

---

[3] We draw heavily in this section from a recent article by Weisburd and Telep (2014) on "what we know and need to know" in hot spots policing.

include community partnerships, checks on probationers and parolees, and using warrant service operations to target wanted offenders.

We also need to know more about the impact of new technologies on the effectiveness of hot spots policing. Lum, Hibdon et al. (2011) for example, found that license plate readers (LPRs) were not effective at reducing overall crime or automobile crime. In contrast, Koper, Taylor, and Woods (2013) found LPRs reduced at least certain crime types when used in a rotating, short-term crackdown fashion as recommended by Sherman (1990). While these two randomized experiments are an important first step in understanding how police technology affects hot spots policing, we still need to know more about whether often costly new technologies can enhance the ability of police to address high-crime places.

Nearly all the experimental and quasi-experimental studies of hot spots policing have been conducted in large cities like Minneapolis (Sherman & Weisburd, 1995), Jersey City (Braga et al., 1999), and Jacksonville (Taylor, Koper & Woods, 2011). This raises questions about how applicable existing hot spots tactics, and the evidence supporting them, are to smaller, less densely populated cities. Even less is known about whether the tactic is applicable in small towns or rural county jurisdictions. As Lum and Koper (2013) find, just one of nearly 120 rigorous policing crime control interventions included as part of the evidence-based policing matrix (Lum, Koper & Telep, 2011) took place in a rural area. Hot spots researchers (like police researchers more generally) have largely ignored smaller cities and towns and rural areas. This is not a minor concern as the vast majority of police agencies in the United States are small to midsized agencies serving smaller cities and towns.

Hot spots policing studies to date have looked only at the short-term benefits of these tactics. Not one of the studies reviewed by Braga, Papachristos, and Hureau (2014) had more than a one-year follow-up period. What this means is that we know little about whether hot spots policing strategies will affect crime in the long run. Can we have long-term impacts on crime at hot spots? What types of strategies are likely to have only short-term benefits? What types of strategies are likely to ameliorate crime in the long run?

Finally, we have little rigorous information on the size of possible jurisdictional impacts of hot spots policing programs. Hot spots policing experiments have randomly allocated hot spots within a single jurisdiction. While this provides for a strong causal test of the impacts of hot spots policing on crime at hot spots, it does not allow us to answer with certainty the question of how large the impact of hot spots policing will be when it is applied broadly across a jurisdiction. The fact that hot spots policing on average leads to a "diffusion of benefits" (Clarke & Weisburd, 1994) to nearby areas suggests that these programs will have jurisdictional impacts. But absent direct studies of this issue, we cannot provide estimates of the magnitude of such impacts. We know of only one study that tried to estimate jurisdictional impacts. Using simulation modelling. Weisburd and colleagues (2017) found that high-intensity hot spots policing, where half the police officers assigned to a beat spent all of their time in the top five hot spots in that beat, reduced the incidence of robbery by 11.7 percent at the borough level, 11.5 percent at the police-beat level, and 77.3 percent at the hot-spot level in comparison to random police patrol.

THE LINK BETWEEN RESEARCH AND PRACTICE

We have so far shown that hot spots policing emerged from theoretical developments in criminology, and basic research indicating a very high concentration of crime at hot spots. Hot spots policing was also subjected to substantial experimental evaluation that showed that it could be an effective policing strategy to prevent crime and disorder. Importantly, it is also the case that this approach had diffused widely in American policing by the turn of the last century. In a 2001 Police Foundation study, more than seven in ten police departments with more than 100 sworn officers reported using crime mapping to identify "crime hot spots" (Weisburd et al., 2001). The 2007 LEMAS survey founds that nearly all police agencies in large metropolitan centers use computers for hot spots identification (Reaves, 2010). In a more recent study of a representative sample of police agencies, the National Police Research Platform reported that 75 percent of the agencies surveyed used the hot spots policing approach (Mastrofski & Fridell n.d., reported in Weisburd & Majmundar, 2018). But the fact that the research literature is supportive of hot spots policing and that police have implemented this approach widely, does not necessarily mean that research strongly impacted police practice. For example, it may be that the police adopted hot spots policing independently and later evidence simply confirmed that the strategy was useful.

While the Minneapolis Hot Spots Experiment is the first example we know of a successful program in which micro-level crime hot spots were systematically identified on a large scale for the purpose of police intervention, it is not the first example of police use of crime mapping to identify crime problems. Police officers have long recognized the importance of place in crime. Hand-developed pin maps have been widely used in police agencies for over half a century (Weisburd & McEwen, 1997). And one can find isolated examples of what today we would define as hot spots policing in earlier periods (e.g., see Weiss, 2001). Moreover, during the 1970s, crime analysts looked for patterns in crime by plotting the locations and times at which crimes were committed to direct patrol officers to the most likely targets (Reinier, 1977), and cutting-edge crime analysts were experimenting with computerized crime mapping before the hot spots studies were well known (Weisburd & Lum, 2005).

Nonetheless, a study by Weisburd and Lum (2005) suggests that the timing of the wide-scale implementation of hot spots policing follows very closely the basic and applied research we have reviewed. The study examined the diffusion of computerized crime mapping in police agencies using data from the National

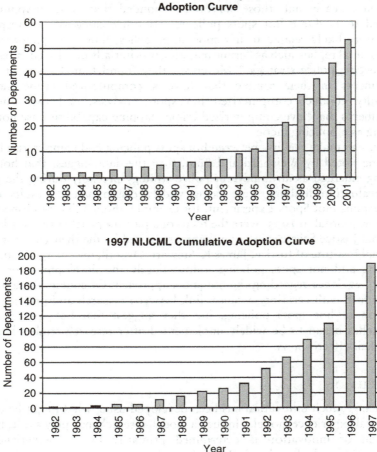

FIGURE 13.3 Cumulative Distribution of Computerized Crime Mapping adopted from the Weisburd et al. Pilot Study and the NIJ CML study
Source: Weisburd and Lum, 2005

Institute of Justice Crime Mapping Laboratory (Mamalian et al., 1999), and a small pilot study of ninety-two police agencies of over 100 sworn officers conducted by Weisburd and Lum. They found that computerized crime mapping in larger police agencies first began to emerge in policing in the 1980s and early 1990s. Adoption began to grow steeply in the mid 1990s with the number of adopters increasing at a large rate after 1995 (see Figure 13.3).

Weisburd and Lum (2005) make a direct link in their survey between the diffusion of innovation in crime mapping and the adoption of hot spots policing. When they asked why departments developed a crime mapping capability, nearly half those surveyed responded that crime mapping was adopted to facilitate hot spots policing. Of other categories of responses, many were likely related to hot spots approaches, though respondents gave more general replies such as "crime mapping was initially developed in response to a specific police strategy." Moreover, they found that 80 percent of the departments in their sample that have a computerized crime mapping capability conduct computerized hot spots analysis, and two thirds of departments that have computerized crime mapping capabilities use hot spots policing as a policing tactic.

If we can make the link between hot spots policing and computerized crime mapping noted by Weisburd and Lum, then the data suggest that hot spots policing emerged as an important police strategy precisely during the period that evaluation findings were being widely disseminated. Results of the Minneapolis Hot Spots Experiment, for example, though first published in an academic journal in 1995, were the focus of a plenary panel at the Academy of Criminal Justice Sciences in 1990 that was chaired by the then-Director of the National Institute of Justice, James K. Stewart. Overall, the emergence of crime mapping and hot spots policing follow closely the development of strong research evidence regarding the hot spots approach. Of course, these data do not confirm with certainty a causal link between research and practice in the adoption of hot spots policing, but they suggest that hot spots policing approaches began to be widely implemented after research studies began to show their effectiveness.

CONCLUSION

In policing, much innovation has been developed using what might be termed a "clinical experience model." In such a model, research may play a role, but the adoption of innovation is determined primarily by the experiences of practitioners and often has little to do with research evidence. Such models often have a weak theoretical basis and it is not uncommon to discover that they have little crime prevention value once they are subjected to serious empirical investigation. Given the importance of policing for public safety, it seems unreasonable that policing should continue to rely on such a model for the development and diffusion of innovation.

Our discussion of hot spots policing suggests an alternative model for police innovation. Hot spots policing was consistent with developing theoretical insights in criminology and was supported by basic criminological research on crime and place. Accordingly, before hot spots policing was to emerge as a coherent strategic approach, there was strong theoretical justification and empirical support for testing the value of this strategy. Hot spots policing was subjected to rigorous empirical investigation before it was widely diffused and adopted by American police agencies. In this sense, hot spots policing suggests that "evidence-based policing," as Lawrence Sherman (1998) has called it (see Part X in this volume), can form the basis for important police innovation. Hot spots policing is a model for the integration of research in the world of policing, and this integration has produced what is, according to empirical evidence, the most effective police innovation of the last few decades.

REFERENCES

Agnew, R. (1992). Foundation for a general strain theory of crime and delinquency. *Criminology, 30,* 47–84.

Agnew, R. (1999). A general strain theory of community differences in crime rates. *Journal of Research in Crime and Delinquency, 36,* 123–155.

Akers, R. (1973). *Deviant Behavior: A Social Learning Approach.* Belmont, CA: Wadsworth Publishing.

Baumer, E., Lauritsen, J., Rosenfeld, R., & Wright, R. (1998). The influence of crack cocaine on robbery, burglary, and homicide rates: A cross-city, longitudinal analysis. *Journal of Research in Crime and Delinquency, 35,* 316–340.

Bayley, D. (1994). *Police for the Future.* New York: Oxford University Press.

Block, C., Dabdoub, M., & Fregly, S. (eds.). (1995). *Crime Analysis through Computer Mapping.* Washington, DC: Police Executive Research Forum.

Braga, A. (2001). The effects of hot spots policing on crime. *Annals of the American Academy of Political and Social Science, 578,* 104–125.

Braga, A. (2005). Hot spots policing and crime prevention: A systematic review of randomized controlled trials. *Journal of Experimental Criminology, 1,* 317–342.

Braga, A., & Bond, B. J. (2008). Policing crime and disorder hot spots: A randomized controlled trial. *Criminology, 46,* 577–608.

Braga, A., & Bond, B. J. (2009). Community perceptions of police crime prevention efforts: Using interviews in small areas to evaluate crime reduction strategies. In J. Knutsson, & N. Tilley (eds.), *Evaluating Crime Reduction Initiatives. Crime Prevention Studies,* vol. 24. Monsey, NY: Criminal Justice Press.

Braga, A., Andresen, M., & Lawton, B. (2017). The law of crime concentration at places: Editors' introduction. *Journal of Quantitative Criminology, 33,* 421–426.

Braga, A., Hureau, D., & Papachristos, A. (2011). An ex-post-facto evaluation framework for place-based police interventions. *Evaluation Review, 35,* 592–626.

Braga, A., Papachristos, A., & Hureau, D. (2014). The effects of hot spots policing on crime: An updated systematic review and meta-analysis. *Justice Quarterly, 31,* 633–663.

Braga, A., Weisburd, D., Waring, E., Mazerolle, L. G., Spelman, W., & Gajewski, F. (1999). Problem oriented policing in violent crime places: A randomized controlled experiment. *Criminology, 37,* 541–580.

Brantingham, P. J., & Brantingham, P. L. (1975). Residential burglary and urban form. *Urban Studies, 12,* 273–284.

Brantingham, P. J., & Brantingham, P. L. (1981). Notes on the geometry of crime. In P. J. Brantingham, & P. L. Brantingham (eds.), *Environmental Criminology.* Beverly Hills, CA: Sage Publications.

Brantingham, P. J., & Brantingham, P. L. (1990). Situational crime prevention in practice. *Canadian Journal of Criminology,* January, 17–40.

Bursik, R. J., Jr., & Grasmick, H. G. (1993). *Neighborhoods and Crime*. San Francisco: Lexington.

Caeti, T. (1999). Houston's targeted beat program: A quasi-experimental test of police patrol strategies. Doctoral dissertation, Sam Houston State University. Ann Arbor, MI: UMI.

Chermak, S., McGarrell, E. F., & Weiss, A. (2001). Citizens' perceptions of aggressive traffic enforcement strategies. *Justice Quarterly, 18*, 365–391.

Clarke, R. V. (1983). Situational crime prevention: Its theoretical basis and practical scope. In M. Tonry, & N. Morris (eds.), *Crime and Justice: An Annual Review of Research*, vol 4 (pp. 225–256). Chicago: University of Chicago Press.

Clarke, R. V. (1992). *Situational Crime Prevention: Successful Case Studies*. Albany, NY: Harrow and Heston.

Clarke, R. V. (1995). Situational crime prevention: Achievements and challenges. In M. Tonry, & D. Farrington (eds.), *Building a Safer Society: Strategic Approaches to Crime Prevention, Crime and Justice: A Review of Research*, 19, 91–150. Chicago: University of Chicago Press.

Clarke, R. V., & Felson, M. (eds.). (1993). *Routine Activity and Rational Choice: Advances in Criminological Theory*, 5, 1–14. New Brunswick, NJ: Transaction Press.

Clarke, R. V., & Weisburd, D. (1994). Diffusion of crime control benefits: Observations on the reverse of displacement. In R. V. Clarke (ed.), *Crime Prevention Studies*, 2 (pp. 165–183). Monsey, NY: Criminal Justice Press.

Cloward, R., & Ohlin, L. (1960). *Delinquency and Opportunity*. Glencoe, IL: Free Press.

Cohen, J., Gorr, W., & Singh, P. (2003). Estimating intervention effects in varying risk settings: Do police raids reduce illegal drug dealing at nuisance bars? *Criminology, 41*, 257–292.

Cohen, L. E., & Felson, M. (1979). Social change and crime rate trends: A routine activity approach. *American Sociological Review, 44*, 588–605.

Cornish, D. B., & Clarke, R. V. (1986). *The Reasoning Criminal: Rational Choice Perspectives on Offending*. New York: Springer-Verlag.

Corsaro, N., Hunt, E. D., Hipple, N. K., & McGarrell, E. F. (2012). The impact of drug market pulling levers policing on neighborhood violence. *Criminology & Public Policy, 11*, 167–199.

Criminal Justice Commission. (1998). *Beenleigh Calls for Service Project: Evaluation Report*. Brisbane, Queensland: Criminal Justice Commission.

DiTella, R., & Schargrodsky, E. (2004). Do police reduce crime? Estimates using the allocation of police forces after a terrorist attack. *American Economic Review, 94*, 115–133.

Duffala, D. C. (1976). Convenience stores, robbery, and physical environmental features. *American Behavioral Scientist, 20*, 227–246.

Eck, J. E., & Weisburd, D. (eds.). (1995). *Crime and Place: Crime Prevention Studies*, vol. 4. Monsey, NY: Criminal Justice Press.

Farrington, D. P. (1983). Offending from 10 to 25 years of age. In K. Van Dusen, & S. A. Mednick (eds.), *Prospective Studies of Crime and Delinquency* (pp. 17–38). Boston: Kluwer-Nijhoff.

Farrington, D. P., Ohlin, L., & Wilson, J. Q. (1986). *Understanding and Controlling Crime*. New York: Springer-Verlag.

Felson, M., & Clarke, R. V. (1998). Opportunity makes the thief: Practical theory for crime prevention. *Police Research Series: Policing and Reducing Crime Unit*, Paper 98. London: Home Office.

Goldstein, H. (1990). *Problem-Oriented Policing*. New York: McGraw-Hill.

Gottfredson, M. R., & Hirschi, T. (1990). *A General Theory of Crime*. Stanford, CA: Stanford University Press.

Green, L. (1996). *Policing Places with Drug Problems*. Thousand Oaks, CA: Sage Publications.

Greenwood, P. J., Petersilia, J., & Chaiken, J. (1977). *The Criminal Investigation Process*. Lexington: D.C. Heath.

Guerry, A. M. (1833). *Essai sur la Statistique morale de la France*. Paris: Crochard.

Hirschi, T. (1969). *Causes of Delinquency*. Berkeley: University of California Press.

Hope, T. (1994). Problem-oriented policing and drug market locations: Three case studies. In R. V. Clarke (eds.), *Crime Prevention Studies* vol. 2 (pp. 5–31). Monsey, NY: Criminal Justice Press.

Hunter, R. D. (1988). Environmental characteristics of convenience store robberies in the state of Florida. Paper presented at the annual meeting of the American Society of Criminology, Chicago.

Kelling, G., Pate, A. M., Dieckman, D., & Brown, C. E. (1974). *The Kansas City Preventive Patrol Experiment: Summary Report*. Washington, DC: The Police Foundation.

Kochel, T. R. (2011). Constructing hot spots policing: Unexamined consequences for disadvantaged populations and for police legitimacy. *Criminal Justice Policy Review*, 22, 350–374.

Kochel, T., & Weisburd, D. (2017). Assessing community consequences of implementing hot spots policing in residential areas: Findings from a randomized field trial. *Journal of Experimental Criminology*, 13, 143–170.

Koper, C. S. (2014). Assessing the practice of hot spots policing: survey results from a national convenience sample of local police agencies. *Journal of Contemporary Criminal Justice*, 30, 123–146.

Koper, C. S., Taylor, B. G., & Woods, D. J. (2013). A randomized test of initial and residual deterrence from directed patrols and use of license plate readers at crime hot spots. *Journal of Experimental Criminology*, 9, 213–244.

Lawton, B., Taylor, R., & Luongo, A. (2005). Police officers on drug corners in Philadelphia, drug crime, and violent crime: Intended, diffusion, and displacement impacts. *Justice Quarterly*, 22, 427–451.

LeBeau, J. (1987). The methods and measures of centrography and the spatial dynamics of rape. *Journal of Quantitative Criminology*, 3, 125–141.

Levine, J. P. (1975). Ineffectiveness of adding police to prevent crime. *Public Policy*, 23, 523–545.

Lipsey, M. W. (1992). Juvenile delinquency treatment: A meta-analytic inquiry into the variability of effects. In T. D. Cook, H. Cooper, D. S. Cordray, H. Hartmann, L. V. Hedges, R. J. Light, T. A. Louis, & F. Mosteller (eds.), *Meta-analysis for explanation: A casebook* (pp. 83–127). New York: Russell Sage Foundation.

Lipsey, M., & Wilson, D. (2001). *Practical Meta-Analysis. Applied Social Research Methods Series*, vol. 49. Thousand Oaks, CA: Sage Publications.

Loftin, C., & Hill, R. (1974). Regional subculture and homicide: An examination of the Gastil-Hackney thesis. *American Sociological Review*, 39, 714–724.

Lum, C., & Koper, C. S. (2013). Evidence-based policing in smaller agencies: Challenges, prospects, and opportunities. *The Police Chief, 80*, 42–47.

Lum, C., Hibdon, J., Cave, B., Koper, C. S., & Merola, L. (2011). License plate reader (LPR) police patrols in crime hot spots: An experimental evaluation in two adjacent jurisdictions. *Journal of Experimental Criminology, 7*, 321–345.

Lum, C., Koper, C. S., & Telep, C. W. (2011). The evidence-based policing matrix. *Journal of Experimental Criminology, 7*, 3–26.

Mamalian, C., LaVigne, N., Groff, E., Loftin, C., & Hill, R. (1999). *The Use of Computerized Crime Mapping by Law Enforcement: Survey Results (NIJ Research Preview)*. Washington, DC: National Institute of Justice. Retrieved from www.ncjrs.org/pdffiles1/fs000237.

Martinson, R. (1974). What works? – Questions and answers about prison reform. *The Public Interest, 35*, 22–54.

Mastrofski, S., & Ritti, R. (2000). Making sense of community policing: A theoretical perspective. *Police Practice and Research Journal, 1*(2), 183–210.

Mastrofski, S. D., & Fridell, L. (n.d.). Police Departments' Adoption of Innovative Practice. National Police Research Platform. Retrieved from http://static1.1.sqspcdn.com/static/f/733761/26580910/1443907094233/Department+Characteristics+Survey.pdf?token=1xxue9jmC71p%2BeA7gpKCf2WEf7U%3D [January2016].

Mayhew, P., Clarke, R. V., Sturman, A., & Hough, M. (1976). *Crime as Opportunity: Home Office Research Study* 34, Longon: H.M. Stationary Office.

Mazerolle, L., Price, J., & Roehl, J. (2000). Civil remedies and drug control: A randomized field trial in Oakland, California. *Evaluation Review, 24*, 212–241.

Merton, R. K. (1968). Social structure and anomie. *American Sociological Review, 3*, 672–682.

Meyer, J., & Rowan, B. (1977). Formal structure as myth. *American Journal of Sociology, 83*, 340–363.

Moffitt, T. (1993). Adolescence-limited and life-course persistent antisocial behavior: A developmental taxonomy. *Psychological Review, 4*, 674.

Nettler, G. (1978). *Explaining Crime*. 2nd ed. New York: McGraw Hill.

Pierce, G. L., Spaar, S., & Briggs, L. R. (1986). *The Character of Police Work: Strategic and Tactical Implications*. Boston, MA: Center for Applied Social Research, Northeastern University.

Quetelet, A. J. (1842). *A Treatise of Man*. Gainesville, FL: Scholar's Facsimiles and Reprints (1969 ed.).

Raine, A. (1993). *The Psychopathy of Crime*. New York: Academic Press.

Ratcliffe, J., Taniguchi, T., Groff, E., & Wood, J. (2011). The Philadelphia foot patrol experiment: A randomized controlled trial of police patrol effectiveness in violent crime hot spots. *Criminology, 49*, 795–831.

Reaves, B. A. (2010). *Local police departments, 2007*. Washington, DC: Bureau of Justice Statistics, US Department of Justice.

Reinier, G. H. (1977). *Crime Analysis in Support of Patrol*. National Evaluation Program: Phase I Report. Washington, DC: US Government Printing Office.

Rengert, G. F. (1980). Theory and practice in urban police response. In D. Georges-Abeyie, & K. Harries (eds.), *Crime: A Spatial Perspective*. New York: Columbia University Press.

Rengert, G. F. (1981). Burglary in Philadelphia: A critique of an opportunity structure model. In P. J. Brantingham, & P. L. Brantingham (eds.), *Environmental Criminology* (pp. 189–201). Beverly Hills, CA: Sage Publications.

Rosenbaum, D. P. (2006). The limits of hot spots policing. In D. L. Weisburd, & A. A. Braga (eds.), *Police Innovation: Contrasting Perspectives* (pp. 245–266). New York: Cambridge University Press.

Sampson, R. J. (1985). Neighborhood and crime: The structural determinants of personal victimization. *Journal of Research in Crime and Delinquency*, 22, 7–40.

Sampson, R. J., & Groves, W. B. (1989). Community structure and crime: Testing social disorganization theory. *American Journal of Sociology*, 94, 774–802.

Sampson, R. J., & Laub, J. H. (1993). *Crime in the Making: Pathways and Turning Points through Life*. Cambridge, MA: Harvard University Press.

Sechrest, L. B., White, S. O., & Brown, E. O. (1979). *The Rehabilitation of Criminal Offenders: Problems and Prospects*. Washington, DC: National Academies of Sciences.

Shaw, C. R., & McKay, H. (1972). *Delinquency and Urban Areas*. Chicago: University of Chicago Press.

Shaw, C. R., & Myers, E. D. (1929). *The juvenile delinquent*. In *Illinois Crime Survey*. Chicago: Illinois Association for Criminal Justice.

Shaw, J. (1995). Community policing against guns: Public opinion of the Kansas City gun experiment. *Justice Quarterly*, 12, 695–710.

Sherman, L. W. (1990). Police crackdowns: Initial and residual deterrence. *Crime and Justice*, 12, 1–48.

Sherman, L. W. (1995). Hot spots of crime and criminal careers of places. In J. E. Eck, & D. Weisburd (eds.), *Crime Prevention Studies*, vol. 4 (pp. 35–52). Monsey, NY: Criminal Justice Press.

Sherman, L. W. (1998). *Evidence-based policing*. Ideas in American policing series. Washington, DC: The Police Foundation.

Sherman, L. W. (1987). *Repeat Calls to the Police in Minneapolis*. Washington, DC: Crime Control Institute.

Sherman, L. W., & Rogan, D. (1995a). Effects of gun seizures on gun violence: Hot spots patrol in Kansas City. *Justice Quarterly*, 12, 673–694.

Sherman, L. W., & Rogan, D. (1995b). Deterrent effects of police raids on crack houses: A randomized controlled experiment. *Justice Quarterly*, 12, 755–782.

Sherman, L. W., & Weisburd, D. (1988). Policing the hot spots of crime: A redesign of the Kansas City Preventive Patrol Experiment. Research proposal submitted to the US National Institute of Justice, Program on Research in Public Safety and Security.

Sherman, L. W., & Weisburd, D. (1995). General deterrent effects of police patrol in crime "hot-spots": A randomized controlled trial. *Justice Quarterly*, 12, 626–648.

Sherman, L. W., Buerger, M. E., & Gartin, P. R. (1989). *Repeat Call Address Policing: The Minneapolis RECAP Experiment. Final Report to the National Institute of Justice*. Washington, DC: Crime Control Institute.

Sherman, L. W., Gartin, P. R., & Buerger, M. E. (1989). Hot spots of predatory crime: Routine activities and the criminology of place. *Criminology*, 27, 27–56.

Skogan, W., & Frydl, K. (eds). (2004). *Fairness and Effectiveness in Policing: The Evidence*. Committee to Review Research on Police Policy and Practices. Washington, DC: National Academies Press.

Spelman, W., & Brown, D. K. (1984). *Calling the police: Citizen reporting of serious crime*. Washington, DC: US Government Printing Office.

Sutherland, E. (1947). *Principals of Criminology*. Chicago: J. B. Lippincott Co.

Sviridoff, M., Sadd, S., Curtis, R., & Grinc, R. (1992). *The Neighborhood Effects of Street-Level Drug Enforcement: Tactical Narcotics Teams in New York*. New York: Vera Institute of Justice.

Taylor, B., Koper, C., & Woods, D. (2011). A randomized controlled trial of different policing strategies at hot spots of violent crime. *Journal of Experimental Criminology*, 7, 149–181.

Taylor, R. (1997). Social order and disorder of street blocks and neighborhoods: Ecology, microecology, and the systemic model of social disorganization. *Journal of Research in Crime and Delinquency*, 34, 113–155.

Telep C. W., & Weisburd, D. (2018). Crime concentrations at place. In S. Johnson, & G. Bruinsma (eds.), *Oxford Handbook of Environmental Criminology*. Oxford: Oxford University Press.

Trasler, G. (1993). Conscience, opportunity, rational choice, and crime. In R. V. Clarke, & M. Felson (eds.), *Routine Activity and Rational Choice: Advances in Criminological Theory*, vol. 5 (pp. 305–322). New Brunswick, NJ: Transaction Publishers.

Visher, C., & Weisburd, D. (1998). Identifying what works: Recent trends in crime prevention strategies. *Crime, Law and Social Change*, 28, 223–242.

Weisburd, D., & Eck, J. E. (2004). What can police do to reduce crime, disorder, and fear? *The Annals of the American Academy of Political and Social Science*, 593, 42–65.

Weisburd, D., & Green, L. (1995). Policing drug hot-spots: The Jersey City drug market analysis experiment. *Justice Quarterly*, 12, 711–735.

Weisburd, D., & Green, L. *(Green-Mazerolle)* (1994). Defining the drug market: The case of the Jersey City DMA system. In D. L. MacKenzie, & C.D. Uchida (eds.), *Drugs and Crime: Evaluating Public Policy Initiatives*. Newbury Park, CA: Sage Publications.

Weisburd, D., & Lum, C. (2005). The diffusion of computerized crime mapping policing: Linking research and practice. *Police Practice and Research*, 6, 433–448.

Weisburd, D., & Majmundar M. (eds.). (2018). *Proactive Policing: Effects on Crime and Communities*. Committee on Proactive Policing: Effects on Crime, Communities, and Civil Liberties. Washington, DC: The National Academies Press.

Weisburd, D., & McEwen, T. (eds.). (1997). *Crime Mapping and Crime Prevention: Crime Prevention Studies*, vol. 8. Monsey, NY: Criminal Justice Press.

Weisburd, D., & Neyroud, P. (2011). *Police Science: Towards a New Paradigm*. Washington: National Institute of Justice.

Weisburd, D., & Telep, C. W. (2014). Hot spots policing what we know and what we need to know. *Journal of Contemporary Criminal Justice*, 30, 200–220.

Weisburd, D., Bushway, S., Lum, C., & Yang, S. M. (2004). Trajectories of crime at places: A longitudinal study of street segments in the city of Seattle. *Criminology*, 42, 283–321.

Weisburd, D. L., Braga, A. A., Groff, E. R., & Wooditch, A. (2017). Can hot spots policing reduce crime in urban areas? An agent-based simulation. *Criminology*, 55, 137–173.

Weisburd, D., Groff, E. R., & Yang, S. M. (2012). *The Criminology of Place: Street Segments and Our Understanding of the Crime Problem*. Oxford: Oxford University Press.

Weisburd, D., Hinkle, J. C., Famega, C., & Ready, J. (2011). The possible "backfire" effects of hot spots policing: An experimental assessment of impacts on legitimacy, fear and collective efficacy. *Journal of Experimental Criminology*, 7, 297–320.

Weisburd, D., Maher, L., & Sherman L.W. (1992). Contrasting crime general and crime specific theory: The case of hot-spots of crime. In *Advances in Criminological Theory*, vol. 4 (pp. 45–70). New Brunswick, NJ: Transaction Press.

Weisburd, D., Mastrofski, S., McNally, A. M., & Greenspan, R. (2001). *Compstat and organizational change: Findings from a national survey*. Washington, DC: The Police Foundation.

Weisburd, D., Mastrofski, S. D., McNally, A. M., Greenspan, R., & Willis, J. J. (2003). Reforming to preserve: Compstat and strategic problem solving in American policing. *Criminology and Public Policy*, 2, 421–456.

Weisburd, D., Wyckoff, L., Ready, J., Eck, J., Hinkle, J., & Gajewski, F. (2006). Does crime just move around the corner? A controlled study of spatial displacement and diffusion of crime control benefits. *Criminology*, 44, 549–592.

Weisburd, D. (2015). The law of crime concentration and the criminology of place. *Criminology*, 53(2), 133–157.

Weisburd, D. (2015a). Small Worlds of Crime and Criminal Justice Interventions: Discovering Crime Hot Spots. In M. Maltz, & S. Rice (eds.), *Envisioning Criminology: Researchers on Research as a Process of Discovery*. New York: Springer Verlag.

Weisburd, D. (2018). Hot spots of crime and place-based prevention. *Criminology and Public Policy*, 17(1): 5–25.

Weiss, A. (2001). The police and road safety. Paper prepared for The National Research Council Committee to Review Research on Police Policy and Practice.

Whitehead, J. T., & Lab, S. P. (1989). A meta-analysis of juvenile correctional treatment. *Journal of Research in Crime and Delinquency*, 26, 276–295.

Willis, J. J., Mastrofski, S. D., & Weisburd, D. (2004). Compstat and bureaucracy: A case study of challenges and opportunities for change. *Justice Quarterly*, 21, 463–496.

Wilson, D. (2001). Meta-analytical methods for criminology. *Annals of the American Academy of Political and Social Science*, 578, 71–89.

Wolfgang, M. E., & Ferracuti, F. (1967). *The Subculture of Violence: Toward an Integrated Theory in Criminology*. New York: Tavistock.

14

Critic

The Limits of Hot Spots Policing

Dennis P. Rosenbaum

INTRODUCTION

I begin this chapter with a brief acknowledgement of the potential benefits of hot spot policing, followed by a serious critique. The thesis of this paper is that, while the concept of hot spots policing is attractive, we should be concerned about how scholars have narrowly defined it in theory and research and how police organizations have narrowly practiced it. While recent experimental tests have improved the situation, in general, the practice of hot spots policing has failed to embody the fundamental principles of problem-oriented policing, community policing and procedural justice, which many scholars believe represent the basic pillars of "good policing" in the twenty-first century. Too often, place-based or hot spots policing fails to specify innovative strategies or tactics for police officers once they arrive at hot spots and the hot spots themselves are poorly specified. Consequently, the reliance on conventional enforcement tactics can lead to collateral damage to the community, especially people of color and those of low income.

Acknowledging the Benefits

The concept of hot spots is indisputable from a criminological perspective. From the very beginning of criminological inquiries in nineteenth century France, scholars have noted that criminal activity is not randomly distributed, but rather varies by geographic area such as regions, states, and communities (see Eck & Weisburd, 1995). More recently, the criminology of place, led by David Weisburd and his colleagues, has advanced beyond this basic premise to discover that crime is especially concentrated at very small "micro" areas, such as specific addresses and street corners, and not just certain police beats, neighborhoods, or larger units of analysis (Weisburd, Groff & Yang, 2012; Weisburd, 2015; Telep &

Weisburd, 2018). Hence, a sensible policy implication is to recommend the concentration of more resources in high-crime areas, including police resources (Sherman, Gartin & Buerger, 1997). The most important question, however, is not whether we should assign more resources to problem areas, but rather, what resources should be deployed, where should they be deployed, and how should they be deployed?

Also, the concept of data-driven policing is difficult to dispute. Relying on information to make decisions about tactics, strategies, and programmatic interventions, assuming the data are accurate and complete, is preferred to making decisions based on personal whim or political pressure. Using experimental designs, hot spots researchers have encouraged the police to focus their attention on geographic areas smaller than police beats that have a high concentration of criminal activity or repeat calls for service (e.g., Sherman et al., 1989; Sherman & Weisburd, 1995). Building on these studies and the revolution in information technology, including mapping programs (Maltz, Gordon & Friedman, 1990; Mamalian & LaVigne, 1999), we have witnessed significant growth in the strategic deployment of police personnel in response to geo-based patterns of crime incidents and calls for service (e.g., Skogan et al., 2002).

Short-Term Localized Impact

Hot spots policing, when implemented under controlled experimental conditions with researchers involved, appears to have some effects on crime and disorder (for reviews, see Sherman, 1997; Taylor, 1998; Weisburd & Eck, 2004; Weisburd et al., 2008; Braga, Papachristos & Hureau, 2014). But the qualifications on this conclusion are extremely important. First, the effects on crime are small and not as consistent as the effects on disorder. Second, and most importantly, the effects dissipate quickly. Sherman's (1990) review of the police crackdown literature indicates that any residual deterrence effect is weak and likely to decay rapidly. The conclusion regarding drug market crackdowns is that they are ineffective in controlling drug hot spots. In one of the stronger experimental tests, crime dropped on targeted blocks in Kansas City after raids of crack houses, but returned within seven days, leading the authors to conclude, "Like aspirin for arthritis, the painkiller does nothing to remedy the underlying condition" (Sherman & Rogan, 1995a: 777). For directed patrols of high-crime locations, the best research suggests a positive relationship between the length of patrol presence at hot spots in Minneapolis and the length of the deterrent effect, up to fifteen minutes, after which time, the effect reverses (Koper, 1995). Third, evidence does not exist to demonstrate that the crime control benefits of hot spots policing reach beyond the small target or proximate areas to help larger beats, neighborhoods, or communities (see draft report from the National Academies of Sciences, Engineering, and Medicine, 2018).

The implication of these findings are that (1) the expense of concentrating police resources, especially for drug market crackdowns, may be difficult to justify given the cost of sustaining the effect; (2) a more sophisticated understanding of deterrence is required before police are ready to implement high-impact "schedules of punishment"; and (3) the absence of larger and more sustained effects suggests the need for a more complete understanding of the criminogenic forces at work in hot spots and the neighborhoods in which they are embedded. Finally, the argument is made that the aggressive policing tactics frequently used in hot spots could undermine the legitimacy of the police, which in turn, could undermine the long-term effectiveness of crime control, given that crime prevention is heavily dependent on the cooperation and law-abiding behavior of the public.

Problem Definition

What follows is a critique of hot spots policing from a problem-oriented and community policing framework, beginning with the definition of the problem. Engaging in "good" hot spot policing is not feasible if the hot spot itself cannot be easily identified or well defined. The definitional problem is complex and involves both conceptual and operational issues. At the conceptual level, we need to ask – how does a particular place achieve the status of being a "hot spot?" And who decides – the police on the street, administrators or politicians, or the community? Generally, the police have decided that a hot spot is a place where there are too many violent crimes, drug deals, or gangs. But why is the definition of "the problem" so narrowly construed? Undoubtedly, urban neighborhoods have hot spots of public fear of crime, hot spots of public hostility toward the police, of slum landlords, homelessness, racial profiling, disorder, weak informal social control, institutional disinvestments, and weak interagency partnership, to name just a few. Yet these problems are not treated as hot spots because they are not typically police priorities, because they are not well measured or understood, and because they do not fit within the traditional definition of the police function. For example, we have proposed that cities measure and map hot spots of procedural injustice or public dissatisfaction with police encounters (McCarthy & Rosenbaum, 2015) because public evaluations of police tactics or public trust in the police, should have equal status with police effectiveness in fighting crime (Lum & Nagin, 2017). Providing yet another angle, Weinborn et al. (2017) have examined the severity of harm rather than simple crime counts, and found that half of all harm is concentrated in only 1 percent of street segments.

The notion of hot spots, even if modified, still limits the definition of the problem to geographically linked phenomenon. This approach overlooks a number of serious crime-related problems that are not structured in this way. Terrorism, cybercrime, economic and international crime, and even drug trafficking are examples of serious problems that stretch beyond small geographic or neighborhood boundaries. Even gang homicide, which is associated with geography, is best understood in terms of social structure of the gang and social interactions rather than location (Papachristos, 2003). In fact, the Boston Gun Project was a big success because it focused on disrupting conflicts between gangs rather than on the places where shots were fired (Braga et al., 2001). Hence, place-based conceptions can sometimes restrict our ability to understand and respond effectively to serious crime problems, even those that cluster in space and time.

Even if we accept the traditional concept of hot spots, we still face serious problems trying to identify and operationally define them. First, the judgments of individual officers about hot spots can be inaccurate if not supported by computer analysis of larger samples. Second, when community input is sought, the police and local residents often disagree when evaluating and prioritizing neighborhood problems (Skogan et al., 2002). Third, when GIS mapping software is employed, the hot spot boundaries can be "fuzzy" (Taylor, 1998). Circles can be imposed over data plots, but in reality, these are somewhat arbitrary cut-offs. Where does one hot spot end and another begin? In high-crime neighborhoods, this can be a serious problem. If a hot spot is enlarged, then what is the benefit of a focused deployment scheme? If the hot spot is circumscribed to a small area, the agency runs the risk of making a false positive identification. Researchers prefer small hot spots, but some problem locations may not be sufficiently stable to warrant that label (i.e., the spot doesn't remain hot). In a similar vein, the selection of places as "hot spots" on the basis of extreme crime scores (e.g., spike in violence during the past month) can lead police managers and researchers to draw false conclusions about the effectiveness of hot spots policing. "Regression to the mean" – a statistical artifact that would show up as a decline in the crime rate regardless of policing efforts – is more likely under these circumstances, so a strong evaluation design is needed to avoid making false causal inferences about the effectiveness of intensive directed policing (see Shadish, Cook & Campbell, 2001). These criticisms aside, the author acknowledges recent evidence of the stability of crime hot spots across time (e.g., Weisburd et al., 2012). Researchers and police officials will need to reach some agreement about the best set of methods to arrive at the most accurate definition of hot spots and deploy police accordingly. At present, we find examples of police engaging in data-driven deployment, but defining hot spots much larger than micro areas, and thus contributing to ineffective policing (e.g., Alderden et al., 2010).

Weak Problem Analysis

Identifying a hot spot is not the same as understanding it. The analysis phase of problem-oriented policing is often lacking in hot spots policing. Too often the data analysis team is satisfied with colorful crime maps as the final product. Rarely do we see a detailed analysis of the characteristics of the hot spot and the nature of the problem. How much can we really learn about the problem from the spatial distribution of calls about drug transactions, crime incidents, or arrests? A thorough and comprehensive analysis of the hot spot would require that these data be placed in the larger environmental context. Knowing the physical and social milieu is critical for understanding the factors that facilitate and constrain hot spot behaviors. Census, housing, and survey data can be used to triangulate police data. Interviews and observations of users of the hot spot environment are essential (see Rosenbaum & Lavrakas, 1995). Also, police officers who walk the beat can gather a wealth of information about the social ecology of hot spots, which should result in fewer inequities in enforcement (cf. Rosenbaum, 2015a). The real problems are hidden behind the calls for service or arrest data. The real story is more complex, more dynamic, and more difficult to summarize. Without digging deeper, the police responses will be standardized and superficial, thus resulting in either short-term impact or no impact at all, and risking collateral damage.

For the modern high-tech police organization, the information managers believe that the most sophisticated type of hot spot analysis involves using real-time data to engage in "crime forecasting" and deployment. Analyses of monthly or weekly data are used to identify emerging hot spots and deploy officers in a proactive manner. Although making this type of prediction can be risky given that estimates can be unstable within small geographic areas using small amounts of data (Spelman, 1995), sophisticated modeling can help police organizations identify the characteristics of places that encourage crime and open-air drug markets. For example, Barnum and his colleagues (2016) determined that place accessibility and security were important to drug dealers. This type of work can lead to proactive policing and other preventative actions (e.g., guardianship, physical design) for specific types of hot spots.

The comorbidity of problems in low-income neighborhoods suggests that police should look beyond crime statistics when planning hot spot policing strategies. Mental health is a good example. Detailed analysis of clinical data collected from 2,805 children in eighty Chicago neighborhoods revealed that mental health problems are much more prevalent in low-income neighborhoods with concentrated disadvantage (Xue et al., 2005). Given that some police departments have been criticized and taken to court for using excessive force with persons experiencing a mental health crisis, the field should be particularly sensitive to use-of-force decisions and other tactics used in hot spots.

Narrow and Predictable Response Options

After the police (and hopefully, the community) identify and analyze the hot spots, they are still facing the problem of what to do about them. On this topic, only rarely have the police followed the guidance of Herman Goldstein (1990: 102), the father of problem-oriented policing: "This requires a process both broad and uninhibited – broad in that it breaks out of the rigid mindset of the past, and uninhibited in that it explores sensible responses without regard, at least initially, to potential impediments to adopting them." Instead, police departments have turned to what they have done for years with drug enforcement: patrols, stakeouts, buy and busts, reverse stings, raids, sweeps, etc. The responses tend to be narrow and predictable – surveillance, stop-question-frisk, and arresting – regardless of the nature and causes of the problem. Braga's (2001) review of nine early evaluations of hot spot policing confirms this tendency to rely on visible patrols and intensive enforcement tactics. Goldstein (1990) encouraged a systematic inquiry into the nature of local problems and the creation of strategic responses that would likely be effective in reducing or eliminating them. Frankly, I do not see this happening in American policing. Problem analysis tends to be superficial, nonexistent, or based on a limited set of specific criteria. Although some agencies engage in exemplary analysis (www.popcenter.org/casestudies/), responses tend to be pre-packaged, cookie-cutter reactions rather than tailored, evidence-based strategic plans for solving or eliminating the problem over the long haul.

The simple fact that crime is concentrated in identifiable locations does not justify the geographic concentration of limited police resources unless the police have a compelling plan for dealing with the problem. What is the plan? What is the "theory of action" behind the plan that would convince others it will work? How long will it work? What are potential adverse effects of the plan? How is "success" defined and when is a problem "solved"? Arguably, short-term reductions in crime and disorder are overrated and give the false impression that the problem has been solved.

The Deterrence Model. One major reason that traditional hot spots policing tactics are not likely to have a *sustained* impact on serious crime is because they are not based on a compelling understanding of criminality or the larger hot spot environment. The importance of place (hot spots) in crime causation and prevention can be viewed through the lenses of rational choice theory (Cornish & Clarke, 1986), routine activity theory (Cohen & Felson, 1979), crime pattern theory (Brantingham & Brantingham, 1993), or social disorganization theory (Bursik & Grasmick, 1993; Sampson, 2002). But hot spots policing, in practice, is not so sophisticated and reflects a basic deterrence model. Directed patrols, undercover intelligence gathering, visible surveillance systems (such as cameras), and various types of aggressive enforcement in the target areas are expected to deter offending by increasing the actual and perceived risk of detection, apprehension, and punishment. The preventative focus of hot spots policing tends to be the potential offender's fear of punishment and not the other elements of criminal opportunity in the environment (e.g., victims, witnesses, social control agents, physical features) that influence offender motivation. Repeat offenders often do not fear punishment and have become increasingly sophisticated in avoiding it. Also, police sanctioning of gang members can be viewed as a "badge of honor" (Klein, 1999). Suffice it to say that subjective assessments of risk by potential offenders (the key element in many hot spots tactics) are based on a variety of factors, including the perceived certainty, severity, and swiftness of punishment (Tittle & Paternoster, 2000). Unfortunately, the criminal justice system has failed to deliver on these threats in a consistent manner and has not demonstrated an understanding of the complexity of the deterrence processes. Challenging this general conclusion is the focused deterrence approach that targets high-risk repeat offenders.

Offender-Centered Policing. For good reason, some hot spots advocates have been critical of offender-focused research and interventions that have dominated criminology for decades and have ignored situational factors in crime. Rather than favoring one over the other, combining offender-based and place-based policing may be a more fruitful approach. For example, giving more attention to high-impact suspects within hot spot areas should produce significant results with less collateral damage than focusing on geography alone. Indeed, in one randomized control trial in Philadelphia, Groff and her colleagues (2015) found that offender-focused policing tactics in hot spot locations, such as having more frequent contact with and arrests of repeat offenders, yielded a 42 percent reduction in all violent crime and a 50 percent reduction in violent felonies relative to control places. Given that a small percentage of all offenders account for a disproportionate amount of crime (Esbensen et al., 2010), targeting the "right" offenders should maximize the impact on crime. In 2017, New York City experienced only 289 homicides (vs 2,262 in 1990), which the NYPD attributes to their new laser-like focus on repeat offenders (see Werner, 2017. For a review of evidence regarding this "pulling levers" approach, see Braga & Weisburd, 2012). In contrast, relying on a non-targeted or zero-tolerance approach that impacts a broad sample of persons living or functioning within a particular hot spot, as too often happens, runs the risk of upsetting law-abiding community members and undermining police legitimacy (more about this issue to follow).

Community and Problem Oriented Approaches. Hot spots policing, in practice, is like old wine in new bottles. Too often, police agencies continue to do what they do best – undercover and visible enforcement activities – but with greater efficiency and focus on specific locations. Police administrators tend to ask themselves, how can we deploy more police officers to these locations to make more arrests and seize more contraband? A better question is – what are the best strategies to combat crime, disorder, and quality of life in these hot spots given all that we know about these problems, these locations, and the many resources that can be leveraged (including non-police resources)?

Theories of community policing (e.g., Rosenbaum, 1994; Greene, 2000; Skogan, 2003), problem oriented policing (Goldstein, 1990), and community crime prevention (Tonry & Farrington, 1995; Rosenbaum et al., 1998) have largely been ignored in hot spots policing, despite advocates' claims to the contrary. These models all suggest that police would be unwise to limit their focus to maps of *where* crime is occurring, and should give more attention to *why* it is occurring and how the police and community can *work together* to address the problem. Hot spots policing somehow leaves the impression that our knowledge of hot spots is limited to GIS plots of crime incidents or calls for service. In fact, we know a lot more about hot spots, and this knowledge could be exploited to develop lasting solutions to neighborhood problems. For example, criminologists have examined the role of the physical environment, families, peers, schools, neighborhood resources, housing policies, labor markets, social organization processes, public attitudes, gun markets, offender re-entry problems, and many other factors that contribute to crime, disorder, and deviance within specific geographies (see Tonry & Farrington, 1995; Tittle & Paternoster, 2000; Welsh et al., 2001; Wilson & Petersilia, 2002). Our knowledge of how to prevent crime is substantial. The only question here is what role the police can play in converting this knowledge into practice?

Police as Experts on Crime

Over the years, police organizations have acquired the image of "the effective crime fighters" and "experts" on crime in general, thus receiving the lion's share of taxpayer dollars for public safety programs. To justify this reputation, law enforcement should demonstrate a deeper knowledge of the forces that contribute to crime and the quality of urban life. Educated people can disagree about whether the police have any responsibility to reach beyond short-term strategies to address the underlying, chronic causes of crime. (Most police officers would say, "That's not our job.") I would argue that police leaders can play an important role by (1) working with criminologists to educate policy makers and the public about what can, and should, be done to prevent crime, (2) creating and leading multi-agency partnerships that have a higher probability of yielding a sustainable impact on crime and disorder, and (3) focusing on comprehensive strategies that attack crime and disorder at all levels (see Rosenbaum, 2002; Schuck & Rosenbaum, 2006; Rosenbaum & Schuck, 2012).

Unfortunately, hot spots policing, if limited to directed patrols and enforcement tactics, can reinforce the persistent public misperception that police can solve the crime problem alone, without the help of the communities they serve, other government agencies, or the private sector. One laudable exception is the work by White and Weisburd (2017) who, after determining that mental health problems were concentrated in small geographic units, worked with the Baltimore Police Department to implement a pilot co-responder program (i.e., police officers paired with mental health professionals) to assist persons experiencing mental health problems at specific hot spot locations. These crisis intervention team (CIT) models have been widely adopted to improve police responses to persons facing a mental health crisis (see Watson et al., 2010), but are not typically implemented around hot spots.

Community policing strategies also remind us that public confidence in the police is an important goal by itself, independent of crime control objectives – something to keep in mind when planning hot spots policing tactics. As discussed below, community-oriented programs can improve the public's perceptions of the police, although what constitutes "community policing" varies considerably (Gill et al., 2014).

A close adherence to the principles of problem-oriented policing would, I believe, lead most police administrators to question current stand-alone hot spot practices. The urban problems of youth violence cannot be explained with simple statements like, "kids make bad choices and they need to pay the price" or "our job is to take the scumbags and gang bangers off the street." The solutions are much more complex. The goal of problem-oriented policing should be to eliminate or permanently reduce the problem, not simply to increase the efficiency of the response. Furthermore, a major goal of community policing is to achieve fair and equitable policing, not just to achieve efficient policing (Eck & Rosenbaum, 1994). Hot spots policing, *as currently practiced*, may be at odds with these goals for reasons I describe later under "Potential Adverse Effects."

I am pleased that since the first publication of this book, we have moved beyond the simple question of how many officers can be sent to hot spots (dosage) to the question of what they will do when they arrive (tactics). Indeed, what officers do in hot spots will influence their effectiveness in preventing crime. In their review, Lum and Nagin (2017) conclude that hot spots policing is more effective when it is focused and tailored via problem-oriented policing, third-party policing, social and situational prevention, or contact with "hot" people, than when it involves unfocused enforcement and arrests. Thus, our knowledge of how hot spots tactics impact crime has improved significantly, but how these tactics impact community members who live and work in these areas remains uncertain and concerning.

POTENTIAL ADVERSE EFFECTS OF HOT SPOTS POLICING

Hot spots policing is potentially harmful to both targeted and non-targeted communities. Some of the potential untoward effects of hot spots policing are discussed in this section.

Displacement Effects

One of the question marks surrounding hot spots policing is about possible displacement effects. If hot spots policing is simply altering criminal activity by location, time, MO, or type of offense, rather than preventing it, then the *collective* benefits to the larger community are limited or nonexistent.

The problem of displacement, if occurring, may indicate that non-targeted residents or locations are suffering *more* because additional criminal activity is being pushed into their environment.

Criminologists are divided on this issue and the evidence is mixed. Most evaluations do not define and measure displacement adequately, if at all, and most research designs are biased in favor of the null hypothesis (Weisburd & Green, 1995a). Some studies suggest evidence of diffusion of crime control *benefits* to nearby areas (see Sherman & Rogan, 1995b; Weisburd & Green, 1995b; Green Mazerolle & Roehl, 1998; Braga et al., 1999), but some of these effects may reflect a mis-specification of the target area boundaries. On the other side of the fence, there is good evidence of spatial displacement of calls or crime incidents as a result of police crackdowns, especially during drug enforcement (e.g., Kleiman, 1988; Potter, Gaines, & Holbrook, 1990; Smith et al., 1992; Uchida, Forst & Annan, 1992; Kennedy, 1993; Hope, 1994; Sherman & Rogan, 1995a; Maher & Dixon, 2001). A meta-analysis by Sherman (1997), however, suggests that displacement effects are not as large as crime prevention effects. Furthermore, recent systematic reviews suggest that hot spots policing, when monitored by researchers, does not displace crime into the immediate surrounding areas (Braga et al., 2014; National Academies of Sciences, Engineering, and Medicine, 2018), but research does not address possible displacement into more distal, non-adjacent areas. Talking with police officers in any large urban jurisdiction will likely produce anecdotal evidence of spatial displacement of specific crime and disorder problems, ranging from prostitution to homeless camps. Clearly, there are many types of displacement that have yet to be carefully measured.

Misuse of Authority

Hot spots policing, because it is often operationally defined as aggressive targeted enforcement, runs the risk of police abuse of authority or corruption. When officers feel pressure from the administration to make arrests, seize drugs, and seize guns, under limited supervision, some will exercise poor judgment or be inclined to cut corners to increase counts, and as a result, every officer's credibility is compromised. Complaints about excessive force and police misconduct are not uncommon in hot spots neighborhoods where police are sometimes viewed as an "occupying force."

One of the most controversial strategies used in hot spots involves Broken Windows policing (Wilson & Kelling, 1982), which relies heavily on arrests for minor infractions to reduce disorder. Over time, this approach has become linked to zero-tolerance policing and involuntary pedestrian stops. The New York Police Department (NYPD) has popularized the "stop-question-frisk" tactic (also called field interviews, investigatory stops or "Terry stops"), which is now institutionalized by American police agencies and believed to be an indispensable tool in controlling crime, drugs, and guns.[1] However, as practiced, these stops have become very controversial both in the community and in the courts because of the amount of police discretion involved and concerns about racial profiling. Critics even maintain that police often develop "reasonable suspicion" after (rather than before) stopping the individual.

The issue of due process is critical to the legitimacy of the criminal justice system. A twenty-year prosecutor summarized the problem for me in this way: "Winking at questionable stops and arrests may serve to get major waves of contraband off the streets for a while but it eventually begins to draw the ire of the judiciary and threatens the credibility of both the police and that of the prosecuting authorities" (Andreou, personal communication, 2003). Indeed, these consequences have come to fruition in several cities. The NYPD, lauded for its effectiveness in reducing crime, took Terry stops to a new level. The number of Terry stops rose from 97,296 in 2002 to 685,724 in 2011 (New York Civil Liberties Union, 2017). Of the 4.4 million stops between 2004 and 2012, only 6 percent resulted in an arrest and 83 percent involved black or Hispanic community members, who represented only about half of the population (New York Times Editorial Board, 2013). Using these statistics, Judge Shira A. Scheindlin ruled in 2013, that NYPD's practice amounted to unconstitutional racial profiling and violated the public's Fourth Amendment protection against unreasonable search and seizure (Savage & Goode, 2013). Relevant to this paper, the stops were carried out in front of private residential buildings at the request of building managers and owners. This court action led to a settlement agreement in 2017 that ended a long series of stop-and-frisk law suits (Mueller, 2017). Terry stops in New York declined to 12,404 in 2016, and yet crime dropped dramatically in 2017.

The Chicago Police Department was also sued over its stop-and-frisk policy (Meisner, 2015). After an ACLU analysis revealed that 72 percent of all stops were of African Americans (who make up only 32 percent of the city's population), the city decided to keep better records on stops and searches by requiring a more detailed contact card after street encounters. In January of 2016, when the new monitoring system was in place, officers completed 79 percent fewer contact cards than the previous year. Whether this drop reflected fewer stops or a lack of report writing is unclear, but some police officers referred to Chicago's dramatic increase in homicides in 2016 as the "ACLU effect" (Main, 2016).

Stigma from Labeling

There is a real risk that neighborhoods and smaller areas identified as hot spots will acquire a more negative image as a result of the labeling process. In some

---

[1] In *Terry v. Ohio* (1968) the Supreme Court allowed police to stop, question, and search someone if the officer has "reasonable suspicion" that the person had committed a crime and is armed.

cases, the stigma of being a hot spot of crime may stimulate greater fear of crime among residents (both inside and outside the neighborhood) and eventually lead to disinvestment, residential transiency, and lower property values. Granted, some hot spots already have a bad reputation, but others on the margins could be further damaged by the labeling process. Yet police face a "catch 22." The adverse effects of labeling would be minimized by keeping the identity of the location confidential and internal to the police, but that would prevent the department from soliciting community support for aggressive police interventions or other prevention initiatives.

Policing Bias by Race and Class

America has a long history of institutional racism, from slavery to Jim Crow enforcement (Kendi, 2017) and, unfortunately, the police functioned as society's instrument of injustice for more than a century (Williams & Murphy, 1990). Today, we still cannot avoid the fact that policing tactics and strategies vary by race and social class. These differences are due, in part, to bias, but also to data-driven deployment of police officers on the basis of known crime hot spots. Violence and illicit drug markets (not drug use) are more prevalent in low-income communities of color, and consequently, these areas receive a disproportionate share of police attention in response to public demand and crime analysis within agencies. By definition, the pressure on the police to reduce crime and disorder is the greatest in these hot spot areas.

The problem is that constitutionally guaranteed civil liberties are more easily jeopardized in low-income neighborhoods of color where residents feel disenfranchised, lack collective efficacy, and do not have easy access to legal remedies when they feel mistreated by authorities. Communities of color are the primary focus of not only drug and gun enforcement, but also minor disorders (e.g., hanging out, public drinking) and various types of traffic enforcement activities. As discussed earlier, police-initiated contacts (often involving minor infractions) are used as a tool to identify weapons, drugs, guns, and persons with outstanding warrants. The research on traffic stops has clearly documented racial disparities in police decision-making (e.g., Lamberth, 1998; Weiss & Rosenbaum, 2009). Blacks and Hispanics are much more likely than whites to be stopped, ticketed, and searched (see Lum & Nagin, 2017 for a review). Furthermore, the "hit rate" for contraband or guns is extremely low, and lower for minorities than whites, so the vast majority of persons who are inconvenienced (if not offended) by these stops are innocent persons of color. (For a closer look at the history and complexities of race/ ethnicity bias in policing, see Rice & White, 2010.)

The problem runs deeper than differential rates of police contact. People of privilege rarely experience the embarrassment and humiliation associated with having their possessions dumped onto the street and searched, being questioned as to where they are going, or having to "assume the position" in front of family, friends, and bystanders. As Epp and colleagues (2014: 15) explain, investigatory stops "have profound consequences for people's sense of their place and status in American society," and can lead to hostility and resentment. Consistent with this statement, a 2011 national contact survey by the Bureau of Justice Statistics of persons stopped by the police (Langton & Durose, 2013) found that Blacks were much less likely than whites to feel that the police officer behaved properly during a traffic stop (37.7 percent vs. 77.6 percent) or that the officer's reason for the stop was legitimate (67.5 percent vs. 83.6 percent). The bottom line is that the legitimacy of American police clearly remains a bigger concern for Blacks and Latinos than for Whites in the United States (see Weitzer & Tuch, 2006).

I should note that traffic stop patterns are sometimes linked to neighborhoods and hot spots and other times are not (e.g., interstate highways), but involuntary pedestrian stops are definitely geo-based contacts. In this vein, some defenders of police action claim that higher stop rates for people of color simply reflect higher crime rates for specific racial/ethnic groups and specific neighborhoods. However, an analysis of 125,000 pedestrian stops in New York by Gelman and his colleagues (2007) revealed that African Americans and Hispanics were stopped more frequently than whites even after controlling for differences in crime rates by precinct and race/ethnicity.

Beyond Terry stop tactics, there is deep and growing concern about police misuse of authority, which is also not randomly distributed. Looking at twenty years of data in New York, one study concluded that police misconduct is higher in neighborhoods with structural disadvantage, population mobility, and increases in the Latino population, among other factors (Kane, 2002). So, these and other data suggest that neighborhoods victimized the most from crime are also areas where the police are more likely to violate policy with limited accountability.

Persistent local and national protests against the police since the 2014 shooting of Michael Brown in Ferguson, Missouri, and the emergence of grassroots organizations like "Black Lives Matter" indicate a growing concern about the use of deadly force against unarmed black men. Consent decrees between the United States Department of Justice (2017) and two dozen US cities since 1994, along with the creation of the President's Task Force on 21st Century Policing (2015), reflect our national apprehension about use-of-force decisions and other police actions that violate citizens' constitutional rights. As researchers, many of us have sought to explain to the public that police use of force and excessive force are extremely rare (and that most people are fond of their local police), but we often fail to mention that black men make up 24 percent of the nearly 1,000 persons shot and killed each year by the police and yet constitute only 6 percent of the nation's population (Sullivan et al., 2017).

When making enforcement decisions, there is little reason to believe that police officers are able to mentally separate small hot spots from the larger neighborhood context in which they are situated because of "ecological contamination" (Werthman & Piliavin, 1967) – i.e., judging an individual based on the socioeconomic characteristics of the neighborhood rather than the individual's own behavior. Research in two major cities has shown that police are more likely to use higher levels of force in disadvantaged neighborhoods and neighborhoods with higher homicide rates, after controlling for situational factors such as the suspect's level of resistance (Terrill & Reisig, 2003). Diverse research in psychology and sociology suggest that concentrated disadvantage shapes the perceptions of threat and bias for both civilians and police (Holmes & Smith, 2008). Thus, hot spots present a host of potential problems for police officers when faced with discretionary enforcement decisions. Whether we define hot spots as small areas (as do many researchers) or as beats and neighborhoods (as do many police agencies), it may not matter because of ecological contamination, where areas are defined as "bad" and threatening and the people within them are assumed to share these characteristics and justify society's response.

The impact of aggressive enforcement in these neighborhoods creates a host of problems for community members that have yet to be fully researched. For example, Fagan (2017) argues that the additional enforcement amounts to a hidden "criminal justice tax" on low-income neighborhoods, including jail time, multiple court dates, fines, and fees. Also, the stigma of a misdemeanor conviction can limit access to housing, employment, and schooling. Thus, Fagan maintains that enforcement effectively contributes to racial and economic segregation: "The combination of criminal sanctions and mounting fees tends to reinforce both social and spatial boundaries, and in turn deepen racial and economic concentrations in 'poverty traps'" (2017: 1).

Since the original publication of this chapter in 2006, there has been growing criticism of hot spots policing as discriminatory. Consequently, Weisburd (2016) has recently argued that this approach does not "inevitably" lead to unfair and abusive police practices, as some critics argue, and the evidence of this effect is limited. He admits that hot spots are usually located in high-crime, low-income neighborhoods with non-White populations, but that an aggressive style of policing is not inevitable. I strongly agree with him. Consistent with recommendations made here, he has proposed (and is field testing) policing strategies that seek to integrate hot spots policing with community-oriented policing and procedural justice approaches designed to reduce crime *and* increase police legitimacy.

Mass Incarceration

The United States leads the world (ahead of China and Russia) in both the volume and rate of incarceration of its citizenry. The National Research Council (2014) found that the United States has approximately one-quarter of the world's prisoners but only 5 percent of the world's population, with a rate of imprisonment that is five to ten times higher than rates in Western Europe and other democracies. Poor, young men of color are being confined and incarcerated at much higher rates than other segments of the population, with about 60 percent of the prison population in 2011 being black or Hispanic. The bottom line, after the criminal justice system has completed its work, is what has been called "disproportionate minority confinement" (Pope et al., 2003). Alexander (2011), in her widely read book, *The New Jim Crow*, argues that despite our claim to "colorblindness," the "mass incarceration" of blacks through the war on drugs has destroyed communities and created a new caste system of racial control and second-class citizens. Indeed, the incarceration rate for drug offenses increased tenfold between 1980 and 2010 (National Research Council, 2014), with rates much higher for blacks and Hispanics.

Inevitably, we must ask ourselves the macro-level question regarding the long-term consequences of applying greater enforcement resources to low-income and non-White communities. The National Research Report (2014) has delineated the numerous adverse consequences of arrest and incarceration on individual health, mental health, employment options, families, and communities. Clearly, the police are the gatekeepers to the criminal justice system and must accept some responsibility for these outcomes. As noted above, American police agencies have continued a heavy dose of drug enforcement in hot spots for more than three decades and are more likely to use force and engage in misconduct in structurally disadvantaged neighborhoods.

In sum, the style and consequences of policing in low-income communities of color are often different than those applied in middle-class neighborhoods and the application of enforcement tactics is increasingly driven by hot spot analyses. Clearly, we need more culturally sensitive, community-oriented and comprehensive approaches to the serious problems that characterize hot spots.

Direct and Opportunity Costs

Although advocates of hot spots policing often tout the efficiencies of this approach, intensifying police resources in hot spots can be expensive in terms of added personnel costs and additional activity for the criminal justice system. The Vera Institute (Henrichson, Rinaldi & Delaney, 2015) noted our prison population is five times larger than it was in the 1970s and our local jail population is four times larger than the 1980s, costing taxpayers billions of additional dollars. In addition, because the effects of hot spots policing tend to be short-lived, the repeated and indefinite deployment of additional police personnel can have a large cumulative impact on taxpayers, something that has not been studied. Overtime is available to 99 percent of officers in the United States and only one-third of agencies nationwide place a limit on the amount of overtime an officer can earn (Reaves, 2015). Furthermore, overtime work can lead to officer fatigue and implicit bias (Maciag, 2017). The options for addressing these additional costs are to increase the police budget, borrow resources from other neighborhoods, or discontinue the program after a short period. Intensive policing may not be affordable in many cases, and, therefore, not sustainable in the absence of careful planning about deployment.

A bigger concern is the opportunity costs associated with hot spots policing. In other words, what are police departments *not* doing because they are involved in hot spots policing? First, there is a tendency to reduce police resources in low and moderate crime neighborhoods by creating special teams, transferring personnel, or redrawing beat boundaries. Sometimes, police are "assigned" to a low crime neighborhood, but are "temporarily" transferred to hot spots. City-wide special units are not really city-wide because they spend most of their time in hot spots. Without knowing it, low and moderate crime communities may be shortchanged and may experience crime increases if policing is reduced below a critical level for an extended period. Second, there may be a tendency to reduce police resources for community policing, problem-oriented policing, or badly needed training in critical areas such as de-escalation, crisis intervention, procedural justice, bias/equity, and crowd control. Preventing crime and effectively addressing social problems that demand police resources, such as the geographic covariation of homelessness and mental illness, will require a substantial investment by police agencies into multi-agency partnerships (Rosenbaum, 2002).

Opportunity costs come in many sizes and shapes. One could argue that the popularity of hot spots policing and other place-based policing models discourages an intelligent public policy debate about long-term solutions to our crime problems. (I saw this occur with the popular but ineffective D.A.R.E. program, which effectively suppressed discussion of other school-based drug prevention; see Rosenbaum, 2007.) As noted earlier, this type of policing is designed to leave the public with the impression that crime is under control, thus contributing to the image of law enforcement agencies as independently effective crime fighting machines with little room for improvement.

Unanticipated Effects on Crime

Arrest (and, for some, conviction and incarceration) does not always have the desired deterrent effects, and may even produce boomerang effects. A couple of examples will suffice. First, there is some evidence that arresting inner city youths can have the criminogenic effect of increasing, rather than reducing, their probability of recidivism (Klein, 1986). Second, there is evidence that having a criminal record reduces one's probability of finding gainful employment (Bushway, 1996). The plight of 600,000 ex-offenders who return from prison each year clearly illustrates the many legal, social, family, and employment obstacles they face to successful reintegration (Travis et al., 2001; National Research Council, 2014), thus explaining why most return to a life of crime. Also, the extent to which law enforcement agencies use technology to track and monitor ex-offenders by address is unprecedented and facilitates the parole violation process.

In sum, our criminal justice system may be having criminogenic effects, making crime more (not less) probable for those who are targeted, arrested, and labeled as "criminals." This is especially troubling for the large volume of incidents involving misdemeanor and non-violent drug offenses and raises the question of whether aggressive enforcement activity in high-crime neighborhoods is helping or hurting public safety in the long run. Over the last decade, various branches of government have sought to reduce the punitiveness and overuse of the criminal justice system, but these promising actions have been challenged in 2017 by the President of the United States and his Attorney General who are starting a new "law and order" campaign against crime, drugs, and immigration (Collinson & Jarrett, 2017).

Collective Efficacy

Neighborhoods with high rates of violent crime that are typically the target of hot spots policing also suffer from social disorganization and a lack of collective efficacy in solving problems (Sampson, Raudenbush & Earls, 1997). "Get tough" policies run the risk of further undermining social control and a community's capacity for self-regulation. By strengthening the hand of the police to solve crime-related problems, without engaging the community, residents may feel less empowered to solve neighborhood problems. Policy makers may need to be reminded that community crime rates, in the final analysis, are influenced more by the social ecology of communities than by formal control mechanisms (Sampson, 2002). Hence, within the community-policing framework, a primary mission of police organizations should be to work with other organizations to design strategies that strengthen community capacity rather than to supplant or weaken the role of community.

Police–Community Relations and Police Legitimacy

Hot spots policing, when operationally defined as aggressive enforcement in specific areas, runs the risk of weakening police–community relations (see Kleiman, 1988; Worden, Bynum & Frank, 1994; Sherman, 1997; Rosenbaum et al., 1998). These tactics, which can include monetary costs to residents and the threat of losing personal freedom, can drive a wedge between the police and the community, as the latter can begin to feel like targets rather than partners in the fight against crime and disorder. When the police decide to focus on removing the "bad element" and serving as the "thin blue line" between "good" and "evil," these strategies can pit one segment of the community against another, as the "good" residents are asked to serve as informants and the "eyes and ears" of police. Parents, siblings, and friends of gang members and persons involved in drug markets can feel a divided loyalty and be caught in the crossfire. This is one reason the "no snitch" culture is strong in some communities.

The success of police organizations in reducing crime is dependent on the cooperation of the citizenry, but this is unlikely when the public's trust and confidence in the police is undermined. The central theme of the President's Task Force report (2015) is that we are facing a new crisis of legitimacy in American policing and something needs to be done about it. The most basic question is – what determines police legitimacy? (i.e., the public's trust in the police and willingness to accept their authority). While police effectiveness in fighting crime and agency transparency are important, a large body of research has consistently shown that procedural justice during the exercise of authority is a primary determinant of police legitimacy (for reviews, see Tyler, 2006; Hinds & Murphy, 2007; Mazerolle et al., 2012; Jackson et al., 2013; Donner et al., 2015). In other words, when the police are respectful to community members, listen to their voices, make decisions that are viewed as fair or neutral, explain their actions, and show compassion/empathy when appropriate, the public is more likely to view the police as a legitimate authority. When the police have legitimacy, the public is more inclined to view them in a positive light, cooperate with them, report crime, and even obey the law more often (e.g., Tyler, 2001; Tyler & Huo, 2002; Tyler & Fagan, 2008; Kochel, Parks & Mastrofski, 2013; Rosenbaum et al., 2017). However, when police are rude, disrespectful, or show bias in their actions during stops or arrests, the opposite response can be expected. As discussed earlier, involuntary stops and tickets can be very upsetting to community members, but we have learned that these negative effects can be dramatically offset when officers act in a procedurally just manner (Rosenbaum et al., 2015). Unfortunately, acting in a procedurally just manner, according to contact surveys, is more difficult for officers in large urban areas than in smaller jurisdictions (Rosenbaum, 2016), perhaps because these officers are more likely to work in hot spots, have more regular contact with residents who dislike the police and respond to more serious calls for service.

We must acknowledge that residents of high-crime areas are very ambivalent about aggressive enforcement. Many demand it and are pleased to see the police, for example, removing guns from the streets (Sherman & Rogan, 1995b; McGarrell et al., 2001). Sadly, surveys also indicate that many urban residents are willing to give up their civil liberties to achieve a better sense of security, however fleeting (Rosenbaum, 1993). Residents will insist on aggressive enforcement up until the point where it adversely affects them, their family, or their friends. However, in this post-Ferguson world, we have learned that communities have an upper limit on their tolerance of aggressive policing tactics when real lives are at stake and when race bias by the police is perceived to be present.

Impact on Police Personnel

In the face of widespread criticism and public protests around police use of force, we should not be surprised that American police officers are feeling attacked, and are less interested now in proactive policing that could put them at risk of discipline or worse (Pew Research Center, 2017). I have suggested here that the aggressive style of policing in hot neighborhoods, encouraged by community members besieged by fear and violence, is partially responsible for this morale problem and sense of injustice inside police organizations. But a decline in proactive policing, especially when directed at serious repeat offenders, could cause a spike in crime (see Lum & Nagin, 2017).

In terms of directed patrols in hot spots, there is also concern that when patrols are limited to small geographic areas (e.g., one block), this type of work can feel very constraining on officers' autonomy. A study by Wain et al. (2017) found that British officers who were required to work in small hot spots for specific time periods under GPS supervision expressed more dissatisfaction with their assignment, less internal procedural justice, and less organizational commitment than officers in parallel patrols without hot spot assignments. Thus, the planning for hot spots policing should consider the needs of police officers. In our research with 100 American police organizations, we found that officers' assessment of "organizational justice" (i.e., the procedural justice they received from leaders and supervisors at work) was positively associated with officers' morale, organizational commitment, and rule compliance (Rosenbaum & McCarty, 2017).

RECENT RESEARCH ON PUBLIC PERCEPTIONS

Since the original publication of this chapter, policing scholars have acknowledged the possibility that hot spots policing could damage police–community relations and undermine police legitimacy (e.g., Kochel, 2011; Kochel & Weisburd, 2017). I have already cited research establishing a connection between hot spots and aggressive tactics, between aggressive tactics and perceived procedural injustice, and growing public discontent with police use of force in the United States. But we now have research that specifically examines the relationship between hot spots policing and public sentiment about the police, as well as perceptions of crime and fear. Two studies by Weisburd and his colleagues have looked at the effects of broken windows (order maintenance) policing on residents. Hinkle and Weisburd (2008) found that an intensive crackdown in Jersey City, NJ, produced a large increase in fear of crime relative to the control group. A subsequent study by Weisburd et al. (2011), a randomized trial in three smaller California cities, did not find this fear effect, but did find residents in the treatment areas perceived higher levels of physical disorder than controls. Police legitimacy and collective efficacy were not impacted; however, this experiment was conducted in relatively low-crime areas, so the types of intensive enforcement and non-white populations that would produce a "backfire" effect would not be present.

In contrast, two other randomized field trials were conducted in urban areas with substantial hot spots. Ratcliffe and his colleagues (2015) tested three distinct tactics in high-crime areas of Philadelphia: foot patrol, problem-oriented policing, and offender-focused policing. They found that none of these policing tactics had a significant effect on community perceptions of crime and disorder, fear of crime, satisfaction with the police or procedural justice. However, the authors admit that the foot patrol and problem-oriented policing programs were weakly implemented, supported by statistics showing no impact on crime. How such programs are implemented (including new training and supervision) would determine any effects on residents' perceptions of the police.

Kochel and Weisburd (2017) conducted a randomized field trial with the St Louis County Police Department to examine the community impact of directed patrol (the most common form of hot spots policing) versus collaborative problem solving or standard policing in seventy-one crime hot spots. Consistent with the arguments put forth here, the researchers found significantly lower levels of procedural justice in the directed patrol condition relative to the problem-solving or standard policing conditions. Furthermore, police legitimacy declined in the directed patrol condition. However, these negative differences disappeared within six to nine months, suggesting no lasting effects, but cumulative effects would take longer to emerge. Our knowledge of the long-term effects of hot spots policing beyond nine months is nonexistent.

The reported upward trend in procedural justice and legitimacy for all three groups from pre-test to post-test is interesting, along with evidence that cooperation increased. Recall that I expressed concern that residents exposed to aggressive hot spots policing would begin to feel like the targets of police rather than partners. This was not true in this RCT, but the findings may be attributable to the local police culture of strategic innovation, including the absence of aggressive enforcement tactics. Indeed, officers in all three conditions made fewer pedestrian and vehicle stops once the program was introduced. The officers in the directed patrol condition spent considerably more time in the hot spots over time, but enforcement activities accounted for only 15 percent of their recorded activities. As the authors noted, officers had more time to engage with community members in non-enforcement activities and casual conversations. Hence, this should not be considered a true test of any "backfire" effects of aggressive enforcement. If anything, it shows what is possible when police officers do not rely on aggressive tactics in hot spots and instead adopt a more community-oriented style of interacting with the public.

A report from the National Academies of Sciences, Engineering, and Medicine (2018: 186) concludes that place-based policing "rarely leads to negative community outcomes," but the committee admits that the extant evaluations are very limited, focusing on short-term effects of hybrid tactics with little attention to what police officers actually did in the hot spots.

In juxtaposition to the hot spots evaluations, research suggests that problem-oriented policing and community policing initiatives can have positive effects on community perceptions with little evidence of "backfire" effects (for reviews, see Lum, Koper & Telep, 2011; Gill et al., 2014). These reviews uncover more than a dozen studies that show increased public satisfaction with the police as a result of problem-oriented policing, including one randomized control trial (Graziano et al., 2014) and one longitudinal study in Chicago (Skogan, 2006). Furthermore, Gill and her colleagues (2014) report "robust evidence" that community policing improves public satisfaction with the police and some evidence that it increased police legitimacy, including longitudinal effects (e.g., see Skogan & Hartnett, 1997; Myhill & Quinton, 2010). However, more controlled evaluations, such as randomized control trials or strong quasi-experiments, are needed of interventions that are clearly defined and consistently applied. At present, police tend to introduce a hybrid of tactics that make evaluation difficult and evaluators rely too often on weak evaluation methods.

Beyond controlled research studies, I encourage evidence-based police agencies to routinely document the effects of their officers'/deputies' actions on community perceptions. Specifically, police organizations could commit to using contact surveys as part of their routine operations to measure the level of public satisfaction and perceptions of procedural justice during police contacts with the public. We have developed a survey for this purpose and have field tested it in fifty-three large American cities (Rosenbaum et al., 2017). Innovative police chiefs and sheriffs who seek to promote evidence-based learning organizations are beginning to measure the quality of service delivery by their sworn personnel. Unless police agencies begin to measure what matters to the public, they will be unable to evaluate their performance and make adjustments as needed. As Lum and Nagin (2017) argue, crime control effectiveness and public trust in the police are equally important and "one should not trump the other."

RETHINKING HOT SPOTS POLICING

Hot spots policing can be effective at reducing crime, but we must pay more attention to how it is executed and minimize any collateral damage to the community. To begin with, if police can rethink the concept of place, the notion of hot spots policing can be given new meaning. I would encourage police departments to adopt a more holistic approach to problems that cluster in space and time, including: (1) conducting an in-depth, comprehensive analysis of the hot spot environment and the many factors that are responsible for making the area "hot"; (2) exploring a wide range of alternative solutions that might reasonably be expected to have either a short-term and/or a long-term impact on the problem. This would include strategies that allow patrol officers to spend additional time at hot spots to identify repeat offenders, thus reducing the collateral damage of stopping, questioning, and searching innocent community members; (3) attempting to build real partnerships among government, private sector, and community organizations that have a stake in public safety; (4) giving more attention to the prevention of crime at the individual, family, and community levels; (5) introducing new police training and supervision around procedural justice, problem solving, community policing, race bias, and de-escalation tactics in hot spots; and (6) measuring both the process and impact of these efforts in the short run and long run in both the targeted areas and more remotely. To their credit, some agencies have sought to achieve some of these objectives by, for example, supplementing traditional hot spots enforcement with community policing and/or problem-oriented policing approaches (e.g., Weisburd & Green, 1995b; Eck & Wartell, 1996; Green Mazerolle & Roehl, 1998; Braga et al., 1999; Kochel & Weisburd, 2017). Unfortunately, commitment to these innovations tends to come and go with each new police chief or sheriff.

I have argued in testimony before the President's Task Force that a new form of foot patrol, where officers "strike up a conversation rather than an investigation," could reduce crime (by having officers become familiar with social ecology of hot spots and engage in problem solving, including surgical arrests of repeat offenders), and at the same time, enhance police legitimacy by acting in procedurally just ways (Rosenbaum, 2015b). In other words, hot spots policing should not be limited to enforcement activities, as progressive police administrators and researchers are beginning to demonstrate.

In this paper, I have suggested that the concept of hot spots, despite its theoretical and empirical appeal, can create problems that were unintended. Police administrators and researchers need to exercise caution when labeling and responding to locations in a narrow manner, given the political and racial/ethnic sensitivities associated with hot spots. Investigatory stops and directed enforcement in hot spots have their place in the toolkit of urban policing, but they should not be used as stand-alone strategies or as society's primary response to concentrated crime or disorder. Also, these strategies and tactics require close supervision of police officers, new training, and regular feedback from the community members to minimize poor discretionary actions and regain public trust and legitimacy. Most importantly, the majority of police resources should be devoted to strategies that (1) show promise for long-term impact on rates of community crime and the quality of community life, (2) reflect the equitable distribution of police resources based on human need, and (3) embody the police organization's constitutional commitment to the fair and impartial treatment of all segments of society. Given what we know today, it is no longer sufficient to simply add more police officers to hot spots – administrators must care about what officers do at these locations and how they do it. Nor is it sufficient to implement effective, targeted strategies in hot spots such as problem solving, third-party policing, social and physical design, or repeat offender contacts. The police must also care about whether the selected policing tactics are being implemented in a manner that is fair, respectful and empathetic toward the people with whom officers are interacting. Police should be judged on whether they can achieve the "4 Es" – Effectiveness, Efficiency, Equity (Eck & Rosenbaum, 1994), and Empathy (Rosenbaum et al., 2017).

In essence, hot spots policing, as currently practiced, does not adequately address the historical, economic, political, social, and cultural dimensions of these target areas, all of which contribute to crime rates. The solution is not as simple as getting local residents, under the threat of arrest, to make better choices or accept responsibility for their behavior. These assumptions are overly simplistic and do not acknowledge the loss of hope and despair among these residents, their disconnection from conventional institutions, the stigma and rejection that result from having a criminal record, the inadequacy of resources to support healthy families, and the fact that dozens of other social problems (beyond crime) cluster in these hot spots. Hence, real solutions in these hot spots will require sophisticated research and intelligence, strategic planning, and comprehensive prevention programs involving many agencies and organizations working in concert. I believe that senior police officials are capable of meeting this challenge by playing a lead role in multi-agency partnerships and accepting the responsibility that comes with being "the crime experts."

Notwithstanding recent gains in knowledge, more research is needed regarding what police actually do in hot spots, how they do it, and how those actions affect the communities they serve. More experimental research is needed to examine the impact of different types and styles of policing in hot spots on community perceptions of the police and willingness to work with the police. The research cited earlier (Hinkle & Weisburd, 2008; Weisburd et al., 2011; Groff et al., 2015; Ratcliffe et al., 2015; Kochel & Weisburd, 2017) represents a laudable move in that direction. Monitoring the type and dosage of police activities in hot spots, as well as their effects on public perceptions is essential. More research is needed on possible long-term, cumulative effects of hot spots policing, both inside and outside designated hot spots. Also, we know very little about whether hot spot tactics affect the public's willingness to work with the police in the future or their level of cynicism toward the law.

In the meantime, police leaders and trainers must be extremely sensitive to the needs of high-crime communities that are defined by a disproportionate number of hot spots. Regardless of cause and effect, high levels of crime, disorder, fear, police enforcement, and negative views of the police tend to covary in the same geographic areas, along with concentrations of low-income families and people of color. As we seek more effective and efficient methods of crime control in hot spots, we must never forget the long and painful history of relations between the Black community and law enforcement, from slavery to this day (see, for example, Wilkerson, 2010). Latinos have their own distressing history with law enforcement and the unique issues they face have only intensified under the current administration's immigration crackdown (Hirschfeld Davis, 2017) and the President's recommendation that police officers be "rough" with people they arrest (Sanchez, 2017). Through oral and written histories, these troubling stories are indelibly recorded in the minds of families of color and passed along to future generations. Keeping all of this in mind, police agencies need to be extremely attentive to procedural justice during all hot spot encounters, not only because such behavior should contribute to public trust in the police, as well as increase cooperation with the police and reduce the need to use force, but because it is the right thing to do.

REFERENCES

Alderden, M. A., Schuck, A. M., Lavery, T. A., Stephens, C. D., Johnston, R. M., & Rosenbaum, D. P. (2010). *Gang Hot Spots Policing in Chicago: An Evaluation of the Deployment Operations Center Process*. Final report to the National Institute of Justice. Chicago: Chicago Police Department and Center for Research in Law and Justice, University of Illinois at Chicago.

Alexander, M. (2011). *The New Jim Crow: Mass Incarceration in the Age of Colorblindness*. New York: The New Press.

Andreou, J. C. (2003). Personal communication.

Barnum, J. D., Campbell, W. L., Trocchio, S., Caplan, J. M., & Kennedy, L. W. (2016). Examining the environmental characteristics of drug dealing locations. *Crime and Delinquency*, 1–26. doi: 10.1177/0011128716649735.

Braga, A. A. (2001). The effects of hot spots policing on crime. *The Annals of American Political and Social Science*, 578, 104–125.

Braga, A. A., Kennedy, D. M., Piehl, A. M., & Waring, E. J. (2001). *Reducing Gun Violence: The Boston Gun Project's Operation Ceasefire*. Washington, DC: Department of Justice, National Institute of Justice.

Braga, A. A., Papachristos, A. V., & Hureau, D. M. (2014). The effects of hot spots policing on crime: An updated systematic review and meta-analysis. *Justice Quarterly*, 31, 633–663.

Braga, A. A., & Weisburd, D. L. (2012). The effects of "pulling levers" focused deterrence strategies on crime. *Campbell Systematic Reviews*, 6.

Braga, A. A., Weisburd, D. L., Waring, E., Green Mazerolle, L., Spelman, W., & Gajewski, F. (1999). Problem-oriented policing in violent crime places: A randomized controlled experiment. *Criminology*, 37(3), 541–580.

Brantingham, P. L., & Brantingham, P. J. (1993). Environment, routine, and situation: Toward a pattern theory of crime. In R.V. Clarke, & M. Felson (eds.), *Routine Activity and Rationale Choice*. Advances in Criminological Theory, Vol. 5. New Brunswick, NJ: Transaction Publications.

Bursik, R. J., Jr., & Grasmick, H. G. (1993). *Neighborhoods and Crime: The Dimensions of Effective Community Control*. New York: Lexington.

Bushway, S. (1996). *The impact of a criminal history record on access to legitimate employment*. Unpublished doctoral dissertation. H. John Heinz School of Public Policy and Management, Carnegie Mellon University.

Cohen, L. E., & Felson, M. (1979). Social change and crime rate trends: A routine activity approach. *American Sociological Review*, 44, 588–605.

Collinson, S., & Jarrett, L. (2017). Trump embraces law and order agenda. *CNN*. Updated 9:47 AM ET, Tue August 29. www.cnn.com/2017/08/29/politics/trump-law-order-jeff-sessions/index.html.

Cornish, D., & Clarke, R. V. (eds.). (1986). *The Reasoning Criminal: Rational Choice Perspectives on Offending*. New York: Springer-Verlag.

Donner, C., Maskaly, J., Fridell, L., & Jennings, W. G. (2015). Policing and procedural justice: A state-of-the-art review. *Policing*, 38(1), 153–172.

Eck, J. E., & Rosenbaum, D. P. (1994). The new police order: Effectiveness, equity, and efficiency in community policing. In D. P. Rosenbaum (ed.), *The Challenge of Community Policing: Testing the Promises* (pp. 3–23). Newbury Park, CA: Sage.

Eck, J. E., & Weisburd, D. (1995). Crime places in crime theory. Crime Prevention Studies, 4, 1–33.

Eck, J. E., & Wartell, J. (1996). *Reducing crime and drug dealing by improving place management: A randomized experiment.* Report to the San Diego Police Department. Washington, DC: Crime Control Institute.

Epp, C. R., Maynard-Moody, S., & Haider-Markek, D. (2014). *Pulled Over: How Police Stops Define Race and Citizenship.* Chicago: University of Chicago Press.

Esbensen, F., Peterson, D., Taylor, T. J., Hawkins, D., & Freng, A. (2010). *Youth Violence: Sex and Race Differences in Offending, Victimization, and Gang Membership* Philadelphia, PA: Temple University Press.

Fagan, J. A. (2017). Policing and segregation. A paper presented at New York University's Furman Center, Dream Revisited series. July. http://furmancenter.org/research/iri/essay/policing-and-segregation.

Gelman, A., Fagan, J., & Kiss, A. (2007). An analysis of the New York City police department's "stop-and-frisk" policy in the context of claims of racial bias. *Journal of the American Statistical Association,* 102(479), 813–823.

Gill, C., Weisburd, D. L., Telep, C.W., Vitter, Z., & Bennett, B. (2014). Community-oriented policing to reduce crime, disorder and fear and increase satisfaction and legitimacy among citizens: A systematic review. *Journal of Experimental Criminology,* 10(4), 399–428.

Goldstein, H. (1990). *Problem-Oriented Policing.* New York: McGraw-Hill.

Graziano, L. M., Rosenbaum, D. P., & Schuck, A. M. (2014). Building group capacity for problem solving and police-community partnerships through survey feedback and training: A Randomized Control Trial within Chicago's community policing program. *Journal of Experimental Criminology,* 10(1), 79–103.

Greene, J. R. (2000). Community policing in America: Changing the nature, structure, and function of the police. In J. Horney, J. Martin, D. L. MacKenzie, R. Peterson, & D. P. Rosenbaum (eds.), *Policies, processes, and decisions of the criminal justice system* (vol. 3, Criminal Justice 2000 series). Washington, DC: US Department of Justice, National Institute of Justice.

Green Mazerolle, L., & Roehl, J. (1998). *Civil Remedies and Crime Prevention.* Monsey, NJ: Criminal Justice Press.

Groff, E. R., Ratcliffe, J. H., Haberman, C. P., Sorg, E. T., Joyce, N. M., & Taylor, R. B. (2015). Does what police do at hot spots matter? The Philadelphia Policing Tactics Experiment. *Criminology,* 53(1), 23–53.

Henrichson, C., Rinaldi, J., & Delaney, R. (2015). *The Price of Jails: Measuring the Taxpayer Cost of Local Incarceration.* New York: Vera Institute of Justice. www.vera.org/price-of-jails.

Hinds, L., & Murphy, K. (2007). Public satisfaction with police: Using procedural justice to improve police legitimacy. *The Australian & New Zealand Journal of Criminology,* 40(1), 27–42.

Hinkle, J. C., & Weisburd, D. L. (2008). The irony of broken windows policing: A micro-place study of the relationship between disorder, focused police crackdowns and fear of crime. *Journal of Criminal Justice,* 36(6), 503–512.

Hirschfeld Davis, J. (2017). Trump to revive push on immigration crackdown on Long Island trip. *New York Times,* July 28. www.nytimes.com/2017/07/28/us/politics/trump-immigration-gangs.html

Holmes, M. D., & Smith, B. W. (2008). *Race and Police Brutality: Roots of an Urban Dilemma.* Albany, NY: State University of New York Press.

Hope, T. (1994). Problem-oriented policing and drug market locations: Three case studies. In R. V. Clarke (ed.), *Crime Prevention Studies*, vol. 2. Monsey, NY: Criminal Justice Press.

Jackson, J., Bradford, B., Stanko, B., & Hohl, K. (2013). *Just Authority? Trust in the Police in England and Wales.* New York: Routledge.

Kane, R. J. (2002). The social ecology of police misconduct. *Criminology*, 40(4), 867–896.

Kendi, I. X. (2017). A history of race and racism in American, in 24 chapters. Book Review, *New York Times*, February 22. www.nytimes.com/2017/02/22/books/review/a-history-of-race-and-racism-in-america-in-24-chapters.html.

Kennedy, D. (1993). *Closing the Market: Controlling the Drug Trade in Tampa, Florida.* NIJ Program Focus. Washington, DC: National Institute of Justice, US Department of Justice.

Kleiman, M. (1988). *Street-Level Drug Enforcement: Examining the Issues.* Washington, DC: National Institute of Justice, US Department of Justice.

Klein, M. W. (1986). Labeling theory and delinquency policy: An empirical test. *Criminal Justice and Behavior*, 13, 47–79.

Klein, M. W. (1999). Attempting gang control by suppression: The misuse of deterrence principles. In L. K. Gaines, & G. W. Cordner (eds.), *Policing Perspectives: An Anthology.* Ch. 18 (pp. 269–282). Los Angeles: Roxbury.

Kochel, T. R. (2011). Constructing hot spots policing: Unexamined consequences for disadvantaged populations and for police legitimacy. *Criminal Justice Policy Review*, 22(3), 350–374.

Kochel, T. R., Parks, R., & Mastrofski, S. D. (2013). Examining police effectiveness as a precursor to legitimacy and cooperation with police. *Justice Quarterly*, 30(5), 895–925.

Kochel, T. R., & Weisburd, D. (2017). Assessing community consequences of implementing hot spots policing in residential areas: Findings from a randomized field trial. *Journal of Experimental Criminology*, 13, 143–170.

Koper, C. (1995). Just enough police presence: Reducing crime and disorderly behavior by optimizing patrol time in crime hot spots. Unpublished paper.

Lamberth, J. (1998). Driving while black: A statistician proves that prejudice still rules the road. *Washington Post*, August 16. Pg. C01.

Langton, L., & Durose, M. R. (2013). Police behavior during traffic and street stops, 2011. *A Special Report.* Bureau of Justice Statistics, Office of Justice Programs, US Department of Justice. NCJ 242937 September.

Lum, C., Koper, C. S., & Telep, C. W. (2011). The evidence-based policing matrix. *Journal of Experimental Criminology*, 7(1), 3–26.

Lum, C., & Nagin, D. S. (2017). Reinventing American policing. *Crime and Justice*, 46 (1), 339–393.

Maciag, M. (2017). The alarming consequences of police working overtime. *Governing: The States and Localities.* October issue. www.governing.com/topics/public-justice-safety/gov-police-officers-overworked-cops.html.

Maher, L., & Dixon, D. (2001). The cost of crackdowns: Policing Cabramatta's heroin market. *Current Issues in Criminal Justice*, 13(1), 5–22.

Main, F. (2016). Street cops say "ACLU effect" drives spike in gun violence. *Chicago Tribune*, January 31, 2016, 8:24 pm. https://chicago.suntimes.com/chicago-politics/street-cops-say-aclu-effect-drives-spike-in-gun-violence/.

Maltz, M., Gordon, A. C., & Friedman, W. (1990). *Mapping Crime in Its Community Setting: Event Geography Analysis*. New York: Springer-Verlag.

Mamalian, C. A., & LaVigne, N. G. (1999). *The Use of Computerized Mapping by Law Enforcement*. Washington, DC: National Institute of Justice, Office of Justice Programs, US Department of Justice.

Mazerolle, L., Bennett, S., Manning, M., Ferguson, P., & Sargeant, E. (2012). *Legitimacy in policing: A systematic review of procedural justice*. Brisbane: Campbell Crime and Justice Group, ARC Centre of Excellence in Policing and Security.

McCarthy, G. F., & Rosenbaum, D. P. (2015). From CompStat to RespectStat: Accountability for respectful policing. *The Police Chief*, August, 76–77.

McGarrell, E. F., Chermak, S., Weiss, A., & Wilson, J. (2001). Reducing firearms violence through directed police patrol. *Criminology and Public Policy*, 1, 119–148.

Meisner, J. (2015). Chicago sued over police department's alleged stop-and-frisk practices. *Chicago Tribune*, April 21.

Mueller, B. (2017). New York Police Dept. agrees to curb Stop-and-Frisk tactics. *New York Times*, February 2, 2017.

Myhill, A., & Quinton, P. (2010). Confidence, neighbourhood policing, and contact: Drawing together the evidence. *Policing: A Journal of Policy and Practice*, 4(3), 273–281. https://doi.org/10.1093/police/paq026.

National Academies of Sciences, Engineering, and Medicine. (2018). *Proactive Policing: Effects on Crime and Communities*. Washington, DC: The National Academies Press. doi: https: doi.org/10.17226/24928.

National Research Council. (2014). *The Growth of Incarceration in the United States: Exploring Causes and Consequences*. Washington, DC: The National Academies Press. https://doi.org/10.17226/18613.

New York Civil Liberties Union. (2017). Stop-and-Frisk Data. www.nyclu.org/en/stop-and-frisk-data Annual Stop-and-Frisk.

New York Times Editorial Board. (2013). Racial discrimination in Stop-and-Frisk. *New York Times*. August 13. www.nytimes.com/2013/08/13/opinion/racial-discrimination-in-stop-and-frisk.html.

Papachristos, A. V. (2003). The social structure of gang homicide in Chicago. Paper presented at the Annual Conference of the American Society of Criminology, November 21, Denver, Colorado.

Pew Research Center (2017). *Behind the Badge: Amid Protests and Calls for Reform, How Police View Their Jobs, Key Issues and Recent Fatal Encounters between Blacks and Police*. Washington, DC: Pew Charitable Trusts. January.

Pope, C., Lovell, R., & Hsia, H. M. (2003). *Disproportionate Minority Confinement: A Review of Research Literature from 1989 to 2001*. Washington, DC: Office of Juvenile Justice and Delinquency Prevention, Office of Justice Programs, US Department of Justice.

Potter, G., Gaines, L., & Holbrook, B. (1990). Blowing smoke: An evaluation of marijuana eradication in Kentucky. *American Journal of Police*, 9(1), 97–116.

President's Task Force on 21st Century Policing (2015). *Final Report of the President's Task Force on 21st Century Policing*. Washington, DC: Office of Community Oriented Policing Services.

Ratcliffe, J. H., Groff, E. R., Sorg, E. T., & Haberman, C. P. (2015). Citizens' reactions to hot spots policing: Impacts on perceptions of crime, disorder, safety and police. *Journal of Experimental Criminology*, 11, 393–417.

Reaves, B. A. (2015). *Local Police Departments, 2013: Personnel, Policies, and Practices*. Washington, DC: US Department of Justice, Office of Justice Programs, Bureau of Justice Statistics. May. NCJ 248677. www.bjs.gov/content/pub/pdf/lpd13ppp.pdf.

Rice, S. K., & White, M. D. (eds.). (2010). *Race, Ethnicity and Policing: New and Essential Readings*. New York: New York University Press.

Rosenbaum, D. P. (1993). Civil liberties and aggressive enforcement: Balancing the rights of individuals and society in the drug war. In R. C. Davis, A. J. Lurigio, & D. P. Rosenbaum (eds.), *Drugs and the Community* (pp. 55–82). Springfield, IL: Charles C. Thomas.

Rosenbaum, D. P. (ed.). (1994). *The Challenge of Community Policing: Testing the Promises*. Newbury Park, CA: Sage.

Rosenbaum, D. P. (2002). Evaluating multi-agency anti-crime partnerships: Theory, design and measurement issues. *Crime Prevention Studies*, 14, 171–225.

Rosenbaum, D. P. (2007). Just say no to D.A.R.E. *Criminology and Public Policy*, 6, 1701–1711.

Rosenbaum, D. P. (2015a). Reflections on the President's Task Force Report: Time to re-think our core crime control strategies in American policing. Plenary Session: President's Task Force on Policing. 2015 Symposium by the George Mason University Center for Evidence-based Crime Policy and the Police Foundation. Washington, DC.

Rosenbaum, D. P. (2015b). Strike up a conversation, not an interrogation: The Respectful Engaged Policing (REP) model. Testimony before the President's Task Force on 21st Century Policing. Phoenix, Arizona, February 13, 2015.

Rosenbaum, D. P. (2016). The National Police Research Platform: Advancing knowledge and practice in American policing. NIJ panel presentation at the annual meeting of the American Society of Criminology, New Orleans.

Rosenbaum, D. P., & Lavrakas, P. J. (1995). Self-reports about place: The application of survey and interview methods to the study of small areas. *Crime Prevention Studies*, 4, 285–314.

Rosenbaum, D. P., Lawrence, D. S., Hartnett, S. M., McDevitt, J., & Posick, C. (2015). Measuring procedural justice and legitimacy at the local level: The Police-Community Interaction Survey. *Journal of Experimental Criminology*, 11(3), 335–366.

Rosenbaum, D. P., Lurigio, A. J., & Davis, R. C. (1998). *The Prevention of Crime: Social and Situational Strategies*. Belmont, CA: Wadsworth.

Rosenbaum, D. P., Maskaly, J., Lawrence, D. S., Escamilla, J. H., Enciso, G., Christoff, T. E., Posick. C. (2017). The Police-Community Interaction Survey: Measuring police performance in new ways. *Policing: An International Journal of Police Strategies & Management*, 40(1), 112–127.

Rosenbaum, D. P., & McCarty, W. P. (2017). Organizational justice and officer "buy in" in American Policing. *Policing: An International Journal of Police Strategies & Management*, 40(1), 11–25.

Rosenbaum, D. P., & Schuck, A. (2012). Comprehensive community partnerships for preventing crime. In B. C. Welsh, & D. P. Farrington (eds.), *The Oxford Handbook on Crime Prevention*. Oxford: Oxford University Press.

Sampson, R. J. (2002). The community. In J. Q. Wilson, & J. Petersilia (eds.), *Crime: Public Policies for Crime Control* (pp. 225–252). Oakland, CA: Institute for Contemporary Studies Press.

Sampson, R. J., Raudenbush, S. W., & Earls, F. (1997). Neighborhoods and violent crime: A multilevel study of collective efficacy. *Science*, 277, 918–924.

Sanchez, R. Police push back against Trump's law-and-order speech. *CNN*, Updated 11:27 PM ET, Sat July 29, 2017.

Savage, C., & Goode, E. (2013). Two powerful signals of a major shift on crime. *New York Times*. August 12, 2013.

Schuck, A. M., & Rosenbaum, D. P. (2006). Promoting safe and healthy neighborhoods: What research tells us about intervention. In K. Fulbright-Anderson (ed.), *Community Change: Theories, Practices and Evidence* (pp. 61–140). Washington, DC: The Aspen Institute.

Shadish, W. R., Cook, T. D., & Campbell, D. T. (2001). *Experimental and quasi-experimental designs for generalized causal inference*. Boston: Houghton Mifflin.

Sherman, L. W. (1990). Police crackdowns: Initial and residual deterrence. In M. Tonry and N. Morris (eds.), *Crime and Justice: A Review of Research*, vol. 12. Chicago: University of Chicago Press.

Sherman, L. W. (1997). Policing for crime prevention. In L. W. Sherman, D. Gottfredson, D. MacKenzie, J. E. Eck, P. Reuter, & S. Bushway (eds.), *Preventing Crime: What Works, What Doesn't, What's Promising*. Ch. 8. Report to the National Institute of Justice, Office of Justice Programs, US Department of Justice. (NCJ 165366).

Sherman, L. W., Gartin, P. R., & Buerger, M. E. (1989). Hot spots of predatory crime: Routine activities and the criminology of place. *Criminology*, 27, 27–55.

Sherman, L. W., Gottfredson, D., MacKenzie, D., Eck, J., Reuter, P., & Bushway, S. (eds.). (1997). *Preventing Crime: What Works, What Doesn't, What's Promising*. Report to the National Institute of Justice, Office of Justice Programs, U. S. Department of Justice (NCJ 165366).

Sherman, L. W., & Rogan, D. P. (1995a). Deterrent effects of police raids on crackdowns: A randomized, controlled experiment. *Justice Quarterly*, 12(4), 755–781.

Sherman, L. W., & Rogan, D. P. (1995b). Effects of gun seizures on gun violence: "Hot spots" patrol in Kansas City. *Justice Quarterly*, 12(4), 673–693.

Sherman, L. W., & Weisburd, D. (1995). General deterrent effects of police patrol in crime "hot spots": A randomized, controlled trial. *Justice Quarterly*, 12(4), 625–648.

Skogan, W. G. (ed.). (2003). *Community Policing: Can It Work?* Belmont, CA: Wadsworth.

Skogan, W. G. (2006). *Police and Community in Chicago: A Tale of Three Cities*. New York: Oxford University Press.

Skogan, W. G., & Hartnett, S. M. (1997). *Community Policing Chicago Style*. New York: Oxford University Press.

Skogan, Wesley G., Steiner, L., Hartnett, S. M., DuBois, J., Bennis, J., Rottinghaus, B., Young Kim, S., Van, K., Rosenbaum, D. P. et al. (2002). *Community Policing in Chicago, Years Eight and Nine: An Evaluation of Chicago's Alternative Policing Strategy and Information Technology Initiative*. Final report to the Illinois Criminal Justice Information Authority. Evanston, IL: Northwestern University, Institute for Policy Research. December.

Smith, M., Sviridoff, M., Sadd, S., Curtis, R., & Grinc, R. (1992). *The Neighborhood Effects of Street-Level Drug Eenforcement. Tactical Narcotics Teams in New York: An evaluation of TNT*. New York: Vera Institute of Justice.

Spelman, W. (1995). Criminal careers of public places. In J. E. Eck, & D. Weisburd (eds.), *Crime and Place, Crime Prevention Studies*, 4 (pp. 115–144).

Sullivan, J., Thebault, R., Tate, J., & Jenkins, J. (2017). Number of fatal shootings by police is nearly identical to last year. *The Washington Post*, July 1.

Taylor, R. B. (1998). Crime and small-scale places: What we know, what we can prevent, and what else we need to know. *Crime and place: Plenary papers of the 1997 conference on criminal justice research and evaluation*. Washington, DC: National Institute of Justice, Office of Justice Programs, US Department of Justice (NIJ 168618).

Telep, C. W., & Weisburd, D. (2018). Crime concentration at place. In S. Johnson, & G. Bruinsma (eds.). *Oxford Handbook of Environmental Criminology*. Oxford: Oxford University Press.

Terrill, W., & Reisig, M. D. (2003). Neighborhood context and police use of force. *Journal of Research in Crime and Delinquency*, 40(3), 291–321.

Tittle, C. R., & Paternoster, R. (2000). *Social Deviance and Crime: An Organizational and Theoretical Approach*. Los Angeles, CA: Roxbury.

Tonry, M., & Farrington, D. P. (1995). Building a safer society: Strategic approaches to crime prevention. *Crime and Justice: A Review of Research*, 19.

Travis, J., Solomon, A. L., & Waul, M. (2001). *From Prison to Home: The Dimensions and Consequences of Prisoner Reentry*. Washington, DC: The Urban Institute.

Tyler, T. R. (2001). Trust and law-abiding behavior: Building better relationships between the police, the courts, and the minority community. *Boston University Law Review*, 81, 361–406.

Tyler, T. R. (2006). *Why People Obey the Law*. Princeton, NJ: Princeton University Press.

Tyler, T. R., & Fagan, J. (2008). Legitimacy and cooperation: Why do people help the police fight crime in their communities? *Ohio State Journal of Criminal Law*, 6, 231–275.

Tyler, T. R., & Huo, Y. J. (2002). *Trust in the Law: Encouraging Public Cooperation with the Police and Courts*. New York: Russell Sage.

Uchida, C., Forst, B., & Annan, S. (1992). *Modern Policing and the Control of Illegal Drugs: Testing New Strategies in Two American Cities*. Washington, DC: National Institute of Justice, Office of Justice Programs, US Department of Justice.

United States Department of Justice. (2017). *The Civil Rights Division's Pattern and Practice Police Reform Work: 1994-Present*. Washington, DC: Civil Rights Division, US Department of Justice. www.justice.gov/crt/file/922421/download.

Wain, N., Ariel, B., & Tankebe, J. (2017). The collateral consequences of GPS-LED supervision in hot spots policing. *Police Practice and Research: An International Journal*, 18(4), 376–390.

Watson, A. C., Ottati, V. C., Morabito, M., Draine, J., Kerr, A. N., & Angell, B. (2010). Outcomes of police contacts with persons with mental illness: The impact of CIT. *Administration and Policy, Mental Health and Mental Health Services Research*, 37 (4), 302–317.

Weinborn, C., Ariel, B., Sherman, L. W., & O' Dwyer, E. (2017). Hotspots vs. harmspots: Shifting the focus from counts to harm in the criminology of place. *Applied Geography*, 86 (September), 226–244.

Weisburd, D. L. (2015). The law of crime concentration and the criminology of place. *Criminology*, 54, 133–157.

Weisburd, D. L. (2016). Does hot spots policing inevitably lead to unfair and abusing policing practices or can we maximize both fairness and effectiveness in the new proactive policing? The University of Chicago Legal Forum. 2016 U. Chi. Legal F. 661.

Weisburd, D. L., & Eck, J. E. (2004). What can police do to reduce crime, disorder and fear? *The Annals of the American Academy of Political and Social Science*, 593, 42–65.

Weisburd, D. L., Eck, J. E., Hinkle, J. C., & Telep, C. W. (2008). Effects of problem-oriented policing on crime and disorder. *Campbell Collaboration Library of Systematic Reviews*. www.campbellcollaboration.org/library.php.

Weisburd, D. L., & Green, L. (1995a). Measuring immediate spatial displacement: Methodological issues and problems. In J. E. Eck, & D. Weisburd (eds.), *Crime and Place, Crime Prevention Studies 4*, 349–361.

Weisburd, D. L., & Green, L. (1995b). Policing drug hot spots: The Jersey City drug market analysis experiment. *Justice Quarterly*, 12(4), 711–735.

Weisburd, D. L., Groff, E. R., & Yang, S. M. (2012). *The Criminology of Place: Street Segments and Our Understanding of the Crime Problem*. New York: Oxford University Press.

Weisburd, D. L., Hinkle, J. C., Famega, C., & Ready, J. (2011). The possible "backfire" effects of hot spots policing: An experimental assessment of impacts on legitimacy, fear and collective efficacy. *Journal of Experimental Criminology*, 7(4), 297–320.

Weiss, A., & Rosenbaum, D. P. (2009). *Illinois Traffic Stop Statistics Study, 2008 Annual Report*. Springfield: Illinois Department of Transportation.

Weitzer, R., & Tuch, S. A. (2006). *Race and Policing in America: Conflicts and Reform*. New York: Cambridge University Press.

Welsh, B. C., Farrington, D. P., & Sherman, L .W. (2001). *Costs and Benefits of Preventing Crime*. Boulder, CO: Westview Press.

Werner, A. (2017). Murder rate in NYC drops to lowest level in decades. *CBS News*. December 29, 2017, 6:38 PM. www.cbsnews.com/news/murder-rate-in-nyc-drops-to-lowest-level-in-decades/.

Werthman, C., & Piliavin, I. (1967). Gang members and the police. In D. Bordua (ed.). *The Police: Six Sociological Essays* (pp. 56–98). New York: John Wiley.

White, C., & Weisburd, D. (2017). A co-responder model of policing mental health problems at crime hot spots: Findings from a pilot study. *Policing: A Journal of Policy and Practice*, 12(2), 194–209.

Wilkerson, I. (2010). *The Warmth of Other Suns: The Epic Story of America's Great Migration*. New York: Vintage Books.

Williams, H., & Murphy, P. V. (1990). The evolving strategy of police: A minority view. Perspectives in Policing, January issue (No. 13). National Institute of Justice, Office of Justice Programs, US Department of Justice.

Wilson, J. Q., & Kelling, G. (1982). Broken windows: The police and neighborhood safety. *Atlantic Monthly*, 249(3), 29–38.

Wilson, J. Q., & Petersilia, J., (eds.). (2002). *Crime: Public Policies for Crime Control*. Oakland, CA: Institute for Contemporary Studies Press.

Worden, R., Bynum, T., & Frank, J. (1994). Police crackdowns on drug abuse and trafficking. In D. McKenzie, & C. Uchida (eds.), *Drugs and Crime: Evaluating Public Policy Initiatives*. Thousand Oaks, CA: Sage.

Xue, Y., Leventhal, T., Brooks-Gunn, J., & Earls, F. J. (2005). Neighborhood residence and mental health problems of 5- to 11-year-olds. *Archives of General Psychiatry*, 62 (5), 554–563.

PART VIII

PREDICTIVE POLICING

Advocate

Predictive Policing

Jerry Ratcliffe

At the First Predictive Policing Symposium held in Los Angeles in 2009, Assistant Attorney General Laurie Robinson noted, "Law enforcement leaders are using predictive techniques in a variety of forms, but we don't necessarily have a handle on all of them." Predictive policing is starting to demonstrate modest positive results; however it is still a nascent field where the dimensions of predictive policing are still not clear. It comprises multiple elements and often means different things to different people.

Predictive policing links two emerging and dynamic strands of modern law enforcement; the development and use of algorithms to estimate a probability of future criminality at places or among high-risk people, and the application of policing strategies to these forecasts in order to prevent or reduce crime. This creates a double challenge for predictive policing in determining (1) accurate crime and criminality prediction, and (2) the choice of an effective prevention strategy based on a forecast.

Given this area is still in its infancy, there are multiple aspects that either require significant development or elicit concerns from outside the field. I will not shy from these anxieties in this "advocate" chapter. As I will explain, however, incorporation and management of these concerns into the future development of predictive policing will enhance what might become a vital element in the future of proactive criminal justice in democracies.

In this chapter, I adopt the perspective that predictive policing may not yet be at the stage where it clearly surpasses other methods of analytically driven policing; however, the potential for substantial benefit exists. I doubt anyone would consider us at the zenith of predictive efficiency. Current algorithms are making use of data that were never collected for this purpose, and have to incorporate flawed temporal and spatial accuracy into the analysis. For example, longer-term prediction models use population census data that are estimated at best once a year, and even those estimates are based on limited samples of five-year rolling data sets. Outside the USA, census updates can be less frequent. These analytic constraints are coupled with a limited evidential base for many of the police strategies that might use forecasts in a preventative way.

But even with inconsistent source data and questions surrounding appropriate tactics, we already recognize the importance of improved targeted and more focused policing. With a more precise focus, there is less inadvertent collateral damage to civilians unconnected to criminality, we benefit from improved efficiency within our criminal justice services, there is greater objectivity, and there may even be increased public trust and law enforcement legitimacy when people see the police are focused on the right people at the right places.

That being said, predictive policing has highlighted a long-simmering debate about the role of the police in our society. Should the police be restricted to a reactive role of just patrol and investigating crime or the provision of more proactive prevention and risk management? This "fundamental and defining tension" (Innes, 2004: 151) is underscored when we operationalize risk forecasts in ways that directly impact citizens. At present, policing seems to be leaning toward the latter, whether the forecasts are clinical (based on a police officer's experience), actuarial (based on a computer algorithm) or a hybrid (such as a crime analyst's interpretation of aggregate mapped crime patterns or other data).

Concerns regarding this new enforcement initiative include issues of accuracy, transparency, and strategy. While these are clearly issues that demand attention, the overall move to more objective targeting of limited police resources feels like an inescapable direction that is likely to be beneficial to society. So while I will argue that we are not there yet, we are on the right track to significant improvement of a major aspect of the criminal justice system; a police crime control effort that is more focused on high-risk people and places and less likely to impact innocent parties.

DEFINING PREDICTIVE POLICING

First, a definition or two to get us on the same page. Reactive policing occurs when police respond to events such as crimes and calls for service. The criminal event has either occurred or is happening right now. With a reactive policing model, departments can choose to triage their response to types of calls, but they tend not to have a significant role in choosing the place and time of their activities. Crime investigation is one example. At its most basic, proactive policing is the reverse of this, and occurs when police try to anticipate the *who* and/or *where* of crime that has yet to transpire, and attempt to shape the situation to prevent or mitigate the expected harm. Proactive policing has been formally defined as "all policing strategies that have as one of their goals the prevention or reduction of crime and disorder and that are not reactive in terms of focusing primarily on uncovering ongoing crime or on investigating or responding to crimes once they have occurred" (Weisburd & Majmundar, 2018: 1–12). Predictive policing attempts to direct this proactive work.

I will assume that as you are reading this scholarly book, you value some form of evidential foundation as the basis of criminal justice decision-making. I will therefore skip the near-obligatory dismissal of crime prediction based on crystal balls, tea leaves, tarot cards, psychic predictions, or any similar *Minority Report*-type nonsense. The future of crime prediction (or more accurately, forecasting) is either *actuarial* and based on an analysis and interpretation of historical data with an associated forward projection of risk probability, or a *hybrid* approach whereby a person (such as a professional crime analyst) works in combination with computer models to refine actuarial forecasts. These are contrasted with the most common approach employed today. Someone in the criminal justice field (such as a probation officer or police sergeant) uses their experience and judgment (sometimes in concert with some basic information) to determine on whom or where the highest risk rests. This *clinical* model remains the dominant model of crime forecasting today.

A common definition of predictive policing comes from the Rand Corporation. While sometimes cited, their definition of predictive policing is both broad and problematic. They suggest it is "the application of analytical techniques – particularly quantitative techniques – to identify likely targets for police intervention and prevent crime or solve past crimes by making statistical predictions" (Perry et al., 2013: xiii). This seems excessively broad, in that it includes the solving of past crimes, which doesn't appear to reflect the focus of current predictive policing attention. It is also problematic because it doesn't actually say anything about policing tactics, strategies, or operational behavior. At a macro level, we might look at FBI city statistics and determine that Chicago or Philadelphia are likely targets for police intervention, but this doesn't recommend how those cities should be policed. In other words, the Rand definition doesn't say anything about the "policing" in predictive policing.

I have previously defined predictive policing in terms of street crime and geographic enforcement activity (Ratcliffe, 2014: 4) and this geographic enforcement model is where current iterations of predictive policing tend to focus (Weisburd & Majmundar, 2018). To adjust this definition to include individual offender forecasting, we might define predictive policing as *the use of historical data to create a forecast of areas of criminality or crime hot spots, or high-risk offender characteristic profiles that will be one component of police resource allocation decisions. The resources will be allocated with the expectation that, with targeted deployment, criminal activity can be prevented, reduced, or disrupted.* The preceding two sentences probably feel pretty wordy; however they incorporate not only the forecasting of people and places but also the associated policing response.[1] It is in the response as much as

---

[1] It should also be noted, that while not common, a predictive reassurance policing approach might attempt to forecast likely victims based on an analysis of current crime victims and offer prevention or anticipate the need for victim support services. But for most predictive policing applications, at the time of writing, hot spots and offenders are the main focus.

the forecasting mechanisms where much of the concern with predictive policing currently lurks, but first we should examine the limits of current forecasting knowledge.

THE TECHNICAL CHALLENGE OF FORECASTING

Spatial Crime Forecasting

Police were putting pins in maps long before I joined the police service in 1984. While the pins showed locations of historical activity, this had a predictive component to it. After all, why do it if you don't think the pins will give you some clue as to future criminality? Pins of course have their limitations and the move to the use of geographic information systems (GIS) has been widespread across policing for many years (Chainey & Ratcliffe, 2005). The pins have been replaced by GIS symbols but the principle remains. This is the simplest form of crime forecasting – where crime has happened before is where it will happen again. I call it the *Groundhog Day* approach to prediction.[2] It's simple, because it only requires identifying current high risk places and bringing an often reasonable suspicion that, absent any intervention, little will change and these locations will continue to be a significant risk to the community.

Researchers seeking more sophistication have sought to identify covariates of crime – characteristics of locations that link to crime risk – and project locations with similar traits as likely high risk, even when they may not have demonstrated criminogenic tendencies to date. While involving a forward projection, these forecasts are still based on an interpretation of historical data.

It should also be noted that a *prediction* is generally considered to be a definitive statement that has only one of two outcomes (right or wrong), while a forecast comes with an associated probability. For the nitpickers among us, this is a cause for gnashing of teeth when predictive policing is mentioned: it should really be *forecast policing*. Predictive policing's alliteration does however sound cooler and has become the commonly used term, so I'll throw in the towel.

There is a theoretical foundation to this new movement. A significant body of research demonstrates that crime is unevenly distributed among places and victims (Felson, 1987; Sherman, Gartin & Buerger, 1989; Weisburd & Eck, 2004), and a number of spatial theories of crime can explain short-term changes in crime risk for small, local areas. Various predictive policing analytical approaches are tied to these theories, such as risk terrain modeling (Caplan, Kennedy & Miller, 2011; Kennedy, Caplan & Piza, 2011; Moreto, Piza &

---

[2] This is a reference to the movie of the same name. If you are unfamiliar with this iconic piece of cinematic history, then you should know that Bill Murray plays Phil Connors, an arrogant weatherman stuck in a time loop in a small Pennsylvania town where he has to repeat the same day over and over again. In case this description has you wondering, it's a comedy.

Caplan, 2014), techniques that utilize short-term event patterns (Johnson et al., 2009; Mohler et al., 2011; Gorr & Lee, 2015), and near repeat patterns (Townsley, Homel & Chaseling, 2003; Johnson et al., 2007; Ratcliffe & Rengert, 2008).

Gorr, Olligschlaeger, and Thompson (2003) have shown that just about any kind of forecasting method is preferable to two traditional *Groundhog Day* approaches: this month's crime rate will be the same as last month, or this month will be the same as the identical month a year ago. There are a variety of techniques that have gained support among the analytical community that have some empirical support in terms of accuracy and precision (Drawve, 2016). Gorr and Lee have suggested that addressing short-term, temporary hot spots can be more effective for crime prevention than large chronic hot spots, and provide for greater equity of crime reduction resources (Gorr & Lee, 2015). This contradicts the view of Sherman who argues for the use of long-term hot spots of at least one year for patrol purposes on the grounds that "predictive policing is premised on the already-falsified claim that hot spots are not stable, and that date-and-time-specific factors must be taken into account to predict reliably where crime will be concentrated in short periods of time" (Sherman et al., 2014: 108).

Taylor and colleagues (2015) have conducted an extensive examination of the communities and crime literature and identified a number of theoretically relevant variables that can predict crime for a forthcoming year, in particular socio-economic status and racial composition. Two aspects of this are important to note. First, their crime-plus-demographics model improves on the *Groundhog Day* model (this year's crime areas will predict next year's crime areas) by adding certain demographic indicators to the crime frequencies in the prediction. These indicators are reflecting ecological crime discontinuities of shifting structural conditions that affect future crime patterns.

Second, the inclusion of racial composition in the prediction improves the model. This may be of concern to some readers, yet it is worth reflecting on two aspects of this. With regard to geographic crime prediction, the algorithms are forecasting patterns of *victimization* and not offending. They therefore help us understand where people are most likely to be a victim of crime, and not where offenders reside. A further consideration is that, at least in the USA, when racial variables (such as the percentage of non-white residents) are significant, they are really reflective of their status as proxy variables representative of decades of social segregation, unequal access to opportunities for advancement, and other measures of structural racism. They are not representing a criminal proclivity among any racial group. But caution regarding the use of race-related variables and how predictions are employed by the criminal justice system are merited, as recognized by the National Academies of Sciences report into proactive policing (Weisburd & Majmundar, 2018).

These analytical advances notwithstanding, the extant research largely suggests that spatial crime forecasting is still not fully formed as a field, with lack of agreement over spatial scale, time frames, or the requisite independent variables. There is also an absence of clarity around how to contrast actuarial, hybrid, and clinical crime forecasts. While we know that officers' (clinical) knowledge of crime patterns varies with crime type (Ratcliffe & McCullagh, 2001) there is still a paucity of detail around the effectiveness of hybrid (crime analysts using analytical software) or actuarial (predictive algorithms) methods.

But while there is little research, there isn't a total absence. Mohler and colleagues (2015) noted that using predictive forecasts in one police department led to an average 7.4 percent reduction in crime compared to the days officers used hot spots that originated from a crime analyst's conventional crime mapping. If the assumption holds that the policing response did not change because of the analytical approach, then this might reflect analytical improvements. During the Philadelphia Predictive Policing Experiment, the HunchLab software predicted twice as much violence and property crime than if the crime were uniformly distributed (Ratcliffe, Taylor & Askey, 2017). And the latest research out of Northern Ireland suggests that (clinical) officer predictions are less effective than a software algorithm (actuarial) when identifying crime and harm hot spots in street segments. The authors also concluded, with regard to a hybrid model, "While it may be true that a combination of statistical and clinical prediction may prove beneficial, in practice there is limited evidence to suggest that this is the case" (Macbeth & Ariel, 2017: 24).

Offender Forecasting

While dating back to at least the 1920s, offender-focused crime forecasting has received less attention from policing than the spatial domain. Within the criminal justice system, prediction can be beneficial to criminal justice practitioners interested in informing decisions around sentencing and parole (Farrington, 1987), and this is where most work has been conducted. To date, it has been challenging to find successful examples of criminal justice forecasting, in part because of the demanding nature of some types of forecast (Berk, 2008). Predicting individual-level criminality would certainly fall into the category of "demanding." That being said, there is strong support for the concentration of criminality within a limited number of offenders. After a meta-analysis of fifteen studies on the prevalence of offending and twenty-seven studies on the frequency of offending, Martinez, Lee, Eck, and O (2017: 13) concluded that "a few people do commit the most crimes, and among offenders, a relatively small group are responsible for most crimes. The policy implications we can draw are obvious: focus attention on the most active offenders."

Given the current political apathy for mass incarceration, decision-makers are interested in improving decisions around deterrence, focused incarceration, or rehabilitative measures in a way that maximizes public safety at least cost. In this vein, Berk and colleagues used nearly half the more than 66,000 cases from the City of Philadelphia's Adult Probation and Parole Department to build a predictive model to estimate who might be charged with murder or attempted murder (Berk et al., 2009). The remainder of the data set was used to evaluate the model. Although the authors claim to "provide a more precise and reliable means to analyze [probation and parole] data" (p. 193). the best model produced about twelve false positive cases for every successful forecast. Yes, you read that right and it isn't a typo. For every correct prediction of an individual who would be charged with murder or attempted murder over a two-year period, the model incorrectly drew attention to about twelve other people who did not.

While this may seem damning, Berk and colleagues (2009: 206) note that while this issue will "raise considerable controversy over the use of such forecasts ... [it] must be addressed in the context of the on-going use of untested and subjective clinical forecasts." In other words, it's pretty bad, but probably less awful than the existing approach of having people in the criminal justice system guess (the clinical model). A recent comparison (also in Philadelphia) asked crime analysts and criminal intelligence officers to list the most harmful gun violence offenders. A computer-generated list significantly outperformed the crime and intelligence analysts on both overall weighted offender harm and the mean number of gun crime episodes in offenders' recent histories (Ratcliffe and Kikuchi, in press).

And herein lies one challenge for both spatio-temporal forecasting and offender forecasting: What is the baseline against which we are trying to improve? Clinical forecasts, or hybrid forecasts where crime analysts or other criminal justice practitioners merge computer models with their subjective experiences, are not only popular but also have the advantage of being accepted as current practice. As such, they are subject to less scrutiny than predictive algorithms.

The Challenge of Uncertainty

Whether offender-focused or place-based, prediction stems from an extrapolation of a probability that a high-risk place or person will have certain propensities. Forecasting future crime from current patterns or criminal records is a univariate approach, whereas incorporating historical criminality and other characteristics (such as land use or demographic characteristics) is a multivariate approach to estimating these propensities. Neither methodology can achieve a perfect prediction, so this leaves us with the challenge of targeting resources with the knowledge that our forecasts are imperfect.

Imperfect forecasts are largely inevitable. The reality of this works thus. If we try and predict which street corners of a city will have a shooting on them in the coming month, we might look at previous shooting patterns. We could incorporate census data in our analysis and notice an increased chance of shootings in areas where people are more likely to rent their homes rather than own, and where they are more transient, frequently living in an area for only a short time. At the street corner level we might see that there is a tendency for these hot spots to have a bar on the corner and be in run-down neighborhoods.

These snippets of information could be gleaned from a regression model; however regression models always include a contemporaneous random perturbation, or in English, a chunk of error. This means there will be some intersections with bars in derelict neighborhoods that have a transient, rental community that *don't* have a history of shootings. Perhaps the bar is well managed and is the focus of a vibrant community life with a strong sense of collective neighborhood cohesion. Or perhaps the bar is right next to a fire station (around which crime doesn't appear to concentrate – see Ratcliffe, 2012). Some of the variation comes from "simple randomness" resulting from a significant number of individual people involved all acting independently (Gorr et al., 2003).

This is the inevitable heterogeneity (variability) of modern life, and is reflected in the R-squared value you might only now be vaguely remembering from your statistics classes. This represents the variance in the crime distribution that is reflected in the statistical model. For example, an R^2 value of 0.60 means that 60 percent of the variation in the crime is represented in the statistical model. The 40 percent that is left is the unexplained portion – the variation that the model cannot fit as well.

What are the consequences of this inevitable variance in crime for predictive policing? It means that if we try and predict crime hot spots (or robbers or murderers), these models will only give us a partial forecast and not a perfect answer. We will inevitably presage some corners that are not going to have shootings, and fail to identify corners that will have shootings. We will predict people who are not murderers, and fail to predict a few people who go on to kill someone. By moving from reactive policing where our response is driven by the deterministic reality that a crime has already occurred to a stochastic possibility that something "might" be going down, we move policing into a situation where activity and life-and-death decisions may be grounded in a forecast that is not perfectly accurate. We could proactively save lives but also inadvertently target people and places that do not pose a threat.

And herein lies one of the cruxes of predictive policing. How comfortable are we with our police targeting people and places based on an algorithm that is not perfect? We live in a world with no apparent tolerance for mistakes, and there is little relief from knowing that some of the algorithms currently available are less subjective than the prevailing methods – the experience or best guesses from police commanders or the hybrid estimates of crime analysts.

Proponents of predictive policing need to help the public realize that if they want the police to be proactive around crime and risk, then that will inevitably involve forecasting high-risk people and places (either offenders for additional attention or victims and places for protection). Forecasts from whatever source (crime analysis, experience, or algorithms) are inevitably imperfect. It will certainly help if the algorithms are at least transparent, but more on that in a bit.

PREDICTIVE POLICING IS FOCUSED POLICING

Predictive policing is inherently focused policing. And while some communities still struggle with this role of the police, there appears to be general agreement that policing should involve some form of proactive activity to prevent crime and provide domestic security. We don't often see calls for the police to remain in their stations until a crime is discovered. What then should be the proactive nature of that activity? In more specific terms, once we have a forecast of high-risk people or places, what do we do with it? Because, absent an operational strategy, we do not have the *policing* part of predictive policing. It is regretfully still the case that, "Currently, the policing aspect is mostly overlooked in evaluations of predictive policing" (Rummens, Hardyns & Pauwels, 2017: 261).

The Kansas City Preventative Patrol Experiment (Kelling et al., 1974) did much to quash the notion that generalized patrol had any benefit (though more replication is long overdue). With improvements in crime mapping, it became possible to map crime hot spots. Focused policing to these hot locations has been so effective that over a decade ago the National Research Council (2004: 250) concluded "studies that focused police resources on crime hot spots provide the strongest collective evidence of police effectiveness that is now available."

Hot spots policing refined the area of focus from the beat to the hot spot, with a concomitant improvement in police effectiveness. If effective, the increased micro-focus of predictive policing grids may increase efficiency further. There are two chapters in this volume that address hot spots policing directly, so I will refer you to the more experienced chapter authors for that review (see Part VIII). What is worth noting is the significant resource commitment that is necessary for a successful hot spots intervention. A Campbell Collaboration review reported that 80 percent of police interventions focused on crime hot spots "reported noteworthy crime and disorder reductions" (Braga, Papachristos & Hureau, 2012: 6); however, a number of the interventions described requiring significant resource commitments from the police department, such as dedicated foot patrols of multiple officers for sixteen hours a day (Ratcliffe et al., 2011), or sufficient directed patrol resources to "saturate" a crime hot spot (Taylor, Koper & Woods, 2011).

Because the response to predictive software is overwhelmingly a police patrol strategy, is there any significant difference between predictive policing and hot spots policing? This question was voiced in the National Academies of Sciences report into proactive policing when we wrote, "the policing tactics adopted appear to be in most locations a traditional patrol response. In other words, rather than new practices and tactics emerging from predictive policing, to date the strategy has consisted of more-honed spatial resource allocation models whose location forecasts are then linked to traditional crime prevention policing activities" (Weisburd & Majmundar, 2018: 4–10). This prompts the pertinent question as to whether there are policing strategies employed in predicted crime areas that are more effective or different from patrol tactics usually employed in hot spots. Both hot spots policing and the geographic application of predictive policing take advantage of what Weisburd calls the "law of crime concentration at places," the realization that crime concentrates at very small units of geography (Weisburd, 2015: 151) – a characteristic first articulated during the Minneapolis (MN) Hot Spots Experiment (Sherman & Weisburd, 1995). The jury is still out, given that the National Academies of Sciences panel concluded that "it is as yet unclear if predictive policing is substantively different from hot spots policing" (Weisburd & Majmundar, 2018: 4–11).

The Philadelphia Predictive Policing Experiment

A recent experiment in Philadelphia sought to coalesce both strands of predictive algorithm and policing response. The Philadelphia Predictive Policing Experiment was designed as a citywide randomized field experiment that explored whether uniform police in marked cars would be more effective at reducing crime in predicted crime areas than officers in plain-clothes – or unmarked – cars (Ratcliffe & Taylor, 2017). Twenty Philadelphia Police districts were randomly selected to one of four conditions. *Awareness districts* just informed officers of the predicted target areas for an eight-hour shift, while in *marked car districts*, supervisors assigned a couple of officers to a uniform patrol car dedicated to working in the grids. *Unmarked car districts* deployed plain-clothes officers in an unmarked police vehicle instead of the marked car. These three experimental conditions were compared to *control districts* where police personnel did not even have access to the crime prediction software and so maintained a standard business-as-usual strategy. These experimental conditions were tested on property crime for three months, and violent crime for a similar period.

The results showed that there was no discernable crime reduction effect from the awareness model where officers were simply informed of the predicted areas. Neither was there any effect with violent crime. However, the marked police car was shown to have some modest crime reduction effect for property crime, an effect that was not noticeable with the unmarked car (Ratcliffe et al., 2017). This suggests that a conspicuous, marked police presence may have some preventative effect when used in predicted crime areas. Of course, this is just one study in one city, but it demonstrates that it is possible to run randomized, controlled experiments that can illuminate predictive policing benefits. "Further academic publications are expected from this project soon. Please search 'Philadelphia Predictive Policing Experiment' for details."

Focused Interventions

The research on focused interventions with offenders identified as high risk is less robust. What is quite clear is that a small percentage of people are responsible for much of the crime. In a recent meta-analysis, Martinez and colleagues (2017) drew on fifteen and twenty-seven studies respectively and calculated a distribution curve of crime by offenders within the overall population, and among just the offending population. The findings were clear. Ten percent of the most active criminals are responsible for about two-thirds of the crime, and among just offenders, the top 15 percent account for half the crime.

What can we do with this knowledge? At the offender level, police might continue to keep surveillance on a known recidivist offender who has recently been released from incarceration, or try and find him access to support services. A combination of stick and carrot is the basis behind one promising approach, *focused deterrence*.

Focused deterrence is a multiphase strategy that involves the identification and notification of a high-risk individual, followed up by either enforcement or service delivery depending on that person's cooperation with the program. A recent report that examined the existing research concluded that while the body of research was insufficient to unequivocally declare focused deterrence was effective at violence reduction, "mostly positive" impacts had been noted at least in the short term (Scott, 2017). The main issue appears to be the absence of rigorous randomized controlled trials. While a systematic review found nine of the ten studies included in the review reported significant reductions in crime, all of them used nonrandomized quasi-experimental designs. This left Braga and Weisburd to conclude that while focused deterrence strategies seem to be effective at reducing crime, caution was necessary when "interpreting these results because of the lack of more rigorous randomized controlled trials in the existing body of scientific evidence on this approach" (Braga & Weisburd, 2012: 6).

How predictive algorithms can help with target identification is still a little unclear, given that "Selecting the right individuals to target requires a blend of documented evidence of prior offenses, law enforcement practitioners' understanding of offenders' motives and social influence, and a deliberate process for choosing from among target candidates" (Scott, 2017: 11).

What focused deterrence and hot spots policing have in common is the targeted nature of police resources. While the evidence for crime concentration in places (Lee et al., 2017) and among people (Martinez et al., 2017) is robust and unequivocal, it is the focused nature of the police activity that has in some cases drawn criticism. It is therefore worth examining these critiques.

CRITIQUES OF PREDICTIVE POLICING

Police Tactics are Damaging to Communities

A common condemnation for focused policing has centered on the corrosive nature of intensive police interventions (Rosenbaum, 2006). In particular, when more aggressive tactics are focused in minority neighborhoods, police legitimacy and public trust can suffer. Predictive policing identifies micro-places (small grids and streets) and focuses police attention to these areas, and without a doubt, there have been egregious examples where aggressive enforcement has aggravated local communities. The subsequent loss of public support has eroded the perceived benefits from any crime reduction. The experiences of communities with stop, question, and frisk in New York City are a good example of the unintended consequences of well-intentioned efforts. While crime did reduce at the micro-level crime hot spots where the tactic was concentrated, the tactic resulted in a growing dissatisfaction with the police and a subsequent successful legal challenge to the legitimacy of stop, question, and frisk (Weisburd, 2016).

There is nothing in the various definitions of predictive policing that suggests what tactics police have to use in predicted areas or toward predicted high-risk offenders. The mistake that is frequently made with regard to proactive or predictive policing is a reluctance of police commanders to move away from traditional tactics. I doubt some of the criticisms of predictive policing would exist if the results of geographic algorithms were used to target the provision of additional childcare or welfare services. And focused deterrence strategies specifically can include mental health counseling, housing and education assistance, and job-interview training (Scott, 2017). Predictive policing identifies the places and people most at risk of future involvement in crime. The challenge for police commanders is to work with community partners to design interventions that boost community support and police legitimacy alongside enhancing crime prevention.

Police Focus on People because They Are Minorities

Scott (2017: 21) summarizes another central critique of focused policing by noting, "Historically, police efforts that target specific individuals for enforcement are subject to criticism as being fundamentally unfair because of the perception that individuals are being targeted for who they are rather than for what they have done." In Philadelphia, the city council's discussions around a risk assessment model based on the work of Richard Berk and his colleagues (mentioned earlier in this chapter) resulted in an online newspaper article with the headline "Philadelphia is grappling with the prospect of a racist computer algorithm" (Reyes, 2016). The ACLU have released a statement voicing a range of predictive policing concerns, including that systems are failing to monitor their racial impact (ACLU, 2016).

While crime prediction tools may be imperfect and vulnerable to false positives and other errors, it is appropriate to consider what they are compared against. Policing doesn't happen in a vacuum and in the absence of analytical tools with a quantitative foundation, police command staff will inevitably have to make subjective decisions regarding whom and what they target. The outcome of these discretionary policing "clinical" forecasts should be just as controversial: "Unmeasured and undocumented racial bias may be just as much – or more – a component of untested clinical forecasting than of a statistical model in which race contributes a little to forecasting accuracy. The democratic virtue of a statistical forecast is that it is transparent and debatable" (Berk et al., 2009: 207).

In other words, if our prediction algorithm and associated data are transparent, they may contain less implicit bias than the subjective judgments of operational police officers or crime analysts. Of course, care should always be taken to think about the types of data that are fed into the prediction engine. For example, it is inadvisable to include the locations of drug arrests because these are generated by police activity more than public complaints and can result in a self-fulfilling prophecy of police targeting an area because they have previously targeted that location. Avoiding the use of police-generated data can defend against some of the criticisms of systematic bias and racism. Relying on complaints from the public as input data can give predictive policing a victim-centered focus that is more democratic.

Furthermore, with regard to focused deterrence, Scott (2017: 21, emphasis added) notes that "*properly administered*, [focused deterrence] can not only escape charges of unfairness but also be perceived as extraordinarily fair, even to the individuals being targeted for attention. When this occurs, overall police–community relations and the public's belief in the legitimacy of the police stand to improve." Properly administered, the targeting of offenders can be based on transparent, objective, and documented criteria established prior to the identification of any person. In essence, a community could agree the terms by which individuals are targeted prior to any police intervention. A key element is therefore transparency in the data, the algorithms, and the overall system.

Lack of Transparency

Continuing this theme of transparency, another concern has been that "a lack of transparency about predictive policing systems prevents a meaningful, well-informed public debate" (ACLU, 2016). This is a legitimate criticism. It certainly doesn't help when evaluators of one predictive policing project noted in a footnote, "The software company refused to give information to the police department about the algorithm employed. The only information provided is that up to two years of past data on the type, time and place of incidents were employed" (Galiani & Jaitman, 2017).

When my colleagues and I developed the PROVE predictive policing software with Azavea and funding from the federal government, we were all adamant that the software, the theories, and our methods would be transparent and publicly available. Likewise, the originators of programs such as Risk

Terrain Modeling and HunchLab have been transparent about the data, theories, and methods they use to generate crime area forecasts.

This transparency is particularly important when software programs use demographic information to predict crime victimization. Demographic indicators related to race and ethnicity, such as the percentage of residents in a census area who are not white, are rife with social meaning dependent on context. Within the community criminology setting, racial composition appears to be a reliable indicator of violent and property crime outcomes (Peterson & Krivo, 2010; Taylor et al., 2015). But what is this saying? Race and socioeconomic status are two of the more reliable indicators, but, as stated earlier, they are proxy measures more reflective of decades of structural inequality. For the residents of those communities, this is an indicator of a historical lack of fairness and equity accessing economic, political, and educational opportunities and equivalency. Predicting crime victimization says a great deal about vulnerability and nothing about offender demographics or characteristics.

In Berk and colleagues' probation and parole models, removing race from consideration increases the error in the Philadelphia probation and parole data by about 2 percent (Berk et al., 2009), and the race variable is not selected in the PROVE geographic prediction software by default (the user has to explicitly choose to include it). Adding the variable in both cases would improve the predictive ability of the algorithms but if at the price of the legitimacy of the organizational entity or the criminal justice system, then that might not be a price worth paying. Unlike with clinical or hybrid decision-making, at least administrators and voters can make an informed decision regarding the algorithms and data that are inputs for predictive policing algorithms.

One Criticism that is Usually Ignored

What is noticeable from the critiques of predictive policing (such as ACLU, 2016) is the absence of concern regarding what predictive policing is replacing. A computer program might be highly technical and a real understanding only available to an esoteric cabal of statisticians,[3] but it is at least replicable and – as long as publicly available – transparent. In other words, if you use a software algorithm to predict crime in a city, you should be able to learn how it works and, in most cases, choose to include (or not) factors of race, if those variables form part of the algorithm. Removing race from the subjective impressions of workers in the criminal justice system might be more challenging. It is certainly harder to confirm.

The predictive side of predictive policing is designed to improve the capacity of the criminal justice system to identify high-risk places and people, and to improve on the subjective and frequently untested estimates of practitioners

---

[3] If there is a more appropriate collective noun, I'm not aware of it.

such as crime analysts and probation and parole agents. While there is an argument that these individuals bring an experience to the role that is difficult for the software to replicate, they can also bring subjectivity, unconscious bias, and differing levels of experience. If they are new to the role they may lack any experience, or what experience they have gleaned is piecemeal and lacks a citywide perspective. This could result in them focusing on the areas they know rather than the most appropriate places and people. When researchers test their prediction algorithms against the work of crime analysts (for example Mohler et al., 2015, Ratcliffe and Kikuchi, in press) an appropriate question is how effective are the crime analysts on which the comparison is based? And what inadvertent biases do they bring to their analysis?

When comparisons have been made between the crime reduction associated with analyst predictions and crime reduction associated with predictive software, little difference has emerged. Scant predictive policing research exists outside developed countries, though a recent study from Montevideo, Uruguay, is a welcome exception (Galiani & Jaitman, 2017). After thirty-one weeks, the researchers concluded "we did not find that the predictive software introduced in the treated areas helped the police do a better job." There were no significant differences in crime level between the precincts patrolling with crime analyst predictions and precincts with algorithmic software predictions.

Does this mean that the software isn't any good, or does it mean that the crime analysts are really effective? Are they tapping into the same data in the same way? Or are there significant differences between the predictions that are washed out because of inefficiencies in the police tactics? These questions were not answered in the research, but demonstrate the challenges of working in this emerging research area. There are simply more questions about predictive policing than we can answer in one go.

FINAL CONSIDERATIONS

I have previously argued that a problem with evaluating predictive policing is, "The efficacy of crime predictions are conflated with the policing response. If a police department adopts a predictive policing strategy but crime does not drop, is this a failure of the predictive algorithm, the choice of response tactic, or the implementation of the response?" (Ratcliffe, 2014: 5). You could replace "predictive algorithm" with "crime analysis" or "probation analysis" and the question remains valid. The difference is that the software algorithm is predictable and usually (outside certain proprietary programs) open for discussion and scientific inquiry.

Probation agents, parole officers, crime analysts, police officers, judges, and just about everyone working in the criminal justice system bring some desire to improve justice and safety. Any biases or errors they introduce to the process are rarely intentional and are frequently the result of differential experiences and exposure to diverse opportunities and situations. Inherently, we recognize this and see in others dissimilar levels of professional experience. It's rare that we take the next step and consider what impact that has on crime and criminal forecasts. But it is this variance in clinical decision-making that has the potential to introduce inaccuracies, inefficiencies, and inequalities into the criminal justice system. The accuracy of crime forecasts across a variety of people and platforms is just one of many areas of policing that has yet to be subjected to rigorous inquiry and scientific study.

Beyond the potential for an improvement in efficiency and accuracy, there is also the opportunity for enhancements to police legitimacy. General patrol inevitably draws police to areas with more non-criminal places and non-offending individuals. Conducting traffic stops and pedestrian investigations of innocent individuals attracts criticism and damages the reputation of police departments. It damages perceptions of police legitimacy and harms community relations. By increasing precision, as long as the analysis is conducted efficiently, predictive policing has the potential to center police on the highest crime areas and most likely offenders.

The field of predictive policing is still under development. Ultimately, we may not see a conflict between a clinical and an actuarial model but rather end up with a hybrid model where crime predictions are recommended to decision-makers who adjust them as necessary or as they see fit (as recommended by Ratcliffe & Kikuchi, in press). That might be a way to retain a human element in the analytical process, as long as we acknowledge that the human element can introduce not only perspective and context, but also bias and error.

To get there, we have to address a number of fundamental concerns that challenge our comfort levels.

- How do we feel about law enforcement taking a proactive role in crime prevention and interdiction rather than just reacting to crime that has been reported?
- Can we accept that some predictive analysis will be inaccurate? Or that it will lack "a human touch"?
- How comfortable are we moving from a clinical or a hybrid model of crime forecasting to an actuarial one?
- How at ease are we with the frequent lack of transparency in assessing crime analysis as it currently stands, and arguably, a lack of accountability?

Reactive policing has a simple certainty to it. Responding to and investigating crime that has happened brings police into contact with the public in situations when they have called and want police attendance. It is specific and targeted, but also reactive. By the time police know where to go, it is too late. As such, there is no evidence that this standard model of policing (reactive investigations and rapid response to calls for service) is anything other than inefficient and ineffective (Weisburd & Eck, 2004). Forecasting crime and criminality and being proactive with these forecasts carries the potential for increased community safety, but also a possibility of sometimes incorrectly targeting places and people. The move from a deterministic inefficiency to a potentially beneficial stochastic efficiency will have to be managed carefully by criminal justice agency managers. But any improvement has to be welcome, and as we move into more open data-driven times, is arguably inevitable. The Philadelphia Predictive Policing Experiment should not be the last word on how we can harness the power of better data analysis with a focused policing response. Hopefully, continued learning and exploring of different strategies will lead to an emergence of new approaches to old crime problems.

REFERENCES

ACLU. (2016, August 31). *Predictive Policing Today: A Shared Statement of Civil Rights Concerns*, 2.

Berk, R. (2008). Forecasting methods in crime and justice. *Annual Review of Law and Social Science*, 4, 219–238.

Berk, R., Sherman, L. W., Barnes, G., Kurtz, E., & Ahlman, L. (2009). Forecasting murder within a population of probationers and parolees: A high stakes application of statistical learning. *Journal of the Royal Statistical Society, Series A*, 172(1), 191–211.

Braga, A. A., Papachristos, A., & Hureau, D. (2012). *Hot Spots Policing Effects on Crime*. Campbell Systematic Reviews: Campbell Collaboration.

Braga, A. A., & Weisburd, D. L. (2012). *The Effects of Pulling Levers Focused Deterrence Strategies on Crime*. Campbell Systematic Reviews: Campbell Collaboration.

Caplan, J. M., Kennedy, L. W., & Miller, J. (2011). Risk terrain modeling: Brokering criminological theory and GIS methods for crime forecasting. *Justice Quarterly*, 28 (2), 381.

Chainey, S., & Ratcliffe, J. H. (2005). *GIS and Crime Mapping*. London: John Wiley and Sons.

Drawve, G. (2016). A metric comparison of predictive hot spot techniques and RTM. *Justice Quarterly*, 33(3), 369–397.

Farrington, D. P. (1987). Predicting individual crime rates. *Crime and Justice*, 9, 55–101.

Felson, M. (1987). Routine activities and crime prevention in the developing metropolis. *Criminology*, 25(4), 911–932.

Galiani, S., & Jaitman, L. (2017). *Predictive policing in a developing country: Experimental evidence from two randomized controlled trials*. Washington, DC: Inter-American Development Bank. Retrieved from https://papers.ssrn.com/sol3/papers.cfm?abstract_id=3009748.

Gorr, W., Olligschlaeger, A., & Thompson, Y. (2003). Short-term forecasting of crime. *International Journal of Forecasting*, 19(4), 594.

Gorr, W. L., & Lee, Y. (2015). Early warning system for temporary crime hot spots. *Journal of Quantitative Criminology*, 31(1), 25–47.

Innes, M. (2004). Reinventing tradition? Reassurance, neighbourhood security and policing. *Criminal Justice*, 4(2), 151–171.

Johnson, S. D., Bernasco, W., Bowers, K. J., Elffers, H., Ratcliffe, J. H., Rengert, G. F., & Townsley, M. (2007). Space-time patterns of risk: A cross national assessment of residential burglary victimization. *Journal of Quantitative Criminology*, 23(3), 201–219.

Johnson, S. D., Bowers, K. J., Birks, D., & Pease, K. (2009). Predictive mapping of crime by ProMap: Accuracy, units of analysis and the environmental backcloth. In D. Weisburd, W. Bernasco, & G. J. N. Bruinsma (eds.), *Putting Crime in Its Place: Units of Analysis in Geographic Criminology* (pp. 171–198). New York: Springer-Verlag.

Kelling, G. L., Pate, T., Dieckman, D., & Brown, C. E. (1974). *The Kansas City Preventative Patrol Experiment: A Summary Report.* Washington, DC: The Police Foundation.

Kennedy, L. W., Caplan, J. M., & Piza, E. (2011). Risk clusters, hotspots, and spatial intelligence: Risk terrain modeling as an algorithm for police resource allocation strategies. *Journal of Quantitative Criminology, 27*(3), 362.

Lee, Y., Eck, J. E., O, S., & Martinez, N. N. (2017). How concentrated is crime at places? A systematic review from 1970 to 2015. *Crime Science, 6*(6), 1–16.

Macbeth, E., & Ariel, B. (2017). Place-based statistical versus clinical predictions of crime hot spots and harm locations in Northern Ireland. *Justice Quarterly,* 1–34.

Martinez, N. N., Lee, Y., Eck, J. E., & O, S. (2017). Ravenous wolves revisited: A systematic review of offending concentration. *Crime Science, 6*(10), 1–16.

Mohler, G. O., Short, M. B., Brantingham, P. J., Schoenberg, F. P., & Tita, G. E. (2011). Self-exciting point process modeling of crime. *Journal of the American Statistical Association, 106*(493), 108.

Mohler, G. O., Short, M. B., Malinowski, S., Johnson, M., Tita, G. E., Bertozzi, A. L., & Brantingham, P. J. (2015). Randomized controlled field trials of predictive policing. *Journal of the American Statistical Association, 110*(512), 1399–1411.

Moreto, W. D., Piza, E. L., & Caplan, J. M. (2014). "A plague on both your houses?": Risks, repeats and reconsiderations of urban residential burglary. *Justice Quarterly, 31*(6), 1102–1126.

National Research Council. (2004). Fairness and Effectiveness in Policing: The Evidence W. Skogan, & K. Frydl (eds.). Washington, DC: Committee to Law and Justice, Division of Behavioral and Social Sciences and Education.

Perry, W. L., McInnis, B., Price, C. C., Smith, S. C., & Hollywood, J. S. (2013). *Predictive Policing: The Role of Crime Forecasting in Law Enforcement Operations.* Washington, DC: Rand Corporation.

Peterson, R. D., & Krivo, L. J. (2010). *Divergent Social Worlds: Neighborhood Crime and the Racial-Spatial Divide.* New York: Russell Sage.

Ratcliffe, J. H. (2012). The spatial extent of criminogenic places: A change-point regression of violence around bars. *Geographical Analysis, 44*(4), 302–320.

Ratcliffe, J. H. (2014). What is the future … of predictive policing? Translational Criminology, (Spring), 4–5.

Ratcliffe, J.H., & Kikuchi, G. (in press). Harm-focused offender triage and prioritization: a Philadelphia case study. Policing: An International Journal.

Ratcliffe, J. H., & McCullagh, M. J. (2001). Chasing ghosts? Police perception of high crime areas. *British Journal of Criminology, 41*(2), 330–341.

Ratcliffe, J. H., & Rengert, G. F. (2008). Near repeat patterns in Philadelphia shootings. *Security Journal, 21*(1–2), 58–76.

Ratcliffe, J. H., Taniguchi, T., Groff, E. R., & Wood, J. D. (2011). The Philadelphia Foot Patrol Experiment: A randomized controlled trial of police patrol effectiveness in violent crime hotspots. *Criminology, 49*(3), 795–831.

Ratcliffe, J. H., & Taylor, R. B. (2017). *The Philadelphia Predictive Policing Experiment: Summary of the Experimental Design*. Philadelphia, PA: Temple University. bit.ly/CSCS_3PE.

Ratcliffe, J. H., Taylor, R. B., & Askey, A. P. (2017). *The Philadelphia Predictive Policing Experiment: Effectiveness of the Prediction Models*. Philadelphia, PA: Temple University. bit.ly/CSCS_3PE.

Ratcliffe, J. H., Taylor, R. B., Askey, A. P., Grasso, J., & Fisher, R. (2017). *The Philadelphia Predictive Policing Experiment: Impacts of Police Cars Assigned to High Crime Grids*. Philadelphia, PA: Temple University. bit.ly/CSCS_3PE.

Reyes, J. (2016, September 16). Philadelphia is grappling with the prospect of a racist computer algorithm. *Technically Philly*. Retrieved from https://technical.ly/philly/2016/09/16/jails-risk-assessment-richard-berk/.

Rosenbaum, D. P. (2006). The limits of hot spots policing. In D. Weisburd, & A. A. Braga (eds.), *Police Innovation: Contrasting Perspectives* (pp. 245–263). New York: Cambridge University Press.

Rummens, A., Hardyns, W., & Pauwels, L. (2017). The use of predictive analysis in spatiotemporal crime forecasting: Building and testing a model in an urban context. *Applied Geography*, 86, 255–261.

Scott, M. S. (2017). *Focused deterrence of high-risk individuals* (13). Problem-Oriented Guides for Police: Response Guides Series: Washington, DC.

Sherman, L. W., Gartin, P., & Buerger, M. E. (1989). Hot spots of predatory crime: Routine activities and the criminology of place. *Criminology*, 27(1), 27–55.

Sherman, L. W., & Weisburd, D. (1995). General deterrent effects of police patrol in crime "hot spots": A randomized, controlled trial. *Justice Quarterly*, 12(4), 625–648.

Sherman, L. W., Williams, S., Ariel, B., Strang, L. R., Wain, N., Slothower, M., & Norton, A. (2014). An integrated theory of hot spots patrol strategy: Implementing prevention by scaling up and feeding back. *Journal of Contemporary Criminal Justice*, 30(2), 95–112.

Taylor, B., Koper, C. S., & Woods, D. J. (2011). A randomized controlled trial of different policing strategies at hot spots of violent crime. *Journal of Experimental Criminology*, 7(2), 149–181.

Taylor, R. B., Ratcliffe, J. H., & Perenzin, A. (2015). Can we predict long-term community crime problems? The estimation of ecological continuity to model risk heterogeneity. *Journal of Research in Crime and Delinquency*, 52(5), 635–657.

Townsley, M., Homel, R., & Chaseling, J. (2003). Infectious burglaries: A test of the near repeat hypothesis. *British Journal of Criminology*, 43(3), 615–633.

Weisburd, D. (2015). The law of crime concentration and the criminology of place. *Criminology*, 53(2), 133–157.

Weisburd, D. (2016). Does hot spots policing inevitably lead to unfair and abusive police practices, or can we maximize both fairness and effectiveness in the new proactive policing? *University of Chicago Legal Forum*, Article 16.

Weisburd, D., & Eck, J. (2004). What can police do to reduce crime, disorder, and fear? *The Annals of the American Academy of Political and Social Science*, 593(1), 43–65.

Weisburd, D., & Majmundar, M. K. (eds.). (2018). *Proactive Policing: Effects on Crime and Communities*. Washington, DC: National Academies of Sciences Consensus Study Report.

16

Critic

Predictive Policing: Where's the Evidence?

Rachel Boba Santos

INTRODUCTION

Crime analysis is a field of study and practice in criminal justice that utilizes various data sources and analytical techniques to support crime prevention, crime reduction, and criminal apprehension efforts of police agencies (International Association of Crime Analysts [IACA], 2014). Crime mapping is a subset of crime analysis that focuses on understanding the geographic nature of crime and other activity and presents results to a wide range of police audiences through published maps (Santos, 2017). Although there have been crime analysts in police departments since the early 1970s (Austin et al., 1973) and researchers who have analyzed crime for centuries (Weisburd & McEwen, 1997), there has been a notable increase in the last twenty years of police agencies implementing crime analysis, purchasing analytical technology and software, and hiring in-house qualified individuals to conduct analysis – crime analysts.

A national survey conducted by the Police Executive Research Forum found that of the 600 randomly selected local police agencies stratified by agency size, type, and geography, that 89 percent either employed a full-time crime analyst or had a staff member whose secondary responsibility was conducting crime analysis (Santos & Taylor, 2014). An examination of the most recent (2013) Law Enforcement Management and Administrative Statistics (LEMAS) shows that crime analysis is becoming common, particularly in medium and large agencies (Bureau of Justice Statistics, 2018). Of the 2,528 agencies surveyed that employed civilian staff, 40 percent (1,130) had civilian employees who performed research, statistics, or crime analysis duties, and an overwhelming majority of those agencies (75 percent) were agencies with more than fifty officers.

In terms of technology, particularly crime mapping software, Weisburd and Lum (2005) illustrate how there was a steep growth curve in the use of computerized crime mapping in police agencies from the late 1980s through the 1990s. While there has been no national survey on crime mapping technology since 1997 (Mamalian & LaVigne, 1997), crime-mapping software is an industry standard in crime analysis. In the last fifteen years, a large number of software solutions have been developed specifically for crime analysis, many of which are based in a geographic information system.

The crime analysis field within policing is relatively new, and it faces a number of challenges, many of which are a direct result of its infancy.[1] In the broadest sense, these challenges are the quantity and quality of data; development of evidence-based crime analysis techniques (i.e., those based in, and tested, by research); recruiting, hiring, and training crime analysts; and the effective use of crime analysis products to guide police operations (Santos, 2017). Even though desktop geographic information systems software, and a handful of other software programs, have been used by crime analysts since the early 1990s (Weisburd & McEwen, 1997), it has been only in the last five to ten years that the federal government, academics, researchers, and private sector software companies have begun to focus on addressing these challenges. While crime analysts serve one another and the profession through training and networking, these other entities seek to improve crime analysis by providing technology and developing new advanced analytical techniques with corresponding software solutions.[2]

I believe this trend has occurred because providing technology and advanced techniques is less difficult for individuals and entities unfamiliar with the practical field of crime analysis. For example, it is straightforward for the federal government to provide police departments funding for geographic information systems or analytical technology. But it is more difficult and complex to assist police departments by educating a cadre of qualified applicants in undergraduate and graduate programs, hiring new analysts, training those in the field, and assisting crime analysts in their day-to-day work.[3]

---

[1] Because there is little research on the crime analysis field, this and other similar conclusions are based on my experience over the last twenty-four years as a local crime analyst, as Director of the Crime Mapping Laboratory at the Police Foundation in Washington, DC, and as an author, instructor, and researcher of crime analysis and evidence-based crime reduction practices.

[2] A review of the International Association of Crime Analysts (www.iaca.net) annual training conference agendas for the last twenty years, shows that many of the presentations (i.e., training) are from working or former crime analysts. The courses in IACA's training series are also primarily conducted by a similar cadre of instructors. Very few have been conducted by researchers, academics, and other established analysis experts.

[3] Seeking to improve the current crime analysis profession in terms of the abilities of crime analysts and the quality and effectiveness of their current methods requires a comprehensive effort. For example, *Crime Analysis with Crime Mapping* (Santos, 2017) is one of the first and only textbooks written specifically to educate college students and practitioners in the history and fundamental processes of crime analysis. The first edition was published in 2005, with three subsequent editions, and there are few, if any, other books on the market that seek to accomplish the same purpose. In addition, it was not until 2012 that the International Association of Crime Analysts

Similarly, it is less arduous for researchers to develop new analytical techniques outside the practical police and crime analysis environment. It takes time for researchers and academics to build relationships and assist police and crime analysts in their everyday operations. By simply requesting data from a police department, researchers can test statistical models based in theory in their own offices at the university with the help of graduate students. Finally, working with researchers or on their own, private companies are able to, independent of crime analysis standards and practice, create new software based on techniques borrowed from other fields and sell products as innovative alternatives to traditional crime analysis. These "off the shelf," more cursory solutions to improving crime analysis often appeal to government officials and police leaders who are looking to implement crime analysis quickly.

When federal funding has been allocated for analytical technology, most of the support has gone to crime mapping hardware and software, as well as spatial techniques, instead of to crime analysis more generally. From 1995 to 2002, the US Department of Justice's Office of Community Oriented Policing Services (COPS Office) directly allocated just over $53 million (ninety individual grants) in funding to crime mapping technology and staff (Santos, 2017). The National Institute of Justice (NIJ) established the Crime Mapping Research Center in 1997 employing full-time governmental staff to assist police departments with crime mapping and allocated millions of dollars for researchers to conduct spatial analysis to develop both techniques and software (National Institute of Justice [NIJ], 2018a). Yet, no funding was provided specifically for crime analysis technology, education for crime analysts, or testing of current crime analysis techniques until the Bureau of Justice Assistance (BJA) established its crime analysis portfolio in 2012. BJA allocated just over two million dollars to understanding the field, developing best practices, and training police executives in crime analysis (Bureau of Justice Assistance, 2018). To date, however, a national "crime analysis center" still does not exist.

Thus, the fundamental argument that frames this chapter is that a predominant trend in advancing the analysis of crime for police is to provide advanced analytical techniques and technological solutions directly to police departments and bypassing the field of crime analysis and crime analysts. Doing this is both simpler for police agencies to implement and more lucrative for those offering the assistance (both in publications for researchers and profit for

published a document on the review of crime analysis courses and programs offered in universities and colleges and recommendations for crime analysis education (IACA, 2012). They subsequently developed an advisory board for crime analysis education that has been slow to get off the ground. While the IACA has begun offering crime analysis training more frequently in recent years, there is no established training program and few standards for qualified instructors or curriculum. The IACA developed a certification program in the last ten years and have certified just seventy-two crime analysts (IACA, 2018) out of the over 2,500 members and thousands of other crime analysts in the United States and internationally.

software developers) than it is to work to improve the quality of crime analyst education and training or current practices in the field.

From my assessment of the policing and crime analysis fields, as well as the popular media, this new trend, in its many different forms (i.e., techniques and software), is being called "predictive policing" (Uchida, 2010). I will not argue in this chapter that developing advanced techniques and/or software specifically for crime analysis is problematic, because both are important and necessary for the field to progress and improve. However, I will critique the current and most prevalent practice of predictive policing as a warning that "quick and easy" ways of seeking to improve police crime analysis that are not supported by evidence-based research cannot result in more efficient or effective policing.

Consequently, this chapter begins with the definition and development of predictive policing followed by a description of the most common predictive policing analytical technique and how it is used by police. I will then present my criticisms of the technique, its application in police practice, and tests of effectiveness. Lastly, I will present some recommendations for improving predictive policing based on my critique.

However, before doing so, I want to emphasize at the outset of this chapter, that after doing an extensive search of research and academic literature on predictive policing, I have found very few publications that explore, describe, or evaluate predictive policing and its analytical or police practices. This is similar to the lack of research and academic publications for crime analysis more generally (Santos, 2017). Consequently, where possible, I discuss what I was able to find, but much of this chapter is based on my own research and experience in crime analysis and policing, as well as what I have found in less academically rigorous sources, such as newspaper and magazine articles.

DEFINITION AND DEVELOPMENT OF PREDICTIVE POLICING

Predictive policing has been defined as "the application of analytical techniques – particularly quantitative techniques – to identify likely targets for police intervention and prevent crime or solve past crimes by making statistical predictions" (Perry et al., 2013: xiii). Development of predictive policing has been supported by federal funding since 2010 (NIJ, 2010; 2018b) and is becoming widely implemented in its various forms in medium to large police agencies in the United States and internationally – for example, in Canada, Europe, South Korea, as well as countries in the Caribbean and South America. Its prevalence in police agencies is likely due to the nature of its development. This is why predictive policing is a new part in the second edition of this book, as the editors believe it is worthy of discussion and debate about its development and relevance to innovative policing.

The initial concept of predictive policing was introduced by William Bratton, formerly the NYPD Commissioner who created CompStat, one of the most significant innovations in policing in the last twenty-five years. At the end of his tenure as Chief of Police in LAPD, Bratton introduced what he called "COMPSTAT Plus" (Bratton & Malinowksi, 2008). Looking forward to the future of Compstat, he mentioned predictive policing for the first time in an academic journal opinion piece, "We [LAPD] will move from near real-time analysis to true real-time analysis and then to a 'predictive policing' posture wherein more accurate and reliable probability modeling will be utilized to forecast potential crime trends over an increasing time span" (Bratton & Malinowski, 2008: 264).

As a result of Bratton's inspiration and leadership, the LAPD partnered with professors at UCLA to develop specific analytical techniques to forecast crime incidents with the purpose of directing patrol officers to areas at high risk for crimes to occur during their shift (Bond-Graham & Winston, 2013; Goldsmith, 2014). With the touted success of LAPD and Chief Bratton standing behind the concept, from 2009 to 2013, the National Institute of Justice allocated 6.6 million dollars for defining, refining, and implementing predictive policing which included: (1) 1.2 million dollars for eight organizations (Boston, New York City, Chicago, Washington DC, Shreveport (LA), and Los Angeles police departments as well as the Los Angeles Police Foundation and Maryland State Police) to plan predictive policing models in their jurisdictions (NIJ, 2018c); (2) over 2 million dollars for Chicago and Shreveport police departments to carry out their predictive policing plans (NIJ, 2018d); (3) just over 1 million dollars for the RAND Corporation to provide analytical and research support to all the agencies through both phases (NIJ, 2018c); and (4) in 2013, around 2.4 million dollars to five research projects to "conduct studies on using geospatial strategies to improve policing" (NIJ, 2018b).

Since 2009, predictive policing has become common nomenclature when discussing crime analysis and police crime reduction efforts, and a critical mass of police agencies have purchased software and/or claim to have implemented or hope to implement predictive policing in some way.[4] In 2016, William Bratton (as NYPD commissioner), when asked about the current state of predictive policing, stated to a reporter, "Predictive policing used to be the future, and now it is the present" (Black, 2016a).

Yet, predictive policing is still in its infancy, and thus is being practiced a variety of ways in police agencies in the United States. The next sections cover the predominant way in which predictive policing is operationalized in police departments as reflected in the research conducted by the RAND corporation (Perry et al., 2013), several academic articles, more than a few newspaper

---

[4] There is currently no research as to the level of adoption, prevalence, or the nature of implementation of predictive policing on a large scale, so this is my own conclusion based on my experience and the research conducted for this chapter. Bond-Graham & Winston (2013), San Francisco investigative reporters, claimed after their intensive research that more than 150 police departments nationally were deploying predictive policing analytics at that time.

articles, and on my own research and work with crime analysts and police departments in the United States and internationally.

PREDICTIVE POLICING ANALYTICAL TECHNIQUES

According to research by RAND (Perry et al., 2013), predictive policing analytical methods are primarily focused on (1) predicting the spatial location of future crime, (2) predicting locations of offenders, (3) predicting perpetrators' identities, and (4) predicting victims of crime. In this chapter, I focus on the first method as this appears to be the method most implemented by police departments as a form of crime analysis and is predominant in the news media.[5] Notably, because this method is predicting the location of crime, the techniques are spatial and corresponding software is embedded into geographic information systems. This continues the trend of the 1990s in which police, the federal government, and software developers focus on crime mapping techniques and technology instead of the entire breadth of crime analysis.

In their examination of predictive policing methods, Perry et al. (2013) found that the four predictive methods utilize sophisticated analytical techniques with large datasets that can only be facilitated through computer software. In addition, the results generated come solely from the computer with little, if any, subsequent examination by an analyst (i.e., maps with predicted crime locations, lists of high risk offenders). The advanced techniques Perry and colleagues (2013) identified, in practice, included originally developed algorithms, risk terrain analysis, near repeat analysis, regression and cluster modeling, geographic profiling tools, and other data-mining techniques. These methods represent a clear distinction from traditional crime analysis techniques that include the analyst critically analyzing and making conclusions based on qualitative efforts such as reading crime and arrest reports, synthesizing intelligence, visually inspect maps, as well as using statistical and mapping techniques, such as percent change, linear regression, and density mapping (Santos, 2017).

There are a number of reputable criminological researchers with expertise in environmental criminology and/or geographic analysis of crime who have begun to develop and test several advanced methods and software for deploying police resources under the auspices of predictive policing, in particular risk terrain modeling (Kennedy, Caplan & Piza, 2011; Drawve & Barnum, 2017; Piza et al., 2017) and near repeat analysis (Johnson et al., 2009; Haberman & Ratcliffe, 2012). Although risk terrain modeling and near repeat analysis may, sometime in the near future, become more common in police practice, they are methods primarily being used by police for research projects

---

[5] I have a Google Alert for "predictive policing" and for the last several years I receive seven to ten alerts a week about predictive policing being implemented in police agencies in the United States and internationally, being criticized, or being advertised.

and have not been integrated into police operations and/or lauded in practitioner conferences or in the media.

On the other hand, a third method is arguably synonymous with predictive policing as its technique has no other name, and its method is represented as predictive policing in the news media as well as in practitioner publications and conferences.[6] In addition, this method has been operationalized into several proprietary software programs that are marketed, sold, and used by many police agencies in the United States and internationally (Bond-Graham & Winston, 2013; Goldsmith, 2014; Benbouzid, 2016). In fact, this method is the technique developed by the researchers at UCLA in partnership with the Los Angeles Police Department and was initial manifestation of predictive policing introduced by Police Chief Bratton (Mohler et al., 2011).

The purpose of this predictive policing analytical technique is to forecast individual crimes in the immediate future in order to direct patrol officers into 500-by-500 foot areas (i.e., boxes) that are at a higher risk of a crime occurring during a particular eight, ten, or twelve-hour shift. Unlike hot spots policing, where long-term hot spots are identified and patrol resources are directed into those areas for a period of several months or longer in order to stop the long-term trend (i.e., many crimes) from continuing (Braga, Papachristos & Hureau, 2014), the objective of this technique is to inform response for the next shift in a small area in order to stop a single crime from happening. For this predictive policing technique, new predictions are created for each shift and may or may not occur in the same 500-by-500 foot areas. The crime reduction objective is for the police officers to respond to the predicted areas multiple times during that shift moving from one area to another between citizen-generated calls for service.

While there are a number of software companies that create similar results, the original algorithm was developed with Los Angeles data and was modeled on seismic aftershock theory that utilizes a self-exciting point process to forecast crime in the immediate future (Mohler et al., 2011). In a recent article that tested the method in two agencies, Los Angeles and Kent, UK, Mohler et al. (2015) use 365 days of data for their ETAS (Epidemic Type Aftershock Sequence) model in which hot spots are estimated from the crime data itself using a stationary Poisson process. The model accounts for "near repeat" or "contagion" effects by computing an exponential decay so that artificially constructed 500-by-500 foot grid cells containing more recent crime events are weighted relatively more than those with fewer recent events (Mohler et al., 2015: 9). The authors state that the ETAS model estimates both long-term and short-term hot spots and their relative contribution to overall risk of a future crime. The model itself is based on earthquake aftershocks in that the "the rate of crime increases locally in space, leading to a contagious sequence of 'aftershock' crimes that eventually

---

[6] From the Google Alerts for "Predictive Policing" over the last several years, I would estimate over 95 percent of the articles have to do with police practice related to this method.

dies out on its own, or is interrupted by police intervention" (Mohler et al., 2015: 10). The method can be applied to different types of crime separately and uses three crime data variables – location, date, and time of the reported crime.

The results of the analysis are created by the software program with no interpretation from a crime analyst since the analysis occurs at the front end. The resulting analytical product is a map of the study area (e.g., beat, neighborhood, districts, or entire jurisdiction) with 500-by-500 foot boxes marked that indicate areas at a "higher risk" for a crime incident in the immediate future (i.e., next few hours) (Mohler et al., 2015). The 500-by-500 foot boxes do not follow any particular geographic feature of a jurisdiction. They are based on an arbitrary grid that the software places over the entire study area to conduct the analysis, similar to the procedure for density mapping (Santos, 2017). The grid size, in this case, was chosen by these researchers to model a city block in the Foothill District of Los Angeles. They use this same sized box for Kent, UK, as well as other jurisdictions where the model has been applied (PredPol, 2018a). In this study, the most recent LAPD crime data were uploaded into the software every day, and maps were generated twice a day for two twelve-hour patrol shifts (Mohler et al., 2015).

A proprietary software program called "PredPol" was subsequently developed and is based on the algorithm used for LAPD (PredPol, 2018a). However, it is not clear from the published research and the software's website whether the software product uses the exact method described in the academic articles. In addition, there are other software companies that have subsequently developed proprietary software products with similar functionalities (i.e., producing maps predicting a crime incident in small boxes within a patrol shift).[7] However, their analytical methods are currently not published in academic journals nor on their websites so cannot be described here.

PREDICTIVE POLICING IMPLEMENTATION

To implement this form of predictive policing, a police department purchases a subscription to the software that is housed on a private server of the software company and allows the company to access the police data directly (Bond-Graham & Winston, 2013; Jackson, 2015; Motorola, 2018; PredPol, 2018a). The software company or police agency personnel prints maps with the 500-by-500 foot boxes for each shift that are distributed to managers or directly to officers in patrol briefings. In either case, officers are then directed to respond in the boxes during their uncommitted time (i.e., when they are not answering service calls) (Bond-Graham & Winston, 2013; Mohler et al., 2015).

---

[7] As of this writing, well-known and large companies such as Motorola (2018), IBM (2017), and Hunchlab (2017) offer similar products. There are a variety of lesser-known companies that are attempting to enter the market as well.

The tactics carried out in the boxes are not clearly defined in practice: for example, in LAPD they were told to just "go to the box" (Mohler et al., 2015). From my experience and observation of police departments with the software, the expectations by police leaders are similar to those of hot spots policing. Patrol officers are to conduct standard patrol techniques and be present periodically in the predicted areas to have a deterrent effect and prevent the predicted crime incident. Ideally, an officer might even observe a crime about to be committed and seek to prevent it or stop it in progress. The predictions are often computed separately by general category of crime (i.e., violent versus property) or by specific crime type (i.e., street robbery, residential burglary). Ideally, different responses could be developed and implemented based on the type of crime.

In terms of diffusion of these predictive policing practices, obviously, LAPD has implemented the approach in this form in some of its districts and has been lauded as a success story by the department itself and the PredPol software company. This execution of predictive policing has been implemented in slightly different forms throughout the United States as well as internationally as evidenced in my research of news articles from around the world. A simple query on Google today on "predictive policing" reveals a plethora of newspaper articles since 2009 about police agencies that have implemented predictive policing. In my conversations with police chiefs, even those who have not yet implemented predictive policing refer to the process described here as the implementation they hope to achieve.

CRITIQUE OF PREDOMINANT PREDICTIVE POLICING PRACTICE

As a researcher and former crime analyst, I am ecstatic about the attention that crime analysis has received in recent years from police leaders, government officials, federal funding sources, and software developers. The field of crime analysis is still young and is in need of professionalization in terms of the positions themselves as well as establishing standards and practices. The concerns with the implementation of predictive policing that I lay out in this section are not unique to predictive policing. I have had the same concerns about crime analysis over the years and have written about the development and use of evidence-based practices specific to clarifying definitions, addressing data quality, developing software, evaluating techniques, and applying relevant analysis for police crime reduction efforts (Santos, 2014; 2017).

My critique follows the form of the previous section, focusing on the definition and development of predictive policing, its techniques and software, and its implementation in police departments. Again, my critique draws from a limited amount of academic literature, some news articles, and much of my own experience and research. In the 2013 report that describes the field of predictive policing, Perry and colleagues laid out a number of pitfalls in the predictive policing approach based on research funded by the National Institute of

Justice's predictive policing portfolio, so those ideas are woven throughout the discussion where relevant.

The "Predictive Policing" Label

In 2012, Haberman and Ratcliffe concluded, "Predictive policing, while remaining largely undefined, is still mostly an analytical challenge and curiosity for crime analysts and computational scientists" (2012: 164). Six years later, however, there is a critical mass of police agencies, federal funding, software companies, and the media that have publicized predictive policing to the point that it dominates the conversation in both crime analysis and police crime reduction. The National Academy of Sciences report on proactive policing has recognized predictive policing as a place-based policing strategy along with hot spots policing (Weisburd & Majmundar, 2018). The panel acknowledges that "predictive policing overlaps with hot spots policing but is generally distinguished by its reliance on sophisticated analytics that are used to predict likelihood of crime incidence within very specific parameters of space and time and for very specific types of crime" (Weisburd & Majmundar, 2018: 36).

Yet, I would argue Haberman and Ratcliffe's conclusion that predictive policing is not clearly defined is still true in terms of its fundamental characteristic – advanced analytics. Even further, this lack of clarity has given police departments, software companies, and others the opportunity to label whatever they are doing as advanced analytics and predictive.[8] The label of "predictive policing" has come to represent proactive, innovative, and a "smart" way of policing using popular rhetoric from the business and technology sectors – "analytics" (Beck & McCue, 2009). Unlike hot spots policing and problem-oriented policing that have specific processes and practices as well as a foundation of evidence based in research (Weisburd & Majmundar, 2018), at this point in time, predictive policing is simply a label used for a variety of analytical practices used to direct a variety of police tactics rather than a comprehensive, evidence-based policing approach to crime reduction.

In fact, I have previously argued that predictive policing is not a policing approach at all but is synonymous with crime analysis, since what is unique is its use of "advanced" methods of predicting future crime, which is what crime analysis does as well (Santos, 2014). In truth, a more appropriate label might be "predictive crime analysis." Even so, most crime analysis is already predictive. So, the question becomes whether predictive policing is a distinct police crime reduction approach or is just an extension of crime analysis, and thus should be

---

[8] I have worked with several agencies that say they are doing predictive policing and once I speak with personnel and observe what they are doing, I see they essentially have hired a crime analyst to do basic crime analysis and nothing more.

treated as such. The following sections delve deeper into these distinctions and their critiques.

Transparency and Academic Rigor of Analytical Techniques

Because predictive policing is primarily manifested in the use of advanced analytics, the most important criticism of the current predictive policing methods is twofold – the lack of transparency and the lack of academic rigor. Both of these are fundamental tenets of evidence-based policing (Sherman, 1998). The first issue of transparency concerns the public availability of the specific predictive analytical techniques. In their research of predictive policing methods, Perry et al. (2013) conclude that the "predictive tools are designed in a way that makes it difficult, if not impossible, to highlight the risk factors present in specific areas" (p. xxi). In my research for this chapter and knowledge of crime analysis and predictive policing methods and technology over the last ten years, I have been unable to find documentation in academic journals, trade journals, practitioner magazines, or on software websites explaining the exact data, formulas, and procedures carried out by the major predictive policing software programs that have been purchased by police departments.

Even though Mohler and colleagues (2011; 2015) describe their formulas in several academic articles published in non-criminological statistical journals, there are important details that are not provided (e.g., whether report date or occurrence date is used; how data quality is managed for such large databases). In addition, the major private-for-profit companies that provide the analytical software to police do not want to share their "secrets" with competitors, so the methods have not been published or provided to customers.[9]

The lack of transparency affects policing and crime analysis in a number of important ways. First, independent researchers are not able to duplicate the methods using different data or test the methods for accuracy (further discussion in next section). Second, crime analysts and police departments cannot determine if the models being applied to their data are actually relevant to their own jurisdiction's environment and levels of crime before or even after they have purchased access to the software. And third, police leaders are spending significant amounts of money on software and subsequently directing their limited resources without knowing how the predictions were developed or what they really mean.

Related to transparency is the lack of academic rigor of these methods. The purpose of the academic process of peer review and publication is for ideas and techniques to be evaluated and tested by other researchers in the field. Empirical

---

[9] A lesser-known company, CivicScape, released its algorithm and data online in March 2017 for experts to evaluate (Miller, 2017). This may or may not become a trend, but at this time none of the major providers for predictive policing software has done the same.

generalizations and evidence-based practices can only come about after a myriad of studies are conducted under a variety of circumstances. Even though predictive policing came about nearly ten years ago, there are only a few academic publications about the techniques used to predict the 500-by-500 foot boxes, most of which are not published in criminology or criminal justice journals.

Mohler et al. (2011) is the foundation for one proprietary software program and was published in a non-criminological statistical journal. I have been unable to find peer-reviewed publications for methods used in the other proprietary software programs. Interestingly, the less popular predictive policing methods mentioned at the outset of the chapter (i.e., risk terrain modeling and near repeat analysis) that have been developed by criminological researchers are published in peer-reviewed criminology and criminal justice journals and are operationalized into free, non-proprietary software (Johnson et al., 2009; Ratcliffe, 2009; Haberman & Ratcliffe, 2012; Caplan, Kennedy, & Piza, 2013; Kennedy et al., 2015; Piza et al., 2016; Drawve & Barnum, 2017).

In conclusion, the main issue with both transparency and academic rigor is that if the police department is paying for a product that does not require a trained analyst, at a minimum, the department should know the exact method being used, how it has been evaluated by experts in the field, and its prediction accuracy. The police profession is becoming more sophisticated and using evidence-based practices is paramount to improving the quality and effectiveness of police crime reduction efforts.

Applicability of Analytical Models

My first criticism related to the predictive policing analytical models is the quality of the crime data used, which is mentioned as a pitfall by Perry et al. (2013). That is, the data is based on reported crime and is subject to victim reporting rates, the imperfect report writing by officers, as well as data collection and quality assurance procedures of each police department. Issues, such as date and time accuracy, geographic accuracy and completeness (i.e., all crimes are mapped), and consistent use of crime codes, are only some of the many data quality concerns that are faced by crime analysts on a daily basis (Santos, 2017), and therefore, by predictive policing as well.

Specific to predictive policing techniques, coding of variables, systematic errors, and other factors may systematically bias the data and may not be transparent in an automatic transfer and analysis of large amounts of data. In fact, officers in one agency complained that "silly" locations like the police department continually come up on the predictive policing maps (Tchekmedyian, 2016). Issues of quality of reported crime data as well as other data used by crime analysis (i.e., calls for service, arrests, and crashes) is unavoidable, which is why it is very common for crime analysts to manually assess their data to ensure their analytical results are accurate. In fact, doing this is a formal step in the crime analysis process called the "data modification sub-cycle" which is the ongoing assessment and improvement of crime analysis data (Santos, 2017: 92–95).

Continual assessment of data quality is difficult when doing automated analysis of large amounts of data, so data integrity issues are even more salient for predictive policing techniques, especially when the most current data (i.e., from the previous day) are included. That is, there are often changes and updates to aspects of a crime after the initial report, especially in the first several days. In addition, predictive policing analytical methods that identify 500-by-500 foot boxes only rely on crime data and more specifically, only three variables within that data – date, time, and location (Jackson, 2015; Motorola, 2018; PredPol, 2018a). Understandably, these are variables that nearly all crime incident databases contain, so an analytical model based on these variables can be used by any police agency with electronic crime data. However, using only date, time, and location of the crime ignores other very important contextual factors such as modus operandi, type of location where the crime occurred, and the qualitative aspects of the crime contained in the report narrative. In addition, the models do not account for arrests, calls for service activity, field intelligence collected by officers, or other types of information used by crime analysts on a daily basis to prioritize and enhance their crime analysis results (Santos, 2017).

That being said, there are particular issues using date and time of the reported crime to predict future occurrences of crime. The first issue is whether these methods consider the reported date or the occurrence date of the crime. These two dates are often not the same, especially for property crime, as citizens may not discover the crime right away, so will report the crime several days after it has occurred. It is not clear which variable these methods use because of the lack of transparency.

The second issue is that exact date and time data are not available for certain types of crimes (typically property crimes) where specific information is not known (i.e., someone broke into my house between 7:00 AM and 5:00 PM when I was at work). Thus, any predictive policing technique must reconcile time span data, and whatever method is used will influence the nature of the predictions. For example, one method for examining time span uses the "split time" to determine when the crime occurred. This method creates one value (i.e., midpoint of the time span) from two (i.e., the beginning and end of the time span). This method is not used in crime analysis because it does not represent the beginning and end or the length of the time span, so the results provide little relevant information. That is, a time span beginning at 4:00 PM and ending at 12:00 AM (eight hours) is very different than one from 7:00 PM to 9:00 PM (two hours) and one from 10 AM to 6 AM the next day (twenty hours), even though they all share the midpoint ("split time") of 8:00 PM. Split time estimates are even more inaccurate for time spans that are longer than twenty-four hours.

Instead, crime analysts use the weighted time span technique for this type of analysis that accounts for both aspects of time spans (Santos, 2017). What method do predictive policing models employ? My guess is that they create a single value (e.g., split time) in order to easily incorporate it into a multivariate analysis. Regardless, the methods are not transparent, so we cannot answer this question for most predictive policing techniques. Also, this issue is particularly salient for predictive policing, not only because time of day is one of only three variables used, but also because the forecasts being made are for the immediate future (i.e., next eight, ten, or twelve-hour shift).

More broadly, there are concerns about the applicability of the analytical models to crime. The predominant form of predictive policing analysis and popular software program uses a model based on seismic aftershock theory (Mohler et al., 2011). In 2016, Bilel Benbouzid, a lecturer at the University of Paris, sought to investigate Mohler and his colleagues' application of earthquake methods to crime prediction. He contacted David Marsan, a professor at the earth sciences laboratory at the University of Savoie, in Chambéry, France, who specializes in the study of earthquake aftershocks and developed the algorithm used by Mohler et al. (2011; 2015). Marsan agreed to test his algorithm using data from Chicago, particularly for burglaries, and draws the following conclusion:

These results cast strong doubts on the capacity of the models proposed here to outperform simple hotspot maps obtained by smoothing, for the dataset analyzed. The triggering contribution to the occurrence of future events is small (it accounts only for 1.7% for the best model). Accounting for memory in the system therefore can only provide a very modest contribution to the effectiveness of the prediction scheme. More importantly, it is assumed that the dynamics of the process stays the same over time. Possible nonstationarity of the process is thus clearly an issue, as it will prevent the use of past information to predict the future. This is for example experienced in this analysis, as 2015 burglary events are clearly not distributed (in time and in space) as they were in 2014. This non stationarity [sic] is likely due to uncontrolled evolutions in the way these acts are performed, but, in situations where new prediction algorithms are set up and exploited by police patrols, could also be a response by burglars to such a change. Unlike natural processes like earthquakes, analyses like the one presented here could therefore have the ability to modify the observed process, making it more difficult to correctly predict future events. (Marsan, 2018: 3)

Marsan's conclusions are cause for concern for any police agency that is paying for and using software based on this method. Irrespective of Marsan's conclusions, this type of discourse is part of the academic rigor that is missing from the predictive policing conversation.[10]

---

[10] Benbouzid (2016) sought out this analysis and published Marsan's note which contains a mathematical analysis of the Mohler et al. (2011; 2015) method in order to start this dialog; however, I did not find any evidence of a response or follow-up by Benbouzid since the publication in October 2016.

Prediction Accuracy

Another criticism of predictive policing analytical practices is the lack of testing the accuracy of the predictions. Berk (2011) discusses the importance of testing predictive accuracy because predicting crime is serious and has consequences for people's lives. He gives the following example:

The outcome to be forecasted is whether an individual on parole or probation will commit a homicide ... A false positive can mean that an individual is incorrectly labeled as "high risk." A false negative can mean that a homicide that might have been prevented is not. There is no reason to assume that the costs of these two outcomes are even approximately the same. Qualitative outcomes can also play a role in predictive policing. (2011: 108)

Perry and his colleagues (2013) identify the lack of accuracy testing as a pitfall of predictive policing and found that in interviews with practitioners, few said they evaluated effectiveness of predictions. That is, they have not determined whether the software they are using actually predicts crime accurately in their own jurisdiction. This is important because if one model is used to predict crime for different crimes in a variety of environments, it would follow that the model's predictive accuracy would vary and be better in some circumstances than others. In other words, even an effective approach is not effective in every situation. Mohler and colleagues' model parameter was to predict 500-by-500 foot boxes because that was the approximate size of a block in the Foothill District in Los Angeles and was relevant for the LAPD patrol practices (Mohler et al., 2015). It is unlikely that this same grid size is relevant across environments and for different jurisdictions. However, without testing the predictive accuracy of the method, we do not know if and when a particular predictive policing method is appropriate.

The lack of testing does seem to be unique to the predictive policing approach, as there have been many studies on the predictive accuracy of traditional crime mapping techniques. Notably, they support my conclusion that nuances of selected parameters and examination in different circumstances yield varying accuracy results. For example, Chainey, Tompson, and Uhlig (2008) tested the predictive spatial (only) accuracy of common spatial analysis techniques used in crime analysis. They compared accuracy of point mapping, thematic mapping of geographic areas, spatial ellipses, grid thematic mapping, and kernel density estimation (KDE) on four type of crimes (burglary, street crime, theft from vehicles, and theft of vehicles). They found that the techniques differ in their prediction abilities with KDE outperforming the others and that street crimes (robbery of personal property and theft from the person) were more accurately predicted than property crime types (Chainey et al., 2008).

As an extension of this study, Tompson and Townsley (2010) tested the accuracy of KDE for predicting both space and time for street crime. They found that using time in addition to the location of the crime enhanced predictability by shift. The method's accuracy was better during the overnight shift than in the afternoon or morning. The researchers attributed this to the fact that overnight activities are more constrained by location because people's activities are limited (i.e., many businesses, offices etc. are closed at night), while in the afternoon people are doing a wide range of things across a larger geographic area.

Hart and Zandbergen (2014) also examined the predictive accuracy of the KDE method by varying components of the technique and the type of crimes using data from one large police department. They found that "depending on the interpolation method employed, considerable difference in the ability of KDE hot spot maps to predict future crime events – based on past events – were evident" (p. 316). Specifically, they found that while the grid cell size did not affect predictive accuracy, there was considerable variation in predictive accuracy when the search radius varied. They also found that violent crimes, such as robbery and aggravated assault, were more successfully predicted than property crimes, such as motor vehicle theft and burglary.

Yet, it does make some sense that police departments are not testing the accuracy of the predictions themselves, because they are paying for the software and analytical service and are focused on responding to crime. If police are relying on the software companies to decide the technique, dictate the way the data are managed, and run the analysis, it follows that the police might expect the software companies to provide evidence of prediction accuracy. I have only found a few examples of studies specifically focused on predictive accuracy; however, none has been conducted by researchers independent from the software companies.

The Mohler et al. (2015) study is the only published study I was able to find that was published in an academic journal, albeit a non-criminological statistical journal. It is important to note that five of the seven authors acknowledge at the end of the article that they "hold stock" in the computer software company that uses the algorithm they are testing (Mohler et al., 2015: 26). That being said, the researchers found using Los Angeles, CA and Kent, UK, combined burglary, car theft, theft from vehicle, and criminal damage data, that their predictions of a crime in the 500-by-500 foot box were accurate 4.7 percent, 6.8 percent, and 9.8 percent of the time in the three different areas they studied. They compared these rates to the accuracy rates of crime analysts working in those departments and found the software accuracy was significantly higher than what the crime analysts predicted.

Unfortunately, because there is not a body of published research on accuracy of predictive policing methods, the only other examples I found come from newspapers and software companies themselves. For example, Deputy Chief Clark of Santa Cruz, CA, police department said the following about his agency's implementation of predictive policing in 2011, "I flip through the stack until I find Linden Street, where, the statistics reveal, there is a 2.06 percent chance of a crime happening today, and 3:1 odds that a crime, should it occur, will be a home break-in versus an auto theft" (Thompson, 2011). In a paper published by a software company about its own product (PublicEngines, 2014), the company (i.e., no credited authors) estimated the accuracy and efficiency of their method by examining true/false positives and negatives. They found their software accurately predicted next-day crime around 30 percent of the time in two cities and that it was better than traditional hot spotting methods.[11]

While the Mohler and the PublicEngines studies are unreliable because of prejudice and/or lack of rigor of the research, the information does beg the question what is an acceptable level of predictive accuracy that warrants spending a significant portion of a police department budget on the software and then directing limited police resources based on its predictions.[12] These two studies highlight that both methods are more accurate than what the local police crime analysts produced. However, this assumes that the crime analysts are well educated, intelligent, adequately trained, and are using appropriate methods for the purpose. In this context, it would be like my stockbroker who was able to get me a 2 percent return on my investment telling me this is a great result because the other stockbroker in the office was only able to get clients a 1 percent return, but never mentioning that the stock market was up 10 percent or that the average for all stockbrokers in the company was 7 percent. A comparison to current crime analysis could be meaningful to determine the utility of such a software solution, but the research would need to be done with a more rigorous and independent approach. Nevertheless, fundamental questions remain: (1) is there independent research on the accuracy of crime predictions that police leaders and their municipal governments can "bank" on, and (2) what prediction accuracy rate is acceptable for police departments to invest a large amount of capital and staffing resources?

In summary, the lack of testing of prediction accuracy, which is the essence of *predictive* policing, may seem strange in an analytical field where statistics, evaluation, and testing are central. Yet, when considering the fact that the methods of predictive policing are proprietary and yield a significant amount of money for both the software companies and some researchers, it is less surprising since independent researchers are not able to access either the methods or the software itself to duplicate and test them.

IMPLEMENTATION OF PREDICTIVE POLICING

There are multiple levels at which any crime reduction approach must be implemented in a police agency, from acquiring data and software,

---

[11] I was not able to find any related information published in a peer-reviewed academic or a police practitioner journal. Note that PublicEngines was recent purchased by Motorola who now sells the software.

[12] For example, the Orange County, FL, Sheriff's Office pays $103,000 a year for its predictive policing analysis (Doornbos, 2016).

conducting and disseminating analysis, to responding and holding individuals accountable for doing so. As noted earlier, many of the police departments that utilize predictive policing software provide their data and rely on the software company to provide analytical maps and other reports on a daily basis or have a researcher or analyst use the software to run the preprogrammed analysis. Either way, the department does not own the software but subscribes to the service and/or access to the software company's server.

Role of Crime Analysis

The predictive policing operationalization of the analysis process is an important shift from current and historical crime analysis practices. Crime analysts primarily use desktop software for analysis, whereas predictive policing analysis is under the total control of the company in both what the methods are and how they are carried out. There are many software companies offering police agencies a similar type of server environment for officers to "look up" and map crimes, but these are not analysis programs but instead are simple mechanisms for searching and visualizing crime data.

Predictive policing, on the other hand, is considered "advanced" analytics which arguably should fall under the direct control and oversight of the working analyst of the police department. My first criticism of predictive policing implementation is addressed to both software companies and the police agencies. That is, they both presume that predictive policing analysis can be automated using one model for many agencies and can take place without a qualified working crime analyst.

Even if we disregard the fact that the analytical models are not systematically or independently tested, as noted earlier, the data and parameters used within a particular method dictate the accuracy of the predictions. Will what worked for LAPD also work in a suburban city or a rural town? One of the important skills of a crime analyst is the ability to take an effective and transparent analytical technique and apply it in the context of his/her jurisdiction's environment. However, if the methods are not transparent, never tested for their accuracy in different environments, then refining and applying the technique is nearly impossible.

Responses by Police

In an approach that uses sophisticated analytical techniques, it is perplexing that the resulting police action is responding to 500-by-500 foot boxes that may make no sense geographically or environmentally. As with density mapping (Santos, 2017), the boxes, created by the software program, are part of an arbitrary grid that is placed on top of the jurisdiction's street layer. The boxes are all exactly the same size, and no matter what lies beneath in the "real world" the prediction is for that box. The arbitrary nature of the box locations causes contextual issues for the predictions themselves since each box does not have the same baseline risk for crime (e.g., boxes on the jurisdiction's borders). It also causes issues for police deployment. Oftentimes officers are given a box in which to respond that does not make geographically sense (e.g., the box cuts across a canal or major thoroughfare). When this happens, police officers attempting to respond will likely question the accuracy and relevance of the analysis results, which can undermine the entire approach.

More importantly, what are officers to do in the box when no context or other information is given? Simply go there? In fact, that is what LAPD told their patrol officers to do: "Patrol officers were directed to use available time to 'get in the box' and police what they saw" (Mohler et al., 2015: 8). But what is there to do in a 500-by-500 foot area, especially when there is no actionable intelligence (Ratcliffe, 2016) or problem analysis (Boba, 2003) on which officers can base their responses?

Problem-oriented policing has been shown to be an effective way to address crime, particularly in hot spots (Weisburd & Majmundar, 2018). In problem analysis of long and even short term hot spots, information about the underlying causes and conditions is provided to those who are responding (Boba, 2003) and proves important for developing effective strategies to address crime (Weisburd et al., 2010). In contrast, the result of predictive policing analysis is simply a set of 500-by-500 foot boxes on a map that is exchanged for a new map with new boxes at the beginning of each shift. The boxes are drawn based on the types of crimes selected (e.g., street robbery or burglaries; violent or property crime), but the results do not provide any contextual information to indicate why the crime will occur there or what/ who to look for.

This is also in contrast to action-oriented products that crime analysts create that guide other crime reduction approaches. For example, to support intelligence-led policing, crime analysts gather and synthesize intelligence information about offenders, victims, etc. collected by officers in the field that is provided to decision-makers (Ratcliffe, 2016). To support short-term tactical responses, a properly trained crime analyst identifies short-term patterns to direct patrol and investigators. The analysis product (i.e., pattern bulletin) includes a summary of the crimes in the pattern, a map with an area to patrol, information about the MO, property taken, persons victimized, offenders living in the area, and any field intelligence that has been collected (Santos, 2017). To support long-term responses, crime analysts also produce problem analysis reports detailing the underlying causes of long-term problems with information about victims, offenders, place managers, and stakeholders (Clarke & Eck, 2005; POP Center, 2018).

Notably, one predictive policing software produces 500-by-500 foot boxes on a map by crime type (PredPol, 2018a). Another software program provides a ranking of the boxes on a map to indicate the order of risk (Jackson, 2015; Motorola, 2018). It does not appear that any of these programs provide a predicted risk value for an individual box. In fact, I was working with a large police agency to test the prediction accuracy of the software they had purchased to produce these maps. When the police department leaders asked the software company for the risk values, they were told that they should just respond to all the boxes, and if they wanted to prioritize patrol efforts, the software could provide fewer boxes each day. The risk values were never provided even though police department leaders (i.e., paying customers) requested them.

The response of this software company leads to one final criticism about implementation of predictive policing, but also about the nature of the crime analysis product that is provided to police. That is, if the software can yield more or fewer boxes each shift, at what point are the risk levels so low that they are no longer meaningful? Should there a minimum threshold risk that the boxes have to meet to be worthy of a police response? That is, does the software produce ten boxes no matter what the crime level and risk in the boxes are? In Mohler and colleagues' experiment (2015), the number of prediction boxes was consistent each day (i.e., twenty, forty, or eighty predictions). This implies that no matter the crime levels or the risks of prediction each day for each shift, the same number of boxes was produced. Without meaningful risk value associated with a predicted area, the police could be responding to areas that are relatively "more" risky than other areas for a crime, but are at an extremely low overall risk for crime. In these cases, it might be that the officer's time is better spent in other areas engaging with the community instead of trying to deter crime where there is not likely to be any.

In summary, predictive policing analysis is appealing to police because it provides clear direction to micro-places where officers should respond based on past crime. However, it does not always provide meaningful areas in which to respond or information that directs officers to employ any particular strategy or to prioritize among the areas. Again, this shows the lack of evidence-based research and transparency of predictive policing methods.

CRIME REDUCTION EFFECTIVENESS RESEARCH AND ANECDOTES

There has been significant research on the effectiveness of proactive police approaches, most of which is discussed in the other chapters of this book. Unfortunately, predictive policing has not been around long enough nor is transparent enough for there to be a body of meaningful and rigorous evaluations. As noted by the National Academy of Sciences panel, there is not sufficient research to reach a conclusion about predictive policing's impact on crime (Weisburd & Majmundar, 2018). However, there have been a few studies conducted by academics and many anecdotes put forth by practitioners and software companies worth discussing.

As of the writing of this chapter, there has been one independent experiment to study the impact of patrol strategies on crime in 500-by-500 foot boxes. Funded by the National Institute of Justice, Temple University worked with the

Philadelphia Police Department in 2015–2016 to randomly assign twenty patrol districts and implemented different responses for three months in order to test the impact on property and violent crime, separately (Ratcliffe & Taylor, 2017). The responses were implemented in 500-by-500 foot boxes predicted by Hunchlab predictive policing software and included (1) standard practice (i.e., control); (2) informing patrol officers about the boxes and asking them to respond during their shift when they can (i.e., awareness response); (3) informing patrol officers and having a dedicated marked patrol car to patrol the predicted areas without answering calls for service (i.e., marked response); and (4) informing patrol officers and having an unmarked car patrol the predicted areas without answering calls for service (i.e., unmarked response) (Ratcliffe & Taylor, 2017).

The researchers did not find reductions in violent crime for any of the responses or in property crime for the "awareness" or "unmarked" responses. They did find that there was a 31 percent reduction in property crime counts in predicted boxes and the area immediate around them, but the results were not statistically significant. Because of the small numbers of crimes (i.e., an average reduction of three crimes over three months in an entire district), the researchers could not make inferences about the experimental effects (Ratcliffe et al., 2017).

The researchers also examined the accuracy of the predictions made in the experiment even though it was not a specific study of prediction accuracy. That is, adjustments were made to the predictions to support the experimental methodology (i.e., not all of the highest crime boxes were used each shift to ensure they were in different areas day to day). The researchers found that "it appears that the software was able to predict twice as much crime as we would expect if crime were spread uniformly across the districts" (Ratcliffe, Taylor & Askey, 2017: 2). Importantly, in the most current preliminary publications about the study, the researchers provide minimal information about the analytical model that was used, "It [Hunchlab] incorporates statistical modeling that considers seasonality, risk terrain modeling, near repeats, and collective efficacy" (p. 1). Thus, similar to other research, verification and replication of the results is not possible. However, I anticipate that the analytical methods will be provided by the researchers in the peer-reviewed publications of these results.

There have also been other experiments conducted under the auspices of predictive policing. Funded by the National Institute of Justice predictive policing portfolio, Hunt, Saunders, and Hollywood (2014) conducted an experiment to test the effectiveness of predictive policing in Shreveport, LA. However, the analytical methods implemented are notably different than those described here, in that they forecasted monthly changes in crime at the district and beat levels (versus daily crime in boxes). That being said, the results showed that the police responses were not implemented as originally intended (i.e., planning meetings did not occur and interventions were implemented haphazardly), and there were no differences in targeted crime (i.e., property crime) between the treatment and control areas (Hunt et al., 2014).

In their 2015 study that tested predictive accuracy of predictive policing software, Mohler et al. conducted an experiment. However, the researchers did not test the effectiveness of a police response in the boxes, but, instead, tested whether patrol response was more effective in reducing crime depending on how the boxes were predicted. Analysis conducted by predictive policing software was the treatment condition and analysis conducted by a crime analyst was the control condition. The type of analysis technique was randomized and given to the same officers in the same districts to implement responses on different days. Notably, the researchers did not standardize the response even though it was supposed to be consistent across both types of analysis. The researchers admit they were "agnostic about the benefits of different tactical choices of officers in the field" (Mohler et al., 2015: 13). Thus, it is not clear from the research what specific responses were conducted as only time in the box was recorded. The researchers did not measure crime occurring in the boxes, but examined crime over the entire study area. Even though they found crime was lower when officers responded to analysis produced by the software than by the analysts, the weakness in the research design and researchers' lack of independence undermines the results.

Additionally, two random controlled trials have been conducted in South America by Laura Jaitman and Sebastian Galiani, two economists. Unfortunately, the studies are so recent, publications about the methodology and results are not yet available, so it is unclear whether these studies examine the methods discussed here (i.e., 500-by-500 foot boxes), examine prediction accuracy and/or test the effect on crime.[13]

Perry and his colleagues recognized in 2013 that predictive policing assessment and evaluation are lacking and underemphasized by police practitioners. Like with prediction accuracy, they found in interviews that few practitioners said they had evaluated the impact of responses directed by advanced predictive policing analysis. Interestingly, there is quite a bit of anecdotal "evidence" presented in the media by police chiefs and by the software companies themselves about the effectiveness of predictive policing in reducing crime. The following are some quotes from police leaders in the media:

- "We use [PredPol] to try to predict crime before it ever occurs and deploy our resources accordingly into those areas to prevent and detect violation of law," Sheriff Demings told commissioners. "That program seems to be going well." (Doornos, 2016)

---

[13] This project titled: "Predictive policing in Latin America: evidence from two randomized controlled trials" (with S. Galiani), noted as a working paper at www.laurajaitman.com/home-1/ (retrieved December 29, 2017).

- "Predictive policing is working from what we can see because, evidently, we've had people in the right places," Merced Police Chief Norm Andrade. (Morgante, 2016)
- "In our first six months, we saw a drop of 28 percent in burglary compared with the same locations and same time in the previous year," Santa Cruz deputy police chief Steve Clark. (Black, 2016b)

The following are a few of the many quotes from one software company's website about the "proven track record of crime reduction" facilitated by their predictive policing software (PredPol, 2018b).[14]

- During Atlanta's initial launch, aggregate crime decreased by 8% and 9% in the two areas that first deployed PredPol in July 2013. Of the four zones where PredPol was not deployed, crime rates increased by 1 to 8% in three and remained flat in one. Due to these successful results, the Atlanta Police Department decided to implement PredPol citywide in November 2013. Atlanta Police Department has seen aggregate crime drop 19% and attribute much of the sustained reduction to PredPol's deployment.
- The Alhambra, CA, Police Department reported a 32% drop in burglaries and a 20% drop in vehicle theft since deploying in January 2013. The city reported its lowest month of crime in history in May 2014.
- The Norcross, GA, Police Department has had a 15–30% reduction in burglaries and robberies just four months after deploying in August 2013, and Captain Bill Grogan has stated that predicted crime is down 22.7% when comparing 10 months using PredPol to the same 10 months before using PredPol.
- The Modesto, CA Police Department recently reported the lowest crime rates in 3 years since deployment in January 2014, including an 18% reduction in residential burglary and a 13% reduction in commercial burglary.

What is interesting is that this particularly company provides incentive for its customers to claim crime reduction and refer other police departments to the company. Through a Freedom of Information Act request, Bond-Graham (2014) was able to obtain a copy of a contract between a software company and a police department that said the following:

In exchange for discounts extended above, Agency agrees to the commitment length and financial terms above and the following additional terms, to the extent reasonable ... provide public testimonials and referrals to other agencies (each successful new referral will result in a 10% additional discount for the following year's annual fee).

Media articles also reveal anecdotal "evidence" that predictive policing may *not* be effective, as a number of police agencies have discontinued its use because they have not seen results:

---

[14] Note that there are no reports or academic publications explaining the analytical methods used to make these conclusions.

- In 2016, the Richmond [CA] Police Department terminated its contract halfway into a three-year program because it found no measurable impact on crime reduction. RPD spokesperson Lieutenant Felix Tan said it was difficult to quantify the software's [PredPol] impact on crime (Thomas, 2016).
- During the January 2015 budgeting planning process he convinced Mayor Libby Schaaf to earmark $150,000 in the city's budget to fund the software over two years. "Maybe we could reduce crime more by using predictive policing, but the unintended consequences [are] even more damaging . . . and it's just not worth it," Tim Birch said [head of planning and research at Oakland, CA, police department] (Thomas, 2016).
- Burbank, CA, police department suspended its deployments based on predictive policing after two years at $15,000 per year. Some officers surveyed felt their intuition and experience was more important than the prediction and that oftentimes the predictions were in obvious areas that they were already aware of or "silly" locations like the police department where citizens report crimes (Tchekmedyian, 2016).

From all this, I think it is safe to conclude that there is just too little evidence to determine whether these predictive policing methods are being effectively used or "work" in reducing crime. However, the anecdotal evidence seems to have had meaningful influence on the adoption of this predictive policing practice.

CIVIL LIBERTIES AND PRIVACY RIGHTS

The last criticism of predictive policing is the issue of civil liberties and privacy rights. American Civil Liberties Union (ACLU) leaders felt compelled to publish a statement of concern in August of 2016 that echoes some of my criticisms in this chapter. These are the key points in the statement:

1 A lack of transparency about predictive policing systems prevents a meaningful, well-informed public debate.
2 Predictive policing systems ignore community needs.
3 Predictive policing systems threaten to undermine the constitutional rights of individuals.
4 Predictive technologies are primarily being used to intensify enforcement, rather than to meet human needs.
5 Police could use predictive tools to anticipate which officers might engage in misconduct, but most departments have not done so.
6 Predictive policing systems are failing to monitor their racial impact. (ACLU, 2016)

Perry and his colleagues (2013: p. xxi) also recognize that predictive policing is "overlooking civil and privacy rights." The three main concerns are (1) if the data are biased, the predictions are biased; (2) the lack of transparency of methods; and (3) what types of enforcement are being used. A recent research publication about predictive policing in Chicago has made a significant splash in the media on this topic. Even though it is on offender-based prediction, the results have been noted extensively in the criticism of biasedness of predictive policing.

Funded by NIJ under the predictive policing research portfolio, Saunders, Hunt, and Hollywood (2016) conducted a quasi-experimental evaluation of Chicago's predictive policing practices. Chicago implemented predictive policing analytics to identify people estimated to be at highest risk of gun violence. Once identified, these individuals were put on a list that was sent to local district commanders. The researchers note, "Commanders were not given specific guidance on what treatments to apply to [those on the list]; instead, they were expected to tailor interventions appropriately" (Saunders et al., 2016: 9). The researchers found that the individuals on the list were no more or less likely to be a victim than those in the comparison group, and the treatment group was more likely to be arrested for a shooting. They conclude that the usefulness of these types of analysis results is not clear and that further discussion and research is necessary.

Ferguson (2012) also discusses the impact of predictive policing analytics on the Fourth Amendment and concludes that they will likely alter the amendment's interpretation for reasonable suspicion analysis, by adding to the totality of circumstances from which courts can find reasonable suspicion for a seizure. Ferguson concludes that while predictive policing results by themselves are not enough for reasonable suspicion, he anticipates courts to begin considering the forecasts as an additional factor. He criticizes the current practices and methods in the context that judges will insist on transparency of both the methods and the data in order to consider predictions in their decisions. In particular, he says this about blind adherence and the Fourth Amendment:

[I]f a particular block suffers a statistically high number of car thefts over a month period, a predictive model might forecast that the same block will be the locus of a subsequent theft. Blind adherence to the predictive forecast might mean that an individual observed with a screwdriver on that block, in combination with the forecast, might result in reasonable suspicion for a stop. However, if prior to the stop police had arrested the gang responsible for all the prior car thefts, improved the lighting in the area, and posted police on the street, reliance on the prediction should be irrelevant. The reason why the future crime is predicted to happen no longer holds. Incorporating predictive policing into the reasonable suspicion analysis of the court then would not be appropriate. (Ferguson, 2012: 314)

In his analysis, Ferguson anticipates the possible legal outcomes of using predictive policing, emphasizing that not only is academic rigor and transparency important for effective police practice, but it also effects other processes within the criminal justice system that start with officer's responses based on predictive policing analytics.

Once again, these potential issues of bias are not unique to predictive policing as standard crime analysis techniques use the same data and attempt to anticipate the future patterns and trends based on past crimes. However, the ACLU has not yet made a statement of concern about crime analysis. I think this is likely because of the aggressive marketing and media attention about crime reduction by the software companies and police departments, respectively. It may also be due to the fact that predictive policing analysis is not transparent and does not include a "human factor" (i.e., crime analyst) through which analytical decisions are made about data, and the appropriateness of analytical techniques are justified.

CONCLUSION

In conclusion, predictive policing appears to be just a label for a new set of advanced techniques that fall within the field of crime analysis and not a representation of an evidence-based policing approach. Importantly, a police agency that implements predictive policing does nothing different organizationally or in its responses, except to direct officers during their shift toward certain areas for patrol in their uncommitted time. It has come to represent innovative and progressive policing and is touted as a quick and easy solution for a police department that wants to implement crime analysis.

With predictive policing software, police departments can literally "pay" for automated analysis, avoid the hassle of hiring and training a crime analyst, and essentially do no structural or functional changes to their agency to be seen as implementing a "proactive" form of crime reduction. This can be particularly attractive to large agencies with massive amounts of data that may not want to invest in crime analysts over sworn police officers. While I agree that finding more efficient and effective ways to deploy patrol resources in an immediate time frame is an important goal for police leaders and researchers, such an approach must be grounded in theory, clearly defined, and evaluated either before or during its widespread adoption.

What is also problematic is that the analytical techniques currently used and advertised as "effective" by both police chiefs and software companies are not evidence-based. The lack of transparency in the methods themselves and lack of rigor in evaluation of their accuracy are the two most important criticisms of this chapter and apply to all forms of predictive analysis as well as general crime analysis. Fortunately, these criticisms can be overcome through the publishing of analytical methods and rigorous independent testing of the models with secondary data from a variety of police agencies. But this will require researchers, police leaders, and government officials to value and seek to employ evidence-based research and practices.

Unfortunately, predictive policing is not there yet, and the incentive to be evidence-based is not strong as police departments are often under pressure to reduce crime quickly, so they are vulnerable to companies that effectively market their untested products for significant profit. In light of this, researchers and federal funding should play a major role in insisting on transparency and conducting independent evaluations.

I end with a few universal recommendations that are applicable to any form of predictive policing, even those not discussed here:

1 Define the term and decide whether predictive policing is a comprehensive crime reduction approach or whether it is set of analytical techniques within police crime analysis. If it is the former, the police strategies and tactics must be defined, not just the analytical methods.

2 Evaluate and publish the methods and results of predictive policing techniques and software in academically rigorous and discipline-relevant publications. This is important for general crime analysis practices as well. It is acceptable for researchers with interests in a software product to conduct research on that product as long as the data and methods are transparent and findings can be replicated.

3 Do not underestimate the importance and value of having a skilled crime analyst conduct both qualitative and quantitative analysis with specific insight to the data and environment of the jurisdiction. This is not to say that current crime analysis practices cannot be improved, only that a software program with advanced statistics cannot replace an effective crime analyst who examines data and applicability of techniques critically. They should complement one another.

4 Educate government officials and police leaders about evidence-based policing and the importance of purchasing technology and implementing strategies that are transparent and have been rigorously tested. That being said, until evidence for predictive policing emerges, police would be more effective identifying and responding to long-term hot spots as a place-based crime reduction approach (Weisburd & Majmundar, 2018).

REFERENCES

Austin, R., Cooper, G., Gagnon, D., Hodges, J., Martensen, K., & O'Neal, M. (1973). *Police Crime Analysis Unit Handbook*. Washington, DC: US Department of Justice, National Institute of Law Enforcement and Criminal Justice.

American Civil Liberties Union (2016, August). *Statement of Concern about Predictive Policing by ACLU and 16 Civil Rights Privacy, Racial Justice, and Technology Organizations*. Retrieved November 21, 2018, from www.aclu.org/other/statement-concern-about-predictive-policing-aclu-and-16-civil-rights-privacy-racial-justice? redirect=hearing-statement/statement-concern-about-predictive-policing-aclu-and-16-civil-rights-privacy.

Beck, C., & McCue, C. (2009, November). Predictive policing: What can we learn from Wal-Mart and Amazon about fighting crime in a recession? *Police Chief Magazine*, 76, 18–20, 22–24.

Benbouzid, B. (2016, October) Who benefits from the crime? *Books and Ideas*. Retrieved November 21, 2018, from www.booksandideas.net/Who-Benefits-from-the-Crime .html.

Berk, R. (2011). Asymmetric loss functions for forecasting in criminal justice settings. *Journal of Quantitative Criminology*, 27, 107–123.

Black, D. (2016a, January). Here comes predictive policing: The next wave of crime fighting technology is being tested in New York City. *New York Daily News*. Retrieved November 21, 2018, from www.nydailynews.com/opinion/david-black-predictive-policing-article-1.2506580.

Black, D. (2016b, Winter). Predictive policing has arrived. Big Data on the Beat. Retrieved November 21, 2018, from www.city-journal.org/html/big-data-beat-14125.html.

Boba, R. (2003). *Problem Analysis in Policing*. Washington, DC: Police Foundation.

Bond-Graham, D. (2014, December) Modesto Police Department correspondence with predictive policing company PredPol, Inc. *Public Intelligence*. Retrieved November 21, 2018, from https://publicintelligence.net/modesto-police-correspondence-with-predpol-inc/.

Bond-Graham, D., & Winston, A. (2013, October). All tomorrow's crimes: The future of policing looks a lot like good branding. *SF Weekly*. Retrieved November 21, 2018, from https://archives.sfweekly.com/sanfrancisco/all-tomorrows-crimes-the-future-of-policing-looks-a-lot-like-good-branding/Content?oid=2827968.

Braga, A. A., Papachristos, A. V., & Hureau, D. M. (2014). The effects of hot spots policing on crime: An updated systematic review and meta-analysis. *Justice Quarterly*, 31(4), 633–663.

Bratton, W. J., & Malinowski, S. W. (2008). Police performance management in practice: Taking COMPSTAT to the next level. *Policing*, 2(3), 259–265.

Bureau of Justice Assistance. (2018). Crime analysis. Retrieved November 21, 2018, from www.bja.gov/ProgramDetails.aspx?Program_ID=113.

Bureau of Justice Statistics. (2018). Law Enforcement Management and Administrative Statistics (LEMAS), 2013. Retrieved November 21, 2018, from www.icpsr.umich .edu/icpsrweb/NACJD/studies/36164.

Caplan, J. M., Kennedy, L. W., & Piza, E. L. (2013). Joint utility of event-dependent and environmental crime analysis techniques for violent crime forecasting. *Crime & Delinquency*, 59(2), 243–270.

Chainey, S., Tompson, L., & Uhlig, S. (2008). The utility of hotspot mapping for predicting spatial patterns of crime. *Security Journal*, 21, 4–28.

Clarke, R. V., & Eck, J. (2005). *Crime Analysis for Problem Solvers: In 60 Small Steps*. Washington, DC: Office of Community Oriented Policing Services.

Doornbos, C. (2016, October). Orange county sheriff's office technology helps predict, prevent crime. *Orlando Sentinel*. Retrieved November 21, 2018, from www .orlandosentinel.com/news/crime/os-predpol-ocso-crime-tech-20161008-story.html.

Drawve, G., & Barnum, J. D. (2017). Place-based risk factors for aggravated assault across police divisions in Little Rock, Arkansas. *Journal of Crime and Justice*. DOI: 10.1080/0735648X.2016.1270849.

Ferguson, A. G. (2012). Predictive policing and reasonable suspicion. *Emory Law Journal*, 62, 259–325.

Goldsmith, S. (2014, August). Predictive tools for public safety. *Digital Transformation: Wiring the responsive city. Civic Report No. 87.* Retrieved November 21, 2018, from http://datasmart.ash.harvard.edu/news/article/predictive-tools-for-public-safety-506.

Haberman, C. P., & Ratcliffe, J. H. (2012). The predictive policing challenges of near repeat armed street robberies. *Policing, 6*(2), 151–166.

Hart, T., & Zandbergen, P. (2014). Kernel density estimation and hotspot mapping: Examining the influence of interpolation method, grid cell size, and bandwidth on crime forecasting. *Policing: An International Journal of Police Strategies & Management, 37*(2), 305–323.

HunchLab. (2018). *Next generation predictive policing software.* Retrieved November 21, 2018, from www.hunchlab.com/.

Hunt, P., Saunders, J., & Hollywood, J. (2014): *Evaluation of the Shreveport Predictive Policing Experiment.* Santa Monica, CA: RAND.

IBM. (2018). *IBM SPSS Crime prediction and prevention.* Retrieved November 21, 2018, from www-01.ibm.com/software/analytics/spss/11/na/cpp/.

International Association of Crime Analysts [IACA]. (2012). Crime analysis education recommendations for colleges and universities (White Paper 2012–02). Overland Park, KS: Author.

International Association of Crime Analysts [IACA]. (2014). Definition and types of crime analysis (White Paper 2014–02). Overland Park, KS: Author.

International Association of Crime Analysts [IACA]. (2018). *Certified law enforcement analyst directory.* Retrieved November 21, 2018, from http://iaca.net/certification_clea_directory.asp.

Jackson, D. (2015, April) Motorola Solutions: Rich Payne discusses predictive-policing capabilities. *Urgent Communications.* Retrieved November 21, 2018, from http://urgentcomm.com/motorola-solutions/motorola-solutions-rich-payne-discusses-predictive-policing-capabilities.

Johnson, S. D., Bowers, K. J., Birks, D. J., & Pease, K. (2009). Predictive mapping of crime by Promap: Accuracy, units of analysis, and the environmental backcloth. In D. Weisburd, W. Bernasco, & G. Bruinsma (eds.), *Putting Crime in Its Place: Units of Analysis in Geographic Criminology* (pp. 171–198). New York: Springer.

Kennedy, L., Caplan, J., & Piza, E. (2011). Risk clusters, hotspots, and spatial intelligence: Risk terrain modeling as an algorithm for police resource allocation strategies. *Journal of Quantitative Criminology, 27*(3), 339–362.

Kennedy, L., Caplan, J., & Piza, E. (2015) A multi-jurisdictional test of risk terrain modeling and place-based evaluation of environmental risk-based patrol deployment strategies. *Results in Brief.* Completed in partial fulfillment of National Institute of Justice (NIJ) award #2012-IJ-CX-0038. Retrieved November 21, 2018, from www.rutgerscps.org/uploads/2/7/3/7/27370595/nij6city_results_inbrief_final.pdf.

Mamalian, C., & LaVigne, N. (1997). The use of computerized crime mapping by law enforcement: Survey results. In *National Institute of Justice Research Preview.* Washington, DC: National Institute of Justice.

Marsan, D. (2018). *La note de David Marsan sur PredPol.* Retrieved November 21, 2018, from www.scribd.com/document/323069015/La-note-de-David-Marsan-sur-PredPol.

Miller, B. (2017, March). Exclusive: Predictive policing startup publishes code online, Seeks to address bias. *Government Technology.* Retrieved December 29, 2017, from www.govtech.com/civic/Predictive-Policing-Startup-Publishes-Code-Online-Seeks-

to-Address-Bias.html?utm_content=buffer63a84&utm_medium=social&utm_source=
twitter.com&utm_campaign=buffer,

Morgante, M. (2016, September). Police chief says "predictive policing" showing results. *Merced Sunstar*. Retrieved November 21, 2018, from www.mercedsunstar.com/news/article103071847.html.

Mohler, G. O., Short, M. B., Brantingham, P. J., Schoenberg, F. P., & Tita, G. E. (2011). Self-exciting point process modeling of crime. *Journal of the American Statistical Association, 106*(493), 100–108.

Mohler, G. O., Short, M. B., Malinowski, S., Johnson, M., Tita, G. E. Bertozzi, A. L., & Brantingham, P. J (2015). Randomized controlled field trials of predictive policing. *Journal of the American Statistical Association, 110*(512), 1399–1411.

Motorola. (2018). *Command central analytics*. Retrieved November 21, 2018, from www.motorolasolutions.com/en_us/products/smart-public-safety-solutions/intelligence-led-public-safety/commandcentral-analytics.html.

National Institute of Justice [NIJ]. (2010). *Predictive policing symposiums*. Retrieved November 21, 2018, from www.ncjrs.gov/pdffiles1/nij/242222and248891.pdf.

National Institute of Justice [NIJ]. (2018a). *Mapping and analysis for public safety*. Retrieved November 21, 2018, from www.nij.gov/topics/technology/maps/pages/welcome.aspx.

National Institute of Justice [NIJ]. (2018b). *Predictive policing*. Retrieved on Retrieved November 21, 2018, from www.nij.gov/topics/law-enforcement/strategies/predictive-policing/Pages/welcome.aspx.

National Institute of Justice [NIJ]. (2018c). *Funding awards, FY 2009*. Retrieved November 21, 2018, from www.nij.gov/funding/awards/Pages/2009.aspx?fiscalyear=2009.

National Institute of Justice [NIJ]. (2018d). *Funding awards, FY 2011*. Retrieved November 21, 2018, from www.nij.gov/funding/awards/Pages/2011.aspx?fiscalyear=2011.

Perry, W. L., McInnis, B., Price, C. C., Smith, S. C., & Hollywood, J. S. (2013) *Predictive Policing: The Role of Crime Forecasting in Law Enforcement Operations*. Santa Monica, CA: RAND.

Piza, E., Feng, S., Kennedy, L., & Caplan, J. (2016). Place-based correlates of motor vehicle theft and recovery: Measuring spatial influence across neighbourhood context. *Urban Studies, 54*(13), 2998–3021.

POP Center. (2018). Problem solving tool guides. Retrieved November 21, 2018, from www.popcenter.org/tools/.

PredPol. (2018a). *PredPol: The predictive policing company*. Retrieved November 21, 2018, from www.predpol.com.

PredPol. (2018b). *Proven crime reduction results*. Retrieved November 21, 2018, from www.predpol.com/results/.

PublicEngines. (2014). *Predictive Analytics vs Hot Spotting: A Study of Crime Prevention Accuracy and Efficiency*. Draper, UT: Author.

Ratcliffe, J. H. (2009). *Near Repeat Calculator* (version 1.3). Philadelphia, PA and Washington, DC: Temple University and National Institute of Justice.

Ratcliffe, J. H. (2016). *Intelligence-Led Policing*. London: Routledge.

Ratcliffe, J. H., & Taylor, R. B. (2017, September). *The Philadelphia Predictive Policing Experiment: Summary of the Experimental Design*. Philadelphia, PA: Center for Crime Science, Temple University.

Ratcliffe, J. H., Taylor, R. B., & Askey, A. P. (2017, September). *The Philadelphia Predictive Policing Experiment: Effectiveness of the Prediction Models*. Philadelphia, PA: Center for Crime Science, Temple University.

Ratcliffe, J. H., Taylor, R. B., Askey, A. P., Grasso, J., & Fisher, R. (2017, September) *The Philadelphia Predictive Policing Experiment: Impacts of Police Cars Assigned to High Crime Grids*. Philadelphia, PA: Center for Crime Science, Temple University.

Santos, R. B. (2014). The effectiveness of crime analysis for crime reduction: Cure or diagnosis? *Journal of Contemporary Criminal Justice, 30*(2), 147–168.

Santos, R. B. (2017). *Crime Analysis with Crime Mapping*. Thousand Oaks, CA: Sage.

Santos, R. B., & Taylor, B. (2014). The integration of crime analysis into police patrol work: Results from a national survey of law enforcement. *Policing: An International Journal of Police Strategies and Management, 37*(3), 501–520.

Saunders, J., Hunt, P., & Hollywood, J. S. (2016). Predictions put into practice: A quasi-experimental evaluation of Chicago's predictive policing pilot. *Journal of Experimental Criminology, 12*(3), 347–371.

Sherman, L. W. (1998). *Evidence-Based Policing: American Ideas in Policing*. Washington, DC: Police Foundation.

Tchekmedyian, A. (2016, September). Burbank police implement changes following survey indicating low morale in department. *LA Times*. Retrieved November 21, 2018, from www.latimes.com/socal/burbank-leader/news/tn-blr-me-survey-changes-20160928-story.html,

Thomas, E. (2016, December). Why Oakland Police turned down predictive policing. *Motherboard*. Retrieved November 21, 2018, from https://motherboard.vice.com/en_us/article/ezp8zp/minority-retort-why-oakland-police-turned-down-predictive-policing.

Thompson, K. (2011, November). The Santa Cruz experiment, *Popular Science*. Retrieved December 29, 2017, from www.popsci.com/science/article/2011-10/santa-cruz-experiment.

Tompson, L., & Townsley, M. (2010). (Looking) back to the future: Using space–time patterns to better predict the location of street crime. *International Journal of Police Science and Management, 12*(1), 23–40.

Uchida, C. (2010). *A National Discussion on Predictive Policing: Defining Our Terms and Mapping Successful Implementation Strategies*. Washington, DC: National Institute of Justice.

Weisburd, D., Telep, C., Hinkle, J., & Eck, J. (2010). Is problem-oriented policing effective in reducing crime and disorder? Findings from a Campbell systematic review. *Criminology & Public Policy, 9*, 139–172.

Weisburd, D., & Lum, C. (2005.). The diffusion of computerized crime mapping in policing: Linking research and practice. *Police Practice and Research, 6*(5), 419–434.

Weisburd, D. L., & Majmundar, M. K. (2018). *Proactive Policing: Effects on Crime and Communities*. Washington, DC: National Academies of Sciences, Engineering, and Medicine.

Weisburd, D., & McEwen, T. (1997). Crime mapping and crime prevention. In D. Weisburd, & T. McEwen (eds.), *Crime Mapping and Crime Prevention* (pp. 1–26). Monsey, NY: Criminal Justice Press.

PART IX

COMPSTAT

17

Advocate

CompStat's Innovation

Eli B. Silverman and John A. Eterno

INTRODUCTION

CompStat tributes are extensive. Compstat has been described as "perhaps the single most important organizational/administrative innovation in policing during the latter half of the 20th century" (Kelling & Sousa, 2001: 6). A *Criminology and Public Policy* journal editor termed Compstat "arguably one of the most significant strategic innovations in policing in the last couple of decades" (Weisburd et al., 2003: 419). The authors of a major study note that Compstat "has already been recognized as a major innovation in American policing" (Weisburd et al., 2003: 422). In 1996, Compstat was awarded the prestigious *Innovations in American Government Award* from the Ford Foundation and the John F. Kennedy School of Government at Harvard University. Former New York City Mayor Giuliani proclaimed Compstat as his administration's "crown jewel" (Giuliani, 2002: 7).

Why the praise, what are they specifically praising, and is this praise warranted? These questions constitute the core of this chapter, which maintains that Compstat praise, criticism, and replication are frequently based on a superficial understanding of its proper development, implementation, and many dimensions. The literature inadequately reflects how Compstat's successful implementation and maintenance is often incomplete when it lacks substantial organizational revamping and proper managerial preparation. This contributes to an insufficient appreciation of Compstat's array of attributes. In addition, there is often a lack of understanding of how any particular Compstat may reflect the organizational and managerial arrangements of an individual law enforcement agency at any specific time.

We stipulate that Compstat is a highly innovative and successful policing system. The National Academy of Science's thorough and rigorous 2017 report on proactive policing did not review Compstat because it did not consider it one of four specific crime prevention strategies (National Academy of Sciences, 2017). While this view is certainly understandable, we strongly suggest that Compstat, when introduced, maintained, and used properly, contributes to efficient and effective law enforcement crime-prevention strategies. This is accomplished, in part, through Compstat's formidable capacity to prevent silo effects (endemic to policing, especially where overlapping jurisdictions exist), in which various units and agencies work in isolation, rather than combining resources and working in unison. Compstat possesses the ability to encourage innovative problem-solving; to incorporate the placed-based approach, the person-focused approach, and the community-based approach at all levels, and to enhance accountability by empowering local area commanders. The Police Executive Research Forum's (PERF) 2014 report of a 2012 study identified Compstat as one in "an endless array of new strategies and new technologies" (Police Executive Research Forum, 2014: 42). Exploration of Compstat's innovation will center on: Compstat's many facets; its origins; the reasons for, and the nature of, its replication in numerous versions and venues; and its very positive strengths, as well as its prospective drawbacks, including implementation and practice.

UNDERSTANDING COMPSTAT

Compstat is most frequently understood by its most visible elements today. These include: up-to-date computerized crime data, crime analysis, and advanced crime mapping as the bases for regularized, interactive strategy meetings which hold managers accountable for specific crime strategies and solutions in their areas. At its best, other agencies and levels of enforcement are invited to these Compstat meetings. Sharing of information, something law enforcement and intelligence agencies are reluctant to do, is thereby encouraged.

Another key to understanding Compstat is seen in its four-part mantra: timely and accurate intelligence, effective tactics, rapid deployment, and relentless follow-up and assessment. This mantra demonstrates Compstat's data-driven, scientific approach with the lynchpin being accurate and timely intelligence.

Familiar Explanations

It is fair to say that the widespread diffusion of Compstat refers to these most noticeable elements. Since Compstat was first unveiled by the New York City Police Department (NYPD) in 1994, a Police Foundation's 1999 survey for the National Institute of Justice (NIJ) revealed that a third of the nation's 515 largest police departments had implemented a Compstat-like program by 2001 and 20 percent were planning to do so. The same survey found that about 70 percent of police departments with Compstat programs reported attending a NYPD Compstat meeting (Weisburd, Mastrofski, McNally & Greenspan 2001). Silverman's (2001) research indicates that very few of the over 250 outsiders who attended Compstat meetings between 1994 and September 1997 were exposed to any Compstat elements other than the meetings (with the exception of a NYPD booklet on Compstat). It is unlikely that the Police Foundation's 70 percent differed much in their exposure to Compstat. (There may, in fact, be some overlap between the two groups.)

This process is continuing. A 2013 PERF survey indicated that Compstat is now ubiquitous. In 2011, the survey was sent to 326 of PERF's member agencies with 166 responding. The survey indicated that 79 percent of the responding agencies utilized Compstat (Bureau of Justice Assistance, Police Executive Research Forum, 2013).

Gootman reported that 219 police agency representatives actually visited NYPD Compstat meetings in 1998, 221 in 1999, and 235 in the first ten months of 2000 (Gootman, 2000: B1). *Attendance at a Compstat meeting, while a useful introduction, does not provide adequate preparation for introducing and establishing Compstat.* In fact, it may be misleading because attendees often become mesmerized by the flashy overhead display of multiple crime maps synchronized with technologically advanced portrayals of computerized crime statistics.

The Lure of Compstat

The first three years of the NYPD's Compstat corresponded with dramatic declines in the City's crime rate. According to the FBI's Unified Crime Reports, the City's 12 percent decline in index crime in1994 (compared to a national drop of less than 2 percent) grew to a 16 percent decline in 1995 and yielded an additional 16 percent decline in 1996. These decreases accounted for more than 60 percent of the national decline during this period. As of June 2017, New York City crime has declined over 76.4 percent since 1993 and homicide declined 82.6 percent (City of New York, NYPD, n.d.).

While these figures, of course, do not prove a causal relationship, they received extraordinary law enforcement and national attention. The New York Model (Compstat) was offered as the road to rapid crime reduction (Gootman, 2000: B1). A *Time Magazine* 1996 observation is still applicable today: "Compstat has become the Lourdes of policing, drawing pilgrim cops from around the world ... for a taste of New York's magic" (Pooley, 1996: 55–56).

Too often, therefore, Compstat has been interpreted as primarily a meeting with a statistical computer program which, when it generates accurate and timely crime statistics, transforms a traditional bureaucracy into a flexible, adaptable police agency geared to effective crime control strategies. In the vernacular, it is only necessary to display computer-generated crime maps and pressure commanders in order "to make the dots go away" (Maple, 1999: 38).

This superficial approach is emblematic of the quick managerial fix, thus contributing to the misunderstanding and misapplication of Compstat.

This CompStat allure of crime reduction through technological advancement is reflected in the in-depth study of the Lowell Police Department's CompStat:

What police department, however, would not want to adopt a program whose clear purpose is to reduce crime through the implementation of a well-defined set of technologies and procedures? The appeal of Compstat's crime fighting goal to the police increases the likelihood that it will endure. (Willis et al., 2004: 11)

THE FULL COMPSTAT

CompStat, however, is a far more complex product of changes in managerial and organizational arrangements including flattening, decentralization, greater personnel authority, discretion and autonomy, geographic managerial accountably, and enhanced problem solving. Based on the New York experience, it is our view that CompStat cannot be a fully viable entity if the above administrative, managerial, and operational activities do not precede it.

It is worthwhile noting that the Police Foundation study's "six key elements" essential to CompStat contain similar components. They are "mission clarification, internal accountability, geographic organization of operational command, organizational flexibility, data driven problem identification and assessment and innovative problem solving tactics, and external information exchange" (Weisburd et al., 2003: 427).

It is equally noteworthy that the Police Foundation study found many of these key elements lacking in many police CompStat programs. In their comparison of CompStat and non-CompStat agencies, the study concludes that the CompStat agencies "have opted for a model much heavier on control than on empowerment" (Weisburd et al., 2003: 448). Moreover, despite its virtues, the authors found that:

Compstat agencies were largely indistinguishable from non-Compstat agencies on measures that gauged geographic organization of command, organizationally flexibility, the time availability of data, and the selection and implementation of innovative strategies and tactics ... Compstat departments are more reluctant to relinquish power that would decentralize some key elements of decision making geographically ... enhance flexibility, and risk going outside of the standard tool kit of police tactics and strategies. The combined effect overall, whether or not intended, is to reinforce a traditional bureaucratic model of command and control. (Weisburd et al., 2003: 448)

But we find this conclusion less than surprising. The study's CompStat programs are self-designated. There is no evidence that these police agencies underwent the self-diagnosis, reengineering, and organizational and managerial overhaul processes that preceded the New York CompStat experience. Additionally, if leadership is inadequate, it does not mean the CompStat innovation is useless. The community policing model, for example, was operationalized in various ways. New York City developed such a model in the 1980s that is generally considered a colossal failure as officers made their own hours and rarely worked when needed – weekends and late at night (Eterno, 2003: 126).

Thus, a more complete understanding of CompStat may be gained through a review of the context and origins of New York's CompStat in order to fully appreciate its positive qualities for modern-day policing. Failure to grasp the differences between popular accounts and CompStat's actual origins can deflect attention away from CompStat's merits while activating undesirable features.

Immediate Origins

In the immediate sense, contrary to a widely held view, CompStat was not a preordained planned system of managerial supervision, accountability, and strategic policing. Its first meeting, as a matter of fact, was almost serendipitous. Upon taking office in 1994, Commissioner Bratton called for a weekly, one-on-one, current events briefing with a representative from each of the NYPD's eight bureaus during the early months of his administration. Deputy Commissioner Maple authorized the head of the Patrol Bureau to discuss crime statistics with the commissioner. A disturbing reality surfaced: the NYPD did not know its current crime statistics; there was a reporting time lag of three to six months.

Maple, in conjunction with other key people, pressed the precincts to generate crime activity statistics on a weekly basis. During the second week of February 1994, all precincts provided a hand count of the seven major crimes for the first six weeks of 1993 compared to the same period in 1994. The Patrol Bureau's staff computerized this crime activity and assembled it into a document referred to as the "CompStat" book. The first CompStat book included current data on a year-to-date basis for crime complaints and arrests for every major felony category, as well as gun arrests, compiled on citywide, patrol borough, and precinct levels.

Contrary to most accounts, the acronym CompStat is not short for "computer statistics." CompStat actually arose from a computer file, "compare stats," in which the data was originally stored. CompStat, then, was simply short for "compare stats." This distinction is not trivial since the "computer statistics" interpretation frequently suggests that an advanced statistical computer program is synonymous with effective crime control, further contributing to CompStat's misapplication.

In fact, at the outset, CompStat was based on an elementary database, created in a set of desktop office software called SmartWare, from Informix. This was later replaced, for a considerable period, by Microsoft's very basic FoxPro database for businesses, to enter all the statistics into files.

In New York, regularized CompStat meetings grew out of a need for a mechanism to ensure precinct Commanding Officers' (CO) accountability and to improve performance. In April 1994, the leadership was searching for ways to sharpen the NYPD's crime-fighting focus. At that time, for example, boroughs held monthly field robbery meetings in which precinct COs and robbery and anti-crime sergeants met with the borough staffs (to whom they reported) to discuss robbery trends.

Top-level executives requested that the Brooklyn North patrol borough hold its monthly robbery meeting at headquarters – One Police Plaza. After the Brooklyn borough CO's overview of special conditions, several precinct COs were called to the front of the room. Their presentations, although suitable for public community council meetings, lacked in-depth analyses of complex crime problems. Dissatisfied, the Chief abruptly terminated the meeting and announced monthly headquarters meetings for each borough. The CompStat process was launched; there was no turning back.

Late in April 1994, the NYPD leadership decided to use these headquarters meetings to link the newly released drug and gun strategies with the CompStat books. Tenacity was essential. The meetings, held twice weekly became mandatory. They began promptly at 7:00 a.m. when there were likely to be few distractions.

Organization and Managerial Foundations

CompStat's roots, however, are far deeper than the scenario described above. Many managerial and organizational interventions laid the foundation for CompStat. The groundwork for CompStat centered on early developments prior to the Bratton administration (Silverman, 1999: 21–66). Even during the Bratton administration, which began in 1994, *all interventions took place before CompStat's introduction*. Early in 1994, the NYPD began to redesign its organizational structure, employing management strategies designed to re-engineer its business processes and create a "flatter" organizational structure based on geographic decentralization, teamwork, information sharing, and managerial accountability (Silverman & O'Connell, 1999).

Information flow, for example, was eased by the elimination of the level of Division, which, prior to 1994, was interposed between the precincts and the boroughs. Each of the twenty-three Divisions was responsible for from two to four precincts. Since the Divisions' responsibilities were primarily administrative, the new organizational arrangement smoothed relationships between newly beefed-up precinct and borough responsibilities and capabilities.

The rapid redesign of the Department's organizational architecture was based upon the concept of continuous performance improvement characterized by clearly delineated objective standards, benchmarking, sharing of "best practices," and the development and analysis of timely and accurate information to manage change.

Modern management provided the orchestral score; "reengineering" was its name. Contemporary management literature (Bratton, 1996: 1) explains that reengineering requires "radical change," a "starting over" throughout the entire organization, nothing less than a "reinvention of how organizations work." Commissioner Bratton insisted: "We reengineered the NYPD into an organization capable of supporting our goals."

Reengineering acted like a booster cable to the NYPD's battery, providing the cranking power needed to activate decentralization and command accountability. Relinquishing control of daily ground operations was the most fundamental yet difficult challenge facing the new administration. Traditionally, the person at the apex of the NYPD pyramid would retain control through standardized procedures and policies. But in order to hold precinct commanders accountable for crime prevention, the new leadership knew the organization must grant them more discretion. Rather than allow headquarters to determine staffing and deployment on a citywide basis, it was decided that reducing crime, fear of crime, and disorder would flow from patrol borough and precinct coordination of selected enforcement efforts.

In essence, the NYPD was able to achieve what Peters and Waterman (1982: 318) label "simultaneous loose-tight properties," meaning the "co-existence of firm central direction and maximum individual autonomy." So while the top NYPD levels were now fortified with greater detail, this knowledge extended beyond activities such as arrest particulars to more informative data such as the characteristics, times, and locations of precinct-selected enforcement strategies and their relationship to crime reduction.

These reengineering structural, operational, and strategic reconfigurations stemmed from a so called "cultural diagnostic" which rested on deliberations emanating from multi-rank and functional NYPD focus groups. These groups examined various dimensions of NYPD missions and strategies and the obstacles that hindered strategy effectiveness and goal achievement.

Consequently, the reengineering reports questioned the NYPD's operating procedures. What current policy yields, they claimed, was inadequate. The precinct organization report, for example, noted:

2 or 3 percent reduction in crime is not good enough. We need to change the organization to do more. The need to reengineer precincts is not immediately apparent. Citywide crime continues to decline year after year. Every annual precinct state of command report, without exception, includes evidence of neighborhood improvements. Bureau and Special Unit Commanders to a man, or a woman, will vigorously defend the effectiveness of the present system. Why fix what's not broken?

The answer is in the new mission of the department to dramatically reduce crime, fear, and disorder. Slow, continuous improvement doesn't cut it, and that is all the present system can deliver ... [R]e-engineering in its simplest forms means starting all over, starting from scratch. (New York City Police Department, 1994: v)

SELLING COMPSTAT

What started out as a computer file and a book to satisfy crime informational needs has evolved and been reconstructed into a multifaceted forum for coordinated, reenergized and accountable organizational crime fighting strategies. To this day, its strength lies in its adaptability and compliance mechanisms. It is vitally important to recognize that CompStat's initial and prime *raison d'être* was and is to measure and hold managers accountable for performance. In Moore's words:

It becomes a powerful managerial system in part because the technical capacity of the system allows it to produce accurate information on important dimensions of performance at a level that coincides with a particular manager's domain of responsibility ... [Compstat] is, in the end, primarily a performance measurement system. (Moore, 2003: 470, 472)

All these characteristics have contributed to its widespread replication in various formats in numerous locations. The claims and counterclaims are numerous and often difficult to evaluate since CompStat has frequently been associated with and introduced at the same time as other law enforcement and societal changes.

The boldest claims assert that CompStat plays a significant role in crime reduction due to its accountability and decentralized components. Kelling and Sousa include CompStat in their analysis of NYPD effective crime reduction policing in six precincts. They conclude that

Both the problem-solving strategy and the notion of accountability came to fruition in weekly NYPD headquarters meetings known as Compstat ... But the true effectiveness of Compstat lies in its ability to drive the development of crime reduction tactics at the precinct level. By making precinct commanders accountable, centralized Compstat allows the problem solving strategy to operate in a decentralized manner. (Kelling & Sousa, 2001: 17)

CompStat crime-reduction efficacy is also frequently advocated by police administrators, several of whom moved from the NYPD to head other city police departments. CompStat's introduction in New Orleans, for example, corresponded with a decline in murders from 421 in 1994, diving 55 percent in 1999 to 162. Minneapolis's CompStat version, CODEFOR (Computer Optimized Deployment-focus on Results), has been credited for a double-digit decrease in homicides, aggravated assaults, robberies, burglaries, and auto thefts between 1998 and 1999 (Anderson, 2001: 4). In 2000, CompStat was introduced in Baltimore by its new chief, a former NYPD Deputy Police Commissioner. By the end of the year, Baltimore experienced its first year of below 300 homicides in twenty years, accompanied by an overall crime drop of 25 percent (Anderson, 2001: 4; Clines, 2001: 15; Weissenstein, 2003: 27). Between 1999 and 2001, Baltimore's overall violent crime declined 24 percent, homicides dropped 15 percent, shootings fell 34 percent, robberies dropped 28 percent, rapes 20 percent, and assaults 21 percent (Henry & Bratton, 2002: 307). Philadelphia's former Police Commissioner, another former NYPD Deputy Police Commissioner, attributed a decline in that city's crime to CompStat-driven policing. "Social conditions in the city have not changed radically in the two years and we have the same police department, the same number officers. Nothing has changed but how we deploy them and utilize them" (Anderson, 2001: 3).

Similar crime reduction assertions have been made for police agencies around the world. Two Australian scholars, for example, published an evaluation of the New South Wales CompStat-modeled Operation and Crime Review (OCM). The authors found that this process was effective in reducing three of the four offence categories studied (Chilvers & Weatherburn, 2004).

Although these claims are repeated elsewhere, some scholars are not convinced. While Eck and Maguire acknowledge that "homicide rates have declined significantly from 1994 to 1997, following the implementation of Compstat" in the United States, they raise serious reservations (Eck & Maguire, 2000: 231). Firstly, they correctly assert that "Compstat was implemented along with a number of changes in the NYPD ... Consequently it is difficult to attribute any reductions in crime to specific police changes" (2000: 230).

Beyond this valid point, the relationships are even more complicated. A full CompStat program, as discussed earlier, rests upon and ultimately encompasses many changes, including police deployment driven by more accurate CompStat crime-mapping. The efficacy of these strategies depends on the extent to which CompStat can permeate the agency's entire operations. So some CompStats may be viewed as "CompStat Lite" while others may be more fully developed, embracing many dimensions of CompStat's crime strategy management. CompStat's prime architect, the late Jack Maple, referred to the pale CompStat imitations as the "knock off versions" whereby administrators "just sit in a circle and chat about the intelligence" (Maple, 1999: 47). This vivid CompStat contrast explains why, in our view, Eck and Maguire are compelled to maintain:

We do not know, however, whether this [homicide] reduction is produced through general deterrence of all those who frequent hot spots, through specific deterrence of hot-spot offenders who come under closer scrutiny of the police, or through incapacitation of repeat offenders following their arrest at these hot spots. So, there is an array of possible mechanisms through which directed patrol can reduce crime at hot spots. (2000: 231)

Finally, Eck and Maguire find that the rate of homicide reductions in other cities does not lend credence to the independent impact of CompStat on homicide rates. Yet they acknowledge that these findings are tenuous.

Our analysis does not find that Compstat is ineffective. These explorations can not be interpreted as a rigorous exploration of Compstat ... It is possible, given the complexity of homicide patterns, that the Compstat process had a subtle and even meaningful but difficult to detect effect on crime in New York. (2000: 235)

As Eck and Maguire (2000) suggest, there are many possible reasons for crime decreases. We do not disagree. However, to suggest that CompStat had no effect on crime whatsoever is an overstatement, at best. Those who claim the drop is due to unemployment, drugs, or macro-economic trends, for example, have legitimate arguments but ultimately these are questionable, especially since CompStat continues to maintain its large decreases in crime. While we do not disagree that these other factors have some influence, it is equally clear that CompStat also has an impact. How much each factor influences the crime rate is clearly controversial. To reject any variable, however, without clear support is, simply put, rhetoric without a scientific underpinning.

The difficulty is to show causality – that is, whether it is CompStat or other variables. Is there one key to the drop in crime? For example, Zimring (2011) suggests the decrease is due completely to the efforts of the NYPD. This is an overstatement as no scientifically sound study clearly demonstrates this. However, CompStat must be considered a critically important variable in the crime decline. To show causality, however, we must have three key elements: that the variable in question comes earlier in time, is associated with the drop in crime, and that no third variable is responsible. CompStat is generally prior in time to the huge decrease in crime but some decreases did occur earlier – under Mayor Dinkins' Safe Cities, Safe Streets program. CompStat is associated with the decrease as well. The vast majority of the decrease did occur when CompStat was adopted at NYPD. The main issue, however, is whether a third variable is responsible. Of course there are many variables that influence crime and it is difficult to parse out the effects of each. We do not dismiss the influence of other variables, although they seem more unlikely as time passes and the crime decreases remain. Ultimately, CompStat must be considered if we are to call ourselves scientists. Thus, we do not quarrel with other explanations but suggest that CompStat is, at a minimum, another variable to be considered.

Additionally, we also maintain that crime control should not be the ultimate measure of the success of CompStat or any police department. Crime is only one measure, albeit an exceedingly faulty one, that we are reluctant to use. This is because: (1) the mission of policing in democratic society is far more complicated than simplistic crime decreases; (2) crime reports are manipulated and subject to other distortions (Eterno & Silverman, 2012; Eterno, Verma & Silverman, 2016); and (3) other variables may be just as, if not more, important (e.g., corruption, police brutality, racism).

Less controversial to government agencies, however, is CompStat's surging popularity and adoption by numerous agencies and jurisdictions seeking to more effectively administer their operations and hold managers accountable. Omaha's one-year-old CompStat was credited with improving cooperation among all units. "Instead of one unit tackling a problem, everyone gets involved ... The entire culture has changed now" (*Law Enforcement News*, 2004: 11).

In 1996, New York City's Corrections Department modeled its TEAMS (Total Efficiency Accountability Management System) program on CompStat with an examination of the department's "most fundamental practices and procedures" (O'Connell, 2001: 17). Again, accountability is a major theme, which, when fused with more accurate and timely statistical reporting and analysis and inter-unit cooperation, has been credited with a dramatic reduction in inmate violence. Between 1995 and 1999, stabbings and slashing declined from 1,093 to 70 (Anderson, 2001: 3).

TEAMS has evolved and now addresses more than just jail violence. Its accountability system has been continually expanded to retrieve and assess almost 600 performance indicators addressing such issues as religious service attendance, maintenance work orders, health care, overtime, compliance with food service regulations, completed searches conducted, and the performance of personnel who have been the subject of the departments' civility tests (O'Connell & Straub, 1999a; 1999b; 1999c).

Since TEAMS is oriented to systemwide innovation, its impact has contributed to a "shift in organizational culture and philosophy" (O'Connell, 2001: 19). A former Commissioner observed:

The key is really the way that it assists us in using proactive and creative management. It expands possibilities and gets more people involved in the decision making process. Our people don't just think of themselves as corrections officers anymore. Now they see themselves as managers. (O' Connell, 2001: 19)

CompStat accountability mechanisms, long a staple of the private sector, have also become increasingly attractive to non-law enforcement public agencies. There are numerous examples. The New York City Department of Parks and Recreation, for instance, developed its own version of CompStat, calling it Parkstat. When Parks officials visited NYPD CompStat meetings in 1997, they realized that they could utilize this system to develop and refine their Parks Inspection Program (PIP) which oversees the maintenance and operation of over 28,000 acres of property throughout New York City. Now Parks department data analysis and managerial accountability are combined with monthly meetings to assess overall conditions, cleanliness of structural features such as benches, fences, sidewalks, play equipment, and landscape features such as trees, athletic fields, and water bodies (O'Connell, 2001: 20). The percentage of parks rated acceptably clean and safe increased from 47 percent in 1993 to 86 percent in 2001 (Webber & Robinson, 2003: 3). One observer's assessment of Parkstat ranks it comparable to CompStat's high rating.

As with Compstat and TEAMS, an emphasis is placed on pattern or trend identification. All performance data are viewed through three lenses, which look for district wide trends, borough wide comparison and trends, and citywide comparison and trends ... Parkstat serves many functions, not the least of which is the fostering of organizational learning. Senior administrators learn about what is occurring in the field at the same time that districts are learning from one another. Effective practices are openly shared and disseminated throughout the entire organization.

The Parkstat program is continually developing. Indeed, the department renamed it Parkstat Plus and has expanded it to include a broader range of performance measures ... relating to personnel, vehicle maintenance, resource allocation and enforce-ment activity to ensure superior service delivery. Parkstat stands as an excellent example of how the Compstat model can be adopted and successfully implemented outside the field of criminal justice. (O' Connell, 2001: 21, 22)

Perhaps the most ambitious extension of CompStat's managerial accountability and informational exchange processes began in the City of Baltimore in mid 2000 when its mayor was delighted with the results of the Baltimore Police Department's first year with CompStat. Baltimore's program, called Citistat, (first developed by CompStat architect, the late Jack Maple) is an attempt to evaluate and coordinate performance on a citywide basis whereby supervisors report every two weeks (as opposed to the previous quarterly basis) on their departments' performance. Citistat's timely data permits the assessment and coordination of diverse social services dealing with graffiti, abandoned vehicles, vacant housing, lead paint abatement, urban blight, drugs, and drug treatment. Discussions are based on up-to-date information. Citistat meetings are similar to those of CompStat whereby data, graphs, and maps are projected to track and display department performance.

So far, the City of Baltimore is pleased with Citistat's development. There has been a 40 percent reduction in payroll overtime with a savings of over $15 million over two years. Its Director of Operations maintains that "the charts, maps and pictures tell a story of performance, and those managers are held accountable" (Webber & Robinson, 2003: 4). The fact that the prestigious *Innovations in American Government Award* was awarded to Baltimore's Citistat ten years after NYPD's CompStat received the same award speaks to the enduring concepts embedded in this managerial and organizational approach. Speaking for Harvard University's Kennedy School, Stephen Goldsmith (2004: 4) stated: "Citistat is a management tool for public officials that translate into real, tangible results for citizens. Government leaders across the country and around the world are taking notice of its success-and for good reason."

Citistat, like most CompStat-type programs, seeks to lower the informational barriers that generally hinder intra- and interagency collaboration. Baltimore is constantly expanding the number of agencies included in the data analyses and its Citistat meetings. It appears that Citistat is the ultimate test of CompStat's ability to serve as the informational cement of reform, the central mechanism that provides communication links to traditionally isolated specialized units. Fragmentation plagues many organizations. Harvard management expert Rosabeth Kanter calls it "segmentalism" and notes, "The failure of many organization-change efforts has more to do with the lack ... of an integrating, institutionalizing mechanism than with inherent problems in an innovation itself" (Kanter, 1983: 301). Without CompStat, fragmentation would continue to rule supreme. CompStat's confrontation of informational splintering can be indispensable to organizational well-being. CompStat can serve as the organizational glue that bonds many changes together. As a policing reform, CompStat can serve as a management system and promote community policing, data sharing, problem-solving, corruption-fighting strategies, and other changes.

MAINTAINING COMPSTAT

Like any administrative-managerial-technological innovation, CompStat is not an unalloyed asset when either of two conditions is not met. The first pertains to the proper and full fundamental organizational and managerial reforms necessary to establish CompStat as an innovation. The absence of these reforms yields a CompStat that is more in name than in substance. The second refers to the obligation to maintain these structural and managerial underpinnings.

Since the first condition was previously discussed, we now turn to the second condition of CompStat maintenance. Just as it mistaken to assume that all CompStats are the same, it is equally erroneous to suppose that all CompStats will receive steady attention to their reform underpinnings. The vitality of a well-functioning CompStat rests on its connections to, indeed its centrality to, a reenergized, restructured, and adaptable problem-solving law enforcement organization.

CompStat's proper introduction should not be confused with long-term preservation. As a study of CompStat and organizational change in one law enforcement agency observed: "police organizations are notoriously resistant to change and any subsequent changes usually require many years to take effect" (Willis et al., 2003: 58). Properly installing and maintaining CompStat, therefore, requires vigilance. Indeed CompStat can serve as one tool used to overcome that resistance through its accountability.

There are serious liabilities when CompStat is not properly implemented and sustained, or even abused. CompStat can be easily engulfed by a culture of top-down directives dominated by numbers reflecting the predominant control system of the particular agency (Eterno & Silverman, 2012).

When CompStat performance and accountability measurement becomes excessively supervised, whether within a highly centralized organization or from external hierarchical organizations, the consequences can be alarming, especially in CompStat's paramilitary setting. Subordinate units will naturally concentrate on those items being measured. Or, as the saying goes, what gets measured gets done. This can lead to crime report manipulation and quota-driven activity such as aggressive stop and frisk. (Eterno & Silverman, 2012; Eterno, Barrow, & Silverman, 2016; Eterno, Verma, & Silverman, 2016) which has been recently been reported in numerous locales including Philadelphia, Atlanta (Hart, 2004: 6), New Orleans (Ritea, 2003a: 1; 2003b: 1), New York (Gardiner & Levitt, 2003: 8; Parascandola & Levitt, 2004: 5), and Broward County, Florida (Hernandez, O'Boye, & O'Neill, 2004: 9). Any performance measurement instrument, including CompStat, has the capacity to aggravate this condition, posing serious problems for law enforcement's statistical accuracy (Manning, 2001: 331–333; Willis et al., 2003: 13).

Thus it is crucial to recognize that CompStat is not some distinct identity isolated from the law enforcement agency in which it functions. Measurement of its success cannot be divorced from the structure in which it operates since it often reflects the prevailing organizational and political climate. To view CompStat in any other way is to reify it and endow it with elements beyond its control.

CompStat's evolving role in department priorities can be observed even in the police departments where it gained the greatest notice. Over the years, the NYPD's CompStat has become increasingly centralized with specialized units more likely directed from above.

In effect a centralization thrust has been superimposed on decentralized reforms. But centralization now has a powerful weapon in its arsenal – CompStat.

CompStat, in many senses, has been turned on its head. Instead of a tool to reevaluate objectives and tactics and scan the environment for future trends, the information from computer-generated comparative statistics is becoming known for only its most visible aspects – crime mapping and deployment activity. Greater information now is used to bear down on the management of many street operations. Numbers, sometimes any numbers, rule the day.

The original technocratic components of CompStat have been reified and duplicated, while its analytical underpinnings dwindle. In this mix, organizational learning often gets lost in the shuffle.

And what happens when painstaking and constant lessons of implementation are neglected for the quick fix? The short-haul dominates (Silverman, 2001: 206–213).

CompStat should not be implemented nor maintained as an exclusively crime control, top-down system. At its finest, CompStat focuses on multiple aspects of policing. Civil liberties, community policing, corruption, and other essential aspects of policing can and should be incorporated into the CompStat model. Unfortunately, the myopic vision of some leaders, who focus almost exclusively on crime control, is detrimental to the police mission – which ultimately rests on the social contract. This means police must protect democracy, work with communities, and safeguard basic rights, as well as prevent crime. This can be accomplished when leaders aim to inspire, not instill fear into, subordinates (Ianone et al., 2009).

CONCLUSION: COMPSTAT AS AN INNOVATION

Despite its liabilities in specific circumstances, CompStat constitutes a significant law enforcement innovation. At its best, CompStat is a unique blending of performance measurement, computer technology, crime mapping, data analysis, information sharing, managerial accountability, interactive strategy meetings and organizational cohesiveness, and learning. It is easy to forget the freshness of Commission Bratton's approach over twenty years ago when entrance to his higher echelon was restricted to commanders committed to double-digit crime reduction. Establishing a specific objective – a 10 percent reduction in crime for 1994 – was the initial propellant for change. While target setting is the norm for the private sector, it usually is anathema for public organizations because it offers a yardstick against which performance can be more accurately measured and, if deficient, condemned.

The need to instill and recognize good performance in public policing is a vital managerial imperative. Certainly, the call for improved police performance grew out of felt necessities. For both real and/or imagined reasons, there was wide discontent with the effectiveness and management of police performance.

For CompStat, the question, then, is not: should performance be measured. The questions are: what performance should be measured?; (Jones & Silverman, 1984) how should performance measurement be implemented, assessed, and maintained?; by whom?; and, more importantly, in what type of organizational and political context?

In New York, as in many other jurisdictions, CompStat originally focused on crime statistics and police arrest and quality-of-life enforcement activities. But CompStat, per se, is not inherently restricted to these measurements. CompStat's beauty lies in its versatility and adaptability. In New York, for example, CompStat, at various times, has included citizen satisfaction survey statistics, precinct commander community meeting activities, citizen complaints, and domestic violence issues and data. Years ago, the NYPD unveiled a system using location technology which queries smartphone users with questions relating to how safe one feels in one's community and how much trust and confidence do they have in the Police Department. The plan was to provide the retrieved data to commanders to assist them in tailoring strategies to address resident concerns (Baker, 2017). Furthermore, as previously discussed, CompStat lends itself to a variety of law enforcement and non-law enforcement contexts. Numerous additional agencies are currently adopting their own versions of CompStat. These include New York's Office of Health Insurance with its Healthstat designed to assist uninsured New Yorkers enroll in publicly funded health insurance programs. "In the first 18 months, participating agencies enrolled about 340,000 eligible New Yorkers" (Webber & Robinson, 2003: 4). The Department of Transportation instituted MOVE, an accountability and performance management system that meets twice a month to assess operational performance. The cities of Miami and Pittsburgh are pursuing comprehensive CompStat-like systems similar to Baltimore's Citistat.

Societal needs for information sharing, data analysis, and effective organizational-managerial performance will only continue to proliferate and even expand CompStat's rapid diffusion. Two and a half years before the 9/11 terrorist attacks on the United States, CompStat's architect, the late Jack Maple, was asked about the future of CompStat. He replied:

This should not be limited to the police department. It should involve every city agency, the fire department, the building department, the transportation department; everybody should be contributing and coordinating. And other law enforcement agencies need to participate fully. The FBI, DEA and ATF offices in a city should be running their own numbers and then bring those to Compstat meetings at the police department. (Dussault, 1999: 2)

Now in this post-9/11 era, there are numerous calls to overcome institutional barriers by federalizing the CompStat process in order to combat terrorism.

The intelligence and accountability mechanism known as CompStat is tailor-made for combating terrorism. Applying this to America's new war, however, requires solving one of the most enduring problems in policing: turf jealousy, especially between the FBI and local law-enforcement agencies.

The FBI's anti-terrorism efforts should be CompStated in every city where the bureau operations. Where a Joint Terrorism Task Force exists, the commanders of the agencies should meet on a biweekly basis to interrogate task force members about the progress of their investigations. Where JTTFs don't exist, the FBI should assemble comparable meetings with all relevant agency heads. The new Fedstat meetings would have two purposes: to ensure that each ongoing investigation is being relentlessly and competently pursued, and to share intelligence (MacDonald, 2001: 27).

CompStat has provided significant advances in policing and organizational performance. It enables key decision-makers to engage in face-to-face discussions of issues and proactive practices that draw upon the collective expertise of the entire organization. It has developed as an interactive management device that enables the organization to learn, teach, supervise, and evaluate personnel in one central forum. CompStat's multifaceted possibilities embrace an array of positive outcomes. It is incumbent upon effective leadership to seize upon this potential.

REFERENCES

Anderson, D. C. (2001). Crime control by the numbers: Compstat yields new lessons for the police and the replication of a good idea. Ford Foundation Report. New York.

Baker, Al. (2017, May 8). Data crunchers ask New Yorkers: "How are the police doing?" *New York Times* B.1.

Bratton, W. (1996, August 1). Management secrets of a crime-fighter extraordinaire. *Bottom Line.*

Bureau of Justice Assistance, Police Executive Research Forum. (2013). Compstat: Its origins, evolution, and future in law enforcement agencies. Retrieved November 13, YEAR? from http://policeforum.org/library/compstat/Compstat.pdf.

Chilvers, M., & Weatherburn, D. (2004). The New South Wales Compstat process: Its impact on crime. *Australian and New Zealand Journal of Criminology.*

City of New York, NYPD. (n.d.) www1.nyc.gov/site/nypd/stats/crime-statistics/citywide-crime-stats.page.

Clines, F. X. (2001, January 3). Baltimore gladly breaks 10-year homicide streak. *New York Times*, A11.

Dussault, R. (1999). Jack Maple: Betting on intelligence. *Internet, govtech.net/publications*, April.

Eck, J. E., & Maguire, E. R. (2000). Have changes in policing reduced violent crime? An assessment of the evidence. In A. Blumstein, & J. Wallman (eds.), *The Crime Drop in America* (pp. 207–265). Cambridge, UK: Cambridge University Press.

Eterno, J. A. (2003). *Policing within the Law: A Case Study of the New York City Police Department*. Westport, CT: Praeger.

Eterno, J. A., & Silverman, E. B. (2012). *The Crime Numbers Game: Management by Manipulation*. Boca Raton, FL: CRC/Taylor and Francis.

Eterno, J. A., Silverman, E. B., & Barrow, C. S. (2016). Forcible stops: Police and citizens speak out. *Public Administration Review*, 7(2), 191–192.

Eterno, J. A., Verma A., & Silverman, E. B. (2016). Police manipulations of crime reporting: Insider's revelations. *Justice Quarterly*, 33(5), 811–833.

Gardiner, S., & Levitt, L. (2003, June 21). NYPD: Some crime stats misclassified. *New York Newsday*, 11.

Giuliani, R. W. (2002). *Leadership*. New York: Hyperion.

Goldsmith, S. (2004, July 28). *The Innovations in American Government Awards.* Cambridge, MA: John F. Kennedy School of Government, Harvard University.

Gootman, E. (2000, October 24). A police department's growing allure: Crime fighters from around world visit for tips. *New York Times*, B1.

Henry, V. E., & Bratton, W. J. (2002). *The Compstat Paradigm: Management Accountability in Policing, Business and the Public Sector*. New York: Looseleaf Law Publications.

Hernandez, J., O'Boye, S., & O'Neill, A. W. (2004, February 25). Sheriff's office scrutinizes its crime data bonuses tied to performance under review. *Sun-Sentinel*, A1, 6.

Iannone, N. E., Iannone, M. D., & Bernsteing, J. (2009). *Supervision of Police*, 7th ed. Upper Saddle River, NJ: Pearson/Prentice Hall.

Jones, S., & Silverman, E. (1984). What price efficiency. *Policing*, 1(1), 31–48.

Kanter, R. M. (1983). *The Change Masters*. New York: Simon and Schuster.

Kelling, G. L., & Sousa, W. H. (2001). *Do Police Matter? An Analysis of the Impact of New York City's Police Reforms*. Civic Report No. 22. New York: Manhattan Institute.

MacDonald, H. (2001). Keeping New York safe from terrorism. *City Journal*. Autumn.

Manning, P. K. (2001). Theorizing policing: The drama and myth of crime control in the NYPD. *Theoretical Criminology*, 5(3), 315–344.

Maple, J. (1999). *The Crime Fighter*. New York: Doubleday.
Moore, M. (2003). Sizing up Compstat: An important administrative innovation in policing. *Criminology and Public Policy*, 2(3), 469–494.
National Academies of Sciences, Engineering, and Medicine. 2017. *Proactive Policing: Effects on Crime and Communities*. Washington, DC. The National Academies Press. doi: https: doi.org/10.17226/24928.
New York City Police Department. (1994). Re-engineering team. *Precinct Organization*. New York.
O'Connell, P. E. (2001). *Using Performance Data for Accountability*. Arlington, VA: Price Waterhouse Coopers, August.
O'Connell, P. E., & Straub, F. (1999a). Why the jails didn't explode. *City Journal*, 2, Spring, 28–37.
O'Connell, P. E., & Straub, F. (1999b). Managing jails with T.E.A.M.S. *American Jail*, March/April, 48–54.
O'Connell, P. E., & Straub, F. (1999c, September 30). For jail management, Compstat's a keeper. *Law Enforcement News*, 9.
Parascandola, R., & Levitt, L. (2004, March 22). Police statistics: Numbers scrutinized. *New York Newsday*, 14.
Peters, T., & Waterman, R. H. (1982). *In Search of Excellence*. New York: Warner.
Police Executive Research Forum. (2014). Washington, DC: Office of Community Oriented Policing Services.
Pooley, E. (1996). One good apple. *Time*, January, 55–56.
Ritea, S. (2003, October 24). Five N.O. officers fired over altered crime stats. *The Times Picayune*, 1.
Ritea, S. (2003, October 25). Crime, coercion and cover-up. *The Times-Picayune*, 1.
Silverman, E. B. (2001). Epilogue. *NYPD Battles Crime: Innovative Strategies in Policing*. Boston: Northeastern University Press.
Silverman, E. B., and O'Connell, P. (1999). Organizational change and decision making in the New York City Police Department. *International Journal of Public Administration*, 22(2).
Webber, R., and Robinson, G. (2003). Compstamania. *Gotham Gazette*. New York: Citizens Union, July 7.
Weisburd, D., Mastrofski, S. D., McNally, A. M., and Greenspan, R. (2001). *Compstat and organizational change: Findings from a national survey*. Report submitted to the National Institute of Justice by the Police Foundation.
Weisburd, D., Mastrofski, S. D., McNally, A. M., Greenspan, R., and Willis, J. J. (2003). Reforming to preserve: Compstat and strategic problem solving in American policing. *Criminology and Public Policy*, 2(3), 421–456.
Weissenstein, M. (2003). Call on NY's top cops: NYPD brass recruited by other cities to lower crime rates. *Newsday*, January 2.
Willis, J. J., Mastrofski, S. D., Weisburd, D., and Greenspan, R. (2004). *Compstat and Organizational Change in the Lowell Police Department: Challenges and Opportunities*. Washington, DC: Police Foundation.
Zimring, F. E. (2011). The City that Became Safe: New York and the Future of Crime Control. Unpublished article. Retrieved May 23, 2017, from www.law.nyu.edu/sites/default/files/siwp/WP9Zimring.pdf.

Critic

Changing Everything so that Everything Can Remain the Same: CompStat and American Policing

David Weisburd, James J. Willis, Stephen D. Mastrofski, and Rosann Greenspan

CompStat emerged in the mid 1990s and quickly came to be seen as a major innovation in American policing. By the turn of the century it had received national awards from Harvard University and former Vice President Gore, and was featured prominently along with William Bratton (the police administrator who created the program) in the national news media. Its originators and proponents gave CompStat credit for impressive reductions in crime and improvements in neighborhood quality of life in a number of cities that had adopted the program (Silverman, 1996; Remnick, 1997; Gurwitt, 1998; Bratton, 1999). And while CompStat was first introduced only in 1994 in New York City, police departments around the country had begun to adopt it or variations of it by the first decade of the new century (Law Enforcement News, 1997; Maas, 1998; McDonald, 1998; Weisburd et al., 2003; Willis, Mastrofski & Kochel, 2010a). Indeed, in a Police Foundation survey conducted only six years after CompStat emerged on the scene in New York City, more than a third of American police agencies with 100 or more sworn officers claimed to have implemented a CompStat-like program (Weisburd et al., 2001). By 2006, Willis, Mastrofski, and Kochel (2010b) reported that about 60 percent of large police agencies had adopted CompStat, and a Police Executive Research Forum membership survey in 2011 reported that 85 percent of 166 responding member agencies reported having adopted or plans to adopt CompStat (Bureau of Justice Assistance & Police Executive Research Forum, 2013). Drawing on this survey and the comments of police leaders, researchers, and others attending a conference on CompStat in 2013, a report on the meeting offered a uniformly positive assessment of CompStat's performance to date, as well as its future potential: "Regardless of how it develops in the future, it is clear that Compstat has become an integral part of policing in the United States by helping agencies become more productive, agile, and effective" (BJA & PERF, 2013: 30).

Drawing from a series of studies we conducted at the Police Foundation and elsewhere (Weisburd et al., 2001; Greenspan, Mastrofski & Weisburd, 2003;

Weisburd et al., 2003; Willis et al., 2004; Willis, Mastrofski & Weisburd, 2004a; 2004b; 2007; Willis, Mastrofski & Kochel, 2010a; 2010b), we will argue in this chapter that there is a wide gap between the promise of CompStat and its implementation in American policing. While CompStat promises to reinvigorate police organizations and to empower them to solve crime problems in America's cities, it appears to be more focused on maintaining and reinforcing the bureaucratic or paramilitary model of police organization (see Goldstein, 1977; Bittner, 1980; Punch, 1983). In turn, we argue that CompStat may inhibit the problem-solving capabilities of police agencies that it is, in theory, meant to foster. This leads us to question whether CompStat is more a reaction than a reform in policing – a program that enables police agencies to claim that much has changed, but in fact allows the police to return to traditional models of police organization.

We begin our chapter by describing the promise of the CompStat model as an innovation in American policing. We then illustrate how specific elements of CompStat that reinforce traditional supervision models of policing have been dominant in its diffusion onto the American police scene, and argue that the CompStat model includes a fundamental tension that may undermine CompStat's promise of strong crime prevention gains. Before concluding, we speculate on the evidence regarding CompStat's crime control effectiveness, and argue that CompStat should be seen more as an organizational strategy to implement crime prevention goals than as a specific innovation to control crime. We also suggest that much more needs to be known about how CompStat may enhance or hinder the implementation of specific evidence-based strategies.

THE PREMISE OF COMPSTAT

In a groundbreaking article written in 1979, Herman Goldstein described an underlying pathology in police agencies that he viewed as a fundamental cause of the malaise that surrounded policing at the time. Police agencies, Goldstein argued, were more concerned with the means of policing than its ends. The police as an institution had, in Goldstein's view, lost its way, and was in need of fundamental change. He began his article with a quote from an English newspaper suggesting just how serious he thought the problem in policing had become:

Complaints from passengers wishing to use the Bagnall to Greenfields bus service that "the drivers were speeding past queues of up to 30 people with a smile and a wave of a hand" have been met by a statement pointing out that "it is impossible for the drivers to keep their timetable if they have to stop for passengers." (Goldstein, 1979: 236)

Just as bus drivers in this English town had in the pursuit of meeting schedules forgotten that the purpose of having a bus route was to pick up passengers, so too Goldstein argued, American police in their efforts to efficiently manage police organization had forgotten that the primary task of policing was to solve community problems.

Though Goldstein's article is often cited for its description of how police strategies could become more "problem oriented," he called more generally for broad organizational and cultural change in policing that would lead to police organizations that could be focused on solving problems. His article was the first step in a wider movement toward problem-oriented policing practices in the United States. However, Goldstein gave little guidance in his article on the fundamental question that he had raised about the reorganization of policing, and this question received little attention in the vast problem-oriented policing literature that was to develop in subsequent years. For scholars, including Goldstein, problem-oriented policing was to become primarily a tactical innovation concerned with how police solve problems and not how the police organization should be managed.

CompStat was a systematic attempt to answer Goldstein's original question about how police organization could be redefined to focus on problem-solving, and, in this sense, represents an important effort to reform American police agencies. CompStat is a policing model that seeks to focus police organization on specific (typically crime) problems and to empower police organizations to identify and solve those problems. For this reason, we have defined CompStat elsewhere as a type of "strategic problem solving" (Weisburd et al., 2003). CompStat, as opposed to problem-oriented policing as it has been traditionally discussed and implemented, takes a "big picture approach," focusing not so much on the specific strategies that police use as the ways in which police agencies can be organized as problem-solving institutions.

But how does CompStat achieve this goal? The impetus behind CompStat's development in New York was Commissioner Bratton's intention to make America's largest police agency, legendary for its resistance to change, responsive to his leadership – a leadership that had clearly staked out crime reduction and improving the quality of life in the neighborhoods of New York City as its top priorities (Bratton, 1999). Strictly speaking, CompStat in New York City referred to a "strategic control system" developed to gather and disseminate information on crime problems and track efforts to deal with them. It has, however, become shorthand for a full range of strategic problem-solving approaches. These elements are most visibly displayed in CompStat meetings during which precinct commanders appear before the department's brass to report on crime problems in their precincts and what they are doing about them.

Drawing from what those who developed CompStat have written (see Bratton, 1996; 1998; 1999; Maple, 1999), as well as what those who have studied CompStat have observed (see: Kelling & Coles, 1996; Silverman, 1999; McDonald, Greenberg & Bratton, 2001), we identify six key elements that have emerged as central to the development of CompStat as a form of strategic problem solving: mission clarification, internal accountability, geographic organization of command, organizational flexibility, data-driven problem identification and assessment, and innovative problem solving. Together they form a comprehensive approach for mobilizing police agencies to identify, analyze, and solve public safety problems.

Mission Clarification

CompStat assumes that police agencies, like military organizations, must have a clearly defined organizational mission in order to function effectively. Top management is responsible for clarifying and exalting the core features of the department's mission that serve as the overarching reasons for the organization's existence. Mission clarification includes a demonstration of management's commitment to specific goals for which the organization and its leaders can be held accountable – such as reducing crime by 10 percent in a year (Bratton, 1998).

Internal Accountability

Internal accountability must be established so that people in the organization are held directly responsible for carrying out organizational goals. CompStat meetings in which operational commanders are held accountable for knowing their commands, being well acquainted with the problems in the command, and accomplishing measurable results in reducing those problems – or at least demonstrating a diligent effort to learn from the experience – form the most visible component of this accountability system. However, while such meetings are the visual embodiment of CompStat, they are part of a more general approach in which police managers are held accountable and can expect consequences if they are not knowledgeable about or have not responded to problems that fit within the mission of the department. As Jack Maple, one of the program's founders in New York, remarked: "Nobody ever got in trouble because crime numbers on their watch went up. I designed the process knowing that an organization as large as the NYPD never gets to Nirvana. Trouble arose only if the commanders didn't know why the numbers were up or didn't have a plan to address the problems" (Maple, 1999: 33). Internal accountability in CompStat establishes middle managers as the central actors in carrying out the organizational mission, and holds them accountable for the actions of their subordinates.

Geographic Organization of Operational Command

While CompStat holds police managers to a high level of accountability, it also gives commanders the authority to carry out the agency's mission. Organizational power is shifted to the commanders of geographic units. Operational command is focused on the policing of territories, so central decision-making authority in police operations is delegated to commanders with territorial responsibility (e.g., precincts). Functionally differentiated units and specialists (e.g., patrol, community police officers, detectives, narcotics, vice, juvenile, traffic, etc.) are placed under the command of the precinct commander, or arrangements are made to facilitate their responsiveness to the commander's needs. Silverman notes that, in New York, "Rather than allow headquarters to determine staffing and deployment on a citywide basis, it was decided that reducing crime, fear of crime, and disorder would flow from patrol borough and precinct coordination of selected enforcement efforts" (Maple, 1999: 85).

Organizational Flexibility

Middle managers are not only empowered with the authority to make decisions in responding to problems, they are also provided with the resources necessary to be successful in their efforts. CompStat requires that the organization develop the capacity and the habit of changing established routines to mobilize resources when and where they are needed for strategic application. For example, in New York City:

Commanding officers (COs) were authorized to allow their anticrime units to perform decoy operations, a function that had previously been left to the City-wide Street Crime Unit. Precinct personnel were permitted to execute felony arrests warrants, and COs could use plainclothes officers for vice enforcement activities. Patrol cops were encouraged to make drug arrests and to enforce quality-of-life laws. (Silverman, 1999: 85)

Data-Driven Problem Identification and Assessment

CompStat requires that data are made available to identify and analyze problems and to track and assess the department's response. Data are expected to be available to all relevant personnel on a timely basis and in a readily usable format. According to Maple, "We needed to gather crime numbers for every precinct daily, not once every six months, to spot problems early. We needed to map the crimes daily too, so we could identify hot spots, patterns, and trends and analyze their underlying causes" (1999: 32).

Innovative Problem-Solving Tactics

The five elements of CompStat described above would have little substance if CompStat did not encourage innovative problem-solving tactics. Such tactics have been the core concern of problem-oriented policing and they are central to the CompStat model (Bratton, 1998). Middle managers are expected to select responses because they offer the best prospects of success, not because they are "what we have always done." Innovation and experimentation are encouraged;

use of "best available knowledge" about practices is expected. In this context, police are expected to look beyond their own department by drawing upon knowledge gained in other departments and from innovations in theory and research about crime prevention.

COMPSTAT AND THE BUREAUCRATIC/ PARAMILITARY MODEL OF CONTROL

CompStat promises a model of policing that is focused on solving problems. Indeed, in the model of CompStat we have just described, policing is not only focused on specific problems, it is organized around the problem-solving process. But what does CompStat actually deliver in police agencies that have implemented CompStat programs?

In a national survey we conducted at the Police Foundation, we tried to assess to what extent agencies that claimed to have implemented CompStat or "CompStat-like" programs carried out the elements of CompStat that we have described (Weisburd et al., 2001). Surveying all US police agencies with over 100 sworn police officers and with municipal policing responsibilities, we examined the extent of implementation of these core elements of CompStat in agencies that claimed to implement a CompStat program, and compared this to that found in agencies that did not claim to implement a CompStat program. The findings of the Police Foundation study are instructive in understanding how police agencies have used the CompStat model.

When the department goals of those who had recently developed a CompStat program were compared with the goals of those that were not intending to develop a CompStat program, the most significant differences were in the areas of mission statements, increased control of managers over field operations, improving rank-and-file policing skills, and improving police morale. Importantly, departments that had claimed to have recently adopted CompStat were more concerned with reducing crime and increasing internal accountability than departments that reported neither having nor planning to develop a CompStat-like program. At the same time, agencies that had adopted CompStat programs were much less likely to focus on improving the skills and morale of street-level officers. This suggests that CompStat represents a departure from the priorities of "bubble-up" community and problem-oriented policing programs, which focus attention on the empowerment and training of street-level police officers. These differences also help explain why CompStat and community policing appear to operate largely independently when implemented in the same police agencies: doing so reduces the possibility of conflicts between them (Willis, Mastrofski & Kochel, 2010b). Indeed, CompStat appears, in this sense, to be modeled more closely on the traditional bureaucratic or paramilitary form of police organization (e.g., see Goldstein 1977; Melnicoe & Menig, 1978; Bittner, 1980; Davis, 1981; Punch, 1983; Weisburd, McElroy & Hardyman, 1988).

Police departments have traditionally relied on a highly articulated set of rules defining what officers should and should not do in various situations to ensure internal control. This supervisory system is strongly hierarchical and essentially negative, relying primarily on sanctions for non-compliance with police rules and regulations. Importantly, this bureaucratic, military model of organization has increasingly come under attack (Greene & Mastrofski, 1988; Goldstein, 1990; Bayley, 1994; Mastrofski, 1998). Innovations such as community-oriented policing and problem-oriented policing (as it was developed outside the CompStat model) included a strong current of dissatisfaction with traditional bureaucratic, top-down command-and-control management (Weisburd et al., 1988; Mastrofski, 1998). They promoted the professionalization of the rank-and-file, who – equipped with the necessary training, education, and motivation to solve problems – are supposed to use their best judgment to make important decisions about how to solve problems and to serve the neighborhoods to which they are assigned. Some scholars have called this a movement toward "decentralization of command" or "debureaucratization" (Skolnick & Bayley, 1987; Mastrofski, 1998).

The Police Foundation study suggests that CompStat works to preserve and reinforce the traditional hierarchical structure of the military model of policing. While fairly strong on elements of mission clarification and internal accountability, CompStat agencies were found to be largely indistinguishable from non-CompStat agencies on measures that gauged geographic organization of command, organizational flexibility, the timely availability of data, and the selection and implementation of innovative strategies and tactics. More generally, the Police Foundation data present a picture of CompStat departments that have embraced control of middle managers, tending to rely more heavily on punitive than on positive consequences. At the same time, CompStat departments were more reluctant to relinquish power that would decentralize some key elements of decision-making geographically (e.g., letting precinct commanders determine beat boundaries and staffing levels), enhance flexibility, and risk going outside the standard tool kit of police tactics and strategies.

But does CompStat empower police organization more generally to solve problems through its emphasis on the accountability of police managers? In theory, the original developers of CompStat did not dispute the community policing view that giving "cops more individual power to make decisions is a good idea" (Bratton, 1998: 198). However, they believed that in the real world of police organization, street-level police officers "were never going to be empowered to follow through" (Bratton, 1998: 199). Moreover, CompStat offered a more efficient approach for large organizations to encourage problem-solving. Middle managers were expected to spearhead the CompStat approach, bringing the CompStat message to the line officers who served under them.

Our intensive field observations in three police agencies that were seen as model CompStat programs, suggest, however, that the rank and file remain largely oblivious to CompStat and that it intrudes little, if at all, into their daily work (Willis, Mastrofski & Weisburd, 2004b). As one patrol officer put it, "If you don't go [to CompStat meetings], you don't know." In that department, in contrast to almost the entire command staff, only two or three patrol officers are present at any given CompStat meeting. They may answer a question or two, and they may give a brief presentation, but they play a peripheral role. A high-ranking officer we interviewed remarked, "patrol officers can hide in the meeting and get away without saying anything."

Whereas members of the command staff in CompStat departments we observed, in particular the sector captains, are expected to respond to the chief's questions, line officers are rarely called upon to explain a particular decision. It is true that a sector captain who has been "roasted" in CompStat for an inadequate strategy may return to his sector and rebuke his line officers, but the force of the message is considerably weakened for three reasons. First, CompStat ultimately holds middle managers, not line officers, accountable. Second, the message that is received by street-level police officers (as opposed to middle managers) is not being delivered by the highest-ranking official in the police department. And third, failure to innovate at the street level does not result in public censure on the same scale as that experienced by middle managers in CompStat meetings (Willis et al., 2004).

These field observations suggest that, in CompStat agencies, the problem-solving processes are principally the work of precinct commanders, their administrative assistants, and crime analysis staff (sometimes available at the precinct level, as well as at headquarters). The pressures on these people can be quite profound. One precinct commander noted that CompStat was "very stressful." Another told us: "We're under constant pressure. It's the toughest job in this department. We're held a little closer to the fire ... I'll go home at night after ten hours at work and keep working – fifty to sixty hours per week on average." His lieutenant reinforced this. "A precinct commander has no life [outside CompStat]." While the early developers of CompStat argued that they did not hold managers accountable for crime rates, but rather that they held them accountable for making efforts to reduce crime rates, more recent research suggests that the pressures of the CompStat process have led to the manipulation of crime reports (Eterno, Verman & Silverman, 2016). While middle managers in CompStat departments commonly expressed this level of intense accountability, nothing remotely resembling this was found at lower levels in the organization, except on the rare occasion when a line officer was required to make a substantial presentation at a department CompStat meeting. Given these limitations, others have proposed redesigned CompStat models to enhance its problem-solving capabilities, but it is unclear to what extent police agencies have adopted these models and whether they are effective (Willis et al., 2010b; Santos, 2013; Braga & Bond, 2015).

In sum, specific components of CompStat that reinforce traditional hierarchical structures of police organization have taken a predominant role in CompStat programs nationally. The predominance of these components, moreover, does not appear to empower police organization more generally toward the goal of problem solving.

INTERNAL CONTRADICTIONS IN THE COMPSTAT MODEL

The fact that police agencies that adopted the CompStat model emphasized elements of command and control over other components of CompStat does not in itself challenge CompStat as a programmatic entity. The problem we have identified so far is one of implementation of CompStat as it has diffused across the United States. The fact that many departments emphasize specific elements of CompStat does not mean that the program is not capable of being implemented more fully. But our research at the Police Foundation suggests that the CompStat model suffers from a more basic contradiction that hampers the ability of the model to achieve its goal of solving crime problems.

We conducted in-depth field observations in three "model" CompStat programs, chosen because they scored high on elements of CompStat implementation in our survey and followed closely the New York Police Department CompStat model (Willis et al., 2004; Willis et al., 2004a; 2004b). Again, as in our survey, we found in these model departments that CompStat's implementation placed the greatest stress on mission clarification and internal accountability. Notably, when we assessed the strength of problem-solving efforts in these agencies we found that CompStat had done very little to change existing crime-fighting strategies.

We did witness some innovation, such as the successful use of a comprehensive and coordinated problem-oriented approach to shutting down a dilapidated, crime-ridden rooming house in one jurisdiction, but this was the exception, not the norm. The vast majority of problem-solving approaches identified in these model CompStat agencies relied on traditional police strategies that had been used before – in particular, asking patrol officers to identify suspects and keep an eye on things, area saturation, stepping up traffic enforcement, "knock-and-talks," and increasing arrests. For example, in response to two unrelated incidents in a particular location (an increase in prostitution and the constant use of a specific pay-phone by suspected drug dealers), one district commander put "extra cruisers" in the area. During another CompStat meeting showing that the street-side windows of several parked cars had been smashed, the chief asked, "What kinds of things have we done in the past?" His deputy suggested that in the past they clamped down on motor vehicle violations: "You know, chief, sometimes you just get lucky. You catch a kid and they just talk. We need to get people in to talk to them." Similarly, when we asked a district commander what he had done regarding a spate of violent crimes within an area of the city, he told us, "good old police work" that included putting extra people in the area, increasing police visibility, sending in the drug unit, etc.

One area where there was greater innovation was in the use of geographic models of policing, in which police activities were concentrated on specific locales identified by the CompStat process. While concentrating on "hot spots" represents an important innovation in policing that has been supported by strong research evidence (see Weisburd & Braga, Chapter 13 this volume), there was little innovation once hot spots were identified. In this sense, there was often innovation in the focusing of police resources, but relatively little innovation in what the police did once they had identified problems.

There did appear to be some very small, but observable differences in each organization's capacity to facilitate innovative problem-solving. For example, one chief strongly encouraged his command staff to share ideas on crime strategies, and in another jurisdiction, task forces provided a similar forum. However, we found that innovative thinking was generally not encouraged at CompStat meetings, in good part because of time constraints. Questions and discussion were generally put off until the end of the meeting. In fact, even when one of the top managers in one agency advocated the creation of a poster delineating the most effective problem-solving strategies at the department's annual command meeting to assess CompStat, his suggestion was opposed; the district commanders responded that they already knew the answers to the problems in their districts.

Our ethnographic field observations suggest that the failure to achieve more in-depth problem-solving in CompStat departments develops in part from a fundamental tension in CompStat's implementation. The pressure of internal accountability strengthened the existing command hierarchy, but appeared to work against two of CompStat's other key elements – innovative problem solving and geographic organization of operational command. For example, officers were reluctant to brainstorm problem-solving approaches during CompStat meetings for fear of undermining the authority of more senior officers. Thus, the reinforcement of the hierarchy in CompStat has the unintended consequence of stifling the kind of creative and open discussion that is essential to creative problem-solving. Since it is the rank hierarchy within the bureaucratic organization that legitimates superior power by providing the foundation for authority relations, any actions that would jeopardize the legitimacy of command are likely to be avoided. Consequently, lower or same-ranking officers are reluctant to question their superiors during CompStat meetings.

In addition, the danger of taking risks and then looking bad in front of superior officers discouraged district commanders from pursuing more creative crime strategies with a higher risk of failure. Similarly, the decision-making authority of middle managers was limited by top management's willingness to question their judgment and to intervene in deployment decisions. And, in this regard, actions that reinforce the legitimacy of the command hierarchy, such as top leadership's involvement in the decisions of their subordinates, are difficult to change. Thus, paradoxically, the strengthening of the command hierarchy under CompStat not only undermines innovative problem-solving, but it also interferes with the decentralization of decision-making authority to middle managers.

There may be no silver bullet for resolving the tension between traditional bureaucratic features and CompStat's core elements; that is, it is zero sum. The arrangement of certain bureaucratic structures and routines, such as hierarchical authority, is necessary for the successful operation of a large administrative apparatus. It is the overdevelopment or underdevelopment of these features that hinders the functioning of the organization (Merton et al., 1952). For example, too much control from top leadership stifles innovation, but too little exposes the organization to excessive risk due to the reckless actions of its employees (Simons, 1995). With this in mind, the challenge for any department that chooses to implement CompStat is picking the compromise that most suits its needs and those of its constituencies. Since there will always be friction between those CompStat elements that conflict with existing bureaucratic features, implementing CompStat resembles driving down the road with one foot on the accelerator and the other on the brake: there is going to be a lot of friction at the wheel.

The proponents of CompStat have seen the reinforcement of traditional hierarchical models of policing as a key component of CompStat's efforts to focus police organization on problem-solving. Our observations suggest that the reality of CompStat in police departments across the country, as well as in model CompStat programs, departs markedly from this promise. Indeed, the emphasis on the hierarchy has led to internal inconsistencies in the CompStat model, which work against successful innovation. CompStat's reinforcement of the bureaucratic hierarchy of policing stifles rather than enhances creative problem-solving approaches. As Braga and Bond (2015: 33) note in their assessment of CompStat as compared to problem solving meetings in Lowell: "The practice of problem-oriented policing is essentially about insight, imagination, and creativity (Goldstein, 1990). These important ingredients to the problem-solving process seem to be minimized in CompStat meeting settings."

DOES COMPSTAT ENHANCE CRIME PREVENTION?

Whatever the internal contradictions of CompStat, from the outset, it has been seen by its originators and proponents as an effective approach to reducing crime in America's cities (e.g., see: Bratton, 1998; Henry, 2002; BJS & PERF, 2013). As early as 1995, an impressive set of statistics had been marshaled to tout the program's effectiveness in New York. Homicide rates were down almost 31 percent from the same period the year before, and crime generally was down 18.4 percent (Bratton, 1998: 289). Henry (2002: 1) reports that by the year 2000, major crimes had declined 57.26 percent from their level in 1993, and murder had declined 65.18 percent. Other cities also attributed crime declines to CompStat (Anderson, 2001).

One problem in evaluating CompStat as a crime prevention approach is that it includes many individual elements that may in themselves be successful in reducing crime. For example, CompStat has become associated with a focused geographic approach to crime problems. Crime mapping has become an integral part of many CompStat programs and, according to our Police Foundation survey, CompStat departments are much more likely to utilize crime mapping and try to identify crime hot spots than are agencies that do not have CompStat programs (Weisburd et al., 2001). Hot spots policing, as we noted earlier, has been found to have significant effects on crime and disorder at the places that are targeted by the police (Weisburd & Braga, Chapter 13 this volume). But clearly police agencies can implement hot spots policing both in the context of CompStat and without it.

Similarly, CompStat in New York has been strongly linked to what has been called disorder or broken windows policing (Wilson & Kelling, 1982; Kelling & Coles, 1996; Bratton, 1998; Kelling & Sousa, 2001). Disorder policing assumes that if the police focus aggressively on less serious crimes that affect the look and feel of neighborhoods, they will, in the long run, affect more serious offenses. This is because a developmental sequence is assumed that begins with disorder on the street and ends with serious criminal predators taking control of the urban environment (Wilson & Kelling, 1982). The effectiveness of disorder policing is much debated and the research evidence supporting this approach is mixed (Kelling & Sousa, 2001; Taylor, 2001; Weisburd & Eck, 2004). A recent National Academies of Sciences review of the literature suggests that the application of aggressive policing practices in a broken windows framework (increasing the misdemeanor arrest rate) yields small-to-no effects on crime when applied broadly, but produces crime prevention gains when geographically focused (Weisburd & Majmundar, 2018: ch. 4). Again, CompStat has been implemented in some police agencies without an emphasis on disorder policing, and disorder policing has been implemented in police agencies without a CompStat program. Thus, any evaluation of the effectiveness of CompStat will be confounded with crime control strategies that are not necessarily part of CompStat. And, unfortunately, the police agencies that have so strongly advocated CompStat as an approach have had little interest in disentangling the complex network of effects that surround this program's impact. This is perhaps not surprising, when so much good news emerged from the simple reporting of official crime rates.

But is there reason to be more sober about the impact of CompStat, even when relying upon such simple descriptive analyses? John Eck and Edward Maguire (2000) suggest this in their analysis of the crime drop in New York. One of the most important pieces of evidence brought by CompStat advocates is the extremely large decline in homicides in New York after CompStat was initiated. But Eck and Maguire show that the trend toward lower homicide

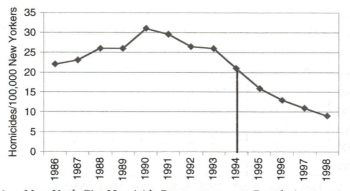

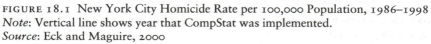

FIGURE 18.1 New York City Homicide Rate per 100,000 Population, 1986–1998
Note: Vertical line shows year that CompStat was implemented.
Source: Eck and Maguire, 2000

rates after 1994, when CompStat was established in New York, follows a similar pattern to that found between 1990 and 1994 (see Figure 18.1). While it is still noteworthy that the homicide rate declined in New York for such a log period of time, the decline began much before the CompStat program was initiated.

Eck and Maguire also examine whether the decline in homicides in New York could have been accelerated by CompStat, even if it did not begin with the program. They do note that homicide rates fell more quickly in New York after than before 1994, when CompStat began. However, they show that states surrounding New York also evidenced more rapid declines in homicide in the latter period. Moreover, in comparing the homicide decline in New York to a series of large cities that did not implement CompStat during the early to mid 1990s, they find that the New York trend is "almost indistinguishable" from that in a number of other cities that they examined.

Our Police Foundation studies did not focus on the crime outcomes associated with CompStat's implementation, but we did examine crime trends before and after the implementation of CompStat in the three model CompStat program cities in which we conducted intensive field observations. As shown in Figure 18.2, our observations follow closely those of Eck and Maguire in New York. Despite the fact that in each of these cities CompStat was given credit, in one form or another, for the declining crime trends observed, we can see an overall decline in index crimes even before CompStat was implemented.

More rigorous attempts to assess CompStat's effectiveness as a crime control strategy do not provide clear and consistent results. Using piece-wise linear growth models, Rosenfeld, Fornango, and Baumer (2005) examined the impact of three law enforcement initiatives, including CompStat, on homicide trends in three cities while making systematic comparisons to crime trends in other cities

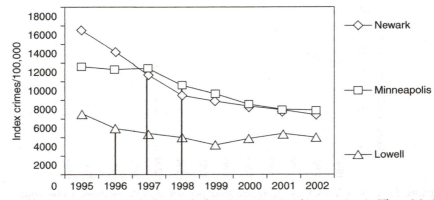

FIGURE 18.2 Crime Rates before and after CompStat Implementation in Three Model
CompStat Departments
Note: Vertical lines show year that CompStat was implemented.

and controlling for other factors influencing crime trends (e.g., measures of
social and economic disadvantage and police density). Based on their analysis,
they concluded that there was insufficient evidence in support of the NYPD
CompStat model's impact on homicide trends. In a sophisticated statistical
analysis of crime trends in New York after the introduction of CompStat that
attempted to overcome methodological limitations of more descriptive studies,
Greenberg (2013) also found little support for the position that CompStat was
responsible for the New York crime decline. Others are also reluctant to suggest
that CompStat's capacity to reduce crime is definitive (Dixon, 1998; Chilvers &
Weatherburn, 2004).

Studies in Queensland, Australia (Mazzerole, Rombouts & McBroom,
2007), Fort Worth, Texas (Jang, Hoover & Hee-Jong, 2010), and Port
St. Lucie, Florida (Santos, 2013), are more optimistic. However, it is
important to note that none of these studies find statistically significant
impacts on violent crimes, despite the fact that the fall in homicides and
violent crimes is a key part of the crime control narrative of CompStat. These
studies use time-series analyses to assess the impact of CompStat on crime.
Using crime data spanning a ten-year period (1995–2004 inclusive), the
Queensland study concluded that CompStat generally reduced reported crime
and was cost effective, but it was most effective at reducing property-related
offenses. Similarly, in Fort Worth, Jang and colleagues find significant impacts
on property crime and total index crimes, but no significant impact on violent
crime. Santos found significant impacts on thefts from vehicles, but did not
examine other crimes.

As a group, these analyses suggest the complexity of making claims of
CompStat's effectiveness. This complexity is a counterweight to the
impressions of police leaders in agencies that have implemented CompStat.

The 2013 PERF membership survey indicated that 86 percent of respondents felt that CompStat had helped the agency achieve a decrease in property crime, while nearly as many (80 percent) felt the same way about violent crime (BJA & PERF, 2013: 38).

But we wonder whether assessing CompStat's crime prevention capabilities confuses the story of CompStat, which is more about organizational change than specific crime prevention outcomes. PERF's 2011 membership survey identified organizational processes as the top reasons for implementing CompStat (BJA & PERF, 2013: 36). The crime prevention capacity of CompStat may be determined in good part by the specific strategic approaches that departments choose to employ. The question we should be asking is whether CompStat enhances the selection of the best strategies for given problems and whether it enhances the crime prevention effectiveness of specific strategies, such as hot spots policing or focused deterrence. We suggested above that the CompStat model may have mixed impacts on problem-oriented policing for example, since it encourages problem-solving on the one hand, but inhibits the creativity and independence that are essential ingredients of problem-oriented policing.

We should be asking how CompStat affects other policing approaches. In this regard, we might expect that CompStat would enhance generalized hot spots policing programs because of its emphasis on managing and controlling police in the field. In this context, CompStat would seem a good organizational mechanism to support hot spots policing. We should be asking more generally, which evidence-based policing innovations are likely to be enhanced by CompStat, and which innovations are likely to be hindered by CompStat.

But whichever directions future evaluations take, it is time to develop experimental evaluations of CompStat programs. One of the key problems in assessing CompStat is that studies have generally been retrospective, or have not had valid comparison groups. In these situations, there are simply too many potential uncontrolled and confounding factors that may influence evaluation results. It is a sobering thought that CompStat has spread so widely across American police agencies absent strong empirical evidence that it actually does something about the crime problem.

CONCLUSION

In a classic Italian novel, *The Leopard* (Di Lampedusa, 1991), about the reunification of Italy in the nineteenth century, we are told about a meeting between the Prince of Salina and his nephew in which the nephew has just told the Prince of his decision to join the republican forces against the King of Salina. The Prince responds, "You're crazy, my son. To go and put yourself with those people ... a Falconeri must be with us, for the King." The nephew, Tancredi Falconeri, answers, "For the King, certainly, but which King? If we're not there with them, that bunch is going to make a republic on us. *If we want everything to remain the same, then everything is going to have to change"* (Di Lampedusa 1991: 40, emphasis added).

In some sense, CompStat in American policing appears to follow Tancredi Falconeri's strategy for retaining the existing order in Italy in the nineteenth century. CompStat promises to enhance police effectiveness by capitalizing on recent police innovations, especially those that have been associated with problem-oriented approaches to policing. Indeed, CompStat, in theory, provides the first real attempt to implement problem-oriented policing at the organizational level, an idea proposed by Herman Goldstein forty years ago, but seemingly forgotten by police scholars, including Goldstein, who focused more on the practice of problem-oriented policing than the nature of police organization.

We have argued that CompStat, as it has actually been implemented by American police agencies, has been focused more on reinforcing and legitimating the traditional bureaucratic military model of police organization than on innovation in the practices of policing. In contrast to reforms such as community policing, which emphasize the importance of challenging the traditional policing models of command and control, CompStat works to reinforce them. In this sense, CompStat can be seen more as a reaction than as a reform in American police organization. It is a return to what is comfortable for American police agencies, and provides a justification for traditional models of police organization that have been under attack by scholars for the last three decades. In this sense, CompStat is indeed a method of changing everything so that everything can remain the same. It is a reform in American policing that allows police agencies to return to what is familiar and comfortable.

If, in doing so, CompStat can reinvigorate conventional police organization for solving problems, then such a reform can, of course, still be seen as innovative in the most positive sense. But we have also shown that CompStat is plagued with a type of internal inconsistency that leads to what might be termed bureaucratic dysfunction. By strengthening the bureaucratic hierarchical model of policing, CompStat agencies impede the ability of police agencies to develop innovative problem-solving approaches. In this sense, the emphasis on command and control found in CompStat departments has the ironic consequence of making it difficult for these agencies to achieve what CompStat is designed to do in the first place.

In the end, the success of CompStat may well be judged on whether its claims of crime control effectiveness are confirmed. The problems we identify do not mean that CompStat programs that are thoughtfully and fully implemented will not be successful in preventing crime. Rather, we think that it is time to recognize that CompStat is not an innovation that advances a particular crime control strategy. Rather it is an organizational reform. In that context, we should assess how CompStat enhances or diminishes the crime prevention effectiveness of specific crime prevention approaches. To date, the data do not allow us to reach a solid conclusion regarding the crime prevention impacts of CompStat.

Given the wide-spread diffusion of CompStat in the landscape of American policing and abroad (de Maillard & Savage, 2017), it is time to develop a series of randomized field trials that would allow us to come to unambiguous conclusions about CompStat's impacts on crime. In turn, it is time to assess, using rigorous evaluations, other programmatic goals that have been associated with CompStat – for example, enhancing community confidence in the police, the conformance of police practices to legal requirements, and the pursuit of procedural justice (Weisburd & Majmundar, 2018).

REFERENCES

Anderson, D. C. (2001). *Crime Control by the Numbers: Compstat Yields New Lessons for the Police and the Replication of a Good Idea. Ford Foundation Report: 5*. New York.

Bayley, D. (1994). *Police for the Future*. New York: Oxford University Press.

Bittner, E. (1980). *The Functions of the Police in Modern Society*. Cambridge, MA: Oelgeschlager, Gunn and Hain.

Braga, A., & Bond, B. (2015). Rethinking the Compstat process to enhance problem-solving responses: insights from a randomized field experiment. *Police Practice and Research*, *16*, 22–35.

Bratton, W. J. (1996). Cutting crime and restoring order: What America can learn from New York's finest. Heritage Foundation *Lectures and Educational Programs*, Heritage Lecture #573. Retrieved from www.nationalsecurity.org/ heritage/library/ categories/crimelaw/lect573.html.

Bratton, W. J. (1998). *Turnaround: How America's Top Cop Reversed the Crime Epidemic*. New York: Random House.

Bratton, W. J. (1999). Great expectations: How higher expectations for police departments can lead to a decrease in crime. In R. H. Langworthy (ed.), *Measuring What Matters: Proceedings from the Policing Research Institute Meetings* (pp. 11–26). Washington, DC: National Institute of Justice.

Bureau of Justice Assistance and Police Executive Research Forum. (2013). *COMPSTAT: Its Origins, Evolution, and Future in Law Enforcement Agencies*. Washington, DC: Police Executive Research Forum.

Chilvers, M., & Weatherburn, D. (2004). The New South Wales "Compstat" process: Its impact on crime. *The Australian and New Zealand Journal of Criminology*, *37*, 22–48.

Davis, E. M. (1981). Professional police principles. In H. W. More, Jr. (ed.), *Critical Issues in Policing*. Cincinnati, OH: Anderson Publishing Company.

Di Lampedusa, G. (1991). *The leopard*. (Translated by Archibald Colquhoun.) New York: Pantheon Books [1960].

De Maillard, J., & Savage, S. P. (2017). Policing as a performing art: The contradictory nature of contemporary police performance management. *Criminology and Criminal Justice*, DOI 10.1177/1748895817718589.

Dixon, D. (1998). Broken windows, zero tolerance and the New York Miracle. *Current Issues in Criminal Justice*, *10*, 96–106.

Eterno, J. A., Verma, A., & Silverman, E. (2016). Police manipulations of crime reporting: Insiders' revelations. *Justice Quarterly*, *33*, 811–835.

Eck, J. E., & Maguire, E. R. (2000). Have changes in policing reduced violent crime? An assessment of the evidence. In A. Blumstein, & J. Wallman (eds.), *The Crime Drop in America* (pp. 207–65). Cambridge: Cambridge University Press.

Goldstein, H. (1977). Toward a community-oriented policing: Potential, basic requirements, and threshold questions. *Crime and Delinquency, 33*(1), 6–30.

Goldstein, H. (1979). Improving policing: A problem oriented approach. *Crime and Delinquency, 24,* 236–258.

Goldstein, H. (1990). *Problem-Oriented Policing.* New York: McGraw-Hill.

Greenberg, D. F. (2013). Studying New York City's crime decline: &<ethodological issues. *Justice Quarterly, 31,* 158–188.

Greene, J. R., & Mastrofski, S. D. (1988). *Community Policing: Rhetoric or Reality.* New York: Praeger.

Greenspan, R., Mastrofski, S. D., & Weisburd, D. (2003). *Compstat and Organizational Change: Short Site Visit Report.* Washington, DC: Police Foundation.

Gurwitt, R. (1998). The comeback of the cops. *Governing,* January, 14–19.

Henry, V. E. (2002). *The COMPSTAT Paradigm: Management Accountability in Policing, Business, and the Public Sector.* New York: Looseleaf Publications.

Jang, H., Hoover, L. T., & Hee-Jong, J. (2010). An evaluation of Compstat's effect on crime: The Fort Worth experience. *Police Quarterly, 13,* 387–412.

Kelling, G. L., & Coles, C. M. (1996). *Fixing broken windows: Restoring order and reducing crime in our communities.* New York: Free Press.

Kelling, G. L., & Sousa, W. H., Jr. (2001). Do police matter? An analysis of the impact of New York City's police reforms. Retrieved from www.manhattan-institute.org/cr 22.pdf.

Law Enforcement News. 1997. NYC's Compstat Continues to Win Admirers. October 13.

Maas, P. (1998). What we're learning from New York City. *Parade,* May 10, 4–6.

Maple, J. (1999). *The Crime Fighter: Putting the Bad Guys out of Business.* New York: Doubleday.

Mastrofski, S. D. (1998). Community policing and police organization structure. In J. P., Brodeur (ed.), *How to Recognize Good Policing: Problems and Issues* (pp. 161–189). Thousand Oaks, CA: Sage Publications.

Mazerolle, L., Rombouts, S., & McBroom, J. (2007). The impact of Compstat on reported crime in Queensland. *Policing: An International Journal of Police Strategies and Management, 30,* 237–256.

McDonald, P. P. (1998). The New York City Crime Control Model: A Guide to Implementation. Unpublished manuscript. Washington, DC.

McDonald, P. P., Greenberg, S., & Bratton, W. J. (2001). *Managing Police Operations: Implementing the NYPD Crime Control Model Using COMPSTAT.* Belmont, CA: Wadsworth Publishing Co.

Melnicoe, W. B., & Menig, J. (1978). *Elements of Police Supervision.* Encino, CA: Glencoe Publishing Company.

Merton, R. K., Gray, A. P., Hockey, B., & Selvin, H. G. (eds.). (1952). *Reader in Bureaucracy.* New York: Free Press.

Punch, M. (1983). Management, supervision and control. In M. Punch (ed.), *Control in the Police Organization.* Cambridge, MA: MIT Press.

Remnick, D. (1997). The crime buster. *The New Yorker,* February 24 & March 3, 94–109.

Rosenfeld, R., Fornango, R., & Baumer, E. (2005). Did Ceasefire, Compstat, and Exile reduce homicide? *Criminology & Public Policy*, 4, 419–449.

Santos, R. B. (2013). Implementation of a police organizational model for crime reduction. *Policing: An International Journal of Police Strategies and Management* 36, 295–311.

Silverman, E. B. (1996). Mapping change: How the New York City police department re-engineered itself to drive down crime. *Law Enforcement News*, December.

Silverman, E. B. (1999). *NYPD Battles Crime: Innovative Strategies in Policing*. Boston, MA: Northeastern University Press.

Simons, R. (1995). Control in an age of empowerment. *Harvard Business Review*, 73, 1–7.

Skolnick, J. H., & Bayley, D. H. (1987). Theme and variation in community policing. In *Crime and Justice*. Washington, DC: National Institute of Justice.

Taylor, R. B. (2001). *Breaking away from Broken Windows: Baltimore Neighborhoods and the Nationwide Fight against Crime, Grime, Fear, and Decline*. Boulder, CO: Westview Press.

Weisburd, D., & Eck, J. (2004). What can police do to reduce crime, disorder, and fear. *Annals of American Political and Social Science*, 593, 42–65.

Weisburd, D., McElroy, J., & Hardyman, P. (1988). Challenges to supervision in community policing: Observations on a pilot project. *American Journal of Police*, 7, 29–50.

Weisburd, D., & Majmundar, M. (eds.). (2018). *Proactive Policing: Effects on Crime and Communities*. Washington, DC: The National Academies Press.

Weisburd, D., Mastrofski, S. D., McNally, A. M., & Greenspan, R. (2001). *Compstat and organizational change: Findings from a national survey*. Report submitted to the National Institute of Justice by the Police Foundation.

Weisburd, D., Mastrofski, S. D., McNally, A. M., Greenspan, R., & Willis, J. J. (2003). Reforming to preserve: Compstat and strategic problem solving in American policing. *Criminology and Public Policy*, 2(3), 421–456.

Willis, J. J., Mastrofski, S. D., Weisburd, D., & Greenspan, R. (2004). *Compstat and Organizational Change in the Lowell Police Department: Challenges and Opportunities*. Washington, DC: Police Foundation. Retrieved from www .policefoundation.org/pdf/compstat.pdf

Willis, J. J., Mastrofski, S. D., & Weisburd, D. (2004a). COMPSTAT and bureaucracy: A case study of challenges and opportunities for change. *Justice Quarterly*, 21(3), 463–496.

Willis, J. J., Mastrofski, S. D., & Weisburd, D. (2004b). *Compstat in Practice: An In-Depth Analysis of Three Cities*. Washington, DC: The Police Foundation.

Willis, J. J., Mastrofski, S. D., & Weisburd, D. (2007). Making sense of Compstat: A theory-based analysis of organizational change in three police departments. *Law and Society Review*, 41, 147–88.

Willis, J. J., Mastrofski, S. D., & Kochel, T. R. (2010a). The co-implementation of Compstat and community policing. *Journal of Criminal Justice*, 38, 969–980.

Willis, J. J., Mastrofski, S. D., & Kochel, T. R. (2010b). *Maximizing the Benefits of Reform: Integrating Compstat and Community Policing*. Washington, DC: Office of Community-Oriented Policing Services, US Department of Justice.

Wilson, J. Q., & Kelling, G. L. (1982). Broken windows: The police and neighborhood safety. *The Atlantic Monthly*, March, 29–38.

PART X

EVIDENCE-BASED/ RISK-FOCUSED POLICING

19

Advocate

Evidence-Based Policing for Crime Prevention

Brandon C. Welsh

INTRODUCTION

In recent weeks Big City has experienced an increase in young people selling drugs on the street. The police chief directs one of his managers to organize a small group of officers to look into the matter and report back with a plan of action. One of these officers is tasked with researching what works to address the problem of street-level drug sales. The officer carries out literature searches, contacts other police departments and police research organizations such as the Police Foundation, and follows up with some of the researchers involved in evaluation studies. The most rigorous evaluations are coded according to the outcomes of interest, results are analyzed, and a report is prepared that shows what type of intervention works best. Detailed observational and other information on the problem gathered by the other officers is used to assess the applicability of the "best practice" to the local context and conditions. On the basis of this information, the chief authorizes the needed resources for a program to be implemented to address street-level drug sales, and introduces a monitoring and evaluation scheme to aid in-house policy and for dissemination purposes.

This fictitious scenario, while brief on details, is an example of evidence-based policing in action. Evidence-based policing involves the police using the highest quality available research evidence on what works best to reduce a specific crime problem and tailoring the intervention to the local context and conditions. This approach likely holds wide appeal. To local government and policymakers, the police may be seen as being efficient in their use of monetary and other resources. To scholars, the police may be seen as acting like scientists – targeting crime problems with accumulated scientific evidence of the highest quality on what works best; here the police are seen as not reinventing the wheel. Evidence-based policing could be another example of, in Bayley's (1998: 174) words, "smarter law enforcement." To citizens, evidence-based policing may also hold appeal because of its commitment to the use of what works best and its clear intent on bringing about positive change. But for some citizens, especially those who reside in high-crime neighborhoods, how the police interact with residents and suspected offenders may ultimately influence their feelings toward evidence-based policing. Arguably, these residents may reserve judgment on all police practices.

This chapter sets out to update an earlier work in support of evidence-based policing (Welsh, 2006). With an additional decade of research, policy developments, and advocacy (see e.g., Braga & Weisburd, 2010; Sherman, 2011; 2013; 2015; Neyroud & Weisburd, 2014; Telep & Lum, 2014; Martin & Mazerolle, 2015; Lum & Koper, 2017; Telep, 2017; Weisburd & Majmundar, 2018), this chapter argues that there is even stronger scientific merit in the police adopting a formalized evidence-based approach to preventing crime and that a great deal of public good can come about from this. This chapter also argues that evidence-based policing holds much promise in making a difference in those very neighborhoods where crime and violence are most intractable and public confidence in the police is lowest. The latter may come about not just because police are using scientific evidence about what works best, but also because police are targeting crime-risk factors and tailoring what works to local context and conditions.

Sherman's (1998) seminal piece, *Evidence-Based Policing*, and his earlier works dating back to his 1992 *Crime and Justice* essay, "Attacking crime: policing and crime control," first spelled out the arguments in support of the police using accumulated scientific evidence on what works best to prevent crime, and set the stage for this approach being acknowledged by police scholars (the editors of the present volume included) as one of the important police innovations of the last two decades. Subsequent works by Sherman, Weisburd, and other police scholars (see e.g., Lum, 2009; Braga & Weisburd, 2010; Sherman, 2013; Neyroud & Weisburd, 2014; Lum & Koper, 2017; Weisburd & Majmundar, 2018) have further elaborated on and elevated the importance of evidence-based policing.[1] Importantly though, evidence-based policing is but one part of a larger evidence-based movement, from which it draws institutional and intellectual support. This may be one feature that distinguishes evidence-based policing from other police innovations.

The chapter is organized as follows. The first part describes the evidence-based model with special reference to evidence-based policing, and overviews the movement that has given rise to its use in the social sciences. It then reviews the state of research on evidence-based policing with a specific focus on the prevention of crime. One of the aims of this part is to address the

---

[1] This includes broader definitions of evidence-based policing. Sherman (2013: 377) defines it as a "method of making decisions about 'what works' in policing: which practices and strategies accomplish police missions most cost–effectively." Lum and Koper (2015: 1) define evidence-based policing as "a law enforcement perspective and philosophy that implicates the use of research, evaluation, analysis, and scientific processes in law-enforcement decision making."

pressing question: Is there sufficient evidence to support the widespread application of evidence-based policing? This is followed by a discussion of whether we can expect the police to use or perhaps institutionalize the evidence-based model to prevent crime. The chapter concludes with a brief discussion on why police agencies should adopt an evidence-based approach to prevent crime.

The Evidence-Based Model and Policing

In characterizing the evidence-based model and policing, it is important to first define what is meant by the term "evidence." Throughout this chapter, evidence is taken to mean scientific, not criminal evidence (see Sherman, 1998: 2, note 1). Evidence introduced in criminal court proceedings, while bound by laws and procedures, is altogether different from scientific evidence (see Zane & Welsh, 2018). The latter "refers to its common usage in science to distinguish data from theory, where evidence is defined as 'facts ... in support of a conclusion, statement or belief'" (*Shorter Oxford English Dictionary*, 2002, as cited in Sherman, 2003: 7).

At the heart of the evidence-based model is the notion that "we are all entitled to our own opinions, but not to our own facts" (Sherman, 1998: 4). Many may be of the opinion that hiring more police officers will yield a reduction in crime rates. However, an examination of the empirical research evidence on the subject reveals that this is not the case (as we shall discuss). Use of opinions instead of facts to guide crime policy has a greater chance to result in harmful or iatrogenic effects (McCord, 2003) or to not work at all, waste scarce public resources (Welsh, Farrington & Gowar, 2015), and divert policy attention from the more important priorities of the day (Mears, 2007; 2010). Moreover, within the evidence-based paradigm, drawing conclusions based on facts calls attention to a number of fundamental issues: the validity of the evidence; the methods used to locate, appraise, and synthesize the evidence; and implementation (Welsh & Farrington, 2011).

In an evidence-based model, the source of scientific evidence is empirical research in the form of high quality evaluations of programs, practices, and policies. An evaluation is considered to be high quality if it possesses a high degree of internal, construct, and statistical conclusion validity (Cook & Campbell, 1979; Shadish, Cook & Campbell, 2002). Internal validity refers to how well the study unambiguously demonstrates that an intervention (e.g., community policing) had an effect on an outcome (e.g., residential burglary). Here, some kind of control condition is necessary to estimate what would have happened to the experimental units (e.g., people or areas) if the intervention had not been applied to them – known as the "counterfactual inference." Construct validity refers to the adequacy of the operational definition and measurement of the theoretical constructs that underlie the intervention and the outcome. Statistical conclusion validity is concerned with whether the relationship between the presumed cause (the intervention) and the presumed effect (the outcome) is statistically reliable.

Put another way, researchers and policymakers can have a great deal of confidence in the observed effects of an intervention if it has been evaluated with a design that controls for the major threats to these three forms of validity. Randomized experiments (see Farrington & Welsh, 2006; Weisburd & Hinkle, 2012) and rigorous quasi-experiments (see Braga & Weisburd, 2013; Nagin & Weisburd, 2013) are the types of evaluation designs that can best achieve high internal validity in particular (i.e., control groups are needed to counter threats to internal validity), and all of these designs matter in evidence-based policing. Moore's (2006) critique of evidence-based policing rightly acknowledges this. While randomized experiments have higher internal validity, quasi-experiments go a long way toward countering many threats to internal validity. Because of this, they are considered the minimum interpretable design for assessing intervention effects (Cook & Campbell, 1979; Shadish et al., 2002).

Just as it is crucial to use the highest quality evaluation designs to generate evidence about the effects of police practices, it is also important to use the most rigorous methods to locate, appraise, and synthesize the available research evidence. The main types of review methods include the single study, narrative, vote-count, systematic, and meta-analytic (Welsh & Farrington, 2006). Single study and narrative reviews are less rigorous than the others, and are not recommended in assessing research evidence. Comprehensiveness, adherence to scientific rules and conventions, and transparency are at the heart of the rigorous review methods.

The question, What does the evidence say?, is in direct reference to existing evaluation studies. Rather than the self-selection of individual studies to substantiate one's position, evidence refers to the accumulated body of studies (published and unpublished) on the subject of interest. This degree of comprehensiveness is one way that the evidence-based model attempts to address researcher or institutional bias. Adherence to scientific rules and conventions is most germane to the use of appropriate quantitative techniques in analyzing results, as well as the presentation of these results. The transparency of search methods, criteria used to include (and exclude) studies, quantitative techniques, and so on is also important in allowing the reviews to be replicated by other researchers (Welsh, van der Laan & Hollis, 2013).

The importance of implementation to the evidence-based model is best captured by the following: "Evidence-based policing assumes that experiments alone are not enough. Putting research into practice requires just as much attention to implementation as it does to controlled evaluations" (Sherman, 1998: 7). Successful implementation calls for taking account of local context and conditions. Some critics of the evidence-based paradigm (Lab, 2003; Sparrow, 2009; Laycock, 2012) claim that it fails to adequately account for local context and conditions in reaching conclusions about what works. The main thrust of this argument is that unless local context and conditions are investigated, undue weight may be ascribed to any effects of the intervention on the outcome of interest. Evidence-based policing has in place the capacity to take account of these features. For example, those tasked with investigating the research evidence on the effectiveness of police practices to deal with a particular crime problem can question the original researchers or solicit unpublished reports to learn about how local context and conditions may have influenced the reported results. This information can then be integrated into the existing profile of the program. This point is overlooked in Sparrow's (2009) critique of evidence-based policing.

Evidence-based policing also has the capacity to appropriately tailor proven strategies or practices to the local setting. While perhaps obvious and supported in research on diffusion of knowledge and replication studies (see Ekblom, 2002; Liddle et al., 2002), not paying attention to this (and using the one-size-fits-all approach) can severely impact implementation as well as the overall effectiveness of the intervention. Hough and Tilley (1998: 28) make clear this point:

Routinely-used techniques often cannot be taken off the shelf and applied mechanically with much real prospect of success. Standard, broad-brush, blockbuster approaches to problems tend to produce disappointing results. Where new approaches are adopted it is likely that adjustments will be needed in the light of early experience. All crime prevention measures work (or fail to do so) according to their appropriateness to the particular problem and its setting.

Detailed observational and other information on the crime problem that is the focus of attention, as well as the setting (e.g., urban density, unemployment rates), can be matched with the proven practice and modifications can then be made as needed.

Another important feature of the evidence-based model is the outcome of interest. While it is acknowledged that evidence-based policing can serve other useful purposes (e.g., improving police training standards, improving police–community relations), the main outcome of interest or bottom line is crime prevention (see Welsh, 2002). The parallel is with evidence-based medicine's primary focus on saving lives or improving the quality of life of those suffering from terminal or chronic illnesses. For evidence-based policing, or evidence-based crime prevention in general, the prevention of crime is a first-tier or primary outcome. This is the focus throughout this chapter.

Part of a Larger Movement

Evidence-based policing is a part of a larger and increasingly expanding evidence-based movement. In general terms, this movement is dedicated to the betterment of society through the utilization of the highest quality scientific evidence on what works best. The evidence-based movement first began in medicine (Millenson, 1997) and was subsequently embraced by social sciences, albeit fairly recently (Mosteller & Boruch, 2002; Sherman, 2003; Sherman et al., 2006).

In 1993, the Cochrane Collaboration, named after the renowned British epidemiologist Sir Archie Cochrane, was established to prepare, maintain, and make accessible systematic reviews of research on the effects of health care and medical interventions. The Cochrane Collaboration established collaborative review groups (CRGs) across the world to oversee the preparation and maintenance of systematic reviews in specific areas, such as heart disease, infectious diseases, and breast cancer. All reviews produced by Cochrane CRGs follow a uniform structure. The same level of detail and consistency of reporting is found in each, and each review is made accessible through the *Cochrane Library*, an electronic publication.

The success of the Cochrane Collaboration in reviewing the effectiveness of medical and health care interventions stimulated international interest in establishing a similar infrastructure for conducting systematic reviews of research on the effects of interventions in the social sciences, including education, social work and social welfare, crime and justice, and, most recently, international development. In 2000, the Campbell Collaboration was established. It is named after the influential experimental psychologist Donald Campbell (see Campbell, 1969). The Collaboration's Crime and Justice Group aims to prepare and maintain systematic reviews of criminological interventions and to make them accessible electronically to practitioners, policymakers, scholars, and the general public (Farrington, Weisburd & Gill, 2011).

The State of Evidence for Evidence-Based Policing

A commonplace critique of evidence-based policing is that there is insufficient research evidence that police agencies can draw upon to guide their practices (Bullock & Tilley, 2009; Laycock, 2012). To address this critique, this section brings together leading reviews on the effectiveness of policing for crime prevention. This serves two main purposes: (a) to take stock of what we know (and do not know) about what works best in policing for crime prevention; and (b) to assess if there is sufficient research evidence to develop evidence-based policing.

Sherman and Eck (2006)
As part of a larger project to assess the scientific evidence on the effectiveness of preventing crime in seven major institutional settings in which crime prevention efforts take place (families, communities, schools, labor markets, places, police agencies, and courts and corrections) in the United States and internationally, Sherman and Eck (2006) undertook a review of police practices. This updates Sherman's (1997) chapter in the influential report prepared for the US Congress,

Preventing Crime: What Works, What Doesn't, What's Promising (Sherman et al., 1997).

On the basis of the highest quality available scientific evidence, the authors identified a total of five police practices that are effective in reducing crime. Most of these practices are highly specific, such as increased directed patrols in street-corner hot spots of crime and arrests of employed suspects for domestic assault. Also important to police managers and other consumers of this research is that this review draws conclusions about what does not work, what is promising, and what is unknown.

One of the first questions that may be asked of these conclusions is: How much confidence can be held in them? This is a critical question in assessing the research evidence, and one that goes to the heart of the underlying methodology employed (e.g., type of evaluation studies included, method used to aggregate results). The saying, "garbage in, garbage out," needs to be kept in mind in judging the results of any single study or review method. As noted above, the evidence-based model is committed to the use of the highest quality available scientific evidence and the most rigorous methods.

Sherman and Eck's (2006) review used what is known as a vote-count methodology. The vote-count method adds a quantitative element to the narrative review, by considering statistical significance (the probability of obtaining the observed effect if the null hypothesis of no relationship were true).[2] In essence, this method tallies-up the "number of studies with statistically significant findings in favor of the hypothesis and the number contrary to the hypothesis (null findings)" (Wilson, 2001: 73). The main problem with using statistical significance is that it depends partly on sample size and partly on effect size. For example, a significant result may reflect a small effect in a large sample or a large effect in a small sample (Farrington et al., 2006).

However, Sherman and Eck's (2006) review adopted a more comprehensive vote-count methodology, first developed by Sherman et al. (1997) and revised by Farrington et al. (2006). In addition to statistical significance, this vote-count method integrates a "scientific methods scale" (SMS) that is largely based on the work of Cook and Campbell (1979), and describes research designs that are

---

[2] Narrative reviews of the literature quite often include many studies and may be comprehensive. The main drawback of the narrative method is researcher bias. This bias, whether intentional or not, typically starts right from the beginning with a less than rigorous methodology for searching for studies. More often than not, the researcher will limit his or her search to published sources or even self-select studies to be included, based on the researcher's familiarity with them, quite possibly leaving many studies out of the review. This can sometimes lead to an incorrect interpretation of the particular intervention's effect on crime; for example, what should have been presented as a desirable effect is instead reported as an uncertain effect (i.e., unclear evidence of an effect). The one main advantage to the narrative review is that the reader can usually glean a great deal more information about individual studies than would otherwise be possible in the more rigorous review methods.

most effective in eliminating threats to internal validity. The scale ranges from level 1 (correlation between a prevention program and a measure of crime at one point in time) to level 5 (random assignment of persons or places to treatment and control conditions), with level 5 being the highest. Only studies with a minimum of a level-3 evaluation design (presence of before and after measures of crime in treatment and comparable control conditions) were included in the review. Importantly, external validity (the generalizability of internally valid results) was addressed to some extent by establishing rules for accumulating evidence.[3]

Eck and McGuire (2006) and Weisburd and Eck (2004)

As part of a larger project to characterize and explain the decline in crime rates in the United States during the 1990s (Blumstein & Wallman, 2006), Eck and Maguire (2006) examined whether the contributions of seven major policing strategies (increase in number of police officers, community policing, zero-tolerance policing, directed patrols in hot spots, firearms enforcement, retail drug market enforcement, and problem-oriented policing) during this period of time reduced violent crime. Their work is relevant here because, in order to do this, Eck and Maguire reviewed the scientific evidence on the effectiveness of these policing strategies. The authors found that some of the policing strategies hold sufficient empirical support to reduce violent crime. These included directed patrols in hot spots, firearms enforcement, retail drug market enforcement (especially when combined with the threat of civil action against property owners), and problem-oriented policing. For the other three strategies, the authors found that the evidence was mixed for increasing the number of police officers, weak for community policing, and nonexistent for zero-tolerance policing.

Weisburd and Eck's (2004) review was carried out as part of a larger National Academies of Sciences panel investigating police policy and practices (Skogan & Frydl, 2004). In reviewing the extant research evidence about what works in policing, the authors set out to address a number of critical questions

---

[3] The aim was to classify all police practices into one of four categories: what works, what does not work, what is promising, and what is unknown. What works: These are programs that prevent crime. Programs coded as working must have at least two level-3 to level-5 evaluations showing statistically significant and desirable results and the preponderance of all available evidence showing effectiveness. What does not work: These are programs that fail to prevent crime. Programs coded as not working must have at least two level-3 to level-5 evaluations with statistical significance tests showing ineffectiveness and the preponderance of all available evidence supporting the same conclusion. What is promising: These are programs wherein the level of certainty from available evidence is too low to support generalizable conclusions, but there is some empirical basis for predicting that further research could support such conclusions. Programs are coded as promising if they were found to be effective in significance tests in one level-3 to level-5 evaluation and in the preponderance of the remaining evidence. What is unknown: Any program not classified in one of the three above categories is defined as having unknown effects.

facing American policing, including "Does the research evidence support the view that standard models of policing are ineffective in combating crime and disorder?" and "Do recent police innovations hold greater promise of increasing community safety, or does the research evidence suggest that they are popular but actually ineffective?" (Weisburd & Eck, 2004: 43).

The authors found that focused (or targeted) police strategies are more likely to yield crime reduction benefits than unfocused (or uniformly applied) strategies. In addition, they found moderate to strong evidence of effectiveness for recent innovations of problem-oriented policing, problem solving in hot spots, focused intensive enforcement, and hot spots patrols. Also revealing was the finding that the standard model of policing (e.g., adding more police, general patrol), which is both unfocused and relies almost exclusively on law enforcement sanctions, is not supported by solid empirical study. On the latter, the authors observe, "While this approach remains in many police agencies the dominant model for combating crime and disorder, we find little empirical evidence for the position that generally applied tactics that are based primarily on the law enforcement powers of the police are effective" (Weisburd & Eck, 2004: 57).

While somewhat different in scope, these two reviews have been grouped together because each reviewed only the most methodologically rigorous studies. They also sought to separate the wheat from the chaff, the former serving as the empirical evidence upon which conclusions are drawn about effectiveness or ineffectiveness.

Campbell Collaboration Systematic Reviews

Under the auspices of the Campbell Collaboration, a total of twenty systematic reviews on policing have been published or completed (and nearing publication) so far (see Table 19.1). Each of these reviews provides evidence that is readily accessible to guide evidence-based policing, and the overwhelming majority (seventeen out of twenty) are focused on the prevention of crime or related outcomes. It is important to note that in their review of systematic reviews of policing, Telep and Weisburd (2016) include several systematic reviews not carried out under the auspices of the Campbell Collaboration.

Compared to the aforementioned reviews, this group of systematic reviews is even more focused on investigating the effectiveness of one particular police practice or strategy, including hot spots policing, community-oriented policing, street-level drug law enforcement, and police diversion programs for youth. This narrow focus is purposeful. Among other reasons, it is meant to enable the researcher to carry out a comprehensive search for relevant studies. Through this, it is hoped that the researcher will uncover all available studies on the subject. This narrow focus is also meant to allow the researcher to look in depth at each study on multiple dimensions (and code them) to assess any potential influence on the observed outcomes.

TABLE 19.1 *Campbell Collaboration Systematic Reviews on Policing*

Topic	Lead Author	Status
1. Legitimacy in policing	Lorraine Mazerolle	Published
2. Police strategies to reduce illegal possession and carrying of firearms	Christopher Koper	Published
3. Hot spots policing	Anthony Braga	Published
4. Pulling levers focused deterrence strategies	Anthony Braga	Published
5. Problem-oriented policing	David Weisburd	Published
6. Street-level drug law enforcement	Lorraine Mazerolle	Published
7. Community-oriented policing	Charlotte Gill	Completed
8. Community-oriented policing in developing countries	Angela Higginson	Completed
9. Broken windows policing	Anthony Braga	Completed
10. Third party policing	Lorraine Mazerolle	Completed
11. Increased police patrol	David Weisburd	Completed
12. Policing school strategies	Anthony Petrosino	Completed
13. Police diversion programs for youth	David Wilson	Completed
14. Geographically focused police initiatives: spatial displacement and diffusion of benefits	Kate Bowers	Published
15. Police body worn cameras	Cynthia Lum	Completed
16. DNA testing in police investigative work	David Wilson	Published
17. Police interview and interrogation methods	Christian Meissner	Published
18. Police stress management interventions	George Patterson	Published
19. Police crisis intervention teams	Sema Taheri	Completed
20. Second responder programs for domestic violence	Robert Davis	Published

Source: Crime and Justice Group, Campbell Collaboration (2018).

The systematic review is the most rigorous method for assessing effectiveness (Chalmers, 2003; Petrosino & Lavenberg, 2007; Welsh et al., 2013). In turn, it has the most to offer to evidence-based policing. It uses rigorous methods for locating, appraising, and synthesizing evidence from prior evaluation studies, and it is reported with the same level of detail that characterizes high quality reports of original research. Systematic reviews, according to Johnson and his colleagues (2000: 35), "essentially take an epidemiological look at the methodology and results sections of a specific population of studies to reach a research-based consensus on a given topic." They have explicit objectives, explicit criteria for including or excluding studies, extensive searches for eligible evaluation studies from across the world, careful extraction and coding of key features of studies, and a structured and detailed report of the methods and conclusions of the review. As noted by Petrosino et al. (2001: 20), "the foremost advantage of systematic reviews is that when done well and with full integrity, they provide the most reliable and comprehensive statement about what works."

With respect to the findings of the systematic reviews, Telep and Weisburd's (2016: 163) "generalizations the police can draw from these reviews" are particularly instructive. The first has to do with the target of police actions. In the words of Telep and Weisburd (2016: 163–164), "the police are most effective when they focus on high-activity people and places." The second generalization has to do with the style of police action: the need for the police to adopt proactive problem-solving. The final generalization speaks to a wider engagement with other community stakeholders (e.g., businesses, resident associations) and crime prevention strategies (e.g., situational, community): "police should, when possible, not rely exclusively on law enforcement and arrest to address crime and disorder" (Telep & Weisburd, 2016: 164).

Weisburd and Majmundar (2018)

The latest review on the effectiveness of policing for crime prevention was carried out by the National Academies of Sciences panel investigating proactive policing (Weisburd & Majmundar, 2018). The report is highly comprehensive in its coverage – taking account of systematic reviews and the latest evaluations – and rigorous in its assessment of the effectiveness of the scientific evidence of the four strategies of proactive policing: (a) place-based (hot spots policing, predictive policing, and closed-circuit television); (b) problem-solving (problem-oriented policing and third party policing); (c) person-focused (focused deterrence and stop-question-frisk); and (d) community-based (community-oriented policing, procedural justice policing, and broken windows policing). Study design and replication were used to rate the strength of causal evidence.

The report found strong evidence in support of effectiveness for three of the techniques (from three different proactive policing strategies): hot spots policing; stop-question-frisk when targeted at hot spots for violent crime; and broken windows policing that use place-based, problem-solving practices. The strength of the evidence for the remainder of the techniques was judged to be a mix of medium and weak. The report's conclusions are equally important in capturing the upward trajectory of policing research and its impact on society:

While the evidence generated by these interventions is far from complete or definitive, the past three decades have been something of a "golden age" for the production of systematic evidence on what works. The police, more than other criminal justice agencies, have been amenable to running field experiments, and even non-experimental interventions are better documented than in the past, due to the increasing quality and quantity of data on crime and police activities. Although the available evidence still has important gaps and contradictions, this recent trend in research is favorable to the ultimate goal of evidence-based crime policy. (Weisburd & Majmundar, 2018: 37; and ch. 4)

Toward Evidence-Based Policing?

Overall, these reviews, using different high-quality methods, demonstrate (with a high degree of concordance) that there are a number of policing practices with robust empirical evidence of effectiveness in preventing crime. These reviews also show (also with a high degree of concordance) that there are some promising practices that police currently employ, and many more that police should consider abandoning or perhaps modifying. It is, of course, recognized that all crime prevention programs, policing included, that become institutionalized and take on brand-name appeal – think of DARE (Drug Abuse Resistance Education) – can be terribly difficult to do away with or even change (see Weiss, Murphy-Graham & Birkeland, 2005).

These reviews of the empirical evidence on policing for crime prevention also suggest that there is sufficient capacity to begin to develop evidence-based policing. Moreover, underlying this aggregate number of effective policing practices are a few important points that speak to the depth and breadth of capacity for the development of evidence-based policing. One is that the effective practices represent a diverse range of policing practices. This is important because different communities have different policing needs. A second and related point is that the effective practices are by no means obscure or relegated to one region or another. Instead, they are used by police departments across the United States and in several other countries.

Another reason to believe there is sufficient capacity to begin to develop evidence-based policing is that there are even more promising practices, or those with moderate evidence of effectiveness, that, with some modest resources directed to replication studies, could conceivably become effective practices. This is by no means a long shot. Few, if any, areas of research in criminal justice, or crime prevention more generally, can boast the level and high-quality nature of experimental evaluation in policing (see Lum & Koper, 2017; Weisburd & Majmundar, 2018). In the words of Sherman and Eck (2006: 321), "It is no small achievement that police crime prevention research has developed to the point of having some conclusions to discard."

Can We Expect the Police to Use the Evidence-Based Model?

If history is any indication, the answer to this question may be mixed. On the one hand, we can look to the widespread adoption of some police innovations in the absence of a link to research evidence, such as community policing (Sherman & Eck, 2006). On the other hand, we can find a connection to the evidence-based paradigm – although perhaps not necessarily conceived of in this form – in the adoption of problem-oriented policing and other targeted police practices that go beyond a reliance on police powers of arrest (Braga & Weisburd, 2010). The good news is that some recent research, organizational developments, and at least one innovative tool have seemingly tipped the scale away from uncertainty and toward a higher likelihood of the police agencies embracing the evidence-based model.

On the research front, this has involved surveys of the receptivity of police officers to evidence-based policing (Telep & Lum, 2014; Telep, 2017). In a survey of four municipal police agencies in the United States, Telep (2017: 995) found that "increasing officer familiarity with EBP [evidence-based policing] and the perceived usefulness of research and researchers can positively impact understanding the evidence base, using research on the streets, and openness to engaging in specific evaluation activities."

Perhaps the most influential organizational development of the last decade has been the rise of professional societies dedicated to the advancement of evidence-based policing. At the time of writing, at least four societies of evidence-based policing have been established, along with a good number of university-affiliated research centers that have as an express mandate the advancement of evidence-based policing. Of the four professional societies, one seeks influence on an international stage (Society of Evidence-Based Policing) and the other three work within the borders of the nation state (Australia/New Zealand, Canada, and United States). For Sherman (2015) this is a direct response to a growing demand of police agencies to embrace the evidence-based model. This is also echoed by supporters of these professional societies (e.g., Martin & Mazerolle, 2015; Huey & Ricciardelli, 2016).

Alongside these other important initiatives has been the development of a rather innovative tool known as the evidence-based policing matrix (Lum, Koper & Telep, 2011). Seen as the "next phase of evidence-based policing," the matrix is designed to aid police agencies in using scientific evidence in a strategic way, by "developing generalizations or principles on the nature of effective police strategies and translating the field of police evaluation research into digestible forms that can be used to alter police tactics, strategies, accountability systems, and training" (Lum et al., 2011: 3). The first test of the matrix reaffirmed some of the scientific evidence on police effectiveness in reducing crime and, importantly, it serves as a key resource for updating the evidence base in a timely manner and tailoring the evidence to the needs of police agencies.

For sure, barriers will always exist to getting the police to use research evidence on what works best in preventing crime. Some of these barriers have already been addressed; others include administrative constraints (e.g., too few resources, need for training of personnel), philosophical differences, and institutional resistance to change. Indeed, a clear lack of imagination and willingness to break down the culture of resistance to change captures much of the criticism of evidence-based policing.

Overcoming disconnect between research evidence and practice may best be achieved through the employment of what Sherman (1998) refers to as an "evidence cop." This individual, ideally working within a police department (for smaller police departments it may be necessary to pool resources), would serve as both a research scientist and manager. In the capacity of a research scientist, the evidence cop would be responsible for keeping up to date on the latest police research findings and coming up with recommendations based on the accumulated research evidence – perhaps drawing upon the evidence-based policing matrix. In the capacity of a manager, the evidence cop's role would be to monitor policing practices in the field to ensure they are adhering to recommendations based on research evidence. Importantly, this role would also be to "redirect practice through compliance rather than punishment" (Sherman, 1998: 3). The police community could learn from similar initiatives that have shown promise in the medical profession (Millenson, 1997) and in agriculture (MacKenzie, 1998).

Why the Police Should Adopt an Evidence-Based Approach

Evidence-based policing brings scientific evidence to center stage in decisions about which police practices should be used to deal with certain crime problems. It also brings to policing a greater focus on the prevention of crime. Improved effectiveness in the prevention of crime, greater efficiency in the use of scarce public resources, and improved relations with the public are some of the outcomes from police adopting an evidence-based approach (Neyroud & Weisburd, 2014). Of course, the police have achieved, and continue to achieve, various degrees of success in these areas through a number of diverse practices.

Returning to the scenario that opened this chapter, a key reason for the police to use an evidence-based approach is that it brings yet another innovative lever to a field of criminal justice that is a leader in innovation. More importantly, evidence-based policing can serve as a catalyst in focusing limited resources on identifiable risks, further developing a knowledge base on what works best, and, in continuing to develop new approaches to crime problems, encouraging police departments to keep an eye on the bottom line of crime prevention effectiveness.

Acknowledgments

I wish to thank Andrea Wexler for excellent research assistance.

REFERENCES

Bayley, D. H. (1998). Introduction: Effective law enforcement. In D. H. Bayley (ed.), *What Works in Policing* (pp. 174–177). New York: Oxford University Press.

Blumstein, A., & Wallman, J. (eds.). (2006). *The Crime Drop in America*, rev. ed. New York: Cambridge University Press.

Braga, A. A., & Weisburd, D. (2010). *Policing Problem Places: Crime Hot Spots and Effective Prevention*. New York: Oxford University Press.

Braga, A. A., & Weisburd, D. (2013). Editors' introduction: Advancing program evaluation methods in criminology and criminal justice. *Evaluation Review*, *37*, 163–169.

Bullock, K., & Tilley, N. (2009). Evidence-based policing and crime reduction. *Policing*, *3*, 381–387.

Campbell, D. T. (1969). Reforms as experiments. *American Psychologist*, *24*, 409–429.

Chalmers, I. (2003). Trying to do more good than harm in policy and practice: The role of rigorous, transparent, up-to-date evaluations. *Annals of the American Academy of Political and Social Science*, *589*, 22–44.

Cook, T. D., & Campbell, D. T. (1979). *Quasi-Experimentation: Design and Analysis Issues for Field Settings.* Chicago: Rand McNally.

Crime and Justice Group, Campbell Collaboration. (2018). Crime and justice reviews. Retrieved January 4, 2018, from www.campbellcollaboration.org/reviews_crime_justice/index.php.

Eck, J. E., & Maguire, E. R. (2006). Have changes in policing reduced violent crime? An assessment of the evidence. In A. Blumstein, & J. Wallman (eds.), *The Crime Drop in America*, rev. ed. (pp. 207–265). New York: Cambridge University Press.

Ekblom, P. (2002). From the source to the mainstream is uphill: The challenge of transferring knowledge of crime prevention through replication, innovation and anticipation. In N. Tilley (ed.), *Analysis for Crime Prevention: Crime Prevention Studies*, vol. 13 (pp. 131–203). Monsey, NY: Criminal Justice Press.

Farrington, D. P., Gottfredson, D. C., Sherman, L. W., & Welsh, B. C. (2006). The Maryland scientific methods scale. In L. W. Sherman, D. P. Farrington, B. C. Welsh, & D. L. MacKenzie (eds.), *Evidence-Based Crime Prevention*, rev. ed. (pp. 13–21). New York: Routledge.

Farrington, D. P., Weisburd, D., & Gill, C. E. (2011). The Campbell Collaboration Crime and Justice Group: A decade of progress. In C. J. Smith, S. X. Zhang, & R. Barberet (eds.), *Routledge Handbook of International Criminology* (pp. 53–63). New York: Routledge.

Farrington, D. P., & Welsh, B. C. (2006). A half century of randomized experiments on crime and justice. In M. Tonry (ed.), *Crime and Justice: A Review of Research*, vol. 34 (pp. 55–132). Chicago: University of Chicago Press.

Hough, M., & Tilley, N. (1998). *Getting the Grease to the Squeak: Research Lessons for Crime Prevention.* Crime Detection and Prevention Series Paper 85. London: Home Office Police Research Group.

Huey, L., & Ricciardelli, R. (2016). From seeds to orchards: Using evidence-based policing to address Canada's policing research needs. *Canadian Journal of Criminology and Criminal Justice*, *58*, 119–131.

Johnson, B. R., De Li, S., Larson, D. B., & McCullough, M. (2000). A systematic review of the religiosity and delinquency literature: A research note. *Journal of Contemporary Criminal Justice*, *16*, 32–52.

Lab, S. P. (2003). Let's put it in context. *Criminology and Public Policy*, *3*, 39–44.

Laycock, G. (2012). Happy birthday? *Policing*, *6*, 101–107.

Liddle, H. A., Rowe, C. L., Quille, T. J., Dakof, G. A., Mills, D. S., Sakran, E., & Biaggi, H. (2002). Transporting a research-based adolescent drug treatment into practice. *Journal of Substance Abuse Treatment*, *22*, 231–243.

Lum, C. (2009). *Translating Police Research into Practice.* Ideas in American policing series. Washington, DC: Police Foundation.

Lum, C., & Koper, C. S. (2015). Evidence-based policing. In R. Dunham, & G. Alpert (eds.), *Critical Issues in Policing*, 7th ed. (pp. 1–15). Longrove, IL: Waveland Press.

Lum, C., & Koper, C. S. (2017). *Evidence-Based Policing: Translating Research into Practice*. New York: Oxford University Press.

Lum, C., Koper, C. S., & Telep, C. W. (2011). The evidence-based policing matrix. *Journal of Experimental Criminology*, 7, 3–26.

MacKenzie, D. L. (1998). Using science and the U.S. land-grant university system to attack this nation's crime problem. *The Criminologist*, 23(2), 1–4.

Martin, P., & Mazerolle, L. (2015). Police leadership in fostering evidence-based agency reform. *Policing*, 10, 34–43.

McCord, J. (2003). Cures that harm: Unanticipated outcomes of crime prevention programs. *Annals of the American Academy of Political and Social Science*, 587, 16–30.

Mears, D. P. (2007). Towards rational and evidence-based crime policy. *Journal of Criminal Justice*, 35, 667–682.

Mears, D. P. (2010). *American Criminal Justice Policy: An Evaluation Approach to Increasing Accountability and Effectiveness*. New York: Cambridge University Press.

Millenson, M. L. (1997). *Demanding Medical Excellence: Doctors and Accountability in the Information Age*. Chicago: University of Chicago Press.

Moore, M. H. (2006). Improving police through expertise, experience, and experiments. In D. Weisburd, & A. A. Braga (eds.), *Police Innovation: Contrasting Perspectives* (pp. 322–338). New York: Cambridge University Press.

Mosteller, F., & Boruch, R. (eds.). (2002). *Evidence Matters: Randomized Trials in Education Research*. Washington, DC: Brookings Institution Press.

Nagin, D. S., & Weisburd, D. (2013). Evidence and public policy: The example of evaluation research in policing. *Criminology and Public Policy*, 12, 651–679.

Neyroud, P., & Weisburd, D. (2014). Transforming the police through science: The challenge of ownership. *Policing*, 4, 287–293.

Petrosino, A., Boruch, R. F., Soydan, H., Duggan, L., & Sanchez-Meca, J. (2001). Meeting the challenges of evidence-based policy: The Campbell Collaboration. *Annals of the American Academy of Political and Social Science*, 578, 14–34.

Petrosino, A., & Lavenberg, J. (2007). Systematic reviews and meta-analyses: Best evidence on "what works" for criminal justice decision makers. *Western Criminology Review*, 8, 1–15.

Shadish, W. R., Cook, T. D., & Campbell, D. T. (2002). *Experimental and Quasi-Experimental Designs for Generalized Causal Inference*. Boston: Houghton Mifflin.

Sherman, L. W. (1992). Attacking crime: Policing and crime control. In M. Tonry, & N. Morris (eds.), *Modern Policing. Crime and Justice: A Review of Research*, vol. 15 (pp. 159–230). Chicago: University of Chicago Press.

Sherman, L. W. (1997). Policing for crime prevention. In L. W. Sherman, D. C. Gottfredson, D. L. MacKenzie, J. E. Eck, P. Reuter, & S. D. Bushway, *Preventing Crime: What Works, What Doesn't, What's Promising* (ch. 8). Washington, DC: Office of Justice Programs, US Department of Justice.

Sherman, L. W. (1998). *Evidence-Based Policing*. Ideas in American policing series. Washington, DC: Police Foundation.

Sherman, L. W. (2003). Misleading evidence and evidence-led policy: Making social science more experimental. *Annals of the American Academy of Political and Social Science*, 589, 6–19.

Sherman, L. W. (2011). Democratic policing on the evidence. In J. Q. Wilson, & J. Petersilia (eds.), *Crime and Public Policy* (pp. 589–618). New York: Oxford University Press.

Sherman, L. W. (2013). The rise of evidence-based policing: Targeting, testing, and tracking. In M. Tonry (ed.), *Crime and Justice in America: 1975–2025. Crime and Justice: A Review of Research*, vol. 42 (pp. 377–451). Chicago: University of Chicago Press.

Sherman, L. W. (2015). A tipping point for "totally evidence policing": Ten ideas for building an evidence-based police agency. *International Criminal Justice Review*, 25, 11–29.

Sherman, L. W., & Eck, J. E. (2006). Policing for crime prevention. In L. W. Sherman, D. P. Farrington, B. C. Welsh, & D. L. MacKenzie (eds.), *Evidence-Based Crime Prevention*, rev. ed. (pp. 295–329). New York: Routledge.

Sherman, L. W., Farrington, D. P., Welsh, B. C., & MacKenzie, D. L. (eds.). (2006). *Evidence-Based Crime Prevention*, rev. ed. New York: Routledge.

Sherman, L. W., Gottfredson, D. C., MacKenzie, D. L., Eck, J. E., Reuter, P., & Bushway, S. D. (1997). *Preventing Crime: What Works, What Doesn't, What's Promising*. Washington, DC: Office of Justice Programs, US Department of Justice.

Skogan, W. G., & Frydl, K. (eds.). (2004). Fairness and effectiveness in policing: The evidence. Committee to Review Research on Police Policy and Practices. Washington, DC: National Academy Press.

Sparrow, M. K. (2009). *One Week in Heron City (case B): A Case Study. New Perspectives in Policing Series.* Cambridge, MA: Harvard University and National Institute of Justice.

Telep, C. W. (2017). Police officer receptivity to research and evidence-based policing: Examining variability within and across agencies. *Crime & Delinquency*, 63, 976–999.

Telep, C. W., & Lum, C. (2014). The receptivity of officers to empirical research and evidence-based policing: An examination of survey data from three agencies. *Police Quarterly*, 17, 359–385.

Telep, C. W., & Weisburd, D. (2016). Policing. In D. Weisburd, D. P. Farrington, & C. E. Gill (eds.), *What Works in Crime Prevention and Rehabilitation: Lessons from Systematic Reviews* (pp. 137–168). New York: Springer.

Weisburd, D., & Eck, J. E. (2004). What can police do to reduce crime, disorder, and fear? *Annals of the American Academy of Political and Social Science*, 593, 42–65.

Weisburd, D., & Hinkle, J. C. (2012). The importance of randomized experiments in evaluating crime prevention. In B. C. Welsh, & D. P. Farrington (eds.), *The Oxford Handbook of Crime Prevention* (pp. 446–465). New York: Oxford University Press.

Weisburd, D., & Majmundar, M. K. (eds.). (2018). *Proactive Policing: Effects on Crime and Communities*. Committee on Proactive Policing: Effects on Crime, Communities, and Civil Liberties. Washington, DC: National Academies Press.

Weiss, C. H., Murphy-Graham, E., & Birkeland, S. (2005). An alternate route to policy influence: How evaluations affect D.A.R.E. *American Journal of Evaluation*, 26, 12–30.

Welsh, B. C. (2002). Technological innovations for policing: Crime prevention as the bottom line. *Criminology and Public Policy*, 2, 129–132.

Welsh, B. C. (2006). Evidence-based policing for crime prevention. In D. Weisburd, & A. A. Braga (eds.), *Police Innovation: Contrasting Perspectives* (pp. 305–321). New York: Cambridge University Press.

Welsh, B. C., & Farrington, D. P. (2006). Evidence-based crime prevention. In B. C. Welsh, & D. P. Farrington (eds.), *Preventing Crime: What Works for Children, Offenders, Victims, and Places* (pp. 1–17). New York: Springer.

Welsh, B. C., & Farrington, D. P. (2011). Evidence-based crime policy. In M. Tonry (ed.), *The Oxford Handbook of Crime and Criminal Justice* (pp. 60–92). New York: Oxford University Press.

Welsh, B. C., Farrington, D. P., & Gowar, B. R. (2015). Benefit-cost analysis of crime prevention programs. In M. Tonry (ed.), *Crime and justice: A review of research*, vol. 44 (pp. 447–516). Chicago: University of Chicago Press.

Welsh, B. C., van der Laan, P. H., & Hollis, M. E. (2013). Systematic reviews and cost-benefit analyses: Toward evidence-based crime policy. In B. C. Welsh, A. A. Braga, & G. J. N. Bruinsma (eds.), *Experimental Criminology: Prospects for Advancing Science and Public Policy* (pp. 253–276). New York: Cambridge University Press.

Wilson, D. B. (2001). Meta-analytic methods for criminology. *Annals of the American Academy of Political and Social Science*, *578*, 71–89.

Zane, S. N., & Welsh, B. C. (2018). Toward an "age of imposed use"? Evidence-based crime policy in a law and social science context. *Criminal Justice Policy Review*, *29*, 280–300.

Critic

Which Evidence? What Knowledge? Broadening Information about the Police and Their Interventions

Jack R. Greene

PREFACE

Observations while attending several crime analysis meetings of a major city police department provide insight into questions of sources and importance of knowledge in policing. This observable knowledge is used by the police as they grapple with the ongoing complexities of public safety, in this case in an urban city.

At each meeting, two forms of knowledge framed discussions of crime and disorder problems. Framing as a sociological and communications theory relies on ideas associated with understanding how attitudes and behavior are shaped by the information or form of knowledge presented (Goffman, 1986; Scheufele & Iyengar, 2014).

In our city, members of the crime analysis unit first framed crime and disorder problems geographically, typically for one police district at each monthly meeting, with reported crime and arrest data from the previous month. Using GIS data, these "maps" were clearly presented, of very high quality, rigorous in the information and analytics that lie behind them, while provoking questions about what was being done to address the identified patterns.

The crime analysts presented information not as criticism or pointed critique, but rather as a review of local safety problems and as a way of describing present problems, including patterns over time. This discussion was not conflictual, rather it approached these questions in a business-like manner, seeking to understand the statistics and their implications. This framing, which might be described as a *business-rational-calculus,* is replicated across the United States in one form or another involving data collected through crime reporting and other police interventions, and requiring considerable analytic skill in building the maps used to prompt these discussions. As this has been in place for some time in this city, those participating in the discussions were indeed thoughtful and neither particularly defensive of the problems they faced nor unimaginative about what they were doing to resolve those problems. Like monthly sales meetings in business, this approach was analytic, systematic and informational; of course, it also prodded commanders for better results, but gently. Sitting in on this discussion one could not help but see the role that scientific-inquiry and data analytics play in better understanding the patterns and problem sets that police leaders confront in their efforts to increase public safety.

Such discussions had the symbolism and *some* of the substance of being evidence-based. Concluding that these analyses contained some of the substance of evidence is predicated on what we know about crime statistics as represented by citizens' reports of crime, and police interventions, all of which are selectively conditioned. Citizens decide whether to call the police or not and police officers decide what calls to validate or what actions to take, if any (Black, 1980). So we should be cautioned that even what we consider to be objective police data has any number of subjective meanings and interpretations underlying crime counts, arrests made, or calls for police assistance.

Following these crime analysis discussions, the review shifted to several specialized units also participating in these meetings and from the commander of the focal police district. External contributions typically involved input from representatives of gang, street crime, juvenile, drug enforcement, school police, license and inspection police who oversee liquor regulations and complaints, park police and transit police, among others. At the same time, the commander of the district *de jour*, would at times introduce the sentiments of community leaders, information collected at community meetings, and collaborations undertaken with other city agencies to address these problems.

Here, the preceding analytic discussion yielded to what might be framed as an *anthropological-qualitative approach* wherein police representatives discussed problem people, families, buildings, bars, and places where deviance, crime, and other social problems tended to congregate. They talked about conversations with school principals, street-workers focused on building community agency, and with gang members and others seen to be associated with the identified problems. Some of these discussions were accompanied by photos of people and places, thereby putting a face on the statistics and patterns previously discussed. First-person accounts of interactions also were brought to bear on understanding the focal problems.

As an aside, but nonetheless very important to these discussions, was the sense of shared meaning and responsibility for better understanding and addressing the subject district's needs. As police districts in this city vary in social composition, commanders often provided "thick descriptions" (see Yin, 2003) of the nature of community and social problems, as well as some depth in programs being implemented to address local concerns. This is part of the process of organizational sense making (Weick, 1995; Maguire & Katz, 2006), wherein those within organizations give meaning to their actions and interpret external stimuli that give rise to, or contradict, those actions. Here meaning was ascendant, such as in "what does this say and what does it mean?"

So, in these crime analysis meetings, scientific facts merged with impressions and interpretations from knowledgeable police officers to form a deeper and more nuanced understanding of the nature of crime and safety problems in targeted areas and what was being done to address them. In some important ways this process could be framed as "Karl Popper meets Margaret Mead," referring to quantitative measurement being illuminated by qualitative observation, or a collision between measurement and meaning (Greene, 2014a). Obviously, seeing or hearing only one part of this discussion diminishes the amount of knowledge being brought to bear on community crime and disorder questions. Each contributed to better understanding the frequency of the problem set, the underlying dynamics of people, places, and situations, as well as potential avenues to address the identified problem and ongoing programs. At the same time, such discussion seemed to bind all present to ownership of the problems defined for the particular district under consideration, while providing pathways for various forms of knowledge to enter and inform the discussion.

These observations help to clarify the question: "What are the tactics" sources of knowledge within policing and how are they brought to bear on community problems and police tactics? This essay seeks to examine this question with the intent of reframing what has become a rather narrow discussion about evidence-based policing favoring one or a few particular sources of knowledge, to embracing a larger understanding of the importance of a wide range of knowledge about communities and the police that can help in designing strategies and tactics to increase public safety and the publics' sense of security. A central issue in this regard is addressing what are considered "wicked problems," that is, problems involving considerable complexity, multiple sources of cause and effect, representing some of the more intractable aspects of communal life, and requiring numerous agency and individual interactions.

This discussion also seeks to more closely apply the medical model of evidence making underlying the evidence-based policing movement. As will be discussed, the practice of medicine is indeed scientifically rooted, but also artfully practiced, and, as such, involves the integration of knowledge from many sources. Part of the reason for this knowledge integration is that evidence-based medicine has recognized three broad knowledge domains for effective medical practice: (1) scientific knowledge, (2) knowledge derived from clinical experience, and (3) the knowledge, perceptions and expectations of patients. As evidence-based medicine has matured, integrating such diverse sources of knowledge has been difficult yet central to the use and impact of medical interventions.

At the onset, it should be noted that this essay is not a critique of all the possible literature that has accumulated around the evidence-based policing movement. Rather, here we consider the importance of multiple sources and types of information to inform police strategies and tactics, just as multiple sources and types of information inform solving wicked problems, and medical practice (Perneger & Agoritsas, 2011).

WICKED PROBLEMS REQUIRE MORE, NOT LESS INFORMATION

Public policy often addresses collective and complex problems. As a shorthand, policy models have shifted from those emphasizing knowledge about the political dimensions of policy processes (Hill, 2014), to incremental decision-making and "the science of muddling through" (Lindblom, 1959), to knowledge derived from positivist planning and rational-technical approaches emphasizing systemic and data-driven policy making (Smith & Larimer, 2017: 119–129). More recently, policy discussions have emphasized a post-positivist framework seeing policy processes as deliberative, highly value-laden, and involving democratic process (Moore, 1997; Smith & Larimore, 2017). Such processes are often focused on wicked problems, characterized as problems involving multiple stakeholders with conflicting interests and value preferences; involving complex inter- and intra-institutional arrangements within and across public and private agencies; and having scientific uncertainty, that is, clear gaps in knowledge about social problems and how to address them, suggesting that many of these problems appear to be rather intractable (Head & Alford, 2013).

It may be the case that wicked problems differ significantly from other problems in that they represent problem sets, that Weber and Khademian (2008) argue are unstructured, cross-cutting, and relentless. As a consequence, trying to address wicked problems requires broader knowledge coming from government, the private sector, civic leadership, and those most affected by these problems, as well as collaboration between and among those having different sources of information, preferences, and premises. In other words, more knowledge rather than less is required in addressing wicked problems.

Crime and public safety are indeed wicked problems: they have many geneses, theoretical understandings, interpretations, and impacts. Crime is about individuals, small groups, communities, and the larger social institutions, including global forces, giving rise to, or trying to, ameliorate these problems. Consequently bringing more, not less, knowledge to the table of improving public safety, reducing crime and fear of crime, and improving community quality of life – all objectives of modern-day policing – invariably requires the synthesis of many sources of knowledge, from the police, from communities, and from other social institutions.

What this shift in policy theory highlights is the many informational or knowledge bases that can be brought to bear on policy questions. Similar to the sources of organizational power or influence that shape individual behavior as posited by French, Raven, and Cartwright (1959), varying sources of knowledge also shape policy and decision-making in policing as well. Knowledge about crime, disorder, policing, and police interventions in communities resides in several places. First, certainly, there is analytic knowledge about crime and social behavior, captured in the hot spots or place-based approaches to crime analysis and their progeny (Lum & Koper, 2017); second, there is the experiential knowledge of police officers who have come to know beat information which shapes their responses to neighborhoods and their residents (Wood et al., 2014); third, there is knowledge stemming from community perceptions and interactions with the police that also shapes the viability and acceptance of police actions (Innes et al., 2009); fourth, there is knowledge from civic and political leaders having influence on police strategies and tactics (Reiner, 2010); and, fifth, there is inter-agency knowledge about underlying community dynamics that may give rise to the wicked problems of crime and social disorder (Robinson & Payton, 2016). With so many sources of knowledge, why a single approach would be more proffered over others is not clear, nor intuitive. All make contributions and all have a place at the table in understanding the police, their impossible mandate (Manning, 1997), their interventions, and the consequences of their interventions, as much of policing involves contingency management (Manning, 2003) in the face of considerable uncertainty.

MULTIPLE SOURCES OF KNOWLEDGE ABOUT THE POLICE

The arc of knowledge about the functioning and impact of the police in the United States and elsewhere is complex and broadly strewn. The police as a social, political, cultural, strategic, and tactical institution have been dissected from many perspectives, separating the formal institution of police (Crank & Langworthy, 1992) from the labyrinth of actors and institutions involved in the web of policing (Brodeur, 2010), while at the same time examining linkages between culture and formal social control (Mears et al., 2017). Knowledge about the police and policing is shared over many disciplines, concepts, theories, and research methods, while also being deeply imbedded in the craft knowledge of the occupation itself (Bayley & Bittner, 1984; Fyfe, 1999; Willis, 2013; Willis & Mastrofski, 2016). Consequently, our acquired knowledge of policing and the police has numerous independent sources.

Audi (2002: 72) suggests that acquired or justified knowledge stems from several basic sources including perception, consciousness (or introspection), memory, and reason (or intuition). With the exception of memory, which Audi sees as a basic source of justification (p. 75), each of these basic knowledge sources yield belief without dependence on another source. That is to say, basic sources of knowledge yield meanings that stand independently from other sources of knowledge. At times, these distinctions have been suggested as a contrast between experience and reason, the former guided by perception, memory, and introspection, and the latter guided by intuition and reason, although Audi is quick to underscore that "it is misleading [to] suggest that experience plays no role in the operation of reason as a source of knowledge" (p. 75).

Applying Audi's ideas to understanding policing places us at the intersection of what Moore (2006) called expertise, experience, and experimentation, each of which shapes our acquired knowledge in this domain. Police knowledge comes from many places, some of which converge and some of which do not. These sources include the norms and mores of the cultural times under consideration (the current or dead hand of history, or both), the formal and informal learning of police officers, the acquisition of data and its analysis, the occupational frameworks of the police (Manning, 1997), and the clinical experiences of the police in field settings. Such epistemological sources of justified knowledge comport well with Audi's framework demonstrating that justifiable knowledge about the police is indeed broadly sourced.

Justifiable knowledge about the police can also be considered by seeing policing as a clinical occupation, consistent with the medical analogy often used in furtherance of the evidence-based policing movement. In many fundamental ways, policing, at its heart, is a clinical occupation, meaning that police operate in a complex social world wherein their treatment of individuals and events is conditioned in part on their observations of situational exigencies and the tailoring of interventions to circumstances observed, and in part by prior learning about the effectiveness of particularly styles of policing or modes of police intervention. Such an approach includes both experience and reason, basic sources of police knowledge. This does not, of course, preclude, demean, or exclude formal analytic information now more present in police routines, but rather requires that such analyses be tempered by their situational applications. It might also be said here that while the analytics undergirding policing help the police to determine where to go, it does not tell them what to do once they arrive.

Whereas police organizations and, indeed, police scholarship, emphasizes social aggregates, much of what presents itself to the police officer is individual, situational, and contextual in nature. Not unlike the general practitioner in medicine, clinical practice requires some science, some experience and some art. Facts, routines, interpretations, and communications are bundled in police actions on the ground; counting cops on dots (a critical interpretation of evidence-based policing) is less sensitive to these concerns (see Haberman, 2015).

In recent years, the "what works," or evidence-based movement in police research has relied on random controlled experiments and quasi-experiments as being the *sin qua non* for what we know about the police and policing (Sherman, 2013; Neyroud & Weisburd, 2014). While thinking and research have certainly moved beyond the initial conceptualization of what works (Nagin & Weisburd, 2013), this movement is largely focused on police tactics and their ability to deter criminality. It is clear that these are important questions, but they reveal only a portion of our understanding of what the police do, what it means to the police and the community, and whether it has its desired effect, without producing unwanted side effects. To be fair, most recently, the evidence-based movement has begun to broaden its focus on other outcomes, including the downstream impacts on community acceptance of the police and police legitimacy (Committee on Proactive Policing, 2017), but, as they acknowledge, much about these downstream effects and their attachments to evidence-based policing remains unknown, owing, in part, to the complexity of these issues and, in part, to only marginal investment in trying to capture this knowledge.

Criticisms of the evidence-based approach include concerns for the size and scale of problems addressed (Hough, 2011); the inability of the police and researchers to communicate effectively about what research is needed and how/when to use police research results (Bradley & Nixon, 2009); how the RCT model tends to be prescriptive, and reductive in terms of understanding how the police solve problems (Tilley, 2006: 2009); and concerns with whether police research looks more like psychiatry rather than pharmacology or general medical practice, that is, where the means and ends are not as clear as they are presented (Maruna & Barber, 2011: 318–334).

Taking a police clinical perspective ultimately means integrating craft-based knowledge with "evidence" of how particular practices work (Willis, 2013). Such ideas are fundamentally rooted in notions about clinical practice and clinical reasoning (Norman, 2005). Such a perspective acknowledges that expertise in medicine (and policing) rests on multiple representations of knowledge; knowing the patient, the patient's history, the diagnosis, and other diagnoses and concurrent ongoing treatments for that patient, the range of prescriptions available to address the illness, and the tolerance of the patient for those prescriptions – these are all part of clinical practice in medicine, as they should be in policing.

In policing, the analogies are rather straightforward. Knowing the community, block group or immediate location, previous problems in these areas, previous interventions, level of public trust and support, other city services or service providers to this location, the nature of the immediate crime or disorder problem, and the range of interventions that might be brought to bear on these problems are sources of knowledge that might greatly affect the quality and effectiveness of policing. Also of concern is public tolerance for certain interventions. More often than not, these are decisions characterized by a mixture of fact-based and normative assessments made by police officers in the field, community members with whom they interact, and in the corridors of police administration. The decisions, of course, are themselves conditioned by fluid or changing social conditions occurring within and across neighborhoods and business/industrial sectors (Weisburd et al., 2012; 2015).

IN HOT PURSUIT OF THE MEDICAL ANALOGY IN POLICING

The use of a medical analogy to enhance police professionalization and decision-making has taken root in most western police agencies. Police policy, like public policy, is thought to be evidence dependent, but where does this evidence reside and how is it produced and reproduced? Developing a simplified process of clinical medical practice results in at least six linkages for considering individuals' medical needs, which can be extrapolated to policing. These stages include presentment and medical history, immediate assessment and diagnosis, prescription and prognosis, treatment and dosage (as well as contraindications of treatments), and follow-up and aftercare. Added to these stages is cost, as resources for public health, like policing, are finite. Each of these stages requires information and knowledge from multiple sources. Some sources are directly linked to the patient (presentment, follow-up, outcome assessment, and individual costs, for example), while others are linked to physician skill and experience (assessment and diagnosis, prescription) and well as broader medical-scientific knowledge (about treatment, dosage and contraindications, systemic and individual outcomes, and larger social and economic costs). Accepting this generalized medical process suggests that for medicine to succeed, many sources of knowledge and evidence are necessary to achieve successful outcomes. No less can be said of policing.

Added to the complexity of varying sources of information to assist medical decision-making is the role of medical theory and biostatistics coupled with clinical experience. As Jenieck (2013: 1–2) suggests,

Medicine means both theory and practice . . . The practice of medicine means actions and processes as exercise as physician's knowledge of both facts and theory and includes both reasoning and actions and their evaluation. Practice of clinical and community medicine becomes not only evidence based but also value based and patient and his or her narratives based.

While these complexities have been clearly outlined and are part of the medical evidence-based discussion, they have not risen to a level of similar consideration in policing. A promising exception to this is the evidence-based matrix for policing created by Lum (2012; also see Lum & Koper, 2017), where there is an attempt to better understand the complexities of units of analysis, variations in treatments, as well as variations in outcomes.

Of course, knowing broadly about what the police are, what they do, and how they are occupationally defined, tells us only part of the information we might need to better understand their interventions. From an analytic perspective, police tactics and their consequences are associated with individual police officer behaviors and decisions, group functions within police agencies (e.g., shifts, patrol, traffic, and the like), organizational specializations (street crime units, community policing officers, and the like), their interactions with the wider environment (e.g., other city agencies,

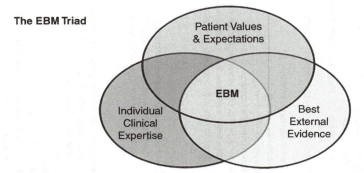

Armstrong, E.C. (2003) Harnessing new technologies while preserving basic values. Fam Sys & Health, (21)4, 351–355.

FIGURE 20.1 The Evidence-Based Medicine Triad

community organizations, civic and religious leaders, and the like), and of course their interactions within and across communities. These units of analysis within policing range from the micro-individual level to the macro-environmental and institutional level (Greene, 1998; 2014b). Such range suggests possible differences in the sources of knowledge about the police at any particular level of inquiry as well as the depth and substance of that knowledge.

Improved thinking about evidence-based medicine (and policing) includes the need to balance several issues thought to impact clinical problem solving which allows the integration of the best available research evidence with clinical expertise and patient values (Sackett et al., 2000: 71). The three major sources of information are depicted in Figure 20.1.

As revealed in Figure 20.1, knowledge frames for evidence-based medicine include patient values and expectations, the best available research evidence, and the clinical experience of individual medical practitioners. Each brings a knowledge set that informs evidence-based medicine; eliminating or discounting any particular source obviously weakens the effectiveness of this approach.

At the same time, invoking the medical process and applying it to policing calls for some attention to the linkages among and between presentment and medical history, immediate assessment and diagnosis, prescription and prognosis, treatment and dosage, follow-up and aftercare, and cost. Figure 20.2 provides a brief depiction of what constitutes stages of police intervention as seen through a medical intervention lens, as well as brief descriptions of the state-of-the-art in knowledge for each stage, and some ideas about the sources and focus of such knowledge for the police. The figure further illustrates the complexity in knowledge and its sources if the police are to fully embrace an evidence-based approach.

Intervention Element	Questions for Police	Current Process and Associated Problems	Knowledge Source and/or Needed Focus
Presentment and History	What circumstances call attention for police intervention into a locality? How is such knowledge brought to the attention of the police?	Much of what passes for understanding community problem presentment is narrow and immediacy focused, although focusing on street segments is quite encouraging.	Crime statistics Calls-for-service Citizen complaints Understanding how communities see these problems
	What do we know about local histories as to previous problems and police interventions?	Some of the problems presented to the police are either too small or too large for police intervention.	Community sense of safety and security
Assessment and Diagnosis	What is the central problem or cluster of problems to be addressed? What community dynamics give rise to public safety problems? And, how and why do they vary?	The range of problems diagnosed by the police are more police serving than community serving, that is they rely on historic police premises, not on systematic diagnosis or community-based models.	Community social Problem Community surveys Community focus groups Stakeholder assessments
Prescription and Prognosis	What types of police interventions are thought to ameliorate what community problems, with what level of anticipated success and for how long?	Police use place-based or person-based interventions largely, and both are tied to ideas about deterrence, not prevention. Impact assessment of these prescriptions is not well established over ranges of problems or ranges of communities.	Knowledge about the validity of a range of police interventions and how they match up with problem sets and community dynamics.
Treatment and Dosage	What should the police actually do to address the problem(s), in what spatial and temporal arrangement, and for how long?	The amount of information on police treatments for defined problems, including information on what the police should/actually do, for how long, and/or in what sequence or combination remains not well understood.	Implementation assessment, including observational assessment of what the police actually do, for how long, and what anticipated effects?
Follow-up and Aftercare	What are the short, intermediate, and long-term effects of the interventions chosen and what is required to sustain the effects achieved over time?	Much of police effort is response focused: aftercare and understanding needs for follow-up are not well understood or measured, nor are they substantially ingrained in police agencies, culture, or leadership.	Knowledge of community change over time, and what needs to be done to sustain any results achieved, victim re-contact, and reassurance policing.
Cost and Consequence	What are the social, financial, and political costs of police interventions?	While there is certainly awareness of the need for police legitimacy, what police interventions strengthen or detract from legitimacy are not well established. Fiscal costs for interventions are not well assessed. Political costs for police interventions are equally not well assessed.	How much? Alternative Costs? Beneficial and less beneficial costs to the police and the community.

FIGURE 20.2 Applying a Medical Intervention Process to Policing

On Presentment and History: Presentment, or how medical or social problems are brought to authority's attention, initiates the process of sorting and addressing problems. History conditions understanding of presentment as it provides some contextual knowledge about previous problems. At the same time, much of the information attendant to presentment comes from the patient, or in the case of the police, from communities. Some of this information is about crime, but in many instances, it is also about order. As Carr (2012) suggests, community order is largely negotiated owing to differing social contexts, structures, and institutional imperatives, attesting to the situational nature of community presentment. So, how communities, currently and historically, articulate their problems, and how the police come to understand these community concerns are central issues in presentment.

Presentment and history for evidence-based police interventions are currently focused primarily on the presence of crime or disorder or patterns thereof, largely drawn from police statistics of crime and disorder. While the problem-oriented policing movement asked police to broadly scan and assess the problems they were trying to address, police shorthand has predominantly relied on crime and disorder, not their genesis, as the focal point for such interventions (Clarke, 1998; Braga, 2014). Even using sophisticated crime analytic tools, much of what passes for problem assessment is rooted in traditional police practices and conceptualizations of crime. While Lum and Koper (2017) point to crime analysis as a means to better outline not-well-understood problems or as a way to implementation innovative programs, much of what constitutes crime analysis is largely rooted in police statistics involving crime and arrests. At the same time, what constitutes community policing efforts to better understand community dynamics and needs are also rather weak in assessing the complexities of community public safety problems (Innes et al., 2009; Cordner, 2014).

In a review of twenty years of police exposure to problem-solving, Scott (2000) identified substantial problems associated with each stage of the problem-solving process. In respect to problem presentment, a critical review of police problem analysis was that it was often broadly focused, thereby diminishing police capacity to address the problem, or more focused on police organizational and occupational needs rather than community needs (Clark, 1998; Scott, 2000), often leading to what Goldstein (1990) defined as a means–ends inversion, where effort (more arrests, citations, and the like) becomes more important than the outcome (public safety).

Questions regarding how residents perceive the dynamics of crime and disorder in their neighborhoods, and what they do to adjust to these circumstances, may provide evidence of potential police responses. Incorporating resident perceptions of the problems and the police can indeed be helpful in understanding how hot spots are policed (Haberman, 2015;

Haberman et al., 2016). Of course, this represents another source of knowledge that can be used to define and address community problems.

These assessments are not simply to create the aggregate pre–post comparison for the assessment of police tactics, typical of much of the evidence-based movement. Rather, the focus on presentment is to generate knowledge to inform the police about the problems to be addressed and their social and contextual anchors, hinting perhaps to the tactics that should/can be deployed (see La Vigne et al., 2017). As part of problem diagnosis, this community-focused information is critical to understand how the community understands the problem, as well as community tolerance for types of interventions (Haberman et al., 2016). Seeing like the citizenry is often difficult for the police (Innes et al., 2009), yet such a vantage point, and the knowledge it produces, is essential for police understanding of the problems besetting a community and what to do to ameliorate those problems. This is equally true of how the police relate to the academic-research community as well (see Cockbain & Knutsson, 2015).

In this regard, Bradley and Nixon (2009) have suggested that many of the interactions between the police and research communities can be seen as a "dialogue of the deaf," meaning that the police and research communities often talk past one another in such discussions, the police perhaps more focused on locality and dynamics, and the research community more focused on outcomes, displacement, or the diffusion of benefits, all different sources of information and knowledge about policing. From the perspective of presentment, this is an important consideration, however, because understanding the initial problem to be addressed, as well as the sources of information about that problem is essential as the first step in much of what we call medical (and police) intervention.

On Assessment and Diagnosis: Similar to the discussion concerning presentment and history, police diagnosis and assessment of troubled places is not particularly focused on social, economic, or cultural dynamics, the underpinning conditions giving rise to problems in these places, although such information was clearly evident during the observed crime analysis meetings previously discussed. Following the medical approach, police, in making choices about tactics and their impact on identified community problems, would want to bring considerable information about these places to the forefront. Here the police may want to consult with other community-serving agencies to better grapple with the nature of underlying problems and how to proceed (Haberman, 2015; Haberman et al., 2016). Or the police may want to compare targeted areas with other areas experiencing similar issues to gain confidence on how to intervene. What is clear is that the front-end work of clinical medicine sets the stage for subsequent interventions and remedies. Of necessity, this stage of intervention attempts to magnify information from as many sources as possible, not restrict it.

Diagnosing crime and safety problems across communities is a complex undertaking. Local crime problems have many geneses. Crime analysis and problem solving are seen as police analytic activities giving greater relevance to first diagnosing and then responding to community problems. But, as Innes (2005) has suggested, there is considerable complexity in sorting out citizen participation in problem-solving from citizen interpretation of signal crime as precursors to more serious crime and risk. Of course, such brief or non-existent assessment makes subsequent diagnosis problematic.

On a broader scale, and taking an institutional perspective, Crank and Langworthy (1992) suggest that public perceptions, like those of the police, are powerfully shaped by institutional myths of the police and their nearly singular role in controlling crime, thereby affording police organizations institutional legitimacy. Following years of conditioning, police and public expectations about what the police are, what they should do, and how they should be assessed reflect such myths and influence current measurement schemes. Gaps between promise and practice result in dissatisfactions among the police and the public. This has analogy in medicine where the imbedded myths of being a physician meet the realities of the role in practice (Dingwall, 2011), often producing occupational dissatisfaction in medicine and frustration in patients.

On Prescription and Prognosis: Prescription in usage here is an authoritative recommendation of a course of action to remediate some situation or problem set. Prescription, of course, is based on knowledge about the effects of the recommended course of action relative to the nature of the problem being addressed. Prescription assumes treatment/intervention fit such that the recommended course of action is likely to produce the needed results. Much of the literature on evidence-based policing can be seen as part of a prescription for what the police should do to address crime, disorder, and public safety problems. Prognosis, on the other hand, is a prediction about the likely outcome of a course of action. Obviously, prescription and prognosis are connected by knowledge.

In many respects, the police treatment or prescription array to address community problems is rather limited, consisting primarily of increased police presence in troubled places, and oftentimes through aggressive police street tactics. The equivalent of take two, or ten, police officers and call me in the morning. More current research has broadened the prescription labels, but they too are elastic, primarily consisting of problem-solving, community policing, or traditional policing, which are meant in part to describe the prescription for increased public safety across any number of community ailments. Yet the evidence supporting these prescriptions is rather mixed, owing in part to the complexities of the problems to be addressed, the places where the problems are located, and, in this case, the broad and rather vague definitions of what the police are to do. It has been argued that there is considerable support for proactive policing, broadly defined (see Committee on Proactive Policing, 2017), but its use by type of policing and where, when, and for how long it should be applied and with what consequences, is less well known or understood. So, in some important ways, the prescription of proactive policing precedes our understanding of the prognosis for the use of varying police proactive techniques.

The nuance of community or crime problem variation is not predominant in the prescriptions of what form of policing to use in what circumstance. The more likely formula is troubled place – increase police presence – decrease trouble. For example, in meta-analyses of the impact of police interventions in hot spots, a wide variety of problems and approaches are often grouped together, that is, the identified prescriptions underlying police interventions. The focus in these studies is on their research design rather than the substance and target of these interventions. Grouped together are studies examining repeat call responses, drug interventions, disorder reduction, gun search and seizures, nuisance bars, and responses following a terrorist attack (Braga et al., 2014), among others. The heterogeneity of these problems, and the corresponding heterogeneity of police interventions present problems for building knowledge on prescriptions and prognoses of such interventions. In medicine, this might look like one vaccination for many or all diseases.

This concern is also relevant to consideration of prognoses about police interventions, other than broad conclusions that in hot spots they reduce problems for some period of time, more often resulting in a diffusion of benefits, and at times cause community reactivity to the treatments applied, such as complaints about the police or larger-scale civil unrest. These are all lines of inquiry in current police research, but the actual knowledge base about these issues remains complex and scant at best. The most recent report by the Committee on Proactive Policing (2017) suggests that there are considerable gaps in knowledge concerning police legality, racially biased policing, and the longer-term outcomes of such practices, which should condition the prescriptive use of proactive policing.

On Treatment and Dosage: What the police do in evidence-based interventions is opaque in current formulations. Should the police invoke stop and frisk, increase high-visibility and aggressive street interventions, go door-to-door to improve police–community interaction, hold stakeholder meetings, coordinate with other agencies both public and private, increase traffic enforcement, increase civil citation, and/or use foot, bike or other forms of patrol, engage in third-party policing, and in what frequency (hourly, daily, monthly) remain open questions for the police. These are not inconsequential questions as police interventions and their dosage have potentially positive and negative consequences, while also being based on differing forms of information and knowledge.

The treatment discussion focuses on a central issue in policing; what to do, and under what circumstances? Unfortunately, much of what we know about the content and substance of police interventions is either masked in studies of hot spots policing, or is taken at a rather high level of definition (see Braga et al., 2014). Moreover, much of the focus on evidence in policing has not produced much knowledge about the practices or impact of investigative activities by the police (Braga et al., 2011). Lastly, even promising schemes seeking to unpack evidence in policing, such as the evidence-based matrix developed by Lum and her colleagues (2011) and Lum and Koper (2017), have difficulty describing or interpreting police interventions in sufficient detail to deepen knowledge about police interventions moving away from broadly stated dichotomies such as reactive/proactive, or general/focused, or in locating their targets (individuals, groups, micro places, neighborhoods, and jurisdictions; Lum & Koper, 2017: 42–50). Such categories mask what the police are actually doing, and, as such, mask understanding about police treatments as well.

Problem-oriented policing as envisioned by Goldstein (1990) was meant to focus more on the means of policing, that is, what the police do to address persistent community, crime, order, fear, and safety concerns, thus producing knowledge about such interventions and their use. Previously, critiques of problem-solving have shown its reliance on existing police practices and tactics, rather than artfully crafting responses to problems that arise, engaging communities purposefully, or relying on collaborations with other social service agencies to identify problems and implement interventions for their amelioration. This ultimately leads to what Weisburd and Braga (2006: 133–152) and Braga and Bond (2009) characterized as "shallow," or thin problem-solving attempts, that is, skipping much of the analysis and rather relying primarily on traditional police interventions (e.g., saturation patrol, aggressive street tactics).

Recent work by Gill and her colleagues (2014: 425) examining the effects of community policing, concluded that understanding community policing effects is similarly complicated by "confusion around the approach [that] has limited the ability of police departments to identify strategies for taking the philosophy of COP through to implementation." Simply put, community policing can be seen as an elastic concept conveying many meanings and encompassing a wide array of police tactics.

Beyond concerns with the treatment knowledge base in policing, there are any number of assessments of implementing police strategies that arrive at similar conclusions to those of Gill and her colleagues (Gill et al., 2014: 413), who suggest in a meta-analysis of community policing,

While fidelity, dosage, and so on are not often reported in evaluation research in criminology ... some authors did note that there was no evidence the police actually carried out the planned activities. Community policing, like hot spots policing, has suffered from definitional and implementation shortcomings, and largely continues to do so.

In addition to concerns with difficulties in specifying treatment regimens for the police, how much treatment should be provided is also a complex undertaking. Relative to hot spots, Koper (1995) suggested that the police could spend as little as ten to fifteen minutes attending to hot spots, thereby increasing police visibility to achieve a deterrent effect. Such treatment specificity has more or less been examined in other settings as well (Lum & Koper, 2017: 69–72). While this is possibly an important set of findings, it remains unclear what the police actually do in these fifteen-minute intervals, as a wide range of interventions (from just being there to the tactics of regular or specialized units, to community or local guardian engagement of one form or another) across a wide range of community problems (drugs, violence, high crime, disorder, unruly bars, domestic violence, and the like) are tangled in these discussions. A fifteen-minute dosage of policing across communities evidencing significant complexity, and with significantly different problems seems rather sweeping.

On the community policing side of the equation, precise knowledge about how the police go about their engagement and interaction with the community and to what end is equally thin. Some of this, no doubt, is an artifact of the ambiguity of community policing (Moore, 1994), that is, the broad philosophic and tactical umbrella that it characterizes. Yet, from a knowledge perspective, the national evaluation of community-oriented policing suggested that, while many police departments benefitted from the considerable funding for these programs, most resulted in programs that were largely extensions of existing police efforts, partnership's between the police and the public remained asymmetric, and crime prevention efforts were mixed, although community satisfaction with the police did improve (Roth et al., 2000). Such findings were essentially replicated in more recent work of Gill and colleagues (2014).

Cumulatively, these findings suggest that understanding what the police do in community settings and with what impacts is a knowledge base on policing that has yet to be fully explored. Returning to our medical model, the absence of clear knowledge about treatments, dosage, and their effects and contraindications reduces the scientific credibility of such interventions.

There is emerging evidence that what is in the "black box" of policing is important to understand. Wood and her colleagues in Philadelphia (2014) found that police officers developed local street knowledge that assisted them in managing their assigned areas, balancing control versus social support tactics, but they also felt constrained by the artificiality of experimental research designs that in part discounted local knowledge in the application of police methods. Groff and her colleagues (2015), after finding that foot patrol and problem-solving appeared to have little effect on violent crime in an RCT study conducted in Philadelphia, acknowledged implementation failure issues as police shifted priorities within and across these targeted communities. Such findings have been associated with changes in police strategies from reactive to proactive policing and the implementation stresses that such changes produce (Bullock, Erol & Tilley, 2006).

More recently, Famega, Hinkle, and Weisburd (2017) opened up the black box of hot spots policing in three California cities by examining police-reported time spent in the designated hot spots noting significant variation. They concluded that significant variation in implementing police engagement in these hot spots impacted the ability of the research to detect outcomes, and that the agencies had failed to take ownership and systematically implement the intervention, even though there was prior agreement about how much time police would stay in the designated areas. Such a finding is consistent with Suchman's (1968) concerns with assessing implementation failure, or the presence or absence of an actual treatment, as opposed to theory failure, or the inappropriate conceptualization of cause and effect. Implementation failure in policing has a long history. Being able to sort the two (theory and implementation failure) is critical to understanding evidence-based policing.

Considering the craft knowledge that police bring to their encounters within communities, Willis (2013) outlines an appropriate merger of knowledge from evidence-based policing, with knowledge stemming from the craft of policing, as a way of improving understanding of the means and the ends of the police. Part of this assessment is rooted in research by Willis and Mastrofski (2016), who asked police officers about how science might improve the craft of policing. Police officers themselves asked that knowledge about a wide range of police responses and the interactional processes undergirding them be expanded. Other important considerations included improving knowledge on police performance measurement, improving police communications skills, and improving knowledge about the police use of discretion. Such police-led inquiry suggests that the clinical practice of policing is clearly underserved and undervalued at the moment.

On Follow-up and Aftercare: How long do police interventions last? How long should they last? At what time do communities show remission and what triggers return to community problems? What are the positive and negative side effects of police interventions? Which police interventions produce what short, intermediate, and long-term effects, both positive and negative? Such questions illustrate the complexities of assessing police interventions, as well as the importance of this information for assessing police practice. All too often, assessment of the effectiveness of police interventions is measured by the police, on the terms of the police – fewer arrests, less reported crime, and the like. Research on community perceptions of the police, fear of crime, and the like should be joined in assessments of police tactics, as at times these assessments contradict what the police are trying to accomplish (Haberman, 2015).

Of course, in using the medical analogy, the concern is with health improvements of the patient. From a policing standpoint, the degree to which the community sees and feels interventions needs strengthening. While community surveys have been abundant in police research, applying them to particular interventions has been less prevalent. Braga and Bond (2009) nicely demonstrate the role that community surveys can play in how police interventions are assessed.

Other aftercare issues include questions about how long the effects of programs designed to reduce crime or improve community safety actually last. An illustration of this is provided for Philadelphia (Sorg et al., 2013), suggesting that foot patrol and crackdowns in hot spot areas are likely short-term in their effects, whereas broader holistic strategies, such as intelligence-led policing, community policing, and problem-solving should be considered as likely having longer-term effects. Improving our understanding of policing interventions and their short- and long-term effects is an area of research sorely in need of expansion.

Aftercare knowledge is extremely important as it has been demonstrated that street segments have life cycles that shift from crime to non-crime and back again over time (Weisburd, Groff & Yang, 2012; Weisburd, 2015). Such knowledge is an important addition to information about how communities or places become engaged with crime, and how they desist from crime. How the police play into the aftercare of communities, can easily be associated with victim re-contact and reassurance policing as outlined by Innes (2004) and Crawford (2007), yet aftercare remains rather elusive in discussion of evidence-based police practice.

On Costs: In many ways, specifying a wide array of costs and benefits of police services has also been elusive. While the absence of crime is seen as the hallmark of the police since the time of Sir Robert Peel, a systematic accounting of what the police actually do across a number of public safety domains remains a moving and unclear target. Moreover, while policing has been formulated around risk and control, there are indeed other ways of thinking about police and social stability, and measuring all that matters in policing provides a much more thorough understanding of police costs (fiscal and social) and benefits. As Schuilenburg, van Steden, and Breuil (2014) suggest, alternatives to crime suppression and population control as means of providing security include increased care and building a sense of belongingness, built on values such as interdependence, inclusion, and cooperation also can reduce insecurity, while strengthening community agency. Ratcliffe (2015) suggests that shifting policing outcomes from risk to harm management opens important sources of knowledge for the police as well as measurements of their effectiveness. And, Langworthy (1999: 3) suggested that measuring what matters in policing includes, the impact domain or measures of what the police are to affect (e.g., crime, fear of crime, and disorder); the organizational health domain focused on the volume of police business and levels of community support, officer job knowledge and satisfaction; a process domain dealing with fairness, civility, equitable service, and ethical service, and, finally the community assessment domain dealing with police abilities and ethical behavior.

Presently, there are numerous programs aimed at increasing police efficiency and effectiveness supported through state and federal initiatives. But, as Harmon (2015) argues, in this case, federal programs being largely assessed in financial terms also produce coercion costs, including increased police intrusiveness, the militarization of the police, and other harmful police actions including the violation of civil rights. Harmon (2015: 960) concludes:

Policing is a crucial and complicated social project. Law enforcement is essential to protecting public order and safeguarding the conditions of liberty, but intrusive and coercive policing also imposes costs on individuals and communities. The legal problem of policing is deciding "how to regulate police officers and departments to protect individual liberty and minimize the social costs the police impose" while promoting the goals of policing: reducing fear, protecting civil order, and facilitating law enforcement.

At the economic level, parsing the fiscal costs for hot spots, community, or other forms of policing is underdeveloped. The costs of policing are complex; they involve budgets distributed over actions taken and results achieved, as well as costs associated with victimization and communal insecurity, among other things.

SOME CONCLUDING OBSERVATIONS

As is the case in many public policy arenas, the complexities of societal, legal system, community values and interpretations, and organizational and work group definitions of role and function intersect in crafting police policy and for its implementation. Broad social expectations about the police are invariably met by police organizational definitions of the role of police in modern society. Legal dictum and processes also influence decisions made by the police. Given ranges in community political and social structures, styles of policing vary by place and are heavily influenced by police organizations and their cultures, resulting in scientific information being coupled with craft knowledge.

At the same time, police work groups and individual police officers breathe life into these definitions or suffocate them as they take up their daily routines and interactions. Moreover, communities receive the benefits or brunt of police actions, such that drawing their experiences into the police knowledge base, most particularly as assessed in evaluation research efforts, needs greater focus (Committee on Proactive Policing, 2017). Policing, then, is an amalgam of many expectations, actions, and results, and, of course, many sources of knowledge.

The resulting proposition from this discussion is that our focus on the police has become too narrow. That is to say, the ways in which police research is framed presently needs reframing. Herman Goldstein (1990) told us that the police had become captives of a means-over-ends inversion, that is, the police were too focused on effort and not particularly well focused on effect or outcome. This, of course, paved the way for problem-oriented policing, crime science, evidence-based policing, and its progeny.

As we have measured "what works" more finitely in the last decade or so, we presently have an ends-over-means inversion. That is to say, we have almost abandoned sorting out what the police actually do, and what such actions actually mean to the communities they serve, instead focusing on outcomes defined as less reported crime or disorder. Weighing these two competing issues will be important to furthering scientific inquiry about the police.

Balancing these definitions can be seen as taking on an art-critic form of evaluation in that the subtleties in hue and contour of policing are often left to the observer, whether that observer calls for Black Lives Matter, or for Support Your Local Police. Both perspectives have validity, yet they are often in opposition. Excluding either diminishes how we have come to know the police and their impact on society.

Guba and Lincoln (1989) introduced the idea of "fourth generation evaluation research" wherein evaluations are undertaken with an explicit concern for "the claims, concerns, and issues of stakeholders" (p. 50), serving as an organizing framework for such efforts. In such a framework, knowledge derived from official records is tempered by stakeholder qualitative assessments of programs and their effects. Moreover, there is a long tradition of implementation research seeking to better understand how the abstract ideas of policy makers are actually put into motion (or not) in action-oriented settings, and, more recently, a revival of wanting to understand what is in the black box of policing (Terpstra & Fyfe, 2015; Famega et al., 2017).

By all accounts, policing is complex, carried out in varying social contexts with varying expectations and varying levels of support for the police. At the same time, police officers should be taken as legal craftspeople, attempting to use legal processes to address what are essentially social, economic, or political problems, imbedded in community settings. Given such complexity broadening the range of useful information on the police and policing seems quite warranted.

REFERENCES

Audi, R. (2002). Sources of knowledge. In P. K. Moser (ed.), *The Oxford Handbook of Epistemology* (pp. 71–94). New York: Oxford University Press.

Black, D. (1980). *The Manners and Customs of the Police.* New York: Academic Press.

Bayley, D. H., & Bittner, E. (1984). Learning the skills of policing. *Law and Contemporary Problems*, 4(4), 35–59.

Braga, A. A. (2014). Problem-oriented policing: principles, practices and crime. In M. D. Reisig, & R. J. Kane (eds.), *The Oxford Handbook of Police and Policing* (pp. 101–121). New York: Oxford University Press.

Braga, A., & Bond, B. J. (2009). Community perceptions of police crime prevention efforts: Using interviews in small areas to evaluate crime reduction strategies. In J. Knutsson, & N. Tilley (eds.), *Evaluating Crime Reduction Initiatives*, vol. 24. Crime Prevention Studies (pp. 87–119). Boulder, CO: Lynne Rienner Publishers.

Braga, A. A., Flynn, E. A., Kelling, G. L., & Cole, C. M. (2011). Moving the work of criminal investigators towards crime control. In *New Perspectives on Policing*. Washington, DC: US Department of Justice, National Institute of Justice.

Braga, A. A., Papachristos, A. V., & Hureau, D. M. (2014). The effects of hot spots policing on crime: An updated systematic review and meta-analysis. *Justice Quarterly*, 31(4), 633–663.

Brodeur, Jean-Paul. (2010). *The Web of Policing.* New York: Oxford University Press.

Bradley, D., & Nixon, C. (2009). Ending the dialogue of the deaf: Evidence and policing policies and practice in an Australian case study. *Police Practice and Research: An International Journal*, 10(5–6), 423–435.

Bullock, K., Erol R., & Tilley, N. (2006). *Problem-Oriented Policing and Partnerships: Implementing an Evidence-Based Approach to Crime Reduction.* Collumpton, UK: Willan.

Carr, P. J. (2012). Citizens, community, and crime control: The problems and prospects for negotiated order. *Criminology & Criminal Justice*, 12(4), 397–412.

Clarke, R. V. (1998). Defining police strategies: problem-solving, problem-oriented policing and community-oriented policing. In T. O'Connor Shelley, & A. C. Grant (eds.), *Problem-Oriented Policing: Crime-Specific Problems, Critical Issues and Making POP Work*. Washington, DC: Police Executive Research Forum.

Cockbain, E., & Knutsson, J. (eds.) (2015). *Applied Police Research: Challenges and Opportunities.* New York: Routledge.

Committee on Proactive Policing. (2017). *Proactive Policing: Effects on Crime and Communities.* Washington, DC: National Institute of Justice and the Laura and John Arnold Foundation. Justice.

Cordner, G. W. (2014). Community policing. In M. D. Reisig, & R. J. Kane (eds.), *The Oxford Handbook of Police and Policing* (pp. 148–171). New York: Oxford University Press.

Crank, J. P., & Langworthy, R. (1992). An institutional perspective on policing. *Journal of Criminal Law & Criminology*, 83, 338–363.

Crawford, A. (2007). Reassurance policing: Feeling is believing. In *Transformations of Policing* (pp. 143–168). Aldershot: Ashgate.

Dingwall, R. (2011). Why are doctors dissatisfied? The role of origin myths. *Journal of Health Services Research & Policy*, 21(1), 67–70.

Famega, C., Hinkle, J. C., & Weisburd, D. (2017). Why getting inside the "Black Box" Is important: Examining treatment implementation and outputs in policing experiments. *Police Quarterly* 20(1), 106–132.

French, J. R. P., Raven, B., & Cartwright, D. (1959). The bases of social power. In D. Cartwright (ed.), *Classics of Organization Theory* (pp. 150–167). Ann Arbor, MI: Institute for Social Research, University of Michigan.

Fyfe, J. J. (1999). Good policing. In S. Stojkovic, J. Klofas, & D. Kalinich (eds.), *The Administration and Management of Criminal Justice Organizations* (3rd ed. pp. 113–133). Prospect Heights, IL: Waveland Press.

Gill, C., Weisburd, D., Telep, C. W., Vitter, Z., & Bennett, T. (2014). Community-oriented policing to reduce crime, disorder and fear and increase satisfaction and legitimacy among citizens: A systematic review. *Journal of Experimental Criminology*, DOI 10.1007/s11292-014-9210-y.

Groff, E. R., Ratcliffe, J. H., Haberman, C. P., Sorg, E. T., Joyce, N. M., & Taylor, R. B. (2015). Does what police do at hot spots matter? The Philadelphia policing tactics experiment. *Criminology*, 53(1), 23–53.

Goffman, E. (1986). *Frame Analysis: An Essay on the Organization of Experience.* Boston: Northeastern University Press.

Goldstein, H. (1990). *Problem-Oriented Policing.* New York: McGraw-Hill.

Greene, J. R. 1998). Evaluating planned change strategies in modern law enforcement. In J.-P. Brodeur (ed.), *How to Recognize Good Policing: Problems and Issues* (pp. 141–160). Thousand Oaks, CA: Sage.

Greene, J. R. (2014a). New directions in policing: Balancing prediction and meaning in police research. *Justice Quarterly*, 31 (2), 193–228.

Greene, J. R. (2014b). The upside and downside of the police epistemic community, *Oxford Journal of Policing*, 8(4), 379–392.

Guba, E. G., & Lincoln, Y. S. (1989). *Fourth Generation Evaluation.* Newbury Park, CA: Sage Publications.

Harmon, R. (2015). Federal programs and the real costs of policing. New York University Law Review, 870–960.

Head, B. W., & Alford, J. (2013). Wicked problems: Implications for public policy and management. *Administration & Society*, 47(6), 711–739.

Haberman, C. P. (2015). Cops on dots doing what? The differential effects of police enforcement actions in hot spots. Dissertation, Philadelphia, PA: Temple University.

Haberman, C. P., Groff, E. R., Ratcliffe, J. H., & Sorg, E. T. (2016). Satisfaction with police in violent crime hot spots: Using community surveys as a guide for selecting hot spots policing tactics. *Crime and Delinquency*, 62(4), 525–557.

Hill, M. (2014). *Policy Process: A Reader.* New York: Routledge.

Hough, M. (2011). Criminology and the role of experimental research. In M. Bosworth, & C. Boyle (eds.), *What Is Criminology?* (pp. 198–210). Oxford, UK: Oxford University Press.

Innes, M. (2004). Reinventing tradition? Reassurance, neighborhood security and policing. *Criminal Justice*, 4(2), 151–171.

Innes, M. (2005). What's your problem? Signal crimes and citizen-focused problem solving. *Criminology & Public Policy*, 4, 187–200.

Innes, M., Abbott, L., Lowe, T., & Roberts, C., (2009). Seeing like a citizen: Field experiments in "community intelligence-led policing." *Police Practice and Research: An International Journal*, 10(2), 99–114.

Jenieck, M. (2013). *A Primer on Clinical Experience in Medicine: Reasoning, Decision Making, and Communication in Health Sciences.* Boca Raton, FL: CRC Press.

Koper, C. S. (1995). Just enough police presence: Reducing crime and disorderly behavior by optimizing patrol time in crime hot spots. *Justice Quarterly,* 12(4), 649–672.

Langworthy, R. (ed.). (1999). *Measuring What Matters.* Washington, DC: US Department of Justice.

La Vigne, N., Fontaine, J., & Dwivedi, A. (2017). *How Do People in High-Crime, Low-Income Communities View the Police?* Washington, DC: Urban Institute.

Lindblom, C. E. (1959). The science of muddling through. *Public Administration Review,* 19, 79–88.

Lum, C. (2012). Incorporating research into daily police practices: The matrix demonstration project. *Translational Criminology,* Fall: 16–17.

Lum, C., & Koper, C. S. (2017). *Evidence-Based Policing: Translating Research into Practice.* New York: Oxford University Press.

Lum, C., Koper, C. S., & Telep, C. W. (2011). The evidence-based policing matrix. *Journal of Experimental Criminology,* 7(1), 3–26.

Maguire, E. R., & Katz, C. M. (2006). Community policing, loose coupling, and sensemaking in American police agencies. *Justice Quarterly,* 19(3), 503–536.

Manning, P. K. (1997). *Police Work: The Social Organization of Policing.* 2nd ed. Homewood, IL: Waveland Press.

Manning, P. K. (2003). *Policing Contingencies.* Chicago: University of Chicago Press.

Maruna, S., & Barber, C. (2011). Why can't criminology be more like medical research? Be careful what you wish for. In M. Bosworth, & C. Boyle (eds.), *What Is Criminology?* (pp. 318–334). Oxford, UK: Oxford University Press.

Mears, D. P., Stewart, E. A., Warren, P. Y., & Simons, R. L. (2017). Culture and formal social control: The effect of the code of the street on police and court decision-making. *Justice Quarterly,* 34(2), 217–247.

Moore, M. H. (1994). Research synthesis and policy implications. In D. Rosenbaum, (ed.), *The Challenge of Community Policing: Testing the Promises* (pp. 285–299). Thousand Oaks, CA: Sage.

Moore, M. H. (1997). *Creating Public Value: Strategic Management in Government.* Cambridge, MA: Harvard University Press.

Moore, M. H. (2006). Improving policing through expertise, experience and experiments. In D. Weisburd, & A. Braga (eds.), *Police Innovation: Contrasting Perspectives* (pp. 17–38). New York: Cambridge University Press.

Nagin, D., & Weisburd, D. (2013). Evidence and public policy: The example of evaluation research in policing. *Criminology and Public Policy,* 12, 651–679.

Neyroud, P., & Weisburd, D. (2014). Transforming the police through science: The challenge of ownership. *Policing,* 8(4), 287–293.

Norman, G. (2005). Research in clinical reasoning: Past history and current trends. *Medical Education,* 39, 418–427.

Perneger, T. V., & Agoritsas, T. (2011). Doctors and patients' susceptibility to framing bias: A randomized trial. *Journal of General Internal Medicine,* 26(12), 1411–1417.

Ratcliffe, J. H. (2015). Towards an index for harm-focused policing. *Policing: A Journal of Policy and Practice,* 9(2), 164–182.

Reiner, R. (2010). *The Politics of the Police.* New York: Oxford University Press.

Robinson, A., & Payton, J. (2016). Independent advocacy and multi-agency responses to domestic violence. In *Domestic Violence* (pp. 249–271). UK: Palgrave Macmillan.

Roth, J. A., Ryan, J. F., Gaffigan, S. J., Koper, C. S., Moore, M. H., Roehl, J. A., Johnson, C. C. et al. (2000). *National Evaluation of the Cops Program*. Title I of the 1994 Crime Act. Series. Washington, DC: National Institute for Justice.

Sackett, D. L., Straus, S. E., Scott Richardson, W., Rosenberg, W., & Haynes, R. B. (2000). *How to Practice and Teach EBM*. Edinburgh: Churchill Livingstone.

Scheufele, D. A., & Iyengar, S. (2014). The state of framing research: A call for new directions. In K. Kenski, & K. Hall Jamieson (eds.), *The Oxford Handbook of Political Communication*. New York: Oxford University Press.

Schuilenburg, M., van Steden, R., & Breuil, B. O. (eds.). (2014). *Positive Criminology: Reflections on Care, Belonging and Security*. The Hague, NL: Eleven International Publishing.

Scott, M. S. (2000). *Problem-Oriented Policing: Reflections on the First 20 Years*. Washington, DC: US Department of Justice, Office of Community Oriented Policing Services.

Sherman, L. W. (2013). The rise of evidence-based policing: Targeting, testing, and tracking. *Crime and Justice*, 42, 377–451.

Smith, K. B., & Larimer, C. W. (2017). *The Public Policy Theory Primer*. 3rd ed. Boulder, CO: Westview Press.

Sorg, E. T., Haberman, C. P., Ratcliffe, J. H., & Groff, E. R. (2013). Foot patrol in violent crime hot spots: The longitudinal impact of deterrence and post treatment effects of displacement. *Criminology*, 51(1), 65–102.

Suchman, E. (1968). *Evaluative Research: Principles and Practices in Public Service and Social Action Programs*. New York: Russell Sage.

Terpstra, J., & Fyfe, N. R. (2015). Mind the implementation gap? Police reform and local policing in the Netherlands and Scotland. *Criminology & Criminal Justice*, 15 (5), 527–544.

Tilley, N. (2006). Knowing and doing: Guidance and good practice in crime prevention. In J. Knutsson, & R. V. Clarke (eds.), *Implementing Situational Prevention and Problem-Oriented Policing*. Crime Prevention Studies, vol. 20. Monsey, NJ: Criminal Justice Press.

Tilley, N. (2009). Sherman vs. Sherman: realism and rhetoric. *Criminology and Criminal Justice*, 9(2), 135–144.

Weber, E. P., & Khademian, A. M. (2008). Wicked problems, knowledge challenges, and collaborative capacity builders in network settings. *Public Administration Review*, 68(2), 334–349.

Weick, K. E. (1995). *Sensemaking in organizations*. Thousand Oaks, CA: Sage.

Weisburd, D., (2015). The law of crime concentration and the criminology of place. *Criminology*, 53(2), 133–157.

Weisburd, D., & Braga, A. (eds.). (2006). *Police Innovation: Contrasting Perspectives*. New York: Cambridge University Press.

Weisburd, D., Groff, E. R., & Yang, S.-M. (2012). *The Criminology of Place: Street Segments and Our Understanding of the Crime Problem*. New York: Oxford University Press.

Willis, J. J. (2013). *Improving Police: What's Craft Got to Do With It?* Ideas in American Policing Series. Washington, DC: Police Foundation.

Willis, J. J., & Mastrofski, S. D. (2016). Improving policing by integrating craft and science: what can patrol officers teach us about good police work? *Policing and Society: An International Journal of Research and Policy*, 1–18.

Wood, J., Sorg, E. T., Groff, E. R., Ratcliffe, J. H., & Taylor, C. J. (2014). Cops as treatment providers: Realities and ironies of police work in a foot patrol experiment. *Policing and Society*, 24(3), 362–379.

Yin, R. K. (2003). *Case Study Research: Design and Methods*. 3rd ed. Thousand Oaks, CA: Sage.

PART XI

TECHNOLOGY POLICING

21

Advocate

Technology in Policing

Barak Ariel

TECHNOLOGY IN POLICING

For nearly forty years, policymakers within law enforcement, commercially motivated interest groups, and scholars have made the case for an augmented implementation of technology in policing, particularly information technologies. The prominent discourse is efficiency and cost-effectiveness of operations, as technology is hypothesized to improve the quality of law enforcement on a wide range of outcomes and outputs. *Prima facie*, technology can revolutionize law enforcement; ample examples indicate where this is the case. Research areas in support of technology in policing include computers, GPS-based technologies, video recording of crime scenes, and forensic evidence, such as DNA testing. Our collective view should be that the pertinent question is one of scale: why not more? Why are information technologies not more pronounced in law enforcement? What stopped the information revolution from establishing a more prominent place in policing?

Law enforcement is steadily becoming a profession characterized as a technologically advanced arena, in part because it has great potential to do so: high-tech companies and senior police officers have been eager to embrace information technology's (IT) advancements with vast quantities of products, services, and innovations. Clearly, key areas in policing, like data collation, management, synthesis, and sharing, significantly lag behind other public-sector professions and certainly vis-à-vis the private sector (see discussion in Ariel, Bland & Sutherland, 2017) yet, technology in policing has made great strides over the years. The average police station is far more technologically sophisticated than at the turn of the twenty-first century, and a common police vehicle is vastly more equipped than the "black and white panda cars" that roamed the streets in the 1980s or 1990s. Special branches, counterterrorism, and counter-insurgency departments maintain considerable amounts of information, employ several layers of data and information technologies, and signals intelligence (SIGINT) collection capabilities are impressive.

To be sure, technology implementation in policing is not usually a smooth process. Scholars have recently unearthed some of the obstacles to modernizing police information technologies (IT) and information systems, including unfitting technologies, objections from frontline as well as back-office personnel, and immature systems that fail to fulfill expectations. "Implementation failures" are greater than successes. Decreased efficiency and effectiveness and the loss of productivity due to the disruption caused by weak implementation have led to highly visible failures even in the most forward-facing law enforcement agencies, and motivated some prominent technology-in-policing scholars to conclude that technology has yet to show that it makes policing more effective (e. g., Manning, 1992; Lum, 2010). Yet, these implementation failures cannot justify halting progress. Quite the opposite. Obstacles ought to motivate us to continue exploring new ways of *appropriately* pushing technology for use in policing.

In support of technology in policing, I investigate information technologies and information systems, rather than technology in the form of devices, tools, or gadgets. Hardware is important, but in and of itself, is not an end goal. Police departments should not procure body-worn cameras, license plate readers, or drones solely for the sake of owning new technologies. Technology's physical tools are not the main issue when considering the role of technology in policing; rather, the (potential) data and information derived from these devices is what we ought to consider. Indeed, technology is the "application of scientific knowledge for practical [law enforcement] purposes" (Oxford Dictionary). Construed this way, then, "technology in policing" is chiefly about the value of information for the benefit of policing, including its inputs, outputs, and outcomes.

This chapter is organized in the following way: first, an overview of the promise of information technologies and information systems in policing will be laid out. Some of the historical context will be presented within this framework along with the prominent research questions associated with the value of technology in policing: efficiency and effectiveness. The main body of this chapter follows with an exposition of the primary areas the value of technology in policing is making the greatest strides: contribution of technology to crime reduction in hot spots; electronic tracking of police resources; big data and machine learning; increasing clearance rates; accountability and transparency; and increasing productivity. These case studies all faced challenges, however, I will defend the view that these claims are not insurmountable; we need more rigorous evaluation research that will promote evidence-based policy, and through testing new technologies prior to deployment, only efficient and cost-effective innovations will be implemented. Finally – and linked to evidence-based policy – implementation failures are discussed, with a call to consider the avenues suitable to ascertain the proper implementation of promising technologies in policing.

THE PROMISE OF INFORMATION TECHNOLOGIES IN POLICING

Policing scholars have long been interested in the potential of information technologies and technology in policing more broadly (e.g., Crowther, 1964; Chaiken & Dormont, 1978; Skogan & Hartnett, 1997: 11; Mastrofski & Willis, 2010). Byrne and Marx (2011: 17) argued that technological innovations are so important to policing that they are the "driving force leading to reform of crime prevention and crime control strategies, both by individual citizens and concerns groups, and by formal police agencies." Even long-time critics of technology's ability to enhance policing would agree that some techniques of crime prevention, including crime analysis, mapping, deployment of resources, and using a targeted approach, can be far-reaching (Manning, 2003: 249–250). Can anyone imagine a police officer today not linked directly to a computer? The genie is already out of the bottle, so the question of technology in policing is therefore about the how and when, rather than the if.

One of the earliest recognitions that IT can benefit policing came in 1967, with US President Johnson's Commission on Law Enforcement and Administration of Justice. The nineteen-member committee concluded that IT can improve efficiency and fairness in policing while maintaining cost-effectiveness. This endorsement was chiefly concerned with computers and electronic systems that would proficiently manage command and control centers to improve the deployment of nearby officers to emergency calls for service. Although we cannot gauge modern policing without a centralized, computerized police dispatch center, the transition was nothing short of revolutionary at the time, with real benefits for members of the public, the police, and law enforcement more broadly (Hickman & Reaves, 2006). From this system, new ways of collating inputs, outputs, and outcomes were quickly developed, consequently increasing the efficacy by which "police data" are synthesized, analyzed, and eventually used. For example, contemporary hot spots policing studies require rather advanced IT systems (Ariel & Partridge, 2016), just as social network analysis (Englefield & Ariel 2017; Denley & Ariel, *forthcoming*), data mining and big data analytics (Oatley, Ewart, & Zeleznikow 2006; Tinati et al., 2014), and machine learning and artificial intelligence programming (Michalski, Carbonell & Mitchell, 2013) are all steadily becoming common features in uber-modern law enforcement. The influx of new technologies is now vastly different from what it was just thirty years ago, when some of the critiques of technology in policing underscored the challenges this field would withstand (e.g., Manning, 1992), that our view of policing has dramatically changed since then.

The future holds even more opportunities in this direction. It is not uncommon for a specific, large police department to hold information on millions of calls for service, with each call broken down into dozens of data points (e.g., spatiotemporal variables, crime categorization, data on the caller/

victim/offender/witness, and a multitude of actionable outputs the police and its partners carried out). Similarly, such a police department may be involved in hundreds of self-initiated daily contacts. As such, for at least two decades both proactive and reactive data have been compiled, with a centralized system of police inputs, outputs, and outcomes likely to include billions of data points. In addition, audial and visual data have recently been added to the mix. As Ridgway (2017: 33) noted, "data volume is simply the magnitude of the data police collect and store. A 30-minute body-worn camera video produces 800 MB of data … A Houston police captain reported that 100 cameras were producing about 1 TB of data per day." The transmission of these data is becoming faster, more reliable, and more secure, providing instantaneous data and reports not only centrally, but also to the individual officers in the field. Consequently, each crime can be linked to a wide range of data sources, thus providing impressive amounts of information that can be used for a myriad of purposes.

Furthermore, technology is not just hardware and new devices; it also incorporates information. Information systems and information technologies are part and parcel of any meaningful conversation about technology and policing, wherein lies incredible promise. We are now seeing the police use more layers of data to manage crime and disorder, precisely the conditions necessary for big data analytics and sophisticated data mining exercises. A recent survey on policing shows that nearly all officers do a background check on suspects or addresses they will visit during the line of duty (Koper et al., 2014). The police can use different data sources as well, such as the New York Police Department's (NYPD) "situational awareness" system, designed so officers can use the data surrounding them (see Levine et al., 2017). Of course, using these systems parallel the recent transition undertaken by the banking industry to investigate fraud and financial crimes more broadly (Hipgrave, 2013): social network analysis, voice recognition technologies, and available socioeconomic data are used to conduct complex fraud investigations (Diniz et al., 2018). Similarly, security services have long tapped into these information domains, with social media a prominent feature in both pre-emptive as well as reactive investigations of "lone wolves" and more organized terrorist threats (Brynielsson et al., 2013; Cardenas, Manadhata & Rajan 2013; Strang & Sun, 2017). Without technological systems that collate, store, synthesize, and provide access to information, the police would be unable to successfully challenge criminals. More than anything, these examples and others illustrate that to the extent that officers *are* using technology, innovations play a large and growing part in modern law enforcement.

To investigate the value of IT and information more broadly on efficiency, productivity, and cost-effectiveness, scholars have undertaken several randomized trials. Rigorous experiments in health studies (e.g., Liu & Wyatt, 2011) have shown that using more information is often met with better outcomes, such as reductions in false positives and false negatives and treatment misalignment, and enhanced prognoses. In law enforcement, studies that focused on IT in policing reported benefits to officers' safety (Garicano & Heaton, 2010), predictive accuracy (Hyatt & Barnes, 2017), tracking of officers (Ariel, Weinborn & Sherman, 2016), with more results explored below. The question that remains, however, is to what extent are these technological advances useful in policing? Officer use of technology does not immediately translate into efficiency, cost-effectiveness, or better policing. Thus, to address this question, six primary areas where the value of technology in policing is making the greatest contributions to crime reduction in hot spots will be explored; advanced crime analysis approaches, specifically CCTV and social network analyses; electronic tracking of police resources; big data and machine learning; increasing clearance rates; accountability and transparency; and increasing productivity.

Contribution of Technology to Crime Reduction in Hot Spots

Technology in policing has seen great benefits for hot spots policing – the idea of positioning police officers in small geographical locations to prevent crime from happening in the first place (Sherman & Weisburd, 1995; see earlier versions of this type of intervention in Scott, 1949: 11). Hot spots policing has been a resounding success in modern policing, with dozens of rigorous evaluations collectively showing its crime suppression benefits (see Braga, Papachristos & Hureau, 2014). The basic science underpinning this modern application of Pareto for crime in place, namely that most criminal events concentrate in a small and identifiable number of places, can be construed as a technological innovation. Some noteworthy impact evaluations, such as those conducted by Jerry Ratcliffe and colleagues (e.g., Ratcliffe et al., 2011; Haberman & Ratcliffe, 2012; Sorg et al., 2014; Groff et al., 2015) are heavily dependent on technology to accurately predict where crime is more likely to take place and, by implication, to be prevented through visible patrols. These hot spots studies and other experiments (e.g., Ariel, Weinborn & Sherman, 2016), are examples of how police use its own data over a long period of time and from multiple sources (e.g., Boyle et al., 2013; Ariel, Weinborn & Boyle, 2015; Sutherland et al., 2017) to both predict where future crimes are more likely to occur and to prevent crime through proactive interventions. For example, and in one of the more innovative experimental designs, Groff et al. (2015) combined data on both crime places as well as offenders to address the vortex of places where, and people who, commit crime. Without information systems, which enabled this approach, the experiment would have been impossible only a few short years ago.

These advancements are not merely back-office functions. In the place-based criminology literature, Weisburd et al. (2010) commented that problem-oriented policing illustrates that technology has led to enhanced efficiency of policing in reducing crime and disorder. Another prominent area is the provision of real-time information to officers about where and when they should target criminogenic places. Koper et al. (2014) show that most officers, more than 80 percent, review historic data on addresses they go to on the job to acquaint themselves with the necessary information about the case. A recent survey by the Police Executive Research Forum (2014) of nearly 200 departments shows that 70 percent use data in a predictive way (what some refer to as predictive policing, which has certainly become a term *de jour* in most police departments), and 100 percent of respondents used technological innovations in their vehicles (see also Weisburd & Braga, 2006; Bratton, Morgan & Malinowski, 2009). We have moved a long way since the well-known Kelling et al. (1974) study on police patrols; Proactive policing within micro-places, such as hot spots, has shown under repeated rigorous evaluation conditions, that it is a valuable crime reduction exercise (see review in Ratcliffe & Sorg, 2017: 7–20). Without data, this theoretical and practical enterprise would not have been available.

Beyond the conceptual novelty, advanced information systems are required to reliably populate data over a relatively long period of time (e.g., Sherman, Gartin & Buerger, 1989). As opposed to crime waves (Newton & Felson, 2015) of a few weeks or even months in duration that do not constitute a hot spot per se, data over longer periods are required for this type of analysis, and therefore mainframes with sufficient computational powers are needed to show, for example, not only that crime concentrates in a small proportion of places, but also that some hot spots are chronic, persistent, and immovable for many years given the ecological features of the criminogenic place (see Ariel, 2011; Weisburd, Groff & Yang, 2012; Weisburd & Amram, 2014; Weinborn et al., 2017). That "law of concentration of crime in place" (Weisburd 2015) exists, meaning data from different police records need to be captured, synthesized, and analyzed, which show that many modern police departments share a similar "data vision." Collection and production of crime statistics on a granular basis are what permit a global analysis of hot spots to be generated in the first place.

Furthermore, technology has been influential in showing that, much like other areas of prediction and actuarial forecasting, machines beat mankind in prediction validity as well as measurement reliability (Meehl, 1954; Tversky & Kahneman, 1975). An illusion of validity exists when humans try to predict, and we are often incorrect in our expectations, at least when compared with algorithmic predictions. Macbeth and Ariel (2017) have recently shown that the same superiority of statistical forecasting over clinical prediction exists in place-based analysis. Experts, i.e., frontline officers, were tasked to predict which geographic areas to target with preventative tactics. These assessments were compared with statistical predictions based on the spatial persistence characteristic of hot spots over time (Weisburd et al., 2012). The comparison between the two systems indicated that while statistical hot spots accurately predict future incidents, the clinical assessment of the experts were nearly always (97 percent) misplaced. This study and others (e.g., Rengert & Pelfrey, 1997; Ratcliffe & McCullagh, 2001; Chainey & Ratcliffe, 2005) show that preventative policing based on statistical forecasting, rather than on professional judgment, should be preferred. Therefore, for hot spots prediction, technology in the form of computer-based systems triumphs over decision-makers.

Thus, modern crime prevention law enforcement, certainly in the context of place-based interventions and other areas of policing as well, is heavily dependent on technology. At its core, the basic patrol function is not only guided by information systems and information technologies, but also cannot function without it. From the emergency call, through to the dispatch call handlers and down to the patrolling officer, every chain is linked to some relevant technological innovation without which the patrol function would be handicapped.

Advanced Crime Analyses Tools

One area where technology has provided a demonstrable advantage to policing was the introduction of sophisticated, advanced, and evidence-based approaches to crime analysis. Two particular examples are noteworthy: the use of CCTV footage in crime analysis and social network analyses used to identify central actors in groups of people.

Surveillance cameras have been in existence even prior to the 1960s. However, only in the last twenty-five years or so have CCTV (closed circuit televisions) devices become an integral part of law enforcement (Goold, 2003). Technological advancement made cameras better, more reliable and substantially less expensive (McCahill & Norris, 2004). Most, if not all, modern police CCTV form an important part of crime investigation, prosecution, and crime deterrence and enhance the public's satisfaction with the police (Ariel, 2016c).

Admittedly – and despite investing billions of dollars on CCTV – the overwhelming evidence is mixed and in the majority of studies the findings are not supportive of this technology. Meta-analyses of the evidence (Welsh & Farrington, 2002; 2009) show that installing CCTV in the public domain causes a modest decrease in crime, compared to similar places without CCTV, particularly when considering the costs of installing, operating, and using CCTV. Dozens of studies of varying methodological rigor and in different locations illustrate that the overall crime reduction effect of CCTV is approximately 16 percent; however, half that reduction is concentrated in car parks, and no significant effect on violent crimes such as assaults, robberies, and similar against-person crimes has been observed. The evidence also tends to show that criminal behavior is displaced to other areas (Ratcliffe, Taniguchi & Taylor, 2009). Likewise, any prolific offender already knows precisely where the blind spots of CCTV cameras are located, and that CCTV does not work well in the dark or when the offender wears a hoodie that creates a shaded and unidentified image instead of a recognizable face. It may also be the case that CCTV has become such a part of everyday life that its presence escapes our conscious attention, and thus cannot deter criminal behavior (van Bommel et al., 2014).

More recent studies, however, suggest otherwise; namely, that CCTV can be used in proactive policing and produces more substantive results. CCTV is an evolving technology, and with this technological development the police can use it in "smarter" ways. For example, Piza, Caplan, Kennedy, and Gilchrist (2015) tested the use of this technology in Newark, New Jersey, with nineteen cameras monitored by a dedicated camera operator and two patrol cars that were exclusively seconded to responding to incidents identified by the camera operator, while nineteen cameras in control areas were used normally, that is, with monitors reporting suspicious activities through a computer-aided dispatch system to patrol officers. This study found up to 48 percent and 49 percent reductions in violent crime and social disorder, respectively, with the use of this approach – distinctively more pronounced results than earlier studies reviewed by Welsh and Farrington (2009). In this respect, Piza and colleagues' (2015) study shows, which is supported by the National Academy of Sciences (Weisburd & Majmundar, 2018: 4–12), that CCTV could be effective "when bundled with other crime prevention measures." This suggests that CCTV may indeed be useful if used appropriately, actively, and alongside other interventions. Even though it may be difficult to single out the effect of these costly CCTV systems from additional interventions (e.g., dedicated officers, lighting typically installed with the cameras – which may be the primary factor that deters offenders – or other apparatuses), as a package, CCTV could be linked to demonstrable utility for crime analysis, prevention, and proactive policing.

Beyond CCTV, social network analysis is another useful piece of technology for crime analysis, particularly when targeting repeat offenders or repeat victims. There are theoretical as well as practical elements here. A central element in most crime theories is that criminal behavior is a skill shared, learned, or transmitted between individuals. Learning theories and differential association (Sutherland, 1947), social disorganization theories (Shaw & McKay, 1942), strain theories (Merton, 1938), culture conflicts (Lewin, 1948), and social bonding theories (see review in Gardner & Shoemaker, 1989) all share a common feature embedded within them, that the "crime idea" is carried between various actors in society. This is where social network analysis comes into play: it is a tool for mapping actors and those relations among the actors (Wasserman & Faust, 1994: 20), particularly in more complicated and long-term criminal networks (Sarnecki, 1990; 2001). In this context, social network analysis allows scholars to understand relationships on a bounded set of actors (see review in Papachristos, 2011), using graph theory, or mathematical models that measure the type and scope of relationships between *nodes*, or actors. Rather sophisticated statistical computations illustrate network parameters such as closeness, proximity, density, betweenness, interdependency, or various types of connections between these actors, in ways that allow scholars to understand group dynamics, structures, relationships between nodes, who are the more dominant nodes in particular settings, and so on – all based on different parameters and assumptions.

Advanced technology is required for these kinds of crime analyses because they require advanced computational powers, and, optimally, a triangulated approach with multiple data sources that may require large data sets. If performed appropriately, social network analysis can be used for crime analysis by identifying high-risk people (who could be both victims and offenders) or to diagnose gang violence problems when implementing focused deterrence strategies, in ways that were not available for scholars and practitioners only two decades ago (see Braga & Weisburd, 2012; Braga, Apel & Welsh, 2013; Braga & Weisburd, 2014; Kennedy, Kleiman & Braga, 2017). Collectively, the use of social networks to analyze organized crime and gangs seems to be the most profound and promising avenue at this stage. The conceptualization of Reiss's (1986) approach to co-offending and other grounded theories of crime can now be operationalized to aid analysts in fresh ways. Understanding street gang structures (McGloin, 2005; Papachristos, 2009), organized crime (Morselli, 2003), heroin trafficking (Natarajan, 2006), suicide attacks and terrorist groups (Pedahzur & Perliger, 2006), opioid distribution on a darknet cryptomarket (Duxbury & Haynie, 2017), serial homicide investigations (Bichler, Lim & Larin, 2017), criminal recruitment (Englefield & Ariel, 2017), and even white collar crime conspiracies (Baker & Faulkner, 2003) are all notable examples of applications of social network analysis. It would be surprising if this approach will not continue to grow in the near future.

Electronic Tracking of Police Resources

Although the notion that hot spots policing reduces in crime is fairly established, the link between treatment dosage within the hot spots, tracking the performance of officers within the targeted areas, and estimating the causal link between the two is underdeveloped. Koper (1995) was among the first to recognize the important connection between outputs (i.e., delivery of the policy) and outcomes (i.e., variations in crime levels) when showing that residual deterrence (Sherman, 1990) is correlated to the time spent in the hot spots. Koper (1995) concluded that fifteen-minute patrols mark the optimal duration in the hot spot, a conclusion that has led to the development of "Koper Minutes" patrols, which are now practiced in many hot spots experiments around the world (e.g., Telep, Weisburd & Mitchell, 2014). With this in mind, however, the rigorous assessment of outcomes alongside outputs is a related area where the benefits of technology in policing are sound, but only recently began to emerge as critical knowledge in the application of technology in policing. Koper (1995) was fortunate to be linked to a major National Institute of Justice grant that monitored hot spots with 7,542 hours of systematic observations. Since such a grand study with its large number of research assistants is not translatable into practice for tracking police resources, technology can assist, using global positioning systems (GPS), automatic vehicle locators (AVL), or WiFi trackers of the officers in the field.

Before elaborating on these innovations, it should be stressed that it would be a mistake to assume that the hierarchical nature and para-militaristic organizational structure of the police profession immediately leads to a complete and perfect execution of policies. Police officers defy, resist, and are often unwilling to execute strategies for a wide range of reasons. Mastrofski and Willis (2010: 91) argued that officers "resist using or actively undermine many of the innovative information technologies." We know, for instance, that the presumption of arrest in domestic violence, that is, the blanket requirement to make an arrest every time a domestic abuse is reported to the police, is only applied in three-quarters of cases in the UK (Beale, 2009). We also learned from studies of body-worn cameras that activation policies are often not followed, despite straightforward guidelines (Ariel et al., 2016a; 2016b). The same disobedience happens in hot spots policing as well, where assigned interventions are usually not followed through for various justified (and unjustified) reasons. Goddard and Ariel (2014) conducted an experiment in Northern Ireland's night-time economy hot spots comparing static presence of officers in hot spots with random patrols of fifteen minutes. While the study was underpowered to form conclusions about the relative effect of each approach, a clear finding emerged for the delivery of the treatment. By using on-officer GPS trackers, it was soon apparent that officers assigned to static patrols were underperforming – often performing less than 10 percent of their assigned patrol dosage – while the random patrol group was equally underdelivering. Underdelivery was also detected in a similar study in Birmingham, UK (Ariel, Weinborn & Sherman, 2016), where GPS trackers indicated that the assigned interventions were not delivered as planned. Collectively, these pieces of evidence illustrate the need to measure performance: simply drafting a protocol is not enough. Relentless tracking of the resources is required.

Electronic tracking in policing combines two interrelated data systems: outputs and outcomes. Tracking of outcomes refers to the consequences of policing actions (or inactions). These can be crime levels, calls for service generated by victims and offenders, witness statements, and recidivism rates, among other things. These are commonly considered the results of impact evaluations, as they provide a bottom line approach to the value of policing for society. When victim-generated crime, such as robberies, burglaries, violence, or domestic abuse are down, one contributing factor is the involvement of police in curbing down criminal activity (although we should admit law enforcement is just one of many factors that contribute to crime patterns and distributions). In this respect, information systems are constantly improving. From paper copies, through purely free-text data points that are difficult to manipulate, to drop-down menus, automated tagging systems, and cross-referencing, outputs are becoming more valid, reliable, and useable for analysis.

Tracking police resources and outputs refers to the activities carried out by the officers themselves: what the organization does, the problems it targets, and the crime types it handles. An evidence-based approach to tracking (Sherman, 2013) incorporates the systematic measurement of police activities, in a consistent, repetitive, and relentless way. For reasons that go beyond the scope of our present interests, the tracking of police resources is not what it should be. Except for human resources data, which are often linked to remunerations, leave days, and pension-related matters, most tracking systems are, generally speaking, handicapped in some form or another. We may know where officers are broadly patrolling, how many jobs each officer has attended, and the ratio of arrests per calls for service, but there are a tremendous number of "hidden figures" in police data. Even the number of officer-involved shootings where the suspects deceased are imprecisely captured in national US databases, with some estimating that up to half the incidents are undercounted (Lartney, 2017). At the local level, police departments are trying to track their patrol cars, individual officers, encounters (e.g., stop-and-frisks), solvability factors, problem-oriented policing outcomes (see Part IV in this book), and victims. But as noted, these are often inexact and at times just anecdotal.

Tracking of police resources in hot spots illustrates that technology can greatly enhance the capacity of police management to assess the use of police resources. Rosenfeld et al.'s (2014) experiment is the only study that has reported accurate account of outputs (e.g., arrests, stop-and-account) with sufficient granularity. Systematic social observations (see Sampson & Raudenbush, 1999) would have been the appropriate approach here, but this methodology exceeds most research budgets in policing. Another notable example is CompStat, informatively discussed in Part IX of this book; however, CompStat is not primarily concerned with tracking at the systematic level to which Sherman (2013) refers. Instead, one keynote area of research that shows the promise of IT and technology more broadly for policing is in "movement tracking" of police resources and where and when they are out there in the field, using GPS tagging. GPS trackers were originally installed to provide personal security of officers and subsequently to allocate officers in real-time settings to calls for service (see Wain & Ariel, 2014). However, GPS technology can be used to measure how much time officers spend in particular areas and how many visits. Every tracker is set to transmit a ping to the satellite with the tracker's spatiotemporal coordinates (latitude, longitude, and a timestamp). The GPS back-office systems can then be used to geo-fence areas of land. And, by counting how many pings the trackers send from within these geo-fenced areas, it is possible to measure with precision and accuracy how many minutes and how many visits each officer has made to these geo-fenced areas. This "point in polygon" analysis can then be applied for various tracking opportunities, as geo-fencing allows the police to measure dosage delivery. For example, Ariel, Weinborn, and Sherman (2016) applied this analysis to a hot spots experiment using "soft policing" approaches. The experiment detected significant treatment effects, but also illustrated precise treatment-to-control treatment delivery at no extra cost. (On the potential backfiring effects of GPS tracking, see Wain, Ariel & Tankebe, 2017.)

Weisburd et al. (2015) have also shown that providing frontline commanders with data on unallocated time and AVL data in hot spots was useful for dispatching officers more efficiently for preventative patrols within the Dallas Police Department's jurisdiction. Giving commanders information about the quantity of unallocated time and the fraction of that time spent in hot spots helps "commanders to reallocate free time to crime prevention activities via directed patrol" (Weisburd et al., 2015: 381). This type of feedback is critical, and future research in this area will undoubtedly unearth additional lessons about the usefulness of tracking data in daily operations (e.g., de Brito & Ariel, 2017).

Big Data and Machine Learning

One of the latest technologies currently in the hands of law enforcement is big data analytics. Ridgway (2017: 34) correctly explains that big data refers to the "[integration of] large data sets from multiple sources with the aim of delivering some new, useful insight from those data"; it can be of massive benefit to policing. The Big Data movement shows not only *tested* utilities, but also the next generation in IT innovations. The major features of big data are its "volume, velocity, and variety" (Laney, 2001, in Ridgway 2017: 35). Unlike local surveys or sample data, big data is the comprehensive and most complete dataset available for police to analyses crime patterns and concentrations or responses to crime at different units of analyses (e.g., individuals, places, tangible matters, or actions). The more data, or the more accurate data, available to police, the more enhanced the validity and reliability of the response to crime would be, including by way of prediction and prevention (e. g., Ariel & Tankebe, 2016).

Predictive validity of risk and harm are particularly enhanced with big data analytics (see Hanson & Morton-Bourgon, 2004; Byrne & Pattavina, 2006; or, on the other hand, see Harris & Lurigio, 2007; Taxman & Caudy, 2015). The ability to detect who is more likely to offend, and the severity of his or her recidivism, has vastly improved over the years as we move into actuarial, statistical, and mathematically oriented computations and away from assessments based on clinical, subjective, and professional judgment. The "clinical versus statistical prediction" debate has been ongoing for more than sixty years (e.g., Meehl, 1954), yet years of evidence (see review in Kahenman, 2011) show that the actuarial/statistical assessment is cheaper, faster, reliable, and more accurate. As such, there is a prevalent transition in law enforcement into a scientific approach to risk assessment: I suspect it will continue to flourish. Data mining and big data analytics (Oatley et al., 2006; Tinati et al., 2014), machine learning, and artificial intelligence programming (Michalski, Carbonell & Mitchell, 2013) all show great promise. (On the wider privacy context of these tools, see Soghoian, 2011.)

Random forest algorithm is one innovative, promising, and tested application of a big data, machine-learning approach to predict risk and harm. It is essentially a classification and forecasting tool, in the form of a sophisticated decision tree classifier (see Berk, 2013). When a decision boundary is complex, random forest modeling that proceeds adaptively from the data dramatically improves forecasting accuracy over more basic prediction tools, such as logistic regressions (Berk & Bleich, 2013). From a statistical perspective, one major advantage is that the overfitting problem does not materially take place when using the random forest algorithm. Another important feature is its ability to identify the most salient variables of the available indicators in the dataset. Thus, it has been used to forecast murder within a population of probationers and parolees (Berk et al., 2009), or recidivism more generally in this population (Hess & Turner, 2013), offenders released from prisons (Duwe & Kim, 2015), or homicide offenders (Neuilly et al., 2011). It can also be used to estimate various social problems as well, such as homelessness estimation (Kriegler & Berk, 2010), decisions to refer a sexual assault case for prosecution (Snodgrass, Rosay & Gover, 2014), and arraignment decisions in domestic violence cases (Berk, Sorenson & Barnes 2016).

The crux of our argument here is that machine learning that incorporates advanced statistical modeling technics, such as random forest modeling (for alternatives to random forest algorithm, see Duwe & Kim, 2015) is part and parcel of technology. With more data, more accurate data, and more reliable data available for these computations, law enforcement will be in a better position to target the most harmful, risky, and dangerous offenders. As big data becomes faster and more approachable, the police can leverage data and apply machine-learning tools to increase productivity, efficiency, and cost-effectiveness.

Increasing Clearance Rates

Koper, Taylor, and Kubu (2009) observed that procurement of technology is a high priority for most law enforcement agencies, with the immediate aim of improving their efficiency and effectiveness. Within these outcomes, a prominent question is whether clearance rates have changed as a result of technology in policing. On the one hand, it is not clear whether IT evolution leads to solvability to increase over time. Braga et al. (2011) show that, in the USA, just less than half of violent crimes and around one-fifth of property crimes are cleared and that these ratios have been somewhat stable over time. Similarly, having innovative emergency command and control centers, such as the 911 system, does not seem to lead to improved offender apprehension rates (Sherman & Eck, 2002: 304–306). Although more (recent) research is needed on a cross-national basis before we can firmly conclude that these rates are decisive, they do suggest that the police are unable to clear most crimes and these limited successes have been consistent over time. However, it is not clear from these figures whether the presence of technology crippled the hands of the police to clear more cases. If technology, per se, is unlikely to have had a suppressive effect on clearance rates, then it can be equally argued that without technology, clearance rates would have been lower. Therefore, one can assume that the concern is less with the technological capacity of the police, and more with the way data are collated in the first place as research shows that eyewitnesses can be unreliable (Chabris & Simons, 2010; Gawrylowicz & Memon, 2014), incriminating confessions are problematic (www.innocenceproject.org), and CSI samples may lead to inconclusive material evidence if handled inappropriately. Similarly, Sherman and Eck's (2002) conclusion may be outdated, as mobile telephones have likely shortened the lag in crime reporting time to the police, thus potentially increasing the likelihood of apprehension of offenders. Therefore, more research is needed to compare technological availability with control conditions before we would conclude that technology makes no difference for clearance rates.

Moreover, these longitudinal yet correlational studies are not causal; they have no control groups. Instead, experiments that evaluated the effect of computerized criminal profiling on burglary arrest rates derived from behavioral profiles for burglary offenses and offenders in active police investigations do show the benefits of information systems (Fox & Farrington, 2015). Fox and Farrington (2015) conducted an experiment where one police agency that used the profiles was compared with three matched police agencies that did not. The outcomes suggested that arrest rates for the computerized system increased by three times when compared with the control agencies. While this study was not a Maryland Level 5 study (i.e., a full randomized controlled trial; see Farrington et al., 2002; see also Johnson et al., 2017 for a recent innovative application of the experimental method to target burglaries in Birmingham), the findings illustrate that computerized criminal profiling can be a useful tool in increasing arrest rates for police in an otherwise stubborn crime to clear.

Finally, an experiment on the value of DNA and fingerprint evidence has shown how innovative evidence collection tools can enhance clearance rates (Antrobus & Pilotto, 2016). The randomized controlled trial illustrated that when using these technological innovations unavailable to police departments two decades ago, scenes attended by experimental officers were significantly more likely to be solved (27 percent of scenes) than scenes attended by control officers (20 percent scenes). Although admittedly the overall clearance rate is low, a 26 percent change attributable to the implementation of technology in crime scene investigations illustrates the potential for improvement using forensic sciences.

Accountability and Transparency

One robust example of the benefits of IT on present-day policing is the use of digital evidence – such as body-worn cameras, interview rooms, dash cameras, and, principally, any videorecording device that populates IT in an audial-visual format – on accountability and transparency of law enforcement. Given space limitations, I will focus strictly on body-worn cameras (BWCs); the professional literature can be consulted on the value of other devices (see Baldwin, 1993 and Dixon, 2013: 302–303; Hoffman, 1992, but see Lassiter et al., 2001 and Welsh & Farrington, 2009).

Ariel, Farrar, and Sutherland's (2015) study with the police department in Rialto, California, was the first published experimental evidence on the effectiveness of BWCs. The original impetus for the study was to transition frontline officers from paper-based reports to dictating events onto video cameras, but the plan was eventually ruled out by the city council. Instead of testing the effect of BWCs on productivity, the new aim was to investigate the extent to which the event's being observed increases accountability and transparency of both offenders and officers' actions in police–public contacts. These outcomes were operationalized for use-of-force complaints filed against the Rialto Police Department as proxies of a civilizing effect the devices would have in police–public encounters (see Coudert, Butin & Le Métayer, 2015). Over the year the experiment ran, use-of-force rates when officers did not use BWCs were more than twice those for interactions when they did, and the number of complaints went down by 90 percent. These studies were then replicated across several tests (Ariel et al., 2016a; 2016b; 2017a; 2017c; see also Drover & Ariel, 2015 and Henstock & Ariel, 2017), as well as longitudinally (Sutherland et al., 2017), using different research methods (Ariel 2016a; 2016b) and, to a large extent, by other researchers (see reviews in Cubitt et al., 2017; Lum et al., 2015; Maskaly et al., 2017).

Yet the routinization of digital evidence in policing is a revolutionizing tool. The American Civil Liberties Union (ACLU) recently noted that "police body-mounted cameras: with right policies in place, a win for all" (Stanley, 2013: 1). In a short time period, BWCs have improved policing in places where training, departmental orders, or external reviews each failed. Across departments and policing cultures, BWCs reduced complaints against the police on average by more than 90 percent, in part because digital evidence is self-actuating (Ariel et al., 2017); generally accepted by officers who use the technology (Jennings, Fridell & Lynch, 2014; Gaub et al., 2016) as opposed to those who do not

(Tankebe & Ariel, 2016); coordinate and control daily operations; and remove uncertainties that characterize unsuccessful implementations of IT systems. Above all, it can be said that the BWCs carry a "contagious accountability" effect on police departments that embraced this technology (Ariel et al., 2017a).

The deterrent effect of BWCs is in their mere presence in police–public interactions, given the self-awareness effect of being watched (Ariel et al., 2017b; 2017d). Social psychology has established that being observed leads to self-awareness, which leads to self-scrutiny (Morin, 2011; Farrar & Ariel, 2013). This means that the camera leads to behavioral modifications. However, the true technological value of the camera is hidden in its back-office functionality by potentially incriminating evidence caught on tape that would lead to transparency and, by implication, to greater accountability (Ariel, 2016c). With BWCs, officers' decisions, actions, and procedural integrity are recorded and can be audited by members of the public, litigants, courts, and the officers' supervisors. The audial and visual big data and the analytics that are linked to this type of evidence are steadily evolving and changing policing (Google Scholar indicates that, since 2015 there had been 366 new patents in this unique research space), not just in dealing with rogue officers, but also to exonerate officers from frivolous claims. As one officer commented, "I would rather leave my gun back in the station than to patrol without my body worn camera" (Tankebe & Ariel, 2016).

Increasing Productivity

Distinct from outcome effectiveness, technology in policing can also increase the output effectiveness, or production. Casady et al.'s (2015) experiment conducted with the Lincoln Police Department in Nebraska shows that once officers are given information about offenders and hot spots on their handheld devices, productivity increases, i.e., more citations and arrests compared with control officers who were not given access to the application. Similar increases were reported in Mesa, Arizona (Taylor et al., 2012): officers used license-plate recognition technology more frequently to investigate suspicious vehicles when compared with manual checks of vehicles. In both experiments, officers' level of interaction with the technology was elevated. Once the officers materially use the applications, productivity increases.

It should be noted, however, that the link between these outputs and outcomes is unclear. Officers often maintain that the "more" they do will lead to more law and order, but this assumption might be an illusion. The Lincoln Police Department and the Mesa Police Department experiments are not necessarily showing that citations and arrests led to a reduction in crime, harm, or fewer victims on the streets. Thus, more productivity (outputs) does not immediately translate into more order and less crime (outcomes). License plate readers (LPR) may lead to more checks, but do not necessarily deter and/ or reduce crime, per se (Lum et al., 2010). One of the better-known examples is *Predpol* (Mohler et al., 2015), a system that applied advanced forecasting models to compete with the prediction made by crime analysts in LA Police Department. Frontline officers were efficiently deployed to the predicted areas based on the statistical forecasting model. However, crime was not significantly reduced. Put differently, PredPol may have improved productivity and enhanced predictive validity, but we have yet to see evidence on its *preventative* value (i.e., outcomes), which is especially problematic since this system or other types of predictive policing platforms are often quite costly.

Of course, embedded in this question of the link between productivity and outcomes is the assumption that officers *use* technology in the first place. An experiment in this area has shown that IT "pushed" to field officers through handheld devices in the Redlands Police Department in California may have its values prima facie, but officers were uninterested in activating the application (Taniguchi & Gill, 2013). A similar problem emerged with an offender-based experiment in Chicago, where a hit list of offenders was provided to the officers in order to actively engage and tackle criminal behavior; however, the officers were generally dismissive and did not use the application (Saunders et al., 2016; see also Papachristos et al., 2012). This issue, as well as others in policing in technology, are discussed more thoroughly in the following section.

Need for Rigorous Impact Evaluations and Valid Official Statistics

The scholastic enterprise on technology in policing is generally limited when compared with evaluation or impact studies in other disciplines. And most so-called impact evaluations are characterized by weak methodologies. Thus, Koper, Lum, and Willis (2014: 212) note, "research on police technology is not well developed." Indeed, IT-in-policing literature to date is often anecdotal, long on localized evidence, and missing a program of rigorous appraisals. This is somewhat surprising, as technological advancements in policing are not new (for a broader review, see Byrne & Rebovich, 2007 and Hummer, 2007): police vehicles (Mastrofski, Weisburd & Braga, 2009); two-way radios (Harris, 2007); emergency command and control centers; DNA testing (Roman et al., 2009; see also systematic review by Wilson, McClure & Weisburd, 2010); license plate reader technologies (Lum et al., 2011); GPS tracking (Hutt et al., 2018; Haggerty & Ericson, 2000); and the use of digital videotaping of crime scenes (Fisher & Fisher, 2012: 68; Ariel, Farrar, and Sutherland 2015; however, cf. Bruce et al., 1999). Except for DNA testing (Wilson et al., 2011), GIS-based hot spots policing (Braga et al., 2014, but see critique in Lum, 2013), and the use of everyday products that have proven themselves as efficient and cost-effective, such as the motor vehicle, emails, and the facsimile, most studies refer to evidence in support of technology in policing in the most anecdotal sense, with usually not more than "after only" or "before–after" so-called impact evaluations. Lacking robust evidence on a wide range of products and IT-enabled services is a concern and requires attention.

Experimental criminology has been on the rise since the turn of the century (Sherman, 2009). There are far more randomized trials published than ever before (Braga et al., 2014), and the appetite for rigorous evaluations by and for criminologists is continuously growing. However, the number of studies dedicated to the study of technology in policing is low because many scholars struggle to contextualize these studies within broader sociological theories. They can, but I would argue that this endeavor is not necessary: assessment of efficiency, efficacy, and cost-effectiveness suffice, just as it is in engineering, medicine, and psychology. The problem is that major journals archaically promote studies on a handful of "big questions" strictly sociologically oriented, and consider studies on technology in policing as a matter best left to professional journals (our publication on the Rialto BWCs experiment was rejected based on these grounds five times). This is a mistake on at least two levels. First, it sends a message to social scientists that technology is not important. Demotivating experimentalists from studying technology in policing is costing law enforcement billions of dollars. Instead, police departments procure technologies that do not work instead of focusing on those successfully shown to enhance policing through impartial rigorous evaluations, so everybody loses. Second, and perhaps more profoundly, technology *can* explain wider theoretical questions. For example, technical breakdowns can predict why applications of deterrence theory do not "work" (e.g., if threatening messages are not applied, we may wrongly conclude that deterrence does not deter); the inability to track officers' behavior in the field with rigor can be linked to levels of police legitimacy; an inefficient IT system in policing can explain the inability to explain crime patterns and concentrations, and, ultimately, an inability to do something about the crime problem. Finally, a theoretical framework that can reasonably predict the odds of success or failure of the desired software or hardware can save millions, if not billions, of dollars in a world of diminishing public funds, is a pretty good reason to invest more in this line of research.

Implementation Failures and the Feedback Loop Strategy

If efficiency and productivity are important in policing, then it will be difficult to argue against the principles of modernization, innovative technologies in the hands of police officers, and IT advancement more broadly. Hence, the counter-arguments against technology have always centered around the inability to implement (Cooper & Zmud, 1990; Dalcher & Gens, 2003) and, to some extent, philosophical ones against data in the hands of the state (see Solove, 2004; and more recently Palmer, 2016). Still, in practical terms, the most common concern with technology in policing is its implementation failures.

Implementation sciences already have a robust and mature history of various models that can be used to explicate the necessary conditions under which technological innovations lead to improved outcomes. For example, the technology acceptance model (TAM) is prominent in studies of the antecedents of IT acceptance; the perceived usefulness and perceived ease of use predict acceptance of any given system (Davis, 1989; Egnoto et al., 2017). As Chaudhry et al. (2006) commented, "limited quantitative and qualitative description of the implementation context significantly hampers how the literature on ... technology can inform decision making by a broad array of stakeholders interested in this field." Criminology is no different, but understanding the underlying mechanisms of these conditions for law enforcement was never part of mainstream criminology, even while there is a critical need to embrace these sorts of questions within criminology and specifically within policing research.

Lessons can be learned from other fields. Reviews of IT implementations in health largely attribute failures to the lack of adaptation, resistance, and cynical or negative views about the introduced technology (LaPointe & Rivard, 2005; Mogard et al., 2006). These issues seem particularly salient in emergency services, such as policing, where the services are inherently complex, time-sensitive, and often require what Kahneman (2011) refers to as System I thinking: intuitive, automatic, fast, frequent, and often emotional. Crucially, emergency services are less predictable than other professions and the job can easily be interrupted (Ren, Chen & Luo, 2008) with more immediate, harmful, risky, or pressurized tasks entering the system. By implication, such a system becomes risk-averse, which leads officers to resist change.

A precursor to implementation failures is the organizational structure of most police departments, which is hierarchical, militaristic, and authoritarian, but glorifies professional judgment, localized knowledge, and a culture of "John Wayne" at the frontline (see more broadly in Boudreau & Robey, 2005). Despite greater accountability and transparency with technology in policing, officers' decisions are nearly never challenged, and ad hoc investigations of officers' decisions seldom reverse the decision. Moreover, officers often prefer to rely on what they learn from their own experiences and vicariously through their peers, rather than external expertise (Sherman, 1998; Bayley, 2008), which may explain why some officers are against technological innovations.

What can be done to deal with future implementation failures in policing technologies? Skogan and Hartnett (2005: 401) argued that successful implementation can be attributed to three elements: "the active role played by the 'evangelist' representing the host department; the fact that access to the system was free; and because it primarily empowered detectives – who enjoy a privileged position in policing – and did not challenge the traditional mission and organization of participating agencies." More recently, Egnoto et al. (2017) added a critical component: technology is more likely to be embraced if its value can materially contribute to officers' behavior. Willis, Koper, and Lum (2017) share a similar view: the availability and compatibility of license plate readers with other information systems, along with their simplicity, were featured as important factors that contributed to their successful infusion in day-to-day policing. Interestingly, Egnoto et al.'s (2017) survey of 101 officers shows that officers were less concerned about error rates (in this study, the false positives of personal radiation detectors), which emphasizes that while compatibility is important, officers accept that technology is not perfect.

Above all, one should be mindful that implementing technology in policing is just like any other tactic or new policy introduced in the organization. Whether BWCs, LPR, or new patrolling tactics or a procedural justice approach (Antrobus, E., Thompson, I., & Ariel, B. (2018). Procedural justice training for police recruits: results of a randomized controlled trial. Journal of Experimental Criminology, 1–25.), the process of implementing is, *mutatis mutandis*, ostensibly similar. As such, we can turn to Sherman et al.'s (2014) concept of feedback, which O'Connor (2016) presented more robustly, as a method to ensure new IT in policing. The idea is to implement a three-stage feedback loop: measurement, feedback, and intervention. The measurement component refers to tracing the extent to which the policy/tactic is being implemented. For example, how often police officers activate their body-worn cameras in police-public interactions, or the number of times officers check license plates using LPR technology. The more precise, rich, and quantitative the data, the better. The feedback element is the information or data provided to the police officers from measurements of their performance. CompStat is an example, however Sherman et al. (2014) and Sherman (2013) call for a much more in-depth, granular feedback at the level of the frontline officer. The feedback ought to be continuous, systematic, impartial, and as accurate as possible. Finally, the intervention stage deals with praise, corrections, or revisions of the frontline officers' behavior when excellence or underperformance is detected. These positive and negative reinforcement tokens are critical but heavily underutilized in policing given that it is quite uncomfortable to have difficult conversations with subordinates; middle managers (e.g., sergeants) are rarely trained in delivering these reviews to their subordinates, if at all. Evidence is accumulating on the role of leadership in proper implementation of technology in policing (Willis et al., 2017); yet, this final stage of leaders intervening when necessary completes the feedback loop and, without it, implementation is likely to be hindered. If the policy penalizes for lack of implementation (as it often does), but no follow-up materializes, then the policy would be considered "toothless" (Ariel, 2012: 39). Brito and Ariel (2017) recently remarked,

Tracking data, in any human service, is merely a starting point. What it provides is a basis for discussing "what's next?" If the tracking evaluations are good, then little needs to be done. But if they are not so good, then a wide range of options must be considered. ... Few police agencies have developed and tested an evidence-based system for improving ... compliance.

One final note is that the use of the feedback loop in the implementation of technologies in policing requires routinization. Organizational routines refer to those repetitive and recognizable patterns within the organization often carried out by multiple agents. Analyzed through the lenses of organizational routines (e.g., Pentland & Feldman, 2005), successful implementation becomes relatively straightforward to quantify: when the seamless adaptation of a technological advancement within the policing takes place, and the technology is accepted and infused within the organization, the odds of its success are increased. The crux of implementation successes or failures, thus, lie within the healthy infusion of the technological advancement in day-to-day core functions. Similar arguments have been made in the past, such as several noteworthy attempts in criminology to consider routines and their role in policing. Beck and McCue (2009) have looked at how the introduction of DNA testing has led to changes in the routine activity of police officers. Wain and Ariel (2014) reviewed how the introduction of GPS tracking has routinized the deployment of police officers in ways that are incredibly different than how officers had been tracked for more than two centuries. Willis, Mastrofski, and Weisburd (2007) discussed the role of routines in the efficient running of CompStat. Sherman (1975; 1980), among others, has argued for some time now that routines and appropriate protocols can be used to professionalize the organizational capability of the police. Future technologies in policing is thus no different: the more that technologies are embedded within the routines, the more the feedback loop becomes part of the organizational DNA of the police, and the less implementation of technology in policing is likely to fail.

REFERENCES

Antrobus, E., & Pilotto, A. (2016). Improving forensic responses to residential burglaries: Results of a randomized controlled field trial. *Journal of Experimental Criminology*, 12(3), 319–345.

Antrobus, E., Thompson, I., & Ariel, B. (2017). Procedural justice training for police recruits: Results of a randomized controlled trial. *Journal of Experimental Criminology*. https://link.springer.com/article/10.1007/s11292-018-9331-9.

Ariel, B. (2011). Hot Dots and Hot Lines: Analysis of Crime in the London Underground. Presented at the Annual American Society of Criminology, Washington, DC, 06 November 2011.

Ariel, B. (2012). Deterrence and moral persuasion effects on corporate tax compliance: Findings from a randomized controlled trial. *Criminology*, 50(1), 27–69.

Ariel, B. (2016a). Increasing cooperation with the police using body worn cameras. *Police Quarterly*, 19(3), 326–362.

Ariel, B. (2016b). Police body cameras in large police departments. *Journal of Criminal Law and Criminology*, 106(4), 729–768.

Ariel, B. (2016c). The puzzle of police body cams. *IEEE Spectrum*, 53(7), 32–37.

Ariel, B., Bland, M., & Sutherland, A. (2017). Lowering the threshold of effective deterrence – Testing the effect of private security agents in public spaces on crime: A randomized controlled trial in a mass transit system. *PLoS one*, 12 (12), e0187392.

Ariel, B., Farrar, W. A., & Sutherland, A. (2015). The effect of police body-worn cameras on use of force and citizens' complaints against the police: A randomized controlled trial. *Journal of Quantitative Criminology*, 31(3), 509–535.

Ariel, B., & Partridge, H. (2016). Predictable policing: Measuring the crime control benefits of hotspots policing at bus stops. *Journal of Quantitative Criminology*, 1–25.

Ariel, B., & Tankebe, J. (2016). Racial stratification and multiple outcomes in police stops and searches. *Policing and Society*, 1–19.

Ariel, B., Sutherland, A., Henstock, D., Young, J., Drover, P., Sykes, J., Megicks, S., & Henderson, R. (2016a). Wearing body cameras increases assaults against officers and does not reduce police use of force: Results from a global multi-site experiment. *European Journal of Criminology*, 13(6), 744–755.

Ariel, B., Sutherland, A., Henstock, D., Young, J., Drover, P., Sykes, J., Megicks, S., & Henderson, R. (2016b). Report: Increases in police use of force in the presence of body-worn cameras are driven by officer discretion: A protocol-based subgroup analysis of ten randomized experiments. *Journal of Experimental Criminology*, 12 (3), 453–463.

Ariel, B., Sutherland, A., Henstock, D., Young, J., Drover, P., Sykes, J., Megicks, S., & Henderson, R. (2017a). "Contagious accountability": A global multisite randomized controlled trial on the effect of police body-worn cameras on citizens' complaints against the police. *Criminal Justice and Behavior*, 44(2), 293–316.

Ariel, B., Sutherland, A., Henstock, D., Young, J., Drover, P., Sykes, J., Megicks, S., & Henderson, R. (2017b). Paradoxical effects of self-awareness of being observed: testing the effect of police body-worn cameras on assaults and aggression against officers. *Journal of Experimental Criminology*, 1–29.

Ariel, B., Sutherland, A., Henstock, D., Young, J., & Sosinski, G. (2017c). The deterrence spectrum: Explaining why police body-worn cameras "work" or "backfire" in aggressive police–public encounters. *Policing: A Journal of Policy and Practice*, 12(1), 6–26.

Ariel, B., Weinborn, C., & Boyle, A. (2015). Can routinely collected ambulance data about assaults contribute to reduction in community violence? *Emerg Med J*, 32(4), 308–313.

Ariel, B., Weinborn, C., & Sherman, L. W. (2016). "Soft" policing at hotspots – do police community support officers work? A randomized controlled trial. *Journal of Experimental Criminology*, 12(3), 277–317.

Baker, W. E., & Faulkner, R. R. (2003). Diffusion of fraud: Intermediate economic crime and investor dynamics. *Criminology*, 41(4), 1173–1206.

Baldwin, J. (1993). Police interview techniques: Establishing truth or proof? *The British Journal of Criminology*, 33(3), 325–352.

Bayley, D. H. (2008). Police reform: Who done it? *Policing & Society*, 18(1), 7–17.

Beale, M. (2009). Understanding Arrest for Domestic Violence in Staffordshire – An Exploratory Analysis. MA dissertation, Cambridge University.

Beck, C., & McCue, C. (2009). Predictive policing: what can we learn from Wal-Mart and Amazon about fighting crime in a recession? *Police Chief*, 76(11), 18.

Berk, R. A. (2013). Algorithmic criminology. *Security Informatics*, 2(1), 5.

Berk, R. A., & Bleich, J. (2013). Statistical procedures for forecasting criminal behavior. *Criminology & Public Policy*, 12(3), 513–544.

Berk, R. A., Sherman, L., Barnes, G., Kurtz, E., & Ahlman, L. (2009). Forecasting murder within a population of probationers and parolees: a high stakes application of statistical learning. *Journal of the Royal Statistical Society: Series A (Statistics in Society)*, 172(1), 191–211.

Berk, R. A., Sorenson, S. B., & Barnes, G. (2016). Forecasting domestic violence: A machine learning approach to help inform arraignment decisions. *Journal of Empirical Legal Studies*, 13(1), 94–115.

Bichler, G., Lim, S., & Larin, E. (2017). Tactical social network analysis: Using affiliation networks to aid serial homicide investigation. *Homicide Studies*, 21(2), 133–158.

Boudreau, M. C., & Robey, D. (2005). Enacting integrated information technology: A human agency perspective. *Organization Science*, 16(1), 3–18.

Boyle, A. A., Snelling, K., White, L., Ariel, B., & Ashelford, L. (2013). External validation of the Cardiff model of information sharing to reduce community violence: Natural experiment. *Emerg Med J*, 30(12), 1020–1023.

Braga, A. A., & Weisburd, D. L. (2012). The effects of focused deterrence strategies on crime: A systematic review and meta-analysis of the empirical evidence. *Journal of Research in Crime and Delinquency*, 49(3), 323–358.

Braga, A. A., & Weisburd, D. L. (2014). Must we settle for less rigorous evaluations in large area-based crime prevention programs? Lessons from a Campbell review of focused deterrence. *Journal of Experimental Criminology*, 10(4), 573–597.

Braga, A. A., Apel, R., & Welsh, B. C. (2013). The spillover effects of focused deterrence on gang violence. *Evaluation Review*, 37(3–4), 314–342.

Braga, A. A., Flynn, E. A., Kelling, G. L., & Cole, C. M. (2011). Moving the work of criminal investigators towards crime control. Executive Session on Policing and Public Safety.

Braga, A. A., Papachristos, A. V., & Hureau, D. M. (2014). The effects of hotspots policing on crime: An updated systematic review and meta-analysis. *Justice Quarterly*, 31(4), 633–663.

Braga, A. A., Welsh, B. C., Papachristos, A. V., Schnell, C., & Grossman, L. (2014). The growth of randomized experiments in policing: The vital few and the salience of mentoring. *Journal of Experimental Criminology*, 10(1), 1–28.

Bratton, W. J., Morgan, J., & Malinowski, S. (2009). Fighting crime in the information age: The promise of predictive policing. Annual Meeting of the American Society of Criminology, Philadelphia, PA.

Bruce, V., Henderson, Z., Greenwood, K., Hancock, P. J., Burton, A. M., & Miller, P. (1999). Verification of face identities from images captured on video. *Journal of Experimental Psychology: Applied*, 5(4), 339.

Brynielsson, J., Horndahl, A., Johansson, F., Kaati, L., Mårtenson, C., & Svenson, P. (2013). Harvesting and analysis of weak signals for detecting lone wolf terrorists. *Security Informatics*, 2(1), 11.

Byrne, J. M., & Rebovich, D. J. (2007). *The New Technology of Crime, Law and Social Control*. Monsey, NY: Criminal Justice Press.

Byrne, J., & Marx, G. (2011). Technological innovations in crime prevention and policing. A review of the research on implementation and impact. *Journal of Police Studies*, 20(3), 17–40.

Byrne, J., & Pattavina, A. (2006). Assessing the role of clinical and actuarial risk assessment in an evidence-based community corrections system: Issues to consider. *Fed. Probation, 70,* 64.

Cardenas, A. A., Manadhata, P. K., & Rajan, S. P. (2013). Big data analytics for security. *IEEE Security & Privacy, 11*(6), 74–76.

Casady, T. K., Cottingham, I., Paulo, J., Ramírez, A. S., Tomkins, A. J., Farrell, K., Hamm J. A., Rosenbaum, D. I., & Shank, N. (2015). A Randomized-Trial Evaluation of a Law Enforcement Application for Smartphones and Laptops that Uses GIS and Location-Based Services' to Pinpoint Persons-of-Interest. Retrieved from www.ncjrs.gov/pdffiles1/nij/grants/248593.pdf.

Chabris, C., & Simons, D. (2010). *The Invisible Gorilla: And Other Ways Our Intuitions Deceive.* HarperCollins.

Chaiken, J. M., & Dormont, P. (1978). A patrol car allocation model: Capabilities and algorithms. *Management Science, 24*(12), 1291–1300.

Chainey, S., & Ratcliffe, J. (2005). Mapping crime with local community data. *GIS and Crime Mapping,* 183–222.

Chowdhury, H. K., Parvin, N., Weitenberner, C., & Becker, M. (2006). Consumer attitude toward mobile advertising in an emerging market: An empirical study. *International Journal of Mobile Marketing, 1*(2).

Cooper, R. B., & Zmud, R. W. (1990). Information technology implementation research: A technological diffusion approach. *Management Science, 36*(2), 123–139.

Coudert, F., Butin, D., & Le Métayer, D. (2015). Body-worn cameras for police accountability: Opportunities and risks. *Computer Law & Security Review, 31*(6), 749–762.

Crowther, R. F. (1964). The use of a computer system for police manpower allocation in St. Louis, Missouri. *Indiana University, Department of Police Administration.*

Cubitt, T. I., Lesic, R., Myers, G. L., & Corry, R. (2017). Body-worn video: A systematic review of literature. *Australian & New Zealand Journal of Criminology, 50*(3), 379–396.

Dalcher, D., & Genus, A. (2003). Introduction: Avoiding IS/IT implementation failure. *Technology Analysis & Strategic Management, 15*(4), 403–407.

Davis, F. D. (1989). Perceived usefulness, perceived ease of use, and user acceptance of information technology. *MIS Quarterly,* 319–340.

Davis, F. D., Bagozzi, R. P., & Warshaw, P. R. (1989). User acceptance of computer technology: a comparison of two theoretical models. *Management Science, 35*(8), 982–1003.

de Brito, C., & Ariel, B. (2017). Does tracking and feedback boost patrol time in hot spots? Two tests. *Cambridge Journal of Evidence-Based Policing, 1*(4), 244–262.

Denley, J., and Ariel, B. (forthcoming). Whom should we target to prevent? Analysis of organized crime in England using intelligence records. *European Journal of Crime, Criminal Law and Criminal Justice.*

Diniz, E. H., Luvizan, S. S., Hino, M. C., & Ferreira, P. C. (2018). Unveiling the big data adoption in banks: Strategizing the implementation of a new technology. In *Digital Technology and Organizational Change* (pp. 149–162). Cham: Springer.

Dixon, D. (2013). Regulating police interrogation. In T. Williamson (ed.) *Investigative Interviewing* (pp. 318–352). New York: Willan Publishing.

Drover, P., & Ariel, B. (2015). Leading an experiment in police body-worn video cameras. *International Criminal Justice Review*, 25(1), 80–97.

Duwe, G., & Kim, K. (2015). Out with the old and in with the new? An empirical comparison of supervised learning algorithms to predict recidivism. *Criminal Justice Policy Review*, 0887403415604899.

Duxbury, S. W., & Haynie, D. L. (2017). The network structure of opioid distribution on a darknet cryptomarket. *Journal of Quantitative Criminology*, 1–21.

Egnoto, M., Egnoto, M., Ackerman, G., Ackerman, G., Iles, I., Iles, I., ... & Liu, B. F. (2017). What motivates the blue line for technology adoption? Insights from a police expert panel and survey. *Policing: An International Journal of Police Strategies & Management*, 40(2), 306–320.

Englefield, A., & Ariel, B. (2017). Searching for influential actors in co-offending networks: The recruiter. *International Journal of Social Science Studies*, 5(5), 24–45.

Farrar, W., & Ariel, B. (2013). Self-awareness to being watched and socially desirable behavior: A field experiment on the effect of body-worn cameras on police use-of-force. Washington, DC: Police Foundation.

Farrington, D. P., Gottfredson, D. C., Sherman, L. W., & Welsh, B. C. (2002). The Maryland scientific methods scale. *Evidence-Based Crime Prevention*, 13–21.

Fisher, B. A., & Fisher, D. R. (2012). *Techniques of Crime Scene Investigation.* CRC Press.

Fox, B. H., & Farrington, D. P. (2015). An experimental evaluation on the utility of burglary profiles applied in active police investigations. *Criminal Justice and Behavior*, 42(2), 156–175.

Gardner, L., & Shoemaker, D. J. (1989). Social bonding and delinquency. *The Sociological Quarterly*, 30(3), 481–500.

Garicano, L., & Heaton, P. (2010). Information technology, organization, and productivity in the public sector: Evidence from police departments. *Journal of Labor Economics*, 28(1), 167–201.

Gaub, J. E., Choate, D. E., Todak, N., Katz, C. M., & White, M. D. (2016). Officer perceptions of body-worn cameras before and after deployment: A study of three departments. *Police Quarterly*, 19(3), 275–302.

Gawrylowicz, J., & Memon, A. (2014). Interviewing Eyewitnesses. In *Encyclopedia of Criminology and Criminal Justice* (pp. 2679–2688). New York: Springer.

Goddard, N., & Ariel, B. (2014). How much time should officers spend in night-time economy hotspots? Lessons from a "Randomized Controlled Trial in Northern Ireland." Presented at the Annual American Society of Criminology (San Francisco, CA, 18–20 November 2014).

Goold, B. J. (2003). Public area surveillance and police work: The impact of CCTV on police behavior and autonomy. *Journal of Surveillance and Society*, 1(2), 191–203.

Groff, E. R., Ratcliffe, J. H., Haberman, C. P., Sorg, E. T., Joyce, N. M., & Taylor, R. B. (2015). Does what police do at hotspots matter? The Philadelphia policing tactics experiment. *Criminology*, 53(1), 23–53.

Haberman, C. P., & Ratcliffe, J. H. (2012). The predictive policing challenges of near repeat armed street robberies. *Policing: A Journal of Policy and Practice*, 6(2), 151–166.

Haggerty, K. D., & Ericson, R. V. (2000). The surveillant assemblage. *The British Journal of Sociology*, 51(4), 605–622.

Hanson, R., & Morton-Bourgon, K. (2004). *Predictors of Sexual Recidivism: An Updated Meta-Analysis*. Ottawa, ON: Public Safety and Emergency Preparedness Canada.

Harris, A., & Lurigio, A. J. (2007). Mental illness and violence: A brief review of research and assessment strategies. *Aggression and Violent Behavior*, 12(5), 542–551.

Harris, C. (2007). Police and soft technology: How information technology contributes to police decision making. *The New Technology of crime, Law and Social Control*, 153–183.

Henstock, D., & Ariel, B. (2017). Testing the effects of police body-worn cameras on use of force during arrests: A randomised controlled trial in a large British police force. *European Journal of Criminology*, 1477370816686120.

Hess, J., & Turner, S. (2013). *Risk Assessment Accuracy in Corrections Population Management: Testing the Promise of Tree Based Ensemble Predictions*. Irvine: Center for Evidence-Based Corrections, University of California.

Hickman, M. J., & Reaves, B. A. (2006). *Bureau of Justice Statistics Special Report*. Washington, DC: US Department of Justice.

Hipgrave, S. (2013). Smarter fraud investigations with big data analytics. *Network Security*, 12, 7–9.

Hoffman, P. (1992). The feds, lies, and videotape: The need for an effective federal role in controlling police abuse in urban America. *S. Cal. L. Rev.*, 66, 1453.

Hutt, O., Bowers, K., Johnson, S., & Davies, T. (2018). Data and evidence challenges facing place-based policing. *Policing: An International Journal of Police Strategies & Management*, 41(3), 339–351.

Hummer, D. (2007). Policing and "hard" technology. In *The New Technology of Crime, Law and Social Control* (pp. 133–152). Monsey, NY: Criminal Justice Press.

Hyatt, J. M., & Barnes, G. C. (2017). An experimental evaluation of the impact of intensive supervision on the recidivism of high-risk probationers. *Crime & Delinquency*, 63(1), 3–38.

Jennings, W. G., Fridell, L. A., & Lynch, M. D. (2014). Cops and cameras: Officer perceptions of the use of body-worn cameras in law enforcement. *Journal of Criminal Justice*, 42(6), 549–556.

Johnson, S. D., Davies, T., Murray, A., Ditta, P., Belur, J., & Bowers, K. (2017). Evaluation of operation swordfish: A near-repeat target-hardening strategy. *Journal of Experimental Criminology*, 1–21.

Kahneman, D., & Egan, P. (2011). *Thinking, fast and slow*. New York: Farrar, Straus and Giroux.

Kelling, G. L., Pate, T., Dieckman, D., & Brown, C. E. (1974). *The Kansas City preventive patrol experiment*. Washington, DC: Police Foundation.

Kennedy, D. M., Kleiman, M. A., & Braga, A. A. (2017). Beyond deterrence. In *Handbook of Crime Prevention and Community Safety*, 157.

Koper, C. S. (1995). Just enough police presence: Reducing crime and disorderly behavior by optimizing patrol time in crime hot spots. *Justice Quarterly*, 12(4), 649–672.

Koper, C. S., Lum, C., & Willis, J. J. (2014). Optimizing the use of technology in policing: Results and implications from a multi-site study of the social, organizational, and behavioral aspects of implementing police technologies. *Policing: A Journal of Policy and Practice*, 8(2), 212–221.

Koper, C. S., Taylor, B. G., & Kubu, B. (2009). *Law Enforcement Technology Needs Assessment: Future Technologies to Address the Operational Needs of Law Enforcement*. Police Executive Research Forum.

Kriegler, B., & Berk, R. (2010). Small area estimation of the homeless in Los Angeles: An application of cost-sensitive stochastic gradient boosting. *The Annals of Applied Statistics*, 1234–1255.

Lapointe, L., & Rivard, S. (2005). A multilevel model of resistance to information technology implementation. *MIS Quarterly*, 461–491.

Lartney, J. (2017). US police killings undercounted by half, study using Guardian data finds. *The Guardian*. Retrieved October 13, 2017, from https://tinyurl.com/y7kzug3 h.

Lassiter, G. D., Munhal, P. J., Geers, A. L., Weiland, P. E., & Handley, I. M. (2001). Accountability and the camera perspective bias in videotaped confessions. *Analyses of Social Issues and Public Policy*, 1(1), 53–70.

Levine, E. S., Tisch, J., Tasso, A., & Joy, M. (2017). The New York City Police Department's Domain Awareness System. *Interfaces*, 47(1), 70–84.

Lewin, K. (1948). Conduct, knowledge, and acceptance of new values. In G. Weis Lewin (ed.) *Resolving Social Conflicts: Selected Papers on Group Dynamics* (pp. 56–68). New York: Harper & Row.

Liu, J. L., & Wyatt, J. C. (2011). The case for randomized controlled trials to assess the impact of clinical information systems. *Journal of the American Medical Informatics Association*, 18(2), 173–180.

Lum, C. (2010). Technology and mythology of progress in American law enforcement. *Science Progress*, Feb 11.

Lum, C. (2013). Is crime analysis evidence-based? *Translational Criminology*, 5, 12–14.

Lum, C., Hibdon, J., Cave, B., Koper, C. S., & Merola, L. (2011). License plate reader (LPR) police patrols in crime hotspots: an experimental evaluation in two adjacent jurisdictions. *Journal of Experimental Criminology*, 7(4), 321–345.

Lum, C., Koper, C. S., Merola, L. M., Scherer, A., & Reioux, A. (2015). *Existing and Ongoing Body Worn Camera Research: Knowledge Gaps and Opportunities*. George Mason University.

Macbeth, E., & Ariel, B. (2017). Place-based statistical versus clinical predictions of crime hotspots and harm locations in Northern Ireland. *Justice Quarterly*, 1–34.

Manning, P. K. (1992). Technological dramas and the police: Statement and counterstatement in organizational analysis. *Criminology*, 30(3), 327–346.

Manning, P. K. (2008). *The Technology of Policing: Crime Mapping, Information Technology, and the Rationality of Crime Control*. New York: New York University Press.

Maskaly, J., Donner, C., Jennings, W. G., Ariel, B., & Sutherland, A. (2017). The effects of body-worn cameras (BWCs) on police and citizen outcomes: A state-of-the-art review. *Policing: An International Journal of Police Strategies & Management*, 40(4), 672–688.

Mastrofski, S. D., Weisburd, D., & Braga, A. A. (2010). Rethinking policing: The policy implications of hot spots of crime. *Contemporary Issues in Criminal Justice Policy*, 251–264.

Mastrofski, S. D., & Willis, J. J. (2010). Police organization continuity and change: Into the twenty-first century. *Crime and Justice*, 39(1), 55–144.

McCahill, M., & Norris, C., (2004). From cameras to control rooms: The mediation of the image by cctv operatives. CCTV and Social Control: The politics and practice of video surveillance. *European and Global Perspectives*, 1.

McGloin, J. (2005). Policy and intervention considerations of a network analysis of street gangs. *Criminology & Public Policy*, 4(3), 607–635.

Meehl, P. E. (1954). *Clinical vs. Statistical Prediction* (pp. 389–391). Minneapolis: University of Minnesota Press.

Merton, R. K. (1938). Social structure and anomie. *American Sociological Review*, 3(5), 672–682.

Michalski, R. S., Carbonell, J. G., & Mitchell, T. M. (eds.). (2013). *Machine Learning: An Artificial Intelligence Approach*. Springer Science & Business Media.

Mohler, G. O., Short, M. B., Malinowski, S., Johnson M., Tita, G E., Bertozzi, A., & Brantingham, P. J. (2015). Randomized controlled field trials of predictive policing. *Journal of the American Statistical Association*, 110(512), 1399–1411.

Morin, A. (2011). Self-awareness part 1: Definition, measures, effects, functions, and antecedents. *Social and Personality Psychology Compass*, 5(10), 807–823.

Morselli, C. (2003). Career opportunities and network-based privileges in the Cosa Nostra. *Crime, Law and Social Change*, 39(4), 383–418.

Natarajan, M. (2006). Understanding the structure of a large heroin distribution network: A quantitative analysis of qualitative data. *Journal of Quantitative Criminology*, 22(2), 171–192.

Neuilly, M. A., Zgoba, K. M., Tita, G. E., & Lee, S. S. (2011). Predicting recidivism in homicide offenders using classification tree analysis. *Homicide sStudies*, 15(2), 154–176.

Newton, A., & Felson, M. (2015). Crime patterns in time and space: The dynamics of crime opportunities in urban areas. *Crime Science*, 4(1), 1–5.

Oatley, G., Ewart, B., & Zeleznikow, J. (2006). Decision support systems for police: Lessons from the application of data mining techniques to "soft" forensic evidence. *Artificial Intelligence and Law*, 14(1–2), 35–100.

Palmer, D. (2016). The mythical properties of police body-worn cameras: A solution in the search of a problem. *Surveillance & Society*, 14(1), 138.

Papachristos, A. V. (2009). Murder by structure: Dominance relations and the social structure of gang homicide. *American Journal of Sociology*, 115(1), 74–128.

Papachristos, A. V. (2011). The coming of a networked criminology. In J. MacDonald (ed.). *Advances in Criminological Theory* (pp. 101–140). New Brunswick, NJ: Transactions Publishers.

Papachristos, A. V., Braga, A. A., & Hureau, D. M. (2012). Social networks and the risk of gunshot injury. *Journal of Urban Health*, 89(6), 992–1003.

Pedahzur, A., & Perliger, A. (2006). The changing nature of suicide attacks: A social network perspective. *Social Forces*, 84(4), 1987–2008.

Pentland, B. T., & Feldman, M. S. (2005). Organizational routines as a unit of analysis. *Industrial and Corporate Change*, 14(5), 793–815.

Piza, E., Caplan, J. M., Kennedy, L. W., & Gilchrist, A. M. (2015). The effects of merging proactive CCTV monitoring with directed police patrol: A randomized controlled trial. *Journal of Experimental Criminology*, 11(1), 43–69.

Police Executive Res. Forum. (2014). *Future Trends in Policing*. Washington, DC: Police Executive Res. Forum.

Ratcliffe, J. H., & McCullagh, M. J. (2001). Chasing ghosts? Police perception of high crime areas. *British Journal of Criminology*, 41(2), 330–341.

Ratcliffe, J. H., & Sorg, E. T. (2017). A history of foot patrol. In *Foot Patrol* (pp. 7–20). Cham: Springer.

Ratcliffe, J. H., Taniguchi, T., & Taylor, R. B. (2009). The crime reduction effects of public CCTV cameras: A multi-method spatial approach. *Justice Quarterly*, 26(4), 746–770.

Ratcliffe, J. H., Taniguchi, T., Groff, E. R., & Wood, J. D. (2011). The Philadelphia foot patrol experiment: A randomized controlled trial of police patrol effectiveness in violent crime hotspots. *Criminology*, 49(3), 795–831.

Reiss Jr, A. J. (1986). Co-offender influences on criminal careers. *Criminal Careers and Career Criminals*, 2, 121–160.

Ren, A., Chen, C., & Luo, Y. (2008). Simulation of emergency evacuation in virtual reality. *Tsinghua Science and Technology*, 13(5), 674–680.

Rengert, G. F., & Pelfrey, W. V. (1997). Cognitive mapping of the city center: Comparative perceptions of dangerous places. *Crime Mapping and Crime Prevention*, 193–218.

Ridgway, G. (2018). Policing in the era of big data. *Annual Review of Criminology*, 1, 401–419.

Roman, J. K., Reid, S. E., Chalfin, A. J., & Knight, C. R. (2009). The DNA field experiment: a randomized trial of the cost-effectiveness of using DNA to solve property crimes. *Journal of Experimental Criminology*, 5(4), 345.

Rosenfeld, R., Deckard, M. J., & Blackburn, E. (2014). The effects of directed patrol and self-initiated enforcement on firearm violence: A randomized controlled study of hot spot policing. *Criminology*, 52(3), 428–449.

Sampson, R. J., & Raudenbush, S. W. (1999). Systematic social observation of public spaces: A new look at disorder in urban neighborhoods. *America Journal of Sociology*, 105(3), 603–651.

Sarnecki, J. (1990). Delinquent networks in Sweden. *Journal of Quantitative Criminology*, 6(1), 31–50.

Sarnecki, J. (2001). *Delinquent Networks: Youth Co-Offending in Stockholm*. Cambridge University Press.

Saunders, J., Hunt, P., & Hollywood, J. S. (2016). Predictions put into practice: a quasi-experimental evaluation of Chicago's predictive policing pilot. *Journal of Experimental Criminology*, 12(3), 347–371.

Scott, H. (1949). *Police Problems of Today* (Vol. 3). Stevens.

Shaw, C. R., & McKay, H. D. (1942). *Juvenile Delinquency and Urban Areas*. Chicago: University of Chicago Press.

Sherman, L. W. (1975). Middle management and police democratization: A reply to John E. Angell. *Criminology*, 12(4), 363–378.

Sherman, L. W. (1980). Causes of police behavior: The current state of quantitative research. *Journal of Research in Crime and Delinquency*, 17(1), 69–100.

Sherman, L. W. (1990). Police crackdowns: Initial and residual deterrence. *Crime and Justice*, 12, 1–48.

Sherman, L. W. (1998). *Evidence-Based Policing*. Washington, DC: Police Foundation.

Sherman, L. W. (2009). Evidence and liberty: The promise of experimental criminology. *Criminology & Criminal Justice*, 9(1), 5–28.

Sherman, L. W. (2013). The rise of evidence-based policing: Targeting, testing, and tracking. *Crime and Justice*, 42(1), 377–451.

Sherman, L. W., & Weisburd, D. (1995). General deterrent effects of police patrol in crime "hotspots": A randomized, controlled trial. *Justice Quarterly*, 12(4), 625–648.

Sherman, L. W., Gartin, P. R., & Buerger, M. E. (1989). Hotspots of predatory crime: Routine activities and the criminology of place. *Criminology*, 27(1), 27–56.

Sherman, L. W., Williams, S., Ariel, B., Strang, L. R., Wain, N., Slothower, M., & Norton, A. (2014). An integrated theory of hotspots patrol strategy: Implementing prevention by scaling up and feeding back. *Journal of Contemporary Criminal Justice*, 30(2), 95–122.

Sherman, L. W., and J. E. Eck (2002). Policing for Crime Prevention. In L. W. Sherman, D. P. Farrington, B. C. Welsh, & D. L. MacKenzie (eds.), *Evidence-Based Crime Prevention* (pp. 295–329). London: Routledge.

Skogan, W. G., & Hartnett, S. M. (1997). *Community Policing, Chicago Style*. New York: Oxford University Press.

Skogan, W. G., & Hartnett, S. M. (2005). The diffusion of information technology in policing. *Police Practice and Research*, 6(5), 401–417.

Snodgrass, G. M., Rosay, A. B., & Gover, A. R. (2014). Modeling the referral decision in sexual assault cases: An application of random forests. *American Journal of Criminal Justice*, 39(2), 267–291.

Soghoian, C. (2011). An end to privacy theater: Exposing and discouraging corporate disclosure of user data to the government. *Minnesota Journal of Law, Science & Technology*, 12, 191.

Solove, D. J. (2004). *The digital person: Technology and privacy in the information age*. New York: New York University Press.

Sorg, E. T., Wood, J. D., Groff, E. R., & Ratcliffe, J. H. (2014). Boundary adherence during place-based policing evaluations: A research note. *Journal of Research in Crime and Delinquency*, 51(3), 377–393.

Stanley, J. (2013). *Police body-mounted cameras: With right policies in place, a win for all*. New York: ACLU. www.aclu.org/sites/default/files/assets/police_body-mounted_cameras.pdf.

Strang, K. D., & Sun, Z. (2017). Analyzing relationships in terrorism big data using hadoop and statistics. *Journal of Computer Information Systems*, 57(1), 67–75.

Sutherland, A., Ariel, B., Farrar, W., & De Anda, R. (2017). Post-experimental follow-ups – Fade-out versus persistence effects: The Rialto police body-worn camera experiment four years on. *Journal of Criminal Justice*. https://doi.org/10.1016/j.jcrimjus.2017.09.008

Sutherland, E. H. (1947). *Principles of Criminology*, 4th ed. Philadelphia: Lippincott.

Taniguchi, T. A., & Gill, C. (2013). The mobilization of crime mapping and intelligence gathering: Evaluating smartphone deployment and custom app development in a mid-size law enforcement agency. Washington, DC: Police Foundation. www.policefoundation.org/content/ mobilization-crime-mapping.

Tankebe, J., & Ariel, B. (2016). Cynicism Towards Change: The Case of Body-Worn Cameras Among Police Officers. Research paper.

Taylor, B., Koper, C. S., & Woods, D. (2012). Combating vehicle theft in arizona: A randomized experiment with license plate recognition technology. *Criminal Justice Review*, 37(1), 24–50.

Taxman, F. S., & Caudy, M. S. (2015). Risk tells us who, but not what or how. *Criminology & Public Policy, 14*(1), 71–103.

Telep, C. W., Mitchell, R. J., & Weisburd, D. (2014). How much time should the police spend at crime hot spots? Answers from a police agency directed randomized field trial in Sacramento, California. *Justice Quarterly, 31*(5), 905–933.

Tinati, R., Halford, S., Carr, L., & Pope, C. (2014). Big data: Methodological challenges and approaches for sociological analysis. *Sociology, 48*(4), 663–681.

Tversky, A., & Kahneman, D. (1975). Judgment under uncertainty: Heuristics and biases. In *Utility, Probability, and Human Decision Making* (pp. 141–162). Netherlands: Springer.

van Bommel, M., van Prooijen, J. W., Elffers, H., & van Lange, P. A. (2014). Intervene to be seen: The power of a camera in attenuating the bystander effect. *Social Psychological and Personality Science, 5*(4), 459–466.

Wain, N., & Ariel, B. (2014). Tracking of police patrol. *Policing: A Journal of Policy and Practice, 8*(3), 274–283.

Wain, N., Ariel, B., & Tankebe, J. (2017). The collateral consequences of GPS-LED supervision in hotspots policing. *Police Practice and Research, 18*(4), 376–390.

Weinborn, C., Ariel, B., Sherman, L. W., & O'Dwyer, E. (2017). Hotspots vs. harmspots: Shifting the focus from counts to harm in the criminology of place. *Applied Geography, 86*, 226–244.

Weisburd, D. (2015). The law of crime concentration and the criminology of place. *Criminology, 53*(2), 133–157.

Weisburd, D., & Majmundar, M. (2018). *Proactive Policing: Effects on Crime and Communities. National Academy of Sciences.* Washington, DC: The National Academies Press.

Weisburd, D., & Amram, S. (2014). The law of concentrations of crime at place: The case of Tel Aviv-Jaffa. *Police Practice and Research, 15*(2), 101–114.

Weisburd, D., Groff, E. R., & Yang, S. M. (2012). *The Criminology of Place: Street Segments and Our Understanding of the Crime Problem.* Oxford University Press.

Weisburd, D., Groff, E. R., Jones, G., Cave, B., Amendola, K. L., Yang, S. M., & Emison, R. F. (2015). The Dallas patrol management experiment: Can AVL technologies be used to harness unallocated patrol time for crime prevention? *Journal of Experimental Criminology, 11*(3), 367–391.

Weisburd, D., Telep, C. W., Hinkle, J. C., & Eck, J. E. (2010). Is problem-oriented policing effective in reducing crime and disorder? *Criminology & Public Policy, 9*(1), 139–172.

Welsh, B. C., & Farrington, D. P. (2002). *Crime Prevention Effects of Closed Circuit Television: A Systematic Review* (vol. 252). London: Home Office.

Welsh, B. C., & Farrington, D. P. (2009). Public area CCTV and crime prevention: An updated systematic review and meta-analysis. *Justice Quarterly, 26*(4), 716–745.

Willis, J. J., Koper, C., & Lum, C. (2017). The adaptation of license-plate readers for investigative purposes: Police technology and innovation re-invention. *Justice Quarterly,* 1–25.

Willis, J. J., Mastrofski, S. D., and Weisburd, D. (2007). Making sense of Compstat: A theory-based analysis of organizational change in three police departments. *Law and Society Review, 41*, 147–188.

Wilson, D. B., McClure, D., & Weisburd, D. (2010). Does forensic DNA help to solve crime? The benefit of sophisticated answers to naive questions. *Journal of Contemporary Criminal Justice*, 26(4), 458–469.

Wilson, D. B., Weisburd, D., McClure, D., & Wilson, D. B. (2011). Use of DNA testing in police investigative work for increasing offender. *Campbell Systematic Reviews*, 7.

22

Critic

The Limits of Police Technology

Christopher S. Koper and Cynthia Lum

Technological advancements have shaped policing in many important ways over the years.[1] One needs only to consider that the primary police strategy for much of the twentieth century – motorized preventive patrol and rapid response to calls for service – was developed in response to the invention and use of the automobile, two-way radio communications, and computer-aided dispatch systems in policing. In recent decades, there have been many significant developments with respect to information technologies, analytic systems, video surveillance systems, license plate readers, DNA testing, body-worn cameras, and other technologies that have had far-reaching effects on police agencies. Technology acquisition and deployment decisions are high priority topics for police (e.g., Koper, Taylor & Kubu, 2009), and law enforcement agencies at all levels of governments are spending vast sums on technology in the hopes of improving agency efficiency and effectiveness.

However, research on police technology is not well developed, and the available evidence suggests that technology's impacts on police effectiveness may be limited considerably by numerous factors. In this chapter, we discuss the potential impacts of technology on policing, what we know about its actual impacts, and what more we need to understand to implement technology in evidence-based ways that facilitate effective policing strategies. We particularly emphasize the intended and unintended ways that technology affects police agencies (for example, in terms of their operations, structure, culture, effectiveness, and legitimacy) and the various contextual aspects of police agencies and their environments that shape the uses and effectiveness of policing technology. Drawing heavily upon our own work on police technology, we highlight four technologies to make our points: information technologies, crime analysis, license plate readers, and body-worn cameras.

---

[1] This chapter is adapted with modifications from *Evidence-Based Policing: Translating Research into Practice* (see chapter 7, "Technology – Evidence-Based Policing Playing Catch-Up") by Cynthia Lum and Christopher S. Koper (Oxford University Press, 2017). It has been reproduced here with permission from Oxford University Press.

TECHNOLOGY AND ITS IMPACT ON POLICING

The current emphasis on police technology reflects a belief among both police and citizens in technology's potential to enhance policing. For example, technology is believed to strengthen crime control by improving the ability of police to identify and monitor offenders (particularly repeat, high-rate offenders); facilitating the identification of places and conditions that contribute disproportionately to crime; speeding the detection of and response to crimes; enhancing evidence collection; improving police deployment and strategies; creating organizational efficiencies that put more officers in the field and for longer periods of time; enhancing communication between police and citizens; increasing perceptions of the certainty of punishment; and strengthening the ability of law enforcement to deal with technologically sophisticated forms of crime (e.g., identity theft and cybercrime) and terrorism. Technological advancements in automobiles, protective gear, weapons, and surveillance capabilities can reduce injuries and deaths to officers, suspects, and bystanders. Pressing operational needs exist in numerous areas to which technology is central, including crime analysis and information-led policing, information technology and database integration, and managing dispatch and calls for service (Koper et al., 2009). And to the extent that technology improves police effectiveness, strengthens communication between police and citizens, reduces negative outcomes from police actions, and increases police accountability, it may also have the added, indirect benefit of enhancing police legitimacy among citizens.

But these are only best guesses and hopes for technology. Because of the scarcity of evaluation research on technology, we do not know whether such outcomes are actually achieved. Much of the research we do have focuses on technology's efficiencies and outputs, rather than its connection to outcomes. While recent technological advances have undoubtedly enhanced policing in many respects (e.g., see Danziger & Kraemer, 1985; Roth et al., 2000; Ioimo & Aronson, 2004; Roman et al., 2008), it is not clear that they have made police more effective (Chan, 2001; Harris, 2007; Garicano & Heaton, 2010; Lum, 2010; Byrne & Marx, 2011; Koper et al., 2015a; National Academies of Sciences, Engineering, and Medicine, 2017). Technology thus presents a paradox; it may operate correctly and speed up various policing activities, but it may not actually lead to outcomes sought by the police or the community.

Take, for example, forensics and surveillance technologies. It is fair to say that forensics technologies have significantly improved and become more available in the last fifty years; these changes include improvements in DNA and fingerprint collection and analysis, as well as the development of mobile devices to make the collection of forensic evidence easier and faster. Surveillance technologies have also improved, with greater use of closed circuit televisions (CCTVs), license plate readers (LPRs), and even technology that can detect gunshots. Police data systems that can be used to identify and locate suspects have also become more extensive and integrated. Yet, despite these improved detection capabilities, national averages of clearance rates for property and violent crimes have remained stubbornly low and stable for the last thirty years, and in the case of homicide, are *declining* (Braga et al., 2011; Lum et al., 2016a; Vovak, 2016). Although there are likely many complex factors that have influenced recent clearance trends, this serves as an example of how advancements in police technology do not always correspond to obvious improvements in police performance.

What might explain these limitations to technology's benefits? For one, technology can produce unintended consequences in police agencies. For instance, while manual report writing is tedious, agencies transitioning from paper reports to records management systems and automated report writing often go through significant growing pains. Officers have to adapt to new systems that may have added reporting requirements and require the use of the internet or wireless technology that is slow or unreliable. All of this may reduce expected gains in efficiency and have other unintended and undesirable consequences (see our discussion of IT to follow). Another example of unintended consequences can be found in the adoption of computer-aided dispatch, or "911," systems in the United States (alternatively, 999 in the United Kingdom). These systems were developed to speed officer responses to calls for service, not only to improve customer service and connectivity with citizens but also to increase the possibility of apprehending offenders. However, the notion that 911 systems improve offender apprehension has been undermined by studies showing that response times have little effect on arrests due to delays in the reporting of crime (Sherman & Eck, 2002). Further, the burden of answering 911 calls, roughly half or more of which are not urgent (Mazerolle et al., 2002: 98), leaves police with less time to engage in proactive or problem-oriented policing, which we now know from research can prevent and reduce crime. As we have argued elsewhere (see Lum, 2010), 911 systems may have thereby reinforced a reactive, incident-based approach that is the standard model of policing, which may have even hindered other innovations (e.g., see Sparrow, Moore & Kennedy, 1990).

In addition, the impact of technology on police effectiveness may be limited or distorted by several factors. These include engineering problems (i.e., whether the technologies work), difficulty in implementing and using a technology, legal or administrative limits on a technology's use, lack of fit between a technology and the tasks for which it is used, interdependencies between different technologies (within and across agencies), ancillary costs associated with using a technology (e.g., costs related to training, technical assistance, and maintenance), and the failure of technologies to provide certain expected benefits like time savings or increased productivity. Studies have produced varied findings on these issues (see, e.g., Kraemer & Danziger, 1984; Nunn, 1994; Frank, Brandl & Watkins, 1997; Koper & Roth, 2000; Roth et al., 2000; Chan et al., 2001; Colvin, 2001; Koper, Moore & Roth,

2002; Nunn & Quintet, 2002; Chan, 2003; Ioimo & Aronson, 2004; Zaworski 2004; Manning, 2008). At the same time, organizational and cultural factors within an organization may play a particularly important role in mediating, in either positive or negative ways, the potential of technology to improve police effectiveness and legitimacy.

For instance, from a crime prevention perspective, new information systems and analytic technologies like crime analysis can help police to more precisely identify the people, places, and problems that contribute most to crime. Yet these advances may have less impact if police managers fail to focus adequate resources on crime hot spots or if the results of crime analysis are not adequately disseminated (or accepted) throughout the agency, particularly among patrol officers and first-line supervisors. Consequently, the effects of these and other technologies may often depend on organizational culture and other organizational changes, such as the adoption of new management systems, the implementation of analytic processes, and changes in deployment. In order to achieve the many improvements to existing police operations that might be sought with new technology, changes may thus be needed in agencies' organizational cultures, practices, and infrastructures (e.g., Chan et al., 2001; Chan, 2003; Zaworski, 2004; Harris, 2007; Garicano & Heaton, 2010; Koper et al., 2015a).[2]

Technological Frames in Policing

Theory and research from other fields also suggests that sociological features of police agencies can be particularly important in shaping technology's outcomes. Technology scholars Orlikowski and Gash (1994) theorize that "technological frames" mediate the impact of technology on outcomes in organizations more generally. Such frames reflect workers' expectations, knowledge, experiences, values, objectives, and roles within an organization, as well as the organization's history of technology use. In turn, these frames can shape technology uses and products in an organization and, therefore, the outcomes associated with those technologies (see also Orlikowski, 1992; Robey, Boudreau & Rose, 2000; Boudreau & Robey, 2005). This perspective thus

---

[2] This idea is related to the notion of "complementarity" (Milgrom & Roberts, 1990) in economics, which suggests that technology may not have much positive impact on its own (or may even have adverse effects) unless it is accompanied by other organizational changes – in work processes, procedures, training, management, organizational structures, and the like – that enable an organization to effectively leverage new technological capabilities. Garicano and Heaton's (2010) research on police performance and IT, which we will discuss, provides one illustration of how this can apply to policing (see Brynjolfsson & Hitt, 2000 for a review of evidence on this issue in the private sector). Yet, efforts to make such organizational changes may be less likely in public sector organizations like police agencies because, as noted by Brown (2015), public sector organizations often adopt technology for social and political reasons (e.g., to appear more competent and legitimate) that are not linked to clear goals for enhancing performance.

highlights the role of human agency and social interpretations as reasons for varying outcomes associated with technology in organizations While technology shapes human actions, people in organizations also enact technology in different intended and unintended ways (e.g., in innovative or perfunctory ways) that can produce varying outcomes, both positive and negative. In this manner, technology and human actors both affect and transform one another in their effects on performance.

Technological frames can also vary across members and units of an organization. Such "incongruence" (Orlikowski & Gash, 1994: 180) can result in conflicts about the development, use, and meaning of technologies in an organization, as well as different outcomes of technology (see Rocheleau, 1993 for further discussion). In the context of policing, for example, a police chief may view a new information system as increasing efficiency and accountability. However, patrol officers and detectives may see the same innovation as threatening their discretion or autonomy, or making their daily work more difficult and time-consuming (e.g., see Manning, 1992; Chan et al., 2001; Harris, 2007).

Frames are important to any discussion of technology as an innovation to improve policing. Manning (2008) argues that the dominant frame in policing reflects a reactive view of policing, characterized and fostered by an incident-based, response-oriented, and procedures-dominated approach. Manning and others (see Harris, 2007; Lum, 2010; Sanders & Henderson, 2013; Sanders, Weston & Schott, 2015) suggest that the technological and organizational frames that are nurtured by this reactive model filter technology adoption. This filtering process influences the way technology is used and the outcomes achieved with technology. In other words, adopting new technologies such as information and records management systems, body-worn cameras, license plate readers, analytic tools, or forensics technologies might produce benefits in administrative efficiency, accuracy and timeliness of crime data, response to calls, and detection capabilities. Yet these changes may not be sufficient to produce substantial improvements in police outcome effectiveness (crime prevention and control, improved relationships with citizens, stronger internal affairs and management, etc.) absent congruent technological frames and practices that promote technology use in these strategic ways.

Police leaders, scholars, and reformers may see technology as a means to facilitate innovations (e.g., problem-solving, community policing, hot spots policing, third party policing, evidence-based policing) that can reduce crime or improve citizen trust, rather than just as a means to react to crime or increase arrests and detections. However, these expectations might be overly optimistic if these objectives are not incorporated into daily policing tasks and expectations that ultimately can create the technological frames of officers, detectives, or supervisors. Hence, technology will not be used in evidence-based ways, if an agency's approach to policing more generally does not involve evidence-based policing.

EXAMINING THE EVIDENCE BASE FOR SELECTED TECHNOLOGIES

The mediating effects of organizational frames on technology's impacts provide a strong justification for improving the evidence base on technology application in policing. Not only do we need to identify how organizational frames and other factors shape technological outcomes, but we also need more evaluation research to discern what those outcomes are and whether they are aligned with broader policing goals. Four examples illustrate our point – information technologies, crime analysis (as a technology), license plate readers, and body-worn cameras.

Information Technologies

Information technology (IT) is arguably the technology category with the most potential to impact police innovation and evidence-based approaches, as it has become well developed and affects almost all aspects of police work and management. IT within police agencies includes a wide array of databases and data systems (and their supporting hardware and software) for storing, managing, retrieving, sharing, and analyzing information both within and across agencies. Common components include records management systems (RMS) that capture criminal incident records; computer-aided dispatch systems that record and assign calls for service; and various other databases that may contain information and/or intelligence on persons, groups, personnel, and other matters. IT systems can also include those fostered by data collection over the internet (such as tiplines or other social media sites), as well as mobile computers and data terminals that give officers wireless access to information in the field and that allow them to file reports remotely.

By improving the ability of police to collect, manage, and analyze data, IT has enhanced the administrative efficiency of police organizations, improved their apprehension capabilities, and given them the ability to more precisely and proactively target the people, places, and problems that contribute most to crime and disorder in their communities (e.g., see Groff & McEwen, 2008). Many police researchers have recognized the centrality of IT to police work and organizational change more generally (e.g., Manning, 1992; Ericson & Haggerty, 1997; Chan, 2001; 2003; Boudreau & Robey, 2005; Harris, 2007; Mastrofski & Willis, 2010). Accordingly, IT has been studied more extensively than other forms of police technology. Yet, this body of research has produced complex and often contradictory findings on IT's impacts.

For example, in a national study of US police agencies over the period of 1987 to 2003, Garicano & Heaton, (2010) found that increases in the use of IT by police were not associated with improvements in case clearance rates or crime rates. Brown (2015) reported similar findings in a national study focusing on more recent changes (2003–2007) in police IT capabilities and clearance rates. However, Garicano and Heaton also found evidence that IT is linked to improved performance (i.e., higher clearance rates and/or lower crime rates) when complemented with other organizational changes including greater use of specialized units, higher educational and training requirements for staff, and managerial practices indicative of CompStat. Other studies of IT in policing have also produced a somewhat clouded picture; while officers generally have positive attitudes toward IT improvements (though exceptions are noted below), the effects of IT have been mixed with respect to improving productivity, case clearances, proactive policing, community policing, problem-solving, and other outcomes (e.g., Palys, Boyanowsky & Dutton, 1984; Danziger & Kraemer, 1985; Rocheleau, 1993; Nunn, 1994; Brown, 2001; Chan et al., 2001; Colvin, 2001; Nunn & Quinet, 2002; Agrawal, Rao & Sanders, 2003; Brown & Brudney, 2003; Ioimo & Aronson, 2003; 2004; Zaworski, 2004; Groff & McEwen, 2008; Koper et al., 2015a; Koper, Lum & Hibdon, 2015b).

In general, these studies highlight a number of factors that can offset the potential benefits of IT for officers. For example, officers may be hampered by technical difficulties and the complexities of using IT systems, particularly when the systems are new (e.g., Koper et al., 2015a). Further, the adoption of new IT systems often leads to more extensive reporting requirements for officers. These factors may negate expected time savings, lessen (or fail to improve) time for interacting with citizens and engaging in proactive work, and create frustration and dissatisfaction for officers (e.g., Chan et al., 2001; Colvin, 2001; Ioimo & Aronson, 2004; Koper et al., 2015a). Surveys and interviews in police agencies illustrate that negative implementation experiences and functionality problems with new technology have important ramifications for the acceptance, uses, and impacts of that technology and can produce negative effects on officers' attitudes and performance (i.e., job satisfaction and productivity) that last for long periods (Koper et al., 2015a; also see Koper, Lum & Willis, 2014). IT may have other unintended consequences that also have negative implications for organizational functioning and performance (e.g., see Chan et al., 2001; Koper et al., 2015a). Examples include reducing time that supervisors spend mentoring officers; worsening perceptions of inequality for line-level staff, particularly patrol officers who may feel heavily burdened and scrutinized by the reporting demands and monitoring that often come with new information and surveillance technologies; and encouraging an overemphasis on technical skills and computer literacy at the expense of skills in dealing with people in the community (on the latter point, see Palys et al., 1984).

Perhaps more importantly, police may also fail to use IT in the most strategically optimal ways for reducing crime. Although research shows that police are most effective in reducing crime when they focus their efforts on high-risk places and groups and use problem-solving strategies tailored to specific issues, police may not regularly employ technology toward these ends in practice. This is because perceptions and uses of technology are highly dependent on the norms and culture of an agency and how officers view their function (i.e., technological "frames" as discussed). And because officers continue to frame policing in terms of reactive response to calls for service, reactive arrest to crimes, and adherence to standard operating procedures, they use and are influenced by technology to achieve these goals (Lum, 2010). Our own research supports this idea (Koper et al., 2015a; also see Koper et al., 2014; Koper et al., 2015b; Lum, Koper & Willis, 2017). In surveys with officers from four agencies, we found that patrol officers were much more likely to use IT to guide and assist them with traditional enforcement-oriented and reactive activities (e.g., identifying persons of interest, running license plate checks, and checking the call history of a location before responding to a call) than for more strategic, proactive tasks (e.g., determining where to patrol between calls or how to respond to a particular crime problem). This likely helps to explain why greater use of IT by patrol officers in the field did not appear to enhance their effectiveness in reducing crime (Koper et al., 2015b).

In addition, we found through interviews and focus groups that officers judged technology against the value (or technological frame) of efficiency, not necessarily outcome effectiveness (Lum et al., 2017). Officers often verbalized these outputs as gaining information "faster" or with "greater ease" when they discussed IT, and they emphasized how technology helped them to accomplish tasks quickly. When these efficiency gains were not achieved, technology was seen more negatively, sometimes leading officers to avoid using it. This mindset affects not only discretionary uses of technology (which in turn impacts outcomes) but also definitions and expectations about outcomes themselves. For example, the term "effectiveness" was most often defined by officers (and used interchangeably) to mean "efficiency," or the ability to respond to crime and to quickly identify suspects, victims, witnesses, and other aspects of crimes to resolve cases. Less often did officers define effectiveness in terms of their ability to achieve specific outcomes of interest to the police department, such as preventing crime or improving relationships with citizens or community groups.

These tendencies are also extended to managers, as we found that supervisors were less likely to use IT to form crime prevention strategies with their subordinates and more likely to use it to check reports and assess performance measures of officers and squads. Supervisors typically provided little in the way of consistent training or direction to officers on ways to optimize technology use in their daily work and deployment habits. Our observations suggest that while technology has fostered strategic innovation and accountability at higher managerial levels in policing (for example, through CompStat-type management processes), the innovative use of technology as a tool by middle- and lower-level supervisors to manage the performance of line-level officers is still neither institutionalized nor clearly understood in many agencies.

All of this suggests that police may not fully capitalize on the aspects of technology that enable them to do things that could optimize their effectiveness.[3] Hence, while basic application of IT might have marginal effects in improving police efficiency, detection capabilities in the field, and officer safety in responding to calls, these improvements may not alone be enough to enhance police performance as measured by crime reduction or even case clearances. This is where we need to strengthen the evidence base in this area.[4]

Crime Analysis

The development and application of analytic technology in policing (i.e., crime analysis) also has a high potential for enhancing police effectiveness and has been strongly linked to that of IT. Despite the mixed findings of prior technology research, innovations like hot spots policing and CompStat have been linked to advances in IT. Strategic use of IT capabilities by police is thus likely central to realizing IT's full potential. One strategic use with demonstrated promise for improving the effectiveness of police is IT's application to crime analysis. As described by Taylor and Boba (2011: 6), "crime analysis involves the use of large amounts of data and modern technology – along with a set of systematic methods and techniques that identify patterns and relationships between crime data and other relevant information sources – to assist police in criminal apprehension, crime and disorder reduction, crime prevention, and evaluation." Common duties for crime analysts involve assisting detectives, mapping crime, identifying crime patterns, conducting network analysis, and compiling data for UCR reporting and managerial meetings (Taylor & Boba, 2011).

The development and adoption of crime analysis have been significant trends in policing over the last few decades, as it has become very common in law enforcement agencies (Burch, 2012; Reaves, 2010; Taylor & Boba, 2011).

---

[3] This tendency is likely reinforced by the limitations of police IT systems, in terms of available data and functionality, for facilitating problem-solving tasks (e.g., Brown, 2001; Nunn & Quinet, 2002; Brown & Brudney, 2003).

[4] Although our focus here is on IT and policing, similar concerns and uncertainties have arisen from efforts to assess the effects of IT on performance and productivity more broadly in the public and private sectors, where studies have yielded mixed results with regard to IT's impacts on aggregate level productivity, organizational performance, and client outcomes (e.g., see Brynjolfsson, 1993; Lehr & Lichtenberg, 1999; Triplett, 1999; Brynjolfsson & Hitt, 2000; Lee & Perry, 2002; Stiroh, 2002; Garg et al., 2005; Goolsbee & Guryan, 2006; Foley & Alfonso, 2009; Garicano & Heaton, 2010; Brown, 2015). Scholars have offered a number of hypotheses for this disconnect, which may also be applicable to police use of IT. Brynjolfsson (1993), for example, has suggested that IT may fail to improve performance or have effects that are difficult to detect for several reasons, including mismeasurement (e.g., technology may improve quality of service in less tangible ways that are not measured by standard performance metrics like crime rates), learning curves that delay technology's impacts, mismanagement of IT implementation (e.g., see Goldfinch, 2007), and the possibility that technology may improve organizational processes without improving outcomes (e.g., improving the speed and accuracy of police reporting without clear effects on crime control; for examples in other public sectors, see Garg et al., 2005; Goolsbee & Guryan, 2006). Also see our discussion of the concept of complementarity in note 2.

Crime analysis is believed to hold great potential for improving the effectiveness of police. While it has perhaps been linked most prominently to hot spots policing and CompStat, crime analysis is also used heavily for investigative work and can be a valuable component of problem-oriented policing (see Taylor, Koper & Woods, 2011a).

However, with the exception of its role in supporting hot spots policing (see, for example, Kennedy, Caplan & Piza, 2015), we are not aware of much evidence demonstrating a clear link between the use of crime analysis and lower rates of crime (Lum, 2013; Santos, 2014).[5] Although this may reflect a lack of study (for example, we have seen no before-and-after assessments evaluating the impact of establishing crime analysis units on crime reduction), it is also likely that, as with other technological and analytical innovations, the potential impact of crime analysis is limited by organizational factors. While agencies are obviously constrained by the sophistication of their crime analysis capabilities (see O'Shea & Nicholls, 2003), other obstacles can also impede effectiveness, such as a police culture that doesn't value analytical work, the reactive nature of policing, and a disregard for crime analysis that is done largely by civilians (Taylor & Boba, 2011; Lum, 2013). In practice, officers may not use products like maps and may find them of little value in their work (Cope, 2004; Paulsen, 2004; Cordner & Biebel, 2005; Koper et al., 2015a). Indeed, crime analysis is largely produced for police managers. Additionally, while managers tend to be the heaviest users of crime analysis, they often focus largely on criminal apprehension and short-term tactical planning rather than long-term strategic planning (O'Shea & Nicholls, 2003; Harris, 2007; Taylor & Boba, 2011).

In our technology fieldwork referenced above, we examined crime analysis in tandem with IT, and our conclusions about its uses and impacts were much the same as those for IT (Koper et al., 2014; 2015a; Lum et al., 2017). Although officers were sometimes instructed to conduct directed patrol in particular areas based on crime analysis (particularly in one agency that had a very advanced crime analysis unit and a strong managerial commitment to its use), they often did not take their own initiative in using crime analysis for self-directed proactive work and problem-solving. Nor did they necessarily understand the value of crime analysis for facilitating such work. Even detectives, who often worked closely with crime analysts, most heavily used and valued crime analysis for tracking leads for cases they were investigating reactively. The use of crime analysis by detectives to anticipate future events using pattern analysis or for other types of proactive decision-making that might help to prevent crime was

---

[5] On a related note, evidence has also been mixed to date on the effects of "predictive policing" efforts which attempt to use advanced statistical modeling to more precisely identify and focus police attention on high-risk locations, times, and people in a preemptive manner (see review in National Academies of Sciences, Engineering, and Medicine, 2017; also see Hunt, Saunders & Hollywood, 2014; Mohler et al., 2015; Jaitman, 2017).

rare. Again, these tendencies varied notably across agencies, but they were apparent among many officers and detectives even in an agency that placed a heavy managerial emphasis on crime analysis and data-driven policing.

These technological frames of officers thereby mediate the relationship between the adoption, implementation, and use of crime analysis, and outcomes sought. Our work, and that of others, suggests that crime analysis can be leveraged to greater effect if police can learn to use it more systematically throughout their organizations to identify crime patterns, respond to crime problems, guide proactive patrol, and facilitate other innovations that are connected to evidence-based policing.

License Plate Readers (LPRs)

Another technology that has been adopted by law enforcement in recent decades to achieve crime control outcomes is license plate reader technology. The story of LPRs is also one of rapid adoption of technology in a low-information environment in which little outcome research was available – but adoption moved forward nonetheless. License plate readers, or LPRs, are both a sensory and an information technology that can be placed on mobile patrol units or in fixed locations to detect stolen automobiles, help with investigations, assist in finding missing people, or for general crime-prevention purposes. Using a high-speed camera and database system, LPRs scan and read the alphanumeric characters of license plates within view of the camera and then automatically (and instantaneously) compare the scanned plates against existing databases of license plates that are of interest to law enforcement. Plates "of interest" might include those associated with stolen vehicles, vehicles of interest to a police investigation, or vehicles linked to registered owners who have open warrants or are being sought by the police. When a match is made, a signal alerts the officer to proceed with further confirmation, investigation, and action. Hundreds of vehicle plates can be scanned in minutes by LPR technology, thereby automating a process that, in the past, was conducted by officers manually, tag-by-tag, and with much discretion. LPR is also an information technology, as these systems can collect and store large amounts of data (plates, dates, times, and locations of vehicles) for future records management, analysis, and dataset linking for investigation and crime prevention. Given these characteristics, LPR has the unique potential to improve police effectiveness by enhancing patrol, investigative, and other security operations.

Although limited by the data it accesses and by the frequency and way that it is used (Lum et al., 2010; 2011; 2016c), LPR technology is seemingly a force-multiplier to many crime prevention and homeland security efforts. Because of its intuitive appeal and fast automation of what was once a slow process, police have expressed high interest in this technology. About a quarter of US police agencies were using LPRs as of 2009 (Roberts & Casanova, 2012), and more than a third of agencies with 100 or more officers were using them by 2010 (Lum et al., 2010; also see Koper et al., 2009). In our most recent national survey of LPR use in the United States (Lum et al., 2016c; 2018), the proportion of agencies with 100 or more officers using LPRs had almost doubled to 59 percent by 2014. This diffusion of LPR technology has not only occurred rapidly but has also changed in nature very quickly. In 2010, most agencies with LPRs had no more than four devices (today, they have eight on average), primarily using them to detect stolen vehicles and tags in patrol. Today, agencies are also using LPRs to varying degrees for a variety of investigative, vehicle enforcement, and counter-terrorism activities (Lum et al., 2018).

Like other technologies (see the discussion of body-worn cameras to follow), this rapid and changing adoption of LPRs has also taken place despite the technology's high cost ($20,000 – $25,000 per unit in its earlier days) and without much research on its crime control impact and cost effectiveness. Prior studies of LPRs conducted in the United Kingdom and North America have focused largely on the accuracy and efficiency of the devices in scanning license plates and on their utility for increasing arrests, recovery of stolen vehicles, and seizure of other contraband (PA Consulting Group, 2003; Maryland State Highway Authority, 2005; Ohio State Highway Patrol, 2005; Patch, 2005; Cohen, Plecas & McCormack, 2007; Taylor, Koper & Woods, 2011b; 2012).[6]

However, there is very limited evidence on whether LPR use actually reduces auto theft or other crimes and what types of LPR uses best achieve those ends. Studies of LPR use and its effects on crime have tested small-scale deployment of LPRs with patrol units. One study that spanned two suburban jurisdictions in Virginia found that thirty-minute LPR patrols conducted once every few days (on average) in randomly selected crime hot spots for a period of two to three months did not reduce auto-related or other forms of crime in the targeted locations (Lum et al., 2010; 2011). Although the experimental dosage was relatively low and the LPR databases were limited to information on stolen vehicles, Lum et al. argued that these conditions reflected the current state of LPR use. The other study testing LPRs was a randomized experiment in Mesa, Arizona (Taylor et al., 2011b; 2012; Koper, Taylor & Woods, 2013). In that study, a small auto theft squad conducted short operations to detect stolen and other vehicles of interest at high-risk road segments that were identified as likely travel routes for auto thieves based on analysis of auto theft and recovery locations (see Lu, 2003) and the input of detectives. As expected, the officers were much more likely to detect and recover stolen vehicles and apprehend auto thieves when using the LPR devices, though the numbers of hits and arrests were small. Further analyses revealed that the patrols produced short-term

---

[6] These sources also provide information on some of the technical limitations of LPRs with regard to issues like misreads, false alarms, and difficulties with reading particular types of license plates or reading plates under particular types of conditions.

reductions in crime at the hot spots in both the LPR and non-LPR modes (Koper et al., 2013), but the study could not definitively isolate the effects of the LPRs from those of the extra patrols more generally, due in part to the low number of LPR arrests (and to the fact that the LPR cameras were mounted on the cars even when not in use, thus potentially creating deterrent effects).

While informative, both the Mesa and Virginia studies were limited by the short duration or low dosage of the interventions, the small numbers of LPRs available, and the limited data fed into the LPR devices (the data consisted largely or entirely of manually downloaded information on stolen vehicles and license plates). Updated studies are thus needed to examine large-scale LPR deployments and LPR operations conducted with access to more extensive data systems.

LPR use has also raised questions about citizen privacy that have also not been fully evaluated. In their study of LPR use in Virginia, Lum et al. (2010) surveyed community residents in one of the study jurisdictions and found that while there was strong support for LPR use in general, this support can vary depending on the types of LPR applications under consideration (see also Merola et al., 2014). For example, using the devices to detect stolen automobiles or criminal behavior received much more community support than using them to detect parking violations. Additionally, the survey revealed that members of the public do not regard all uses as equivalent, but rather make significant distinctions in their concerns based upon the way in which systems are deployed. Several factors corresponded with decreased support for the technology, including using LPR in ways unrelated to serious crimes (e.g., to detect parking violations) or for prolonged storage of information. Merola and Lum (2013) also found that support for an agency's use of technology depended on how much legitimacy and trust a person affords to the police. Those with more trust tend to support the use of LPRs more than those with less.

Improving apprehensions and deterrence with LPRs will also depend on many other operational decisions about how and where to deploy LPRs. With regard to the former, police currently deploy more than half their LPRs on patrol vehicles, and deploy most of the remainder in fixed locations (Lum et al., 2018). However, the relative pros and cons of mobile versus fixed LPR deployments have yet to be studied. Decisions about where to deploy LPRs are especially critical from an evidence-based perspective, given the importance of place-based policing strategies as discussed elsewhere in this volume. Our sense is that many agencies deploy their LPRs with no particular strategy. LPR technology is often treated as a resource that has to be divided equally among administrative units (e.g., districts or divisions) within the agency, rather than allocated based on needs assessment. Assignment of LPRs to officers might similarly be made with no particular strategy nor any guidance for the officers. Indeed, in our national survey, 59 percent of agencies using LPRs in patrol gave officers full discretion over how they use their LPR units. About a third provided some direction to patrol officers on where to patrol with LPRs, while only 5 percent almost always provided such direction (Lum et al., 2018). Further, most agencies using LPRs did not collect performance measures associated with LPR use. All of this is consistent with the technological frames (as discussed) that arise from a reactive and procedures-oriented mindset toward policing.

In contrast, a more strategic, evidence-based approach to using LPRs is to deploy them to crime hot spots and other locations (like highly traveled roads) where the risk of detecting stolen vehicles and other vehicles of interest will be higher (e.g., see the Mesa and Virginia studies discussed). Agencies might also conduct their own pilot tests to determine optimal places and methods for LPR deployment based on sound analysis. For example, police in Surrey, British Columbia (Canada) conducted pilot tests with LPRs by assessing the number, rate, and types of LPR hits they could obtain on various roadways in the jurisdiction at different times of day (Cohen et al., 2007). This established baseline data for the agency that could guide LPR deployment and be used to evaluate trends over time. Another example comes from the Ohio State Highway Patrol (2005), which tested three modes of LPR deployment: fixed use at tollbooths on a major turnpike, mobile deployment on marked police cars on the same turnpike, and mobile deployment on an unmarked police vehicle in a high-crime area. They compared these modes of deployment with respect to technical performance (number and accuracy of reads), hits (including an assessment of the validity of those hits), arrests, and stolen vehicle recoveries (results were most promising for the mobile deployment in the high-crime area).

In sum, LPR technology has been rapidly embraced by police because it fits well into the dominant technical frame of efficiency and rapid reaction to crimes. However, much more research about the crime control, legitimacy, and privacy impacts of LPR is needed to inform law enforcement leaders about the acquisition and use of LPRs. In the case of this and many other technologies, adoption came before outcome evaluation and relied almost exclusively on technical tests of the technology. An evidence-based approach to LPRs requires not only increasing knowledge of the technical capabilities of this technology, but also using it to maximize the potential for LPRs to increase both criminal apprehension and deterrence while minimizing negative impacts on the community. More attention to strategic deployment and in-depth program evaluation of LPRs can assist with this goal.[7]

Body-Worn Cameras (BWCs)

Body-worn cameras (BWCs) provide another very contemporary example of a rapidly spreading technology that may have complex and unintended effects

---

[7] More recent studies of LPR use in patrol and investigations continue to show null or inconclusive results even for large-scale LPR deployment (Koper et al., 2018).

in policing. As of this writing, recently publicized and controversial use-of-force events in Ferguson (Missouri), New York City, South Carolina, Baltimore, and elsewhere have led law enforcement agencies, citizens, civil rights groups, and city councils to push for the rapid adoption of BWC technology. The US Department of Justice has dedicated $20 million to fund the purchase of, and technical assistance for, BWCs. Proponents of BWCs believe that these devices will deter problem conduct in police–citizen contacts (on the part of both police and citizens) and provide better evidence on police–citizen encounters that will foster public transparency and accountability in the handling of cases that do result in citizen complaints and/or use of police force. If achieved, these benefits could increase citizens' trust and confidence in the police.

As with LPRs, this rapid adoption of BWCs has occurred within a low-evidence-based environment; researchers are only beginning to develop knowledge about the effects, both intentional and unintentional, of this technology. But in contrast to developments surrounding LPRs, there has been a rapid push in generating research evidence on BWCs, primarily spearheaded by the Laura and John Arnold Foundation as well as the National Institute of Justice. In a recent study led by the authors (Lum et al., 2015), we examined both the existing and ongoing BWC research to identify existing gaps in the knowledge necessary to build the evidence-base of this rapidly diffusing technology.

At the time of our review, we found over a dozen completed empirical studies of BWCs and thirty ongoing research projects, many of which were randomized controlled experiments and high-quality quasi-experimental studies.[8] This level of evidence generation for a law enforcement technology is unprecedented in the history of police technology adoption. In many ways, it reflects greater recognition of the importance of developing better evidence on the impacts of new policing technologies. Our survey of existing and ongoing research on BWCs also highlighted issues that are receiving significant research attention, as well as knowledge gaps in need of more attention.

We found that the most common research that has been or is being conducted explores questions related to the impact of BWCs on the quality of officer–citizen interactions (including, for example, the nature of the interaction/communication, displays of procedural justice and professionalism, and misconduct or corruption), as often measured by complaints and/or surveys. Also highly researched is the related issue of the impact of BWCs on officer use of force during these interactions. Other relatively common research topics include officer attitudes about cameras, the impact of BWCs on citizen satisfaction with police encounters, the broader

---

[8] To view all of these studies in this report, go to http://cebcp.org/wp-content/technology/BodyWornCameraResearch.pdf. Since the writing of this chapter, we have conducted an updated review of seventy BWC studies, which largely reinforces the general themes and conclusions stated here (Lum et al., 2019).

impacts of BWCs on community attitudes and perceptions of the police and their legitimacy, the effects of BWCs on officer discretion (especially to arrest or cite individuals), and the impact of BWCs on suspect compliance to commands (and relatedly, assaults on officers). While findings are not definitive, they illustrate the complexity of questions that research needs to address given the rapid adoption of this technology and its potential to affect the behaviors of both police and citizens.

For example, early results suggest that BWCs may reduce complaints against the police (see Goodall, 2007; Farrar & Ariel, 2013; Katz et al., 2014; Ariel, Farrar & Sutherland, 2015) or result in quicker resolution of complaints (see ODS Consulting, 2011; Katz et al., 2014). However, whether or not that signals increased accountability, improved citizen satisfaction, and/or improved police or citizen behavior is still uncertain. There are signs that BWCs also reduce use of force by police but with caveats. For instance, Ariel et al. (2015) find that BWCs reduce use-of-force incidents, but Katz, Kurtenbach, Choate, and White (2015) find that arrest activity increases for officers wearing BWCs (Owens, Mann & Mckenna, 2014, also seem to find similar impacts on individuals being charged). Interestingly, Ready and Young (2015) seem to find that officers wearing cameras, while less likely to perform stop-and-frisks or make arrests, are more likely to give citations. In a recent review of ten experiments in the United States and the United Kingdom, Ariel et al. (2016) found that BWCs may only reduce use of force if officers do not have much discretion on when to turn cameras on and off. These initial findings suggest that BWCs can at least discourage negative behaviors by officers; however, deeper research will be needed to determine if BWCs prompt more fundamental changes in officers' attitudes and behaviors as police learn to better utilize this technology for training, supervision, accountability systems, and self-learning (e.g., see Koen, 2016).[9]

Many other important questions also warrant attention. For instance, will BWCs change discretionary officer behaviors by affecting officers' propensity to engage in proactive activities, issue citations, or make arrests? To the extent that officers frame BWCs as a tool for monitoring them, it might conceivably make them less likely to engage in proactive contacts out of fear that their actions will result in greater scrutiny, particularly if encounters go badly. This same concern might also prompt them to take a more legalistic approach in situations where they have discretion over issuing citations or making arrests (thus resulting in

---

[9] For example, Koen's (2016) research in a medium-sized suburban agency suggests that reductions in citizen complaints and police use of force associated with the use of BWCs may arise from a complex mix of deterrence (for both police and citizens), citizen reassurance (i.e., the cameras may cause them to feel more at ease in their interactions with police), dropped complaints (i.e., citizens may drop complaints when they are given an opportunity to view their own behavior as captured by BWCs), improvements in training and officer selection, improvements in supervision and coaching, and self-improvement (i.e., officers learn from reviewing their own work as captured by BWCs).

more minor citations and arrests). Substantial changes in officer behavior either way could then have ramifications, both good and bad, for police crime-control efforts as well as police–citizen interactions and relationships. Studies are underway on this issue, but it is an area that arguably needs further research emphasis (Lum et al., 2015).

There is then the question of how BWCs affect citizens' views and behaviors. The decline in citizen complaints found in BWC studies to date is encouraging, but it may not mean that citizens are more satisfied with police contacts in general. Citizens' views of police more generally may also not change if the adoption of BWCs doesn't seem to bring changes in police accountability and actions. Indeed, if police come to frame BWCs as a tool for protecting themselves and gathering evidence on citizens (e.g., Koen, 2016), acceptance of BWCs may grow among police, but citizens may come to view BWCs in an antagonistic manner rather than as tools for their protection or as a means to improve police service and accountability. BWCs could also have unintended effects on citizens' actions. For example, might fear of being recorded on a police BWC discourage some people from contacting the police or cooperating with police as victims, witnesses, or informants? Also, might police adoption of BWCs worsen citizens' perceptions of the police due to privacy concerns? Some of these issues are currently under study, while others need attention.

Other significant research gaps also remain. While much of the existing and ongoing research focuses on officer behavior, this research tends to focus on police professionalism, use of force, and misconduct. However, BWC adoption has also been spurred on by more critical and hard-to-measure concerns, including whether BWCs can reduce implicit or explicit bias among police and differential police treatment based on race, sex, age, ethnicity, or other extralegal characteristics. Additional questions of misconduct or professionalism concern the potential impact of BWCs on officer compliance with 4th Amendment standards during stop-question-and-frisk encounters – another area not yet examined. In a similar vein, while ongoing research is examining officer attitudes about BWCs, other measures of these attitudes, such as job satisfaction and retention, have not been investigated. Finally, several organizational issues warrant attention, including whether BWCs can facilitate the investigation of critical incidents such as officer-involved shootings; improve training and affect policy changes; or impact the accountability, supervision, management, and disciplinary systems of an organization, including those related to internal investigations.

Thus, like LPRs, BWCs were adopted with relatively little understanding of their effects. In a period of only a few years, tens of millions of dollars (and perhaps more) have been spent on their acquisition. Of course, law enforcement cannot always wait for research before making a policy or technology decision. In the current environment, police agencies felt they needed to do something to improve their legitimacy with citizens as well as to protect themselves against unjustified complaints. And in fairness, unlike LPRs, the push to create an evidence-base for this technology is stronger, due to a greater level of commitment and funding for research on BWCs by both the US Department of Justice and the Laura and John Arnold Foundation. Nonetheless, BWCs provide another example of how police can sometimes move quickly to adopt an innovation despite a lack of knowledge about the consequences of that innovation. This stands in contrast to experience with other innovations, such as problem-solving, community policing, hot spots policing, and other forms of targeted policing. The uptake on these strategic innovations has been much slower even though we have much research knowledge to guide these practices. Politics, a belief that an innovation is "common sense" or straightforward, and the ease with which an innovation fits into policing's tasks, functions, and existing technological frames all contribute to this state of affairs.

BETTER INTEGRATING TECHNOLOGY AND EVIDENCE-BASED POLICING

We recognize that technology adoption is sometimes viewed outside the realm of evidence-based policing and other substantive policing innovations; in some cases, adoption of technology is a reflection of modernizing the police force, increasing job satisfaction, and just making certain processes easier. But to *optimize* the use of technology to improve the quality of policing requires a different discussion. Agencies may already have acquired LPRs and BWCs and want to know how to use them in ways that lead to outcomes that they seek, including not angering the communities in which they operate. Technologies such as crime analysis and information technologies have already been well integrated into many police agencies, but thinking about how they are currently used and what organizational factors shape those uses is essential when agencies consider how to optimize technology use. Research knowledge on police strategies and tactics, technological frames, and outcome research on technology are all important parts of the evidence base for technology that can contribute to optimizing its use.

Based on our fieldwork in this area, we have suggested several recommendations for agencies to optimize their adoption and use of technology within an evidence-based policing framework. We provide a summary version of those recommendations here, drawing upon our work with James Willis as discussed in Koper et al. (2014; 2015a).

For starters, there are a number of ways that police can potentially smooth the process of technological change and increase receptivity to new technology. For one, police managers should allow for a broad base of participation in the technology implementation process by various personnel who will be affected by the technology. This process should provide ample opportunities for pilot testing early versions of a technology for both technical assessment and outcome effectiveness, and soliciting input that can be incorporated into its final design. This process can be helpful in identifying and correcting technical problems with a technology and for determining its most effective applications. Staff at various levels should also have opportunities to offer insights on how technologies like IT, crime analysis, LPRs, and BWCs might be best integrated into assessments of performance. Allowing those who are being assessed to participate rather than simply imposing new requirements upon them will likely increase levels of understanding and acceptance of the technology being used in this way (Mastrofski & Wadman, 1991).

Proper levels of training are also essential, especially for the most difficult technological changes. For example, learning how to use an IT system properly, in terms of both input and use of output, requires extensive training, follow-up, and consistent adjustment. Moreover, once basic training is done, agencies should prepare a systematic and continuous approach to follow-up, in-service training, reinforcement, ongoing technical support, and adaptation to new lessons. This should include dissemination of information about effective practices, success stories, and tips for easier or faster use of technology (such techniques are often discovered by individuals but not shared widely or systematically).

However, to reap the full potential benefits of technology in an evidence-based framework, police must also arguably address traditional and long-standing philosophical and cultural norms about the role of law enforcement (Lum, 2010). For example, research indicates that from a policy and practice perspective, adjusting organizational factors and frames may be just as useful as adjusting the use of the technologies themselves. Technological adoption is not only a long and continuous process of its own, but one that is highly connected to many other aspects of policing, including daily routines and deployments, job satisfaction, interaction with the community, internal relationships, and crime control outcomes. Thus, managing technological change in policing is challenging and closely connected to managing other organizational reforms (such as improving professionalism, reducing misconduct, and adopting community, problem-solving, or evidence-based policing). Accordingly, strategizing about technology application is essential and should involve careful consideration of the specific ways in which new and existing technologies can be deployed and used at all levels of the organization to meet goals for improving efficiency, effectiveness, and agency management. Research evidence can provide knowledge to assist agencies with this task.

Most fundamentally, training about proactive and evidence-based strategies – and how technology can be used in support of those strategies – is needed. As we have discussed elsewhere (Lum & Koper, 2017), police are most effective in reducing crime when their strategies are proactive, focused (both on high-risk places and groups), and oriented toward problem-solving and prevention. In our experience, however, officers often seem to have a limited understanding of how technology might help them in these regards, and their agencies typically lack reward systems to encourage innovative responses to crime. As discussed earlier, officers generally focus on using technology in support of answering calls and other traditional enforcement and surveillance activities. Given that an agency is trying to reduce, prevent, and control crime (rather than just react and respond to it), training regarding technology or other tools needs to incorporate how technology might be used more comprehensively for these goals. How, for example, can officers use their agency's information systems and crime analysis to guide their patrol activities between calls for service, identify and address problems at hot spot locations, and monitor high-risk people in their areas of responsibility? At the same time, how can managers use these technologies to encourage such work by their subordinates?

Training on the use of technology for evidence-based practices should also extend to the enhancement of police legitimacy in the community, for example, to include the application of procedural justice (e.g., Mazerolle et al., 2013). Officers working with video and audio recorders in their car or on their person might benefit from training on how these technologies can reduce the chances of conflict in citizen encounters and maximize citizens' sense that they have been treated respectfully and fairly. Training might also emphasize issues such as how officers can use their technologies (such as information systems) to be more helpful to citizens in their encounters and how they might explain the purpose and uses of surveillance technologies (like LPR) that may arouse privacy concerns.

Finally, there is a need for both police and researchers to make a greater commitment to a strong research and development agenda regarding technology. This is currently lacking, as police often adopt new forms of technology like LPRs and BWCs before their impacts and effectiveness have been demonstrated and understood. Practitioners should review existing research about the uses, consequences, and effectiveness of technologies and also consider conducting their own pilot testing and evaluation of these technologies before making substantial investments in them (e.g., Ohio State Highway Patrol, 2005; Cohen et al., 2007).

A related point is that police managers should do more to systematically track the ways that new technologies are used and the outcomes of those uses. This is particularly applicable to technologies like LPRs, which are typically deployed with no systematic tracking of how they are being used and with what results. In the case of LPRs, managers could track the specific areas in which LPRs have been deployed; how specifically LPRs have been deployed (e.g., fixed or on patrol cars); the number, nature, and results of license plate matches achieved with the LPRs (e.g., vehicles recovered and arrests made); the number and outcomes of investigations for which LPRs or LPR data have been used; and whether crime was reduced in areas where LPRs were deployed. Agencies can then use these results to refine their use of this technology. One could envision similar forms of tracking and evaluation for other technologies like in-car and body cameras and new forensics technologies, to name a few. This would help police to evaluate the benefits of new technologies relative to their costs – an important consideration given the costs of many new technologies and the general fiscal pressures faced by police agencies – and inform their assessments of which technologies are most beneficial.

Researchers can assist practitioners in these endeavors by collaborating on evaluation studies that carefully assess the theories behind technology adoption (i.e., how and why is a particular technology expected to improve police effectiveness), the ways in which technology is used in police agencies, the variety of organizational and community impacts that technology may produce (both intended and unintended), and the cost efficiency of technology. Additionally, research is needed to clarify what organizational strategies – with respect to training, implementation, management, and evaluation – are most effective for achieving desired outcomes with technology and avoiding potentially negative unintended consequences. In all of these ways, greater attention to technology implementation and evaluation can help police agencies optimize technology decisions and fully realize the potential benefits of technology for policing within an evidence-based framework.

REFERENCES

Agrawal, M., Rao, R. H., & Sanders, L. G. (2003). Impact of mobile computing terminals in police work. *Journal of Organizational Computing and Electronic Commerce*, 13(2), 73–89.

Ariel, B., Farrar, W. A., & Sutherland, A. (2015). The effect of police body-worn cameras on use of force and citizens' complaints against the police: A randomized controlled trial. *Journal of Quantitative Criminology*, 31(3), 509–535.

Ariel, B., Sutherland, A. Henstock, D., Young, J., Drover, P., Sykes, J., Megicks, S., & Henderson, R. (2016). Report: Increases in police use of force in the presence of body-worn cameras are driven by officer discretion: A protocol-based subgroup analysis of ten randomized experiments. *Journal of Experimental Criminology*, 12 (3), 453–463.

Boudreau, M.-C., & Robey, D. (2005). Enacting integrated information technology: A human agency perspective. *Organization Science*, 16(1), 3–18.

Braga, A. A., Flynn, E. A., Kelling, G. L., & Cole, C. M. (2011). Moving the work of criminal investigators toward crime control. *New Perspectives in Policing*. Washington, DC: National Institute of Justice.

Brown, M. M. (2001). The benefits and costs of information technology innovations: An empirical assessment of a local government agency. *Public Performance & Management Review*, 24(4), 351–366.

Brown, M. M. (2015). Revisiting the It productivity paradox. *The American Review of Public Administration*, 45(5), 565–583.

Brown, M. M., & Brudney, J. L. (2003). Learning organizations in the public sector? A study of police agencies employing information and technology to advance knowledge. *Public Administration Review*, 63(1), 30–43.

Brynjolfsson, E. (1993). The productivity paradox of information technology. *Communications of the ACM*, 36(12), 67–77.

Brynjolfsson, E., & Witt, L. M. (2000). Beyond computation: Information technology, organizational transformation and business performance. *Journal of Economic Perspectives*, 14(4), 23–48.

Burch, A. M. (2012). *Sheriffs' Offices, 2007 – Statistical Tables*. Washington, DC: Bureau of Justice Statistics.

Byrne, J., & Marx, G. (2011). Technological innovations in crime prevention and policing. A review of the research on implementation and impact. *Journal of Police Studies*, 20(3), 17–40.

Chan, J. (2001). The technological game: How information technology is transforming police practice. *Criminology and Criminal Justice*, 1(2), 139–159.

Chan, J. (2003). Police and new technologies. In T. Newburn (ed.), *Handbook of Policing* (pp. 655–679). Portland: Willan Publishing.

Chan, J., Brereton, D., Legosz, M., & Doran, S. (2001). *E-Policing: The Impact of Information Technology on Police Practices*. Brisbane: Criminal Justice Commission.

Cohen, I. M., Plecas, D., & McCormick, A. V. (2007). *A Report on the Utility of the Automated License Plate Recognition System in British Columbia*. Abbotsford, British Columbia: School of Criminology and Criminal Justice, University College of the Fraser Valley.

Colvin, C. (2001). *Evaluation of innovative technology: implications for the community policing roles of law enforcement officers*. San Francisco: Psychology Department, San Francisco State University.

Cope, N. (2004). Intelligence led policing or policing led intelligence? Integrating volume crime analysis into policing. *British Journal of Criminology*, 44(2), 188–203.

Cordner, G., & Biebel, E. P. (2005). Problem-oriented policing in practice. *Criminology & Public Policy*, 4(2), 155–80.

Danziger, J. N., & Kraemer, K. L. (1985). Computerized data-based systems and productivity among professional workers: The case of detectives. *Public Administration Review* (January/February), 196–209.

Ericson, R. V., & Haggerty, K. D. (1997). *Policing the Risk Society*. Toronto: University of Toronto Press.

Farrar, W. A., & Ariel, B. (2013). *Self-Awareness to Being Watched and Socially-Desirable Behavior: A Field Experiment on the Effect of Body-Worn Cameras on Police Use of Force*. Washington, DC: Police Foundation.

Frank, J., Brandl, S. G., & Watkins, R. C. (1997). The content of community policing: A comparison of the daily activities of community and "beat" officers. *Policing: An International Journal of Police Strategies & Management*, 20(4), 716–728.

Foley, P., & Alfonso, X. (2009). eGovernment and the transformation agenda. *Public Administration*, 87(2), 371–396.

Garg, A. X., Adhikari, N. K. J., McDonald, H., Rosas-Arellano, M. P., Devereaux, P. J., Beyene, J., Sam, J., & Haynes, R. B. (2005). Effects of computerized clinical decision support systems on practitioner performance and patient outcomes: A systematic review. *JAMA*, 293(10), 1223–1238.

Garicano, L., & Heaton, P. (2010). Information technology, organization, and productivity in the public sector: Evidence from police departments. *Journal of Labor Economics*, 28(1), 167–201.

Goodall, M. (2007). *Guidance for the Police Use of Body-Worn Video Devices*. London: Home Office.

Goldfinch, S. (2007). Pessimism, computer failure, and information systems development in the public sector. *Public Administration Review*, 67(5), 917–929.

Goolsbee, A., & Guryan, J. (2006). The impact of internet subsidies in public schools. *The Review of Economics and Statistics*, 88(2), 336–347.

Groff, E. R., & McEwen, T. (2008). *Identifying and Measuring the Effects of Information Technologies on Law Enforcement Agencies*. Washington, DC: Office of Community Oriented Policing Services; Alexandria, VA: Institute for Law and Justice.

Harris, C. J. (2007). The police and soft technology: How information technology contributes to police decision making. In J. M. Byrne, & D. J. Rebovich (eds.), *The New Technology of Crime, Law and Social Control* (pp. 153–183). Monsey, NY: Criminal Justice Press.

Hunt, P., Saunders, J., & Hollywood, J. (2014). *Evaluation of the Shreveport Predictive Policing Experiment*. Santa Monica, CA: RAND Corporation.

Ioimo, R. E., & Aronson, J. E. (2003). The benefits of police field mobile computing realized by non-patrol sections of a police department. *International Journal of Police Science & Management*, 5(3), 195–206.

Ioimo, R. E., & Aronson, J. E. (2004). Police field mobile computing: Applying the theory of task-technology fit. *Police Quarterly*, 7(4), 403–428.

Jaitman, L. (2017). *Evaluating Predictive Policing in Latin America*. Presentation at the Center for Evidence-Based Crime Policy annual symposium. Arlington, Virginia.

Katz, C. M., Choate, D. E., Ready, J. R., & Nuño, L. (2014). *Evaluating the Impact of Officer Worn Body Cameras in the Phoenix Police Department*. Phoenix: Center for Violence Prevention & Community Safety, Arizona State University.

Katz, C. M., Kurtenbach, M., Choate, D. E., & White, M. D. (2015). *Phoenix, Arizona, Smart Policing Initiative: Evaluating the Impact of Police Officer Body-Worn Cameras*. Washington, DC: Bureau of Justice Assistance.

Kennedy, L., Caplan, J., & Piza, E. (2015). *A Multi-Jurisdictional Test of Risk Terrain Modeling and a Place-Based Evaluation of Environmental Risk-Based Patrol Deployment Strategies*. Newark, NJ: Rutgers Center on Public Security, Rutgers University.

Koen, M. (2016). *Technological Frames: Making Sense of Body-Worn Cameras in a Police Organization*. PhD Dissertation, George Mason University.

Koper, C. S., Lum, C., & Hibdon, J. (2015b). The uses and impacts of mobile computing technology in hot spots policing. *Evaluation Review*, 39(6), 587–624.

Koper, C. S., Lum, C., & Willis, J. J. (2014). Optimizing the use of technology in policing: results and implications from a multi-site study of the social, organizational, and behavioral aspects of implementing police technologies. *Policing: A Journal of Policy and Practice*, 8(2), 212–221.

Koper, C. S., Lum, C., Willis, J. J., Happeny, S., Johnson, W. D., Nichols, J., Stoltz, M., Vovak, H., Wu, X., & Nagin, D. (2018). *Evaluating the Crime Control and Cost-Benefit Effectiveness of License Plate Reader Technology*. Report to the National Institute of Justice, US Department of Justice. Fairfax, VA: Center for Evidence-Based Crime Policy, George Mason University.

Koper, C. S., Lum, C., Willis, J. J., Woods, D. J., & Hibdon, J. (2015a). *Realizing the Potential of Technology in Policing: A Multi-Site Study of the Social, Organizational, and Behavioral Aspects of Implementing Policing Technologies.* Report to the National Institute of Justice. Fairfax, VA: Center for Evidence-Based Crime Policy, George Mason University and Police Executive Research Forum.

Koper, C. S., Moore, G. E., & Roth, J. A. (2002). *Putting 100,000 Officers on the Street: A Survey-Based Assessment of the Federal Cops Program.* Washington, DC: The Urban Institute.

Koper, C. S., & Roth, J. A. (2000). Putting 100,000 Officers on the Street: Progress as of 1998 and Preliminary Projections Through 2003. In J. A. Roth, J. F. Ryan et al. (eds.). *National Evaluation of the COPS Program – Title I of the 1994 Crime Act.* Research Report (pp. 149–178). Washington, DC: US Department of Justice.

Koper, C. S., Taylor, B. G., & Kubu, B. E. (2009). *Law Enforcement Technology Needs Assessment: Future Technologies to Address the Operational Needs of Law Enforcement.* Washington, DC: Police Executive Research Forum and the Lockheed Martin Corporation.

Koper, C. S., Taylor, B. G., & Woods, D. J. (2013). A randomized test of initial and residual deterrence from directed patrols and use of license plate readers at crime hot spots. *Journal of Experimental Criminology,* 9(2), 213–244.

Kraemer, K. L., & Danziger, J. N. (1984). Computers and control in the work environment. *Public Administration Review,* 44(1), 32–42.

Lee, G., & Perry, J. L. (2002). Are computers boosting productivity? A test of the paradox in state governments. *Journal of Public Administration Research and Theory,* 12(1), 77–102.

Lehr, B., & Lichtenberg, F. (1999). Information technology and its impact on productivity: Firm-level evidence from government and private data sources, 1977–1993. *Canadian Journal of Economics,* 32(2), 335–362.

Lu, Y. (2003). Getting away with the stolen vehicle: An investigation of journey-after-crime. *The Professional Geographer,* 55(4), 422–433.

Lum, C. (2010). Technology and the Mythology of Progress in American Law Enforcement. Science Progress (Center for American Progress). Feb. 11. Retrieved from www.Scienceprogress.Org/2010/02/Police-Technology/.

Lum, C. (2013). Is crime analysis evidence-based? *Translational Criminology,* (Fall), 12–14.

Lum, C., & Koper, C. S. (2017). *Evidence-Based Policing: Translating Research into Practice.* Oxford, UK: Oxford University Press.

Lum, C., Koper, C. S., Merola, L. M., Scherer, A., & Reioux, A. (2015). *Existing and Ongoing Body Worn Camera Research: Knowledge Gaps and Opportunities.* Report for the Laura and John Arnold Foundation. Fairfax, VA: Center for Evidence-Based Crime Policy, George Mason University.

Lum, C., Koper, C. S., & Willis, J. (2017). Understanding the limits of technology's impact on police effectiveness. *Police Quarterly,* 20(2), 135–163.

Lum, C., Koper, C. S., Willis, J., Happeny, S., Vovak, H., & Nichols, J. (2016c). *The Rapid Diffusion of License Plate Readers in U.S. Law Enforcement Agencies: A National Survey.* Report to the National Institute of Justice, US Department of Justice. Fairfax, VA: Center for Evidence-Based Crime Policy, George Mason University.

Lum, C., Koper, C. S., Willis, J., Happeny, S., Vovak, H., & Nichols, J. (2018). The rapid diffusion of license plate readers in US law enforcement agencies. *Policing:*

An International Journal of Police Strategies and Management, DOI 10.1108/PIJPSM-04-2018-0054.

Lum, C., Merola, L., Willis (Hibdon), J., & Cave, B. (2010). *License Plate Recognition Technology: Impact Evaluation and Community Assessment*. Final Report to SPAWAR and the National Institute of Justice. Fairfax, VA: Center for Evidence-Based Crime Policy, George Mason University.

Lum, C., Stoltz, M., Koper, C. S., & Scherer, J. A. (2019, forthcoming). Research on body worn cameras: What we know, what we need to know. *Criminology and Public Policy*, 18(1).

Lum, C., Wellford, C., Scott, T., & Vovak, H. (2016a). *Trajectories of U.S. Crime Clearance Rates*. Report for the Laura and John Arnold Foundation. Fairfax, VA: Center for Evidence-Based Crime Policy, George Mason University.

Lum, C., Willis (Hibdon), J., Cave, B., Koper, C. S., & Merola, L. (2011). License plate reader (lpr) police patrols in crime hot spots: An experimental evaluation in two adjacent jurisdictions. *Journal of Experimental Criminology*, 7(4), 321–345.

Manning, P. K. (1992). Technological dramas and the police: Statement and counterstatement in organizational analysis. *Criminology*, 30(3), 327–346.

Manning, P. K. (2008). *The Technology of Policing*. New York, NY: NYU Press.

Maryland State Highway Authority. (2005). *Evaluation of the License Plate Recognition System*. Retrieved from the American Association of State Highway and Transportation Officials at Http://Ssom.Transportation.Org/Documents/Lpr_Report_Part3.Pdf

Mastrofski, S. D., & Wadman, R. (1991). Personnel and agency performance measurement. In B. L. Garmire (ed.), *Local Government Police Management* (pp. 363–397). Washington, DC: International City Management Association.

Mastrofski, S. D., & Willis, J. J. (2010). Police organization continuity and change: Into the twenty-first century. *Crime and Justice*, 39(1), 55–144.

Merola, L. M., & C. Lum. (2013). Predicting public support for the use of license plate recognition technology by police. *Police Practice and Research: An International Journal*, DOI: 10.1080/15614263.2013.814906.

Merola, L. M., Lum, C., Cave, B., & Hibdon, J. (2014). Community support for the use of license plate recognition by police. *Policing: An International Journal of Police Strategies and Management*, 37(1), 30–51.

Mazerolle, L., Bennett, S., Manning, M., Davis, J., & Sargeant, E. (2013). Legitimacy in policing: A systematic review. *Campbell Systematic Reviews*, No. 1 (January).

Mazerolle, L., Rogan, D., Frank, J., Famega, C., & Eck, J. E. (2002). Managing citizen calls to the police: The impact of Baltimore's 3-1-1 call system. *Criminology & Public Policy*, 2(1), 97–124.

Milgrom, P., & Roberts, J. (1990). The economics of modern manufacturing: Technology, strategy, and organization. *The American Economic Review*, 80(3), 511–528.

Mohler, G. O., Short, M. B., Malinowski, S., Johnson M., Tita, G E., Bertozzi, A., & Brantingham, P. J. (2015). Randomized controlled field trials of predictive policing. *Journal of the American Statistical Association*, 110 (512), 1399–1411.

National Academies of Sciences, Engineering, and Medicine. (2017). *Proactive Policing: Effects on Crime and Communities*. Washington, DC: The National Academies Press. doi: https: doi.org/10.17226/24928.

Nunn, S. (1994). How capital technologies affect municipal service outcomes: The case of police mobile digital terminals and stolen vehicle recoveries. *Journal of Policy Analysis and Management*, 13(3), 539–559.

Nunn, S., & Quinet, K. (2002). Evaluating the effects of information technology on problem-oriented-policing: If it doesn't fit, must we quit? *Evaluation Review*, 26(1), 81–108.

ODS Consulting. (2011). *Body Worn Video Projects in Paisley and Aberdeen, Self Evaluation*. Glasgow: ODS Consulting.

Ohio State Highway Patrol. (2005). *Automatic Plate Reader Technology*. Ohio Planning Services Section, Research and Development Unit.

Orlikowski, W. J. (1992). The duality of technology: Rethinking the concept of technology in organizations. *Organization Science*, 3(3), 398–427.

Orlikowski, W. J., & Gash, D. C. (1994). Technological frames: Making sense of information technology in organizations. *ACM Transactions on Information Systems (TOIS)*, 12(2), 174–207.

O'Shea, T., & Nicholls, K. (2003). Police crime analysis: A survey of US police departments with 100 or more sworn personnel. *Police Practice and Research*, 4(3), 233–250.

Owens, C., Mann, D., & Mckenna, R. (2014). *The Essex BWV Trial: The Impact of BWV on Criminal Justice Outcomes of Domestic Abuse Incidents*. London, United Kingdom: College of Policing.

Pa Consulting Group. (2003). *Engaging Criminality – Denying Criminals Use of the Roads*. London: Author.

Palys, T. S., Boyanowsky, E. O., & Dutton, D. G. (1984). Mobile data access terminals and their implications for policing. *Journal of Social Issues*, 40(3), 113–127.

Patch, D. (2005). *License Plate Scanners Lead to Recovery of Stolen Vehicles*. Toledoblade.Com. Retrieved January 11, 2007, from Http://Toledoblade.Com/Apps/Pbcs.Dll/Article?Aid=/20050105/News11/501050412.

Paulsen, D. J. (2004). To map or not to map: Assessing the impact of crime maps on police officer perceptions of crime. *International Journal of Police Science & Management*, 6(4), 234–246.

Ready, J. T., & Young, J. T. (2015). The impact of on-officer video cameras on police-citizen contacts: Findings from a controlled experiment in Mesa, AZ. *Journal of Experimental Criminology*, 11(3), 445–458.

Reaves, B. A. (2010). *Local Police Departments, 2007*. Washington, DC: Bureau of Justice Statistics.

Robey, D., Boudreau, M.-C., & Rose, G. M. (2000). Information technology and organizational learning: A review and assessment of research. *Accounting, Management and Information Technologies*, 10(2), 125–155.

Roberts, D. J., & Casanova, M. (2012). *Automated License Plate Recognition (ALPR) Systems: Policy and Operational Guidance for Law Enforcement*. Alexandria, VA: International Association of Chiefs of Police.

Rocheleau, B. (1993). Evaluating public sector information systems: Satisfaction versus impact. *Evaluation and Program Planning*, 16(2), 119–129.

Roman, J. K., Reid, S., Reid, J., Chalfin, A., Adams, W., & Knight, C. (2008). *The DNA Field Experiment: Cost-Effectiveness Analysis of the Use of DNA in the Investigation of High-Volume Crimes*. Washington, DC: The Urban Institute.

Roth, J. A., Ryan, J. F., Gaffigan, S. J., Koper, C. S., Moore, M. H., Roehl, J. A., Johnson, C. C. et al. (2000). *National Evaluation of the Cops Program Title I of the 1994 Crime Act.* Washington, DC: National Institute of Justice.

Sanders, C. B., & Henderson, S. (2013). Police "empires" and information technologies: Uncovering material and organisational barriers to information sharing in Canadian police services. *Policing and Society,* 23(2), 243–260.

Sanders, C. B., Weston, C., & Schott, N. (2015). Police innovations, "secret squirrels" and accountability: Empirically studying intelligence-led policing in Canada. *British Journal of Criminology,* 55(4), 711–729.

Santos, R. Boba. (2014). The effectiveness of crime analysis for crime reduction: Cure or diagnosis? *Journal of Contemporary Criminal Justice,* 30(2), 147–168.

Sherman, L, W., & Eck, J. E. (2002). Policing for crime prevention. In L. W. Sherman, D. P. Farrington, B. C. Welsh, & D. L. MacKenzie, *Evidence-Based Crime Prevention* (pp. 295–329). London, UK: Routledge.

Sparrow, M. K., Moore, M. H., & Kennedy, D. M. (1990). *Beyond 9-1-1: A New Era for Policing.* New York: Basic Books.

Stiroh, K. J. (2002). Information technology and the US productivity revival: What do the industry data say? *The American Economic Review,* 92(5), 1559–1576.

Taylor, B., & Boba, R. (2011: updated in 2013). *The Integration of Crime Analysis into Patrol Work: A Guidebook.* Washington, DC: Office of Community Oriented Policing Services.

Taylor, B., Koper, C. S., & Woods, D. (2011a). A randomized controlled trial of different policing strategies at hot spots of violent crime. *Journal of Experimental Criminology,* 7(2), 149–181.

Taylor, B., Koper, C. S., & Woods, D. (2011b). *Combating Auto Theft in Arizona: A Randomized Experiment with License Plate Recognition Technology.* Final Report to the National Institute of Justice, US Department of Justice. Washington, DC: Police Executive Research Forum.

Taylor, B., Koper, C. S., & Woods, D. (2012). Combating vehicle theft in arizona: A randomized experiment with license plate recognition technology. *Criminal Justice Review,* 37(1), 24–50.

Triplett, J. E. (1999). The Solow productivity paradox: What do computers do to productivity? *Canadian Journal of Economics,* 32(2), 309–334.

Vovak, H. (2016). *Examining the Relationship between Crime Rates and Clearance Rates Using Dual Trajectory Analysis.* PhD Dissertation, George Mason University.

Zaworski, M. J. (2004). *Assessing an Automated, Information Sharing Technology in the Post "9-11" Era – Do Local Law Enforcement Officers Think It Meets Their Needs?* PhD Dissertation, Florida International University.

Conclusion

Police Innovation and the Future of Policing

Anthony A. Braga and David Weisburd

In this volume, a group of leading scholars presented contrasting perspectives on eleven major innovations in American policing developed over the course of the last three decades. Police departments needed to improve their performance and relationships with the community and innovation provided the opportunity to make these improvements. These innovations represent fundamental changes to the business of policing. However, as many of our authors point out, improving police performance through innovation is often not straightforward. Police departments are highly resistant to change and police officers often experience difficulty in implementing new programs (Sparrow, Moore, & Kennedy, 1990; Bayley & Nixon, 2010; Maguire, 2014; Lum & Koper, 2017). The available evidence on key dimensions of police performance associated with these innovations, such as crime control effectiveness and community satisfaction with services provided, is sometimes limited. These observations are not unique to the policing field. For example, as Elmore (1997) suggests, the field of education was awash in innovation during the 1990s, but there is little evidence examining whether those innovations advanced the performance of schools, students, or graduates.

While our knowledge about the effects of these innovations on police performance is still developing, we think there is reason for optimism about the future of policing. This period of innovation has demonstrated that police can prevent crime and can improve their relationships with the communities they serve. In this concluding chapter, we begin by categorizing the directions of police innovation. We then summarize how these innovations have affected crime and communities, and discuss challenges to their implementation in police agencies. Finally, in concluding, we turn to challenges that have emerged for policing in the new century, and how they have impacted and will continue to impact the direction of innovation in policing.

CATEGORIZING RECENT POLICE INNOVATIONS

Moore, Sparrow, and Spelman (1997) suggest four distinct categories of police innovation: programmatic, administrative, technological, and strategic. These categories are not clearly separated from each other and, as Moore and his colleagues admit (1997), assigning any one innovation to one category over another is often a judgment call. Programmatic innovations establish new operational methods of using the resources of an organization to achieve particular results. These programs can include arresting fences as a way to discourage burglary, using police officers to provide drug education in schools, and offering victim-resistance training to women. Administrative innovations are changes in how police organizations prepare themselves to conduct operations or account for their achievements. These include new ways of measuring the performance of an individual officer or the overall department, as well as changes in personnel policies and practices such as new recruiting techniques, new training approaches, and new supervisory relations. Technological innovations depend on the acquisition or use of some new piece of capital equipment such as non-lethal weapons, DNA typing, or crime-mapping software.

Strategic innovations represent a fundamental change in the overall philosophy and orientation of the organization (Moore, Sparrow & Spelman, 1997). These changes involve important redefinitions of the primary objectives of policing, the range of services and activities supplied by police departments, the means through which police officers achieve their goals, and the key internal and external relationships that are developed and maintained by the police. Strategic innovations include shifting from "law enforcement" to "problem solving" as a means of resolving incidents, forming working relationships with community groups as a tactic in dealing with drug markets, and recognizing citizen satisfaction as an important performance measure. These innovations are strategic because they involve changing some of the basic understandings about the ends or means of policing or the key structures of accountability that shaped overall police efforts under the standard model of policing (Moore, Sparrow & Spelman, 1997). We think that the innovations described in this volume represent related attempts to change the ends and means of policing, and therefore, should be regarded as strategic innovations. However, it is important to note that a few of these reforms, most significantly CompStat and evidence-based policing, are organizational reforms that seek to advance strategic innovations. We reviewed technological innovations in Section XI, though the approach of our advocate and critic was to consider the more general influences of technology on evidence-based practices and advancing the strategic goals of policing.

Weisburd and Eck (2004) suggest that recent strategic innovations expand policing beyond standard practices along two dimensions: *diversity of approaches* and *level of focus* (see Figure C.1). The "diversity of approaches"

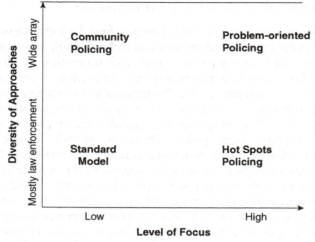

FIGURE C.1 Dimensions of Policing Strategies
Source: Adapted from Weisburd and Eck, 2004

dimension represents the content of the practices employed or tools used by the police. As represented by the vertical axis, tools can range from mostly traditional law enforcement to a wide array of alternative approaches. The horizontal axis represents the extent to which police practices are focused or targeted. Weisburd and Eck (2004) contrast standard police practices with hot spots policing, problem-oriented policing, and community policing. The standard model of policing, with its emphasis on enforcing the law and its generalized application of law enforcement powers, scores low on both dimensions. Hot spots policing (carried out simply as standard increases in patrol) scores high on focus, but low on the diversity of tools used to control hot spot locations. Problem-oriented policing rates high on diversity of tools and focus as the approach challenges police officers to implement strategies designed to deal with the underlying conditions that give rise to discrete crime problems. Community policing, where police draw on a wider array of resources to prevent crime and engage the community in defining and dealing with problems, scores high on diversity of approaches. However, when implemented without problem-oriented policing, the approach is not well focused on crime problems and provides a common set of services throughout a jurisdiction.

Another dimension that could be added to Weisburd and Eck's (2004) classification of police practices is the degree to which the innovations change the goals of policing. Under the standard model, police departments were mostly focused on preventing serious crime by deterring and apprehending criminal offenders, serving justice by holding offenders accountable for their crimes, rendering immediate aid to people in crisis, and providing non-emergency services such as controlling traffic (Eck & Rosenbaum, 1994). While the eleven innovations described in this book do not remove any of these goals from the tasks of policing, the new strategies rearrange the priorities among the goals and add new ones.

Non-criminal and non-emergency quality-of-life problems receive much more attention from the new police strategies. Community and problem-oriented policing, and procedural justice policing represent the most radical departures from standard police work. Community policing, in its various manifestations, challenges police officers to work with citizens to deal with a broader range of concerns, most notably fear of crime and social and physical disorder (Skogan, Chapter 1 in this volume). Procedural justice policing does not seek directly to affect crime outcomes, but looks instead to affect citizens' evaluations of the legitimacy of the police (Tyler & Meares, Chapter 3 in this volume). Problem-oriented policing also adds new goals to policing. It can focus on crimes, or disorder, or other problems that are concerns of the public. But more central to problem-oriented policing is that it reorganizes police actions from focusing on incidents as units of work to focusing on classes of problems to be addressed by responses that can be quite different from routine police activities (Eck, Chapter 7 in this volume). Other innovations represent less dramatic changes to standard police goals. For example, broken windows policing, if engaged without community and problem-oriented policing, expands the police mandate to include social and physical disorder but does not radically change the tactics engaged by the police to deal with these problems (Sousa & Kelling, Chapter 5 in this volume; Taylor, Chapter 6 in this volume).

CRIME AND DISORDER CONTROL EFFECTIVENESS

How do these new directions in policing impact upon crime and disorder? A recent National Academies of Sciences committee on proactive policing allows us to consider this question in the context of eight of the eleven police innovations that we review in this volume (Weisburd & Majmundar, 2018).[1] In Table C.1, we summarize the overall findings of the panel concerning the extent of focus of innovations and the expansion of the tools of policing beyond traditional law enforcement. What we learn reinforces the conclusions that Weisburd and Eck (2004; see also Skogan & Frydl, 2004) reached more than a decade ago, though now there are many more studies that inform our understanding of these questions.

The innovations that emphasize focus as the key element of reform are most likely to evidence crime prevention benefits. Hot spots policing, for example, first proposed by Sherman and Weisburd (1995), has now been found to have strong crime prevention benefits across a large number of studies (see Weisburd

---

[1] Both of us were members of the NAS panel, and Weisburd chaired the committee.

TABLE C.1 *Crime Outcomes of Police Innovations*[2]

Innovation	Primary Type of Innovation	Do Studies Show Crime Prevention Benefits	Strength of the Evidence
Hot Spots Policing	Increase in focus	Yes	A large number of strong experimental and quasi-experimental studies
Predictive Policing	Increase in focus	No	Evidence base is small
Focused Deterrence	Increase in focus and expansion of tools	Yes	A number of strong quasi-experimental studies
Third-Party Policing	Increase in focus and expansion of tools	Yes	A small number of strong experimental and quasi-experimental studies
Problem-Oriented Policing	Increase in focus and expansion of tools	Yes	A small number of strong experimental and quasi-experimental studies
Broken Windows Policing – Type I ("zero tolerance" unfocused)	Neither an increase in focus nor expansion of tools	No	A small number of rigorous studies.
Windows – Type II (focused disorder policing)	Increase in focus	Yes	A small number of strong experimental and quasi-experimental studies
Community Policing	Expansion of tools	No	A number of strong quasi-experimental and fewer experimental studies
Procedural Justice Policing	Expansion of tools	No	A small number of rigorous studies showing mixed outcomes

---

[2] We draw from the NAS Proactive Policing Report (Weisburd & Majmundar, 2018) for Outcomes, except as noted in the table.

TABLE C.1 *(continued)*

Innovation	Primary Type of Innovation	Do Studies Show Crime Prevention Benefits	Strength of the Evidence
INNOVATIONS NOT REVIEWED BY THE NAS COMMITTEE			
CompStat	Organizational reform	No	Outcomes of studies are mixed; A small number of observational studies
Evidence-Based Policing	Organizational reform	No	Absence of empirical studies to date

We do not summarize the evidence on Technology Policing because of the diversity of approaches included in this category (see note 3).

& Braga, Chapter 13 in this volume). Many of these studies are randomized field experiments, and accordingly allow us to draw strong causal conclusions about the effectiveness of hot spots policing. In turn, the evidence base suggests that focusing in on hot spots does not just move crime "around the corner" (see Weisburd et al., 2004). Indeed, the evidence to date suggests that hot spots policing is more likely to lead to a "diffusion of crime control benefits" to areas nearby, than displacement of crime. We do not have enough studies of predictive policing to add to the hot spots findings more generally.

When police innovations focus on high-risk people, they are also likely to yield crime prevention benefits. The strongest example of this is found in the case of "focused deterrence policing." Focusing on very high-rate violent offenders has been found to be a strong approach for crime prevention. While there are no randomized field trials in this area, the National Academies of Sciences committee concluded that the quasi-experimental studies were persuasive, and that focused deterrence policing has strong impacts on crime.

It does not appear to be the case that innovations that simply expand the toolbox of policing lead to crime prevention benefits. For example, community policing has not been found to be effective on its own in producing prevention outcomes. Indeed, the NAS committee concluded that departments that seek to focus on crime control should not see community policing as a direct method of doing this. The same is true of procedural justice policing. We do not have evidence yet that it will produce short-term or long-term crime prevention gains. This is an important conclusion given the strong support for programs that promise to increase popular legitimacy and through such changes reduce crime (President's Task Force on 21st Century Policing, 2015). While we need more study of these questions, we think at this juncture it is reasonable to conclude that community policing and procedural justice policing on their own are not proven crime prevention approaches.

One key reason for this may be an issue we raised earlier. Some of these innovations do not necessarily focus directly on crime. As Skogan (Chapter 1 in this volume) notes, community policing was not developed originally as a crime prevention approach. Rather, it was seen as way of redirecting the goals of policing. Community policing, in and of itself, developed as an innovation that would strengthen the ties between the police and the public. It is perhaps not surprising that when programs focus primarily on that goal, they are not robust in producing prevention gains. At the same time, as we note below, they lead to positive community outcomes. Similarly, procedural justice policing was meant to increase police legitimacy in the community. Crime control is claimed by advocates of this innovation as a long-term outcome, but again the fact that it may not have short-term crime prevention outcomes is consistent with its primary goals.

In this context, expanding the diversity of the tools of policing to prevent crime has been found to be effective. Problem oriented policing, which is often focused on specific places where crime occurs but expands the toolbox of policing, was found to have consistent crime prevention outcomes, though the number of rigorous studies available is still small. Similarly, though again based on a small number of studies, third-party policing, which also relies on the problem-solving model, is noted as effective by the NAS committee. Moreover, the evidence here supports Weisburd and Eck's (2004) original proposition that a combination of focus and expansion of the tools of policing will lead to the strongest crime prevention benefits. In Braga and colleagues' (2014) meta-analysis on hot spots policing, they found that hot spots policing programs that utilized problem solving produced much larger crime prevention gains than those that did not. Similarly, the effects of focused deterrence programs, which utilize both focus and a "pulling levers" approach, increasing the diversity of tools of policing beyond traditional law enforcement, shows perhaps the strongest crime prevention impacts of any innovation we examine in this volume. Though some caution should be exercised in drawing this conclusion given the absence of randomized experiments (and prior studies that show that quasi-experimental designs tend to produce stronger outcomes than experimental evaluations, see Weisburd, Lum & Petrosino, 2001), the trend of the evidence supports the original proposal of Weisburd and Eck.

The evidence on broken windows policing supports our more general explanation as well. As we noted earlier, broken windows policing often relies on traditional law enforcement tools, such as crackdowns or arrests. When applied with focus at specific places, it has strong prevention outcomes. Unfocused, it does not lead to crime control benefits. Accordingly, though broken windows policing seeks to change the community in the long run, its short-term tactics reinforce the place focus conclusions we have noted.

Turning to innovations not reviewed by the NAS committee, our advocates and critics agree that evaluation studies do not allow us to draw conclusions about the crime prevention effectiveness of CompStat or evidence-based policing.[3] Weisburd et al. (Chapter 18 in this volume) note that the evidence for CompStat is mixed. However, more importantly, they argue that CompStat is an organizational reform that seek to support strategic objectives. The question should not be whether CompStat is effective, but rather whether CompStat is effective in leading to more successful implementation of other innovations in crime prevention. Evidence-based policing follows a similar approach to reform (see Welsh, Chapter 19 in this volume). It is not about the introduction of a specific strategy but rather about organizational reform that would advance the use of evidence in developing and implementing police practices. The truth is that we know little about whether evidence based policing is effective as an organizational strategy. There is much reason for supporting evidence based policing, especially given the evidence base on innovation that we review in this volume (see also Lum and Koper, 2017). However, as Lum and Koper observe, researchers are going to have to develop a more "practice oriented" criminology if they are going to help make evidence based policing a reality. Researchers have focused on specific innovations; they have seldom considered in detail how police agencies must change to successfully implement evidence based policing as an institutional reform. Similarly, we do not have solid knowledge about CompStat because scholars have often failed to recognize that it is not a specific strategic approach, but rather an approach to implementing innovation in policing. We know too little about organizational reforms that seek to advance strategic innovations in policing. It is certainly time to invest in this type of research.

While recognizing these gaps, we think the overall evidence on recent innovations in policing leads to an optimistic sense of what the police can do to prevent crime. The assumptions prevalent in the 1990s that the police could not prevent crime (Gottfredson and Hirschi, 1990; Bayley, 1994) are simply wrong. There is much the police can do to successfully prevent crime. Not every innovation has shown prevention success, but a series of strategies have. In this sense, a number of the innovations that developed at the end of the last century as a reaction to the crisis of police legitimacy, at least in terms of crime control, have fulfilled, to a great degree, the promise of their originators.

COMMUNITY REACTION TO INNOVATIVE POLICE STRATEGIES

In addition to concerns over the crime control effectiveness of the standard model of policing, police innovation in the 1980s and 1990s was also driven by

---

[3] We do not review the crime control outcomes of what we term "technology policing" in Section XI because the approaches differ widely, as do the outcomes. We do not think this area of innovation is consistent enough to review under a single heading.

TABLE C.2 *Effects of Police Innovation on Communities*[4]

Police Innovation	Is it Primarily Focused on Crime Control?	Does it Have Positive Community Outcomes?	Does it Have Negative Community Outcomes?	What is the Strength of the Evidence?
Hot Spots Policing	Yes	No	No	A small number of rigorous studies
Predictive Policing	Yes	—	—	No studies
Focused Deterrence	Yes	—	—	No studies
Third-Party Policing	Yes	—	—	Little information on community outcomes
Problem-Oriented Policing	Yes	Yes	No	A small number of rigorous studies
Broken Windows Policing	Yes	No	SQFs and similar aggressive tactics have been found to lead to negative outcomes for individuals	A small number of rigorous studies
Community Policing	No	Yes	No	A number of strong quasi-experimental and a few experimental studies
Procedural Justice Policing	No	No	No	A limited number of studies available to date

INNOVATIONS REVIEWED BY THE NAS COMMITTEE

CompStat	Yes	–	–	No rigorous studies
Evidence-Based Policing	Yes	–	–	No rigorous studies

We do not summarize the evidence on Technology Policing because of the diversity of approaches included.

[4] Based on NAS Committee Report.

high levels of community dissatisfaction with police services and a growing recognition that citizens had other concerns that required police action, such as fear of crime. Again, we rely on the recent National Academies of Sciences committee report (Weisburd & Majmundar, 2018) on proactive policing to assess the impacts of police innovations on communities (see Table C.2).

Since citizen involvement in policing is a core element of community policing programs (Skogan, Chapter 1 in this volume), it is not surprising that we know most about citizen reaction to these types of programs. The findings of the NAS report suggest that community policing, which began as an innovation to improve relationships between the police and the public, can do so (see Table C.2). Community policing strategies that entail direct involvement of citizens and police, such as police community stations, citizen contract patrol, and coordinated community policing improve citizen attitudes toward the police. In turn, they also have been found to reduce fear of crime among individuals and decrease individual concern about crime in neighborhoods (Pate & Skogan, 1985; Wycoff & Skogan, 1986; Brown & Wycoff, 1986). Interestingly, the evidence base is mixed on whether community policing increases cooperation between the police and the public. This is important because it may, in some sense, explain the lack of crime prevention outcomes for community policing programs that are implemented primarily to engage the public and improve police–citizen relationships. The mechanism for crime control in these cases would seem to rely on increased citizen involvement in reporting crime to the police, and cooperation with the police in responding to crime. These elements, which would support crime control, have not been found to be a clear outcome of community policing programs.

While community policing has been found to impact positively on communities, other strategies that have looked to impact on communities have not been shown to be effective. Advocates of procedural justice policing argue that this approach will change the way citizens view the police, and that police behavior toward citizens that they have contact with will affect the broader community's evaluations of the police (Tyler & Meares, Chapter 3 in this volume). This is an important hypothesis to examine, but one that has not been confirmed in research to date. Some studies do suggest that treating citizens in procedurally just ways will lead to more positive evaluations of police legitimacy among those who have contact with the police (Mazerolle et al., 2013; Sahin et al., 2017), but others do not (e.g., see MacQueen & Bradford, 2015). The National Academies of Sciences committee argued that research in other fields like the courts, does suggest that procedurally just policing will lead to higher evaluations of police legitimacy. Despite the support this approach has gained (e.g., see President's Task Force on 21st Century Policing, 2015), there is not a strong evidence base in policing to date supporting such impacts.

And indeed, there are reasons to believe that procedural justice, while a positive goal for policing in itself, may not very strongly affect attitudes in minority and disadvantaged communities. Some scholars have argued recently that this perspective fails to recognize the historical and social context of policing in the United States (e.g., see Nagin & Telep, 2017). More than a decade ago, Jerome Skolnick (2007: 65) encouraged researchers to situate discussions of modern policing within the broader sociohistorical context of US race relations, reminding us that policing in the Jim Crow South often functioned as a form of racialized social control, designed to keep "the Negro in his place." The recent National Academies of Sciences report on proactive policing notes in this regard:

In sum, while there have been important changes in the scope for racial bias and animus in policing, with respect to the impact of proactive policing on racial bias and disparate outcomes, law enforcement in the United States does not start with a clean slate. As noted by Chief Terrence M. Cunningham in his presidential address to the International Association of Chiefs of Police, "this dark side of our shared history has created a generational – almost inherited – mistrust between many non-White communities and the law enforcement agencies that serve them." (Weisburd & Majmundar, 2018: 271)

Perceptions of the police may be rooted in broader perspectives of the law, justice, and historical treatment that are rarely captured and measured in research on attitudes of the police. Nagin and Telep (2017: 13) argue that "evidence of exogenous manipulations affecting citizens' perceptions and behavior is in short supply" and research has failed to examine the broader social context of people's lives and how this shapes perceptions.

Broken windows policing has also failed to produce the kind of changes in communities that its originators suggested. The broken windows policing model relies on a developmental sequence that begins with police responding to disorder, but leads in the long run to lower levels of fear in the community and heightened collective efficacy. These changes in the community, which enhance informal social controls, are expected to reduce crime more generally. However, there is simply little evidence that broken windows policing reduces fear of crime, and even less that it increases collective efficacy (see Weisburd et al., 2015).

Most of the effective crime control strategies that are identified by the National Academies of Sciences committee have little impact on community attitudes (see Table C.2). Hot spots policing for example, has not been found to lead to negative community reactions. This in itself is important, because of a growing narrative among scholars and the public that these types of effective policing approaches lead to negative outcomes in the community (e.g., see Rosenbaum, Chapter 14 in this volume). At the same time, it is noteworthy that most of these strategies effective in terms of crime control show little evidence of improving citizen attitudes toward the police, or improving cooperation with the police. This is true in the case of hot spots policing, third-party policing, and focused deterrence policing, all of which have robust impacts upon crime. If police leaders look to effective crime control to enhance evaluations of the police, the evidence does not support this approach.

At the same time, the case of problem-oriented policing suggests that police may gain the most benefits both in terms of crime and in terms of improving their standing in the community by combining community policing with innovations that have shown strong crime prevention benefits. The NAS committee noted, "(s)tudies show consistent small-to-moderate, positive impacts of problem-solving interventions on short-term community satisfaction with the police." This dual impact seems to be due to the strong reliance of problem-oriented policing on collaborative community problem solving. This, of course, is a key element of community policing. We believe that there is much promise in combining community-based approaches with focused crime prevention approaches. This should be a key part of police innovation over the next decade.

POLICE REACTION TO INNOVATIVE STRATEGIES

The eleven innovations differed in their degree of departure from the standard model of policing. The police most easily adopt innovations that require the least radical departures from their hierarchical paramilitary organizational structures, continue incident-driven and reactive strategies, and maintain police sovereignty over crime issues. This is certainly the case for many of the innovations in technology that are reviewed in Part XI of this book. At the same time, both Koper and Lum (Chapter 22 in this volume) and Ariel (Chapter 21 in this volume) emphasize the importance of changing aspects of police organization and culture if technology is to advance the goals of police agencies. Indeed, they argue that the successful use of technological innovations to improve policing is often hampered by traditional structures of police organization.

In its most basic form, hot spots policing simply concentrates traditional enforcement activity at high crime places. The familiarity of the approach is straightforward to police as they have a long history of temporarily heightening enforcement levels in problem areas. While law enforcement tools are deployed in a new way, the pulling levers, focused deterrence strategy targets existing criminal justice activities on groups of chronic offenders. Broken windows policing involves making arrests of minor offenders to control disorder and, as an end product, reduce more-serious crime. As Kennedy (Chapter 9 in this volume) observes, "law enforcement likes enforcing the law." Strategies such as hot spots policing, broken windows, and pulling levers policing appeal to law enforcement practitioners primarily because they allow mostly traditional tactics to be deployed in new ways with the promise of considerably greater results.

While all major American police agencies report some form of community policing as an important component of their operations (see Skogan, Chapter 1 in this volume), the police have been generally resistant to its adoption. This is not surprising since community policing involves the most radical change to existing police organizations. Skogan (Chapter 1 in this volume) and Mastrofski (Chapter 2 in this volume) report many shortcomings in the practical application of its three core elements: citizen involvement, problem-solving, and decentralization. Citizens are generally used as information sources rather than engaged as partners in producing public safety. Officers prefer law enforcement strategies to developing and implementing alternative problem-oriented responses. Most "community-oriented" police agencies have not made the organizational changes necessary to decentralize decision-making authority to the neighborhood level. Similarly, the available research on problem-oriented policing suggests that police officers experience difficulty during all stages of the problem-oriented process (Braga & Weisburd, Chapter 8 in this volume). Problem analysis is generally weak and implemented responses largely consist of traditional enforcement activities. Problem-oriented policing as practiced in the field is but a shallow version of the process recommended by Herman Goldstein (1990). Given its close relationship to problem-oriented policing, it seems likely that police departments engaging third-party policing will encounter similar practical problems.

It is not remarkable that the strategies that require the most radical changes to existing police practices and structures report the greatest difficulties in implementation. Nonetheless, the available evidence indicates a gradual transformation in police attitudes toward adopting these new strategies. In addition to the widespread reporting of innovative police practices across the United States, police officers' views toward the community and problem-oriented policing philosophy are becoming more positive. As summarized by Skogan (Chapter 1 in this volume), studies point to positive changes in officers' views once they are involved in community policing, positive findings with respect to job satisfaction and views of the community, and growing support for community policing in districts that engage the strategy compared to districts that maintain traditional activities. Police history shows that it takes a long time for new models of policing to develop fully. The standard model of policing was itself a reform in reaction to corrupt and brutal police practices during the so-called "political era" of policing (Walker, 1992). Initially, the reform movement progressed very slowly; in 1920, only a few departments could be labeled "professional" or engaging in the basic tenets of the standard model. It was not until the 1950s that virtually all American police departments were organized around the principles set forth by O. W. Wilson, August Vollmer, and other reformers (Walker, 1992).

We think that it is particularly important for police scholars and practitioners to focus more attention on how the police can implement evidence-based approaches. Lawrence Sherman and colleagues make this point directly, in a critique of research on hot spots policing. They argue that "(d)espite a flourishing body of research (if not formal theory) on the effects of hot spots policing (Braga et al., 2012), there is neither theory nor evidence on what actions police leaders should take to create and maintain the causes of a successful hot spots patrol strategy" (Sherman et al., 2014: 95; see also Weisburd et al., 2015). Police scholars have paid too little attention to the organization structures that would facilitate or inhibit strategic innovations in policing.

Weisburd et al. (Chapter 18 in this volume) describe CompStat as precisely this type of innovation in policing. It was developed more to facilitate specific types of strategic innovations in policing, and particularly problem-solving approaches, than as a specific strategic approach. However, research suggests that CompStat may hinder rather than facilitate problem-solving because of its reinforcement of the traditional standard hierarchical structure of policing. Weisburd et al. argue that more research is needed to understand how CompStat may facilitate or hinder other strategic innovations in policing. Evidence based policing should also be seen in this context. As Lum and Koper (2017) have argued, there is need to work not simply on what evidence-based policies are, but the processes and practices that will make it possible for them to be successfully implemented in policing.

THE FUTURE OF POLICING

What will the future bring? Will the police continue to innovate at a rapid pace? When we published our first edition of this volume in 2006, we argued that we did not expect a new wave of strategic police innovation in the near future. The context of policing at that time suggested that future innovation would be incremental in nature. The conditions in the 1980s and 1990s that created the pressure for innovation simply no longer exist. Indeed, the atmosphere was precisely the opposite of earlier decades. Crime was down and federal funds available for demonstration projects to spur innovation were limited. While the available research evidence was not as strong as some police executives believed, there was a general sense that these police innovations worked in preventing crime and satisfying community concerns.

This perspective on the crime control effectiveness of new police practices was reinforced by the research reviewed in this volume, and by a cursory examination of crime trends at that time and more recently (see Figure C.2). The Federal Bureau of Investigation's Uniform Crime Reports showed declining crime trends from the early 1990s through the new century. And in this regard, the crime statistics continued to point to strong declines through 2016. The crisis of rising crime rates is no longer a reality of American life. Indeed, some scholars have argued that crime control is simply not a central problem for the police as we approach the end of the second decade of the twenty-first century (Tyler, Jackson & Mentovich, 2015).

While no single factor, including innovative policing, can be invoked as the cause of the crime decline of the 1990s (Blumstein & Wallman, 2000), the "nothing works" view of policing in the 1970s and 1980s described in our introduction is no longer a topic of discussion in most policing circles. Indeed,

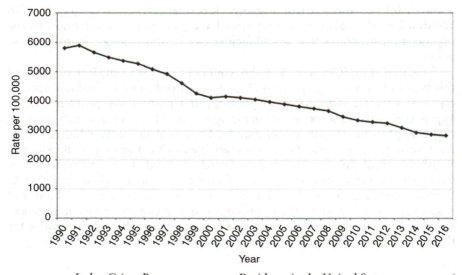

FIGURE C.2 Index Crime Rates per 100,000 Residents in the United States, 1990–2016
Source: Federal Bureau of Investigation, Uniform Crime Reports (accessed January 24, 2018)

the recent National Academies of Sciences committee report on proactive policing reinforces what police have been saying. Police innovation over the last three decades has led to the development of effective evidence-based crime control strategies (Weisburd & Majmundar, 2018).

In concluding our first edition, we noted the challenges of homeland security concerns that emerged after 9/11. We argued that American police departments would be challenged to maintain their current trajectory by the new set of homeland security demands created in the wake of the 9/11 tragedy. In many ways, this was a new crisis for police departments, as their goals were further expanded by a new focus on preventing future terrorist attacks and dealing with potentially catastrophic events. We questioned whether this new set of demands, with its emphasis on collecting intelligence on terrorist networks, apprehending terror operatives, and protecting likely targets, might push policing back to a more professional model that is distant from the community. Or whether this crisis would create a new source for innovation as police departments would strive to continue their recent success in dealing with crime and community concerns.

It is certainly true that the new set of demands on policing put pressure on the ability of police agencies to innovate or even to sustain innovative practices (Chappell & Gibson, 2009). The financial crisis of 2007 and 2008, and the slow recovery of the American economy over the last decade, created additional challenges for police agencies. Not only were the police expected to deal with a new set of security concerns, but they also faced decreasing budgets at the same time. As a result, many police agencies cut special units and innovative new programs. But at the same time, it led to a recognition that the police must carefully choose crime control policies, and consider not only effectiveness but the efficiency of their choices. This led, to some extent, to the reinforcement of using evidence to make decisions about the allocation of police resources (Neyroud & Weisburd, 2014), and in turn strengthened the relevance of innovation and testing in policing (Sherman, 2013).

We do not think that the rush to respond to homeland security concerns had very strong impact on the development and implementation of new innovations in police agencies. Exceptions to this can be found. For example, the development of "intelligence led policing" appeared to be spurred by homeland security concerns, as was the appearance of fusion centers across the United States, supported by the federal government to allow integration of data across police agencies (see McGarrell, Frielich & Chermak, 2007; Ratcliffe, 2016). However, most American cities were not directly impacted by large-scale security threats. Outside major population centers such as New York or Los Angeles, terrorism was not a major concern. Although there have been isolated incidents in smaller cities over time, the job of policing in the United States has, for the most part, continued to be focused on local crime problems.

While the need to be responsive to homeland security concerns has not impacted innovation in American policing to the extent that might have been predicted a decade ago, a new set of concerns has emerged onto the American police scene that is reminiscent of the crisis of confidence of the 1970s and 1980s in policing that led to much of the police innovation described in this volume. Recent events involving police shootings or perceived police misbehavior, especially involving minority communities, and subsequent riots and disorder in a number of American cities, have led national police leaders and scholars to be concerned about the issue of public trust. An example of that effort is the recent report of the President's Task Force on 21st Century Policing (2015), which made perceived legitimacy a core theme in its discussion of policing. The report noted that recent events "have exposed rifts in the relationships between the local police and the communities they protect and serve" (2015: 1). The emergence of procedural justice policing, which seeks to improve perceptions of police legitimacy is a direct response to this set of concerns.

Some police scholars have begun to argue that public trust in the police rather than crime control should be the central concern of police innovation over the next decade (Tyler, Jackson & Mentovich, 2015; Tyler, 2017). Tyler, Jackson and Mentovich wrote in 2015:

We argue that these changing goals and style reflect a fundamental tension between two models of policing: the currently dominant proactive risk management model, which focuses on policing to prevent crimes and makes promises of short-term security through the professional management of crime risks, and a model that focuses on building popular legitimacy by enhancing the relationship between the police and the public and thereby promoting the long-term goal of police–community solidarity and, through that, public–police cooperation in addressing issues of crime and community order. (2015: 3)

Decreasing crime rates across many American cities have contributed to this perspective. As we noted earlier, some argue simply that crime is not a problem any longer and should take a back seat to the development of stronger relationships between the police and the public.

We disagree with this "either/ or" portrait of innovation in American policing. We do not see crime control and improved police legitimacy as in tension, but rather as something that police need to achieve simultaneously. We have already discussed how community collaboration in problem-oriented policing appears to lead to both more positive evaluations of policing and to strong crime prevention gains. We think that the task of police innovation over the next decade is to strive to develop programs that can simultaneously improve public perceptions of the police and prevent crime. We also think that it is important to recognize that the key goal of policing is not to be perceived as legitimate. This is a secondary goal that comes in the pursuit of other objectives. The police are created to prevent crime, to respond to crimes, or to ensure order in the community, and so forth. In doing these jobs, we want the police to be perceived as legitimate. This is a key element of policing in a democratic society. However, it is a mistake to emphasize police legitimacy absent the essential goals of policing. We have a police force to achieve these goals, not to have itself defined as legitimate. Nevertheless, we expect police in achieving these goals to behave in ways that are procedurally just and that encourage citizens to trust police and to accept their authority and behavior as legitimate.

CONCLUSIONS

Over the last three decades, the police industry has undergone radical changes in the ends and means of policing. This period of innovation has yielded a set of very promising strategies that can improve the ability of the police to prevent crime and enhance their relationships with the communities they serve. Each new decade presents new challenges to the police. Today, we think the key challenges follow that which informed policing at the end of the last century. The challenge at that time was to reduce crime and to improve relationships with communities. While both of these goals were emphasized in policing, they were generally developed in distinct innovations. The growing concerns about trust in the police over the last decade suggest that a new approach may be necessary. That new approach would seek to integrate more directly the key goals of policing. Having advanced policing greatly over the last few decades, it is time to consolidate the gains of police innovation and to experiment with programs that simultaneously seek to reduce crime and increase collaboration and cooperation with communities.

REFERENCES

Bayley, D. H. (1994). *Police for the Future*. New York: Oxford University Press.

Bayley, D. H., & Nixon, C. (2010). *The Changing Environment for Policing, 1985–2008*. Cambridge, MA: Harvard Kennedy School Program in Criminal Justice Policy and Management.

Blumstein, A., and Wallman, J. (2000). The recent rise and fall of American violence. In A. Blumstein, & J. Wallman (eds.), *The Crime Drop in America*. New York: Cambridge University Press.

Braga, A. A., Papachristos, A. V., & Hureau, D. M. (2014). The effects of hot spots policing on crime: An updated systematic review and meta-analysis. *Justice Quarterly, 31*, 633–663.

Braga, A., Papachristos, A., & Hureau, D. (2012). Hot spots policing effects on crime. *Campbell Systematic Reviews, 8*, 1–96.

Chappell, A. T., & Gibson, S. A. (2009). Community policing and homeland security policing: Friend or foe?. *Criminal Justice Policy Review, 20*, 326–343.

Eck, J., & Rosenbaum, D. (1994). The new police order: Effectiveness, equity, and efficiency in community policing. In D. Rosenbaum (ed.), *The Challenge of Community Policing: Testing the Promises*. Thousand Oaks, CA: Sage Publications.

Elmore, R. (1997). The paradox of innovation in education: Cycles of reform and the resilience of teaching. In A. Altshuler, & R. Behn (eds.), *Innovations in American Government: Challenges, Opportunities, and Dilemmas*. Washington, DC: Brookings Institution Press.

Goldstein, H. (1990). *Problem-Oriented Policing*. Philadelphia, PA: Temple University Press.

Gottfredson, M. R., & Hirschi, T. (1990). *A General Theory of Crime*. Stanford, CA: Stanford University Press.

Jackman, T. (2016). U.S. police chiefs group apologizes for "historical mistreatment" of minorities. *Washington Post*, October 17. Retrieved January 2017 from www.washingtonpost.com/news/true-crime/wp/2016/10/17/head-of-u-s-policechiefs-apologizes-for-historic-mistreatment-of-minorities/?utm_term=.80737fdao070.

Lum, C., & Koper, C. S. (2017). *Evidence-Based Policing: Translating Research into Practice*. Oxford, UK: Oxford University Press.

MacQueen, S., & Bradford, B. (2015). Enhancing public trust and police legitimacy during road traffic encounters: Results from randomized controlled trial in Scotland. *Journal of Experimental Criminology, 11*, 419–443.

Maguire, E. (2014). Police organizations and the iron cage of rationality. In M. Reisig, & R. Kane (eds.), *Oxford Handbook on Police and Policing*. New York: Oxford University Press.

Mazerolle, L., Antrobus, E., Bennett, S., & Tyler, T. (2013). Shaping citizen perceptions of police legitimacy: A randomized field trial of procedural justice. *Criminology, 51*, 33–64.

McGarrell, E. F., Freilich, J. D., & Chermak, S. M. (2007). Intelligence-led policing as a framework for responding to terrorism. *Journal of Contemporary Criminal Justice, 23*, 142–158.

Moore, M., Sparrow, M., & Spelman, W. (1997). Innovations in policing: From production lines to job shops. In A. Altshuler, & R. Behn (eds.), *Innovations in*

American Government: Challenges, Opportunities, and Dilemmas. Washington, DC: Brookings Institution Press.

Nagin, D., & Telep, C. (2017). Procedural justice and legal compliance. *Annual Review of Law and Social Science, 13,* 5–28.

Neyroud, P., & Weisburd, D. (2014). Transforming the police through science: Some new thoughts on the controversy and challenge of translation. Translational Criminology, Spring, 16–18.

Pate, T., & Skogan, W. (1985). *Coordinated community policing: The Newark experience.* Technical Report. Washington, DC: Police Foundation.

President's Task Force on 21st Century Policing (2015). *Final report of the President's Task Force on 21st Century Policing.* Washington, DC: Office of Community Oriented Policing Services, U.S. Department of Justice.

Ratcliffe, J. 2016. *Intelligence-Led Policing.* 2nd ed. Portland, OR: Willan.

Sahin, N., Braga, A., Apel, R., & Brunson, R. (2017). The impact of procedurally just policing on citizen perceptions of police during traffic stops: The Adana randomized controlled trial. *Journal of Quantitative Criminology, 33,* 701–726.

Sherman, L. W. (2013). The rise of evidence-based policing: Targeting, testing, and tracking. *Crime and Justice, 42,* 377–451.

Sherman, L. W., & Weisburd, D. (1995). General deterrent effects of police patrol in crime "hot spots": A randomized, controlled trial. *Justice Quarterly, 12,* 625–648.

Sherman, L. W., Williams, S., Ariel, B., Strang, L. R., Wain, N., Slothower, M., & Norton, A. (2014). An integrated theory of hot spots patrol strategy: implementing prevention by scaling up and feeding back. *Journal of Contemporary Criminal Justice,* 30, 95–122.

Skogan, W., & Frydl, K. (2004). *Fairness and Effectiveness in Policing: The Evidence.* Washington, DC: The National Academies Press.

Skolnick, J. H. (2007). Racial profiling – Then and now. *Criminology & Public Policy, 6,* 65–70.

Sparrow, M. K., Moore, M. H., & Kennedy, D. M. (1990). *Beyond 911: A New Era for Policing.* New York: Basic Books.

Tyler, T. (2017). Procedural justice and policing: A rush to judgment? *Annual Review of Law and Social Science, 13,* 29–53.

Tyler, T. R., Jackson, J., & Mentovich, A. (2015). The consequences of being an object of suspicion: Potential pitfalls of proactive police contact. *Journal of Empirical Legal Studies, 12,* 602–636.

Walker, S. (1992). *The Police in America: An Introduction.* 2nd ed. New York: McGraw-Hill.

Weisburd, D., & Eck, J. (2004). What can police do to reduce crime, disorder, and fear? *Annals of the American Academy of Political and Social Science, 593,* 42–65.

Weisburd, D., & Majmundar, M. (eds.). (2018). *Proactive Policing: Effects on Crime and Communities.* Washington, DC: The National Academies Press.

Weisburd, D., Hinkle, J., Braga, A., & Wooditch, A. (2015). Understanding the mechanisms underlying broken windows policing. *Journal of Research in Crime and Delinquency, 52,* 589–608.

Weisburd, D., Lum, C. M., & Petrosino, A. (2001). Does research design affect study outcomes in criminal justice? *The Annals of the American Academy of Political and Social Science, 578,* 50–70.

Weisburd, D., Wyckoff, L. A., Ready, J., Eck, J. E., Hinkle, J. C., & Gajewski, F. (2004). *Does crime just move around the corner? A study of displacement and diffusion in Jersey City, NJ*. US Department of Justice National Institute of Justice.

Wycoff, M., & Skogan, W. (1986). Storefront police offices: The Houston field test. In D. Rosenbaum (ed.), *Community Crime Prevention: Does It Work?* Thousand Oaks, CA: Sage Publications.

Index